Beautiful

ALSO BY STEPHEN MICHAEL SHEARER

Patricia Neal: An Unquiet Life

Beautiful

The Life of Hedy Lamarr

STEPHEN MICHAEL SHEARER

Thomas Dunne Books

St. Martin's Press ≋ New York

THOMAS DUNNE BOOKS.

An imprint of St. Martin's Press.

BEAUTIFUL. Copyright © 2010 by Stephen Michael Shearer.

Foreword copyright © 2010 by Robert Osborne. All rights reserved.

Printed in the United States of America. For information, address

St. Martin's Press, 175 Fifth Avenue, New York, N.Y. 10010.

www.thomasdunnebooks.com

www.stmartins.com

Frontispiece: Denise Loder-DeLuca Collection

Book design by Michelle McMillian

Library of Congress Cataloging-in-Publication Data

Shearer, Stephen Michael, 1951–

 Beautiful : the life of Hedy Lamarr / Stephen Michael Shearer.—1st ed.

  p. cm.

 Includes bibliographical references and index.

 ISBN 978-0-312-55098-1

 1. Lamarr, Hedy, 1913–2000. 2. Actors—United States—Biography. I. Title.

 PN2287.L24S54 2010

 791.430'28092—dc22

 [B]   2010013058

First Edition: October 2010

10 9 8 7 6 5 4 3 2 1

FOR

M.P.W.

M.E.W. AND M.E.W.

Contents

Foreword
Regarding Hedy Lamarr

Hedy Lamarr came into my life—unexpectedly, that's for sure—one day in the early 1960s. From the minute she greeted me at her front door, I also knew she was a True Original. Hanging prominently on a wall behind her was the ugliest painting I'd ever seen, a wild mix of grays, blacks, and blues, liberally doused with what looked like sand amid colors that seemed to swirl like water circling a drain. I must have blanched, which she interpreted as dumbfounded approval of what I was looking at on that wall. "I painted it," she said with great pride. "I call it 'Umbilical Cord.'" I ask you: Who wouldn't adore an amateur artist who chose as a subject not apples, boats, or trees, but an umbilical cord? I suspected we would become great friends, and we did.

From that moment on we spent a great deal of time together. What surprised me most about Hedy is that she was nothing like the glamorous, mysterious image she projected on screen. She dressed simply. Loved to kick off the shoes. Liked simple foods. Laughed often. Adored charade parties, although game playing was definitely not her strong suit. She liked to do simple things. Picnics. Walks on the beach. Riding bicycles.

Many of the most memorable times I had in Hollywood during my early years there were connected to Hedy, good and bad. Her arrest and trial: bad. A birthday party she gave for me soon afterward: good. The pain on her face when people seemed surprised that at the age of forty-seven she didn't look exactly as she did at twenty-four: bad. The way the old M-G-M guard was always there for support whenever trouble loomed: good.

The Hedy Lamarr I knew was a blithe spirit, a woman with enormous energy, curiosity, intelligence, and sweetness. If there is any tinge of tragedy connected to her it comes from the fact that, having been blessed with probably the most beautiful face that ever stood in front of a movie camera, this was the only thing people were interested in. Mention her name, and no one ever said, "How is she?" or "Is she well? Is she happy?" It was always, "How does she look?" Hers was, no question, the face of faces, but there was so much more to her than that. Indeed, I feel very privileged to have known her.

—Robert Osborne, prime-time host,
Turner Classic Movies television network

SHE WALKS IN BEAUTY

She walks in beauty, like the night
Of cloudless climes and starry skies;
And all that's best of dark and bright
Meet in her aspect and her eyes:

. . .

Which waves in every raven tress,
Or softly lightens o'er her face;

. . .

A mind at peace with all below,
A heart whose love is innocent!

—Lord Byron

Beautiful

Introduction

*I*t is said that beauty lies in the eye of the beholder. When the young Viennese film actress Hedy Kiesler landed on American shores, she was already heralded as "the most beautiful girl in the world." Later, her Hollywood studio boss, Louis B. Mayer, and the Metro-Goldwyn-Mayer publicity mill perpetuated that image. To Depression-weary movie audiences, she was the most beautiful and most glamorous new film actress of the era.

Few American filmgoers in 1937 would associate the young European actress who cavorted nude in the outdoors and unabashedly simulated sexual passion in facial close-ups in the controversial 1933 picture *Ecstasy* with M-G-M's new star. Most Americans never saw that Czechoslovakian film. What they *did* see (and in droves) was Hedy's first American picture, *Algiers*. And as a result, a fresh, new screen favorite—mysterious and alluring—was born.

The respected film critic Parker Tyler once commented about Lamarr's beauty, "Miss Lamarr doesn't have to say 'Yes,' all she has to do is yawn. . . . In her perfect will-lessness, Miss Lamarr is, indeed, identified *metaphysically* with her mesmeric midnight captor, the loving male."[1]

"Of all the glamour queens, surely none was more glamorous than Hedy Lamarr," wrote the social historian Diane Negra. "She seemed the definition of the word. Of all the stars of the forties and early fifties, she was probably the most classically beautiful, with those huge, marbly eyes, the porcelain skin, the dreamy little smile, and the exotic voice that was an artful combination of Old Vienna and the MGM speech school."[2]

Rechristened Hedy Lamarr, and early on a particular favorite of Metro boss Mayer, beginning in 1937 and up to the early 1950s the breathtakingly exotic actress was meticulously coiffed, gorgeously gowned, and exquisitely photographed in one major film after another, costarring opposite almost Hollywood's all of M-G-M's most important leading men.

However, Metro and Mayer did not know exactly what to do with Lamarr. The late British film historian John Kobal wrote:

> During her years at MGM, the challenge, the opportunity her mesmerizing appearance offered as a catalyst—if not for art at least for compelling drama—was continually fumbled. Confronted by a priceless object, everybody wanted her, but having got her they were at a loss to know what to do next, which may have been why the powers at MGM kept casting her as a kept woman, repeating her first successful role until inspiration might strike.[3]

It never did.

In her first American film, *Algiers* (1938), Lamarr created a national sensation. Billie Melba Fuller, the author's mother, recalled that in March 1939, when she was fourteen years old, she was seated in a darkened movie theatre in Ottawa, Illinois, to see the latest picture of her favorite star, Charles Boyer. Like other moviegoers, she was there to also witness Hedy Lamarr's Hollywood screen debut. Billie would never forget the reaction of the audience to the "unknown" actress's very first entrance in the film. Hedy Lamarr is photographed at a distance at the start of the scene, approaching the camera in shadow and profile. Suddenly, when she is about to walk off the screen, Lamarr turns her face toward the camera in a stunning close-up.

"One could feel the audience's anticipation of seeing her face for the first time," Billie said recently. "It was palpable. Sitting there in the dark, when the shadowed image of Hedy Lamarr suddenly turns her face full to the camera, the impact was audible. *Everyone* gasped. That's the *only* time in my whole life I have ever heard an audience do that at the first sight of an actress in a movie. Hedy Lamarr's beauty literally took one's breath away!"[4]

In *Algiers* a new kind of love goddess emerged in film. Usually portraying a vamp, but surprisingly also playing a variety of roles most actresses would never attempt, Lamarr was perpetually typecast as dangerously tempting yet unattainable. Her best film role was in 1941's *H.M. Pulham, Esq.* But it would be as Delilah in Cecil B. DeMille's 1949 hit *Samson and Delilah* that she will arguably be remembered in motion pictures.

It is almost inconceivable today to comprehend the public and private role of women of her era. In the 1940s, when an attractive actress appeared on the screen, she was little more than set decoration. Nothing was expected of her; only her appearance mattered. (Certainly such female film powerhouses as Bette Davis and Joan Crawford were often filmed attractively. But they were never successfully promoted as appearing "beautiful.") It was the physical glamour that brought Lamarr to international attention and fame.

But in Hedy's personal life that same allure brought disillusionment and heartbreak. By her own admission, her many lovers and numerous husbands were mesmerized and trapped by the image and not by the intelligent, sensitive, and romantic individual who struggled within. Lamarr's beauty was also her burden, and from it she would never escape.

Hedy Lamarr once commented, "My face has been my misfortune . . . a mask I cannot remove: I must live with it. I curse it."[5] Yet she also ambitiously bought into its appeal. She was smart in that respect. Even as a child Hedy realized what her visual attributes could achieve for her. But when her physical and professional image began to fade, she was adrift in a world of harsh reality. For Lamarr was indeed a product of her time and environment. Pampered and spoiled as an only child of an affluent family, raised in posh Viennese society, Hedy used her keen mind and remarkable appearance to her advantage, and she exhibited undeniable ambition.

Yet surprisingly always, until the day she died, Hedy Lamarr remained a simple Austrian girl, full of romantic ideals and dreams. In reality she was a very normal human being.

Throughout her life she experienced episodes of unimaginable drama and intrigue, some of which touched upon moments of historical significance. She was always in pursuit of her destiny. She lived in the present, and yet in some ways she was always attempting to escape her past.

Not satisfied with the facts of her life, and certainly not with the religious and political background she inherited, the M-G-M publicity machine embellished and rewrote Lamarr's biography to such an extent that even she began to believe its mythology. In her often-questionable, ghostwritten "autobiogra-phy," *Ecstasy and Me* (1966), Lamarr's life story was never truthfully examined or fully realized. When *Ecstasy and Me* was published it caused yet another sensation. The consequences of this fiction haunted her for the rest of her life—a cloak of exaggerations and inaccuracies that sadly became the "truth." Mystery can be damning.

In the mid-1940s, with the world at war, by necessity the role of women in society changed considerably from what it had been. By the end of World War II the exotically mysterious Hedy Lamarr, the *image* she represented, was passé in motion pictures. In her movies, her lilting Viennese accent undermined an acute acting ability that was never totally exploited on film. Indeed, in her early American pictures, when she was still learning English, she often did not even know what she was saying and consequently recited her lines phonetically.

To filmgoers and critics of that era Hedy Lamarr was considered little more than an exquisite mannequin, not much of an actress, and void of innate intel-ligence or depth of emotion. In hindsight, her film work begs for reevaluation. In a vast array of surprisingly varied characterizations, there is poignancy and understanding behind her eyes, even if her accent clouds the dialogue. And more important, she was box office; reviews of her work were for the most part positive.

Yet the goddess image distanced Lamarr from personal and professional fulfillment. Louis B. Mayer quickly lost interest in her when her films, though turning profits, did not make back the massive amounts of money he had in-vested in her. And Mayer failed to offer her appropriate roles and to properly promote her. He simply did not have a clue exactly what to do with this woman. The studio chief was more familiar with how to turn a midwestern shopgirl, Joan Crawford for instance, into a glamorous imitation blue blood for the screen. Rarely was he able to create a motion picture star out of a genuine aristocrat. Hedy intimidated Mayer. For Mayer and a couple of her husbands, there re-mained a question as to *who* Hedy Lamarr really was. What was behind that astounding, seemingly unattainable image? And what was the real truth about the life she lived?

Hedy Lamarr led many lives. As an only child she was Princess Hedy, or Hedylendelein, so called by her parents. Early on she evolved into Hedwig Kiesler—artist (perhaps her most *real* persona), an up-and-coming young ac-tress. Living a pampered and posh life in Vienna and Salzburg in the early

1930s as Madame Mandl, Hedy possessed wealth and status, all the while encircled by political intrigue and ominous danger. She finally made an escape to freedom in 1937. Arriving in Hollywood with a new name, she became Hedy Lamarr, international film star, and was set to uphold the moniker of "the most beautiful girl in the world," given to her by the legendary theatrical impresario Max Reinhardt.

Sadly, her life became cluttered with drama and literally dozens of distasteful lawsuits, all making for nasty tabloid headlines. Her very name was effectively made into a joke as a result of Mel Brooks's 1974 comedy film, *Blazing Saddles.* Then, quite unexpectedly, after the world had largely forgotten and lost sight of Hedy Lamarr, a light shone at the end of the tunnel.

In a startling announcement made just three years before her death in 2000, Hedy Lamarr was awarded an acknowledgment of her true legacy as an inventor of great technological consequence.

No other film star has led such an existence. There were certainly better movie actresses. There were certainly more impressive film careers. Yet Lamarr was unique. She possessed not only that rare quality heralded as glamour but also a brilliant, creative, and sometimes self-destructive mind. Yet she was also a simple, romantic Viennese girl. Hedy Lamarr was a complicated woman born of an era when the circumstances that gave birth to the actress also helped to destroy the woman.

In 2000, the film historian Jeanine Basinger said about Hedy Lamarr, "She herself created her own legend. . . . She was the last of a movie star type in which we never really knew what her story is."[6]

This is the life story of Hedy Lamarr.

1

Austria

To understand the life of Hedy Lamarr, it is important to understand the world in which she was born. Austria is the heartland of Europe. Vienna, Austria's capital, was and still is its largest city, located at the northeast end of the Alps and on the right bank of the Danube River. The city has for centuries been renowned for its museums; theatre and opera; the Romanesque architecture of the Ruprechtskirche and the baroque architecture of the Karlskirche; cuisine of schnitzel, pastries, and goulash; and a rich heritage of music, from Tyrolean bands and gypsy *Schrammelmusik* to the stirring strains of Mozart and the lilting waltzes of Strauss.

At the end of the gilded age, the belle époque, Vienna in 1913 was the grandest city in all of Austria, its population numbering over two million. In Europe at the turn of the last century, Vienna was the magnet to which those seeking better economic and cultural lives were drawn. On April 13, 1913, *The New York Times* dedicated a full page to the metropolis, entitled "The Gayest City in Europe—Not Paris, but Vienna." It is a colorful homage by the American music critic and correspondent James Huneker, who wrote lovingly of Vienna as "the gayest city I have ever lived in . . . ," one where city life "is not feverish as in the French Capital, but natural and continuous. . . . The Viennese man is an optimist. He regards life not so steadily, or as a whole, but as a gay fragment. Clouds gather, the storm breaks, then the rain stops and the sun floats once more into the blue."[1]

Vienna's thousands of European exiles before World War I, many of them disenfranchised Jews, adopted all things German, from its culture (the music of Richard Wagner and Gustav Mahler, for example) to its economic structure and its language. The integration of the country was important to its society. By 1900, the expression "Jewish intelligence" was well known in Vienna, causing the writer Hermann Bahr to joke that any aristocrat "who is a little bit smart or has some kind of talent, is immediately considered a Jew; they have no other explanation for it."[2]

This world of gayety, peace, and tranquility was forever changed when, on June 28, 1914, in Sarajevo, the capital of the Austro-Hungarian province of Bosnia and Herzegovina, Archduke Franz Ferdinand of Austria was brutally assassinated. This singular event effectively ignited World War I. Fighting began on August 4, when German troops, allied with Austria-Hungary, invaded Belgium. The Russian leaders saw the war as advantageous, while the German emperor, Kaiser Wilhelm II, found the war inevitable.

But Vienna . . . it still danced. As war clouds loomed on the horizon, the city was enchanted with its music, arts, and financial security. In 1914 Vienna, life was good. Into this world was born Hedwig Eva Maria Kiesler on Sunday, November 9, 1914.

Her parents came from humble birth. Emil Kiesler was born into a Jewish family in L'viv (Lemberg), in the West Ukraine on December 27, 1876. As a young man, Emil was extremely handsome, tall (six feet four), had blue-gray eyes, and was athletically inclined. He loved sports, especially skiing and rowing. Kiesler was also an intelligent and ambitious man who, after completing his education in Russia, sought his future and fortune in banking in Vienna around 1900. Emil became the manager of the Kreditanstalt Bankverein, a leading bank in the city. Though a strict and sometimes stern boss, he was respected and admired by his fellow employees.

In October 1913, in honor of his forthcoming marriage, his colleagues gave Emil a silver cigarette case with his signature engraved on the outside. Inside, each bank employee had etched his own name. For his bride Emil chose an attractive and vivacious Jewish-born Hungarian girl. She was a practicing Christian, having converted to Catholicism. In Austria, this marriage was considered "mixed," religiously. But this was quite common in Vienna and presented no social taboo at the time.[3]

Her name was Gertrud, called Trude, and she was born to Karl and Rosa Lichtwitz in Budapest, Hungary, on February 3, 1897. She was a bright and attractive girl with blue eyes, her hair fair and slightly russet. The lively young woman married Emil when still in her teens. Within months of their marriage, Trude was pregnant. Giving up her dreams of a promising career as a concert pianist, she would instill a love of music and the arts in her only child.

The Kieslers lived at 2b Osterleitengasse, in one of six apartments in a four-storey stucco building located on a narrow street in a fashionable area of Vienna. Hedy's father would affectionately nickname her Hedylendelein and Princess Hedy. Her mother called her Hedl. When she learned to talk, Hedy could not pronounce *Hedwig*, and so she would say "Hedy" (pronounced "hay-dee.") It became her first name.

The family soon moved to a modest yet luxurious home, a nine-room apartment in the hills on Peter Jordan Strasse in the residential area of Vienna (now part of Währing), the 19th District. From birth the young Hedy would want for little, except possibly the attention of her parents. She was surrounded by adults— a parlor maid, a cook, and a nurse. But her socially mobile parents were seldom home in the evenings, instead enjoying the opera, theatre, and Vienna nightlife.

Hedy would later relate that as a child she suffered from nightmares. "When I was four years old I remember them. The most horrible, horrible nightmares." In these nightmares, she would try to have "tea parties" for her dolls. But when she would pour the hot water into their mouths, their plastic doll faces would become soft and begin to melt. Ugliness terrified the little girl. "Nightmares of things so shapeless I could not say of what horror they were made but only that they were horrible," she continued. "I can so well remember nights when Mother and Father were out, and I was in bed, cozy and safe in my room. But it would be dark. And I would doze and at once I would see faces, enormous ugly faces and enormous black or purple hands coming for me. I would scream and the nurse would come running. She would pet me and pat me and tuck me in again and tell me that I had eaten too many pastries for dinner. But I knew that was not so."[4]

Hedy always recalled her father lovingly. "I remember him as a kindly man who wouldn't deny me anything," she recounted years later. "The memory of him will always be beautiful."[5] Emil also had a sense of humor. "He was very farsighted," she would tell a journalist, "and I remember he had to hold a letter or paper at a distance in order to read it. 'Oh, I can see all right,' he'd say, 'only my arms are too short!'"[6]

Emil would encourage physical activity and take his daughter on long walks in the Vienna woods, a place she always held dear. Sometimes she went with her parents on their travels outside Austria. They would take her on sojourns to Lake Geneva, to the opera in Rome, and on walks in the "English countryside, the Irish lake district, the Swiss Alps, and the Paris Boulevards." Hedy's father liked to play make-believe with her. Hedy would remark years later, "My mother was not so imaginative, but she did not mind that I tore up the library to act out *Hansel and Gretel*."[7]

About her daughter, Hedy's mother told *Silver Screen* magazine in 1942, "She has always had everything. She never had to long for anything. First there was her father who, of course, adored her, and was very proud of her. He gave her all the comforts, pretty clothes, a fine home, parties, schools, sports. He looked always for the sports for her, and music. . . . We had a good life together."[8]

Hedy recalled that as a child she would study her mother. "When I was tiny I loved to watch her dress her hair, use her scents and powders, try on this gown and that until she had found the one which suited her mood for the evening," Hedy told a writer many years later. "So early on I learned the value of pretty things . . . to love the feel of soft fabrics against me; delicate laces, lush velvets, and fine linens. I loved always to have my rooms dainty around me, with flowers in them, smelling sweet. People called me 'a fastidious little thing.'"[9]

"I watch her and I'm afraid," Emil Kiesler once told his wife, worried that Hedy's spoiled behavior might cause her harm.[10] Realizing that her child possessed an uncanny beauty even at an early age, Trude stressed that the family not flatter Hedy. Instead, she insisted that Hedy be allowed to enjoy the simple things in life in an attempt to ground her. During the spring the family took their suppers outside under the shade trees. Hedy was allowed to have a dog and was assigned chores around the house, including caring for the family's birdcage.

As was customary in European society, Gertrud Kiesler started preparing her daughter for marriage before Hedy had started school. Trude would enroll her in ballet and piano lessons, which ingrained a love of music that Hedy sustained for the rest of her life. A governess by the name of Nicolette, or Nixy as Hedy called her, taught her German, French, and Italian. Nixy would become the one constantly present adult whom Hedy could rely on for advice and security during her childhood.

"My parents did not know any actors," Hedy would recall years later. "They did not (often) take me to theatres, but mostly to concerts and to operas. There were never any theatrical people in our home."[11] The Kieslers were prominent in Vienna society and would often entertain the city's elite as well as businessmen, local politicians, and even occasionally royalty. But they were not impossibly wealthy. As Oleg Cassini, one of Hedy's suitors, would later recall, "Hedy, of course, was not born with a gold spoon in her mouth, although it must have been sterling silver."[12]

Hedy's first memories were of her father telling her stories. "He'd unfold his hand, as if it were a book, look at his palm and begin his story," she told a columnist. "He would stop to explain something to me, then say: 'Where was I?' and hunt through his open hand to find his place. I was enchanted."[13] She would recall her father reading to her by the fireplace in the library or while tucking her in bed at night, always licking his index finger and thumb before turning the pages of a book. These books likely included *Grimm's Fairy Tales*; Johanna Spyri's *Heidi*; *Max und Moritz*, a book in cartoons and verse; and the strange *Struwwelpeter*, which dealt with cruel and gruesome punishment bestowed on naughty young people. Like most children in Austria and Germany, Hedy was mesmerized by these stories of princesses and monsters, sentiment and horror, magic and superstition.

"The mind of every German child is crammed with music, and song, legends, folklore and fairy stories, a carnival of the tawdry and the epic, freaks and fairies, wolves and Easter bunnies, the savage and the saccharine," wrote Angela Lambert in her biography of Adolf Hitler's mistress and wife, Eva Braun, a contemporary of Hedy.[14] "They are first met in the nursery, through haunting melodies and verses whose underlying theme is often violence. The forest, swirling with fog and darkness, populated by wolves, dwarves, witches and satanic figures all looking for small children to waylay—these provide a wonderful insight to the German soul and justify dwelling on them at some length."

Hedy remembered once when she was three that her father became cross with her. "[I] put on a pretty new hair ribbon which I thought would please him, but it seems he hated bows and he got very angry," she wrote in *Look* magazine.[15] "I ran like mad and he chased me and hit me. I could never forget this." She would often run away from home, but only for a few hours. These were the first of many attempted escapes she would make during her lifetime.

Emil told his daughter that if she learned languages and was active in sports, then everything else in life would fall into place. And he would also spend hours patiently explaining to his daughter how things worked, "from printing presses to streetcars," fostering her inquisitive mind.[16]

At age five she began to read. Hedy would devour movie magazines and pretend she was an actress, "like [her] favorites, Norma Talmadge, Gloria Swanson, and Alice White."[17] And she would often practice her dramatics. "I had a little stage under my father's desk where I would act out fairy tales," she wrote. "When someone would come into the room they would think my mind was really wandering. I was always talking to myself."[18]

Once Trude promised Hedy that if she was good, Hedy would be rewarded with a nice present, a visit to a theatre. "I saw a stage play for the first time," Hedy later recalled. "I was thrilled and speechless. I don't remember the play, its title or anything about it. But I never forgot the first general impression."[19] After that experience, she eagerly took part in school plays and in musical festivals.

Hedy's favorite playmate was a doll with curly blond hair she named Beccacine. "My pet things were dolls . . . I loved being with them," Hedy once told a magazine journalist.[20] In Hedy's solitary youth, often spent playacting, Beccacine became her companion and a fellow thespian. "One day my uncle made fun of me and said, 'Hedy, it's only a doll. Don't be so serious,'" she recalled. "I hated him after that because [the doll] was my only child."[21] Hedy cherished Beccacine and carried it "all over the world" with her well into adulthood.[22]

When she was of age, Hedy was enrolled into private elementary school. "Those school days," she told the writer Gene Ringgold in 1965, "were happy ones. I was both foolish and fanciful and fascinated by the cinema . . . I vowed to everyone that someday I would be a star."[23] Hedy was always dreaming. And she longed to escape into the world of movies. "As a little child, she would dress up in my clothes and in her father's suits and hats," her mother said, and continued: "When she came home from the movies she would act everything she saw there."[24]

Hedy's maternal grandfather, Karl Lichtwitz, supported her artistic merits. "Grandfather was perhaps the only one who ever encouraged me," Hedy said in 1938. "He could play the piano, and to his music I danced. It was awkward, my dancing. But he said he thought it was beautiful. The rest of the family gave me little encouragement."[25]

At the end of school terms, Hedy could look forward to vacations at the family summer home in Salzburg. The Kieslers would also take weekend trips to the country lakes to ski, play tennis, and swim. During the winter they would enjoy such outdoor sports as snow skiing and ice-skating and indoor activities like dancing. "The winters we spent in Switzerland were the happiest in my life," Hedy later said.[26]

As a privileged child living in an insulated world, young Hedy always dressed properly in her blue school uniform and was instructed in her mother's Catholic faith, most likely at Saint Stephan's Cathedral, home of the famed Vienna Boys' Choir.

At the end of the war in 1918, Vienna remained largely untouched and much the same as it had been before 1914. After 1919, however, when the Hapsburg monarchy was ended with the signing of the Treaty of Saint Germaine and when the Republic of Austria was established, there followed two decades that saw the steady rise of political strife and poverty. Anti-Semitism was on the increase. The Kieslers' anxieties for their daughter began to grow.

By 1925, Hedy had developed into a lovely young girl with seductive green eyes and lush dark hair. Since she was a baby, people had remarked on her beauty. "People would flatter me," Hedy would tell the columnist Gladys Hall in 1941. "In order to overcome that, my mother would tell me about everything I did that was just 'all right,' and no more than that. She meant well. She wanted me to be modest."[27]

Hedy was soon becoming a chameleon, willing to change herself to please others. When a boy she was once pursuing eventually took notice of her, she quickly dropped him. "I knew he was in love with me; yes, even when I was ten," she once told a journalist. "I was at an age when I was dreaming of princes and warriors and heroes and such as I read about in books. And so I just took him for granted. And because I took him for granted, I think I lost something very precious and very real."[28]

Sometimes, though, her allure would have consequences. Years later, while undergoing analysis, Hedy dredged up a particular incident that occurred when she was fourteen years old. The laundryman her family employed in Vienna had at one time tried to rape her. A second time he succeeded, and, according to Hedy's account, she broke a miniature ivory statue and struck him with it. She did not tell her parents what had happened. According to Hedy, her mother slapped her for not explaining to them why the expensive statue was broken. Hedy held this "pain-shame" memory within her.[29] It would affect her whole life, though in her youth she told no one about the incident. She appeared outwardly a normal, ambitious teenage girl.

During the summer of 1929, at her family's vacation home in Salzburg, fourteen-year-old Hedy fell "in love" for the first time with a young man of twenty-five named Hans, the son of a wealthy family in Vienna, "a Russian boy, very intense about the new ideas and experiments of his country," Hedy's mother Trude told a journalist.[30] Hans was dating Hedy's best girlfriend and neighbor Hansi Weiler. As Hedy would remember, "when he saw me at a party, he started paying attention to me, too . . . I thought he was wonderful. I thought and thought about him in such an idealistic way."[31]

Confronted by both girls, Hedy and Hansi, and forced to choose, Hans made his choice. "It was a very tense moment. He chose me. I was in heaven," Hedy said. "We had secret meetings, it was all so exciting and romantic, and I was a wiz at deceiving my parents. Once, though, my father caught me coming home late—it must have been nine-thirty."[32] Ever headstrong when it came to "love," Hedy responded to her mother's request that she go to her father and apologize by declaring, "I will apologize, I will say the words, but—the thoughts are free!"[33]

That year, 1929, Hedy was sent to a private *pension*, a girls' finishing school, in Lucerne, Switzerland. Here she would learn discipline and social graces. Students were required to wear black-and-white uniforms and to follow orders. "The rules were strict [and] we made our own beds, kept our own rooms neat and our own clothes in order. The discipline was rigid and good for me," she told a Warner Bros. publicist in 1944.[34] But at the time Hedy was miserable. She was not a poor student, but she was not interested in scholastics either. She would often run away, only to be found and brought, miserable, back to school.

"The headmistress had a sour face and pulled her hair up so," Hedy once demonstrated to a writer in 1938. "She liked rhubarb and so we had it every night for supper. I didn't like the stuff and refused it. They told me I would get nothing else to eat unless I did. So I ran away." Hedy had a friend in Vienna wire the school in her parents' names to claim that she was needed home. Because the headmistress had guardianship of her money, Hedy booked third-class passage on a train to Vienna and departed with no money for food. There was a fire onboard on the night passage to Vienna, and Hedy claimed later that her legs were slightly burned.[35]

Back in the security of her beloved Vienna home and attended to by her parents, Hedy proceeded to successfully convince them to end her schooling in Switzerland. "By now I was dreaming of being an actress," she would write.

"All my life I had loved to play-act and pretend."[36] Hedy would spend hours in local cinemas and all her pocket money on movie magazines.

And Hedy loved not only Hollywood but everything American. "There was a little music shop in Austria," she would later tell a film-magazine writer. "Every day I used to go in there and ask, 'Have you any new importations from America? Did any new stuff arrive today?' I knew so much American music, the shopkeeper called me the 'Hot Austrian.'"[37]

Like most teenage girls Hedy was self-conscious about her appearance. At age fourteen, Hedy felt she was overweight. Given this perception, and because she longed to crash the movie-studio gate at Sascha-Film and become a film actress, she took matters into her own hands. A girlfriend of hers at school gave Hedy a thyroid compound, which she enthusiastically took. In an accidental overdose of the stimulant, she suffered a serious seizure that weakened her heart.

In early 1929, Hedy's grandmother Rosa died, and Trude, in deep mourning for her mother, was not as watchful of Hedy as she would have been. Unattended, Hedy entered a beauty contest and won. "After that," Trude later told a reporter,

> there could have been no stopping her. From that time on she made her own money, bought her first fur coat. . . . She always knew what she wanted. What she wanted was not, always, what we wanted for her. The stage for example. Her father did not want that for her, and later, I did not either. But she did not ask advice or, I must admit, permission. She did not need to, I suppose, because she always knew where she was going. And where she was going, from the beginning, was the stage.[38]

Her parents were against her becoming an actress, and so Hedy was enrolled in yet another school, the Doebling Academy in Vienna. At the academy she would study art and design, "to occupy my 'waiting time' before acting," Hedy told *Picturegoer* magazine in 1941.[39] Trude recalled: "At school in Vienna, I told the professor, 'You have to be stern with her, show her no special favors.' And he said, 'When she walks towards me, and looks at me, I can do nothing.'"[40]

On her way to school once, Hedy saw something she would never forget. "I had a long walk," she told a journalist, "and I passed a beautiful villa. On this day, they were shooting moving pictures at the villa and I stood there watching. The people had on lovely white wigs and old-fashioned costumes. I could not take my eyes away."[41]

In Vienna parents were required to sign absentee slips for every hour their child missed at school. One day in early 1930, Hedy asked her mother to write her an excuse from school for one hour so that she could run an errand. "She did and I put a '0' after the '1' and gave it to my teacher," Hedy later recalled. "'This is for ten hours—two full days,' she said. 'Yes,' I said. 'I know.' That was no lie. I did know. So, that afternoon after school I went to the Sascha Studios."[42]

Hedy would pass the Sascha-Film Studio, located in the 19th District, called Sievering, every day on her way to classes. Built in 1916, Sascha-Film was Vienna's first film studio. Here was where such classic silent pictures as *Sodom und Gomorrha* (1922) and *Die Sklavenkönigin* (1924) were filmed. On August 23, 1930, *G'schichten aus der Steiermark*, Austria's first sound film, was released by another film company. Later that same year, in order to also make sound films, Sascha joined with Tobis Studio, to create Sascha-Tobis-Film.

Approaching the studio's entrance that afternoon, Hedy gathered her courage, took a deep breath, and snuck onto the lot. Telling the employment manager of the studio she wanted a job as a script girl, the man asked her, "Have you had any experience?" As she wrote later, she confidently replied, "Yes. I have often watched script clerks at work." Surprised by her remark, he laughed and said he'd give her a try. She was told to return the following day. "I had only ten hours in which to make good. Just two small days," she continued. "But, youth is always confident and I thought it was possible. People say that success requires a great deal of luck, and I agree. I was lucky that day . . ."[43]

She reported for work at Sascha-Film Studio the following morning. "Once inside I kept my ears open," she wrote. "As luck would have it, I overheard [the studio film] director Alexis Granowsky discuss the casting of a bit. . . . I applied for a reading—and was terrible. Only, Granowsky felt that I had just enough potential to be coached into this part in the silent film, for the sake of 'development.'"[44] She was rewarded that very day—with a bit as an extra donned in a couture black evening gown that featured her sitting at a table in a nightclub scene.

At day's end, Hedy returned home and explained to her parents that she was going to continue working at the film studio. "It meant persuading my parents," Hedy would later write. "They were much more difficult to persuade . . . because it meant dropping school. But at last they agreed. My father . . . reasoned that I would soon enough quit on my own accord and go back to school."[45] The picture's director, Georg Jacoby, who had noticed Hedy's enthusiasm during the shooting of her one scene, kept her on as a script girl during the rest of the filming of *Geld auf der Strasse* (*Money on the Street*).

The picture *Geld auf der Strasse* was filmed as a silent. On the merger of Sascha and Tobis studios, limited dialogue and a couple of songs, including "Lach mich nicht, weil ich Dir so true bin!" were added. The story told of a runaway bride, Dodo (Lydia Pollmann). She meets the amiable ne'er-do-well Peter Paul Lutz (Georg Alexander), who tells her that luck and wealth can be found lying in the street. The lovers eventually marry and become rich.

A simple trifle of a film, its theme of optimism was common among many Austrian films of the day. But, nevertheless, *Geld auf der Strasse* is an important picture.[46] It was Sascha-Tobis-Film's first sound film. Its director, Jacoby, would later specialize in light, fluffy musicals throughout the Third Reich, most starring his wife, the popular Marika Rökk.

The eighty-five-minute *Geld auf der Strasse* premiered on November 11, 1930, and was released in Germany on December 5, 1930. It became a minor success. Soon after its completion, Hedy was offered an actual role, that of a secretary, in the film *Sturm im Wasserglas* (*Storm in a Water Glass*), also known as *Die Blumenfrau von Lindenau* (*The Flower Woman of Lindenau*). Based on a play by Bruno Frank, it starred Hansi Niese and also featured Harald Paulsen and Renate Müller.[47] Production began in late 1930 at the studio of Sascha-Tobis-Film.

The picture's plot dealt with the trials of a flower seller, Frau Vogel (Niese), who cannot make ends meet and is faced with losing her only companion, her dog. At the home of her alderman, Dr. Thoss (Paul Otto), who is running for mayor, she is sympathetically offered tea by his wife, Victoria (Müller), and a visiting newspaperman named Burdach (Paulsen). Dr. Thoss arrives home and tells Frau Vogel that the law will take its course, and he abruptly dismisses her. Burdach writes a story in the newspaper on Frau Vogel along with an interview with Dr. Thoss. The public is swayed by Frau Vogel's plight and votes against Dr. Thoss's bid for mayor. Victoria divorces Dr. Thoss after he has an affair with Lisa (Grete Maren). Burdach loses his job with the paper but marries Victoria. Frau Vogel's dog is returned to her; she is awarded 1,600 deutsche marks; and subsequently she marries the local dogcatcher.

Completed in early 1931, *Sturm im Wasserglas* was also directed by Georg

Jacoby. Felix Salten, author of the children's classic *Bambi*, wrote the film's dialogue. It premiered on April 21, 1931, at the UFA–Theater Universum on Lehniner Plaza in Berlin. *Sturm im Wasserglas* was a popular hit in Europe. When it opened at the Little Carnegie Playhouse in New York on July 7, 1932, critics praised the film. Hedy Kiesler was not mentioned in any of the reviews, and she was discouraged that leading roles would not come her way.

Hedy's parents began to encourage her to study her chosen craft, and she realized that she should take her career seriously. It was a wise move that would ultimately change her life, for now Hedy wanted to study in Berlin. Yet there were possibly other forces that influenced her decision to leave home, which was ultimately fraught with tragedy.

While she was still attending school in Vienna in 1930, she went on a hiking trip in the Swiss Alps with her classmates and met a handsome young Austrian officer, Ritter Franz von Hochestetten, a nobleman and scion of a wealthy, prominent Bavarian family.[48] The couple began seeing each other, and the sensitive young man pleaded with Hedy to marry him. They became engaged. But Hedy refused to relinquish her dreams of becoming a film actress. After a heated argument one evening, Hedy broke off the engagement, and, according to later accounts, the young man returned to his home and killed himself.[49]

Devastated by this, Hedy concentrated her energies on her ambitions. Because of her work at Sascha-Tobis-Film and her association with Alexis Granowsky, Hedy petitioned the director for an introduction to the Deutsches Theater in Berlin, where she hoped to perform. She was determined to study drama with the already legendary theatrical producer Max Reinhardt at his school in Berlin. Gaining her parents' financial support, she left for Germany. (She did not receive a graduating diploma from the academy in Vienna.)

Arriving in Berlin during the fall of 1930 with the sole purpose of breaking into theater, Hedy soon realized that it would not be easy. Though she was enrolled in the energetic and competitive Max Reinhardt School, Hedy made no headway in achieving her dreams of stardom. "All German actors wanted to work for Reinhardt," writes Scott Eyman in his biography of Ernst Lubitsch, "[w]hich meant that just getting an audition was extraordinarily difficult. For a young [person] whose only stage experience was in school plays, it was impossible."[50] But not entirely impossible for Hedy.

She dutifully attended classes. Her two most influential instructors at the

Reinhardt School were Professor Ernst Arndt and Dr. Stephan Hock. Hedy applied herself to her studies and was rewarded. Her two professors helped her gain entry into a rehearsal of a play Reinhardt was preparing to mount, the French dramatist Édouard Bourdet's social satire, *The Weaker Sex* (*Le sexe faible*).

Reinhardt's protégé, the future film director Otto Preminger, recalls his first meeting with the young Hedy Kiesler. "One afternoon I was sitting in my office," Preminger wrote in his autobiography, "[M]y secretary, Miss Holmann, brought in a girl with a letter of introduction from a friend of mine, the Hungarian playwright Geza Hereczeg. The girl told me shyly that her name was Hedwig Kiesler, that she was called Hedy, that she was seventeen and wanted to act. I took her downstairs to the stage to meet Reinhardt."[51] Dressed in a trench coat and carrying her schoolbooks, Hedy looked even younger than she actually was.

Leading her by the arm, Preminger escorted Hedy down to the theatre auditorium, offered her an empty seat, and departed. Reinhardt was pacing back and forth across the stage, his hands clasped behind his back. Unfortunately for her, Reinhardt hated to have people watching his rehearsals. When he noticed Hedy sitting in the back of the theatre alone, he called her on the stage. "I just wanted to watch a rehearsal," Hedy recalled telling him. "I watched one in Salzburg, and I watched *The Dying Swan*, and I would like to see you direct, if you don't mind."[52] In 1933 she told a reporter what happened next: "'My name is Reinhardt' [he told me], and I answered, 'And mine is Kiesler.' 'Do you speak English?' he asked, and I answered in the affirmative. And I got a small part in *Das schwächere Geschlecht*."[53]

Taken with her obvious beauty and her fearless determination, Reinhardt cast Hedy in the small role of "2nd American Girl" in *Das schwächere Geschlecht* (*The Weaker Sex*). Hedy opened and performed the role briefly in Berlin. Reinhardt then abruptly left Germany to stage the production in Vienna. Hedy was frustrated because she had such a small part. She would write home to her parents to let them know how happy she was to be working as an actress. But often she would suggest that she was lonely.

Berlin at this time was teeming with nightlife, glittering beer halls and watering holes such as the Café am Zoo. Hedy reveled in this nightlife, and she began dating again. Her new beau was Count Blücher von Wahlstatt, a descendant of a famous Prussian officer who had fought opposite Napoleon's army. In 1931, not long after meeting each other, they announced their engagement. Wahlstatt too began suggesting that Hedy give up her fledgling acting career, and soon enough she broke off the engagement.

Neither romance nor her career seemed to be working out. As she would do so many times in her life, Hedy chose to make a clean break of it. Torn between remaining in Berlin and continuing her studies, she chose to follow her famed director and her ambitions to Vienna, back to her family, back to her roots.

2

Reinhardt

The theatrical impresario Max Reinhardt was born Max Goldmann in 1873 in the Austrian city of Baden, the son of poor Jewish parents. Raised in Vienna, he received his theatrical training at the Sulkowsky Theater in Matzleinsdorf. In 1893, he was hired as assistant director by the Stadtheater in Salzburg, and the following year he moved on to the Deutsches Theater in Berlin. Over the next several years, he successfully introduced a new style of dramatic acting that used a more simplified and naturalistic approach to performance than the declamatory style so prevalent in the nineteenth century.

By 1905 Reinhardt managed the Kleines Theater (Small Theater) and Neues Theater (now the Berliner Ensemble) in Berlin, where he staged a spectacular production of William Shakespeare's *A Midsummer Night's Dream*. Following World War I in 1920, along with Richard Strauss and the playwright Hugo von Hoffmannsthal, Reinhardt revived the Salzburg Festival. The Salzburg Festival was begun in 1877 and discontinued in 1910. It was a five-week summer celebration of music and drama held annually in Salzburg, Austria, the birthplace of Wolfgang Amadeus Mozart.

Influenced strongly by the theatrical works of the playwright August Strindberg and by the operatic ideal of Richard Wagner, Reinhardt believed in theatre as spectacle, in the elaborate use of staging and set design to achieve dramatic impact with minimal stage effects. He taught his students that exceptional acting was the most important element of theatre and that the actor was only as good as his or her knowledge of all aspects of stagecraft. This maxim led to Reinhardt's reputation as a master of stage direction.

"When Reinhardt's method of production worked, the play was the star; when it didn't, Reinhardt was the star, one eminently worth watching," wrote the biographer Scott Eyman.[1] Reinhardt was called on in 1929 to establish a drama seminar in Vienna, which was initially taught at the Schönbrunner Schlosstheater, the imperial theatre in Schönbrunn Palace. It was called the Max Reinhardt Seminar, an academy for theatrical training.

Hedy left her Berlin role in *Das schwächere Geschlect* in early 1931, determined to work with Reinhardt in the new staging of the play in Vienna. Welcomed warmly back by her family, Hedy set out to the Theater in der Josefstadt where Reinhardt was preparing the production. "The Herr Professor hardly seemed to remember giving her permission to withdraw from the Berlin company," wrote the future Pulitzer Prize–winning American journalist George Weller, who, as another young acting student in Reinhardt's theatre company, was cast as "An American Man" in the Vienna production. "All [Reinhardt] said was, 'Are you here, too, Fraulein Kiesler? Are you living with your family? All right, you can be the Americaness again.' "[2]

Reinhardt loved his actors. And yet on at least one occasion with Hedy he was blunt. "He was a gentleman," she told Eyman. However, "I remember one sentence. [My character] had been talking about my idea of luxury, to travel unimpeded but to wake up with the clothes and food and belongings of whatever country I happened to be in. And Reinhardt said, 'Why don't you try acting?' "[3]

Before the Vienna premiere of *Das schwächere Geschlect*, Hedy returned to Sascha-Tobis-Film Studio and took a small role in Alexis Granowsky's film *Die Koffer des Herrn O.F.* (*The Trunks of Mr. O.F.*), which began shooting in the summer of 1931. Called "a fairy tale for adults," the story was about thirteen trunks owned by a Mr. O. F. that were mysteriously delivered to a small-town hotel in the fictitious town of Ostend. The hotel's proprietor (Ludwig Stössel), thinking Mr. O. F. must be a wealthy man, has his hostelry renovated, and the shops along main street follow suit.[4]

The editor of the local newspaper (Peter Lorre) suggests that Mr. O. F. is a millionaire planning to invest in the small town. After weeks of no appearance of Mr. O. F., the hotel owner substitutes someone to pretend he is Mr. O. F., and then puts this man under a doctor's care. Suddenly the town experiences a boom and becomes a city. After a year, the hotelier's ruse is discovered, but

everyone has forgotten the mysterious Mr. O. F. when an international economic conference is held in the thriving city of Ostend.

The star of the picture was Peter Lorre, celebrated at the time for his performance in the 1930 film *M*, wherein he portrayed a child murderer. For a
needed change of pace, Lorre was cast in this light comedy set with music. Also
in the picture was Harald Paulsen, who had appeared in *Sturm im Wasserglas*.
Hedy was cast in the small role of the mayor's daughter, opposite Paulsen. In
an even smaller role was the twenty-six-year-old actor Aribert Mog, who would
fall in love with the young Hedy during the filming.

Hedy performed in the picture during the day, and in the evening she would
rehearse her stage role in *Das schwächere Geschlecht*. Filming concluded on
Die Koffer des Herrn O.F. in October.

The plot of the comedy *Das schwächere Geschlect*, Reinhardt's first play
staged in Vienna, is actually quite similar to that of another then-popular play,
Grand Hotel. It tells an overlong tale of a clever Argentine matriarch who has
raised her two sons to prey on rich women vacationing on the Riviera.

"Within the play we were both playing at being Americans," Weller recounted
in a magazine piece. "Hedy had only the vaguest ideas of what the United States
were, except that they were grouped around Hollywood." The two young actors
were each paid the humble amount of seven Austrian schillings a day. "We were
supposed to be the stock figures of the tasteless, whooping North Americans,
indispensable buffoons for the European stage which even then had little else
that was safe to laugh at. We had several lines of sappy *Snobismus*."[5]

Reinhardt told the young Weller to teach Hedy some American songs. Immediately, Weller was criticized by Hedy for the way he danced. For her he
danced much too fast. In Berlin she danced much slower with her partner, "a
movie extra from Dusseldorf," she proudly boasted. During rehearsals Hedy
would softly whisper in Weller's ear, "A little slower, please. We might dance
right off the stage into the orchestra. The Herr Professor doesn't expect us to
be so much like American as that."[6]

Together Weller and Hedy studied American songs, Hedy writing down
the English lyrics in notebooks. Like many Viennese of that day, Hedy loved the
sentimental "Sonny Boy" made popular by Al Jolson in his 1928 film *The Singing
Fool*, and she frequently took the opportunity to give her rendition. "In Act III
there was a place where we Americans were supposed to break out in a ribald
song, spoiling a tender Franco-Argentine marriage contract with our western

animal spirits," wrote Weller.[7] "Every night, at this point in the drama, the Viennese public heard either 'Yes Sir, That's My Baby' or 'Yes, We Have No Bananas.' At matinees it had to be 'Sonny Boy'. . . . When we told all those Viennese women to '*nevah mind thuh gre-ey skies*,' even the other actors stood in the wings and listened to us. All Vienna, the old Austrian Vienna, loved 'Sonny Boy.'"[8]

When *Das schwächere Geschlecht* opened in mid-November, 1931, it enjoyed a modest run. However, Reinhardt was already in Budapest preparing to open the play there. He then returned to Vienna at the end of the month and offered Hedy a larger, more substantial role in Noël Coward's *Private Lives,* his next production.

A work Coward had written in just four days in Shanghai while he was recovering from the flu, *Private Lives* successfully premiered in London's West End in 1930. Its two stars were its playwright Coward and the luminous Gertrude Lawrence. The plot revolves around just four characters, two couples: Amanda Prynne, on her second honeymoon with her new husband, the gullible Victor, and the insecure Sibyl Chase, on honeymoon with her new husband, Elyot.

As the story opens it is discovered that Amanda and Elyot were once married, and it is only after the two couples check in to the same French hotel do they realize their respective rooms are side by side. Amanda and Elyot soon understand that, though they cannot live together, they cannot live without each other.

Hedy was cast in the role of Sibyl. In the role of Amanda's husband, Victor, was cast George Weller. Weller recalled an important moment that occurred during rehearsals of the play, a moment that would dramatically affect and define Hedy's life and future career forever.

"It was at a rehearsal of a café scene," in which the couple danced, Weller recalled:

> There were Viennese newspapermen watching. Suddenly Herr Professor, a man not given to superlatives, turned to the reporters and succinctly pronounced these words: "Hedy Kiesler is the most beautiful girl in the world." Instantly the reporters put it down. In five minutes the Herr Professor's sentence, utter and absolute, had been telephoned to the newspapers of the Innere Stadt, to be dispatched by press services to other newspapers, other capitals, countries, continents.[9]

By the time the play opened, in January 1932, theatergoers were anxious to get a look at this girl.

During the production of *Private Lives*, Hedy fell in love, albeit unrequited, with one of Reinhardt's favorite students, who was not in the play. "I think that the first man who gave me a clean, happy feeling like that was one of Max Reinhardt's actors, Wolfgang Albach-Retty," Hedy would later write. "He was devilishly fascinating."[10] Her infatuation with the handsome actor perhaps enhanced her stage role.

The Viennese production of Noël Coward's *Private Lives* enjoyed a dignified run. As it drew to a close, another play, *Film und Liebe*, went into production, again directed by Reinhardt. George Weller was cast as its leading man, a Hollywood director. But Hedy was not offered the lead female role, that of an actress. Instead, because of her ability to recite English by rote, she was offered a minor role—that of an American heiress. She declined the part.

Meanwhile, *Die Koffer des Herrn O.F.* opened to glowing reviews on November 25, 1931, and was popularly released on December 5. The film was heralded throughout Europe, capturing the hearts and the imagination of the Depression-era audiences of its day. Delighted with its reception, Hedy later acknowledged, "This time I learned something about light comic acting."[11]

The *Kinematograph* reviewer wrote, "Alfred Abel . . . should be singled out. His cute little daughter is Hedy Kiesler, Peter Lorre's journalist is comical as the script requires, and Harald Paulsen is an amiable, sympathetic architect."[12] Officially premiering in Berlin on January 17, 1932, *Die Koffer des Herrn O.F.* proved to be a huge success. Reporting for *The New York Times* that day, the Berlin correspondent, C. Hooper Trask, wrote, "*Die Koffer des Herrn O.F.* is a film that nobody should miss who is interested in the screen's future. There are moments in it where the stylization is successful and points new paths for the screen."[13]

The following year, the recently appointed Nazi Party in Germany ordered the picture drastically cut. All political references, specification of production personnel, and most of the songs by Erich Kästner were eliminated from the screen. Even the performances of the Jewish actors were pared down into a much-truncated version of the film, retitled *Bauen und Heiraten* (*Building and Marriages*). Restored today to its original length of eighty minutes, *Die Koffer des Herrn O.F.* remains enjoyable to watch. Hedy's appearance is brief, her voice perhaps a bit too high. But she photographed beautifully. The performances sparkle overall, the images captivate, the message is clear.

As 1932 blossomed, Hedy found herself in a favorable position when Sascha-Tobis-Film offered her a starring role opposite one of Germany's most popular leading men, the thirty-year-old actor Heinz Rühmann.[14] The studio's new production, *Mein braucht kein Geld* (*His Majesty, King Ballyhoo* in the United States), also known as *Wir brachen kein Geld* (*We Need No Money*), had actually begun shooting on December 31, 1931, while Hedy was still appearing in *Private Lives*.

Directed by Karl Boese, the brisk story line follows the antics of the Chicagoan Thomas Hoffman (Hans Moser), who tells the residents of a small town he is a millionaire, even though he only has a ten-dollar gold piece in his pocket.[15] Also in the film was the immensely popular character actor Kurt Gerron, who in 1928 had introduced the song "Mack the Knife" in the original Kurt Weill–Bertolt Brecht production of *Die Dreigroschenoper* (*The Three Penny Opera*).[16] Completed in less than four weeks, the eighty-seven-minute *Mein braucht kein Geld* was rushed into theatres to capitalize on the popularity of its two romantic stars. It premiered on February 5, 1932, at the Capital Theatre in Berlin.

Hedy received charming reviews, though her voice still registered a little high, and her lines were perhaps a bit rushed. *Mein braucht kein Geld* opened in Vienna on March 22, 1932, and premiered in New York on November 15, 1932. The critic for *The New York American*, Regina Crewe, wrote, "Hedy Kiesler, an easy-to-look-at Viennese player, is decorative as the ingénue."[17] Chiming in with agreement was the critic for *The New York Sun*: "The acting is typically Germanic, slow and clumsy for this sort of thing—the only bright spot . . . being the general attractiveness of a new Teutonic miss, Hedy Kiesler."[18] And *The New York Times* raved: "Excellent work by a cast of familiar German actors, reinforced by Hedy Kiesler, a charming Austrian girl, and fine photography and sound reproduction make the effort thoroughly enjoyable."[19]

After the filming of *Mein braucht kein Geld*, Hedy went directly into a new play, another comedy, entitled *Intimitaten* (*Intimacies*). She would later recall of these early days on the stage, "I was imbued with the confidence of youth and a belief that ultimate fame and fortune was just around the corner. And kind, gentle Max Reinhardt was always on my side. I didn't do too badly in those plays."[20]

Certainly Hedy Kiesler's star was on the rise. But, in true fashion, she turned her back on her promising future and followed her heart—to Prague, Czechoslovakia, where she had been offered another leading film role. She had also fallen in love again. As George Weller would later tell the writer Jeffrey Donovan in 2000, "She was already fixed up sexually with a very 'actory' actor."[21]

Some accounts have concluded that the "actory" actor was twenty-five-year-old Alfred (Fred) Döderlein, who portrayed Alexander in *Die Koffer des Herrn O.F.*, and with whom Hedy had allegedly been briefly engaged.[22] But more probably the fellow was the thirty-year-old Englishman Charles Guy Fulke Greville, the 7th Earl of Warwick, 4th Earl Brook, known simply as the sometime-actor Michael Brooke.[23] One clue comes from a *Picture Play* magazine report that stated that, while skiing in Prague with Brooke, Hedy took a bad fall but recovered in time to accept her next film role.[24]

"I went [to Prague] because I was in love with somebody," Hedy told a reporter in 1970.[25] There, the new script offered to her contained a mere five pages of dialogue. Filmed the summer of 1932, the production was directed by the noted Czech film director Gustav Machatý. As the female lead, Hedy was paid a total salary of $5,000. The picture was called *Extaze,* or *Ecstasy,* as it would be more commonly known. It would define Hedy's screen image and impact her life to the end of her days.

3

Ecstasy

The respected thirty-two-year-old film director Gustav Machatý wrote the screenplay for *Extaze* (*Symphonie der Liebe*), as it was titled for German release. Its plot is simple. A young woman, Eva (Hedy), has married Emil Jerman (Zvonimir Rogoz), a wealthy, much older man who is set in his ways. Their wedding night at his luxurious Prague apartment is not consummated, and Emil's physical disinterest in his young wife leaves her frustrated and heartbroken. She returns to the country estate of her father (Leopold Kramer) to request his help in seeking a divorce. One afternoon, she mounts her horse and rides to a secluded pond, where she impulsively takes a swim au naturel. Her horse runs off with her clothing and catches the eye of a road construction manager, Adam (Aribert Mog), who chases the animal, only to discover the nude Eva cowering in the foliage. Adam is all that Emil is not—young, virile and strong, sensitive and gentle.

Eva pursues Adam to his cottage in the woods one evening. It storms that night, and, confined to his cottage, Eva becomes his lover. Eva learns what true passion and love are about. Emil comes to Eva's father to plead his cause, but to no avail. Eva confronts her husband.

"What more do you want from me?" Eva asks Emil.

"You," he replies.

"It's too late," she tells him.

While returning by car to Prague, Emil picks up Adam on the road and gives him a ride to the city. Emil soon realizes that Adam is Eva's lover but says nothing to the younger man as they check into an inn for the evening. Eva comes again to Adam at the inn. Upstairs in his room, Emil commits suicide as the couple, unaware, dance to music below.

Eva knows that her actions are to blame for her husband's death. As the two lovers wait at a train station, Adam falls asleep, and Eva realizes she must leave him. Adam returns to his job and envisions his lost love, Eva, with a baby.

Because of its erotic story line, written with very limited dialogue, and its dramatic photography, *Extaze* has become a historically important Czech film. Its mature central theme was considered daring in its day but not shocking in its execution.

Hedy was not the first actress to be considered for the role of Eva. According to the Mexican film star Lupita Tovar, it was she who was offered the role of Eva first. Tovar, who had starred in the 1931 Spanish-language version of *Dracula* filmed at Universal Studios, was known as Mexico's Sweetheart. Engaged to Paul Kohner, who in 1932 was a foreign sales agent for Universal in Berlin, she had to turn the part down when he read that Lupita was required to appear nude in one scene.[1] Machatý then at some point offered the role to Hedy, and she agreed to do the picture.

"After we were married we went to Prague to visit the set," Tovar recalled. "And I remember Hedy Kiesler playing the piano [for a scene]. . . . She was very shy."[2] Hedy's shyness may have been a result of the pending nude scene.

The brief nude sequence apparently caused no concern for her at the time, since she later wrote, "There was no reason for me to be apprehensive about the movie."[3] But there also would be another scene that did not call for nudity but was very graphic and sensual, in which Adam makes love to Eva, which Hedy may have been anxious about. By the time both of these sequences were filmed, Hedy was involved with her leading man, Aribert Mog, the same young German film actor who had fallen in love with her during the filming of *Die Koffer des Herrn O.F.*

At twenty-seven years of age, the handsome, masculine, Teutonic (and as "Aryan" as Nature could allow) Aribert Mog had become somewhat of a matinee idol, displaying a passable amount of talent with an abundance of brawny sex appeal. It was not unthinkable that Hedy would be attracted to him, though their affair barely lasted the duration of the filming.

Mog's most important work would come in 1936 in the classic German film *Fährmann Maria* (*Ferryman Maria*), which starred Sybille Schmitz. As a soldier in the Nazi services during World War II, Mog would tragically be killed on October 2, 1941, while in action in Nova Trojanova, then the Soviet Union, during the early days of Germany's war against Russia.

The scenes of Eva swimming au naturel in the pond, running nude through the woods when her horse takes off, and being discovered by Adam were filmed without event. Hedy later wrote, "I remember it was windy but warm, and the breeze was refreshing on my body as I undressed gingerly behind the broadest tree I could find. Then I gave my signal . . . and the director gave his. . . . One deep breath, and I ran zigzagging from tree to tree and into the lake. My only thought was 'I hope they get the splash.'"[4]

Later, when she came to the United States in 1937, Hedy would deny her willing participation in the filming, saying that she was unaware of the nude scenes when she signed the contract. Another writer, however, put it more clearly: "She was ambitious and reasoned that if the picture was well received her career would be made."[5] Certainly, she knew the scenes were in the script. According to film-genre writer Jan Christopher Horak, quoting the film's cinematographer: "Cameraman Jan Stallich substantiates her eagerness to please; 'As the star of the picture, she knew she would have to appear naked in some scenes. She never made a fuss about it during production.'"[6]

Hedy later wrote that she argued with Machatý about the inclusion of the nude scene but that he threatened her into submission. Taking a different tack, she also said that because of her naïveté and youth, she did the swim and the run au naturel but with the understanding that the photographer would be positioned far away and would be using a zoom lens only for her close-up shot after she took cover.

When *Extaze* is viewed today in its most restored version, it is obvious that Hedy was relaxed and quite aware of where the camera was at all times. Her excuses explaining away her youthful "impropriety" made good copy when she arrived in America. But they simply were not true. She would *not* have disagreed with Machatý. He was much too important a director at the time. (Later, in Hollywood, they were great friends.) Add this to the fact that the scenes were shot repeatedly and actor Mog was used in them and that there were several close-ups and stills made between takes.

The cinema historian Patrick Robertson wrote in *Film Facts* in 2001, "Curiously, *Ecstasy* is celebrated as the first motion picture containing a nude scene, which it is not, rather than the first to show sexual intercourse, which it was."[7] And it is that one scene in the film that created the most controversy. When Eva comes to Adam's cottage in the woods, it is storming outside, and they make love for the first time. Symbolism permeates throughout the scene. The photography is stylized and romantic. As Eva succumbs to Adam's lustful charms, she lays back on his bed, her string of pearls breaking and falling to the floor. In angled close-ups of her ecstatic face, Eva experiences the first deep, satisfying waves of sexual fulfillment.

"I was told to lie down with my hands above my head while Aribert Mog whispered in my ear and then kissed me in the most uninhibited fashion," Hedy wrote. "When Aribert slipped down and out of camera, I just closed my eyes."[8] According to Hedy, as soon as Mog made his move, symbolizing his making love to her, Machatý stuck a safety pin repeatedly into her buttocks to achieve the close-up facial expressions the cinematographer captured.

It was reported in the press in 1966 that the film studio producer Josef Auerbach ordered more than 25,000 feet of the love scene in *Extaze* cut and burned before the picture was released. He considered those scenes "too sexy" and sizzling. "The love scenes were real," Auerbach said in 1952, "since Hedy was engaged to the leading man at the time."[9]

Hedy took offense at this remark and refuted Auerbach in later years. She did, however, concede about her sensually handsome leading man: "Aribert had what would be called today 'Actors Studio' realism. I do not deny that there were other shots when his vibrations of actual sex proved highly contagious . . . and I ended up 'winging it' too."[10]

Extaze was released in Europe by Slavia Films. The running time for most copies is approximately eighty-five minutes, depending on the edited version. However, there was also a French-language version shot simultaneously, with some scenes employing different actors. The French version, which is known to have also included an extended, longer tracking shot of Hedy's nude run, was called *Extase* in France and premiered in Paris on March 28, 1933. It ran ninety-five minutes in length, nearly ten minutes longer than today's definitive, restored print, indicating possibly additional scenes. (The original negative of the film was destroyed when the Russians invaded Budapest, Hungary, in 1956, according to Hedy.)

For the more conservative German censors, the nude scenes were alternately filmed with strategically placed bushes and trees shadowing Hedy's body. Cuts were made in part because of Hedy's Jewish heritage. (The German version of the film was banned for over two years.)

By the time production was completed on *Extaze* at the end of the summer of 1932, Hedy's affair with Aribert Mog had quietly run its course. With no new romance on the horizon, she returned to Vienna. Apparently, possibly realizing that in *Extaze* she was a bit heavy, Hedy may have repeated her earlier dieting regime, though not with the same stimulant. In the fall of 1932, she became seriously ill once again, resulting in a drastic weight loss and the decline of her health. In a newspaper interview in early 1933, she told the reporter that after she completed *Extaze*, "I became really ill with an intestinal infection. . . ."[11] Whatever the illness, it left her reed thin.

In Vienna Hedy told a reporter that she had been offered a contract by Paramount Pictures. "My mother and I will be traveling to Hollywood in the middle of May," she proudly announced. "The free time till then I will spend with sports. I am proud of my awards in tennis, skiing, and swimming."[12] A contract from Paramount indeed had been offered Hedy, but she did not sign it immediately.

In Austria, small yet dramatic social changes were taking place, and a current of unrest permeated the status-quo tranquility of peace. Throughout Europe the long-standing existing governments were threatened by totalitarian dictatorships—already established by the Fascist Benito Mussolini in Italy, the Bolshevik Joseph Stalin in the Soviet Union, and the sudden rise of Adolf Hitler in Germany. Vienna, relentlessly content with holding on to its past, was beginning to feel political agitation emanating from its neighbors.

By the spring of 1932, in Germany the Weimar Republic was falling apart. "From midsummer that year," wrote the reporting correspondent for the *Chicago Tribune* at the time, William L. Shirer, "the Reichstag was shorn of its constitutional powers, as the elected body representing the people, to govern the country."[13]

By New Year's Day 1933, there was ever-present alarm in Austria that if Hitler took over the chaotic government in Germany, the first thing he would do would be to annex Austria to the German Third Reich, a plan he had clearly spelled out in the first paragraph of his ominous manifesto, *Mein Kampf.* Despite the conflict brewing in Germany, Vienna had just experienced a peaceful and tranquil year in 1932. Then, on January 30, 1933, Hitler was appointed chancellor of Germany.

Ten days before, on January 20, *Extaze* had made its world premiere in Prague. It was immediately hailed a masterpiece, with much praise for its cinematography and orchestral musical score. "By now my parents were proud of me," Hedy would write. "Their little princess was a real movie star."[14] They had not, however, seen the picture yet. Hedy prepared her parents for the Vienna premiere, scheduled for the following month, by telling them that *Extaze* was an "artistic" film.

On February 14, 1933, *Extaze* opened in Vienna. Emil and Trude were excited at the prospect of seeing their daughter starring in a major motion picture. After the stage show, Hedy remembered sitting in the dark with them, eagerly anticipating her first scene in the picture. "The film began, and 'the' scenes approached," Hedy wrote later. " 'It's artistic,' I whispered to my parents nervously. . . . The next moment I was running nude through the trees. . . . The swimming scene was quick, but not quick enough. . . . I wanted to run and hide. My father solved the predicament. He simply rose, and said grimly, 'We will go.' I gathered my belongings in one grab. My mother seemed angry, but somehow reluctant to walk out. Nevertheless, walk out we did."[15]

Emil was shocked that his daughter would indecently expose herself and disgrace the family in such a manner. "I had a very strict upbringing," Hedy said.[16] Hedy wrote that she was so embarrassed and humiliated by her parents' reaction that she stayed in her room for a week. She promised them that she would never work in films again.

The rest of the European general public, however, took little offense at the two controversial sequences. On March 12, *Extaze* opened at the Tivoli Theatre in London. The reviewer in *The Times* focused on the elements of the film: "*Ekstase* . . . sets out to make the most of musical accompaniment and cut down the use of speech to a minimum. . . . Some of the photography, however, is beautiful in its feeling for air and sunlight, and Haidee Tiesler [sic] gives a sensitive and imaginative performance as a wife who is denied life by her husband and seeks it at the hands of a young man who is everything her husband is not."[17]

There was no mention of the two "scandalous" scenes in the review. When the picture in its most complete form opened in France, critics and audiences alike hailed it a classic. *Extaze* would only become notorious later in the year, when Germany censored it primarily because many of the film's participants were Jewish. The film was, however, publicly condemned in the *L'osservatore romano* by Pope Pius XI, who called it indecent, and it was denied presentation in the United States. Not surprisingly, *Extaze* was considered a masterpiece in Czechoslovakia upon its release there. It would win the Prague State Prize for Excellence in 1934, as well as attract the largest crowd and second prize (losing the prized Mussolini Cup to *Man of Aran,* a documentary) on August 2, 1934, at the Venice Film Festival, where Gustav Machatý was nominated best director.

Viewed today, *Extaze* is a beautifully produced motion picture. Prominent among its many cinematic virtues is its key element—the almost total lack of dialogue. A sweeping musical score by Giuseppe Becca, set designs by Bohumil Hes and Stepan Kopecky, framed by the magnificent photography of Jan Stallich and Hans Androschin—all contribute in making *Extaze* an impressively important film.

In the picture, Hedy is mesmerizing to watch. Her scenes with Aribert Mog are kinetic and sensual. Fraught with symbolism throughout, *Extaze* does not deserve the crude attention or the lingering notoriety it later generated when finally released in the United States. Publicity bordering on slander could not prevent the critics even then from recognizing the minor gem *Extaze* truly is or the respectable performance given by its feminine star. But conservative tastes, including those of Hedy's parents, condemned the picture from the start.

Now dutifully living at home with her parents in 1933, Hedy was asked to replace the German actress Paula Wessely in the successful run of Fritz Kreisler's musical-comedy operetta, *Sissy, the Rose of Bavaria Land*, playing at the ornate Theater an der Wien.[18] The musical was based on a comic play, *Sissy Brautfahrt* (roughly translated *Sissy's Engagement*).

Renowned for her breathtaking beauty, Empress Elisabeth of Austria's story took on heroically romantic overtones shortly after her death at age sixty in September 1898 at the hands of an assassin. Revered and loved by Austrians, Elisabeth's fairy-tale life was popular fodder for the imaginations of young Austro-German girls for many generations. Her life was filmed in Germany in 1931 as *Elisabeth von Österreich* (*Elisabeth of Austria*), a popular early sound film starring Lil Dagover. The theatrical production *Sissy*, directed by Otto Langer, opened on December 23, 1932.

Sissy tells of the courtship of the young Austrian emperor, Franz Josef (Hans Jaray), and Elisabeth (Hedy), the sixteen-year-old daughter of the Duke of Bavaria (Hubert Marischka). The operetta begins at the Possenhofen Castle on Lake Starnberg, with three other scenes occurring at the emperor's villa and at the Golden Ox Inn. There was an intermission between the second and third acts, at which time was projected a short ten-minute film by the thirty-three-year-old Berlin silhouette artist Lotte Reiniger.[19] Fritz Kreisler himself conducted the music for this, his second, operetta (the first being *Apple Blossoms*, which had been a hit musical on Broadway in 1919 starring Fred and Adele Astaire).[20]

Hedy was approached to join the cast of *Sissy* sometime in mid-February 1933, no doubt because she was visible again in Vienna, enjoying the social rounds of the theatrical set. With her new svelte, almost frail figure, Hedy was stunningly beautiful, as production pictures from her period in *Sissy* attest. Starring on the stage in *Sissy* was a redemption of sorts for Hedy. She would be delightfully directed and presented in the best professional light.

Stepping out into the footlights at the Theater an der Wien for the first time in March 1933, Hedy glided through her role as the young Elisabeth with confidence and surety. It was repeatedly said that Hedy's visual appearance in *Sissy* was likened to "a porcelain doll" by Austria's archduke, Max, the brother of Kaiser Karl. This was a high honor indeed, and Hedy performed in *Sissy* throughout the summer of 1933. (In 1955, the first of three "Sissy" films was filmed in Germany in Agfacolor and directed by Ernst Marischka. Collectively they made an international film star out of the young Romy Schneider, the daughter of Hedy's one-time "love," Wolf Albach-Retty.)

During the run of *Sissy*, Hedy was seen in the company of Otto Preminger, who, in the summer of 1933, before leaving Berlin, had succeeded Max Reinhardt as director of the Theater in der Josefstadt. The thirty-two-year-old film producer Sam Spiegel, to whom Hedy was introduced shortly after his escape from Germany in mid-May, would often squire Hedy and Preminger about town in his limousine. Rumors spread throughout Vienna that Hedy had conducted a torrid affair with Spiegel on a train. They were probably not true, since Spiegel was married and the father of a child.[21]

Ominous events occurring in Germany and threatening Vienna were whispered about among the affluent Jewish. Emil was a major player in the banking world of Vienna. His position was long held assured with the Kreditanstalt Bankverein (Credit Bank Corporation). Prominent though they were, the Kieslers too faced the threat of anti-Jewish persecution if Austria was annexed. They were well aware of the humiliating discriminations inflicted on the Jews in Germany. And, as a result, Emil started suffering recurring migraines. It was becoming more and more difficult for him to function normally. His stress was becoming unbearable.

For Hedy, thoughts of the future were better left to others. During the spring and summer of 1933, while she appeared in *Sissy*, there were many stage-door Johnnies wishing to court her. They came and they went. But, beginning in May, one suitor made his intentions known. Hedy's admirer sent endless flowers, each accompanied by a simple card signed Fritz Mandl. (One evening, after a performance, ushers actually carried several flower displays down the aisle and delivered them to Hedy on stage.) Finally, Mandl presented himself backstage, and Hedy saw something attractive about the man. Sensuously masculine, he also was comfortable with himself and the effect he knew he had on the young woman. It was also appealing that Fritz's determination equaled her own.

Born in Vienna on February 9, 1900, Friedrich "Fritz" Alexander Maria Mandl was the son of Dr. Alexander Mandl, an Austrian Jewish industrialist, whose father, Sigmund Mandl, founded the sprawling Hirtenberg cartridges factory in 1870 on the banks of the Triestine River, near the Vienna forest. Mandl's family was affluent and well assimilated in the Christian Austrian society. Throughout his lifetime, Fritz Mandl hid his Jewish origins, and he would convert to Catholicism under apparent pressure from his mother.

In 1921 Fritz took his first wife, the popular Viennese stage actress Helene "Hella" Strauss. They were married by a rabbi. Giving up her career for marriage, the young Hella soon realized that life as the wife of a munitions king was not without its consequences. Boredom permeated the marriage, and in 1923 the couple divorced in the civil court of Vienna. (In June 1945, Hella sued her ex-husband, then living in Argentina, for $80,000 in back alimony.)[22]

"In Vienna of the 1920s he [Mandl] acquired notoriety as a young *viveur* who gambled for high stakes, and kept fancy apartments," was how the press described Fritz during that time.[23] With chiseled features and a suave and sophisticated demeanor, Mandl cut an irresistible figure in Viennese society. Upon his divorce from Hella, Fritz wasted little time in romancing other beautiful young actresses and squiring them about to the best restaurants and theatres in the capital.

In 1924, Fritz was tragically involved with his cousin Eva May, the daughter of the pioneering Austrian film director Joe May.[24] Temperamental and unstable, Eva had begun acting in films at the age of fifteen, in 1917, and she became a successful screen actress. Her first marriage was to Ring-Film studio manager Manfred Liebenau, who was several years her senior. Divorced in 1922, Eva then wed the young German film director Lothar Mendes, another former Reinhardt student. They divorced within a year, and then Eva married a third time to the director Manfred Noa. Not surprisingly, this marriage too proved a disaster. Growing increasingly erratic, Eva began a fateful affair with her cousin Fritz. Soon she was telling people they would wed.

Her father had been directing her in recent films, and her family grew concerned over her destructive lifestyle. They voiced disapproval of her growing obsession with her cousin Fritz, and Eva's life began a downward spiral. Eventually, at a champagne party, Fritz in private refused to marry her. She checked herself into the Herzoghof Hotel at Baden on September 8, 1924. The following morning around eight o'clock, Eva retired to her bedroom suite on the top floor and shot herself through her temple. Clutched in her hand was a photograph of the handsome Fritz.

Eva had tried suicide the previous year and had staged another "rehearsal" just days before her suicide. Though she was unknown in the United States, her unusual death merited a brief paragraph in the *Los Angeles Times*: "Eva was desperate because the rich family of her betrothed, Fritz Mandl, opposed the marriage. Now the family states that Eva misunderstood, as their objection was not irrevocable."[25]

Fritz's doomed affair with Eva May was quickly hushed up in polite circles. He curbed his café-society lifestyle and concentrated on his work. In 1933 the driven, erudite young man took over from his father the position of chairman of the Hirtenberg factory, as well as the cartridge factory of Lichtenwörth and the Grünbacher Steinkohlenbergbau coal mine, creating the Hirtenberger-Patronen-Fabrik.

By the early to mid-1930s, Fritz Mandl had become the third richest man in Austria. In 1932 the questionable business dealings of Mandl were made public. Through his Hirtenberger-Patronen-Fabrik's production plant, Mandl was supplying weaponry (which some say included grenades and airplanes) to various European nations. Mandl had also befriended two major political allies—the Austrian politician Prince Ernst Rüdiger Camillo Maria von Starhemberg (sometimes spelled Stahremberg) and Italy's fascist dictator, Benito Mussolini. An Austro-Fascist himself, Mandl was prominent in European political circles, making both public and secretive munitions deals.

With the political events in Germany threatening Austria with annexation,

Mussolini's alliance and support of Austria's independence was important. Mandl had already secured an alliance of shipping agreements with Hungary's general dictator, Gyula Gömbös von Jákfa, as well as with the Heimwehr's chief of staff, German-born Major Waldemar Pabst.

But after a branch of the Heimwehr, the Austrian home resistance, failed to seize control of Vienna by force in 1931, Prince von Starhemberg's reputation was damaged. However, when the Austrian Christian Socialist Engelbert Dollfuss became chancellor of Austria the following year, Starhemberg soon came into public favor again and was credited with creating the powerful Fatherland Front, which brought the right-wing groups together.

So it was a great embarrassment in 1932 when a railroad shipment of Hirtenberg arms traveling through Austria, in direct defiance of existing international peace treaties, was inadvertently diverted and exposed by railway workers. The incident, known as the Hirtenberger Waffenaffare, was eventually swallowed up by political events, and it became a solid black mark against both Starhemberg and Mandl. "Some observers claim," wrote the historian Rob Walters, "that the Hirtenberg scandal led indirectly to the dissolution of the Austrian National Council in March 1933 and to Austria's transformation into an authoritarian state."[26]

That same year saw the exodus from Germany of Max Reinhardt, Otto Preminger, Billy Wilder, Sam Spiegel, and thousands more Jewish artists. Many came directly to Hollywood to reinvent their careers. Others migrated to neutral countries in Europe. Those Jewish artists would eventually be swallowed up in the coming Holocaust. Hitler clearly defined his hatred of all Jews in *Mein Kampf,* in which he specifically referred to those Jews in his native country of Austria and *especially* targeted those Jews living in Vienna. The growing storm forced many to take action and flee Europe. Others were sadly paralyzed into denial.

Hedy paid little attention to political events and rumors. Her romantic notions were triggered by the flowers and gifts showered upon her by her determined suitor. Though she later stated that at first she did not want to meet him, Hedy was still intrigued. Mandl, for his part, had already beseeched her parents for an introduction. When he showed up backstage after Hedy consented to meet him, the confident, imposing Mandl was said to have asked, "I suppose you have heard a lot about me?" To which Hedy was reported to have replied, "Yes, but nothing good."[27]

Nevertheless, Hedy arranged the next afternoon for Fritz to formally meet her parents. Emil also knew that Mandl was a power in Austria. "It was said of him that he could break a prime minister faster than he could snap a toothpick in half," wrote one journalist of Mandl during this period.[28]

Mandl had acquired millions, albeit through shady dealings with Fascist sympathizers. Surrounded by chauffeurs and servants, he owned a large and luxurious apartment in Vienna and a modest castle in Schwarzenburg. Mandl's religious upbringing and background were similar to those of Hedy's. So it was with little hesitation that Emil strongly suggested to his daughter that she consider Mandl as a husband.

Hedy saw in Fritz a man who knew what he wanted. And as she was learning about him, besides being impressed with his affluent lifestyle, she was also drawn to his masculine sexuality and social power. "We drove everywhere in a black chauffeured limousine," she would later relate. "One day he whirled me up to his hunting estate, presented me with seventeen dogs and a friendly little staff of household companions that included cooks, butlers, gardeners, an upstairs maid and a downstairs maid. And finally, he asked—demanded that I marry him."[29]

Wanting to please her parents and already intoxicated by Mandl's wealth and promised security, Hedy accepted his proposal. After eight brief weeks of courtship, they married. He called her Hansi ("Little Bunny"). And he would sign his cards and letters to her Bunny. He promised a marriage that would last forever. Hedy represented what Fritz socially needed at that point in his life and career, a beautiful young wife. For her part, Hedy agreed to give up her career, and she subsequently declined the Paramount Pictures contract. At the end of July, Hedy left the cast of *Sissy*.

Attended by over two hundred people, the crème of Vienna's artistic and political society, the wedding of Hedwig Kiesler and Friedrich Mandl in the tiny chapel of the elaborately baroque Karlskirche took place on August 10, 1933. Wearing a black-and-white print dress and carrying a bouquet of white orchids, Hedy became Madame Fritz Mandl. The couple honeymooned for a few weeks on the Lido in Italy.

As political events in Europe threatened the very existence of Vienna, Hedy's life was consumed by a man who promised her luxury, security, and leisure. His promises, though, would come at a dangerous price.

4

Mandl

To nineteen-year-old Hedy's way of thinking, marriage was like playacting. Along with luxurious furs and an extensive wardrobe, Fritz had given his wife an eleven-carat diamond-and-gold ring, which she flashed proudly about. "When I got it, I used to fuss with my hair, pose my hand on my cheeks, anything to make sure everyone would see it," she told a magazine reporter some time later. "I thought it would be wonderful to wear the gold ring and to have waiters address me as 'Frau' instead of 'Fraulein.'"[1]

Ensconced in a sumptuous ten-room apartment in a prominent section of Vienna, Hedy had seven servants there to attend her every need. She and Fritz were driven about in one of nine chauffeured automobiles. At their country home in Schwarzenburg, the Castle Schwarzenau, dinners were served on plates of gold, allegedly stolen in recent rioting in Vienna and acquired by Mandl. "I felt like Cinderella," Hedy once remarked about dining off of them.[2]

Along with the Vienna apartment and the twenty-five-room hunting "lodge," during the Mandl's marriage the couple also acquired a place in the Austrian Alps and another on the Riviera. Early in their marriage, Hedy was content. "We were entertaining morning, noon, and night," she once told a writer. "We had two butlers, a huge staff of servants. There seldom were less than 30 people at a meal. Our guests ranged from industrialists to royalty."[3]

And a list of those guests is intriguing. Hedy and Fritz entertained the socially important, both in the arts and in politics, of Vienna. Hedy also dined with and entertained her husband's closest friend, Vice Chancellor Prince Ernst Rüdiger von Starhemberg, and the country's two federal chancellors, Engelbert Dollfuss and Kurt von Schuschnigg. "The Mandl guest list often included such names as Prince Gustav of Denmark, Prince Nicholas of Greece . . . Madame Schiaparelli," wrote the biographer Christopher Young, and the list also included the "Hungarian playwright Odeon von Horvath, and writer Franz Werfel and his wife, who was the widow of composer Gustav Mahler."[4] Other royal visitors included Albrecht, Prince of Bavaria, and his wife, Maria, as well as their niece, the young Dorothea Theresa of Bavaria (later Archduchess Gottfried of Austria). Notably, Hedy once dined with the Italian dictator Benito Mussolini. Bowing and kissing her hand, Il Duce had insisted on being seated next to Hedy at the supper table.

At those dinner soirées that the Mandls hosted for members of the board of his company and their wives, Fritz would preside at the head of the table. Hedy sat glitteringly gowned and bejeweled among the priceless paintings and sculptures that Fritz and she had collected. Though bored by table talk, Hedy would listen to the conversations carefully nonetheless.

Hedy kept in contact with her mentor, Max Reinhardt, who now lived in Austria, as well as other "respectable" people of that artistic milieu. Occasionally there would be a dinner guest in the arts of whom Hedy was particularly fond, like a female star of the state opera and her companion or the young painter Georg Kirsta and his motherly wife. Once even the aging Sigmund Freud and his daughter dined with the Mandls.

In the early days of their marriage, Fritz was proud of and attentive to his lovely wife both in private and at public affairs. But his mind was continuously fixed on business. "I would drag him to a theatre or the opera," Hedy told an American magazine writer in 1939. "And Fritz would be thinking of time bombs or gas masks. He was oh so much for business that husband of mine."[5] They would dress immaculately, Fritz in white tie and tails, always sporting a boutonniere, and Hedy ravishingly displayed in designer gowns and jewels. She became the "trophy wife" that Fritz had desired, another one of his many possessions.

They would travel together to Paris, London, Monte Carlo, and Venice, and in the early days of their marriage they were relatively happy. On one of their trips to Paris, the couple strolled by Cartier on the Place Vendôme. Gazing into the display window of the internationally renowned jeweler, they viewed magnificent diamonds, emeralds, rubies, and pearls, all set in gold, silver, and platinum. "Do you like them?" Fritz asked his young bride. Hedy nodded yes, and Fritz bought the complete display for her. Back in Vienna, alone in her room, Hedy would showcase and play with her gems as if they were dolls, her only playmates.[6]

Hedy realized that her position in Fritz's life was absolute. He demanded her attention and companionship only on his terms and timetable. "Mandl carried a solid gold stop watch, and each minute was scheduled," she would later write.[7] And more telling than this was Fritz's growing jealousy. Hedy attracted male attention, some of it none too discreet.

Hedy was drifting. Lonely, she would visit her parents in Vienna and plead with them to allow her to come home. They would send her back to Fritz, convinced she should honor her marriage vows.

Regarding the political events and the individuals she met, Hedy would later comment, "All the time I was blind to the intrigue going on all around me. I found my only real happiness in the comparative privacy of our hunting lodge away from Vienna."[8] Yet catastrophic and dangerous social upheavals were igniting unrest in Europe. Hedy would soon realize that she was in the middle of more than just routine politics.

In February 1934, Nazi agents within the security forces in Austria provoked the arrest of Austrian Social Democrats of the outlawed political party Republikanischer Schutzbund. Because Chancellor Engelbert Dollfuss was against them, the Social Democrats declared a nationwide resistance against the government. Civil war was waged between February 12 through 15, with fierce fighting primarily in eastern parts of the country, in the outer Vienna districts, and in the province of Styria, where the Nazis conducted a massive bloodbath between security forces and workers' militias. The conflict was subsequently squelched by Ernst Rüdiger von Starhemberg. Eventually the Social Democrats were outlawed, and they either were imprisoned or fled the country.

Under the leadership of Dollfuss, a new Austrian constitution took effect on May 1, 1934, effectively abolishing democracy and the political system of the first Austrian Republic. The social tranquility of Austria came to an end when the Nazis decided it was time for their own putsch. Led by Theo Habicht, who had been expelled by Dollfuss, and who had met with Hitler in June in Berlin, eight Austrian Socialists seized the chancellery building in an attempted coup d'état on July 25. There they stumbled upon Chancellor Engelbert Dollfuss and brutally assassinated him.

Hedy recalled those cataclysmic events of July 1934 years later. When asked in an interview in the 1940s what the most exciting moment in her life had been, without hesitation she replied, "The putsch in Vienna when Dollfuss was killed. I was driving into the city and did not know whom I would find in control when I arrived."[9]

The financial institutions throughout Austria, especially the banks based in Vienna, suffered a backlash because of the unstable government. Emil's firm in particular was experiencing reversals of fortune, which trickled down to the Kiesler household. Servants were let go, and expenditures were tightened. For Hedy's father and mother this was an extremely bleak and stressful period.

Life continued extravagantly, however, for the Mandls. When Hedy married Fritz he gave her charge accounts at some of Vienna's smartest shops and boutiques. After a brief burst of extravagance, Fritz cut off her credit and placed her on a limited account. Soon Hedy began hoarding her allowance. Unrest in Europe and the threat of Nazi domination, coupled with Hedy's uneasiness about her future, all began to weigh on her young shoulders. Gloom was slowly settling in as Hedy came to the sad realization that her happiness was not to be with Fritz.

Mandl was possessive. He even forbade Hedy to swim alone. There were seven keys to lock and unlock the doors at their apartment in Vienna. Those were given to the staff to see that Hedy was safely kept home. Though allowed freedom to visit her family in Vienna and to enjoy the hunting lodge with her dogs as companions, Hedy was not allowed the opportunity to socialize unchaperoned or to be left to her own devices. Marriage to Mandl became a prison sentence.

To relieve the heavy strain of being Madame Mandl, Hedy reverted to simpler pleasures in her everyday life. She once told a story to the actor Farley Granger about an incident that occurred at the Mandls' lakeside country home: "One day she decided to entertain herself by taking all sixteen toilet seats from the house out on the lawn that swept down to the lake to paint them in the sun," wrote Granger in his memoirs. "As she was beginning the last one, she spotted a long line of black Mercedes limos in the distance coming up the long drive to the house. Her husband had not bothered to call and warn her that he was bringing important guests for the weekend. Hedy laughed, 'I took one look at his thundercloud of a face when he got out of the lead car and knew I was going to revive that Hollywood offer.'"[10]

Some temporary relief came late in the summer of 1934, when Hedy and

Fritz were invited to Salzburg as guests of Max Reinhardt at his baronial estate, the Schloss Leopoldskron (which would soon be confiscated by the Nazis as "Jewish property").[11] There she would meet a man who would have more influence on her life than any other.

In the third week of July, as Austria suffered its political crisis, the powerful Hollywood film mogul Louis B. Mayer embarked on his annual combined vacation and talent search abroad. Mayer was encouraged by his former mistress, Adeline (Ad) Schulberg, the wife of Paramount Studio's boss B. P. Schulberg, to seek out artists and actors who were more often than not of Jewish heritage. By having these creative individuals contract with his studio Metro-Goldwyn-Mayer, usually at bargain rates, Mayer may have inadvertently rescued many Jewish artists from certain death.

Accompanying Mayer as usual on this trip was his wife, Margaret, and the M-G-M publicist Howard Strickling. Margaret had many symptomatic ailments (it would be discovered later she suffered from ovarian cancer), so it was decided she should take the cure in the healing waters of the various health spas on the Continent. And in a quite perverse move, traveling separately on the ship was Mayer's current mistress, the actress Jean Howard, who was accompanied by the actress Ethel Borden.

The trip proved to be a nightmare for Mayer. On the voyage over, Margaret came down with a malady described as "pneumonia." She remained ill in bed in their London hotel suite the full ten days they were there. Leaving London and moving on to Paris, Mayer focused on business. In France he contracted the witty Polish-born musical composer Bronislau Kaper and the gifted Austrian Walter Jurmann, whose songs were the rage in Europe that season.

While in the "City of Lights," Mayer learned from hired detectives that his mistress, Jean Howard, was conducting a romance with the powerful Hollywood talent agent Charles Feldman, whom she was also seeing in Paris. Mayer was devastated, pacing his George V hotel suite "like a caged animal."[12]

Margaret was admitted to the American Hospital at Neuilly, where she underwent a radical hysterectomy. Mayer left abruptly for the Richmond Park Hotel in Carlsbad, Germany, allegedly to "take the cure" himself. While there he learned that Howard had married Feldman on August 25.

Suffering from depression, Mayer accepted an invitation at the end of August to visit Reinhardt at his home in Salzburg. Reinhardt had also requested the presence of Hedy and Mandl. It is quite possible that Reinhardt was using the gathering as an opportunity for Mayer to offer his former protégée a film contract. Hedy certainly dressed for the occasion, since she surely knew who Louis B. Mayer was. (Strangely, Hedy does not mention this 1934 encounter with Mayer in any later accounts.) And Mayer also knew that Madame Mandl had been a film actress. He had once actually screened a print of *Extaze* and pronounced it "dirty."

No doubt it was Reinhardt himself who asked Mayer at the dinner table for his casual opinion of Madame Mandl's prospects for a career in American films. (Hedy would not have brought the subject up in front of Fritz; and, no doubt, Fritz was unhappy about the direction the conversation took.) Mayer tactfully told his host and Hedy that it would be virtually impossible for him to make her a star in Hollywood after she had appeared in the raw in a movie. That went against moral propriety in the United States. And though Hedy was certainly lovely and charming, he reassured her, she spoke no English. End of discussion. The first week of September, Mayer returned to London and sailed on the French liner *Paris* back to New York on October 30.

Eventually the security of the Mandl marriage was tested in late 1934, when Fritz finally viewed *Extaze*, which was then in preparation for distribution in Germany and the United States and was meeting with censorship problems. "One night Mandl arranged a screening in a private projection room," Hedy recalled. "The viewers were just Mandl, his most trusted lieutenants, and I. He knew from the publicity what he was about to see, yet I knew it would infuriate him." Silently he watched his wife in the nude, in "those scenes." Hedy continued, "When the lights went on, his face was red. I looked away."[13]

Fritz then ordered his lieutenants to buy up every print of the picture in existence, including the negative. "I don't care how much you have to pay," he told them.[14] And for the next two years, they attempted to do just that, sometimes paying up to $60,000 per print. (It was said that Mussolini owned a copy of *Extaze* but would not hand it over to Mandl at *any* price.) Mandl, as it turned out, could not stop its distribution.

Samuel Cummins, described as "a bustling gentleman, who imports and [distributes] pictures like *Hitler's Reign of Terror* and *Man of Courage* (*Man of Aran*)," had paid Josef Auerbach, *Extaze*'s owner, $12,500 in Vienna and an equal amount in New York, plus royalties, for the U.S. distribution rights of the film.

On November 2, 1934, the film-import company Eureka Productions Inc.

attempted to release the film as *Ecstasy* in the United States. Nudity and the suggestion of sex, however, were unequivocally not allowed to be displayed on American movie screens. The film was impounded by New York customs authorities not only because of its condemnation by Pope Pius XI but also because of its public denouncement by Mandl. Thus, one of the first tests of the newly formed Hawley-Smoot Tariff Act, signed into effect in 1930 to increase record-high tariffs on imported goods into the United States, was the question of admittance of *Ecstasy* into the country for public distribution.

After a viewing by the Treasury Department, its jury declining comment during deliberation, the newspapers picked up the story. The *Los Angeles Times* correspondent wrote, "The film, starring Hedy Kiesler . . . has been described by foreign critics as 'extremely audacious,' although virtually all critics agree that the photography is excellent."[15]

On January 7, the U.S. State Department slapped a ban on the public exhibition of *Ecstasy*, calling it indecent. This decision was surprising because it "was the first time the Treasury Department has ever taken official interest in a moving picture," wrote Ruth McKenney.[16] According to *The New York Times*, "Senator [Henry] Morgenthau [Jr.] said he had not seen the film himself but had approved the recommendations of his commissioner of customs and of the chief counsel of the department. Mrs. Morgenthau viewed the picture here."[17] Former governor of New York Al Smith, on behalf of the Legion of Decency and the Catholic Church, protested the picture, stating that, if shown, it would "loosen the bars on moving pictures in general."[18]

In a review hearing where another print, this one a different version of the picture, was screened on July 15, New York's federal district court judge John C. Knox once more found *Ecstasy* to be "obscene, indecent, immoral and impure."[19] That print "was burned on July 27 by government agents on an order signed by Federal Judge John C. Knox."[20]

A third print of the film, the same as the first one, was eventually brought over from Europe by Cummins himself at great risk. "I had to go to Berlin to get it. And my life in Berlin after my Hitler picture is worth just this," Cummins said, snapping his finger. By the end of November, Cummins, who had decided to fight the ban "until Hedy was an old woman," had won his appeal, and the film was reviewed once again. Cummins told the press, "Boy, I'll bet that munitions maker is plenty sore now."[21]

Though Mandl would later deny trying to buy up all the copies of *Extaze*, it is true he tried. He eventually spent over $300,000 (worth several times that amount today) in a futile attempt to stop its distribution. Many years later, Hedy told the actor Farley Granger, "He had no more luck with that than he did turning me into a contented mistress of his fancy country mansion."[22]

Ecstasy opened in the United States in the spring of 1936. The National Legion of Decency naturally condemned it. *The Boston Globe* said, on April 23, 1936, "One cannot say that the picture is vulgar, because it has been quite tastefully and honestly directed. . . . As for nudity—there are a dozen pictures made every year in Hollywood which are far more suggestive in their veiled and brief glimpses of America's best-known stars taking shower baths or undressing in their boudoirs."[23]

Fred Stein, in his review in the *Hollywood Spectator* on May 18, raved,

We are at a loss for words with which to convey the qualities of *Ecstasy*. It is a pictorial poem, a symphony in moods and movement expressed in the most evanescent overtones of sight and sound. . . . No picture we have seen has so completely realized the cinema as an independent art form. . . . No doubt this picture should not be seen by those who are too young to know what life is about. . . . To the rest of us *Ecstasy* can be nothing less than a great artistic experience.[24]

On Thursday, February 14, 1935, Emil Kiesler was found dead at home by his wife Gertrud. Devastated by personal financial losses and worried about the increasing fear of the Nazi menace in neighboring Germany, Emil suffered a massive heart attack while resting in Hedy's former bedroom. He was fifty-eight years old. When Gertrud telephoned Hedy with the news, she told her daughter, "He spoke of you with his last breath. How he loved you."[25]

The newspapers reported Emil Kiesler's death the following week. There was a private burial for the director of the Vienna Bank Association on Saturday, February 16, 1935.[26] Hedy, overcome with grief, did not attend the funeral. Years later, Hedy's daughter said of her mother, "She was really devastated by Emil's death. She loved her father, and told me that many, many times."[27]

During the following months, Hedy spent a great deal of time with her mother, telling Trude of her troubles in her marriage. "'*Ach, es ist taurig!* It is so sad that which has come upon you,' she would say," Hedy told the journalist Marian Rhea in early 1939. "And then she would add, 'Hedy, *liebschen*, whatever you do,

I shall understand.' She begged me, though, not to tell her of my plans. Because, she explained to me then, when Herr Mandl questioned her, she could truthfully say, '*Ich weiss nicht*. I know nothing of what Hedy has done.'"[28]

Hedy later said about those difficult years with Fritz, "But how different everything was, now . . . different because my heart had changed. I no longer idolized him. I no longer lived to gratify his every wish. I no longer was content with his companionship alone."[29] Shortly after her father's death, Hedy began planning her escape.

Sometime during that spring of 1935, Mandl entertained an English colonel as a guest to their home in Vienna. At dinner that evening, so Hedy wrote, "Colonel Righter [as she called him in her book] was particularly attentive [to me], even in front of Mandl. He was openly critical of the Nazi movement. I sensed a fellow conspirator."[30] The colonel, a smoker of long, thin cigarettes, ran out of his brand during the course of the evening's conversation. Fritz offered to bring him some of his own. When her husband retired to his den to bring his guest the cigarettes, Hedy made her move. She wrote in her book:

> As soon as he left, I moved a chair near Colonel Righter, and whispered frantically, "Can you help me escape from Vienna? I'm virtually a prisoner here at my home and in this country. Can you please help me?"
>
> He seemed to think I had been struck mad. "What is the problem?"
>
> "Where are you staying?" I countered quickly, desperate to arrange things before Mandl returned.
>
> He gave me his hotel's name.
>
> "I must escape," I said. "My husband has servants watching me and the surveillance gets more cruel all the time."
>
> Colonel Righter was very nervous. "Contact me," he said after a pause. "I will help you somehow."[31]

Fritz returned to the couple, and for the rest of the visit he and Hedy played the perfect hosts. At the end of the evening, with the servants dismissed for the night, Hedy was in her boudoir brushing her hair when Mandl knocked at her door and entered. He had a record with him that he told her was of a Strauss waltz. When he placed it on her Victrola, the music began. But then her voice was heard: "Can you help me escape from Vienna? I'm virtually a prisoner . . ." Her blood ran cold.

"My dear, it's necessary in business to know what's going on everywhere," Fritz cruelly explained. "Then I can better evaluate the situation. Now your Colonel, for instance. He won't help you because he is on my payroll." Mandl paused. "Righter's one weakness has always been beautiful women. But you see he's too selfish to accept a number two position."

He kissed me on the forehead and said goodnight. "Of course I will have to increase your guard. And perhaps for a little while you should confine your activities to your suite." And he left.[32]

Mandl bought Hedy more furs and jewels and expensive gifts to compensate for his actions, including a luxuriously appointed 1935 Mercedes (which, years later, sold for over $200,000). Fritz had been making innumerable business trips without Hedy throughout their marriage. Now he began taking his wife with him more often. When he was forced to leave her alone in Austria, her actions were meticulously monitored.

In February 1936, *The New York Times* ran a major feature article on Austria's energetic vice chancellor, Ernst Rüdiger von Starhemberg. "No politician in Europe is more active these days," the paper said. "He has a regular luncheon day with his closest and most powerful business associate, Fritz Mandl, the munitions king, the man who rearmed Austria."[33] Heavily emphasized in the telling piece was Starhemberg's pro-monarchist stance as well as Mandl's participation in the government's internal operations.

That spring, Austria's new chancellor, Kurt von Schuschnigg, believed he had allied Mussolini with Austria. Mussolini, however, was dependent on Germany and Hitler for military and diplomatic power in Italy's fight against Ethiopia. "It was during March 1936 that von Schuschnigg discovered this closeness with Mussolini and Hitler, when he was told by the former in no uncertain terms to come to an agreement with Germany," wrote the historian Gertrude Schneider in 1995. "Von Schuschnigg reluctantly did so and was forced to accept several Nazis into his government. They in turn prepared the way for the triumphant entrance of Hitler into Austria and the subsequent *Anschluss*."[34]

By May, Starhemberg was no longer vice chancellor. On May 21, 1936, Dr. Kurt von Schuschnigg proclaimed himself sole dictator of Austria. *The New York Times* announced on May 23 that the newly proclaimed dictator Schuschnigg was threatening to take over the Austrian arms industry. "This is a direct threat to the man behind the Heimwehr—Fritz Mandl, Austrian 'munitions king' who is a friend of . . . the present Financial Minister, Dr. Ludwig Draxler." Published the previous Wednesday in the *Weltblatt* (*International Press*) was an article approved by Schuschnigg that advocated the nationalization of the munitions works. "The article contained a paragraph declaring Austrian armament manufacturers had frequently tried to get foreign participation in their concerns in order to be sure of foreign protests against eventual nationalization. This is precisely what Mr. Mandl is believed to be doing in Rome," said *The New York Times*.[35]

Fritz brought Hedy along with him to the Lido in Venice later that summer, and they stayed at the Hotel Excelsior. He seldom let Hedy leave his sight unless he was taking his afternoon siesta. Back in Vienna, and once again defying Fritz, Hedy began a reckless affair with the former vice chancellor of Austria, and Fritz's best friend, Prince Ernst Rüdiger von Starhemberg. With the world caving in about them, this most dangerous and volatile romance was potentially fatal for both of them.

The prince gave Hedy a private key to his palace in Vienna, and, when Fritz was out of town, she several times slipped in at night to be with him. Hedy had devised a plan to flee Vienna, and she needed Starhemberg's help. Boarding the Vienna-Budapest train, Hedy and her lover traveled to Budapest, where the prince had offered to introduce Hedy to theatrical producers. Mandl, in Rome yet again on business, was notified by his spies of the intrigue and took a plane that night to intercept the couple in Budapest. When the train arrived at the station, Mandl confronted them, his face red with anger.

As they stepped off the platform in shock, Mandl ignored his friend Starhemberg at first and addressed his wife. "His voice was soft and silky, but his eyes were blazing in anger," Hedy told a magazine columnist in 1939. "'You will come home with me, my Hedy. Then, of course, there will be no scandal.' And so, bowing to the inevitable, knowing his great power . . . I returned with him. My beautiful plan had failed. I was heartsick."[36]

It was reported in the New York *Daily News* at the time that Fritz then confronted Ernst, stating, "If this keeps up, our friendship ends here."[37] Starhemberg capitulated. Heartbroken and thwarted yet again, Hedy threw the key her lover had given her to his palace into the Danube Canal.

That fall, Fritz sought to appease his wife by contracting with the Viennese

architect Walter Sobotka to sketch and design a $25,000 addition onto the
Mandl hunting lodge in the Austrian Alps near Vienna. These plans interestingly specified a nursery in the wing.

The summer of 1937 in Austria was the last peaceful one for the fairy-tale
country before the war. It was also the last summer of the Mandl marriage.
The Salzburg Festival was held every summer, and it had gained international
recognition. The 1937 Salzburg Festival focused on presenting musical works
by Mozart and Strauss, but it was also the premier venue for operatic, dramatic, and classical music presentations. (In 1936 the Trapp Family Singers
had performed at the festival.)

That summer of 1937 saw the masterful recording of Mozart's *Le nozze di
Figaro* with Ezio Pinza, Giuseppe Nessi, Esther Rethy, and Mariano Stabile
performing and Bruno Walter conducting the Vienna Philharmonic Orchestra. Conductor Herbert von Karajan was the festival's musical director. That
year, 1937, would long be recalled as one of the most memorable of all the festivals. (The following year the Salzburg Festival would be annexed by the Germans during the *Anschluss*.)

Hedy and Fritz had planned to vacation that summer in Antibes, but at the
last moment they accepted an invitation from Max Reinhardt, now married to
the actress Helene Thimig, to visit his Salzburg home as guests during the festival in August. Fritz and Hedy were photographed arriving for a musical performance, and both looked stunningly attractive. But the image is equally
jarring. The dapper, magnificently groomed Fritz, his mouth firmly set, is to
the far right of the picture. Two unidentified women separate the couple. To
the far left is the winsomely beautiful Hedy. There is a distinct air of gloom on
their faces. In fact, Fritz and Hedy were barely speaking with each other at this
point.

Alone with the great director at his home, sitting in front of a fire after dinner, Hedy unburdened herself to her mentor, telling him about her troubled
marriage and her desire to return to work. "My dear, you never will. It's all
talk," he told her unsympathetically.[38]

Upon their return to Vienna, the Mandls resumed their lifestyle. Slowly
Hedy was becoming aware of the dangers and threats closing in on her. For endless hours Fritz and his cronies—builders, weapons developers, and buyers—
would talk about military supremacy and armaments. Fritz specialized in shells
and grenades. He manufactured military aircraft as well, and the conversation

often turned to discussions of varying types of radio-control systems and the research currently being conducted by the Third Reich.

Hedy would ask Fritz about his numerous trips, and he would change the subject. At one long and dull dinner in their Vienna apartment, surrounded by powerful men in the armament industry, Hedy listened patiently at the table, taking in what was being said. With increasing shock and disbelief she realized that Fritz was now making arms agreements with the Nazis.[39] At once, she was shocked and terrified as the reality of the moment struck home.

In effect, Fritz had become an "honorary Aryan," "a special status created by [the German propaganda leader Joseph] Goebbels for Jewish people who served Hitler personally."[40] Realizing her husband's dangerous position, Hedy was truly frightened.

Recklessly, she began another affair, which was talked about in Vienna and became the final rift in the Mandl marriage. Thoroughly disgusted with Fritz and wanting desperately out of the marriage, Hedy threw all caution to the wind. Her new lover was the famed athlete and mountain climber Count Max Hardegg. Together he and Hedy publicly made the café rounds and created a momentous scandal. Hedy had been offered a lead role in a Viennese production of Clare Boothe Luce's caustic comedy *The Women*. The play was set to begin rehearsals that fall. According to a New York *Daily News* article at the time, both Hedy's ambitions and her affair with Hardegg were cut short. "When Mandl heard about it, he forbade his wife to visit the theatre and even ordered her not to leave the house."[41]

Hedy planned her next escape carefully. As a ruse to impress a dignitary (most probably Starhemberg) who was coming to dinner, Hedy approached Fritz with the idea of bedecking herself with her most costly and flashy jewels. Fritz, who controlled the only key to the safe, thought the idea splendid and retrieved the gems for Hedy to select. At the end of the evening Hedy returned the glittering jewels back to her husband but cleverly concealed the most expensive pieces. She then wired money she had hoarded from her allowance and mailed some of her jewels to a trusted friend in Paris. Soon afterward, Gertrud was visiting and watched tearfully as Hedy packed her clothes and her remaining jewels in anticipation of departure.

Hedy's chance came quickly. One Thursday in late August, Fritz departed for a hunting trip in the country. With the help of her faithful maid Laura, that evening Hedy dressed as a servant and, with suitcases and passport in hand, quietly slipped out of the apartment.[42] After she and Laura drove to the Haupt-bahnhof on the Mariahilfer Strasse, Hedy was forced to wait an hour, in what must have been crushing fear, for the arrival of the Trans-Europe Express to Paris. Bidding farewell to Laura, she sat rigidly in her compartment until the train departed the station. At dawn the express crossed the Czechoslovakia border, then continued into Germany, and finally it reached the border of France, eventually pulling into Paris.

Hedy had booked accommodations in advance, but waiting for her at the hotel was a cable from Laura. Mandl was on his way to bring her home. Im-mediately, without even unpacking her clothes, Hedy caught a cab and within a half hour was on the train to Calais to catch a channel vessel to England. Ar-riving safely in London, she checked into the Hotel Regent Palace in the center of Piccadilly Circus.

Mandl did not pursue Hedy across the English Channel. By this time Fritz might have had enough as well. On September 18, 1937, the New York *Daily News* announced from Vienna that Hedy and Fritz had filed for a mutual di-vorce action.[43]

Through friends Hedy was advised that M-G-M mogul Louis B. Mayer had also been in London to begin his annual European tour. Mayer was just completing the last of his talent hunts in Europe before the start of World War II. He would ostensibly be back in England for the opening of Metro's new M-G-M–British Denham Studios production *A Yank at Oxford* (1938), star-ring Robert Taylor and Vivien Leigh, which had just completed shooting.

On this trip, Mayer reconnected with his former mistress Ad Schulberg, who now had talent agencies in Hollywood, New York, and London. Accord-ing to the biographer Charles Higham, there were again more than superficial reasons for the annual talent searches during the 1930s. "Of a strong liberal per-suasion, Mrs. Schulberg now represented as agent a number of significant Euro-pean Jewish and non-Jewish writers and actors," wrote Higham. "She saw Mayer, who was always looking for new talent, as a way of rescuing those artists who might be threatened by Hitler in the future. She was careful not to emphasize to Mayer the liberal leanings which some of them showed; by stressing that they were Jewish, or sympathetic to Jews, she ingeniously ensured his support."[44]

His European contract list that year included director Walter Reisch, Polish-born opera coloratura Miliza Korjus, as well as services secured in Lon-don of the Gaumont Films producer-director Victor Saville and actress Greer

Garson; in Austria, actress Rose Stradner (she had been Hedy's replacement in *Sissy* and later married Joseph L. Mankiewicz), dancer Tilly Losch, the Hungarian-born Ilona Hajmassey, and writer-director Rheinhold Schünzel; and in Paris, film director Julien Duvivier (who directed *Pépé le Moko*) and actresses Jacqueline Laurent and Mireille Balin.

After several days in London, Hedy, moving quickly, arranged a meeting with the M-G-M talent scout Robert Ritchie, who had seen *Extaze* in Europe. He agreed to represent Hedy as her agent. Through his London office Ritchie contacted Mayer, who, before returning to London, was then in Vienna. Ritchie secured an appointment for Hedy to meet Mayer when he arrived back in town at the Claridge Hotel. "She's not only gorgeous, but she can act," Ritchie told Mayer. "You can make her a big star at MGM."[45] When Ad Schulberg also notified Mayer of Hedy's presence in London, the mogul listened.

When the day arrived for her meeting with Mayer, Hedy selected her best ensemble to impress the mogul. After greeting her, Mayer motioned for Hedy to sit down; pulled himself up straight to look taller; and, with the occasional help of a translator, reminded Hedy of the discussion he had with her just three years earlier at the home of Reinhardt. "You're lovely, my dear, but I have the family point of view," he said. "At MGM we make clean pictures. We want our stars to lead clean lives. I don't like what people would think about a girl who flits bare-assed around the screen."[46]

Hedy carefully explained to Mayer in fractured English that she had been very young when she made *Ecstasy* and that she had been forced into doing "those scenes." She told him she wanted to prove herself a good actress. She rose to leave, but Mayer stopped her and suggested that if she paid her own way to Hollywood, he would offer her a six-month standard studio contract at $125 a week. Hedy Kiesler was already an established star in Europe, and that, along with her own strong sense of self-worth, made her decline his offer. "Mayer's behavior may not have offended her, but his offer certainly did. She turned him down flat," wrote social historians Raymond Sarlot and Fred E. Basten. "Speaking in her most precise broken English, which was horrendous at best, she refused to be intimidated or bamboozled into accepting 'a cheap contract.' There was more to this girl than her luscious looks, Mayer had to admit. 'You have spirit,' he said playfully. 'I like that.'"[47]

Leaving Mayer's hotel suite, Hedy met with Ritchie at Sylvan's restaurant for coffee. An hour later she had changed her mind, with a little advice from her European lawyer, Paul Koretz, who would eventually negotiate her contract with Metro before he too came to the United States in 1939. Hedy was now prepared to accept the offer from Mayer. But he was leaving the next day to France to sail to America on the French superliner *Normandie*, and Hedy would not be able to see him. Checking the French Line reservations desk, Ritchie found the ship was completely booked. Struck with an idea, Ritchie suggested that Hedy take the crossing posing as the nanny of another one of his clients, the fourteen-year-old American violinist prodigy Grisha Goluboff, who was returning to the United States after a successful European concert tour. She agreed. (Mayer would incorrectly and repeatedly advise the press later that Goluboff was Hedy's "protégé.")

Crossing the channel again to France and boarding the *Normandie* in Le Havre as Hedwig Mandl, the name on her passport, Hedy had little to no luggage with her—just some street wear and a designer gown by Alix, a well-known European couture. On boarding the ship, she wore a simple gray tailored suit, a pair of gloves, and carried $900 in her handbag. She had sold most of her jewels to cover her fare.

In the Mayer party were his wife, Margaret, who had joined him from a sanitarium in France, Ad Schulberg, the newly contracted writer Walter Reisch, and the M-G-M executive publicists Benny Thau and Howard Strickling. Also sailing on board were the rakishly handsome Douglas Fairbanks Jr., the most recent lover of Marlene Dietrich; Fernand Gravet (who would star in Metro's *The Great Waltz* with Miliza Korjus the following year); and Elisabeth Rethberg and Ezio Pinza, both of the Metropolitan Opera company, returning from their 1937 European concert tour.

Just outside of Le Havre the liner lost a propeller and was forced to return to port. While repairs were being made, Mayer hosted a party, which included Hedy and her "protégé." Recognizing the effect she had on the other male passengers, Mayer offered Hedy a seven-year contract beginning at $550 a week with options, which she accepted with the understanding that she would properly learn English. (When she was just twelve, Hedy had been instructed in English for only one year.)

On the resumed Atlantic crossing, Hedy's beauty caught everyone's attention, including Mayer's. He was enamored with her. She was recognized by some as the star of *Ecstasy*. But for the rest, she was merely hypnotically captivating.

Two days out of Southampton, the ship ran into a storm. Summoning Walter Reisch to his stateroom, Mayer told the writer he needed to come up with a new name for Hedy Kiesler. Around the A-deck ping-pong table the following day with Reisch, Thau, and Strickling, Mayer remembered the tragically beautiful film actress Barbara La Marr, "the girl who was too beautiful." La Marr died in 1926 from tuberculosis and alleged drug addiction.[48] Hedy Kiesler would become Hedy Lamarr. (Hedy would categorically state until the end of her days that it was *she* who renamed herself Lamarr, because the French words for "the sea" are *la mer*.) "Mayer sent her to E-deck, where [international coutouriers] Dior and Chanel had boutiques," wrote Charles Higham. "She was allowed to charge her clothes to the studio; she was also permitted to buy a matching set of expensive suitcases."[49] By the time the *Normandie* docked in New York, Mayer, his mood much improved and his professional prospects brightened, had signed the boy prodigy Goluboff to a Metro contract as well.

The *Normandie* docked in New York on September 30. Mayer gave a brief interview on deck to the awaiting press and told the reporters about his new discoveries. He had already renamed the beautiful Ilona Hajmassey as Ilona Massey and, privately, had sent Robert Ritchie a wire to cinch the deals offered the opera diva Miliza Korjus and Rose Stradner. The New York press then photographed and interviewed Hedy, dressed unflatteringly, sporting a large orchidlike corsage and looking rather heavily made up.

The ship's news reporters embarrassed her by asking questions about *Ecstasy*. They referred to her as "The *Ecstasy* lady," and "the brunette Hedy Kiesler," to which Hedy told them, "Please call me Hedy *Lamarr*." In response to her film *Ecstasy*, she told the reporters that she saw nothing wrong with the picture's nudity. "I don't know why the censors banned it," she said. "Men look at women all the time and undress them with their eyes." One reporter asked if she intended to appear nude in American pictures. To which she replied, with a smile, that she had no intention of doing so. After refusing to confirm or deny she was in America to divorce her munitions-magnate husband, her English giving her trouble, the M-G-M publicist Howard Dietz, whom Mayer had summoned to New York to promote her to the public, fielded the remaining questions. As Dietz led Hedy to an awaiting limousine, she told him, "I don't know what Mr. Mayer is going to say when he reads the newspapers tomorrow."[50]

After delivering Hedy to the Plaza Hotel, Dietz departed and went downtown. Once back in his office, his phone rang. It was Louis B. Mayer. Wrote Dietz in his autobiography, " 'I have a hysterical star on my hands,' [Mayer] said. 'Come up and save the situation.' " Dietz knew that both Hedy and his boss were sensitive to references made to Hedy's nude appearance in *Ecstasy*. The American press had considerably unnerved her.

Dietz continued in his book:

I hot-footed it to the Plaza and went in to see Hedy.

"You Americans are terrible," she said through her tears, "you have no artistic appreciation."

"Did you appear in the nude?" I asked.

"Yes," Miss Lamarr replied.

"Did you look good?"

"Of course."

"Then it's all right," I assured her, "no damage has been done." I convinced her that all Americans care about is success. If you're successful nude, you're ahead of the game.[51]

That next day at Grand Central Terminal, Hedy boarded the train for Los Angeles. During the long journey across the country, she prepared for her arrival in California by taking in everything her new boss and his staff had told her about the world she was now entering. Studying English and working on her appearance, her hair, her makeup, her wardrobe, her diet, her "look," Hedy was determined to make an impression on arrival in Hollywood. Hedy Kiesler was re-creating herself.

As Hedy Lamarr her life would change forever.

5

Hollywood

When the newly rechristened Hedy Lamarr stepped onto the railroad platform at Los Angeles's Union Station on October 4, 1937, the press saw a smartly dressed, attractive young woman wearing a light-colored, conservative, three-quarter-length skirt and matching jacket, bearing a small corsage of flowers. On her shoulder-length dark tresses she wore a stylish late-1930s beret. Her appearance was quite a contrast from the high-gloss, heavily made-up exotic who had descended the French Line gangway in New York just five days earlier. Hedy had listened to what her new boss had told her about her appearance, as rude as he may have been.

A Metro publicist had accompanied Hedy on the cross-country journey aboard the City of Los Angeles. He oversaw her "look" for her arrival into Los Angeles. She was in America on a visitor's permit, and the press quickly picked up on the fact that she could speak virtually no English. Once again, Hedy did not understand many of the news reporters' questions. However, one she did. It was about her nude appearance in *Ecstasy*, to which she replied that, if they used their imagination, they could look at any actress and see her nude. She hoped to make them use their imagination.

Mayer sent another M-G-M publicist to bring her to the studio. He carried a bouquet of long-stemmed red roses with a hand-signed welcoming card from Mayer himself. Told to look for "the most beautiful creature on earth" by the boss, in the glare of morning sunlight, the young publicist had little trouble spotting her. "The jet black shoulder-length hair, the exquisitely refined features, the flawless complexion," wrote biographers Sarlot and Basten about Lamarr's arrival into Hollywood, proved to the publicist that "[s]he was even more magnificent than he had been led to believe."[1]

After welcoming her, the publicist nervously whisked Hedy off to the Metro-Goldwyn-Mayer Studios on Constellation Boulevard to meet with the boss. Mayer had arrived in Los Angeles the day before by plane and enthused to the press in glowing tones about his plans for Greer Garson, whom he wished to make into the studio's resident grande dame. Shuffled into Mayer's office, Hedy was left with the film mogul for several minutes. It was with caution that Mayer had signed her, he reminded her. Within minutes he then summoned the studio's chief of publicity, Howard Strickling, into his office to discuss Metro's immediate plans for Hedy Lamarr.

With Strickling present, Mayer resumed his talk: "You'll find we run a clean ship. Our reputation for morality is never questioned," he said. "At MGM we try very hard to maintain our stars' images. Be sure and read your morals clause in your contract. Don't talk to reporters or allow pictures to be taken unless you're with an MGM publicist. If you have any questions, come to me."[2] Mayer advised Hedy to obtain a Hollywood agent, learn English, begin diction lessons, and even study dance.

Hedy knew better than to attempt to speak with her new boss in his own language. Nonetheless, when Mayer asked his new "discovery" how she liked Hollywood so far, Hedy surprised him by frankly stating that she was rather let down. Usually Mayer was answered with gushing words of appreciation by his young hopefuls. But with Hedy he was confronted by a lady of class, and her response threw him.

Mayer had no project for Hedy until she perfected her English. He did promise her that Metro would find her a small bungalow or apartment to share with another contract actress. Yes, the studio had great plans for her, but she needed to do her homework in the meantime. Perfunctorily dismissing her and Strickling, Mayer then turned his attention to other matters, mainly Greer Garson.

And Mayer also had other pressing issues on his mind that fall of 1937. His production chief, Irving Thalberg, had died quite suddenly at the age of thirty-seven just the year before. A man of extremely fine taste, Thalberg had supervised some of the best and most profitable films M-G-M ever produced. Well respected by Metro stars and employees alike, Thalberg was an invaluable force at Metro, but he seldom saw eye to eye with his older boss. Now Mayer was in complete control of the studio.

As he did annually, Mayer began to voice his desire to leave the studio to his boss, Joseph Schenck, in New York, saying that many of his producers were not giving him their support and so forth. Mayer also threatened that, if he left the studio, many of his loyal executives would follow him. Schenck was familiar with Mayer's tactics, since they usually were preliminaries for contract renegotiation.

In Palm Springs late that fall, the two industry giants met and compromised. Mayer's new contract, when renewed, would run from December 1, 1939, for five years, at $3,000 a week. It would also give him 6.77 percent of the net profits of Loew's, Inc., M-G-M's parent company based in New York, computed after a minimum-annual-dividend deduction on the common stock. In 1938, the studio chief would lead the list of the twenty-five highest corporate salaries, with annual earnings of $688,369.[3]

Strickling's staff consisted of thirty-five dedicated men and women who oversaw the well-being and needs of the contract players, each of whom was assigned an aide. That afternoon, Hedy's aide comforted and reassured her as he showed her around the Metro lot. The first film star she recognized that day was the British actor Reginald Gardiner.

The publicist then took her to the studio commissary for lunch. Dutifully, she ordered the famous chicken soup Mayer always recommended, as well as a steak sandwich named after one of her favorite film actors, Clark Gable. Hedy recalled that she was shown indifference by those around her until the publicist told them that she was "the girl who had posed nude in *Ecstasy*."[4] Suddenly Hedy became the focus of everyone's attention.

By the end of of the day she was exhausted. Mayer had reserved a private suite for her at the Chateau Marmont. By the time she arrived there, she appeared, as one observer recalled, "rather befuddled."[5] Hedy was asked to sign one of the hotel's registration cards. "She shifted the wilting roses from one arm to another and reached for a pen," wrote the hotel's historians. "She started to write, then paused, her expression blank. She turned to the man from M-G-M, as if awaiting a cue, but none came. She lowered the pen once more, fixing her eyes on the small card at her fingertips. Then slowly, in childlike block letters, she painstakingly wrote for the very first time: *H-E-D-Y*

L-A-M-A-R. Louis B. Mayer had given her a new name, but he hadn't taught her how to spell it."[6]

Hedy did know that her work was cut out for her. She realized that she had to learn and understand English as soon as possible. She also knew that she could never eradicate her past, and she did not know why she should she feel ashamed of it.

With her signature on the Metro-Goldwyn-Mayer contract, Hedy was joining the ranks of a very special world, a dream factory where "one entered it at the risk of forgetting what reality was," wrote one film historian.[7] The studio was a factory that proudly boasted having under contract "more stars than there are in heaven." In 1937 those luminaries included Norma Shearer, Clark Gable, Spencer Tracy, Luise Rainer, William Powell, Myrna Loy, Greta Garbo, Joan Crawford, Robert Taylor, James Stewart, and Mickey Rooney.

M-G-M was the richest and most efficient motion picture studio of them all. The studio planned at least fifty-two productions each year to give its movie theatres a new film every week. Metro's parent company, Loew's, Inc., owned hundreds of theatres nationwide, and the studio had instituted the method of mass booking its product a year in advance, thus guaranteeing the supply of films. To produce such an output of motion pictures, Metro had 140 different departments at its disposal on the lot, efficiently running like clockwork—a makeup department that would handle more than twelve hundred makeups an hour, costume designers, songwriters, screenwriters (with thousands of novels, plays, and short stories at their disposal), set designers, carpenters, directors, producers, musicians, contract players, electricians, medical staff, and so on.

Metro-Goldwyn-Mayer also had an immense photography system. Each one of their twenty-five major stars between 1937 and 1940 was extensively photographed for at least five thousand portraits every year. The top stars received an average of one portrait sitting a month. M-G-M sent more than one million photographs a year to magazines and newspapers, gleaned from over 200,000 selected negatives taken on the set, in sittings, and for fashion shoots. Prints from those negatives cost Metro approximately $100,000 (in 1930s dollars) each year. For every big film M-G-M produced during its heyday, over six hundred stills were taken during production.[8]

After a few days' stay at the Chateau Marmont, Hedy contacted Ilona Massey, who had just arrived in Hollywood from Europe. "I telephoned her and she invited me to share her apartment until I could get my bearings," Hedy told a magazine correspondent. "This I did gladly, and we spent many pleasant weeks together, trying to perfect our English, laughing at our mistakes, attending countless motion pictures, sometimes seeing a film repeatedly, that we might learn proper intonation and diction."[9] About Massey, Hedy once jokingly remarked, "She buried the English language after I murdered it."[10] Mayer had specifically insisted that they *not* accept radio work and be closely supervised at premieres and public functions.

Eventually the studio found Hedy a six-room hilltop bungalow at 1807 Benedict Canyon, complete with a tiny garden, which she filled with potted petunias and Snow White and the Seven Dwarfs figurines. The cottage cost $100 a month (deducted from her paycheck). She stocked the grounds with chickens, rabbits, and other small barnyard animals and acquired a Packard car. On the studio lot everyone Hedy came in contact with or spoke to "fed" her progress back to Mayer. She attended parties and also went to movies.

Max Reinhardt's son Gottfried had recently contracted with M-G-M as a story writer and was in Hollywood at this time. Because of Mayer's attention to Hedy, Massey, and Rose Stradner—all of whom young Reinhardt knew personally—he assumed they were "Mayer's property."[11] It is highly unlikely Hedy was aware that she was perceived as such.

"She was so lonesome that the publicity gals at MGM inveigled their brothers into stepping out with her now and then," wrote one film magazine writer about rumors surrounding Hedy.[12] The columnist Sheilah Graham wrote that one Saturday evening in the winter of 1937 she and her lover, F. Scott Fitzgerald, were at the Beverly Hills Brown Derby and noticed the new Metro contractee dining across the room by herself. " 'How typical of Hollywood,' said Scott, 'the most beautiful girl in the world alone on a Saturday night.' "[13]

Shortly after settling in to her new lodgings, Hedy began searching for art pieces to furnish it. Hedy once said that to her a good painting was like a friend. It supplied her with inspiration, comfort, and company. At a gallery in Laguna, she ran into Reginald Gardiner, whom she had seen on her first day on the Metro lot.

When Hedy met Gardiner, rumors of her loneliness stopped. The attractive thirty-four-year-old British comedian, who was currently working at Metro in *Everybody Sing* with young Judy Garland, was taken by Hedy's elegance and beauty, and she with his humor and wit. Reggie delighted and pleased Hedy. His manner was easy, his interest in her thoughts and opinions sincere. She was flattered, and in turn she relaxed in his company. Seldom was Hedy without the company of the affable Gardiner.

Hedy did attend some Hollywood soirées but would leave frustrated. "I hated the parties," she would later say. "I would be completely dizzy when I came home. When a person was on the fifth sentence, I would still be digesting the first one."[14] Hedy spent long evenings at home when not with Gardiner, and she often listened to "Whispering" Jack Smith on the radio to improve and understand her newly adopted language.

Hedy's persistent requests to the studio for film assignments fell on deaf ears. She kept in constant contact with Mayer's office, insisting on a script. Ida Koverman, Mayer's longtime secretary, eventually became a staunch ally. Mayer was at a loss, however, on how to present Hedy to American screen audiences. So the press went to work. There was mention in the *Los Angeles Times* that Paramount might borrow her from Metro for a remake of their 1929 film *The Letter*, which had starred Jeanne Eagels.

Hedy also acquired an agent to guide her career. His name was Arthur Lyons, and in 1937 he represented such noted celebrities as Jack Benny, Ray Milland, Judy Garland, Joan Crawford, and Cole Porter.

Finally, good news came from the studio—Hedy was going to be screen-tested. Reginald told her that they would not test an actress unless they were preparing to use her in a film. When the day arrived, Mayer himself came down to the set to manage the test of his latest discovery: "This is just routine. It is meaningless," he told her. "Relax. No one will ever look at the test. It is filed for the future to see how you change and how you improve."[15] Of course once the test was edited and ready to be viewed, Mayer called in all his executives and screened it. Hedy had sailed confidently through it (paired with Henry Daniell), her photographed image stunningly captured on celluloid. But, to her surprise, nothing happened.

Meanwhile, Hedy continued to collect her weekly $550 paycheck. She was assigned to study at M-G-M with an acting coach, Phyllis Loughton, wife of the writer-director George Seaton. Still, she fretted over not being cast in a film. Her contract held a six-month option, and the months were ticking by. She was worried, and with good cause. Her Metro option would be up in April 1938, and it was agonizing for Hedy that her fellow two "Neglected Imports" were now hard at work on the Metro lot—Miliza Korjus was in *The Great Waltz* (for which she would garner a Best Supporting Actress Oscar nomination the following year), and Ilona Massey was in *Rosalie*. Most of Mayer's other 1937 discoveries were also already cast in Metro films—Rose Stradner was starring opposite Edward G. Robinson and James Stewart in *The Last Gangster*, and Jacqueline Laurent was in *Judge Hardy's Children*, opposite Mickey Rooney.

Earlier that year, Louis B. Mayer had, interestingly, contracted Hedy's *Ecstasy* director, Gustav Machatý, who had helped direct, uncredited, portions of the studio's *The Good Earth* and *Conquest*. With hopes of reteaming himself with Hedy in a new film, *Within the Law*, Machatý viewed Hedy's English-speaking screen test and found it was lacking. Ruth Hussey was given the part.

Mayer then offered to loan Hedy to Paramount for *If I Were King*, but they passed. He even suggested her to Samuel Goldwyn for his action film *The Adventures of Marco Polo*, opposite Gary Cooper. Goldwyn too passed, and the role went to Sigrid Gurie.[16]

Metro then considered her to star opposite Melvyn Douglas in *Frou Frou*. Hedy was actually only used as a threat to the studio's Oscar-winning Viennese actress Luise Rainer, who eventually accepted the part in that picture, released as *The Toy Wife*. Meanwhile, *The New York Times* on February 10 announced that Metro was again attempting to match director Machatý with Hedy opposite Robert Montgomery in *One Minute Alone*, with a screenplay by Dalton Trumbo. That picture was never made.

The following year Mayer's son-in-law, David O. Selznick, showed interest in Hedy during his preparations for *Gone with the Wind*. In one of his numerous memos to his associate Harry Ginsberg, dated August 10, 1938, Selznick wrote, "I think we are going to pass up a fortune if we lose our chance to get Hedy Lamarr for a picture . . . I think the best and almost only opportunity that we have to use her is opposite [Ronald] Colman in 'Second Meeting.'"[17]

As frustrating as her prospects with the studio were, Hedy was finding solace with Reginald Gardiner, who had more or less moved in with her by this time. She did have a full-time secretary companion/cook/housekeeper/chauffeur—a Frenchwoman named Ericka Manthey. Reggie helped Hedy decorate her modest home and built for her a full-service black and red bar, though Hedy did not drink. Initialed *HL*, it was a most impressive piece. Gardiner was also an accomplished artist, and he gifted Hedy with several paintings that he had made of her.

Hedy often dressed in casual slacks or dirndls when home, and she would wear delicate sandals on her feet. She would accentuate her casual attire with an expensive jewel or bauble. She looked effortlessly immaculate, her hair beautifully coiffed, her nails painted in rich, lustrous reds. Hedy also insisted there be fresh flowers around her house at all times, and she loved American foods, especially ice cream.

As anxious as Hedy was about her career, her fears would end the third week in February 1938, when she and Reggie attended a party where the French actor Charles Boyer and the highly successful independent film producer Walter Wanger were among the guests. The thirty-seven-year-old Boyer was enjoying a tremendous success as a romantic leading man in American films at the time. And all the news around town was about his upcoming picture.

It was pouring rain that evening. Just the thought of another typical Hollywood party, with its ceaseless shoptalk, promised to be yet one more crashing bore for Hedy. She barely understood English, and at these events she would often withdraw and simply observe. At one point during that particular evening Hedy overheard the deep resonating voice of Boyer in conversation with Reggie. Behind her, Boyer had remarked in French that *"elle doit être une belle femme"* ("she must be a beautiful woman"), forcing Hedy to turn around and face him, smiling her most charming smile. After a few words of small talk in French, Boyer, obviously enchanted with her beauty, asked Hedy if she would consider "making a picture with me?"[18] Cautiously, she nodded yes. Taking her by the arm, he guided her across the room and introduced her to his producer, Walter Wanger.

Lamarr wrote:

Wanger stared at me. "Say a few sentences."

"I was happy at home painting in the rain," I improvised, "and now I am wondering whether it was wise to leave. I am very bad at small talk and my English is still very hard to handle."

Wanger nodded, "Yes, it could be. Could be. . . . You have the beauty, Miss Lamarr, and I would guess that if that pirate Louis B. Mayer put you under contract you can act."

"I am a good actress," I told him. . . . Later I heard the two men talking when they didn't know I was there. Wanger was saying, "She has small tits but a magnificent face."[19]

Walter Wanger, who had produced *Going Hollywood* in 1933, featuring Bing Crosby and Marion Davies, and *Queen Christina*, starring Greta Garbo, both for Metro, had recently independently financed *Vogues of 1938* in Technicolor for his paramour, the actress Joan Bennett. Wanger viewed the test footage of Hedy and liked the results. Subsequently, he asked Metro for her services. Wanger originally wanted her for the supporting female role in his film. But after viewing Lamarr's image on the screen, he was prepared to cast her in the female lead opposite Boyer.

Summoning Hedy into his office shortly after negotiations were made with Wanger and the production contracts signed, Mayer announced his plans to loan her to United Artists for the role of Gaby in *Algiers*, a remake of the highly successful French film *Pépé le Moko,* which had starred Jean Gabin the year before.

Ironically, the director-screenwriter Julien Duvivier, currently under a one-picture deal with Metro, had previously offered Boyer the starring role of the charming thief Pépé le Moko in the French production. Boyer, however, felt that the character was more thief than charming and declined the offer. Thus, the ruggedly attractive Jean Gabin stepped in, helping in no small part to make *Pépé le Moko* a huge success in Europe.

The story line of *Algiers* tells of a handsome French thief, Pepe le Moko (Charles Boyer), who hides deep inside the Casbah, the mysterious quarter of Algiers in northern Africa. The Casbah is a labyrinth of crowded streets, and Pepe is housed, fed, and protected from the local police by the residents and riffraff who dwell deep within its teeming neighborhood. A beautiful French tourist, Gaby (Hedy), is introduced to the infamous Pepe. They are attracted to each other, he for the lost beauty of Paris he sees in her, and she for the romance and adventure that her life is sadly missing. Eventually, a murder takes place, and Pepe must leave the Casbah. He hopes to pursue Gaby and begin life anew in Paris. Through deceptions and lies, the lovers do not meet a happy end.

By loaning Hedy to Wanger, Mayer effectively abandoned his policy of not lending his foreign stars to other studios. Three days after Hedy was signed by Wanger, Mayer lent Rose Stradner to R-K-O for *The Saint in New York*.

After attending the Paris premiere of *Pépé le Moko* in early 1937, the former silent-film director Erich von Stroheim cabled Mayer's executive Eddie Mannix to encourage Mayer to buy the rights to the film for an American remake *and* to sign the picture's director, Julien Duvivier, and its stars, Jean Gabin and

Mireille Balin. Negotiations were begun. Mayer acquired the rights to the film for one million French francs (about US$38,000 at the time).

On his 1937 European talent search, Mayer also signed to Metro contracts both Duvivier, to direct the remake, and actress Mireille Balin. However, the mogul did not get Jean Gabin. Gabin would later remark rather facetiously that, like a certain French wine he particularly liked, he too did not travel well. Duvivier was not assigned the remake of his film as promised. Instead, he directed *The Great Waltz*, which won three Oscar nominations the following year. Mireille Balin was forced to sit out her contract with Metro without ever landing an American film role. They both returned to Europe. (Duvivier subsequently directed *La fin du jour*—"to get *The Great Waltz* out of my system," he smugly confessed.)[20]

Louis B. Mayer had by then discovered the story line of *Pépé le Moko* was too risky to attempt to pass the Hays Office censorship. For one thing, the connubial relationship between Pepe and the gypsy, Ines, was "illicit." So Mayer sold it to Walter Wanger, who also bought the distribution rights of the French film to eliminate competition with his American remake.

Thus in one fell swoop Mayer bought a highly successful European film for a remake he would never produce; sold it (at a profit) to a competitor; held the film's director for a one-picture deal by assigning him another project; signed the leading lady of said film, whom he never put in front of a camera during the duration of her contract; and loaned out to his competitor an exotically ravishing beauty that he had no immediate plans to use. Was Mayer cautious or clever?

For her work in *Algiers*, Mayer continued to pay Hedy her weekly contracted salary of $550. In return for her services to Wanger, Mayer would receive $1,500 a week, giving the Metro chief a neat $950-a-week profit. He actually owed Wanger a loan-out. Just the year before, Metro had borrowed Boyer (for $125,000) from Wanger to portray Napoleon Bonaparte in *Conquest*, opposite Greta Garbo. The picture did not earn back its cost in this country but was a *huge* moneymaker overseas, eventually becoming one of the studio's highest-grossing pictures of the year. It was also one of the only films where the great Garbo "supported" her leading man. (In return for Boyer's services, Wanger had originally requested the use of another of Metro's biggest stars, Myrna Loy, to which Mayer responded by throwing Wanger off the lot.)[21]

Based on a novel by Detective Roger D'Ashelbe (a former commissioner of the Paris police), with an original screenplay by D'Ashelbe and Julien Duvivier, the script of *Pépé le Moko* was translated and rewritten by John Howard Lawson and James M. Cain, who was briefly hired to rearrange scenes and help soften the seamy relationships to appease the censors. The final film version of *Algiers* was not a shot-for-shot remake of *Pépé le Moko*, though the sets were re-created faithfully and the photography emulated the low-key lighting and soft focus of the original French version.

That January a translated, prepared script was readied. On February 17, Wanger's secretary, Rosemary Foley, sent two copies of the English version of the script and a cover letter to the production-code censorship office, the Breen Office, for approval. Changes were made, and on April 15 the Breen Office approved the ending of the film.

Dolores del Rio had turned down the role of Gaby early in discussions. Sylvia Sidney was offered the role of Ines. (Sidney was the former mistress of Paramount executive B. P. Schulberg, husband of Ad Schulberg.) The veteran actress knew very well that it would be Hedy's beauty that would steal the picture. She also believed the role of the native Ines was just "another tenement girl—this time in spangles."[22] Sidney, a major film star at this time, balked at supporting the glamorous newcomer Lamarr. Wanger promptly let Sidney go.

Wanger had initially tempted Sidney into accepting the supporting role of Ines by offering her the part of Cathy in his upcoming production of *Wuthering Heights*. After Wanger suggested adding humor to the script of *Wuthering Heights*, the writers, Ben Hecht and Charles MacArthur, begged Samuel Goldwyn to buy the property, and in the exchange Goldwyn lent Wanger Sigrid Gurie, who then assumed the role of Ines.

Production started on *Algiers* on April 1, 1938, at the Warner Bros. Studios on Dijon Street, in Los Angeles. It was shot completely within the confines of the soundstages. The fifty-year-old John Cromwell, who helmed such classic films as *Of Human Bondage* (R-K-O, 1934) and *The Prisoner of Zenda* (Selznick-International, 1937), was assigned to direct.

Cromwell held true to the original structure of the film. Boyer complained later that the director "would run a scene from the original and insist we do it exactly that way . . . terrible, a perfectly terrible way to work . . . an actor never likes to copy another's style, and here I was copying Jean Gabin, one of the best."[23] However, by copying the original, Cromwell saved time and money. It also inspired David Selznick to follow suit the following year when he introduced the Swedish actress Ingrid Bergman to American audiences in his scene-for-scene remake of *Intermezzo*.

"In the early rushes, Miss Lamarr didn't even suggest the Dream of All Time," wrote *Screenland* magazine's William Lynch Vallee. "But cameraman James Wong Howe calmed his frantic overlords by explaining that contrast was what he was aiming at with his gifted Bell & Howell."[24] By generating a mysterious shadow over Lamarr's hauntingly beautiful eyes, he was able to provide startling close-ups.

"When they finally came to the scene where the wallop was needed he gave it to them," wrote the magazine journalist Kyle Chrichton. "It's the scene where she leans back and a mysterious shadow plays over her eyes. At the opening night there was the sound of popping hearts all over the house when that part arrived."[25] Howe would receive the first of his ten Oscar nominations for Best Cinematography for *Algiers*.

Of all Lamarr's films, it is *Algiers* that would make the most impact on her early Hollywood career. Its importance in film history in connection with the actress is without question. Lamarr's keen intelligence guided her instinctively through the mechanics of making this film, though most of the time she was challenged by the language and those around her.

But she did find some technicalities daunting. "I was new to pictures and the mechanics of a scene confused me," she told *Movieland* magazine. "I must open a closet door while speaking a line, take down a coat, put on a hat, still carrying on a conversation, glancing at another character, then picking up something, crossing the room as I continued speaking my lines would end as I reached the door. It was very difficult."[26]

At the end of April, Hedy and Reginald attended a party that included Ira Gershwin, Joseph Schildkraut, Peter Lorre, Margo, Lillian Hellman and Dashiell Hammett, and the directors Fritz Lang, Ernst Lubitsch, William Wyler, William Dieterle, and Otto Preminger. The largely European crowd reminisced about their lives in old Vienna.

What had been happening to Jewish film artists in Europe since January 30, 1933, was harrowing. In Berlin Josef Goebbels, the Nazi propaganda minister, effectively took over the German film industry. The composer Frederick Hollander, actor Peter Lorre (who had been filming in Vienna), writer-director Billy Wilder, director Henry Koster, and Viennese composer Erich Wolfgang

Korngold fled to Paris. After the *Anschluss* of 1938, Korngold's wife, Luzi, commented, "We thought of ourselves as Viennese. Hitler made us Jewish."[27]

After Hitler took power, between 1933 and 1940 over eight hundred Jewish and non-Jewish film professionals would flee persecution in Europe. With the ever-increasing influx of talented European Jewish émigrés into the film colony, work became scarcer.

The screenwriter Salka Viertel, in Hollywood since 1928, would entertain the growing number of Europeans in Hollywood, even boarding refugees at her Santa Monica home during the exodus. And so did Marlene Dietrich, whose own sister and brother-in-law were Nazi party sympathizers. Los Angeles soon became known as the Weimar of the Pacific.

Many exiles would succeed in Hollywood. But some would not. They found that, in Hollywood, little, if anything, was even made of their being either Jewish or Christian. But everything German was unpopular. As Hedy had done, they stopped speaking German completely, watched English-language films, read newspapers, and studied comic strips, not only to learn and understand the language but also to assimilate into the American culture quickly.[28]

By the late 1930s the European exiles Lotte Lenya, Kurt Weill, Fritz Lang, Billy Wilder, Peter Lorre, Otto Preminger, Jean Gabin, Lilli Palmer, Jean Renoir, Robert Siodmak, and Hedy all lived within ten square miles of one another.

Meanwhile, progress on *Algiers* continued. Charles Boyer was debatably not as good an actor as Jean Gabin. He nonetheless exuded a charisma that complemented the classic beauty of his costar, Hedy. But he complained to his superiors throughout the filming that Hedy could not act and that she was delivering her lines phonetically. This was typical of Boyer. He was a complainer.

As Gaby, Hedy was merely a magnificently beautiful cipher whose sole purpose in the picture was to listen, enraptured at Pepe's mournful longings of his home, his lovely Paris. Hedy knew that her best ploy was to try *not* to act. She was confident of her natural beauty and the fact that the audience would read mystery and desire in her face. "I just did my job the best way I knew how under particular circumstances," she later wrote. "And I was always serious about work."[29]

Hedy enjoyed working with wardrobe on selecting the clothing her character would wear in the film. Her costumes were designed by the screen fashion designer Irene (Gibbons). Hedy suggested that she wanted to vary Gaby's wardrobe with an array of turbans, in particular a white one worn for a splash of sophistication. She was already recognized as an elegant clotheshorse long before landing in Hollywood, and so Hedy joined in with Irene to develop fashions that would set trends for years to come.

Filming on *Algiers* was completed in May 1938, and so enthusiastic over the rushes of the picture was Wanger that he advised that the film be quickly edited and prepared for release. But on June 14, the French government argued that they opposed its title, not wanting French Algiers to be associated with the criminal scenario of the picture. Said Wanger, "The majority of Americans do not know where Algiers is and this picture will be of the greatest value in publicizing the name and locale. I am sure those who see it will want to go to Algiers and look for the counterparts of Hedy La Marr [sic] and Charles Boyer."[30]

After finishing her scenes in *Algiers*, Hedy took an unpublicized break from Hollywood. In mid-June she briefly resided in Ensenada, Mexico, while awaiting her immigration visa at the United States consulate there; she was joined by the English actor Aubrey Mather and Jane Renouardt (the wife of Fernand Gravet, star of M-G-M's *The Great Waltz*, which was in production at the time). More than likely at this juncture Hedy acquired her divorce from Fritz. Later articles state that the divorce was finalized in Mexico, but the exact location and date are not known. Nevertheless, by the time Hedy returned to Los Angeles, she was legally recognized as a free woman. And now both her personal life and her career looked promising.

In Austria, where Hedy's mother remained, the political crisis came to a head. Chancellor Kurt Schuschnigg reneged on his earlier promises of allegiance to Hitler, stating that his country "would never voluntarily surrender its independence."[31] Enraged, Hitler massed his troops on the Austrian border.

On March 11, 1938, Schuschnigg was forced to resign, and Hitler's troops stormed into Austria, meeting with no resistance and signaling the start of the *Anschluss*, or the bloodless invasion of Austria, truly the first victim of World War II. Austria was declared a province of Germany on March 13. This was Hitler's first move beyond Germany's borders, as neighboring countries Czechoslovakia, France, the Soviet Union, and Great Britain stood by and watched. "Not realized by most of the observers, the *Anschluss* signaled the end of the Jewish community in Austria," wrote the social historian Gertrude Schneider. "Two-thirds of its number went into exile. One-third, however, fell victim to the 'Final Solution.'"[32] The persecution of the Jews was effectively begun in earnest.

Hedy's heart was broken when news arrived in America about Austria's annexation to the Third Reich. Hitler's prophesies were coming true. Hedy's beloved Vienna was lost. She wept bitterly when she heard the news.

On May 6, *The Washington Post* carried the story about Hedy's thirty-eight-year-old former husband, Fritz Mandl, who had been relieved of his resources and properties in Germany, valued at excess of $60 million. *The New York Times* picked the story up three days later, stating that the National Socialist State Treasury "has made claims against the Hirtenberg ammunition factory, for tax arrears of about $70,000, for the satisfaction of which it has seized mortgages that he gave to several firms. Since Herr Mandl is absent from the country, a receiver has been appointed."[33]

Fritz had for years been funneling large amounts of funds from the Hirtenberg industries into various Swiss bank accounts and firms, wisely revealing this from a safe distance. The German National Socialists could do nothing unless they created problems with neutral Switzerland. At Zurich's Dolder Hotel, they negotiated with Mandl to release his father, Alexander, whom they had held captive, giving Mandl in return a healthy monthly pension.

Mandl's association with his close friend, Prince Ernst Rüdiger von Starhemberg, had proved fatal to his industrial empire. After Starhemberg's downfall, "Herr Mandl considered his position unstable and began transferring his activities to South America sometime in early January, effectively severing his ties and interests with the Hirtenberg factory," continued *The New York Times* article.[34]

No longer considered an "honorary Aryan," Fritz attempted to build up a Portuguese ammunitions factory for the war ministry, but lobbyists did not want the Jewish Mandl, and the project was given to the Fritz Werner AG in Berlin. This was possibly the last example of the breakup of Mandl's political power. In Italy he had lost the approval of Mussolini. Before the *Anschluss*, Fritz tried to improve his relationship with the Third Reich by rallying his Hirtenberg workers to vote for annexation. And in possibly his most damning and desperate move, Fritz Mandl denied his heritage, stating he was actually the son of an extramarital affair his mother had consummated with a Catholic bishop.

After exiling himself to France in 1938, the following year Fritz traveled to Brazil before finally settling in Argentina in 1940, where he astonishingly attempted yet another communiqué with Nazi commander Hermann Göring's office to negotiate the possibility of a joint iron-production venture. Göring showed interest. But then Mandl realized that the transport of iron across the

Atlantic was too uncertain. He cut off all exchange of letters with the Third Reich.

There was no question why the American film studios, United Artists and M-G-M, were quick to silence press discussion of Hedy's ancestry and her marriage to the former munitions czar. The true status of her marriage to Mandl in early reports suggests that Hedy had divorced him sometime in 1937, possibly in Paris. She had not. Hedy had indeed petitioned for a divorce from Mandl, possibly in Europe at one point. She had also applied to the Holy Rota for an annulment in 1937, which was apparently granted, freeing both parties to marry again in the Catholic Church. By all social standards, in 1938 Hedy was a free woman.

Algiers was previewed at the Fox Wilshire Theatre on Thursday evening, June 23, 1938, to unanimously positive reviews. *Daily Variety* on June 24 reported, "Hedy Lamarr's quiet but provocative and intense projection allure in the love scenes with Boyer is a superb piece of acting, richly emotional and highly skillful."[35] *The Hollywood Reporter* was in accord: "She has more sex [appeal], more rare beauty, than the screen has seen for many days, and with it, definite artistry that will merit the best that MGM (her present studio) has to offer."[36]

The world premiere of *Algiers* took place on the evening of Wednesday, July 13, 1938, at the Four Star Theatre in Hollywood. Hedy took a snapshot of the marquee with her name in lights to send to her mother. The star-studded evening was the last gala event of the summer. Hedy arrived that evening wearing a chinchilla cape over a purple orchid-print evening gown, on the arm of Reggie Gardiner. She was photographed and interviewed in front of the theatre by the Mutual Network radio (reading a prepared speech). Beforehand she told Reggie, "If it goes badly, I will go home and cry. And you must permit it."[37] Throughout the screening, she held Reggie's hand, squeezing so tightly she left marks.

After the premiere, she and Reggie drove to his hideaway house high above Malibu Beach. "Now this is my moment. Tell me everything I want to hear," she told him. "Tell me about the picture, my performance, and my beauty. I do not want to be modest now at this wonderful moment. And talk slowly." Under the moonlight, they drank lavender sherry and made passionate love throughout the night and well into the next day. Hedy's dream of becoming an international film star had become a reality.[38]

The following day the columnist Elena Binckley wrote, "The new face is Hedy LaMarr [sic] who gives a fresh and exciting slant on continental glamour. She is young, vital, and sure to be a sensation. One doesn't really notice if she can act—she's that beautiful! But actress or not, she manages to steal every scene in which she appears, effortlessly and with hardly a flicker of winter-weight eyelashes."[39] Later, New York's Hollywood columnist, Ed Sullivan, would rave, "Most gorgeous item to come to the films in the past year is Hedy Lamarr. . . . Wait until you get a load of this lovely number in Wanger's 'Algiers.' . . . She'll create more talk than any performer in seasons. . . . TERRIFIC!"[40]

Hedy was ecstatic with her reception. "I'm so lucky, I'm afraid," she told a *Los Angeles Times* reporter at her Beverly Hills bungalow a few days later. Hedy said that Mayer had attended the premiere and that afterward everyone complimented her except him. She told the writer that she approached her boss and "asked him, 'Were you pleased with me?'" Mayer's reply was typical, "'Sure, you were great,' he replied." She went on to say, "my happiness was complete. Now, too, my salary will be better.'"[41]

After *Algiers* opened in New York at Radio City Music Hall on July 14, *Time* magazine hailed its leading lady: "But best of all is the smoldering, velvet-voiced, wanton-mouthed, *femme fatale* of *Algiers*, black-haired, hazel-eyed Viennese actress Hedy Kiesler (Hollywood name: Hedy Lamarr)."[42] *The New York World-Tribune* said, "Hedy Lamarr gives a vivid and forthright performance. But whether she is a good actress or not will make practically no difference at all once you get an eyeful of her brunette beauty. It's exactly what the doctor ordered in the way of glamour, and for once the west coast critics weren't exaggerating when they called her a knockout."[43]

Viewed today, the ninety-five-minute-long *Algiers* still has impact.[44] The picture is visually dark and moody, full of mystery and exoticism. The thirty-nine-year-old Boyer in this, his last, Walter Wanger outing is powerful. For his role as Pepe, he would earn the second of two consecutive Best Actor Oscar nominations, the first for *Conquest*. Dressed in black throughout most of the film, Boyer's personal vanity seems apparent, especially in his close-ups. But to his credit it is his underlying understanding of and compassion for his character that elevates his performance into classic proportions.

Hedy's image was carefully created in her first American picture. Richard Hanley of *The New York Times* noted in his 1976 obituary of James Wong

Howe that the cinematographer strove for visual realism in all his pictures, stating, "Perhaps his most widely acclaimed specialty was his ability to make actresses appear to be unusually beautiful."[45] It is with little surprise that the third-billed Hedy Lamarr, as the sultry *Parisienne* Gaby, comes across in the picture sympathetically, though she had only six key scenes.

From her first entrance, costumed in a clinging black dress and sporting a long-sleeved, white-caped bolero jacket, her magnificent face surrounded by lush, dark, shoulder-length hair parted in the middle and accentuated with dangling jeweled earrings adorned with large gem-encrusted bracelets on her wrists and a double-strand pearl necklace around her neck, Lamarr is all style and cool elegance. Throughout the film she is sensual, sexual, and mysterious. She wears a white hat with a net veil in one scene and two turbans in others to accentuate the perfect structure of her face. Through her wardrobe alone she made her screen time count. And female filmgoers paid attention.

To seasoned fans of the day, Hedy represented a certain glamour and sophistication that had been missing from the screen since the days of Gloria Swanson and Pola Negri. Wrote the film costume historian Margaret J. Bailey,

> After her first appearance on the screen in *Algiers*, drugstores experienced a run on hair dyes, and soon everybody, including starlets and established luminaries like Crawford and Joan Bennett, had changed their locks from blonde or brown to jet black. The Lamarr hairdo with the part in the middle and the tall Lamarr look became the new standard of glamour. Shock waves were felt not only in personal beauty, but also in the realm of fashion, in particularly, the hat. Somehow that three letter word seems inadequate when describing what Lamarr wore in her first films. Lamarr veils, snoods, turbans, and such swept the fashion world and millinery companies would overnight fill the hunger for the new cinema image. Not everyone could affect the Lamarr styles, but just about everyone tried. Turbans and snoods became the fashion for Forties headgear.[46]

Suddenly, Hedy's image was everywhere. Reams of Metro publicity were released. On July 17, Reggie and Hedy attended a formal dinner party with a polo motif at the new home of Joan Bennett, celebrating the birthday of Walter Wanger. On July 18, she and Reggie were spotted at the Trocadero. And on July

23, escorted again by Reggie, Hedy attended the opening of Max Reinhardt's production of *Faust* at the Pilgrimage Theater in the Hollywood Hills.

By the fall of 1938, the name of Hedy Lamarr was known by almost every English-language movie fan around the world. "Come wiz me to the Casbah" (a line *never* uttered in the film) became a national catchphrase. As a direct result of the immense sensation she created in *Algiers*, according to two of the most revered of American film historians, Richard Griffith and Arthur Mayer, Hedy Lamarr was unequivocally the "only big new star to emerge at the end of the Thirties."[47]

In turn, Hedy became the most coveted and valuable commodity in the Metro stable of stars. Mayer's gambit had paid off in spades. He must have been highly pleased with himself. He had had nothing to lose, and now he would reap the rewards. *Algiers* proved to be the sleeper hit of 1938, and in no small part because of Lamarr's presence.

Overnight, because of that very success, Hedy Lamarr became a bona fide film star. Now girded with a renewed self-confidence, she would challenge Louis B. Mayer on his turf and on her terms.

6

Stardom

ilmgoers, men and women alike, fell in love with Hedy Lamarr. "We have gone through an arid spate of years in which
women have become economically independent and as flat,
erotically, as the flat-soled shoes we wear," wrote a fan-magazine journalist in
late 1938. "We have forgotten perfumes and laces and spangled fans and
beauty spots and lovers who die for love for us and laces and jewels and veils
and those immortal lilies who toil not, nor do they spin. . . . LaMarr [sic] is
making us remember."[1] According to the film biographer Larry Swindell,
Hedy's impact on the film industry was major: "She was the sensation of the
age, and possibly of all time in films."[2]

Regarding new film roles, Hedy boldly advised the press, "I will not accept
any part unless it is good theater."[3] Arriving back onto the M-G-M lot that late
summer of 1938, she later wrote, "I returned in triumph. The praise gave me
great courage. Without calling or announcing myself I walked past Mr. Mayer's two secretaries and strolled into the great man's office. I was dressed beautifully and confidence flowed in my veins."[4] There were business executives in
Mayer's office, and L. B. quickly introduced Hedy to them.

Mayer prided himself in the knowledge that he had cleverly manipulated
the making of a new star. Now he needed just the right vehicle for Hedy to star
in to maintain her momentum. Mayer envisioned Hedy as the next Garbo or
Dietrich, realizing that the primary commodity he needed to exploit was her
stunning appearance.

According to Hedy, after she was greeted by Mayer, he made introductions and told her his plans for her future. "My dear Hedy," he said, "your next picture at MGM must be better than *Algiers*. If it isn't, we won't make it. Your next picture must be an artistic triumph, a picture that will make *Algiers* look small. We are now going to give you the biggest stars, the finest writers, and the most talented directors."[5]

The only property Mayer could find for Hedy was one called *A New York Cinderella*. To that end, Mayer had commissioned Charles MacArthur, one of the most expensive screenwriters in Hollywood, to develop the screenplay, and Josef von Sternberg, Marlene Dietrich's "Svengali," to direct and showcase Hedy in her first Metro picture. Mayer budgeted the project at approximately $700,000.

The studio also announced that Hedy would star in a remake of *Flesh and the Devil*, which had starred Greta Garbo and John Gilbert in 1927. Dutifully, Hedy sat through several of Garbo's films at studio screenings and firmly advised L. B. that she did not envision herself "doing another Garbo. . . . That is, keeping her incommunicado where the press is concerned, forbidding her to give out interviews, veiling her in mystery and secrecy and silence."[6]

Mayer felt that *A New York Cinderella* should be a major film for the studio. Taking unusual interest in this project, he called on thirty-nine-year-old Spencer Tracy to star opposite Metro's newest and brightest star. The recipient earlier that year of the Best Actor Academy Award for his role in *Captains Courageous*, Tracy would win the award again the following year for his just-completed performance in *Boys Town*, making him the first actor to win two consecutive Best Actor Oscars.

Spencer Bonaventure Tracy was born in Milwaukee, Wisconsin, and as an actor toured the country in the early 1920s, eventually landing on Broadway in 1922 in the play *R.U.R.* He followed that with five more New York productions during that decade, culminating with his biggest stage success, *The Last Mile*, in 1930, the year he went to Hollywood. Signing with Fox, Tracy starred in such pictures as *Goldie*, with Jean Harlow, and *A Man's Castle*, with Loretta Young (with whom he had a disastrous affair). He contracted with Metro after his 1935 success in *Whipsaw*, with Myrna Loy.

Tracy was Catholic and a deeply troubled man. He was an alcoholic, yet a consummate actor. Though he fought his demons, one of which was his inability to divorce his wife, the former actress Louise Treadwell, and another of which was his sense of guilt over the hearing disability since birth of his son John, Tracy was extremely difficult to deal with both on and off the set.

In late 1938, Tracy was hoping to follow *Boys Town* with his next project for Metro, *Northwest Passage,* a mammoth Technicolor film version of Kenneth Robert's historical novel. But it was not yet ready to roll. Instead, Mayer chose to lend Tracy to Twentieth Century–Fox for *Stanley and Livingston* in exchange for Tyrone Power, who would star opposite Norma Shearer in *Marie Antoinette*.[7] However, *Stanley and Livingston* would not be ready to shoot for several months, so for the moment Tracy was available.

When Mayer told the unpredictable Tracy he was to star in "my Hedy Lamarr picture," Tracy balked.[8] He had no desire to support his boss's latest find. But Mayer was persistent, finally convincing Tracy and everyone else that *A New York Cinderella* would be an important picture. (Although unbeknownst to Tracy, Mayer had advised MacArthur to expand Hedy's part and make it larger than Tracy's.)

Hedy was now called "The Dream Girl of 50,000,000 Men."[9] Regarding her sudden rise to popularity, she told *Movie Mirror*, "I cannot yet believe that my apparent good fortune is real . . . that the name, Hedy Lamarr, that I see blazoned over movie marquees is my own. Perhaps it is only a dream and I shall wake one day to find glory vanished and failure confronting me, after all."[10]

Pleased though she was with the buildup Mayer was now giving her, Hedy was distracted by the plight of her mother in Austria. She had been corresponding with Trude until the *Anschluss* in Austria earlier that year. She feared for her mother's safety in Vienna now that the Nazis occupied the country. And so, thanks to Hedy's elevated status at the studio, efforts were made to evacuate Trude to London, most probably through Mayer's connections.

In Hollywood, Hedy remained attached to Reggie Gardiner; he was her best beau. Wrote Gladys Hall for *Motion Picture* magazine, "Reginald Gardiner, the only man with whom Hedy has gone out with in Hollywood thus far, keeps her house filled with flowers, always her favorite tuberoses, of course. And he usually brings cartons of ice cream [her favorite flavors were coffee and pecan crunch] when he comes to the house."[11] On one occasion, Reggie entered Hedy's home, deposited the ice cream on the living room table, struck his chest dramatically, and cried out, "The things I do for Austria!"[12]

Hedy, remarkably, maintained close communication with Fritz, who was then residing in France. She corresponded frequently with him. "For he is still her friend," reported Gladys Hall. "He is a fine friend, she will tell you, a much better friend than when he was her husband and those two sharp-cutting spirits came into intimate contact. He writes her constantly. He asks her when they may meet again. . . . Recently I am told Mandl sent her a little matter of $10,000 . . . Mandl need not have made a single financial gesture toward Hedy since it was she who left him. But he is her friend and he did what he wanted to do."[13]

Hedy now purchased a new home in September, a small white ranch house with a stone gate located in Beverly Hills, where, Reggie told the press, he would install a swimming pool by Christmas. The pool never happened, but Reggie did successfully complete a club room, which he designed and decorated.

In an economic purge at Metro, Mayer let studio drama coach Phyllis Loughton go. Hedy had been studying with Loughton for the past six months, and yet no amount of pleading on Hedy's part could convince Mayer to bring Loughton back. Hedy's confidence was rattled.

A New York Cinderella began production on October 18. Immediately, there were problems. The temperamental director Josef von Sternberg hated the script. Within days of the start of shooting, Hedda Hopper wrote of Hedy, "She's already started 'New York Cinderella' with Spencer Tracy. Story might have been tailor-made for Joan Crawford, but, from what I hear, is totally unsuited to Hedy."[14]

The plot of *A New York Cinderella* follows the journey of Georgi Gragore (Hedy), who works in the fashion trade in New York. She has been jilted in South America by her married lover, Phil Mayberry (Walter Pidgeon). Returning on a steamer bound for the United States, the depressed Georgi prepares to jump over the side of the ship but is rescued by Dr. Karl Decker (Spencer Tracy), who has been doing medical research abroad. When the vessel docks in New York, Dr. Karl suggests to Georgi that she find some kind of serious work to do.

Georgi starts helping him in his clinic, which aids the poor. Karl falls in love with her and they marry, though she still loves Phil. Karl decides to quit his clinic in the tenement and become a society doctor to give his wife luxuries. Pleased with his decision, Georgi sees Phil secretly, even as she makes plans for a second honeymoon with her husband. Karl leaves her when he finds out she has seen Phil. At the clinic, a young intern bungles a diagnosis, and the patient dies. Dr. Karl, not caring what happens to himself, takes the blame but is exonerated. Karl realizes that his place is at his clinic helping the poor. Back at the clinic, he finds Georgi, who realizes that her place is beside her husband. Also cast in the film were Adrienne Ames, Laraine Johnson

(Day), Jack Carson, Louis Calhern, and the Ziegfeld comedienne Fanny Brice as Madame Marcesca.

Dorothy Ducas visited the film set and reported in the New York *Daily News* that Sternberg was very considerate of Hedy. Wrote the columnist, "You are aware you are watching something extra-special, for even von Sternberg says, 'Do you like that one, Hedy? You do? Well, print that.' The girl has the movie world in the palm of her hand." Ducas continued, "Walter Pidgeon says he never put his arm around an actress in any picture without hitting shoulder bones— until he encircled Hedy. Spencer Tracy . . . refused to do a sequence in which he socks Hedy on the jaw. 'She's too lovely to hit,' he declared."[15]

Unfortunately, the screenplay for *A New York Cinderella* might be the worst script ever penned by the high-priced MacArthur, husband of Helen Hayes. Perhaps he wrote it in spite. MacArthur had been a close friend of the late Irving Thalberg. It was alleged that Mayer's ruthlessness may have quickened the demise of the frail Thalberg. Whatever the reason for its shortcomings, MacArthur's screenplay was truly appalling.

Difficulties soon began to arise on the set. Tracy, it was said, was stunned that Hedy performed in some scenes as if she were reciting her lines by rote. However, the most damning problem with the filming was due to Sternberg, who clashed with Mayer.

This was the only time Mayer ever personally produced a motion picture for Metro-Goldwyn-Mayer, with the possible exception of 1924's *Ben-Hur* (Mayer went uncredited). According to the studio biographer Peter Hay, the picture "soon acquired the sobriquet 'Mayer's Folly.'"[16] Mayer was continuously taking charge of photography, direction, and anything pertaining to Hedy's performance. There were even a couple of times when Mayer attempted to tell Tracy how to play a scene. On November 5, after two weeks of fighting and screaming and of Mayer's constant presence on the set, Sternberg abruptly quit. Filming on *A New York Cinderella* came to a halt.

Mayer would always insist that he had fired the director. According to Swindell, "Mayer went through all of the footage and scrapped everything except a few well-photographed studies of Miss Lamarr. He said it was all lousy, and Sternberg would probably have agreed."[17]

"The boys at Metro take themselves very seriously, and more than a faint suspicion lurked in their minds that von Sternberg was making fun of them," wrote Douglas W. Churchill in *The New York Times*. "On one occasion he wore knitted ear-muffs, so he could not hear the actors. Nothing personal; it was just that all actors annoy him. Whenever a take was spoiled by a noise or the failure of a lamp, he would have the film printed to show the executives the difficulties under which he worked."[18]

On November 6, Frank Borzage, under contract with Metro since 1937, was assigned to direct on the picture. He didn't want the job. By the time he reported to the set of the newly retitled *I Take This Woman*, the overworked Borzage "looked like a whipped dog."[19]

In November, Hopper announced in her column that Hedy and Joan Crawford were both being considered by the Metro director Clarence Brown for "the naughtiest woman" role in the upcoming *The Women*.[20] Crawford got the part. And on November 10, 1938, the *Los Angeles Times* announced that Hedy would star with Robert Taylor in the studio's *Lady of the Tropics,* set to begin filming in February. It was to be directed by Josef von Sternberg, whose problems on the set of *I Take This Woman* had been with Mayer, not Lamarr. (*Lady of the Tropics* had been originally announced in January as a property for Isa Miranda.)

After a two-week delay, while Borzage labored with both the script and Mayer, on November 21 filming commenced again on the troubled picture. Things did not improve. As Borzage attempted to take control of the production, Mayer remained on the set, continually interfering. He would not let go.

In the early days of the second filming of *I Take This Woman* it was rumored that Hedy and Tracy had a clandestine affair, beginning in October 1938 and ending in February 1939. It is possible, but what is certain is that Tracy did not enjoy his assignment opposite Hedy. And her feelings about Tracy were never warm. "We were seated around a table one day, rehearsing our lines," Hedy told *The New York Times*. At the time she was still learning English. She continued: "When Spencer turned to me and said, briskly, 'Get me a taxi,' I obligingly arose and started to walk toward the sound-stage door, not realizing that it was the next line in the script. He was a great actor, but there were times when he made me cry. He was not precisely my favorite person."[21]

On the set things were falling apart. Hopper wrote that the actress Ina Claire, who had replaced Fanny Brice, "jittered" through a scene and that Hedy was heard to say, "I wouldn't worry. No matter how it goes it always comes out all right." To which the indomitable Claire replied, "Yeah? I always remember what my grandmother used to say to me—you can't make a silk purse out of a sow's ear."[22]

In December 1938, Hedy was named Glamour Girl of 1938 by the popular press. It did not help the progress of the picture. Now the screenwriter Ben Hecht was brought in to do an extensive reworking of the convoluted script of *I Take This Woman*. By the end of January he had completed a forty-nine-page revision. The filming continued to stumble along until time ran out.

At one point in the difficult production, Mayer again suggested to Tracy how to interpret a particular scene. Tracy stood back and stared silently at Mayer, who finally took the hint and began standing off to the sidelines.

Tracy was scheduled to begin *Stanley and Livingston* for Fox and would be officially off the picture on February 1. Despite recasting and innumerable daily rewrites, *I Take This Woman* came to a complete standstill on January 30, 1939, and was shelved. Some $900,000 had been spent on it, and the industry was abuzz with rumors. Hopper reported, "The town's been ringing with conflicting stories as to why Hedy Lamarr's picture 'I Take This Woman' was shelved after they'd spent nearly a million dollars. . . . Well, let's just stop right here. . . . There must have been something wrong with the script if they could replace Fannie Brice with Ina Claire. And there was!"[23]

Hopper was sympathetic to Hedy, noting in her column, "I think we ought to straighten out the little matter of 'I Take This Woman' once and for all. The impression seems to have gone out that Hedy Lamarr can't act. Also, that Spencer Tracy didn't want to play with her. Spencer would love to do another picture with her. But he never did like the story, or the part. Nor did Ina Claire, nor did Hedy."[24] Hopper followed up on her observations in a subsequent column: "And that, my friends, was 'The New York Cinderella,' renamed 'I Take This Woman' and was dreamed up, I actually believe, by Charlie MacArthur's diabolical sense of humor as a joke on Hollywood. Now his side-kick, Ben Hecht, is trying to make something out of the mess. But I give Metro credit for one thing—keeping it off the screen!"[25]

Martha Kerr, a journalist for *Modern Screen* magazine, reported on the film's shelving as well, but she was brutal on Hedy: "There are those who say that Hedy Lamarr just wasn't ready for the responsibility of carrying such an important role. There are those who say that the story was so bad that even Bette Davis could have done nothing with it. Others say that on the day of the shelving Hedy was presented with a diction teacher and dramatic coach."[26]

Hedy, who was by then earning $750 a week after her contract was renegotiated on October 4, 1938, was quickly mentioned for other film projects. On

March 21, *The New York Times* announced that Robert Taylor and Hedy would star in a romantic musical called *Guns and Fiddles,* which featured a screenplay by Walter Reisch and Samuel Hoffenstein and was set to begin shooting before *Lady of the Tropics*. But Mayer had both the script for *Lady of the Tropics* and Taylor ready and available. *Guns and Fiddles* was rescheduled to follow.[27]

Back on January 28, Read Kendall of the *Los Angeles Times* had broken the news that "[f]our nights in a row Hedy Lamarr and (film producer) Gene Markey were a twosome at Marcel La Maze's."[28] A week later, February 7, the couple was spotted back at the popular Hollywood nightspot.[29] According to Hopper, Markey had even dissuaded Hedy from her plans to vacation in Sun Valley.[30]

February proved a visible month for Hedy. Just as *I Take This Woman* was shelved and she awaited her next picture, she was named by Columbia University seniors as "the woman they would most like to be stranded on a desert island with."[31] (The following year the new 1940 class of seniors would vote Hedy their choice of Oomph Girl.) And, once more, Hedy was seen with Gene Markey, who escorted her to the annual Academy Awards party hosted by Darryl F. Zanuck and his wife.

Hopper was keeping score. "Some of our glamour boys could take lessons from Gene Markey," she wrote in her daily column. "One night he gives a birthday dinner to our beautiful Chatterbox, Barbara Trippet. The next two he's hand-holding with Hedy Lamarr, and in between acts as escort for his ex-wife Joan Bennett. I wonder if he remembers the time when he was Ina Claire's shadow? But he's a swell guy, and they're all lucky."[32] Apparently Hedy thought so too. On March 4, 1939, she eloped with Gene Markey.

Born Eugene Lawrence Markey Jr. in Jackson, Michigan, on December 11, 1895, Gene Markey graduated from Dartmouth College in 1918. During World War I, he was a lieutenant in the infantry at the Battle of Belleau Wood. After the war, he joined the naval reserve and became a moderately successful novelist, arriving in Hollywood in 1929 to become a screenwriter. He was once engaged to Ina Claire. Markey's screen-writing credits include *As You Desire Me* (M-G-M, 1932); *Baby Face* (Warner, 1933); and *On the Avenue* (Twentieth Century–Fox, 1937), which he also produced; as well as such other pictures as *Wee Willie Winkie* (1937), with Shirley Temple, and *Suez* (1938), with Tyrone Power, both for Twentieth Century–Fox.

Tall and not terribly handsome, Markey was nonetheless a great conversationalist, attractive in ways not necessarily physical. In 1932 he married twenty-two-year-old actress Joan Bennett. In February 1934, Joan gave birth to their daughter, Melinda. (Bennett's older daughter by her first marriage was adopted by Markey.) In 1937 Gene and Joan divorced. Bennett was then dating Walter Wanger, and they would eventually marry in January 1940.

It came as a surprise to Hollywood when Hedy not only separated from Reggie but then wed Markey after knowing him just over four weeks. In her book, Hedy explained that at a boring preview one evening with Reggie, she left the theatre and stepped outside, only to encounter Markey. After a brief conversation, the two walked to a nearby bar and talked. (Hedy wrote they married that night. But this is untrue. Actually Hedy had first met Markey at the wedding of actress Virginia Bruce to screenwriter J. Walter Ruben, on December 18, 1937.)

Hedy and Gene drove as far as San Diego on Friday night, March 3, and took separate rooms at the Grant Hotel. Besieged by reporters the next morning as they departed, the couple then motored down the coast to Mexicali, the capital of the northern state of Baja California in Mexico. "As Markey's sleek limousine, driven by his chauffeur Jose Fuentes, approached the governor's palace," noted *The Los Angeles Examiner*, "scores of Mexicans screamed excited greetings to the bridal pair."[33]

They wed the afternoon of March 4 at the governor's palace, the service performed by the Mexican civil magistrate Apolonio Nunez. The ceremony was witnessed by Gustavo Padres Jr., the Mexican counsel at Calexico, California (who translated for them); Raul Mateus of the El Centro Police Department; and Jimmy Alvarez, manager of a local tavern. After the ceremony, Nunez gave Hedy a restrained kiss. Markey wore a simple gray business suit, and Hedy, carrying a small purple bouquet, was dressed in a dark dress, accentuated by a woven four-strand, gold-chain necklace. (Though it was a hot day, Hedy draped a mink coat over her shoulders before and after the ceremony.)

"Following a Mexican custom," wrote the *Los Angeles Times*, "Miss Lamarr did not speak to her husband until they had left the building."[34] After a small party, the couple drove back to Los Angeles, where they had to report to their respective studios the following day. They planned to move into Hedy's new home by the end of the following week.

Hedy told the press, "We decided to get married, Mr. Markey and I, while we were having dinner last night. Mr. Markey has to start work on a picture at the studio where he is a producer. I go into a picture Monday. We thought we had better get married right away, for if we waited it might be weeks before we again had time."[35]

One should never underestimate the power the gossip columnists had over the Hollywood community. Hopper was furious that she had not been advised of the elopement in advance. Rival columnist Louella Parsons had gotten the jump on Hopper, reporting the marriage that day in *The Los Angeles Examiner*. In her March 7 column, Hopper rehashed Markey's jilted romance with Ina Claire and nastily threw in at the end of her summary, "I'm wondering if Mrs. Gene Markey will have the same glamour as Hedy Lamarr?"[36]

Markey's response was quick in coming. On Twentieth Century–Fox stationery, dated March 8, he wrote the angered columnist his abject apologies for not giving her the news sooner. "I had no idea that such an unpleasant situation would develop out of our hasty elopement . . . and both Hedy and I are deeply distressed about it," he wrote. Explaining to Hopper that his obligation had been to advise Parsons as soon as the couple made the decision to wed, but Hedy forgot to notify Hopper, though they had sent a wire to her as soon as they reached San Diego. Markey even included a copy of that wire with the letter.[37]

"If you are angry with me, I am sorry. I need not tell you how fond of you I have been, even before I came here to live. However, if you choose to be unfriendly about it, there is unfortunately nothing I can do. . . . Hedy likes you very much—and is extremely unhappy over the whole thing. All I can say is that she tried to keep her promise to you—and the fact that you didn't get the word in time should not be held against her. Knowing how fair you are, I am sure you will see the truth of this."[38] Unfortunately for Hedy, Hopper never forgot a slight.

Gene and Hedy moved into Hedy's home, located at 2727 Benedict Canyon Drive in Beverly Hills, the following week. "It's a little house on a hill," Hedy said at the time. "Gene and I will be happy forever."[39]

At the end of March, Gene's mother passed away. Wrote Parsons in *Photoplay*, "Mrs. Markey was devoted to Joan [Bennett] and her little granddaughter. When she lay so seriously ill, close to death, it was for Joan she asked. Hedy and Gene were there too, but Hedy waited outside in the hospital corridor while Joan and Gene were at his mother's bedside."[40]

Shouldering the loss of his mother with Hedy, Gene appreciatively gave his new wife a huge Great Dane, which they named Prince and later called Donner. Eventually their menagerie would include two Scotties named Jack and Jill and a cat they called Mitzi. The couple was very happy the first months of their marriage. They arose early every morning and would take breakfast in bed.

They had three servants, two Filipino men who had long been under Markey's employ and Hedy's maid, Blanche Williams, who had once worked for the late actress Jean Harlow. During the afternoons Gene and Hedy would drive miles to be with each other for lunch. More often than not, Gene, who it seemed was seldom at the studio, would lie around the pool tanning all day. Decorating their home by herself, Hedy appeared to be very much the hausfrau. She would take long walks with the dogs through the lilac-covered hills of Benedict Canyon. She longed for children, she told reporters, and the couple decided to build an addition, a "playroom" as they told the press, onto their one-storey white farmhouse.

Hedy was also a terrific bridge player. She liked to golf and enjoyed entertaining such friends as the film producer Arthur Hornblow Jr. and his actress-wife Myrna Loy. She understood a story line quickly and would often lend advice to Gene when he was writing. Hedy still preferred dressing in Austrian peasant outfits, usually dirndls, and she enjoyed her home. She was superstitious and would not get out of bed on Friday the thirteenth. She believed strongly in astrology, and she loved going to the movies.

Hedy still longed for her film career to take off. At the end of March the papers reported that director Gustav Machatý had just made an agreement with the French producer Julius Assenberg to make a sequel to *Ecstasy*. It would be called *The Girl of Ecstasy* and would be filmed in either Hollywood or England. (Nothing came of it.)[41]

Once again, Hedy's association with that film was in the news. Tired of the controversy, Hedy told the writer Kyle Chrichton about her participation in the Czech film: " 'I read the part and I liked it,' she says. 'There was nothing wrong in it to which anyone might object. But when the picture was filmed, those other scenes were in the part and I played them.' At this point she shrugs and makes a gesture of resignation with her hands. . . . 'Too much has been made of it.' "[42] Hedy hoped that the film would just go away.

Metro was anxious to get Hedy working as soon as possible, announcing that *I Take This Woman* would resume production as soon as her next project, *Lady of the Tropics,* now in early production, wrapped.

Eager to begin *Lady of the Tropics*, Hedy was advised her costumes would be fabricated by M-G-M's legendary studio fashion designer Adrian. One ensemble, it was reported, would be an elaborate twenty-five-pound gown made entirely of jewels, which Hedy was to wear during a temple scene in which she was required to dance. "It took three weeks to finish the affair with 25 girls working night and day," wrote Jimmie Fidler in his column. "More than 12,000 jewels, 10 bunches of gold spangles, each numbering 2,000 strands with each strand holding 1,000 spangles to total 2,000,000 and 300 yards of gold bullion went into the making of the costume."[43] This was obvious Hollywood ballyhoo, but it made the project sound very exciting.

Metro's stalwart, utilitarian director Jack Conway was set to helm *Lady of the Tropics,* with an original screenplay by Ben Hecht. It was pure soap opera, telling the story of Manon De Vargnes (Hedy), an exotic, biracial woman in Saigon, who meets playboy Bill Carey (Robert Taylor) when he leaves his wealthy fiancée, Dolly Harrison (Mary Taylor) in Saigon. Manon, engaged to a never-seen wealthy Asian nobleman, Kim Kahoon, dreams of going to Paris to escape her tortured existence. Meeting Bill, who falls in love with her, Manon at first believes that, if she marries him, he could be her ticket out of Saigon. However, she is denied a passport by the maniacal Pierre Delaroch (Joseph Schildkraut), who desires Manon for his own.

Manon falls in love with Bill and marries him. She manages to secure a job for Bill from Delaroch on his rubber plantation. Knowing that Delaroch is a politically powerful man, Manon pleads with him for a passport and promises to marry *him* to avoid his advances, though she is already wed. Bill is sent away to the plantation to work. He leaves it, though, when he learns that Delaroch and Manon have attended a performance of Puccini's opera *Manon Lescaut* together. At first Bill believes the incident is innocent, until Manon tells him that she has received her passport to leave Saigon. He then discovers Delaroch's cigar case in Manon's belongings and threatens to kill the man. Manon, however, succeeds in doing that herself. She then shoots herself. Bill rushes to her and begs her to leave Saigon with him before she is arrested. But he is too late, and Manon dies in his arms, knowing that he has forgiven her. Bleak stuff, for sure.

Cameras began to roll on *Lady of the Tropics* on April 24, and filming proceeded with no incidents. Meanwhile, the press continued to suggest more roles for Hedy. *The New York Times* reported on May 12 that Metro had purchased *They Call It Glamour,* by John Larkin and Jerry Horwin, in order to costar Hedy with Taylor once again. (Metro would make *These Glamour Girls* in June of 1939, film it very quickly, and release it in August 1939. It starred Lana Turner.)

On May 14 it was announced that Hedy was considered to star opposite Clark Gable in *Old New Orleans*, with an "all-star" dream cast that would include Jeanette MacDonald, Nelson Eddy, and Mae West. But *Old New Orleans* would not be made.

Hedy's leading man in *Lady of the Tropics* was twenty-six-year-old Nebraskan Robert Taylor, born Spangler Arlington Brugh. Spotted in 1932 by an M-G-M talent scout while he was performing in Pomona College stage productions, the handsome Taylor signed with M-G-M and quickly became a star after his appearances in Universal's *Magnificent Obsession* in late 1935, which he made on loan-out, and in Metro's *Camille* in 1937, opposite Garbo. His perfect looks and masculine voice often threatened to surpass the beauty and talents of his leading ladies. Highly bankable for the studio, Taylor's total 1938 film income would be $184,833, which made him a huge star at Metro.

Taylor was at the time romantically involved with Barbara Stanwyck. He was also a devoted "mother's boy," and marriage to Stanwyck had not been a priority until journalist Kirtley Baskette wrote in *Photoplay* in December 1938 an article entitled "Hollywood's Unmarried Husbands and Wives" about Hollywood's unwed couples, which included Taylor and Stanwyck, Constance Bennett and Gilbert Roland, and Clark Gable and Carole Lombard.

Mayer wisely halted production on *Lady of the Tropics* on Saturday, May 13, 1939, so that Taylor and Stanwyck could be married in a civil ceremony before a municipal judge in San Diego (though after midnight, making it the fourteenth, the thirteenth being unlucky). The next day Stanwyck reported back to Columbia Studios for *Golden Boy*, and Taylor went back to Metro to film the wedding scene in *Lady of the Tropics*.[44]

While working with Taylor, Hedy recalled, "One evening I came home and saw my spouse (Gene) staring at a magazine and turning it every which way, and chuckling. I asked him what the joke was, and he replied that he was trying to decide which of us, Bob or I, was more beautiful. . . . I also remember teaching Bob Taylor how to kiss more convincingly for the movie cameras, because his usual kiss seemed to me more like a school-boy smooch when photographed in close-up."[45]

Jack Conway seemed to be getting what he wanted from Hedy for *Lady of the Tropics*, and the film's producer, Sam Zimbalist, was pleased with her work. "Somewhat bowled over himself, [he] observed: 'Hedy is a nice girl, not at all vain, and a hard worker,'" reported *Time* magazine. "'She has a natural allure. . . . If anything, we've attempted to tone down the sex appeal she exudes. . . . All through the picture she is covered from head to toe."[46]

Filming concluded on June 26, and Hedy's first Metro picture was in the can. For *Lady of the Tropics*, Phyllis Loughton had been brought back by Mayer to guide Hedy. At the wrap party, Hedy gifted her drama coach, who was pregnant at the time, with an English convertible baby carriage, and the crew gave Hedy flowers.

Metro was planning on revamping *I Take This Woman*, but Tracy declared he would not participate. When he finished *Stanley and Livingston* for Fox in April, Hedy was filming *Lady of the Tropics*. So that May, Tracy and his family sailed to Europe for a vacation before his July commitment for *Northwest Passage*. While awaiting a decision to come down from Mayer regarding her next project, Hedy and Gene spent time on Markey's boat, the *Melinda*.

Hedy had posed for the Icelandic-American sculptress Lady Nina Saemundsson during the filming of *Lady of the Tropics*. The finished work, an ethereal bust of Lamarr, was exhibited at the Swedish-American Art Society of the West Show State Building of Exposition Park at the 1939–40 New York World's Fair. It won first prize.

Gossip and speculation were swirling about Hollywood as Hedy's Metro debut continued to be delayed. The magazine writer Adele Whitely Fletcher wrote, "Right now, unquestionably, Hedy needs all her attention. Hedy, at the moment, is something of a pain to Leo, the MGM lion . . . 'Algiers' put Hedy on a spot. And a spot is notably a bad place from which to work. This, in a measure, may explain why 'I Take This Woman,' the picture Hedy made following her skyrocketing fame, fell so far below expectations that you may never see it."[47]

Photoplay came to Hedy's defense with a brief editorial: "Apropos of Lamarr, it is very funny the way the other girls are going around and whispering that the reason Metro couldn't complete 'I Take This Woman' is that Hedy can't read lines . . . well, the public read Hedy's lines in 'Algiers' and was more than satisfied . . . so just leave the acting up to Bette Davis and give us some more of the same Hedy that 'Algiers' showed and we'll be quite content."[48]

The final analysis would rest in the hands of the fans. Jimmie Fidler, never a champion of Hedy's before, wrote in his column for the *Los Angeles Times* on June 8, "It would have been fairer to Hedy Lamarr, who, given time and experience should be a great star, had the studio soft-pedaled the advance sales campaign and given the audience time to form their own conclusions. As it is she must be miraculously good now or be blasted permanently by disillusioned fans."[49]

On August 4, 1939, *Lady of the Tropics* premiered in Hollywood to mixed reviews. Hedy appeared for the ceremony and was greeted by screaming fans. Gene Markey was not with his wife that evening but was recovering from a bout of pneumonia at the Good Samaritan Hospital. (Hedy would take a room at the hospital later that evening to be with him.)

Previewed by *The Hollywood-Citizen News*, the critic saved the kudos for Hedy: "Hedy Lamarr's beauty, and not Ben Hecht's screen play, is the picture's stock in trade. She is ravishingly gowned; she is a better actress than you thought she'd be, and she has animated moments in which she becomes the complete and captivating coquette."[50] And Louella Parsons raved, "Jack Conway . . . not only sees that Hedy Lamarr fulfills all her glamorous promise of 'Algiers' but he gives her a chance to act. Don't think for a moment that Hedy is just a beautiful statue. She does several scenes that call for real dramatic ability."

It was left to the *Film Bulletin* critic to ask, "This marks the long delayed reappearance of Hedy Lamarr on the screen. The point to be answered is 'Did MGM shelve the wrong picture?' It would be hard to imagine anything much worse than 'Lady of the Tropics.'"[51] Yet in March of 1940, *Lady of the Tropics* would be voted one of the best pictures of 1939 by *Photoplay* magazine.

"'Lady of the Tropics' turned hot and cold," Hedda Hopper wrote in her column. "Hot for Hedy Lamarr, cold for Bob Taylor, who was handed the worst part of his life. . . . The story is yardage of tripe. But from the moment Hedy made her Mona Lisa entrance to her final fadeout in her death scene, which incidentally she did darned well (and they're hard to do in case you haven't tried one), she made you realize that girls can dye until they're black in the head. But they'll never look like her."[52]

Later that morning, after she had read Hedda's column, Hedy sent the following wire to the columnist:

> *Dear Hedda*
> *I have been waiting a long time for a few kind words but this*
> *morning they were well worth the waiting for and made me*

*terribly happy. One of these days when you aren't too busy I
would like to talk with you. Love*

Hedy.[53]

Seen today, *Lady of the Tropics* is an interestingly bad film. Production values are lush, the direction plausible, the acting passable, but the screenplay is unbearably dreadful. Truly, perhaps the only reason for watching the picture today is to view the beauty of its two stars. Norbert Brodine, an uncredited photographer, was nominated for Best Black-and-White Cinematography for his work on *Lady of the Tropics*, securing the picture's only Oscar nod. Hedy is dressed by Adrian in flatteringly draped hats, in flowing capes, and (always) in long sleeves and skirts. In one scene she sports the mandatory white turban. The camera loves her face.

It was, however, the Viennese-born stage and screen actor Joseph Schildkraut who walks away with the acting honors in the film. Robert Taylor's posturing and bad acting far surpass the weaknesses of his role. (There is one redeeming moment for Taylor in the film when he becomes an actor: when Bill realizes that Manon has duped him.) The beauty of Lamarr is made evident in her every scene. Her lines are delivered sincerely, and her acting is controlled, though the script has a near total lack of believability.

Lady of the Tropics did make a bundle of money for the studio. It was just a bad film. Immediately, Metro started feeding the press new properties they were projecting for Hedy, including a dusting-off of *Pocahontas*, which was to be shot in Technicolor. Reports suggested the role of Captain John Smith for the British actor Robert Donat, who would win that year's Best Actor Oscar for Metro's *Goodbye, Mr. Chips*. Later, M-G-M would consider both Spencer Tracy and Clark Gable for the part.[54] Mercifully, Metro did not make the film.

In early August Metro announced that Hedy would star in the upcoming *Ziegfeld Girl*, along with Margaret Sullavan, Lana Turner, and possibly James Stewart. Jimmie Fidler wrote, "I can't understand this debate over Hedy Lamarr's future fate. It may be a fact that the lady can't act."[55]

Still not knowing how to handle this rare beauty, personally or professionally, Mayer determinedly resolved to give *I Take This Woman* another try. What both Metro and Hedy needed at the moment was a hit film.

7

Glamour

On October 2, 1939, Hedy dropped a bombshell on Metro-Goldwyn-Mayer. She was unhappy with the studio, considered herself underpaid and overworked, and blamed Mayer in particular with trying to sabotage her film career. Through her agent, Arthur Lyons, she gave official notice that she regarded her contract canceled because certain contractual agreements were not fulfilled by Metro. Mayer had raised Hedy's salary to $750 a week after her success in *Algiers*. According to court papers supplied by her attorney, Barry Brennan, in the renegotiated contract Hedy had been guaranteed forty weeks' work. But her contracted period with Metro had been exceeded by studio demands and stretched out without sufficient notice for layoff or for compensation. Adding insult to injury, Lyons had repeatedly attempted to adjust Hedy's salary with the studio, and now Metro was not answering his calls.

Under her revised contract, Hedy had asked Metro to arrange to pay her $575 a week over a fifty-two-week period, although she had only worked twenty-seven weeks at the studio. Claiming that since July the studio had failed to pay her in accordance with that stipulation, she considered her contract null and void and that the pact had been broken by M-G-M. Negotiations were under way, said her attorney, to place Hedy with another studio guaranteeing her $125,000 for her first two pictures and $150,000 for a third, plus 10 percent of distributor's gross. Metro, however, considered the contract ironclad.

On October 12 Jimmie Fidler announced, "Odes to the insidious power of publicity: Hedy Lamarr, with only one picture to her credit, demanding a pay increase of 1,000 per cent!"[1] More accurately, Fidler announced two weeks later that retakes for *I Take This Woman* would begin as soon as possible. An undisclosed agreement had been made. But still a rift had occurred, and Mayer realized that he had mishandled his first attempt to establish Hedy's film career in America.

Driven to regain the near $1 million already invested in *I Take This Woman*, by the end of the year Mayer assigned James Kevin McGuinness, a screenwriter, to revamp the damnable script and make the characters more sympathetic. By eliminating specific scenes, changing others, and again recasting the film, Mayer advised the press on September 22 that the picture would resume production and be completed within ten days. The next day, papers reported that Mayer had assigned the studio's most efficient and profitable director, W. S. "Woody" Van Dyke II, to replace Frank Borzage.

The actor Walter Pidgeon encountered shooting conflicts with his loan-out to Republic Pictures and the filming of *Dark Command*, and he was replaced by Kent Taylor. Ina Claire was replaced by Verree Teasdale, and Adrienne Ames was replaced by Mona Barrie.

When told of Mayer's plan to complete *I Take This Woman* (or, as it was more commonly called about town, *I Re-Take This Woman*), Tracy was not happy. With Borzage now off the picture, Tracy told intimates that he had no intention of going back to work on it.

While Metro juggled filming schedules around and Hollywood remained absorbed with issues of motion pictures and make-believe, there were some very serious events taking place in Europe. The *Anschluss* of Austria, which occurred on March 12, 1938, was followed by the horrors of *Kristallnacht* ("The Night of Broken Glass"), when the Nazis organized the destruction and ransacking of Jewish-owned businesses and synagogues in Germany on November 9–10 and over ninety Jews were murdered. On that one night between 25,000 and 30,000 Jews were arrested and deported to concentration camps. These two events marked the start of the planned elimination of the Jews by the Third Reich.

On September 1, 1939, Germany invaded Poland. Two days later England, France, New Zealand, and Australia declared war on Germany. Europe was at war.

Throughout the early part of the conflict, Hedy feared for her mother

Trude's safety. Their communication with each other was often censored and erratic. By 1940 Hedy's mother was living in London. Seeking Trude's papers and safe passage to America became one of Hedy's main concerns. Hedy was determined to have Trude come to America and live with her.

During her marriage to Gene, Hedy learned to cook breakfast for her husband occasionally, usually ham or bacon with eggs and fruit. A sign reading "Hedgerow Farm" hung over the outside gate of their home, which was decorated inside with plain white walls, accented with red carpets and fresh flowers. In the living room there was a fireplace with two comfortable chairs on either side of it. There were deep-cushioned divans, one for their Great Dane, and linen draperies. In one corner of the room was a large radio-phonograph. All the wooden furniture was white, including the beds and desks. The library had floor-to-ceiling paneled walls with built-in bookshelves to house books and Hedy's ever-growing collection of china miniatures. To the world, and to each other, the couple seemed to embody contentment and happiness.

With the restart date for *I Take This Woman* now set for December, Hedy began negotiations with the producer Luther Greene to appear in the New York stage production of *Salome*. Greene had opened offices in Hollywood at the Guaranty Building with James Struthers and had plans to produce the play that fall. Hedy walked out on her M-G-M contract on September 20, believing she was free to work on the stage.

Arthur Lyons announced Hedy's intentions to appear on stage in *Salome*. Said *The New York Times*, "A decision on the project is expected by tomorrow. It would be presented here under Luther Greene's management, with Otto Ludwig Preminger suggested as director."[2]

The following day, the *Los Angeles Times* announced Hedy had been forbidden to perform in *Salome* by Judge Emmet H. Wilson and given until November 20 to show just cause why she should be allowed to do the play. The injunction against the play's producer, Luther Greene, was filed by Nicholas Nayfack, treasurer of Metro-Goldwyn-Mayer's parent company, Loew's, Inc., after Hedy's agent, Lyons, had informed Nayfack of her intentions. According to Nayfack, Hedy's contract, renegotiated on October 4, specifically gave her exclusive services to Loew's, Inc. Mayer was beside himself dealing with his rebellious star's behavior.

Hedda Hopper told her readers that Hedy's projected role in the upcoming

Ziegfeld Girl for Metro was being recast with an unknown film newcomer, the ballerina Irina Baronova.[3] Fidler, also possibly to chastise Hedy, wrote in his column that Metro had acquired the services of Baronova, "a great dancer and even greater beauty," as a threat, stating, "[Hedy] should consider carefully before refusing Metro offers to kiss and make up. There is room on the lot for only one star of her type, and it would be unfortunate if she were to seek a reconciliation too late—after someone else had usurped her place."[4] Subterfuge and smoke—these quips were simply another of Mayer's ploys to keep Hedy in line. Baronova never made a picture for the studio.

It is surprising that Hedy remained in good standing with the studio, although she did not with Mayer. She did not directly communicate with her angered boss during this ordeal. She had lunch, however, with his executive secretary, Ida Koverman, several times. What might have transpired between the two women or between Hedy and other studio executives is unclear. But on November 24, Hedy settled with Metro for a new salary of $2,500 a week and gave up her plans to appear in the stage production of *Salome*. Hollywood was a company town after all.

It was reported in the *Los Angeles Times* the following day, "W. S. Van Dyke . . . will dust off 'I Take This Woman,' which was shelved through the brunette's defection, and will resume directing Miss Lamarr and Spencer Tracy."[5] Wrote the *Los Angeles Times*, "Absent for many weeks because of a contract dispute, Miss Lamarr yesterday agreed to 'unconditionally resume her contractual obligations,' the studio announced."[6] Everything now was hearts and roses, and Hedy reported back to work on the Metro lot that same day.

Privately Hedy was frustrated she could not become pregnant. This situation and her professional woes were putting a strain on the marriage. And so Gene and Hedy decided to adopt a child. The columnist Louella Parsons gleefully informed her readers: "On October 16, 1939, fat, chubby, little Jimmy, who is one of those adorable babies with personality, came to live with Hedy and Gene, and it seemed that their cup of happiness was overflowing."[7]

Gene and Hedy took out adoption papers on the baby, who, according to the City of Los Angeles birth records, was born at 10:30 A.M. the morning of March 6, 1939, in Los Angeles County. They named him James "Jamesie" Lamarr Markey. When Hedy brought the seven-month-old home to Hedgerow Farm, she chose the wallpaper for his nursery and saw that he was cared for by a nanny when she resumed work on *I Take This Woman*. Hedy's new cat, named Gertrud, would become his companion.

During her marriage to Gene Markey, Hedy rarely mentioned Jamesie in the press, and he was never photographed. Though Markey showed affection for the boy, he was decidedly more devoted to his daughter Melinda. Compounding the couple's difficulties, Gene was having problems at Twentieth Century–Fox, caused by the long and costly filming of *Lillian Russell*. That, plus Hedy's continual ordeal with Metro and *I Take This Woman*, created cracks in the marriage that were now beginning to show.

Filming began for the final time on the troubled but refreshed *I Take This Woman* on December 4, 1939. Known as "One Take Woody" because of his speedy filming techniques, W. S. Van Dyke (who had filled the studio's coffers with the quickly shot *The Thin Man* films) retained but two of Borzage's scenes (including a couple of Sternberg's close-ups of Hedy). According to Larry Swindell in his Tracy biography, everyone worked hard to put life into the production, "but the set never lost its gloom." When asked during filming how things were coming along, Van Dyke dryly commented, "This is the funniest thing in Hollywood since Jean Harlow died."[8]

There is no doubt that Mayer's persuasive tactics finally coerced Tracy into completing the highly financed production. He was still under contract with Metro after all. But Tracy hated completing the picture. When greeted in the M-G-M commissary during filming shortly before the holidays, someone asked, "What's new, Spencer?" Tracy was heard to reply, "Well, I'm not going to send Charles MacArthur a Christmas card. That's new."[9] Woody Van Dyke completed the film in just twenty-three days, wrapping it up just before Christmas 1939. *I Take This Woman* cost the studio $1.3 million all told.

During the monthlong filming, Mayer was rarely seen around the set. After the response to the screening, the release, and the reviews of *Lady of the Tropics*, he had become disenchanted with his "American Garbo." And Hedy continued to challenge his authority. Perhaps at this point of his professional life, he was becoming exhausted as well. In the coming years, Mayer would turn his energies more and more to the racetrack and horses and women, which diverted his attention away from M-G-M.

Soon after completion of *I Take This Woman*, Gene and Hedy traveled by train to New York. Though worried about the critical reception of *I Take This*

Woman, Hedy's spirits were high. She was pleased to have been recently called by the famed orchestra leader Guy Lombardo "Heaven with an accent."[10]

The Markeys were accompanying Gene's boss, Darryl F. Zanuck; his wife; and the United Artists chief, Joseph M. Schenck (brother of Nicholas Schenck, head of Loew's, Inc.) to New York for the East Coast premieres of Twentieth Century–Fox's two most recent films, *The Grapes of Wrath* and *The Blue Bird,* on which Gene was listed as associate producer. While there, Gene and Hedy took in the Algonquin's Supper Club one evening to cheer on Hedy's old friend from Vienna, chanteuse Greta Keller.

In New York on January 19, 1940, the Markeys attended the film premiere of the Technicolor fantasy *The Blue Bird.* A remake of the Maurice Maeterlinck classic children's novel, *The Blue Bird* starred eleven-year-old movie moppet Shirley Temple. The biggest film star in the motion picture industry during the decade of the 1930s, Temple was under contract with Twentieth Century–Fox, providing hit after hit. But time was her enemy, and unfortunately little Shirley was growing up. Cute just was not working anymore. Upon its release, *The Blue Bird* laid a resounding egg.

When *I Take This Woman* was released on January 26, 1940, it too tanked at the box office. Billed as a romantic comedy, the ninety-six-minute-long picture opened to decidedly negative reviews. Too much studio hype and excessively confusing media attention made for less than objective criticism. "The studio's worries were, I think, largely needless," wrote Philip K. Scheuer for the *Los Angeles Times*; "[it] proved to be neither a very bad picture, as feared, nor a very good one . . . Tracy couldn't fall down if he tried and Miss Lamarr is there beside him to help make the inexplicable believable—or almost."[11] Richard Griffith reported in the *Los Angeles Times*, "'I Take This Woman' is a comparative flop at Radio City Music Hall. . . . The film leaves Hedy Lamarr in the same doubtful position she has occupied for more than a year."[12]

I Take This Woman promised a sterling cast, fine performances, gorgeous photography and production values, superb technicians, an excellent director, beautiful costumes, and lovely musical score.[13] But without a decent script it fell apart. The story goes nowhere, and the film is simply boring—one starts counting the several times Lamarr's hairstyle is short when she enters a room but has grown past her shoulders before she sits down. It becomes a game to figure out in what year each scene was made.

Sadly Mayer and the studio did not learn from their own mistakes. Hedy was typecast by Metro in subsequent films. The social historian Diane Negra commented, "*I Take This Woman* established a pattern which would continue through much of Lamarr's career in which she is placed as an exotic reward for a virtuous, white American male."[14]

I Take This Woman ranks as one of the worst films M-G-M ever produced during the "Golden Era" of Hollywood. Shirking his own responsibility for its failure, Mayer raged, "I told them they were making a lousy picture, but they wouldn't listen to me!" So much smoke. Spencer Tracy was "on to the old man" after *I Take This Woman* and never listened to Mayer again. "After that the two men, who had seldom been together before, hardly met at all, and almost never spoke," wrote Larry Swindell.[15]

The picture's failure sealed Mayer's loss of faith in Hedy. "In time Hedy proved that she had something that was marketable, and possibly a little talent, but she would make it on her own, with little help from L. B. Mayer,"[16] wrote Swindell.

In his column in March, Edwin Schallert wrote that *Box Office Digest* had just published their list of top moneymaking films for 1939–40, which rated over 100 percent in their return. These included *Gone with the Wind* (M-G-M), *Pinocchio* (Disney), *His Girl Friday* (Columbia), *Little Old New York* (Fox), and, most surprisingly, *I Take This Woman*.[17] *I Take This Woman* eventually made back its investment for M-G-M—just not fast enough for Mayer. Hedy's marquee value was still important enough to have Darryl F. Zanuck over at Twentieth Century–Fox consider her for the role of the temptress opposite Henry Fonda in *Chad Hanna*. (The part was given to Dorothy Lamour instead.)

The acerbic Fidler reported in his column on February 28 that while Metro was attempting to recoup their $1 million spent on *I Take This Woman*, they might better try and protect the $10 million spent on Hedy Lamarr, an investment that was now in serious jeopardy of having been wasted. "Given the right vehicles Hedy could be one of the greatest box-office stars in picture history," advised Fidler. "Given a few more duds like 'I Take This Woman,' and she will be box-office poison in spite of all the glamour-girl publicity Hollywood genius can concoct."[18]

At the same time, Hedy's first husband, Fritz Mandl, again made news in the United States. He had been in New York on the café-society circuit with his new wife, the blond, Viennese-born, twenty-nine-year-old Baroness Herta Schneider, a former actress whom Fritz had married before a Baptist minister in Elkton, Maryland, on November 24, 1939. His purpose in coming to America was to purchase machinery for his South American steelworks.

Interviewed and photographed at the nightclub Monte Carlo in Manhattan on New Year's Eve, Mandl was questioned about *Ecstasy*. He boldly told reporters, "I did not see the picture. I never spent money buying prints. It was a ridiculous publicity stunt to say I did." A buzz of whispers was heard throughout the club that evening, as Mandl coolly paid his check with a thousand-dollar bill. Before leaving, he taunted the press, asserting, "We may go to Hollywood, and I hope to introduce Hedy to Mrs. Mandl. We may even buy a house in the movie colony."[19]

Later that week, Fritz "lunched with a friend at the swank Colony Club and tossed a $100 bill on the waiter's tray," wrote one observer. "He talked of costly improvements recently made at his villa at Cap d'Antibe, of an elaborate hacienda at Buenos Aires, of his desire to buy a Hollywood mansion." Mandl would remain in New York until late April.[20]

Hedy now fought for her next film role. Her memoirs state that she demanded from Louis B. Mayer a supporting role in the upcoming *Boom Town* (based on the James Edward Grant story "A Lady Comes to Burkburnett"), which was announced to commence shooting with Clark Gable and Spencer Tracy. It is highly improbable that Hedy was in a position to "demand" anything from Mayer at this juncture of her problematic career. He was focusing his attention on Greer Garson. Instead, Mayer suggested to Hedy the possibility of loaning her to Warner Bros. for an Errol Flynn picture. She countered immediately with the request to test for the supporting role of Karen Vanmeer in *Boom Town*.

Mayer agreed to let Hedy test for the second female lead, since he knew that Gable and Tracy would carry the picture. (Young Rita Hayworth was brought over from Twentieth Century–Fox and also tested for the part, but she lacked the necessary acting ability. Also, according to Hedy's book, Gable went to bat for her. This was possibly true.) On February 9, it was announced that the two female leads in *Boom Town* would be Claudette Colbert and Hedy Lamarr. What Mayer had not expected was that Hedy would steal the film away from Colbert.

Boom Town's star, Clark Gable, was one of Metro-Goldwyn-Mayer's biggest moneymakers, even before his 1939 performance in *Gone with the Wind*. Born William Clark Gable on February 1, 1901, in Cadiz, Ohio, Gable's real rough-and-tumble life included working the oil fields in Oklahoma during the 1920s.

He was married twice to much older women who helped him advance in the acting profession. In 1931 Gable came to the attention of Metro after his Los Angeles stage performance in *The Last Mile* as Killer John Mears, the role Spencer Tracy had originated on Broadway. Winning the 1934 Best Actor Oscar while on loan to Columbia for the Frank Capra comedy classic *It Happened One Night* opposite Claudette Colbert (she won the Best Actress Oscar for the same film), and after the success of *Gone with the Wind*, Gable was at the pinnacle of his career, and was crowned "the King of Hollywood" by the New York columnist Ed Sullivan.[21] A solid megastar in 1940, Gable held clout with the studio.

Filming of *Boom Town* began at M-G-M on March 9, 1940. From the start it was apparent the production was going to be a hit. *Boom Town* was undeniably a "man's picture," with a long, action-filled screenplay by John Lee Mahin. Gable and Tracy had previously costarred together in Metro's *San Francisco* (1936) and *Test Pilot* (1938). Colbert was loaned out by Paramount to play in what was the second of her only three films for M-G-M.

The plot of *Boom Town* concerns the adventures of two oil barons, Big John McMasters (Gable) and Square John Sand (Tracy), wildcatting in Burkburnett, Texas, in 1918. On the day McMasters's first well comes in, Elizabeth "Betsy" Bartlett (Colbert) arrives in town. She is planning to marry her boyfriend, Square John, but meets his partner, Big John, and falls instantly in love with him. Though it hurts Square John, Betsy marries Big John, who soon, it seems to some, treats Betsy poorly. Angered at this, Square John and Big John flip a coin for the ownership of the well, and Square John wins. Later, Big John hits it big in the Oklahoma oil fields and becomes a major power in the oil industry.

Big John partners with the disreputable Harry Compton (Lionel Atwill) and his companion Karen Vanmeer (Hedy) and agrees to develop and expand his investments back East. He soon has an affair with Karen. Square John sees how Big John neglects Betsy and their young son Jack (Casey Johnson), and he teams with Compton in bringing Big John's unscrupulous dealings to the attention of the United States government. At the trial, Square John then comes to Big John's defense, realizing what Big John's attempts for the oil industry were truly all about, and Big John is vindicated. Big John returns to Betsy and, with his old partner, Square John, begins wildcatting again. Man's stuff.

In *Boom Town* Hedy displayed a different side of the Lamarr mystique. This time her character was surprisingly sympathetic. For her role, Hedy wore modern outfits that were again created by Adrian. One particularly stunning costume was a tailored black velvet lounging pajama with white satin jacket and matching trim. Her appearance in the film was noticed.

For the picture, Hedy's luxurious long tresses were shortened into a fashionable, and even more flattering, hairstyle. Hedy herself had taken the initiative. "For four years I wore my hair down to my shoulders," she told a magazine writer shortly before filming started. "The other night, I got tired of it. I took Gene's paper scissors and cut it, and curled up the ends . . . Gene says I look about eighteen. . . . For better or worse, it will have to stay this way now for *Boom Town*. I think it will fit the character."[22]

The filming went smoothly under the competent hands of director Jack Conway. Budgeted at $2 million, a complete town representing Burkburnett, Texas, including fifty buildings, a railroad yard, and rain-soaked streets of mud, was constructed on the Culver City back lot. Location shots were filmed in Bakersfield and Taft, California.[23]

Gable was guaranteed $7,500 a week and top billing. But Tracy found it demeaning for him to costar again with the virile "movie star" Clark Gable. To Tracy this was just another Gable film.

Hedy did not enjoy working with Tracy. She found him aloof. Fireworks between Hedy and Colbert were predicted by the press, but the two women were nothing but cordial to each other. However, Mrs. Clark Gable, the beautiful actress Carole Lombard, came to the set the day of the filming of Hedy's big love scene with Gable. Dressed to the nines—looking "like four million bucks," said the crew—Lombard need not have worried. Wrote one Gable biographer, "Carole knew the type of woman who appealed to Clark, and Hedy wasn't it."[24]

During the production, Gable and Tracy had a fight scene that was rehearsed on the set before it was filmed. Gable was sparring with Tracy's stand-in, and the overzealous fellow landed a punch to the star's million-dollar face, breaking the upper plate of Gable's false teeth and busting his lip open in the process. Days later, wearing temporary dentures while his new ones were being made, Gable returned to the set to film a kissing scene with Colbert. She kissed him so hard his temporary teeth broke, and the actor was removed to the dentist for repairs. The film was shut down until Gable secured new dentures and healed, adding another $50,000 to the cost of the production.

Marital problems between Gene and Hedy continued at Hedgerow. On March 12 Fidler advised his readers, "I have received an inside tip that all is not well in the Hedy Lamarr–Gene Markey household. One source tells me they haven't been on the best of terms for days. From another source close to Miss Lamarr comes information that Hedy has definitely said she will leave her husband." To which Markey fired back a heated wire to Fidler:

> *Fidler, your report that Miss Lamarr and I are separating is absolutely unfounded. Why don't you check with me when you want the truth concerning Hedy and myself? Telephone me when you return to Hollywood as I want to talk this over with you personally.*[25]

Louella O. Parsons, always one to take the high road when sources did not feed her the dirt first, wrote in her March 19 column, "Take it from me, the most ridiculous rumor in Hollywood is the gossip that Hedy Lamarr and Gene Markey are planning a divorce. I do not know any people more in love and happier. Hedy even offered to give up her screen career to look after Gene and their recently adopted baby."[26]

With positive reaction to the *Boom Town* rushes, Mayer finally saw that Hedy could deliver a solid acting performance. But what to cast her in next presented a problem. The press continually announced projects for Hedy. In April Hopper wrote that Hedy was certain to go over to R-K-O Radio for the film version of the recent Broadway hit *Too Many Girls* (the part went to Lucille Ball). The long-awaited lensing of Metro's *Guns and Fiddles*, now set to star Robert Taylor and Hedy with Robert Young and Miliza Korjus, was once again announced to begin, this time in early June.

But on May 28, 1940, the picture was halted indefinitely when Korjus was involved in a serious automobile accident, crushing one of her legs so severely that doctors considered amputation. (The leg was saved, and she eventually recovered.) But *Guns and Fiddles* had been planned as a musical, and without the soprano there was no film. The film was never made.

Fidler wrote in his column that April, "How come Metro finds such difficulty in fitting Hedy Lamarr with a story? The biography of Lola Montez has never been screened."[27] And no doubt Hedy read his column, for shortly afterward she mentioned Lola Montez in an interview. "I would love to do the story of Lola Montez, the dancer of the early California days, during the gold rush," she told the journalist James Reid. "I used to dance, in Europe. . . . But, I am not *planning* to do Lola Montez. I am superstitious about planning."[28] And

Hedy herself expressed interest, along with Joan Crawford, Greer Garson, and Ilona Massey, in portraying Countess Ruby in Metro's upcoming film *Escape*. Norma Shearer would take the part.

Metro finally announced that Hedy's next film vehicle, *Come Live with Me*, with James Stewart, was set to begin shooting at the end of the summer. On April 26 it was announced again that Hedy would then star in *Ziegfeld Girl* with Eleanor Powell, Lana Turner, Walter Pidgeon, Frank Morgan, and George Murphy following the completion of *Come Live with Me*. The cameras were to begin rolling on *Ziegfeld Girl* on June 15.

Hedy and Gene had reached a stalemate in their marriage. On July 6, 1940, Hedy consulted the attorney Lester W. Roth. The following day the *Los Angeles Times* announced that Gene and Hedy had separated after sixteen months of marriage, and that he had moved out of their house two days earlier and was staying at his father's home in Hollywood. Reported the paper, " 'Yes,' [Hedy] said yesterday on the lot at Metro-Goldwyn-Mayer Studio, 'it is true we have separated. For many months we have been incompatible and have considered this step. I feel it is best for both of us."[29]

Sidney Skolsky commented in the *New York Post*, "She wants security, and she wants fame, and she is ambitious. She imagines she is a much better actress than she really is, and if you start to tell her otherwise you're in for a family quarrel. She wants freedom. And she's not accustomed to the Hollywood social way of life. . . . Don't get the impression that she is a party girl. She isn't. Many an evening she and Markey would go for a long stroll through Beverly Hills and then drop in on their friends, Arthur Hornblow Jr. and Myrna Loy."[30]

Hedy spoke with a magazine writer who wrote, "Gene was all the things she desired in a man, witty, urbane, a celebrity in his own right, intelligent, a little unhappy. She was madly in love with him and misunderstood him completely, for she thought that the things he most wanted were a home and children. She did not know until after the marriage that he was really married to his job and that her attraction for him was only her beauty and glamour, both of which bore her."[31]

Hedy was always fodder for the gossip gristmills. Gene may have been threatening to take Jamesie away from Hedy, since her concerns now focused on keeping the boy. She worried that the courts required a period of time, sometimes years, before granting custody to a single parent after divorce. In the interim, before a ruling could be handed down, Hedy was allowed to keep the boy in her custody.

Louella Parsons adapted a motherly attitude about the impending divorce and custody issue, reporting,

"Why didn't you wait, Hedy?" I asked. "It was such a short time more and you could have saved yourself so much of the heartache."

"I couldn't," she said. "We tried, Gene and I. I feel nothing but the deepest fondness for him. I respect him so much. But it was the only honest thing for both of us to admit that we were unable to make a go of it. I will just have to fight it out this way—the honest way. Surely The Children's Society will understand. They must realize that this thing that happened to Gene and me cannot in any way affect the way we feel about the baby. I'm still as good a mother to him as I ever was. Better perhaps, because the fight for his custody made me realize deeper than ever how much he means to me."[32]

At the end of July, Fidler wrote in his column, "Hedy Lamarr's statement she'll be able to keep the baby she and Gene Markey intended to adopt before they separated is premature; the home that provided the child may fight the move."[33]

By the end of the summer, Hedy was living quietly with Jamesie at Hedgerow Farm. As divorce proceedings approached, she was faced with mixed emotions. Her career after two dreadful pictures for Metro was about to take an upswing as positive buzz about *Boom Town* grew. Mayer was again searching for strong picture scripts for her, one a possible reteaming with Gable. Hedy's foothold in the movies was more assured than ever.

Hedy focused on preparing for her future. Recently she had read in *Esquire* magazine about glandular analysis (endocrinology), which held a particular fascination for her. She could have also possibly read the "Chatterbox" column in the June 17 *Los Angeles Times*, which mentioned, "George Antheil—who is not only one of the six leading American composers, but also a gland specialist of note—leaves Wednesday for Palo Alto where he will take over a music course for the summer."[34]

Two of Hedy's closest friends were the designer Adrian (Greenberg) and his actress-wife Janet Gaynor (the very first Best Actress Oscar–winner in 1928). Adrian had been one of the 1930s' most influential couture designers in films. Under contract with Metro, his frilly, feminine fashions in contemporary films were coveted among the female filmgoers of the day. His extravagant designs in such period pictures as *The Great Ziegfeld,* where he literally out-Ziegfelded Ziegfeld's renowned designers, and *Marie Antoinette* were remarkable.

Adrian had designed costumes for Hedy already in 1939 and 1940. But in 1941 Greta Garbo, for whom he had created beautiful and flattering outfits in films throughout the preceding decade, complained to Mayer about his sketches for her latest, and last, film, the disastrous *Two-Faced Woman.* With that affront, Adrian would abruptly leave the studio.

A fateful dinner was arranged by Adrian and Gaynor late that summer of 1940, shortly before the release of *Boom Town,* to introduce the beautiful actress Hedy Lamarr to the eccentric George Antheil. Their meeting would take place during a tremendously turbulent period in world history. The importance of that meeting would produce long-lasting results.

8

Discovery

*L*ouis B. Mayer, in his own professional and sometimes crude manner, had once suggested to Hedy that she do something about the size of her less-than-substantial breasts. In fact, Hedy's breast size was actually fine, and seldom in film did she require any type of "padding." Hedy's height was five feet seven, and her measurements at the time were 33B-23-35. Still, Mayer's comment must have hurt. Certainly, it made Hedy consider doing something about it.

In 1936 *Esquire* magazine had run a series of three articles ("Glands on a Hobby Horse," "Glandbook for the Questing Male," and "The Glandbook in Practical Use"), written, strangely enough, by a music composer, George Antheil. In 1940 Antheil was composing musical scores for films, notably at Paramount for Cecil B. DeMille's *The Plainsman* and *The Buccaneer.* Also at the time he was scoring *Angels over Broadway* for Twentieth Century–Fox. As an avocation Antheil had taken up criminal endocrinology.

In 1937 he wrote a book entitled *Every Man His Own Detective: A Study of Glandular Criminology,* more or less a thesis on how one's glandular development might influence one's criminal tendencies. Though this might sound ridiculous in theory, it nevertheless was popular fodder of the day. Hedy was most interested in speaking with the man who wrote that book.

George Carl Johann Antheil was born on June 8, 1900, in Trenton, New Jersey. As a youth he studied music in Philadelphia. A former child piano prodigy, at the age of twenty-one Antheil sailed for Europe to give concerts.

His notorious recitals usually ended with "ultramodern" works that often led to riots. His music was unapologetically avant-garde. Such original pieces as *Mechanisms, Sonata Sauvage,* and *Death of the Machines* were radical departures from the norm and extremely advanced for the era.

Settling in Paris, Antheil moved into a small apartment owned by Sylvia Beach in the Latin Quarter, above the famed Shakespeare and Company bookstore, with his fiancée, Boski Markus, the niece of Viennese writer Arthur Schnitzler. Befriending such members of the popular Parisian literati as Jean Cocteau, Ernest Hemingway, James Joyce, and Ezra Pound led to Antheil's acceptance into society. On October 4, 1923, Antheil became a sensation in Paris after his acclaimed concert at the Champs-Élysées Theatre, when, once again, rioting broke out in the middle of his performance of *Mechanisms*.

In 1924 he composed what has become possibly his best-known work, the spectacular *Ballet mécanique*. Originally written as a solo Pianola piece, it was a thirty-minute composition that required a film projector and accompanying film and was intended for performance in small salons. However, Antheil expanded on the work and, to accompany it, used multiple pianos in a cacophonous orchestral symphony, steeped with such sound effects as doorbells, automobile horns, and airplane propellers (in 1953, he added the sound of jet engines).

The sixteen-minute film *Ballet mécanique,* today completely restored after an original 35mm version was discovered in a closet in Germany in 1975, was shot in 1924 by Dudley Murphy, Fernand Léger, and Man Ray. Antheil then put the piece to music. In an unusual twist of fate, the world premiere of the film *Ballet mécanique* in Vienna on September 24, 1924, was arranged by the celebrated Viennese theatre designer, artist, and architect, Frederick John Kiesler, a second cousin of Hedy's father.[1]

Antheil's *Ballet mécanique* premiered in France at the Champs-Élysées Theatre in Paris on June 19, 1926. Experimental and certainly different, his music was more than simple noise. The Grammy Award–winning choral composer and conductor Gregg Smith said, "His [Antheil's] early music was oftentimes very atonal, avant-garde. But it was still understandable. I wouldn't call it dissonant. It [the *Ballet mécanique*] was a wonderful work, very exciting. Bombastic in many ways. I would definitely say he was influenced by the work of [Igor] Stravinsky with his use of several pianos and percussion instruments."[2]

In New York, *Ballet mécanique* debuted at Carnegie Hall on April 10, 1927, and it created a major uproar. The airplane propellers unfortunately blew the hats and toupees off some of the male audience members, and scuffles ensued. Antheil was given the moniker of the Bad Boy of Music.

Now married to Boski, he eventually fathered two sons. His first, Peter, was born in 1936. Antheil then began a very prolific period of composing. After briefly residing in New York, where he and the Juilliard School president and writer John Erskine collaborated on the opera *Helen Retires* (1934), Antheil and his family settled in Hollywood in 1937. Given a job by his friend Ben Hecht, Antheil started working for the film studios. Still considered a bit of a maverick in the industry, Antheil kept a low profile in Hollywood, though he and Boski were sought after by the intelligentsia.

In June 1939 Antheil penned a prophetic article, again for *Esquire* magazine, published that November, called "Germany Never Had a Chance." It was expanded into a book, published anonymously in late 1940, titled *The Shape of the War to Come* and set in the future year of 1950. Anticipating the coming conflict with Germany, Antheil predicted with uncanny accuracy the events of World War II and its outcome, including Hitler's defeat. Antheil's beloved brother, Henry, employed at that time as a cipher clerk at the U.S. Legation in Finland, aided George in his research.

According to his 1945 autobiography, over the Easter weekend of 1939 in Trenton, New Jersey, Antheil asked his brother his thoughts about Hitler's chances of victory: "'Will Hitler win?' 'No, he'll have his teeth kicked in,' Henry had replied. 'The reason is that the damned fool will attack Russia. That's his idea, first and last. This may finish him off, but I'm afraid not. I think we'll eventually have to get in. Russia's strong, but not quite strong enough. Hitler is going to go a long way into Europe and Russia before we start rolling him back. But he's going to get his teeth kicked in.'"[3] On June 14, 1940, Henry was traveling in a plane that exploded in midair shortly after leaving Tallinn, Estonia, for Helsinki.

Teaching music that summer at Stanford University, George found himself alone and grieving. He and his wife were then residing at the Hollywood-Franklin Hotel. Boski had gone back East to attend to George's bereft parents. The designer Adrian and his wife, attending to Antheil, planned a dinner and told George that Hedy Lamarr wanted to meet him to discuss her glands. He was intrigued.

On the night of the dinner the following week, Antheil arrived late. "They were already sitting at the dining table, one of green onyx splashed with golden silverware," Antheil wrote in his book. "I sat down and turned my eyes upon Hedy Lamarr. My eyeballs sizzled, but I could not take them away. Here, undoubtedly, was the most beautiful woman on earth. Most movie queens don't look so good when you see them in the flesh, but this one looked infinitely better than on screen. Her breasts were fine too, real postpituitary."[4]

The conversation began at the dinner table. Antheil glanced down at Hedy's breasts and was at a loss for words.

"But your breasts," I stuttered, "your breasts . . ."

She whipped out a notebook and pencil. "Yes, yes," she said breathlessly, "my breasts?"

"They are too small." (I just said that to lead her on; every movie star wants larger bosoms.) Hedy made a note in her book.

"Go on," she said, not unkindly.

"Well," I said . . . "well, they don't really *have* to be, you know." She made another note, taking some time to do it. The butler took away my untouched hors d'oeuvres. Silence reigned, and I knew more was expected of me. "You are a thymocentric, or the anterior-pituitary variety, what I call a 'prepit-thymus,'" I volunteered.

Hedy Lamarr kept on writing for a moment, and then said, "I know it, I've studied your charts in *Esquire*. Now what I want to know is, what shall I do about it? Adrian says you're wonderful . . . the thing is can they be made *bigger*?"

"Yes," I said, "much, much bigger!"

"Bigger than this—" I was afraid for a moment to look, but saw that she did not intend to take off her beautiful Hungarian blouse. She was just thrusting out her chest.

"Yes, yes, yes, yes, yes!" I cried.[5]

Hedy left the party before George, and the next day he noticed that she had scrawled with her lipstick her unlisted telephone number on his car window. When he telephoned, she told him that their discussion the night before had been "most stimulating." And she invited him over to her Benedict Canyon home for dinner that evening. Dressed in his best suit, Antheil was admittedly nervous. Hedy's butler served them dinner, and the discussion returned to the quality of Hedy's breasts.

Hedy put him at ease with her straightforward inquiry, and the two discussed the various glandular extracts that, when taken by injection, would supposedly inflate and stimulate the breasts. "By the way," Antheil asked her. "You
can sue me for this, but from where I sit you look about perfect. Why do you
want to know all this?" Her reply was expected. "Oh, just for a friend."

As the evening progressed, their discussion turned to the possibility that the
United States would enter the war. During the preceding September of 1939, the
Holland-America liner *Volendam,* carrying child war refugees, was fired on by
a German submarine in the mid-Atlantic. A torpedo hit and entered the side of
the ship, but it was a dud and did not explode. The capture of that torpedo and
others like it became the basis of the study of electric models developed later in
the war by the Westinghouse Electronic Corporation, which pioneered electri-
cal transmission in the United States. Hedy spoke at length to Antheil that
night about conversations her ex-husband Fritz had had with his colleagues
at those long, boring dinners, about the "aimlessness" of these missiles and
their thoughts and proposed methods on how Germany was planning to correct them. Hedy had ideas as well. And by 1940 these ideas were at a premium.

That summer America's entry into the conflict looked inevitable. According to Antheil, Hedy felt that she should be doing something other than making movies in Hollywood. "She said she knew a good deal about new munitions
and various secret weapons, some of which she had invented herself, and that
she was thinking seriously of quitting M.G.M. and going to Washington, D.C., to
offer her services to the newly established Inventors' Council," Antheil wrote.[6]

" 'They could just have me around,' she explained, 'and ask me questions,' " Hedy told him. And she was dead serious. As he recalled it, "The fact
of the matter was that Hedy had a flair for inventing new war weapons—a
flair she had acquired years ago when she was the wife of Fritz Mandel [sic],
who used to own the largest munitions works in Austria. Time and time
again she had overheard him and his experts discussing new devices, and she
retained these ideas in basic form in her beautiful beringleted head—while
all the time clever Fritz Mandel [sic] didn't think she knew A from Z. One of
her ideas was so good that I suggested she patent it and give it to the United
States Government."[7]

That idea was for a radio-directed torpedo. Over the course of the following
weeks, Hedy and Antheil brainstormed their thoughts, using the technology
that Hedy recalled from those endless hours sitting with Fritz and his cronies

while they discussed Hitler's plans for wireless communication. Because torpedoes in particular were often missing their mark during seafaring conflicts, these two unlikely yet brilliantly creative individuals, the music composer and the film actress, worked out a system to direct these underwater missiles using a method of wireless communication.

Hedy once said, "People seem to think because I have a pretty face I'm stupid. . . . I have to work twice as hard as anyone else to convince people I have something resembling a brain."[8] And her input was ingenious—a secured torpedo-guidance system that would consist of a transmitter programmed with a frequency that was fixed, continuously shifting, and random, and of a secured guidance receiver, which would shift its frequency to match that of the transmitter. Thus, the receiver could be made to pick up the guidance instructions without difficulty, making it impossible for any eavesdropper to interpret. Hedy called this "frequency-hopping." Antheil's contribution to the project was the use of a quick-learning piano-playing system he had developed years before, called See Note. By the use of two player-piano rolls, consisting of eighty-eight keys and punched with the identical pattern of random holes, the transmitter and the receiver could be controlled using eighty-eight different, shifting frequencies.

By the end of September 1940, Antheil suggested they patent their idea and give it to the government as part of their contribution for the war effort. They sent it to the director of the National Inventors Council, Charles Kettering, who was also the head of the General Motors research division (and later its director), who may have also suggested they patent it.

After Antheil worked out some technical problems with Assistant Professor Samuel Stuart Mackowen from California Technical Institute, the project, called Secret Communication System, was submitted to the government for a U.S. patent. Hedy's name on the submission is Hedy Kiesler Markey, which indicates the invention was possibly submitted before the first week in October, when Hedy's divorce was made final. According to the patent record, however, the submission was made in June the following year. And for the time being Hedy and George would have to play the waiting game.

In Hollywood, where it was business as usual, studio boss Louis B. Mayer had realized in viewing the rushes of *Boom Town* that the chemistry between Hedy and Clark Gable was potent enough to warrant a quick recoupling of the two in yet another picture. In early May, Herman Mankiewicz was tabbed to write the screenplay for the new project.

While shooting *Boom Town*, Hedy had suffered a minor bout with influenza and was confined to her dressing room when not on the set filming her scenes. She had noticed a change in her boss, Louis B. Mayer: "He was once more a father figure, even to the point of sending me chicken soup to my dressing room when I had a cold," she wrote. "He told me at one brief meeting, 'Don't throw all your resources into film making. Make a life for yourself. Have a real home, with children. And you will be a better actress for it.' "[9]

At the end of August 1940, *Boom Town* opened nationally. Louella Parsons led the reviews: "Hedy Lamarr is breathtaking in her beauty. She is without a doubt the most beautiful woman in motion pictures. Her part is less important than the other three, but you carry away the memory of that face and that loveliness which will always make her acting a secondary asset. I do not mean to say that she isn't good, for this is one of Hedy's best performances, but her beauty excludes all else when she is on the screen."[10] But the *Los Angeles Times* critic Philip K. Scheuer remained skeptical of Hedy's talent: "And . . . Hedy! No acting ability; only an aura. But what an aura!"[11]

Boom Town would become one of the biggest moneymakers of 1940, earning the studio $4,586,000 in the United States alone. It would earn three Academy Award nominations in 1941, for Best Black-and-White Cinematography, Best Special Effects, and Best Sound. The Institute of Public Opinion would list *Boom Town* as the most liked motion picture of 1940 after a year long survey.

The 119-minute-long film opens with the credits blazing across the screen from right to left, as had been done with *Gone with the Wind* the year before. With Franz Waxman's dramatic musical score heralding its importance, one knows immediately that this picture is special. *Boom Town* today is acknowledged as the precursor of the 1956 epic film *Giant*, released by Warner Bros. It ushered in the era of "the new Hollywood."

Boom Town moves along at a brisk pace; however, M-G-M's remarkable production values threaten to distract the viewer from the script and the action. Clever acting by the stellar cast saves the production from appearing "overproduced." As Lawrence J. Quirk wrote in his biography of Claudette Colbert, "Director Jack Conway gave his best efforts to inject his trademark elements—snap, punch, and pace—into the story, and John Lee Mahin's screen treatment of the James Edward Grant story kept things busy. But there was an aura of superficiality over it all, glossed-up glamorously in the best MGM style."[12]

Hedy, as Karen Vanmeer, makes her entrance into the picture one hour and fifteen minutes into the action. Her first appearance, dressed in that Adrian-designed silk pajama outfit, is startling. Her costumes are in sharp contrast to those designed for Colbert's character, Betsy. Hers, also by Adrian, were not at all exotic but rather plain and somewhat dowdy (busy prints and large bows). Colbert once said about her participation in *Boom Town*, "I honestly don't know what I was doing in that one."[13]

Hedy, in each of her seven scenes, was beautifully photographed, and her performance was very effective. Pleased with the results of her work, Mayer met with Eddie Mannix and had Hedy's contract renegotiated to guarantee her $25,000 a picture instead of a weekly salary, plus a hairdresser, secretary, script girl, and lunch in her dressing room. Hedy had arrived.

In mid-August, *The New York Times* announced M-G-M's purchase of *Some Day I'll Find You*, by Charles Hoffman, for $35,000.[14] Metro had hoped to reteam Hedy with Gable and Tracy. (Gable would later do the picture in 1942, but with Lana Turner. It was released as *Somewhere I'll Find You*.) Mayer actually owned a property, Henryk Sienkiewicz's sweeping biblical epic *Quo Vadis*, in which he was eager to star Hedy, in glorious Technicolor. (When World War II intervened, the *Quo Vadis* script was shelved until 1951. Then it starred Robert Taylor, Deborah Kerr, and Marina Berti in the role intended for Hedy.)

Mayer then had the screenwriter Walter Reisch, who had cowritten the script for the studio's 1939 smash *Ninotchka*, do the story for a new project meant for Hedy and Gable. In turn, Ben Hecht and Charles Lederer transformed Reisch's work into a script. On August 21 Hedy was assigned the female starring role opposite Clark Gable in *Comrade X*, scheduled to roll on Monday, August 25.

The story line of *Comrade X* was similar to the highly successful *Ninotchka*, in which Garbo had parlayed her title role into an Oscar-nominated performance. Both films were comedies that took potshots at Russian Socialism. *Comrade X*'s action takes place within a forty-eight-hour period. In Moscow the Soviet chief of police, Commissar Vasiliev (Oscar Homolka) advises foreign newspaper correspondents that, until he discovers the identity of a certain reporter known only as Comrade X, who has been discrediting Russia, all news reports from the Kremlin would be censored or stopped.

The news reporter McKinley B. Thompson (Gable) witnesses and photographs an assassination attempt on Vasiliev at the funeral of his predecessor. A porter, Vanya (portrayed by Felix Bressart, who was also in *Ninotchka*), discovers that Thompson is actually Comrade X and threatens to expose him if he does not agree to escort Vanya's daughter, Theodore (Hedy), a streetcar conductor, out of the country because her Communist ideals may lead to her execution. Thompson meets Theodore, convinces her that he too is a Communist, and marries her.

However, she soon learns of Thompson's lie and intends to turn him in, when she, her father, and Thompson are arrested because a hidden camera is discovered in Vanya's room. Thompson sends word to Vasiliev that he has taken a picture of the man who has tried to assassinate him, and he is taken to the police chief, where he learns that Vasiliev has been "eliminated." The new commissar is none other than the man who had attempted to kill Vasiliev at the funeral—the same man Thompson had photographed, Michael Bastakoff (Vladimir Sokoloff). Escaping execution, and outwitting the police, Thompson escapes with Theodore and her father across the border into Hungary in a stolen tank.

Other than ridiculing the Soviets, there is little that *Comrade X* has in common with *Ninotchka*. As in *Ninotchka*, a staunch Russian girl is transformed at the end of the film by the love of a likable American man. But Hedy made no attempt to imitate Garbo's character. In fact, *Comrade X* was a remake of Metro's *Clear All Wires* (1933), written by Bella and Sam Spewack. Said *The New York Times* of the screenplay, "The studio says that it has been altered so radically that even its authors, the Spewacks, would never recognize it."[15]

Gottfried Reinhardt, son of Hedy's beloved mentor Max Reinhardt, was making his film producer debut with *Comrade X*. The picture was directed by King Vidor, fresh from his magnificent job on *Northwest Passage*.[16] The production was quickly and efficiently photographed throughout September 1940. "Hedy prided herself on being Viennese, but she was far more naïve than sophisticated," Vidor would remember. "She was a peasant type, really. She had one of the most beautiful faces ever seen, but not the figure to go with it. She didn't have any natural talent and was inclined to be nervous. You had to nurse her along."[17]

At the end of the first day of shooting, Gable noticed Hedy's nervousness, took her hand, and said, "You're doing great, kid. You're gonna knock 'em dead."[18] Hedy found Clark very warm and "one of the nicest people I'd met."[19] Rumors persisted that Clark and Hedy were having an affair. If that was indeed so, it is surprising that Hedy would often later say that she never understood Gable's sex appeal.

Jean Garceau, longtime friend and secretary to Clark Gable, wrote in her loving biography of her boss:

> Clark thought Hedy was beautiful, liked her very much, and ribbed her unmercifully because she spent so much time on her face and clothes. "Come on," he'd say to her, "forget your face—let's do some acting."
>
> When she arrived in the morning without make-up, Stan [Campbell, Gable's make-up man] would say, "She was so beautiful that I felt it was a shame to have to make that face up." Hedy was new to American picture methods, and was still very unsure of herself. Clark and director King Vidor were very patient with her, trying to put her to ease.[20]

Hedy had tired of her image, though, and when the writer David Hough visited the set of *Comrade X,* she told him that, somehow, the director would work her profile into the coming sequence. "In this coming scene I must show my profile again and say 'Ah, what does it matter?'" she said. "How can you show off your profile in a dungeon?" he asked. "Don't worry, they'll find a way," she replied.[21]

When it was time for the take, Gable took his place on the set, and Hedy, as she walked to her spot, muttered to Hough, "This is going to be silly." Hough wrote, "She was right, about the profile. The director had her sit up very straight against the wall. Then he tilted her head, and they adjusted the lights—and there it was. The profile."[22]

On July 9, it was announced that *Come Live with Me* would now be Hedy's next film, costarring her and James Stewart. The film's assigned director, Clarence Brown, had already flown to New York to secure location shooting in Central Park. While preproduction moved along on the project, Hedy was deeply embroiled in her divorce action against Gene Markey.

On Wednesday, September 4, Hedy petitioned for divorce in Hollywood from Gene, charging cruelty. In her two-page complaint, filed by her attorney, Lester W. Roth, Hedy charged Gene had treated her with extreme cruelty since the day they wed, causing her grievous mental anguish (this was the usual reason given in those days, though in most cases, Hedy's included, it was probably not true). Hedy stated that on August 12 the two had signed a property-settlement agreement, which she was now asking the court to approve. On September 13 Markey filed an "appearance" document, which served the purpose of notifying the court that he acknowledged the divorce action but did not intend to answer the charges. The petition for the final decree was presented to the court by Markey's attorney, Neil S. McCarthy.

What had gone wrong? Hedy would tell a journalist some years later, "First his mother and father died and then he had pneumonia. . . . Our home life was so constantly interrupted with my work and his outside happenings that the first thing we knew it was all over."[23]

In court, Hedy, adorned with a single strand of pearls, hatless, and wearing a pink and white print dress and a bright red camel-hair coat, testified to Superior Judge William S. Baird that during the sixteen months of their marriage, they had spent only four evenings alone together at home. "When we were first married," Hedy animatedly told the court, "I used to tell him the little things that happened to me during the day and I thought it was natural for him to do the same, but he never did. When I asked him casually why he never told me about his own experiences he would say, 'Well, I might bore you—besides I forget. I guess I'll write them down next time.' . . . He avoided talking to me about private affairs. Therefore we had people at home or went out to parties and to movies—anything to avoid that. He always invited the guests."[24]

Hedy told the court what had transpired their last evening together. Wrote the *Los Angeles Times*,

> "We were alone that evening," Miss Lamarr began, taking a deep breath. "We were sitting in the living room and he said, 'What if we would play a game?' Knowing Mr. Markey loathed games, I was amazed, but I asked, 'Well, what is it?'
>
> "He said, 'Why don't we each take a sheet of paper and write down what is wrong about us. You write down what is wrong about me and vice versa.' I said, 'I'll answer whatever question you want to ask. I don't think we need to play games, we might as well talk frankly. It is enough now of this game business.' And so we told each other and it ended up in a rather unpleasant feeling and that night he left me."[25]

Before granting Hedy her decree, Judge Baird asked, "How long had you known him before you were married?" Hedy replied, "Much too short—about four weeks." To which the judge observed, "I think that's the answer to your troubles."[26] Hedy was granted the divorce from Gene Markey on Friday, September 27.[27] She was awarded outright title of Hedgerow Farm, and Gene was allowed to remove only certain furnishings he owned before the marriage. The final decree was awarded to Hedy on October 3, 1940. The issue regarding custody of Jamesie was not mentioned in the press.

Hedy's first date after her divorce was with Woolworth Donahue, heir to the Woolworth millions, whom Hedy had met with friends at Ciro's. Jimmie Fidler reported, "Hear tell Mrs. Donahue, who has millions, is frowning on son Woolworth's romance with Hedy Lamarr."[28] The affair with Donahue did not last. Hedy was soon seen around Hollywood with Anatole Litvak, the director from Warner Bros.

Hedy then met actor John Howard, and for a brief time the two were seriously involved. Howard was a thirty-seven-year-old Ohio native then working at Metro in *The Philadelphia Story,* portraying Katharine Hepburn's jilted fiancé. He was charming, available, and a breath of fresh air. And, like Reggie, he made her laugh. On one of their first dates, they were spotted dining on hamburgers at the Los Feliz Brown Derby "car café."

Hedy enjoyed Howard's robust manliness as well as his mind, and often she would listen to his advice regarding her career. Inspired by her good notices for *Boom Town,* and knowing full well that *Comrade X* was going to be a hit, Hedy started once again expressing to the press her desire to do better projects. In 1940 she announced her longing to play Maria in the screen version of *For Whom the Bell Tolls,* based on Ernest Hemingway's 1940 novel of the Spanish civil war, opposite Gary Cooper.

That part would have been an interesting possibility for Hedy. And indeed she *had* been considered for it. But Maria went instead to actress-ballerina Vera Zorina, the wife of George Balanchine. When Zorina failed to impress in the rushes, the director Sam Wood cast about for a replacement. Eventually, Ingrid Bergman secured the part. That loss would be the first of several important leading roles for which Hedy was considered that Bergman would take instead.

The noted drama critic Edwin Schallert wrote that Metro was finally realizing profitability in Hedy, and plans for her future projects continued, including (again) a remake of *Flesh and the Devil*. Philip K. Scheuer, in the *Los Angeles Times*, remarked, "Miss Lamarr is still her own best argument—and the final word is still to be spoken."[29]

Metro announced on September 23 that Hedy would still star in the upcoming *Ziegfeld Girl*; however, *Come Live with Me* was set to begin filming first, once James Stewart returned from New York. Stewart's contract had been renewed with a substantial pay increase because of his brilliant performance in the as yet unreleased *The Philadelphia Story*.

It was apparent to many that the United States' entry into the war was imminent, and James Stewart was one of the first patriotic actors to volunteer his services. *Come Live with Me* would be the first of three "quickie" films Stewart would complete in rapid succession before his announced entry into the armed forces.

The affable and competent thirty-two-year-old Stewart was reaching the ranks of major stardom in 1940. Born in Pennsylvania, he had attended Princeton University, where he studied architecture and graduated class of 1932. After performing in summer stock from 1932 to 1934, the six-foot-three actor achieved minor success on Broadway, where he was spotted by the M-G-M talent scout Bill Grady in 1935 and signed to a contract for $350 a week.

Obtaining agent Leland Hayward, Stewart subsequently enjoyed a string of major box-office hits, including two directed by Frank Capra for Columbia, *You Can't Take It with You* (Best Picture of 1938) and *Mr. Smith Goes to Washington* in 1939 (for which he earned an Oscar nomination), and Universal's *Destry Rides Again* that same year. Metro was eager to capitalize on Stewart after these loan-outs and promptly handed him the second male lead after Cary Grant in *The Philadelphia Story*. The film made James Stewart a major commodity at M-G-M.

On October 7, 1940, Stewart and Hedy stepped before the cameras for *Come Live with Me*. In the cast was the octogenarian actress Adeline de Walt Reynolds, making her film debut. Much was made of this, her first screen role. Hedda Hopper, then no spring chicken herself, informed her readers, "Grandma is played by 82-year-old Adeline de Walt Reynolds, and her performance will just about clean out all the old ladies' homes, 'cause when they see her, the old gals will say, 'If she can do it, I can do it.'"[30]

Unfortunately, when filming began Stewart was suffering a bad cold, and this would affect his performance. *Come Live with Me*, with an original story by

Virginia Van Upp and screenplay by Patterson McNutt, told the story of Johanna Janns (Hedy), a recent refugee to America, who begins a romance with the married publisher Barton Kendrick (Ian Hunter), whose "modern" marriage with his wife, Diana (Verree Teasdale), allows them both their freedom.

When "Johnny Jones," as Johanna calls herself, finds that she is being deported, she asks a penniless writer, Bill Smith (James Stewart), to marry her and offers to pay him to do so. Under the condition that he not ask where she lives, Bill agrees. Bill writes a story about the arrangement and unknowingly sends his manuscript to the publisher Kendrick, who recognizes that it is *his* story. He buys the book and sends Bill an advance. Now that she will not be deported, Johnny then serves Bill with divorce papers.

Appearing at Johnny's address, which he finds on the papers, Bill agrees to the divorce under the condition that Johnny spend the weekend with him on a farm. Johnny calls Kendrick at the Indian Inn roadhouse café (from a pay phone inside the women's room, marked "Pocahontas"). She asks him to come to her rescue but realizes at the end of the day that she is in love with Bill. The publisher arrives, and Bill thinks Kendrick is there about his book. Bill soon realizes that he is the other man in Johnny's life and leaves the farmhouse in anger. Johnny tells Kendrick that she is in love with Bill, and she remains there waiting for Bill when he returns.

Filming progressed smoothly on *Come Live with Me*, since Hedy and Stewart liked each other immensely. Between takes they would enjoy rounds of Chinese checkers. Clarence Brown tried to infuse some life and sparkle into the project, but Stewart suffered his lingering cold throughout the filming, and his energy level was obviously low.

Not only was Stewart ill but Hedy had impacted wisdom teeth during the early days of filming. She had lost a great deal of weight because of it, and, during breaks in the filming of the rainstorm sequences, she took to her dressing room. According to Stewart, Hedy insisted on doing her own stunts. Because of her admirable fortitude, Stewart would always remain respectful of Hedy.

Hedy would remark that, of all her costars, Stewart was her favorite to work with, probably for no other reason than he put her at ease. She said he was "one of the sweetest men in the world."[31] The feeling was mutual, though some biographers have erroneously stated that Stewart claimed he did not care for her. Stewart's own gracious remarks about knowing and working with Hedy say otherwise. He was a true gentleman and would remain Hedy's favorite leading man.[32]

Metro continued their search for a vehicle to reunite Hedy with Robert Taylor and announced that the screenwriter Howard Emmett Rogers had been assigned to do the scenario for *Episode in Lisbon*, for a reteaming of the two.

In the days building up to America's entry into World War II, Hedy was busy multitasking even in her most prolific period of filmmaking. She actively sought to develop more ideas with Antheil to contribute to the government. At the same time, she fretted about the pending adoption request she had tendered to secure Jamesie in her care. And she was most concerned about the safety of her mother, Trude, in London.

Even as late as 1940, most Americans were fairly apathetic about the war raging in Europe. Hedy would read the papers and buy foreign publications from New York to learn about the growing crisis abroad. Daily she called George Antheil to discuss their project for a "radio-directed torpedo," and she continuously made sure he attended appointments and meetings with proper authorities to expedite their projected patent.

Hedy and Antheil spent many an evening sprawled out on the floor, with Antheil taking notes and diagramming Hedy's ideas into his spiral notebook—always working out their invention, either at her house or his. In time Hedy and Antheil's wife, Boski, both Austrian, became good friends. After visiting a Mr. Reynolds at The National Inventors Council, Department of Commerce, in Washington, D.C., in October 1940, Antheil sent the man a registered letter dated November 8 outlining and explaining another of his and Hedy's prospective inventions—an antiaircraft shell device. Antheil wrote:

> Finally, Mr. Reynolds, if your department decides that there is anything whatsoever in this shell, Miss Lamarr and myself would be more than delighted to send you further and more elaborate sketches and descriptions of same—however might I please ask you to do me one favor—would you please answer me soon concerning it, and, if you can, "yes" or "no," in accordance with your interest.

Antheil added, "Miss Lamarr is a very great friend of ours, and is really a very talented girl."[33]

In December Hedy and Antheil sent a detailed description of their secret communications device in full to the National Inventors Council. Of the some

625,000 ideas and suggestions submitted to the council before its demise in 1974, few were accepted for patent. But Hedy and Antheil's Secret Communication System caused quite a bit of excitement. The council's chairman, Kettering, directed the government's improvements on the idea. Their plan had been accepted as viable. But they were told work needed to be done on it.

Meanwhile, film projects loomed on the horizon for Hedy, and some not necessarily with her own studio. One tempting offer came from Darryl F. Zanuck at Twentieth Century–Fox, who wanted Hedy for his planned remake of *Blood and Sand* with Tyrone Power. As late as December 1940 the columnist Edwin Schallert advised his readers that Hedy would play the role of Dona Sol in the Technicolor production, with a screenplay by Jo Swerling. On January 20, 1941, M-G-M officially refused Hedy's loan-out, and the part eventually went to Rita Hayworth.

Final retakes were done on *Comrade X* on November 19. Throughout that month *Come Live with Me* was filming. The actor Ian Hunter, who was doing such a sterling job in *Come Live with Me*, was announced on November 10 as joining the company of the upcoming *Ziegfeld Girl*, now a glittering all-star production, with Hedy, Judy Garland, and Lana Turner in the female leads. Hunter would be the last actor cast in a major role for that film.

Jimmie Fidler began the ballyhoo for *Comrade X* on November 26: "Hedy had no lion's share of the picture, but her love scenes with Gable caused the hair on the back of my neck to bristle. . . . Miss Lamarr, having more beauty and sex appeal . . . than either Miss Loy or Miss Colbert, should bring out the maximum of Clark's masculine magnetism."[34] *Film Daily* commented, "Miss Lamarr essays a comedy role with swell results. Her acting talents assume a new stature and she definitely proves her ability as a comedienne."[35] The critic of *The Hollywood Reporter* wrote, "The surprise of the picture is Hedy Lamarr. This gal has found herself or better, M-G-M has found her for M-G-M, for she simply knocks over her role of Theodore, looks ravishing and is the top ingredient of the show."[36] And Edwin Schallert, in the *Los Angeles Times*, gave Hedy a thumbs-up as well, "Triumphantly the feature proves the talents of Miss Lamarr as a screen actress. She is given her chance to be something other than beautiful and adorning, which she is essentially. . . . She is required to characterize and succeeds admirably. In fact, this production endows her with true stellar attributes at last."[37]

Comrade X is a joy to watch today. Here were the two most attractive and bankable M-G-M stars of the moment, Gable and Lamarr, enjoying themselves immensely in a simple comedy, complemented by some of Hollywood's best character and supporting actors. Natasha Lytess (who would later become an acting coach for Marilyn Monroe) handed in a brilliant performance. Hedy's fight with Lytess's character, Olga, was hilariously staged and played.

Adrian is credited, as in almost all the Metro pictures of the era, as designer of the costumes for *Comrade X*. Aside from her plain Soviet-inspired motor-woman outfit, there was only one truly feminine costume that Hedy wore in the entire film, a very modest negligée that within minutes is covered by a soiled overcoat that Hedy wears for the remainder of the picture. (Except for the final scene at the baseball game where Hedy sports an absurd white outfit with an astoundingly hideous hat, which Adrian, uncharacteristically, truly struck out with.)

Comrade X was a hit. Walter Reisch's original story for the eighty-seven-minute film garnered an Academy Award nomination in 1941. That year would prove to be Hedy's most productive. And it would also bring her happiness in her personal life. She would fall in love.

9

Career

All her life Hedy believed in astrology. And if she did not actually follow the stars as many assumed she did, Hedy was at least typical of her astrological sign, Scorpio: She was talented, intelligent, romantic, sensual, headstrong, and often recklessly irresponsible.

In early January 1941, impatient and selfish, Hedy sent an accusatory letter to her friend George Antheil, complaining that she had not been advised of progress on another of their inventions by the government. This hurt Antheil, and, in a rush of emotions, on January 10 he dashed off a response.

> I, it was agreed, was to handle entirely the matter of the anti-aircraft shell. I did handle it as well as I knew how. It has not been my fault that (a) it has not developed as I hoped, and (b) that they in Washington have not sent you personal notice of it. . . .
>
> I can only say that I have found you to be by far one of the most wonderful persons I have ever known, and I more than regret the turn of events which possibly could have been switched in time, and for the great good of everybody.[1]

When confronted by her own often irrational behavior, Hedy would apologize. She and Antheil would eventually make amends. As this played itself out, she was busy finishing her work on *Come Live with Me*, even as *Comrade X* ground to a halt. At times Hedy would actually go from one set to the other during the day, performing in both pictures. With the James Stewart picture nearly complete, production of *Ziegfeld Girl* was gearing up, and Hedy found herself again going from one soundstage to another during the final shooting days of *Come Live with Me,* which eventually ended on November 30.

Ziegfeld Girl began production in October, and filming commenced on November 4, 1940. It was produced by Pandro S. Berman, his first M-G-M assignment after his tenure at R-K-O. Photography, shot in sepia tone, was handled by Ray June.

Though both Stewart and Hedy were called for costume, makeup tests, and a few key scenes before the completion of *Come Live with Me,* many of the early days of production of *Ziegfeld Girl* were spent on musical rehearsals requiring only Garland and Tony Martin, while Lana Turner was on the set acting in scenes that did not require her character's romantic interest, Stewart. The studio's stalwart director, Robert Z. Leonard, was assigned the plum spot of the season. Leonard had also directed the studio's *The Great Ziegfeld* (Best Picture winner of 1936). The *Ziegfeld Girl* script was by William Anthony McGuire, who had also written *The Great Ziegfeld*'s Oscar-nominated screenplay. (McGuire sadly died in September 1940 before *Ziegfeld Girl* began shooting.)

Stewart was billed in *Ziegfeld Girl* after Judy Garland but before Hedy, who was followed by Lana Turner. He had not planned on being available for the film since he was scheduled for an army physical the same day that filming commenced. He was quickly given a deferment and believed Mayer was preventing him from enlisting. Mayer wanted Stewart to remain at Metro, especially after his performance in *The Philadelphia Story,* which would soon win Stewart the Best Actor Oscar for 1940.

When he was given his physical, Stewart was told that he did not meet the weight-height restrictions. Indeed, he weighed in at only 130 pounds, and, at six foot three, was ten pounds too thin. "If he looked a bit distracted during the making of *Ziegfeld Girl,*" wrote one Stewart biographer, "it was because all his concentration and energy went toward gaining weight."[2]

Hedy was an ideal and inspirational choice for *Ziegfeld Girl.* She had just recently been voted the year's Favorite Movie Actress by the graduating class of New York University's Washington Square College of Arts and Sciences. (Robert Taylor was voted their Favorite Movie Actor.) Though *Ziegfeld Girl* was technically a musical, Hedy petitioned Mayer for the part, insisting she be cast in the picture as a change of pace.

Hedy once said, "Any girl can be glamorous—all she has to do is stand still and look stupid."[3] And for *Ziegfeld Girl*, Hedy knew just what to do. Ironically, her publicity at this time made constant reference to her non-glamour-girl lifestyle and her love of nature, children, and animals. These characteristics were actually true. But, cleverly, Hedy knew how to capitalize on her looks.

The plot of *Ziegfeld Girl* "was really a granddaughter of *Sally, Irene and Mary* [1925] with (inevitably) three showgirls coming to customary fates," wrote the M-G-M biographer John Douglas Eames.[4] No attempt was made to film the picture as a period piece. The women all sport 1940 hairstyles and outfits. Chronicling the rise of three young beauties, Susan Gallagher (Judy Garland); Sheila Regan, later renamed Hale (Lana Turner); and Sandra Kolter (Hedy), to the heights of stardom on Broadway on the legendary stage of the producer Florenz Ziegfeld, the picture was originally meant as a showpiece for a now grown-up Judy Garland. As filming progressed, however, Turner's performance gained her more attention, and the script took on a completely different slant. Though not denigrating the performances offered by Garland or Lamarr, Turner's histrionics awarded her more screen time and favorable reviews.

Sandra is the beautiful wife of Franz Kolter (Philip Dorn), a talented but unemployed concert violinist; Susan is a vaudevillian like her father, "Pop" Gallagher (Charles Winninger); and Sheila is an elevator operator whose boyfriend, Gilbert "Gil" Young (Stewart), is a truck driver. (Gil strangely calls Sheila "Red" throughout the picture, though Turner's hair was already bleached blond.) The three girls are discovered by the theatrical impresario Florenz Ziegfeld (never seen) through his talent liaison Noble Sage (Edward Everett Horton) and are glorified in his "Ziegfeld Follies."

Their rise to the top is cleverly dramatized. Sandra becomes infatuated with the show's handsome leading man, the singer Frank Merton (Tony Martin), after Franz challenges her to choose him or her career. Susan, who was cast originally as a dancer, suddenly becomes the "Ziegfeld Follies" star singer and sees her father reunite with his former partner, Al Shean (played by the legendary early vaudevillian himself) in the show. Sheila and Gil break up as she takes to wealthy men, riches, and booze. (In one particular scene, Sheila takes a fall during a huge musical production number, an incident that actually echoed that of the real-life Follies showgirl Lillian Lorraine, who fell into an orchestra pit when she was drunk.) Interspersed within the story line are various musical numbers, all staged by the incomparable Busby Berkeley.

By the end of the picture, Susan has become the star of the "Ziegfeld Follies," and is shown sitting atop a massive revolving pedestal (the filmed sequence was actually taken from the finale of *The Great Ziegfeld*). Sandra quits the show when she and Franz are reunited and he lands a job in the orchestra. And Sheila takes a tumble a few more times—on stage while inebriated; while tripping over a fur; and, just for good measure, as she descends a flight of stairs in the finale, giving the picture its one big dramatic moment. All ends in Lana's favor, though, after her character reconciles with Gil right before the fade-out. Not much substance, but lots to see and hear.

As filming moved along on *Ziegfeld Girl*, Stewart started filming another picture at United Artists with Paulette Goddard. "I was going back and forth between *Ziegfeld Girl* and *Pot o' Gold* all the time," Stewart joked. "One day I got to MGM and heard that Lana's character was dead, and really couldn't remember whether my character had been responsible for that."[5] Stewart once again had little time to settle into his character because of his frequent runs between studios during the filming of *Ziegfeld Girl*. He simply just did not grasp the fellow's complexities. The acting kudos all went to Lana Turner.

Among the other principals in *Ziegfeld Girl* were Eve Arden (as Patsy Dixon) and Felix Bressart (Mischa), both fresh from *Comrade X*. Borrowed from Warner Bros. was the lovely model-actress Georgia Carroll. Carroll, who would later marry the comic bandleader Kay Kyser, recalled in 2008 that Hedy was a very private, shy person during the filming of *Ziegfeld Girl*. Much warmer was nineteen-year-old Lana Turner, who was at that time getting the big push by the studio. Photographs used for publicity of the film with Hedy, Lana, and Judy were taken on December 11, 1940. Judy and Hedy would remain life-long friends, though Hedy's friendship with Lana would remain cordial at best.

Turner was indeed elevated to stardom upon the release of *Ziegfeld Girl*. Coming into her own, she exhibited the fun-loving enthusiasm that was once characteristic of Jean Harlow. The studio's stars and grips alike enjoyed working with Turner. The original ending of the *Ziegfeld Girl* had Sheila dying (no doubt of "old movie disease"—simply never diagnosed in the film). That's what bad girls had to do in those days. They had to die. "I'm two people," her character says at one point in the film, "neither one of them good." But when previews indicated the public preferred that Sheila repent and live, the film ended with her sighing in the arms of James Stewart.

In *Ziegfeld Girl*, Turner's descending the stairs during the film's finale, done to the distant lilting music of "You Stepped Out of a Dream," and her collapse at the bottom of them secured her film immortality. "One big moment like this is enough to clinch any career. And Lana knew it," wrote Jeanine Basinger. "In *Ziegfeld Girl*, she walked into a lifetime of super-stardom."[6] And Lana was having the time of her life personally. Seldom declining favors if she liked a man, Turner was also a mainstay on the Hollywood nightlife scene, and she dated constantly, seeing, among others, Tony Martin, at the time recently divorced from the Twentieth Century–Fox star Alice Faye.

Martin was a successful radio singer in the 1930s and had dabbled in movies in 1936, including appearing with the young Garland in *Pigskin Parade* at Fox. "The studio [M-G-M] was going to make a film called *Ziegfeld Girl*, and they had a big production number and they thought I should do it," Martin wrote in his 1976 autobiography. "I had a what-the-hell way of looking at things then. . . . So I . . . reported to MGM, and Busby Berkeley handed me a song to sing . . . called 'You Stepped Out of a Dream.' It was a beautiful song—and it's become a standard—and the scene worked out well."[7]

Tony Martin recalled working with Hedy, though he did not know her well. "She was a very lovely lady," he said in 2007. "She carried herself with dignity all the time."[8] For her part, Judy Garland thought being thrust into a picture featuring the most glamorous women Metro could muster a bit daunting. She found Lamarr to be the most beautiful of all Metro actresses, "very nice but very shy."[9] And Turner, who had successfully grabbed Andy Hardy's (Mickey Rooney's) attention away from (Garland's) Betsy Booth in *Love Finds Andy Hardy* (1938), was also ravishing in *Ziegfeld Girl*. Garland would often repeat a story: When Lana would come bouncing onto the set the technicians would whistle. When Hedy would pass through, they would sigh and stare longingly. When Judy would appear it would be a simple hello.

Apparently during the filming there was difficulty among the actresses. Hedy remained distant and apart from it all throughout the shooting, as recalled by Jackie Cooper, who played Turner's younger brother, Jerry: "Between all the preparation for the big production numbers and all the bitching on the set, there was a hell of a lot of downtime," recalled Cooper.[10] Garland found no consolation in being top billed over Stewart, Lamarr, and Turner. "Her nerves were further strained by the fact that Turner, already separated from Artie Shaw (whom Judy had been in love with), was conducting a none-too-private romance with Tony Martin, to whom Garland was also attracted," wrote David Shipman in his Garland biography.[11]

"Lana, for instance, was a real expert at announcing that she was having her period so [she] needed three or four days at home," said Cooper. "A lot of actresses worked that one, but none of them better than Turner. Then Judy got into the act, and it really disappointed me that she was buying into the same star-attitude thing. Something always seemed to be bothering her and slowing things down. Most of it was Turner, and how Tony Martin seemed to pay more attention to Turner than her. At least when Jimmy was around there was a sense of professionalism."[12]

Costumes for the picture were created by Adrian. And extravagant they were for *Ziegfeld Girl*. For the "You Stepped Out of a Dream" number, Adrian pulled out all the stops in creating erotic fantasy fashions for the female stars and Follies girls. He dressed the showgirls in "see-through" chiffon with strategically placed sequins and feathers over their breasts and elsewhere. Hedy's costume for the number was extraordinary. Gowned in a flowing long-sleeved, high-necked, shimmering white sheath, Hedy sported a shower of stars and sparkles that surrounded her shoulder-length, center-parted signature hairstyle. She wore a dozen other Adrian-designed costumes in *Ziegfeld Girl*. And Hedy was dressed in what was fast becoming her trademark fashion—angular blacks and whites, long-sleeved, clinging garments with high necklines and bejeweled or pearl accessories.

Filming was completed on *Ziegfeld Girl* at the end of January, with a couple of pickup shots added in February. Somehow in all this activity, Hedy found time to petition the federal court, on February 5, to legally change her name from Hedwig Eva Maria Kiesler to Hedy Lamarr.

Hedy during this time was still seeing John Howard, although the press made note he was also dating actress Wanda McKay. In an interview, Hedy told a reporter that Howard surprised her by possessing a beautiful singing voice. She encouraged him to seek singing lessons, which he did. Hedy was unusually candid when she spoke about her beaus. "I went to see 'The Great Dictator,'" she told a journalist. "I went with Reginald Gardiner, my old friend and still my friend, I am happy to say. We sat in the same row with Gene [Markey] in the theatre, which was a coincidence, but a nice, pleasant one. . . . Gene and I also are very friendly. . . . [O]n my last birthday, my first husband, Fritz Mandl, called me on the telephone. . . . He calls me every birthday and last time we talked for an hour. We keep in touch."[13]

On January 29 *Come Live with Me* opened to wonderful reviews. Hedda Hopper said of Hedy's performance, "In 'Come Live with Me' she romped through like a veteran, and now I'll be darned if her acting ability doesn't match her beauty. When you've said that, that's all there is—there isn't any more."[14]

The New York *Daily News* reviewer wrote, "The doubters will be converted after seeing Hedy Lamarr in this picture. . . . Here, she takes off the glamorous mask and, more than ever, gives a touching performance with all the varying facial expressions necessary to make her characterization sympathetic and human."[15] The actor Curt Bois, one of Europe's cinema exiles, was heard to comment about his friend Hedy in *Come Live with Me*, "Hedy Lamarr runs the gamut of emotions from A to X-stasy!"[16]

Come Live with Me is a highly enjoyable film. The story line is light, but the picture's two stars—Hedy, more beautiful than ever, and Stewart, rail thin and yet equally attractive—make an unusual teaming and work very nicely together. Stewart is hammy in his early scenes, possibly because of his intense filming schedule, which gave him little time to develop his character. Yet it is the picture's supporting actors who save the day by springing up at every turn and giving immensely funny bits of business. Donald Meek has a stellar turn as a panhandler, and both Verree Teasdale and Ian Hunter give fine support.

Hedy sported only six Adrian-designed outfits throughout the picture, including the obligatory white turban to allow for an extremely brief and obviously gratuitous close-up. One stunning gown was a misty white organza creation called Summer Moment, with hundreds of handmade loops on the skirt. Hedy's hair remained parted in the middle and shoulder length. During the filming she wore as a good-luck charm a glass locket framed in gold, which she adorned herself with a bracelet. In it was a four-leaf clover her mother had found in the grass at Trafalgar Square in London and sent her in a letter.

Hedy wrote briefly of the film in her book: "Jimmy and I seemed an unlikely romantic pair, *Come Live with Me* pleased audiences, made some money . . . and increased my bargaining power at the studio."[17]

On February 12, because of illness, Hedy withdrew from the picture *The Uniform,* starring Clark Gable, and directed by Clarence Brown, which was set to begin the following day. She had lost twenty pounds over the past six months, and she needed rest. Louis B. Mayer sensed she was becoming temperamental. The role in *The Uniform* was quickly recast with Rosalind Russell after Lana Turner was considered for the part. It was retitled *They Met in Bombay* and released that June. On March 12 the screenwriter Albert Mannheimer was assigned Hedy's next project, *Episode in Lisbon*, to costar Hedy and Robert Taylor again. The project was eventually shelved.

Hedy's illness became a layoff from the studio. Negotiations between the Metro executive Eddie Mannix for an increase in Hedy's salary plus picture approval bogged down completely. So to avoid the fight becoming public, Hedy accepted the layoff without pay. The scripts the studio was offering her were not to her liking, and, at this point in her career, she expected a better arrangement. Hedy's "behavior" was called on the carpet.

As difficult as her life had become professionally, Hedy at this same time was still attempting to gain custody of little Jamesie. She was also trying to secure safe passage from London for her mother so she could be with her. And, most amazing of all, it was during all of this that she and George Antheil were developing various other inventions as America's entry into the war was becoming inevitable.

In March, Jimmie Fidler announced that Howard Hughes had "found" Hedy Lamarr.[18] And to that end, Hughes had generously "lent Hedy a pair of chemists to help her develop a bouillon-like cube which when mixed with water, would create a soft drink similar to Coca-Cola. 'It was a flop.' Hedy said [later] with a laugh."[19] When Hughes offered her $10,000 to pose for a rubber dummy he wanted to mold of her and then sleep with, she asked, "Why not sleep with me, the real thing?" "Because you are too good for me," he replied.[20]

"[Hughes] absolutely proposed to everyone," the actress Paulette Goddard told her biographer, Julie Gilbert. "He knocked them all off—Hedy Lamarr, Jean Peters, Katharine Hepburn, Norma Shearer."[21] (Before their marriages to Goddard, Charles Chaplin, Burgess Meredith, *and* Erich Maria Remarque would all have affairs with Hedy.) When Hughes offered marriage, Hedy understood his complexities and graciously declined. She would later confide to several close friends that Hughes was the worst lover she had ever known.

After a misunderstanding with John Howard, and following a brief fling with the playboy Jock Whitney, Hedy was seen about Hollywood with Reggie Gardiner once more. He was always there to support her. With the dependable Reggie by her side, Hedy felt safe. However, to the press at the end of March, she announced they were "just pals."[22]

Ziegfeld Girl was released on April 17, 1941, and it clearly showed the picture's $1.9 million budget was not wasted. It also became an unqualified hit. *Variety* commented, "Miss Lamarr's dramatic adventure is subordinate to the other two, but provides sufficient footage to present her widely publicized and accepted glamour."[23] Hedda Hopper announced that the "picture is startlingly beautiful—makes you ill that it's not in color. . . . Hedy Lamarr has little to do except be decorative."[24] The film critic of *The Philadelphia Evening Public Ledger* wrote, "As for Miss Lamarr—well, she remains histrionically unobtrusive but she really looks like the most Ziegfeldian showgirl of the lot."[25] And *The New York Times* reported accurately, "Hedy Lamarr is still the show's most expensive single bit of décor."[26]

Dated somewhat today, *Ziegfeld Girl* is stupendous for its production numbers and glorious to view in sepia-toned black-and-white. The cinematography is crisp and clean. For Garland fans, it is another chance to watch their waiflike Judy do what she did best—sing, cry, and break your heart. Lana Turner secured her future with Metro with this one picture, and there would be no stopping her ascent to superstardom. Though Hedy was cast opposite the dull Philip Dorn as her spineless husband, she still managed to make it look as though her character adored him. And though she garnered only about thirty minutes of film time, Hedy, in her brief scene with Rose Hobart (Mrs. Merton), is brilliantly handled, as she carefully underplays the sequence.

The original finale musical number, with Garland and Martin singing "We Must Have Music," was considered lame after Lana's dramatic fall, and so it was cut. Thus the inclusion of the wedding cake finale and a couple of other brief musical clips, lifted directly from *The Great Ziegfeld*, were sloppily pasted into the last reel with new footage of Garland, the camera pulling away from her close-up and dissolving into the original sequence. Sadly it becomes a major letdown for viewers, after having viewed the other spectacular *original* numbers in the picture. *Ziegfeld Girl* borders on becoming a great picture. But its finale stops it dead in its tracks.

There is that one saving grace—what truly is *the* most spectacular production piece in *Ziegfeld Girl*—the six-minute-long "You Stepped Out of a Dream" sequence. It begins with Tony Martin crooning longingly to one of the showgirls, her eyes and smile fixed in close-up. The orchestral strings and angelic choir then take over for Martin as Berkeley's fluid camerawork glides from one half-clad showgirl and principal to another.

Fascinating in its execution, this number gives Lamarr, Garland, and Turner iconically memorable moments. (Tony Martin never looked more gorgeous himself.) It is perhaps the 1940s' quintessential moment of glamorous screen fantasy. "Each girl emerged from a misty cloud effect, dripping with silver sequins," recalled Busby Berkeley. "With all due respect to the master, Ziegfeld could never have done on stage what we did."[27]

As the showgirls begin their walks up and down those sweepingly perilous steps, it is only when Hedy Lamarr comes into view that one's breath stops for a moment. She is mesmerizing. Dressed like a dream, Hedy begins her walk to the lilting music, looking straight ahead, slowly stepping up sixteen smaller and smaller steps in sync with the music, her arms outstretched, self-assured as she comes to a stop atop a small triangle of a pedestal, and the camera glides in for its glorious close-up.

Judy Garland, draped in shoulder-to-ankle tinsel, does not have it easier, as she maneuvers her moment with a half-dozen other similarly attired showgirls descending steps to the music. But for the finish no one can walk as does Lana Turner, bedecked in tulle and sparkles, her beautiful legs in full view (to accentuate her height) as she flows down some thirty steps—eyes and smile transfixed straight ahead, leading a line of showgirls. It is an unforgettable moment.

"When I see those infinite stairs in that lavish production number that out-Metro's even Metro, I break up," Hedy recalled years later about her torturous walk.

The director, Robert Z. Leonard, had instructed me to walk . . . regally. . . . I was to float erect, arms disdainfully away from my body in the accepted Ziegfeld manner, and never, but never, look down to see where I was going. The fact that I couldn't see in the blinding lights, even straight ahead, was small consolation.

And so I descended [actually, she ascended], teetering [up] what felt like millions of steps, in a glorious Adrian costume encrusted with enough twinkling stars to make Neil Armstrong jealous. Out of camera range, a board was strapped on my back, and part of the headdress was attached to this apparatus. Also out of camera range, my bosom was taped from behind and I felt a little like some religious penitent in the 13th century walking in a torture procession.

And so I came, smilingly, my back top-heavy, and as I paraded gingerly [up] each stair, I had to dispel thoughts of losing my balance and toppling headlong down an entire set to the ground miles below—board, tapes, twinkling stars and all."[28]

Ziegfeld Girl made Lana Turner a star, pulled Judy Garland into adult roles, and glorified Hedy Lamarr's breathtaking beauty. But as much as *Ziegfeld Girl* was equally Hedy's picture, she did not get the salary boost she had anticipated. Her fellow inventor was having no better a time of it.

George Antheil would write, "Now here in early 1941, I could at last label myself a complete failure."[29] (Antheil's film score for *Angels over Broadway* would be his last for almost seven years.) His desire to compose serious music was severely jeopardized by the lack of a steady income. Antheil was barely able to pay off bills by composing stock film music. Relief would eventually come in checks from his dead brother Henry's estate. Antheil and Hedy's relationship would become strained periodically. Her constant badgering about their government submissions and the way her inventing ideas came faster than he was able to act on them were certainly distracting Antheil from his own work.

The torpedo project needed work. "The invention used slotted paper rolls similar to player-piano rolls to synchronize the frequency changes in transmitter and receiver, and even called for exactly eighty-eight frequencies, the number of keys on a piano," wrote Karin Hanta in the May 1997 issue of *Austria Kultur* magazine. "Unfortunately, American warlords did not take the inventors' idea, contending that the mechanism would be too bulky to fit into a torpedo."[30]

"In our patent Hedy and I attempted to better elucidate our mechanism by explaining that certain parts of it worked like the fundamental mechanism of a player-piano," Antheil said. "Here, undoubtedly, we made our mistake. The reverend and brass-headed gentlemen in Washington examined our invention read no further than the words 'player-piano.' 'My god,' I can see them saying, 'we shall put a player-piano in a torpedo.'"[31] Antheil stalled Hedy as much as he could as he worked to make the device small enough to fit into a watch. Then, it was ready.

On June 10, 1941, George Antheil and Hedy Kiesler Markey, the names applied to the patent submission, applied for a patent for their invention, which they called the Secret Communication System. That step completed, Hedy turned her attentions to her mother's plight.

Gertrude Kiesler had escaped the dangerous conditions of war-torn London after years of experiencing the nightly fears and terrors of German air-raid bombings. She now stayed with friends in Canada until she could obtain clearance and passage into America.

Just as she was able to stop worrying about her mother's security, Hedy became the subject of an extortion attempt. She had been receiving ominous warn-ings through the mail. In early May, two letters were delivered to her in the mail that were written in longhand, demanding $500 "or else." Hedy was told to leave the money near a gutter at First and Main Streets in downtown Los Angeles. If she failed to do so, one letter read, "You'll be so scarred up you'll never see your-self in pictures again."[32] Signed "Unemployed Bud," the letters were postmarked in Los Angeles.

Hedy thought the first letter was a joke. But then, when the second arrived, she quickly turned both letters over to FBI authorities, upon the advice of Metro's legal team. On July 3, twenty-two-year-old Santa Monica aircraft me-chanic Sidney M. Buchanan, an army deserter, was arrested in Baltimore and charged with extortion. He had been stationed in California, where he mailed the letters, then was transferred to Maryland, where he deserted. Upon Bu-chanan's arrest, a writ was signed to bring him back to Los Angeles to face federal charges. (On November 21, after pleading guilty, he was sentenced by Judge Paul J. McCormick to eighteen months in federal jail.)

Hedy, after having handled that situation, considered her future with Metro and sensed Mayer had again lost interest in her. Jimmie Fidler informed his read-ers: "Hedy Lamarr, now on layoff as provided in her contract, may be suspended any minute for fractious behavior at M.G.M.; not even her boy friends know her new phone number, which IS news."[33] (Only the studio and Reggie were privy to it.) It was apparent Fidler was being handed inside information from the studio. His remarks were often specifically designed to pull stars into line.

During this period Hedy relied on her own intuition to make decisions. "My hunches are always right," she told the journalist Gladys Hall. "I am a hunch-player. I play hunches because I believe in mine. It is not just hunches, however. They are more than that. It is like someone guiding me right. *Some One.* I really believe that. I would never describe myself as religious in the sense that I believe in one creed, or go to any one church, but—*I believe.*"[34]

That summer of 1941 Hedy was seated to the left of King Vidor, the director of *Comrade X,* at a fashionable dinner party. As the evening progressed the discussion turned to Vidor's newest project for Metro, a film version of John P. Marquand's recent novel *H.M. Pulham, Esq.,* which M-G-M had purchased in April for $50,000. Sensing that their hostess's seating arrangement was prear-ranged, Vidor told Hedy straight out that she was not right for any part in the script, which was being prepared by Elizabeth Hill, Vidor's wife.

Hedy smiled pleasantly back at the director, feigning absolute indifference to the project. She then received at her home the following day a dozen roses and a note from Vidor requesting that she join him for lunch to discuss the picture. Meeting at Romanoff's later that week, Vidor offered Hedy the role of the heroine of the book.[35] Vidor's clout with Metro at that time was powerful. If he thought Hedy was appropriate, Mayer was not going to debate the issue.

Hedy was tested in early July for the role of Marvin Miles ("Myles" in the film) Ransome. Lew Ayres was also tested and was presumably considered for the second male lead of Bill King in the film. (Later that month the veteran actor Herbert Marshall was a serious contender for the lead role. At one point, the role of Pulham was also discussed for Robert Taylor and that of Pulham's wife for Myrna Loy.) On July 25 it was announced that Hedy had won the part and that Van Heflin would appear as Bill King, Ruth Hussey as Kay Motford Pulham, and Robert Young as the lead character, H. M. Pulham Jr.[36]

But before filming commenced on *H.M. Pulham, Esq.*, Hedy was finally allowed to make her first appearance on a national radio program, in an adaptation of *Algiers* with Charles Boyer for *The Lux Radio Theater*, broadcast from Hollywood on CBS. The show was hosted by Cecil B. DeMille. *The Lux Radio Theater,* which had begun in New York in 1936, had become the most popular and successful weekly radio anthology in history and would draw an estimated 40 million listeners every Monday night.

Algiers would be both Boyer's and Hedy's first *Lux Radio Theater* performance and also the last radio play of the show's seventh successful season. Hedy sounded enormously confident in her performance.

Immediately after the broadcast, Hedy made a quick trip to New York. While she was at a party held at the plush apartment of Cornelius Vanderbilt "Sonny" Whitney, the young actor Macdonald Carey sat at her feet throughout the evening singing "Das ist die liebe der Matrosen," the only song in German he knew. He recalled that Hedy's eyes misted over with emotion, her longing for Vienna apparent as she quietly sang along with him. (It was at this party that Darryl Zanuck spotted Carey and offered him a Fox screen test the following day.)[37] By the end of the week Hedy left New York, boarding a train for California.

Arriving in Chicago aboard the 20th Century Limited to make her connection, Hedy then switched to the Super Chief for the remainder of the journey to the coast. Also on the train were the publicist Milton Weiss, accompanying a newly signed M-G-M starlet, eighteen-year-old Ava Lavinia Gardner (discovered by Metro talent scout Barney Duhan), and her older sister, Beatrice, who was known as "Bappie." Bappie remarked to Ava when she heard that Hedy Lamarr was on the same train, "That makes two movie queens on board."[38] (Young Ava Gardner would make a brief appearance in *H.M. Pulham, Esq.* before meeting and marrying Metro's biggest box-office star Mickey Rooney.)

Production began on *H.M. Pulham, Esq.* on July 30, with actual filming starting on August 2. The story, adapted from Marquand's then-bestselling novel, which sold 200,000 copies in its first six months, tells the story of Harry Moulton Pulham Jr. (Robert Young), a Back Bay Bostonian. He leads an average and somewhat affluent life in Boston and has been married twenty years to the former Cornelia "Kay" Motford (Ruth Hussey). While working on his biography for his twenty-fifth class reunion, Pulham looks back on his life in a series of flashbacks. As a young man he had returned to New York after serving in the war. There he met the beautiful copywriter Marvin Myles (Hedy) at J. T. Bullards, Inc., an advertising agency where he worked.

The two fell in love, but Pulham's father, Harry Sr. (Charles Coburn), sadly died, and Harry had to return to the stuffy confines of his wealthy family in Boston. Marvin pleaded with him to stay in New York with her, but he could not. Marvin told Harry she would always wait for him. The years slip by, and now he is preparing his biography. Suddenly, Marvin happens to contact Harry while she is visiting Boston. The two meet, and she is older but just as beautiful as ever. They realize they still love each other, but time cannot change things. They bid farewell once again, and Harry returns to the comfortable life and love of his wife.

Metro carefully designed this picture to elevate Robert Young to stardom. The thirty-four-year-old Young had already proven himself over the years a durable and competent actor for the studio in such films as *The Sin of Madelon Claudet* (1931), *Three Comrades* and *The Toy Wife* (both 1938), *Northwest Passage* and *The Mortal Storm* (both 1940). Recently he had starred in *Lady Be Good*, with Hedy's best friend Ann Sothern. Now in *H.M. Pulham, Esq.* Young was given the strongest role of his career.

Under Vidor's direction, Hedy gave a brilliant performance, guided by a man who knew how to bring an understanding of her character out of her, as he had done in *Comrade X*. Nearly everyone in the picture, especially Robert Young and Hedy, would receive possibly the best reviews of their respective film careers.

10

Actress

From Newburyport, Massachusetts, on August 18, 1941, the novelist John P. Marquand, the author of *H.M. Pulham, Esquire,* wrote his friends King and Elizabeth "Betty" (Hill) Vidor. "I am also wondering," he asked, questioning the casting of Hedy, "although I knew you were leaning that way, whether you are seriously going to have Hedy Lamarr play Marvin Miles or whether this is merely an artistic impulse which you are reconsidering?"[1]

Indeed Vidor was going to use Hedy in his twenty-second motion picture for M-G-M. Vidor knew, as did other directors, that if she was handled properly he could pull an intelligent performance from her. Hedy respected Vidor and worked hard to perfect her characterization of Marvin. She would later praise Vidor, stating he was a "wonderful, wonderful director!"[2] Vidor explained his selection of Hedy by saying that he needed her to contrast with Ruth Hussey, who could very well have played either female lead. Hedy's beauty was the key to her selection.

Marvin was written as an American girl, and New York and Hollywood gossips sat in wait for Hedy to fall on her celebrated face. "What the town has considered the major miscasting of the year," wrote the critic Douglas W. Churchill in *The New York Times,* "[is] the placing of Hedy Lamarr in the role of an efficient American business woman in an advertising agency."[3] Because the Vidors were friends of his and he trusted their judgment, Marquand's only comment was, "It is an interesting idea, and not bad, if you can make Miss

Lamarr into a young American business woman. She is certainly the sort of person a man might remember for twenty years."[4]

Hedy knew Vidor was taking a chance in his casting, as did the dependable actor Robert Young, who also was well aware of the opportunity the studio was giving him by starring him in this picture. "I'm glad I had to wait ten years for this break," he said, "because it is going to take every bit of experience I managed to get in that time to play it."[5]

The screenplay only varied from the novel by leaving out the affair between Kay and Bill King. This omission eliminated a possible clash between the studio and the Hays Office. The novelist had shown the Vidors about Boston. For weeks they lived and breathed everything "Bostonia" and studied all the traditions and facets of Harvard University and the city. For four months Vidor diligently prepared his work before shooting began.

Later, during the filming, he brought a metronome to the set. Because the character of Pulham was a studied individual, Young was required to enact his middle-aged scenes to the beat of the metronome—one six-minute sequence took 720 beats of time, 120 beats to the minute. "An example of this is the first breakfast sequence," wrote Vidor in an extensive outline, "Notes on Techniques Employed in 'H.M. Pulham, Esquire,'" "where the whole meal is performed and consumed in timing to the metronome."[6]

Vidor instructed the cinematographer Ray June to use fluid camera work and continuous movement, especially in the outdoor sequences. There are virtually no close-ups in the picture. Also, Vidor insisted on several scenes without a single cut or dissolve, for instance in the transition from Marvin's apartment to the roof garden. "The camera centers on the back of Harry's coat as they [he and Marvin] are dancing in her apartment and when the camera pulls back again from Harry's coat we see the Roof Garden," Vidor explained in his outline.[7] There were sixty-two sets constructed for the picture, all meticulously detailed down to the reproduction of the American landscape artist George Innes's painting, so frequently mentioned in the book.

H.M. Pulham, Esq. is a story told in first person, parts of it using voice-over, much as Eugene O'Neill had successfully done in his *Strange Interlude*. Vidor attempted to capture the feel of reflective haziness to match the vagueness of a person's thoughts. Much of the picture was also structured in flashbacks, a technique quite similar to one used by Orson Welles that same year in his landmark R-K-O film *Citizen Kane*. During the production of *H.M. Pulham,*

Esq. Vidor also insisted on filming extensive makeup tests of his stars to determine just the correct aging images they would require, all the while stressing mannerisms over makeup.

A lengthy film, 119 minutes, *H.M. Pulham, Esq.* was budgeted at $734,676.90, less salaries. Young received $2,750 weekly per his contract, Hedy a total of $17,083.32. Vidor received $130,424.99 total for his bringing the production in within its forty-two allotted production days. The final cost of *H.M. Pulham, Esq.* was $3,818,000. Filming was completed on September 19, 1941.

In early October, Metro announced another plan to star Robert Taylor and Hedy, in a story about Alexander Hamilton by Dorothy Thompson and Fritz Kortner entitled *The Dawn's Early Light*. Purchased by the studio two years before as a project in which Spencer Tracy would be cast as Thomas Jefferson, Robert Young as Aaron Burr, and Laraine Day as Betsy Bowen, the title was then changed to *The Gentleman from the West Indies*. It was to be produced by Sam Zimbalist, with Hedy now in the starring role of Madame Le Croix, opposite Taylor's Hamilton. *The Gentleman from the West Indies* never materialized past the talk stage.

After trying again and spending an extremely unsuccessful holiday together, Hedy and John Howard stopped dating. When asked if she would ever marry an actor, Hedy replied, "I am NEVER going to marry an actor. You can quote me. You can quote me as saying I WILL NEVER MARRY an ACTOR!"[8]

Hedy by then was a big box-office draw, and that September she was listed among the top fourteen film favorite stars voted for by *Young America,* a national weekly, by thirteen-year-old students polled around the nation.

One project Hedy originally did not want to do was *Tortilla Flat,* which Metro had lined up for her next film. Its star would be Spencer Tracy. Hedy did not like working with Tracy, and she did not feel she was right for the part of Dolores "Sweets" Ramirez, a displaced Mexican migrant worker. With her recent pay increase denied by the studio, and what she interpreted as an inferior script, Hedy flatly refused the part. The powers that be at Metro retaliated with leaks to the gossip columnists.

Hedda Hopper kicked off her July 21 column with, "That lovely Inez Cooper, discovered by Mervyn Leroy, and looks like Hedy Lamarr with ammunition, is being considered for the lead in 'Tortilla Flat' with Spencer Tracy. Here's hoping she'll get it."[9] Hedy reconsidered the role, not just to spite Hedda but possibly because she understood that the challenge of portraying an ethnic character at this juncture might enhance her career.

Hedy cared about the quality of her work (it was reported that while watching the rushes of *H.M. Pulham, Esq.*, Hedy had torn her handkerchief to shreds as she dissected her performance). Yet the indifferent *Los Angeles Times* gossip columnist Jimmie Fidler felt it necessary to remind her that Metro had signed Inez Cooper because the "studio is grooming her for your shoes should you misbehave."[10]

At the same time *The Hollywood Citizen-News* surprised the film community with the headline "Hedy Comes Up with Idea for U.S. Defense" on September 30, 1941, and further reported, "From the decorative head of Hedy Lamarr has come an idea which has 'great potential value' to the United States." This was revealed by Colonel L. B. Lent, the chief engineer of the National Inventors Council of the Department of Commerce, at a press conference held at the Roosevelt Hotel in Hollywood. Hedy played down her accomplishment for the press: "The idea just came to me. . . . I never thought of such a thing before and probably never shall again."[11]

The following day, October 1, *The New York Times* wrote, "HEDY LAMARR INVENTOR—Actress Devises 'Red-Hot' Apparatus for Use in Defense." The article said, "So vital is her discovery to national defense that government officials will not allow publication of its details. Colonel L. B. Lent, chief engineer of the National Inventors Council, classed Miss Lamarr's invention as in the 'red hot' category. The only inkling of what it might be was the announcement that it was related to remote control of apparatus employed in warfare."[12]

The *Los Angeles Times* then picked up the story, repeating that Hedy's invention was "red-hot" and developed for the National Inventors Council, for which more than 30,000 ideas had already been submitted, although little more than one hundred actually had been accepted, and only about a half dozen of those were considered "red-hot." Few took the news seriously, though. Hedy's fortune was in her looks.

And Hedy's beautiful face was a cameraman's dream to work with. She was photographed once behind the steering wheel of her car at her home by the noted photographer Peter Stackpole, and when Clarence Sinclair Bull, one of Hollywood's leading portrait photographers (he had been Greta Garbo's favorite) called upon Hedy at Hedgerow Farm for a casual sitting, she prepared him lunch by the kitchen sink. "This is the first time a star's ever done this for me," he remarked. "Oh, I always fix my lunch by the kitchen sink when I'm alone. It's easier," she said.[13] Hedy was always gracious with studio employees and technicians.

She was also photographed by Man Ray and Trude Fleischman, who had taken museum-quality portraits of Hedy in Europe. The famed artist James Montgomery Flagg once painted her and said of her in his book *Roses and Buckshot* that only a blind or a deaf man could not fall in love with her.

Yet Hedy had her detractors. The Hungarian photographer Laszlo Willinger left Germany when Hitler came to power and fled to Vienna, where he also photographed young Hedy Kiesler. Willinger did not like her. "How do you make Hedy Lamarr sexy?" he complained. "She has nothing to give. It wasn't as simple as showing legs or cleavage. She was not very adept at posing. She was just . . . She felt if she sat there, that was enough. You try to bring it to some life by changing the lighting, moving in closer to the head, whatever, because nothing changed her face. It never occurred to me that one could wake her up . . . and nobody ever did."[14]

The legendary photographer George Hurrell felt much the same way. Hurrell first photographed Hedy when she arrived in Hollywood. "I didn't get too much out of Hedy because she was so static," he told the late film historian John Kobal. "Stunning. But it was the nature of her, she was so phlegmatic, she didn't project anything. It was just a mood thing. And she had just one style. It didn't vary particularly. She had a pretty good body. But she wouldn't dress for it. She was always dressing in black. She liked suits. You can't do anything—a woman in a suit is a dead duck."[15] By 1941 Hedy was more confident, and her static period was over. Suits and basic black were quickly becoming fashions of the past as her tastes began to evolve.

Hedy was granted full custody of little Jamesie on November 3, 1941. Appearing in court with the little boy, she testified that she had met his birth mother shortly before his delivery, and when the mother died Hedy took the baby home. She named Mary Ford, who was the wife of the director John Ford, as Jamesie's godmother. Jamesie retained the Markey surname.

M-G-M purchased a screen story by Eleanore Griffin and William Rankin entitled *The Harvey Girls,* an adventure about five waitresses during the development of the Harvey railroad restaurant chain. The projected film was slated to star Hedy with Lana Turner, Ruth Hussey, Patricia Dane, and Marsha Hunt.

But it never happened for Hedy. Then on November 6, Hedy and Joan Crawford both turned down Metro's planned remake of *Her Cardboard Lover,* and
Norma Shearer took the part.

On Sunday at 8 PM, November 30, 1941, Hedy appeared for the first time on
The Edgar Bergen / Charlie McCarthy Show (formerly called *The Chase and Sanborn Program*), broadcast over NBC. The extremely popular show was hosted
by Bergen, a ventriloquist, and his wise-cracking wooden dummy, Charlie Mc-
Carthy. It featured guest appearances by some of Hollywood's brightest stars,
comedians, and popular singers.

Hedy confessed in an interview, "I suffer from mike fright, underline my
part in a radio script in red pencil and have the pages mounted on cardboard,
so that they won't rustle in my hands."[16] But from the start she thoroughly enjoyed her work on the show.

Meanwhile, *Tortilla Flat* had begun filming on November 23, with Spencer
Tracy and Hedy in the lead roles. As added box-office insurance the young
stage and film actor John Garfield, born on New York's Lower East Side, was
borrowed from Warner Bros. to play Danny. All three incongruously portrayed poor Hispanic Californians living in Northern California, as did the
character actor John Qualen, who specialized in playing Swedes. Based on
the bestselling 1935 novel by John Steinbeck, with screen adaptation by John
Lee Mahin and Benjamin Glazer, *Tortilla Flat* was assigned to the rugged
Metro director Victor Fleming. M-G-M had bought the rights to the project
for $65,000 on April 8, 1940, announcing it as a vehicle for Tracy. Steinbeck,
fearing that his beloved *paisano* characters would be patronized and made
quaint, offered to purchase the rights of his story back from M-G-M for $10,000.
When Sam Zimbalist, the producer, and Mahin met with Steinbeck at a Monterey bar with their treatment of the story, he asked them, "What are you doing
to my story?" They replied, "We've butched it up plenty." They then ordered
drinks and sat until three in the morning discussing the screenplay.[17]

At one point, while Hedy dragged her heels before accepting the role, Metro
had wanted to secure the services of Rita Hayworth, now a huge star at Columbia Pictures, for the part of Sweets Ramirez. Former child actress Margaret
O'Brien recalled that M-G-M had also offered the role of Sweets to her aunt,
the beautiful Marissa Flores, who once was the lead flamenco dancer with
Xavier Cugat's band and coincidentally resembled Hedy.

In the early 1940s, when M-G-M signed little Margaret O'Brien to a long-term contract, Margaret's mother (who also somewhat resembled Hedy and for whom Mayer had a particular fondness) mentioned that the studio should also sign her sister Marissa, who was not only beautiful but talented as well. Metro agreed and promised Marissa a brilliant career. Instead, Flores was used as a bargaining tool to force the reluctant Lamarr to take the role of Sweets. "Which sort of ruined the career of a look-a-like," O'Brien recalled. Regarding her aunt, O'Brien sighed, "They used her as a threat . . . my aunt was told she was going to do *Tortilla Flat*. She tested for it. . . . and they were going to give her the part. And she was all set for it with all the costumes. . . . And Hedy came back and that was the end of that. . . . I don't think my aunt ever got over that."[18] Flores would eventually appear in only one film, on loan to Twentieth Century–Fox, *To the Shores of Tripoli* (1942).

In the Steinbeck novel, the story's narration contributes to its charm. Fleming was faced with transforming the book into a rural film, made completely on the vast soundstages of Metro-Goldwyn-Mayer. For the filming of *Tortilla Flat*, Metro constructed an immense set on its largest soundstage, which covered three acres, complete with various poultry, livestock, and a dozen hounds, at a cost of $30,000.

Unfortunately, along with a leading cast that was truly more out of place than the Hispanic bit players, the released film still projected a definite sound-stage quality. Yet somehow Fleming, working in tandem with the screenwriters, who were faithful to the novel's use of lingo and mood, managed to pull it together. (In the original story, Dolores "Sweets" Ramirez was but a minor character. For cinematic purposes her character's importance was built up.)

The story revolves around the lives of poor, impoverished Mexican *paisanos* who live in a Northern California coastal fishing village just north of Monterey called Tortilla Flat. Pilon (Tracy) and Pablo (Akim Tamiroff) are but a couple of the wanderers and scoundrels who populate the village. The other *paisanos* who follow Pilon, the ringleader, are Portegee Joe (Staten Island–born Allen Jenkins), Jose Maria Corcoran (John Qualen), and Danny Alvarez (John Garfield). Sweets Ramirez is the town beauty.

Unexpectedly Danny (Garfield) inherits two houses and a watch. He generously rents one of the houses to his pals for $15 a month and keeps the other house for himself. He sells his watch for money to buy wine and rejoins the group in their wasteful laziness. He is soon drawn to the beautiful cannery worker Dolores.

Pilon wants Pablo to stay with him, charging him $15 a month to make the rent, and soon Portegee Joe and Jose move in too. One day the eccentric Pirate (Frank Morgan) comes into town with his five dogs—Enrique, Sir Alex Thompson, Frog, Pirito, and Rudolph. Pilon plans a way to buy wine by befriending Pirate, who supposedly has money. Pilon invites Pirate to live with him and his group of ne'er-do-wells, and Pirate entrusts Pilon with a bag of money for safe-keeping. Pirate then informs Pilon that the money is meant to be used for a golden candlestick for Saint Francis, whom he believes once saved one of his dogs from death. Thwarted in his original plan, Pilon helps Pirate's dream come true and becomes a better man because of it.

Pilon has, however, created trouble between Danny and Dolores. After a fire destroys one of Danny's houses, a fight between Danny and the cannery workers breaks out. Danny is critically injured and taken to a hospital. Dolores rightfully blames Pilon for all that has happened. After praying in church for Danny's recovery, Pilon now realizes the importance of friendship. He finds a job cutting heads off of squid. Danny miraculously recovers, and he and Dolores marry. There is a public raffle to buy a new fishing boat for Danny. But unbeknownst to everyone, it is Pilon's money that pays for the boat, money he saved for Danny to help him escape the lifestyle that exists in Tortilla Flat. After Danny and Dolores leave, Pilon reasons that it was Danny's houses that were the source of all his woes. A carelessly discarded match eliminates the *paisanos'* problems.

This was a simple tale about simple people. The story of *Tortilla Flat* did not have the same universal appeal of Steinbeck's earlier filmed novels, *Of Mice and Men* and *The Grapes of Wrath*, which became tremendous box-office bonanzas. But M-G-M took a chance with this early work of the author, and the filmed version proved a moving and sincerely made project that surprisingly was sensitive and lovingly executed.

Garfield enjoyed working with Hedy in their love scenes, calling her Wild Cat Lamarr, and she relished the opportunity of not having to glamorize her character. She wore ten-cent lipstick and rubbed grease on her body to darken her porcelain skin. Tracy called her costumes her "dime-store wardrobe." One of her outfits cost a total of $3.95.

Fleming had a penchant for calling his leading ladies Angel, and Hedy took this as quite a compliment until she realized he also called the extra girls the same. Coached by the studio's "co-ordinator of speech," Dr. Simon Mitchneck,

Hedy was able to pitch her voice down to a lower, middle register, which effectively aided her characterization. In one particular scene, filmed at the fish cannery, Hedy actually worked on a fish-canning line, sweating real sweat and packing real fish. She loved that she was required to be smelly and dirty, and she took special pleasure in doing that particular scene.

Hedy also enjoyed working with Garfield. Together they projected remarkable screen chemistry. Hedy took delight in Garfield's stories of riding the rails as a hobo when he was a youngster, before becoming an actor. There was something very Steinbeckian in his persona. Hedy loved adventure, and her romantic fantasies were whetted by his tales. This time around Hedy liked working with Tracy as well. When the day came for the last scene of the picture to be shot, Hedy told a journalist, "I guess this is the only movie in which the last scene was actually shot last. The reason is that the set was burned up, goes away in flames. Spencer and I watched it burn, our Tortilla Flat where we had been happy."[19]

When a movie was in production during the 1930s and 1940s, filming would continue on weekends and on Sundays, and actors would literally be on call twenty-four hours a day. And so it was on Sunday morning, December 7, 1941, as Tracy, Garfield, and Hedy were gathered together rehearsing a scene with Fleming on the vast soundstage on the Metro lot, that the country was forced into World War II.

The *Los Angeles Times* that morning had published in its movie listings Metro-Goldwyn-Mayer's weekly Lion's Roar column, heralding the arrival of *H.M. Pulham, Esq.* "You'll pull for *Pulham*" was the tagline.[20] In Los Angeles that sunny morning, a radio concert was in progress (the pianist Arthur Rubinstein just completing Tchaikovsky's Piano Concerto No. 1). Suddenly it was interrupted by an important news message. Japanese airplanes and submarines had attacked and sunk the American fleet in Pearl Harbor.

Immediately news permeated the confines of the Metro soundstages, where in only minutes the doors were scheduled to be sealed tight to eliminate intrusion on the filming. Hedy excused herself to a dark corner of the set and softly wept. Within hours of the attack, President Franklin D. Roosevelt announced the country's entry into the war. On December 11, Germany also declared war on the United States.

Later that week Hedy conferred with Mayer and Metro officials, begging them to expedite her mother's emigration from Canada. They promised their immediate attention. Hedy's working relationship with George Antheil resumed once more with mutual purpose. Her overwhelming desire to combat the enemy in whatever arena she could was now at fever pitch. And still, to her continuous frustration, there was no news from the government regarding their "red-hot" invention.

H.M. Pulham, Esq. had previewed on November 8, 1941. Immediately, word of mouth spread regarding Hedy's performance. *Daily Variety* raved, "Hedy Lamarr has a role which suits her personality well, and she emphatically demonstrates her ability as an actress."[21] *The Hollywood Reporter* was equally enthusiastic, "Hedy Lamarr undertakes the assignment of a business girl, Marvin Myles, and pre-production critics were quick to voice their objections to her so-called miscasting. The manner in which Miss Lamarr comes through puts to a glorious end all the controversy, leaving her critics with a lot of words to eat. She does Marvin Myles . . . so that it is impossible to imagine any other actress in the part—that's how excellent she is."[22]

As the country reeled from the attack on Pearl Harbor and prepared for war, M-G-M released *H.M. Pulham, Esq.* nationally. The timing, through no fault of the studio's, could not have been worse. America was not in the mood for a period picture reflecting a romantic era gone by. *H.M. Pulham, Esq.* was lost at the box office. But the reviews, nonetheless, were superb. The important Bosley Crowther of *The New York Times* raved, "In brief, Mr. Vidor has . . . got from Miss Lamarr one of the sharpest and most insinuating performances of her career."[23] And the *PM* critic agreed, "Hedy Lamarr as the woman in his [Pulham's] life is astonishing: she's wonderful. Freed here of the rigid mask of glamour, she's human, warm, beautiful and responsive."[24]

The film critic of *Movie-Radio Guide* was enchanted with Hedy's performance, raving, "Hedy Lamarr becomes a great actress in *H.M. Pulham, Esq.* . . . Hedy does take her longest step upward from the nautilus-shell of sheer feminine glamour. She loosens up more than ever before and turns in a grand performance. . . . Her role may not win her an Oscar. But it will undoubtedly go a long way toward establishing her as the outstanding actress she yearns to be."[25] *H.M. Pulham, Esq.* would eventually pull in a profit for Metro, but not as quickly as had been anticipated.

Despite box-office apathy, *H.M. Pulham, Esq.* provided film audiences with the best the studio had to offer. The story transports the viewer to a specific era of time, carefully re-created by King Vidor. With a sterling cast and a compelling story line, *H.M. Pulham, Esq.* moves at a brisk clip. Hedy is dressed by

Robert Kalloch in twelve different costumes, accentuated more often than not with pearls. She wears upsweep period hairstyles throughout the picture. Her own performance is quietly underplayed and quite effective—especially in two key scenes, one in a Greenwich Village café, and the other in an unusually tender moment with Pulham at her apartment, photographed in dark shadows. For many, *H.M. Pulham, Esq.* would give Hedy her finest cinematic moment. And garbed in period costumes and hairstyles, Hedy never looked lovelier.

Regarding the Lamarr style, it was possibly most significantly influenced by M-G-M's new costume designer Robert Kalloch, for whom *H.M. Pulham, Esq.* would be the first of four films he would design for Hedy. Kalloch, whose tenure with the studio lasted only two years, had designed for B movies at Columbia Pictures until 1941. He signed with Metro just as long-term costume designer Adrian was departing.

Taking over as the chief fashion designer for the studio, Kalloch created the Lamarr look. His penchant for straight and angular designs for her—long sleeves; high-necked and often bejeweled collars; simple, sleek, and clinging long- and short-skirted fashions—was his defining contribution to contemporary couture style. Hedy's face was her fortune, and Kalloch made no attempt to distract from its allure. Instead, he fashioned hats and costumes, jewelry and accessories, to flatter her natural beauty, not to overenhance it. His designs were almost masculine in their concepts in order to emphasize Hedy's overpowering feminine beauty. His impact on Hedy's look can not be understated—it is timeless. By 1943 Kalloch was gone from Metro, retiring from film work, returning to design gowns for only two more films before his death in 1947.

As 1941 came to a close Hedy once more appeared on *The Lux Radio Theater,* on December 29, in a comedy called "The Bride Came C.O.D." with Bob Hope. They made a delightful duo, and Hedy was relaxed and comfortable as a slapstick heiress, a role not as well handled by Bette Davis in the Warner Bros. film version released in July. In the midst of the radio play, Hope's character offhandedly asks Hedy's character, "Who do you think you are, Hedy Lamarr?"

One day outside her home during the filming of *Tortilla Flat,* Hedy noticed men working on the manhole and stepped outside to watch. There she met the young actor George Montgomery as he was driving by. (One story says they met at a tennis party at the home of Fred MacMurray and his wife.) The two talked and made a date before he drove off. Montgomery was then working at Twentieth Century–Fox in *Ten Gentleman from West Point.*

A former stunt double, the six-feet-three, twenty-six-year-old Montgomery (real name George Montgomery Letz) had been in motion pictures since 1935. He was primarily considered a Western film actor. But Montgomery was also featured in several contemporary pictures, including *Orchestra Wives* for Fox in 1942, arguably his best cinematic role. Relatively unknown when he met Hedy, Montgomery was handsome and terribly appealing. Soon he was photographed with Hedy, who was slightly older than he, on the set of *Tortilla Flat* before its wrap on February 12. The couple quickly became an item in the columns.

Toward the end of January Metro announced its plan to reteam Robert Taylor and Hedy yet again. Taylor's sexuality, though he was married to Barbara Stanwyck at this time, was always the subject of debate around town. In the studio's effort to "masculinize" the handsome actor, all stops were pulled to team him with the studio's sexiest and most beautiful female stars. He had just played opposite Lana Turner ("Taylor and Turner are *T'N'T!*" shouted the publicity) in Metro's *Johnny Eager.* Unfortunately, he played a dandy opposite Norma Shearer in his next film, *Her Cardboard Lover,* a huge Metro flop. It was time for damage control.

Now faced with Taylor entering the U.S. Army Air Corps, the studio was desperate to "butch up" his image and keep his career going. The project they chose for him and Hedy was *Distant Valley,* a screenplay adaptation of Mildred Cram's novel *Forever,* a sensitive story about two lovers who knew each other in past lives. It possibly could have worked. Hedda Hopper had championed *Forever* in her column as far back as that February. She called it "the prize story of the last three years."[26]

The property had been bought by the actress Janet Gaynor in the 1930s, and she eventually sold it to M-G-M in 1940 for around $6,500. Norma Shearer was interested in starring in a film version. But with the title changed to *Distant Valley,* it was revamped for Hedy and Taylor. Hedy passed on it.[27]

Some good news finally came when Trude Kiesler arrived in New York in late January. After departing England and eventually landing in Canada, Trude had disembarked off a Greek troop transport, which had been at sea for weeks zigzagging through submarine-infested waters. Following a wait in Canada, it took three days for her to make the cross-country train trip to California. Arriving at Pasadena's Union Station on Monday, February 2, Trude, carrying her dark Scottie terrier, Cherie, was met by her daughter and a flood of photographers.

Hedy was heard to exclaim, "Mother!" to which Trude cried, "It is so wonderful to be here." Both women wept with joy. It had been almost five years since they had seen each other.

Hedy acquired a maid, named Mary, and a cook, whom Hedy requested shop at Elgee Meats for exclusive Eastern cuts for her mother. Hedy was happy to be reunited with Trude, and every morning the two women would take a fifteen-minute swim in the pool before breakfast.

Hedy told the journalist Gladys Hall, "No-one knows more of what war can do than my mother. She is like a little soldier. She has been through two wars, you might say, the *Anschluss* in Austria, then four years in England where every night, every night, she went through the bombings and, all the time, through privations. When, at last, it was made possible for her to come over here she went through an ordeal that would have broken a less gallant woman."[28]

On February 5 Hedy was assigned the film *Crossroads* opposite Metro's forty-nine-year-old William Powell (Nick Charles of *The Thin Man* series). *Crossroads* was a remake of the 1938 French film *Carrefour,* which was directed by Curtis Bernhardt and written by Hans Cafka (John Kafka). For the new film, Edwin Knopf was made producer, and on February 6 Jack Conway was assigned as director. Filming commenced two weeks later.

The film, originally titled *Crossroads*, later called *Till I Return* and then *The Man Who Lost His Way*, was in early March again titled *Crossroads*. It told an intriguing story. In Paris in 1935, David Talbot (William Powell), who works for the French government and is up for the position of ambassador to Brazil, and his new wife, Lucienne (Hedy), receive a note demanding David repay a million-franc loan. The Talbots know nothing about this debt. David had received a head injury on March 27, 1922, when the Marseilles-Paris Express he was traveling on was wrecked, and he now has no memory of his life before that. The accuser, Carlos Le Duc (Vladimir Sokoloff), testifies in court that the debt is owed by David and that David is really Jean Pelletier, a criminal who borrowed the money and then suddenly disappeared. Michele Allaine (Claire Trevor) substantiates his testimony by testifying that David is indeed Pelletier and that he had been her lover.

Henri Sarrou (Basil Rathbone) throws a wrench into the proceedings when he testifies in court that he had actually been with Pelletier the night he died. Le Duc is found guilty of extortion and is sent to prison, and David is set free. Later Sarrou tells David his testimony was a lie and that David *is* Pelletier; that he, Sarrou, had been David's accomplice; and that the million francs are now due him for a robbery/murder the two have committed. David begins to believe the story and then is shown a picture of him with Michele in an intimate pose. Lucienne feels she must help David and asks Dr. Andre Tessier (Felix Bressart) to speak with her husband. He does, encouraging David to act on his suspicions. After David cleverly traps the true accomplices with the help of the police, Michele breaks down and confesses she has lied.

Three days after the *Crossroads* cameras began to turn, Hedy was a guest on *The Edgar Bergen / Charlie McCarthy Show* again. She followed this radio show just two weeks later with another, "Too Many Husbands" for *The Screen Guild Players*, broadcast over WABC from Los Angeles on March 8. Hedy starred opposite Bing Crosby and again with Bob Hope. "Too Many Husbands" was a brisk thirty-minute condensation of the popular 1940 Columbia Pictures comedy.

Hedy also appeared with Milton Berle for his *Three Ring Time* program and again in April on the Armed Forces Network's *Command Performance,* hosted by Edward G. Robinson. She was becoming comfortable doing these radio shows, and they were making her an extremely well-known personality. Meanwhile, briskly shot in just six weeks, filming concluded on *Crossroads* in April.

That spring Hedy was seen about Hollywood on the arm of George Montgomery. They were photographed everywhere, and Montgomery's studio began planning big things for the young actor. Together Hedy and George attended the annual Academy Awards ceremony, though they were dressed down in respect of war. At the clubs, which were still actively in full force, the two were always the most beautiful couple present. While Reginald Gardiner used to bring Hedy jewelry and rings, George Montgomery would give her orchids.

George called Hedy Penny for some reason. But it made Hedy smile. "I am so happy I am dizzy," Hedy told her friends. "It is unbelievable that one girl could be so in love. . . . I have never been in love like this before."[29] Montgomery also gifted Hedy with a large sweater of his and a $100 bottle of Shalimar perfume, plus a silver bracelet from Olvera Street and a clay Popeye he had won for throwing baseballs in an arcade at a popular nightspot. Montgomery's parents embraced Hedy when he first introduced them to her, and she spent the evening conversing with them in their native Russian.

It was announced that Hedy, Luise Rainer, and Greer Garson were being considered for the starring role of Jade in Metro's upcoming production of

Dragon Seed, based on a novel by Pearl S. Buck, and a sort of companion piece to the studio's big 1937 blockbuster *The Good Earth,* also by Buck. Katharine Hepburn was the "dark horse" in the running for the coveted role. It was scheduled to begin production immediately after *Crossroads* concluded, but plans fell through, and it was shelved until April 1944, when Hepburn took the role as Jade.

It did not surprise the film community when, on March 24, Hedy, sporting a diamond ring, appeared on the Metro lot and announced her engagement to George Montgomery. Although she didn't set a specific date for them to wed, she was heard to remark "sometime this summer." Suddenly the name George Montgomery was on the lips of every gossip in Hollywood. Immediately, Hedy enrolled the gangly Montana cowboy-actor into a dance school, as reported by Hedda Hopper, "and the other night at the Mocambo he and the little woman put on a rumba that had the customers gaping!"[30] On April 12, public interest peaked about the impending nuptials when columnist Read Kendall of the *Los Angeles Times* speculated that the couple would wed in Las Vegas by that coming weekend, as the wedding-license clerk in Gretna Green, Nevada, had received a wire from Hedy reputedly telling him to expect them.

Then *The New York Times* printed a sterling four-column piece about the life and rise of George Montgomery. In the article "Up from the Range," the columnist observed, "For an ex-cowpuncher, George Montgomery isn't doing badly at all. . . . Only incidentally, of course, Mr. Montgomery recently sealed his intentions of becoming Hedy Lamarr's next husband. What it all adds up to, in short, is that Mr. Montgomery has arrived."[31]

Trude too was excited at the prospect of her daughter's impending marriage. "I am glad, now, that she plans to marry young George Montgomery," Trude told Gladys Hall. "He is a cheerful boy. Hedy loves to laugh and, I feel, needs to laugh. For all she has had in her short, full life, I do not think she has had enough laughter. They are children together which, in love, is a happy good thing. . . . [Hedy] loves him for himself and not for any power or prestige he may have, or anything material he gives her."[32] At the same time Hedy's former beaus were ever faithful, and Trude herself even kept in touch with Fritz Mandl in South America. Just that week, Trude told Hall, Gene Markey had come by to see Jamesie. Reggie would stop by, and Trude said she had also met John Howard's mother at the beauty salon.

In the same interview Hall asked Hedy about George and her engagement, "Why did I fall in love with George in the beginning? His sense of humor . . .

Now, when people are all so worried, it is refreshing to find someone who worries, too, of course, but keeps his head above it. Yes, we are planning to be married, soon, as soon as possible. But the war is sort of doing things to us all. We are all a bit hysterical. These boys, like George, have doubts and fears."[33]

By the time Hall's piece appeared in *Silver Screen* magazine in August, Hedy and George were no more. On May 29, Hedy gave George back his engagement ring.

When asked by the reporter Kay Proctor, "What happened to George Montgomery?" Hedy's reply was to the point: "Hollywood."[34] One journalist wrote,

> She was ready to elope the week after they met. She was overjoyed when they announced their engagement. She planned a brilliant, dramatic future for them. She dreamed of having numerous children. She would have gladly given up her career. . . . She nearly took the count when she heard that George had been instructed to court her, on the grounds that this would give him lots of space in all the newspapers.[35]

Years later Hedy wrote,

> George [like Reginald Gardiner] is one of the men whom I almost married, whom everybody thought I was going to marry, and whom perhaps I *should* have married. He was versatile (not only a fine actor, but a furniture craftsman who could have made a living from his hobby) and handsome. When he went off to war in khaki, he was even more attractive than in any of his Hollywood roles.
>
> We had made some vows, but we both had a faculty for seeing through sham and hypocrisy. . . . In any case we couldn't fool each other, and we both realized deep inside that we weren't sure *enough* about each other.[36]

At the time Hedy was deeply hurt and humiliated. She had allowed herself to fall in love, foolishly and with abandon, and she had been duped. Immediately after their breakup, Montgomery was seen about town with the lovely twenty-four-year-old Metro starlet Kay Williams (she would become the last wife of Clark Gable). "I must see Kay Williams. See what she looks like," Hedy told a studio employee. Glimpsing the pretty blonde sitting in the studio commissary, Hedy looked a long time at her and quietly commented, "She is very lovely."[37]

On May 18, *Tortilla Flat* opened nationally. *Variety* enthusiastically raved, "Hedy Lamarr not only looks stunning as the Portuguese girl, but gives easily her best dramatic performance so far."[38] On May 21, *The New York Sunday Mirror* christened *Tortilla Flat* "Movie of the Week." "Hedy Lamarr, doubtless to the surprise of those who have neglected to keep track of the fact that careful direction and intelligent application has been gradually making an actress out of this beautiful female, is both charming and convincing as the fiery Dolores (though, if there is a gal who can look like that and still work in a fish canning factory, she's wasting her time)."[39]

Bosley Crowther of *The New York Times* noted, "Victor Fleming has directed with deep understanding. And all of the actors—yes, all of them—have delineated robust characters . . . and Hedy Lamarr is remarkably easy to take as Sweets."[40] In Hollywood Louella Parsons praised Hedy's work in her column, "Hedy Lamarr, the Portuguese girl who is different, keeps her house tidy, works in the cannery and proves that she has more than just glamour. She wears the simplest of clothes and makes no effort to appeal to the fans through any physical attributes. Her performance is a revelation, in that she gives a really splendid dramatic characterization."[41]

Much of the acting kudos for *Tortilla Flat* were rightfully handed to Frank Morgan, who pleasingly delivered a sensitive and well-tuned performance as Pirate. The fifty-one-year-old Morgan, long a dependable character actor in Metro's stable of stars (he *was* the Wizard of Oz), would win a second Best Supporting Actor Oscar nomination for his sensitive work.

In view of today's political correctness, *Tortilla Flat* is a bit difficult to watch objectively. But it is a charming film and one that should be seen. There are sequences that are marvelously played by Frank Morgan and Spencer Tracy—especially the Saint Francis scene in the redwoods. Equally appealing are the moments with Garfield and Hedy. One particular vignette, when Dolores feeds a sickly baby, is tenderly photographed by Karl Freund. And Hedy's fight scene with Garfield is amazing to watch. One cannot believe this is the same actress who was once the static mannequin of *Lady of the Tropics*. It is no wonder Hedy stunned critics with her performance. Garfield truly brought her acting "up" in their tightly played moments together.

Unfortunately, because *Tortilla Flat* had so passive a story line, box-office earnings were again less than Metro had anticipated. It remains a touching treatment of a (cinematically) tough property. Indeed, it was Metro-Goldwyn-Mayer at its best—despite itself. About her role, Hedy would say later, "It was an honest part. . . . and I was glad to get away from glamour."[42]

What *could* have been the film that would have solidified Hedy Lamarr as a lasting film icon turned out to be another she was not allowed by Louis B. Mayer to do—*Casablanca*. An inquiry was made for her to be loaned out. In a Warner Bros. interoffice memo dated February 23, 1942, the chief director of casting, Steve Trilling, advised the producer, Hal B. Wallis, that M-G-M's executive Benny Thau was almost positive that Mayer would not lend Hedy to Warner for the picture since he "is opposed to loaning her out to anybody."[43]

Casablanca, which would win the Best Picture Oscar the following year, was set to go with Humphrey Bogart as Rick. Wallis then considered casting Ann Sheridan, Tamara Toumanova, or Michelle Morgan for the part of Ilsa, before Ingrid Bergman, on loan from David O. Selznick for $25,000, was awarded the role.[44]

What *could* have been sadly was not. Louis B. Mayer, true to his consistent mishandling of Hedy's career, instead, on April 16, assigned her the role of the African Congo biracial Tondelayo in a misfire of a production, the turgid *White Cargo*. After her magnificent performances in *H.M. Pulham, Esq.* and *Tortilla Flat,* one wonders what Mayer's motivation was. Whatever the intent, the result very nearly put an end to Hedy's credibilty as an actress and quite possibly could have ended her career.

11

Battle

The original stage version of *White Cargo,* produced by the musical-revue impresario Earl Carroll, premiered at the Greenwich Village Theater in New York on November 5, 1923. Scandalous for its time, its heroine, Tondelayo, was an African black woman, referred to in the play as a "negress," who seduces and cohabitates with a white man. *White Cargo* was written and staged by twenty-eight-year-old Leon Gordon and was based on an equally scandalous 1912 novel, *Hell's Playground,* by Ida Vera Simonton. The production, not too surprisingly, had a strong run of 257 performances.

At the time there stood an MPAA (Motion Picture Association of America) agreement with the U.S. film studios of self-imposed censorship. The MPAA head, Will Hays, who found the play unacceptable for motion picture production, banned it from being adapted for the screen. However, a British film version of *White Cargo* was made and released in the United Kingdom in 1929. When it premiered in the United States the following year, there was an indignant uproar over its content and its direct challenge to the MPAA ruling.

Attempting to change the Hays ruling, in the early 1930s a couple of American film studios inquired about possibly filming a domestic screen version but still found it a difficult sell. In a memo from the Samuel Goldwyn, Inc., film studio dated May 17, 1932, Jason S. Joy offered the property up as available. It eventually came into the hands of Selznick International, which was advised in a memo from Val Lewton on April 12, 1939, that it was still listed on the Legion of Decency's condemned list.[1]

R-K-O then secured the services of the playwright Leon Gordon, who in his revised treatment made Tondelayo half-Egyptian, half-Arab. After that move the project was given an approval certificate. But still, censorship problems plagued the project. It did not help matters that Earl Carroll in his recent *Vanities* of 1940 offered up the play parody "The Song of the Sarong" with a nude actress who gleefully advised the audience, "I am Tondelayo." Nor did it lend to the reputation of Hedy or the Metro film version of *White Cargo* after its release in late 1942 that the stripper Ann Corio bared her assets in a theatrical production of the play somewhere in the Bronx.

In mid-June 1941, Joseph I. Breen held a conference with Leon Gordon and the screenwriter Kenneth McKenna at the request of Louis B. Mayer to discuss the play as a possible project for Hedy, who, according to a Metro memo to the MPAA's current director, Geoffrey Shurlock, would give the project box-office allure. Production-code approval was given to Mayer. After major concessions and revisions, on October 13, 1941, McKenna submitted the final treatment of *White Cargo* to Shurlock for approval. Metro got the green light. (Gordon would eventually earn more than $1 million in royalties alone for the various incarnations of his play.)

Metro's film version of *White Cargo* concerned the travails of Harry Witzel (Walter Pidgeon), who oversees a rubber plantation in the African Congo in 1910. His assistant, Wilber Ashley (Bramwell Fletcher), has deteriorated both in mind and body, his ability to work and his very moral fiber destroyed by drink and by his lust for the wanton Tondelayo (Hedy), and Witzel must replace him. Ashley is sent away, and a new recruit appears on the scene, handsome young Langford (Richard Carlson), who is determined not to let the bleak conditions in Africa get to him. He swears he will maintain propriety. Witzel warns him, however, about the beautiful native girl Tondelayo, who is known to be a seductress. "She knows how to purr her way into your mind and scratch her way out," he says.

Tondelayo, called a "chocolate Cleopatra" by one character, finds out about the new overseer Langford and is later discovered in his bungalow and sent away by Witzel. Langford finds he cannot get any work out of the natives, and his resolve breaks. When Tondelayo returns to seduce him, he becomes enamored of her charms and (per moral-code standards) decides to marry her. Witzel tries to dissuade the young man, realizing that Langford is falling apart. It then is revealed that Tondelayo is actually a white woman, the daughter of an Egyptian woman and a Portuguese father. That allows (per moral-code standards again) the couple free to marry.

Soon Tondelayo is bored with Langford and starts a flirtation with Witzel, who shuns her. Tondelayo taunts Witzel, "Why you no ever come see Awila [Langford]? Why you no ever come see—me?" To which Witzel sarcastically replies, "For the same reason I don't tread on snakes!"

Langford is stricken with a sudden illness, and the doctor (Frank Morgan) cannot diagnose it. Witzel discovers that Tondelayo has begun poisoning her husband and forces her to drink the poison, and she runs into the jungle to die. Langford recovers and is sent home. Now Witzel must break in a new man. The tawdry story ends, and the screen fades to black.

Like it or not, Hedy had to make the film. On accepting the potentially damaging part, Hedy remarked, "There was so much sex in it I couldn't resist the temptation to kill the 'marble goddess image' for good!"[2] And so on May 18, 1942, the same day Metro nationally released *Tortilla Flat,* Hedy stepped before the cameras as Tondelayo in *White Cargo.*

The genial forty-four-year-old, six-foot-two, Canadian-born Walter Pidgeon had been cast in the aborted first filming of *I Take This Woman* in 1938. Having signed with Metro in the mid-1930s, he had just completed his most memorable role for the studio, that of Clem Miniver in the magnificent *Mrs. Miniver,* which would win Best Picture of 1942, and earn Pidgeon a Best Actor Oscar nomination. (Pidgeon had also starred in the previous year's Best Picture, Twentieth Century–Fox's *How Green Was My Valley.*) His relationship with Louis B. Mayer was good, though in later years Pidgeon would remark, "I was like a kept woman during my twenty-one years with MGM."[3]

Production of *White Cargo* moved along rapidly throughout the summer of 1942. It was reported that the director, Richard Thorpe, used two hundred "native" extras in the picture. (This effectively meant that the African-American Screen Actors Guild community was allowed to work in something other than a Tarzan movie.) *Hollywood* magazine reported:

M-G-M wanted to make use of Hedy Lamarr's high voltage, and *Tondelayo* was the role that could do it. . . . Hedy wouldn't allow any visitors on the set the first ten days. Usually amiable about having spectators around, this started the rumor that she was moody about her broken engagement to George Montgomery and wanted to be left alone. Somehow the tale got to her and she laughed. "That isn't the reason at all. I feel a little self-conscious wearing so little and I want time to get used to it. Besides, I'm afraid my costume might fall down on me."[4]

Metro meanwhile announced a trio of future projects intended for Hedy after she completed *White Cargo.* The first would star her as a Russian guerilla in *Scorched Earth,* based on a story by Leo Mittler, Victor Trivas, and Guy Endore and with a screenplay by Anna Louise Strong, to be produced by Joe Pasternak. Later the title would be changed to *Russia,* and Gregory Ratoff made producer. Now it would star Hedy opposite Walter Pidgeon, with Paul Jarrico and Richard Collins writing the screenplay, and would incorporate music by Pyotr Ilich Tchaikovsky. The film *would* eventually be filmed in 1944 as *The Song of Russia* with Robert Taylor and Susan Peters.

The second production was to have been *The Last Time I Saw Paris,* based on the Elliott Paul novel. Hedy was considered for the lead after Myrna Loy turned it down. Only the title of the project would be retained for Metro's eventual 1952 film, which starred Van Johnson and Elizabeth Taylor. The third picture would have been a new teaming of Hedy with Clark Gable, in a film of Marguerite Steen's sweeping twelve-hundred-page novel *The Sun Is My Undoing,* with an adaptation by Marguerite Roberts. Steen had sold the book to Metro in March for approximately $50,000.

The Sun Is My Undoing was yet another story of miscegenation. Its producer, Pandro S. Berman, was hard at work trying to eliminate censorship problems. Again the feminine lead, Sheba (in the novel another "negress"), is sold into slavery. Her marriage to Matthew Flood (Gable) would become legitimate when it is discovered she is actually an Arab and (surprise!) a white woman. Sheba dies in childbirth, thus eliminating two generations from the original novel. *The Sun Is My Undoing* was not made. Gable had just lost his wife, Carole Lombard, in February in an airplane crash in Nevada after she completed a warbond rally in Indianapolis. He would complete his current film, *Somewhere I'll Find You,* with Lana Turner, and join the U.S. Army Air Corps for the duration of the war.

For its last radio play of its eighth season, *The Lux Radio Theater* presented *H.M. Pulham, Esq.* on July 13. Hedy and Robert Young reprised their original film roles, and Josephine Hutchinson performed the part of Kay Motford. This was Robert Young's first appearance on *The Lux Radio Theater*. The host, Cecil B. DeMille, asked Hedy, "Now, Hedy, suppose the Treasury Department asked you to go out and sell some bonds. How would you do it?" The following exchange ensued:

> Hedy: I might say, "Please, mister. Will you buy a bond?"
>
> Robert Young: Hedy, you've talked me into it.
>
> Hedy: But I don't think I'd say that. I think I'd say, "Mister, I personally have seen the Nazis at work in their own country. And believe me, it's worth every dollar you've got to wipe them off the face of the earth. But all our government asks is ten percent of your income invested in bonds and stamps."

The Treasury Department would indeed ask Hedy to sell bonds, and she gladly accepted.

When *Crossroads* ("Where Women Wait to Seal Your Fate!" tempted the movie poster) opened in New York on July 23, the New York *Daily Mirror* said, "There's some fine acting all the way; but Hedy Lamarr is the big special. She's superb—and looks it."[5] And the critic for the *New York Herald Tribune* wrote, "William Powell . . . succeeds in inspiring Hedy Lamarr. . . . She is far more persuasive than I have ever seen her."[6]

The cinematography by Joseph Ruttenberg flattered Hedy and William Powell. They look beautifully ethereal, and Claire Trevor, who was on loan-out from Columbia, was more than happy with the way she appeared in *Crossroads*. Interestingly, Trevor was not the first actress considered for the role of Michele Allaine. It was originally offered to Marlene Dietrich, who, after being told the film would star Hedy Lamarr, allegedly replied, "I'll share glamour with nobody!"[7]

Crossroads is an effective psychological mystery, with a most complicated plot. It embraces many of the film-noir elements of pre–World War II German cinema. Hedy's costumes for this black-and-white film were peak Robert Kalloch. One gown was of shimmering black velvet with a large beaded collar; another was a periwinkle-blue velvet negligé with gold-leaf embroidery. And a daytime outfit was of a two-tone raspberry—a light top and darker skirt.

Adding intrigue and suspense are the art and set designs for the film, especially the cavernous government office where characters dart in and out of shadows at night, played with no music or sound. *Crossroads* was an offbeat picture for M-G-M, and it did moderately profitable business at the box office. (*The Lux Radio Theater* would present *Crossroads* as a radio play on March 23, 1943, starring Jean-Pierre Aumont and Lana Turner.)

At the end of July, *White Cargo* wrapped. And curiously during this period in Hedy's life and film career, she began dating a man from her past, another European exile new to Hollywood—the producer Samuel P. Spiegel. She was prominently on his arm the evening of Wednesday, August 5, when they attended the premiere of *Tales of Manhattan,* which Spiegel had produced at Twentieth Century–Fox.

On August 11, 1942, the United States Commissioner of Patents and Trademarks issued patent number 2,292,387 to Hedy K. Markey and George Antheil for their invention called Secret Communication System. Immediately, Hedy and Antheil offered their patent to the U.S. government. (The two had realized its importance and significance, but the government simply did not know what to do with it.) Inspired about the invention's prospects, Hedy again offered to quit films and lend her services to the government. But because she was an actress, the government felt she could do more for the war effort by selling bonds and advised her so.

The setback was frustrating. Hedy remained full of inventive ideas. She had already worked on the idea for bouillon cubes for multiflavored drinks and soda with an endowment given to her by Howard Hughes. Laboring at a lathe between takes at the studio's laboratory, Hedy was eager to create something practical for the cause. Perhaps because of her admiration for Antheil, Hedy even tried her hand at composing a popular song in 1941, with the help of the Metro music staff's Red Ruthven. Their result was "Believe in Me," for which Hedy wrote the words and music. Judy Garland was supposed to include it in one of her films but did not.

"We were now in the war and a terrible time it was," wrote Hedy. "I was an actress . . . yet I could feel there were more important things in the world at that time than motion pictures."[8] Still, Louis B. Mayer and Loew's, Inc., were not interested in whatever the pretty actress wanted to contribute to the government. They were interested solely in studio profits and producing successful pictures. Wartime film attendance was at an all-time high. If Hedy bucked the system, they would retaliate.

On the Metro lot, Hedy was introduced to the new contract player Jean-Pierre Aumont. The thirty-one-year-old Aumont was recently divorced and himself a Jewish refugee from Europe. He had come to fame in Jean Cocteau's 1934 play *La machine infernale* (*The Infernal Machine*). After the Germans marched into Paris in 1940, he arrived in New York and eventually signed with Metro. He soon voiced to the studio his discontent with making films while his countrymen overseas were being killed. His political activism eventually brought a quick end to his early Hollywood career.

Hedy sang "The Last Time I Saw Paris" to Aumont on their first date, and the two became fast friends. Hedy was infatuated with the handsome, wavy-haired Frenchman, and the two were quite an item during that late summer of 1942. "We go to movies and sometimes we hold hands, but romance? No!" Hedy told the press.[9] Around this time she also casually dated John Howard yet again, the real estate man George Gregson, and Charles "Charlie" Chaplin.

At the suggestion of the U.S. Treasury, Hedy departed for the East Coast in late August by train to aid the war effort. The month of September would be called Salute to Our Heroes Month and be devoted to the first national $1 billion war-bond drive. And Stars over America, teams of motion picture players, were scheduled to tour 210 of the nation's cities holding war-bond rallies to raise money for the effort. Arriving in Washington, D.C., were Bud Abbott and Lou Costello, Charles Laughton, James Cagney, Martha Scott, and Bing Crosby. Hedy later arrived at Union Station from New York aboard the Capitol, Ltd., along with Irene Dunne, Ann Rutherford, Edward Arnold, Greer Garson, Bob Hope, and Virginia Gilmore.

On August 30, 1942, all these stars appeared on *Command Performance,* a show broadcast on short-wave radio for the men and women overseas, which was followed by a luncheon hosted by Senator Henry Morgenthau in his private dining room at the Treasury. Selected from the various Hollywood studios to take the first ten-day tour were Hedy, Ronald Colman, Herbert Marshall, Lynn Bari, Gene Tierney, Joan Leslie, Ralph Bellamy, and Walter Able.

The campaign kicked off on Monday, August 31, in the afternoon on the steps of the Treasury Department and was broadcast on a national radio hookup and filmed by the newsreels. Hosted by Senator Morgenthau, the event was a mass patriotic rally, with music provided by Bing Crosby and Kay Kyser and appearances and speeches by the dozens of stars gathered. James Cagney gave a rousing rally, and then to applause and whistles Morgenthau introduced Hedy, who gave a stirring appeal.

Dressed in a three-quarter-sleeved, lightweight print dress and elegantly accessorized, her long, dark hair wafting gently in the breeze, Hedy was audibly and visibly emotional as she spoke from her heart: "I don't want to make this long. I just want to say that I'm very proud and happy that I too can do my bit in the war effort."[10] To thunderous applause, she was ushered off the podium to the music of "Buy a Share of Freedom Today."

Hedy sat at a table beside Kay Kyser and cheerfully signed autographs for some of the estimated 30,000 war-bond buyers there that day. All told, $1.5 million's worth of bonds were purchased in that one day alone. On this particular campaign, Hedy became the featured attraction. The following day she sold $4,567,000 in F and G bonds in Philadelphia at a luncheon held by a small group of businessmen and labor and social leaders. That evening she appeared at a huge victory show at the Academy of Music, where an additional $2,250,000 was pledged and $7,500 more was collected from admirers who did not attend either function, bringing the total amount in just one day to $6,804,850.

At that luncheon Hedy addressed the crowd, " 'I am just a plain gold-digger for Uncle Sam. . . . I'm here to help win the war. I think you're here to see what that Lamarr dame looks like.' " In a serious vein she continued, "We should be here for the same purpose. What you think Hedy Lamarr looks like doesn't worry me as much as what Hirohito and Hitler are doing. Every time you dig into your pocketbooks you tell those two rotten men the Yanks are coming. Let's make the end of the war come soon. Don't think about what the other fellow is doing. You buy bonds!"[11]

Hedy's train pulled into Newark, New Jersey, on September 4, taking the town by storm. When she left the Robert Treat Hotel over 7,000 fans blocked her path, and when she spoke at Military Park police had to control crowds estimated at between 15,000 and 20,000. In Trenton, New Jersey, Hedy appeared on the stage of the State Theater, accompanied by the United States Military Band, which was introduced by the then-fledgling announcer Walter Cronkite. At the York Safe and Lock Company naval-ordnance plant (its buildings made up part of the Harley-Davidson Springettsbury Township complex) in York, Pennsylvania, 1,000 employees pledged $25 of their wages to buy bonds because of her visit. Hedy shook hands with every one of them to express her gratitude.

In York and Trenton the bond sales reached almost $4 million, and in Essex County, New Jersey, they topped $3.4 million thanks to her appearing there. In New York on September 11, Hedy held a ten-minute private talk, in German, with the city's mayor, Fiorello La Guardia, who announced the following week to be Carole Lombard Memorial Week in honor of the late actress, who had preceded Hedy in war-bond activities. That day, Hedy helped raise an additional $991,377 for the war effort. (Lana Turner sold only $4,000 worth of bonds during her tour, reported one Philadelphia reporter.)[12] Hedy had originally been nervous at the prospect of speaking publicly. But she became a forceful and compelling orator as her confidence grew.

When asked by the newspapers to write about her experiences on the tour, she told the readers,

> I want to tell you about my experiences as a salesman for Uncle Sam— selling War Bonds—and then perhaps you will understand something of what I feel since the United States is my adopted country. At times I'm sure I know more about the freedom we are fighting for than millions who were born in the United States and who have come to accept liberty as their rightful heritage. I have seen enough in Europe to know that freedom isn't a heritage. It must be fought for, won and then cherished. America is the last stop for freedom. We've got to fight to protect it— and that is why I was glad to help in the government's campaign to sell a billion dollars' worth of War Bonds.[13]

In Elizabeth, New Jersey, Hedy, dressed in a long-sleeved print dress and flashing the V-for-victory sign, was introduced at a $1,000-a-plate war-bond luncheon by the master of ceremonies as Miss Lamour. Silence came over the crowd as she took her place before them. "My friends, Lamour or Lamarr—as long as you're healthy—and we are!" she cheerfully acknowledged to thunderous applause. One stalwart gentleman in attendance stood and announced, "I will give Miss Lamarr an extra $1,000 Bond if she will sing, 'Jingle, Jangle, Jingle.'" Hedy did not know it, but replied, "Wait. Why can't I do a song that I can really do justice to!" and she then proceeded to do every verse of "God Bless America," with the crowd joining in.[14]

Following its inception on May 1, 1941, over $54 billion in Series E Defense Bonds, or war bonds, were sold before the end of World War II. Hedy's own contribution to the war effort, as well as those efforts of all the motion picture stars who participated in the numerous war-bond campaigns, cannot be underestimated.

After the grueling ten-day, sixteen-city tour, Hedy returned to New York and finally boarded the train back to California, stepping off the Santa Fe Chief on September 14, tired but happy after selling nearly $25 million in war bonds. Dressed stylishly in a tailored suit, she was asked by reporters how she felt, and replied, "Wonderful—how soon can I do it again?" She continued, "It's hard work, harder than anything I've done—traveling and rushing around and keeping on the go, but I'm proud and happy that I could do it. . . . Just as soon as I get a little rest, I hope they'll send me out again."[15]

On her return to Metro, Hedy filmed a brief introduction for a newsreel for the Hearst Company, released through M-G-M, in a segment entitled "Shangri-La War Stamp Campaign." Shortly after, she was admitted to a hospital for a sprained back she sustained during her tour. After having a few vertebrae adjusted, Hedy had Reggie drive her to a sanitarium for a rest.

She recovered quickly and, on September 27, appeared for the third time on *The Edgar Bergen / Charlie McCarthy Show*. And she starred on *The Lux Radio Theater* on October 5, opposite William Powell in an adaptation of the actor's 1941 hit film *Love Crazy*. Hedy was very good in this production, and it was well received by listeners. On radio Hedy proved how versatile she was when a role truly suited her. What the moviegoing public got from Metro was Tondelayo.

The catchphrase for *White Cargo* read, "Hedy Lamarr Was Never More Exotic or Ravishing." Robert Kalloch had designed for Hedy's Tondelayo a series of padded bikini brassieres and long, clinging, wraparound, side-split skirts, creating what M-G-M ballyhooed as the "lurong." The film's promotion was obviously testosterone driven: "90% allure, 10% sarong—adds up to LU-RONG!" and, "She rings the GONG in her LURONG," read the newspaper ads. Had the studio seriously wanted to promote *White Cargo* as a major drama—and it obviously knew it could not—it would never have used such preposterous and lewdly juvenile taglines. *White Cargo* was aimed strictly at the male libido, and all art was cast aside.

Nevertheless *The Hollywood Reporter* reviewer praised the work of the actors, "No better cast has ever performed 'White Cargo' in its lengthy history. If it were merely intended as a demonstration of Hedy Lamarr's versatility, that point is herewith firmly established."[16] *Variety* prophesied, "The promise of Hedy Lamarr in a sarong and sultry copper makeup should alone underwrite the b.o. of 'White Cargo.' . . . Miss Lamarr as the only femme in the film is doing her best acting to date."[17] However, *The New York Times* cut to basics: "As the gentleman [in the film] keep telling one another, the dry rot has set in—on the Capitol screen. Or is it damp rot? We can't remember. But it is some kind of rot; that much is sure."[18]

Said *The New York Times*'s Bosley Crowther, "Miss Lamarr, stained the color of a bookcase, is nôt much more exciting than same . . . the film is just old-fashioned twaddle."[19] The critic George Jean Nathan allegedly responded to Tondelayo's introductory lines, "'Me Tondelayo. Me stay,'" by standing up at a screening and announcing, "'Me George Jean Nathan. Me go,'" and then walking out of the theatre.[20]

After all the effort the studio took to distance Hedy from her participation in *Ecstasy,* Mayer then shoved her into *White Cargo.* One wonders, Why? Possibly with thousands of young men in the armed forces, Metro felt it was doing the country a service by supplying the boys with Lamarr in a lurong. At the time, the picture made money, lots of money. But it did nothing to substantiate Hedy's career.

The film is tame when viewed today, but during the war it was scandalous. Darkly photographed with heavy use of shadows playing across her face and body (Tondelayo is never seen in the daylight), there is one particularly erotic shot as Hedy moves into extreme close-up, her eyes closing and her lips parting, filling the screen with promises untold. There are also some very strong sadomasochistic overtones in the film.

When Witzel forces Tondelayo to drink the poison in graphic close-up, the brutality of the sequence is difficult to take. *White Cargo* as a whole is obviously a titillating exercise of 1940s eroticism at its most vulgar. Yet Hedy's acting, much to her credit, is purposeful, and she is extremely animated and convincing as the heartless Tondelayo.

White Cargo was naturally given a condemned rating by the National Legion of Decency, with obvious objections to its suggestive and seductive sequences, dialogue, and costuming. It advised that no children be allowed to see the film.

As for her performance in *White Cargo,* Hedy said, "I had to get up with the chickens to have that dark make-up put all over my body. I was proud of my authentic African dance, which I rehearsed for weeks, and which gave me splinters in my feet. It was done with a bed showing in the background, and it was so sexy almost all of the scene was cut."[21] In the released picture, the dance was indeed short, with long close-ups of Richard Carlson nodding his head in carnal approval. "I thought with some interesting makeup, a sarong, and some hip-swinging, I would be a memorable nymphomaniac," Hedy wrote.[22] Hedy had agreed to do the film at Mayer's insistence, causing the M-G-M historian Peter Hay to later write, "In certain instances, she sabotaged her own career, with a little help from MGM."[23]

At the end of the year, on December 27, Theodore Strauss of *The New York Times* observed 1942 had been a good year for bad pictures. *White Cargo* was placed on the *Times*'s Ten Worst Films of the Year list, sharing the dubious honor with three other Metro pictures, *I Married an Angel* (the last of the Jeanette MacDonald–Nelson Eddy teamings), *Two-Faced Woman* (Garbo's last film), and *Her Cardboard Lover* (Norma Shearer's last film). It was only *White Cargo* among those ten films that made a profit (of $2.8 million), and no doubt it was because of Hedy Lamarr and that sarong. American males queued up to see the film, and the line "I am Tondelayo" became a household catchphrase.

Metro was at that time preparing the novel *Vengeance of the Earth* by Erskine Caldwell as a vehicle for Hedy and Jean-Pierre Aumont, and the picture was set to roll in December. The as yet unpublished novel was originally purchased by the studio for Spencer Tracy and Wallace Beery in July. But it was changed to focus on the husband and wife characters, Sergei and Natascha, freedom fighters behind enemy lines, to be portrayed by Hedy and Aumont. Hedy and Jean-Pierre at the time were considered by Metro to be "a very warm combination."[24] The project fell through when Aumont quit Hollywood.[25]

Metro had no other property immediately ready for Hedy, so she enlisted her patriotic energies and offered to help out at the newly opened Hollywood Canteen. Its finance committee was spearheaded by Bette Davis, John Garfield, and Jules Stein, president of MCA (Music Corporation of America). It operated at 1451 Cahuenga Boulevard in Hollywood throughout the war, its doors open to all servicemen and women on their way overseas, offering them food, dancing, and an opportunity to see and be entertained by over 3,000 stars in the industry who staffed the canteen, gladly volunteering their time.[26]

Hedy offered to work, at first every Friday night, then twice a week. There were two shifts—one beginning at 7:00 P.M. for two and a half hours, the second at 9:30 P.M. until closing at midnight. Hedy would help out in the kitchen washing dishes or making sandwiches, clean up the bar, or dance with the visiting servicemen and hand out autographs. The average weeknight crowd usually numbered 1,500, and on weekends that count would frequently double. The stars would entertain, and the singers would serenade. Comedians would tell jokes, and sometimes such legendary conductors as Leopold Stokowski would give a classical concert leading the eighty-piece Hollywood Canteen Orchestra. It was a patriotic and exciting time in history, and Hedy looked forward to working at the Canteen, often doing both shifts.

Friday nights became known as Hedy Lamarr Night, and very often Hedy would dance endlessly with the servicemen. "I want to serve coffee," she would tell them, and then she would spend most of the rest of the evening dancing. "It's cute the way the boys rotate for dances," Hedy told a journalist. "The Canteen rules say we can only dance for ten minutes—then we must change partners. That enables the boys to meet all the girls and vice versa. The boys take the girls away from boys by tapping on the shoulder and saying, 'Praise the Lord and Pass Your Ammunition!'"[27]

With the holidays upon her and still no project ready for her at the studio, Hedy threw herself into activities at the Canteen. She never missed a Friday, and, despite the pouring rain, on Christmas Day 1942 she was there working. The place was fully packed. There was nowhere else in Hollywood for servicemen and women to gather.

The Canteen Orchestra played "Jingle Bells" and "White Christmas" that evening as Hedy, dressed in a black dress with burgundy accents and sitting behind the snack bar signing autographs on papers, pictures, caps, handkerchiefs, anything the soldiers handed her, was reintroduced to a handsome, six-foot-three Englishman serving that night as busboy. He was the only actor working the shift. Hedy had first met him at a dinner party given by Bette Davis earlier in the year, and afterward they had run into each other casually at various functions. His name was John Loder.[28]

Loder was born John Muir Lowe in York, England, on January 3, 1898, into a wealthy and distinguished family. Loder's maternal grandfather was Sicilian but became a British subject. His parents were British Major General Sir William and Lady Frances Lowe. John took Loder as his stage name, rationalizing that, if he were a failure, he would not disgrace the family name. By taking his mother's maiden name, he also did not have to change his initials.

He was educated at Eton and attended the Royal Military Academy, following his father into the army upon England's entry into World War I. Loder himself accepted the surrender of Patrick Pearse, the leader of the 1916 Irish rebellion, in front of the General Post Office in Dublin, Easter week, 1916, on behalf of his father, General Lowe. For that service John was later knighted. He then served in Gallipoli as a second lieutenant with the 15th Hussars and was eventually captured and imprisoned by the Germans.

On his release, he remained in Germany, taking an interest in acting and appearing in German silent films. In Alexander Korda's 1925 UFA picture *Der Tänzer meiner Frau (Madam Wants No Children)* he was a dance extra with Marlene Dietrich. Because of his good looks Loder was featured in eleven German films but had little success before coming to England to work in early British talkies. He failed to become a star in Great Britain.

Trying his luck in America, Loder was seen with Corinne Griffith in First National's *Lilies of the Field* in 1930. Returning to England he had much better success in *The Private Life of Henry VIII* (1933), again directed by Korda, and in Gaumont's 1936 thriller *Sabotage,* directed by Alfred Hitchcock. When war broke out, Loder returned to Hollywood and was featured in *How Green Was My Valley,* with Walter Pidgeon, and in Universal's *Eagle Squadron* (1942), with Robert Stack and Diana Barrymore.

Loder had been married twice before, first to Sophie Kabel, with whom he had a grown son named Robin, who lived in England.[29] His second marriage in London in 1936 was to the actress Micheline Cheirel, with whom he fathered a daughter, Danielle. When Loder met Hedy, he was in Hollywood awaiting final divorce papers and filming *Old Acquaintance* at Warner Bros. with Bette Davis. The day before Christmas, Davis told him the Hollywood Canteen was going to be extremely busy on Christmas Day and asked if he could help out. "I've made no particular plans," John told Bette. "I'll be glad to work."[30]

As Loder attempted to catch Hedy's eye, working his way through a sea of khaki, he was finally able to ask her, "How do you happen to be here?" She smiled at him.[31] Hedy could not help but notice how handsome the dignified, soft-spoken Brit was, with his dark brown hair and wide-set hazel eyes.

Hedy had dishwashing duties for the second shift. "What lovely hands you have," Loder remarked to her as they began their sink duties side by side. Before the evening was over, he had made a date. She bid him good night with,

"See you next Friday night at the Canteen."[32] Hedy later invited Loder to her home in Benedict Canyon for dinner, and soon they were dining there every night. As Loder boastfully wrote in his autobiography, "Within a matter of days tongues were wagging all over Hollywood."[33]

Hedy and Loder were drawn to each other. They had much in common, both having come from proper families and having lost loved ones in Europe during the war—Hedy's friends and relatives and John's sister who was killed in the London blitz. They complemented each other, Hedy talkative and outspoken, John passive and reserved. So proper was Loder in fact, Hedy noticed, that during their courtship he wore shorts underneath his pajamas.

One topic of conversation among those in the film colony in January 1943 was President Franklin Roosevelt's recent decision to top off the yearly income of all high-salaried individuals in or out of the film industry at $25,000, the balance of their salaries to be held back by their employers for the war effort, to be reimbursed to them later. After intensely serious meetings at Hedgerow Farm, numerous members of the industry unofficially appointed Hedy their spokesperson.

On January 6, Hedy sued Loew's, Inc., parent company of Metro-Goldwyn-Mayer, appealing to the California Supreme Court because of the misinterpretation of her contract in regard to capping her yearly salary at $25,000 a year. According to Hedy's contract with Metro, she was to receive a $500-a-week increase as of September 30, 1942, bringing her salary up to $2,000 a week. M-G-M paid her $1,500, challenging that the federal government's limit allowed them to pay her this amount to meet the $25,000 cap. Her suit maintained that she should be paid her contractual amount by the studio, and that *she* be allowed to pay the government anything over her earnings as part of her personal-loan effort.

Under her original contract, dated September 30, 1937, Hedy's salary was to commence at $550 a week, with six yearly increases of $500 additional a week. Metro failed to honor this agreement and exercise her option, according to Hedy, and through her attorney, A. Ronald Button, she now asked the court to decree the contract at an end. Hedy's action became the first suit of its kind filed in the state of California.

On January 25, because of a motion by defense attorneys for Loew's, Inc., Hedy's action was transferred to federal court by Judge Frank G. Swain. The defense argued that because Loew's, Inc., was a Delaware-based company, the case should be tried in federal court. It was taken into submission on February 2 by Judge Harry A. Hollzer. For the time being, Hedy would remain on strike with M-G-M.

Hedy's lawsuit was sent back to the federal court on February 23 after a lengthy ruling by Judge Hollzer stating that her employer, Loew's, Inc., had obtained permission to transfer the action under the assumption that Hedy was a U.S. citizen, which she was not. Hedy could not even apply for her citizenship papers until June, after which she would have been in the country five years. The proceedings reached a stalemate.

It was a foregone conclusion that Hedy would not portray the plum role penciled in for her in *Cry 'Havoc'* because of her pending lawsuit. Metro had denied Hedy a loan-out to Warner Bros. for *Casablanca* and would continue to veto her employment by any other studio. So as much as the studio was claiming damage as a result of Hedy's action, they in turn were denying her work. Records show that M-G-M–Loew's profits for 1942 had reached an all-time high of $12 million, in no small credit to Hedy's appeal at the box office.

At the same time, the studio and its parent company, Loew's, Inc., were trying to muscle the courts into making a decision in their favor regarding Hedy's suit. Judge Swain denied their motions and set the trial to begin on April 23. Loew's, Inc., and Metro-Goldwyn-Mayer were facing a losing battle.

Just as the case started to reach a settlement out of court, Congress lifted its stabilized salary limit, and the studio was obligated to pay Hedy her contractual fee. Another of Hedy's attorneys, Leonard F. Herzog, filed a motion on her behalf to dismiss the suit. A new contract by Metro was drawn up for Hedy guaranteeing her the agreed-on salary of $2,000 a week. Hedda Hopper broke the news on April 15: "Hedy Lamarr finally kissed and made up with Metro and will star in 'The Heavenly Body.'"[34]

Production began on *The Heavenly Body* (once called *Starlight,* then *The Stars Are Bright*). Arthur Hornblow Jr. was set as producer, and Columbia Pictures director Alexander Hall was loaned to Metro to helm the project. The capable forty-nine-year-old Hall had, just the year before, been nominated for a Best Director Oscar for *Here Comes Mr. Jordan.*

The studio fashion designer Irene (Lentz) had worked with Hedy on *Algiers.* For *The Heavenly Body,* Irene made a more contemporary and contrasting fashion statement and designed numerous costumes for Hedy that were ambitious in their intent. One was a short, belted swagger coat of black-and-white checkered wool with a black velveteen collar. And Irene also created a stunning slip of flowing baby-blue silk with a matching chiffon negligé to wear over it. "Hedy is so beautiful she doesn't have to worry about clothes," the designer once remarked. "So she doesn't worry. If I were as beautiful as she I wouldn't worry about clothes either. You could stand her in a gunny sack and she'd still be gorgeous."[35]

Filming began on *The Heavenly Body* on May 4, 1943. It was but another trifle of a story, yet it was also an opportunity for Hedy and Powell to lighten up for war-weary audiences. Just the year before Powell had tragically lost his two former wives—Carole Lombard and Eileen Wilson, the mother of his son, William David Powell. He had been off the screen for eighteen months. *The Heavenly Body* would be a refreshing departure from the gloom that surrounded the actor. Its comic plot was simple.

Professor William S. Whitley (William Powell) is an astronomer who spends every night at the Mount Jefferson Observatory investigating a new comet headed for the moon, leaving his beautiful wife, Vicky (Hedy), alone all night at their home. When Vicky visits an astrologer, Margaret Sibyll (Fay Bainter), at the encouragement of her scatterbrained neighbor, Nancy Potter (Spring Byington), she is told that she will meet a very-well-traveled suitor with whom she will fall in love on the twenty-second of the month. Vicky tells her husband, Bill, about the prediction. He tells her it is rubbish, and, upset that his wife so strongly believes in astrology, he takes off for an indefinite stay at his observatory.

On the twenty-second, Vicky waits patiently until the end of the day, when nothing has happened. She calls Bill and admits her foolishness and asks him to return home. As midnight approaches, Vicky is approached by air-raid warden Lloyd Hunter (James Craig), who admits to being well traveled. He admonishes Vicky for leaving her bedroom light on at night when she is next door visiting her neighbor, a breach of blackout regulations. As Hunter is leaving, Bill arrives home.

The next day Bill asks Lloyd to change his district, but the warden tells Bill he will not and that he has fallen in love with Vicky. Fate keeps bringing Vicky and Lloyd together. Bill goes to Margaret Sibyll and blackmails her into backing him up by telling Vicky he faces imminent death. Bill feigns illness, but Vicky learns of the ruse. He leaves for the observatory once again. Lloyd is misdirected by his air-raid chief to check out Whitley's cabin on Mount Ross, where Vicky has retreated. When Margaret Sibyll is found to be a rations hoarder (a bad thing during the war), Vicky realizes she is a fake. Vicky also realizes she loves her husband and, at the last minute, they reconcile.

As the picture was nearing completion, Hall was called back to Columbia to direct *Once Upon a Time*. So, with just three weeks left of filming, Metro studio director Vincente Minnelli, before he had been given his first full picture to direct (*Cabin in the Sky*), was assigned to bring *The Heavenly Body* in on schedule.

Speculation buzzed about Hollywood as to whether and when Hedy and Loder would marry. The problem delaying them was their respective shooting schedules. John was expected at Warner Bros. to work in *One More Tomorrow*, which had been temporarily on hold because of script problems, and Hedy had to complete *The Heavenly Body*. In early May the papers stated the couple would wed in Mexico. On Tuesday, May 25, the two applied for a marriage license in Santa Monica and announced their engagement and decision to marry as soon as they could obtain short leaves from their studios. Hedy gave her age as twenty-eight, which she was. Loder gave his age as forty-two, which he was not.

Problems delaying the nuptials were also caused by the legality of Loder's divorce from Micheline Cheirel. The Beverly Hills judge Charles Griffin, who had represented Ms. Cheirel, told the press, "Mr. Loder was so anxious to marry Miss Lamarr that he asked my client to get a divorce in Mexico, although she had already obtained her divorce in California, which wouldn't be final for a year. He did go to Juarez and got a divorce, but she wanted the property settlement clarified, so she asked me to get a second decree here, too."[36]

Loder told one journalist he had been in love before, "But it was never this kind of love."[37] Then, according to his autobiography, he received a letter from Hedy with a bill for $350 to cover the cost of the dinners he had shared with her at Hedgerow Farm. "She said it was exactly half the price of the food and wine we had consumed together," he wrote, "and explained that she had divided her cook's wages in half for the month that I had been dining at her house. I was somewhat taken aback." Even more inauspiciously, later that evening he met up with Errol Flynn at the Polo Bar in Beverly Hills, and the handsome Australian warned him, "I suppose you realize, old boy, from tomorrow on you'll be known as Mr. Lamarr."[38]

On Thursday, May 27, 1943, Loder telephoned the makeup department at Warner Bros. to advise them he was shaving off his mustache, which he had grown for his role in *One More Tomorrow*.[39] "Hedy insisted that I shave off my mustache," he told them. "I understand the picture starts re-shooting in a few days. Make up a prop mustache for me. I'm getting married tonight and won't have time to grow one."[40]

John, driving through the gates of Metro to pick Hedy up at 6:30 P.M. and wearing a double-breasted blue suit, strolled to Hedy's dressing room. She was waiting for him, dressed in a plain black velvet suit and white silk blouse, accentuated with white silk gloves and small pearl earrings and a single-strand pearl necklace. She wore black patent leather shoes and, instead of a hat, donned a dark snood covered with small daisies.

Though it was erroneously announced that the wedding would take place at Hedgerow Farm, it was actually held at the apartment home of Hedy and John's friend Mrs. Lily Veidt, the recent widow of the actor Conrad Veidt. (Veidt had suddenly died of a heart attack just the month before.) After arriving at Lily's apartment at 7:15 P.M., the ceremony commenced and was presided over by Judge Cecil D. Holland of the Beverly Hills Justice Court. Hedy's matron of honor was Mrs. Elsie Mendl, and her husband, Sir Charles Mendl, was John's best man. The only other witnesses were Hedy's mother, Trude, and John's friends Bill Gerard from M-G-M and Sam Pierce.

Hedy was anxious. "'Give me my ring,' she insisted like a schoolgirl. 'I won't wait. Let's hurry and get married.'"[41] For the brief double–gold ring ceremony Hedy held a bouquet of roses, all white but for a red rose in the center. At 7:45 P.M. the service was over and champagne was served. The following day, Hedy reported back to work on the Metro lot. Hedy and John's honeymoon would have to wait.

12

Marriage

Hedy and John eventually honeymooned at Big Bear Lake, a resort high up in the San Bernardino Mountains, where they rented a log cabin for four idyllic days and nights. Hedy had brought food supplies, including a fresh chicken, and on arrival asked the elderly proprietor to show her how to cook on the rather primitive stove in their cabin. "You just put your hand inside, Ma'am, and if it's so hot that it burns you, put your chicken in," was his reply. Despite that, Hedy managed to impress her husband with her culinary ability.[1]

Hedy spoke about her honeymoon with *Family Circle* magazine writer Kitty Callahan. "It was simply heavenly," she said. "You know, when you pass a certain point high in the mountains, a beautiful calm comes over you. We had a tiny cabin. It was fun going to Mrs. Burke's little store nearby for milk and eggs, and fun not being dressed up all the time. I love blue jeans. Already they have that well worn look." Hedy told the journalist, "I love nature. Really love it. I'm like Ferdinand. I love to sit under the trees and smell the flowers. I honestly think that if more people loved nature and music the world would be happier."[2]

Back in Hollywood, Hedy's obvious beauty always overshadowed her intelligence, and people meeting her for the first time were often stunned by the real woman. In 1942 Diana Barrymore, the daughter of John Barrymore and niece to Ethel and Lionel, came to California ready to show the world yet another acting legend, or so she thought. Not much of a film actress, Diana was nonetheless gifted and headstrong, but also troubled. In July 1942 she married the British actor Bramwell Fletcher, a good friend of John Loder's and one of Hedy's costars in *White Cargo*.

Barrymore wrote in her autobiography (cowritten with Gerold Frank), "John Loder brought beautiful Hedy Lamarr to visit us. As a gift she gave me a copy of Philip Wylie's newest book [*A Generation of Vipers*]. I'd read reviews of it. 'My God, Hedy,' I exclaimed. 'What an extraordinary gift for you to give me. With that face of yours I didn't think you had a brain in your head.' She managed to laugh."[3]

John rented an apartment in Hollywood at Peyton Hall before relocating to the Beverly Hills Hotel, just two miles from Hedy's home. Upon their return from Big Bear, he permanently moved into Hedgerow Farm with Hedy and Jamesie.

Jamesie, when he was a year and a half old, feared the darkness, just as Hedy had when she was a child. And so she spent time with the boy just before nightfall, playing a music box for him until he felt safe. Jamesie as a baby had been pale and sickly, and Hedy took her motherly duties seriously. She once told a journalist, "I believe raising a child should be an enormous source of pleasure to a mother. Furthermore, that pleasure should be realized day by day from the simplest contacts with the child. . . . I want my child to be physically, mentally and spiritually independent."[4]

Hedy's familial responsibilities also extended to caring for her mother. By this time she was also renting an apartment for Trude, allowing her to maintain a certain amount of independence. Each month Trude would hand over her bills to Hedy, including gratuity receipts from when she dined out. Hedy always found Trude's tipping to be extravagant, and it was usually over this issue, according to Loder, that an argument between the two women would ensue.

Loder was impressed with Hedy's domestic side. On the cook's night off, she would do the food preparation and proved she was quite good at it. Hedy preferred to stay home instead of going to parties, and she rarely drank. She was an excellent conversationalist and yet enjoyed simple tastes. She "was a typical hausfrau," he recalled.[5]

Loder was depressed and remorseful over his two previous failed marriages. And Hedy was sympathetic to this. She wanted to give John a successful union. And in time John and Jamesie warmed toward each other, and John took steps to adopt the boy.

"I was working on a new public image for myself, one that would make me more comfortable," Hedy wrote in her book.[6] And indeed in her personal life

Hedwig Eva Maria Kiesler, c. 1916
(Denise Loder-DeLuca Collection)

Five year-old "Hedylendelein" and her
father, Emil Kiesler, c. 1919
(Denise Loder-DeLuca Collection)

Gertrud "Trude" Lichwitz Kiesler, Hedy's mother,
c. 1921 (Denise Loder-DeLuca Collection)

Backpacking with her family, c. 1920 (Denise Loder-DeLuca Collection)

Hedy Kiesler in *Geld auf der Strasse*, 1930 (Author Collection)

Hedy and her mother, Trude, home in Vienna, c. 1930 (Denise Loder-DeLuca Collection)

Hedy as a young student in Vienna, 1930 (Author Collection)

Hedy Kiesler in *Die Koffer des Herrn O.F.*, 1932 (Author Collection)

With Fred Doderlein in Vienna during the filming of *Die Koffer des Herrn O.F.*, 1932
(Author Collection)

Hedy Kiesler, film actress,
c. 1932 (Author Collection)

The virile Aribert Mog, up-and-coming
UFA film star, c. 1931 (Author
Collection)

Hedy Kiesler as the title character in *Sissi*,
1933 (Denise Loder-DeLuca Collection)

Hedy Kiesler in *Extaze*, 1932 (Author
Collection)

Fritz Mandl, c. 1939 (PHOTOFEST)

The newly rechristened, Hollywood-chic Hedy Lamarr's arrival into Los Angeles, October 4, 1937. (AUTHOR COLLECTION)

Hedy's Euro-chic arrival in New York on board the *Normandie*, September 30, 1937 (AUTHOR COLLECTION)

LEFT: M-G-M began the publicity immediately upon Hedy's arrival, 1937 RIGHT: Hedy in 1937 (AUTHOR COLLECTION)

With future costar James Stewart, c. 1938 (AUTHOR COLLECTION)

Hedy Lamarr (*center*) in *Algiers*, her first Hollywood film appearance, 1938 (AUTHOR COLLECTION)

On the town with Reginald Gardiner, c. 1938 (AUTHOR COLLECTION)

With Charles Boyer in *Algiers*, 1938 (Author Collection)

A rare cheesecake photograph of Hedy, c. 1939 (Author Collection)

LEFT: With Robert Taylor in *Lady of the Tropics*, 1939. RIGHT: Newlyweds Hedy and Gene Markey, with their Great Dane, Donner, March 8, 1939 (AUTHOR COLLECTION)

Filming on the set of *I Take This Woman*, c. 1939, with Spencer Tracy and director W. S. Van Dyke (*standing*) (AUTHOR COLLECTION)

The cast of *Boom Town*, 1940 (*left to right*): Spencer Tracy, Hedy, Frank Morgan, Claudette Colbert, Clark Gable (AUTHOR COLLECTION)

With Clark Gable, *Comrade X*, 1940
(DENISE LODER-DELUCA COLLECTION)

LEFT: George Antheil, the "Bad Boy of Music," c. 1930s. RIGHT: With James Stewart in *Come Live with Me*, 1941 (AUTHOR COLLECTION)

Robert Young and Hedy in perhaps her best film performance, *H.M. Pulham, Esq.*, 1941 (AUTHOR COLLECTION)

Top: Tony Martin singing "You Stepped Out of a Dream" to Hedy in *Ziegfeld Girl*, 1941 (AUTHOR COLLECTION)

Bottom: On the set of *Ziegfeld Girl*, 1941: Lana Turner, Judy Garland, Hedy seated center; showgirl Georgia Carroll standing, on the left. (AUTHOR COLLECTION)

Hedy Lamarr, M-G-M star, c. 1941 (Author Collection)

Hedy greeting her mother upon Trude's arrival in Pasadena, February 1942 (Denise Loder-DeLuca Collection)

With William Powell in *Crossroads*, 1942 (Denise Loder-DeLuca Collection)

With John Garfield in *Tortilla Flat*, 1942 (Author Collection)

As Tondelayo in *White Cargo*, 1942 (AUTHOR COLLECTION)

she achieved that. But because of the extended shooting schedule of *The Heavenly Body,* Hedy lost out on other projects that could have possibly prolonged her career.

Hedy would always say that one of her of deepest regrets was not being cast as Clio in the Warner Bros. film adaptation of Edna Ferber's sweeping novel *Saratoga Trunk,* opposite Gary Cooper. After Bette Davis and Vivien Leigh both turned it down, the role went to Ingrid Bergman. (The picture would not be released until 1945.)

Warner Bros. had also requested Hedy for the part of Fanny in *Mr. Skeffington,* the story about a renowned beauty at the turn of the century who is consumed by her own vanity to the point of the ruination of her marriage to her husband, who suffers miserably because of Fanny's behavior. In the film, Fanny ages dramatically.

Hedy found this distasteful (she had an aversion to anything ugly), and possibly to her great relief Metro once again declined to loan her out. Bette Davis joyfully took the role, giving her yet another chance to chew up the scenery. *Mr. Skeffington* would earn Davis an Oscar nod for Best Actress in 1944.

Hedy said that she turned down Otto Preminger's request to star her in *Laura* for Twentieth Century–Fox. "Otto Preminger, whom I had known way back in Vienna, gave me the script for 'Laura,'" she told a journalist. "I didn't think it was very good then, and I still don't."[7] The haunting musical theme from the film, by the composer David Raksin, became a classic, and several years later she was asked again why she turned the role down, and she replied, "Because they sent me the script instead of the score."[8]

Also on the list of roles for which Hedy was seriously considered was the part of Paula Alquist, opposite Charles Boyer in Metro's remake of *Gaslight.* Hedy was now a star at the studio, and she did not favor second billing to Boyer. And Boyer would accept nothing less. Hedy would have been ideal in the part, and though she said she had been sick and "declined" it, the fact was that Metro was losing faith in her dramatic potential. Again the part was given to Ingrid Bergman, who didn't give a damn about billing. Her performance in *Gaslight* won her the 1944 Best Actress Oscar. Hedy's work at the studio, however, remained on course.

Years later Hedy recalled her life at Metro-Goldwyn-Mayer: "It was generally very friendly at Metro, rather like a great big party, like a little family, you know," Hedy told *The New York Times* journalist Bob Edison in 1974. She continued:

I'd be strolling down a street at morning, feeling fit and fiddle, and it was invariably, "Hi, Mickey; Hi, Judy; Hi, Greer." . . . You have to realize these people were all folk I'd see almost daily, just like you work with anybody in the world itself. And, as in the business world, naturally there were some I was a lot fonder of than others! . . . Well, it seems people have this weird idea of what it was like under the star system. Believe me, the work in those days was generally confining. It was indoors for the most part, inside those soundstages, and we seldom got a chance to get outside into the fresh air. . . . We usually didn't know half the time what hour it was, let alone the day of the week, working weekends and all that. It could be rather numbing, to say the least. And it was ghastly having to get up at 5:30 in the morning with the chicks, and having to sit there in an evening gown by 9 A.M. completely made up and well into a sizzling love scene. . . . Sure, there were many times when, in order to be on an early call from the night before, I'd sleep right over. It was hard work, let me tell you; I guess for some they were the Golden Days, but for me they're mostly happy memories, and that's it.[9]

Hedy completed her scenes in *The Heavenly Body* the first week of August. On August 2, John and Hedy worked together for the first time on *The Lady Esther Screen Guild Theater,* sponsored by Lady Esther Cosmetics and hosted by Truman Bradley for ABC radio. They starred in a thirty-minute adaptation of *Come Live with Me* with Vincent Price.

They next were scheduled to take to the stage for the Naval Aid Auxiliary in mid-August, cast opposite each other in *Play Time.* The revue was an evening of five one-act plays performed by several film stars and the Brentwood Service Players, with all salaries and production profits given to the charitable auxiliary. Hedy and John were to have costarred in the Hungarian playwright Ferenc Molnár's *Marshall.* For whatever reasons, most likely because of the drawn-out filming of *The Heavenly Body,* they did not perform in the production.

In late August Hedy and John headed to Mexico City at the request of Louis B. Mayer, with whom John, according to his account, had become a good friend and horse-riding partner. Because of the high quality of motion pictures Metro-Goldwyn-Mayer had recently released, in particular *Mrs. Miniver* in 1942 and *Madame Curie* in 1943, both of which starred Greer Garson and the latter of which also starred Margaret O'Brien, Mayer, along with Walt Disney, was being honored. "'L.B.' invited me to accompany him . . . to receive the Order of the Aztec Eagle, Mexico's highest decoration," wrote Loder. "What a trip that was, red carpets all the way."[10]

The event was held at the Foreign Office in Mexico City. Mayer, Disney, and the Metro travelogue filmmaker James A. Fitzpatrick were each presented with the highest civilian award given in Mexico by its foreign minister Ezequiel Padilla. John and Hedy were in attendance, along with Walter Pidgeon and Robert Vogel, who had been in charge of the arrangements. The Hearst newsreels were there to capture the event.

Loder told of an incident that happened while they were still in Mexico City. He had picked out a raincoat he liked and was preparing to pay five hundred pesos for it when Hedy addressed the shopkeeper and told him the coat was only worth two hundred pesos. After much squabbling, Hedy got the coat reduced down to three hundred pesos, much to John's embarrassment.

Back in Hollywood, Hedy agreed to participate in the third war-bond drive, the Hollywood Cavalcade, along with other Hollywood stars, which was scheduled to tour the country. Its financial goal was set at $5 billion.

Among those who would make the three-week, fifteen-city tour with Hedy were Edward Arnold, Judy Garland, Cary Grant, Lucille Ball, James Cagney, Mickey Rooney, Walter Pidgeon, Myrna Loy, Dick Powell, Red Skelton, and Kay Kyser. The stars traveled by private railroad car, and the tour's first stop was Washington, D.C., on September 8, followed by a huge rally at Madison Square Garden in New York on September 11, where admission for the 18,500 seats would be the purchase of war bonds.

Hedy was happy to be doing the tour, but during it she missed her son. She had told the press just two years before, "I adore him. But I shall not spoil him. I want him to be my friend as well as my son. In so far as I can, I will devote my life to him. I want him to be a good man, a good American."[11] Now that she and Loder were married, John would begin steps to adopt the child and change the boy's name permanently to James Lamarr Loder.

Late that September, Hedy appeared on *The Edgar Bergen / Charlie McCarthy Show,* much to the delight of listening radio audiences so familiar now with the peccadilloes of America's best-loved ventriloquist and his dummy.

The divorce decree ending the marriage of Loder and Micheline Cheirel became official on September 27. When Hedy and John married there were still four months yet to elapse before it was legal for them to wed. "However, just prior to his marriage to Miss Lamarr," said the *Los Angeles Times*, "Loder obtained a divorce from Miss Cheirel in Juarez, Mex."[12]

As Metro searched for a new property for her, Hedy told Edwin Schallert of the *Los Angeles Times* that she still felt that she had not yet found the perfect film role for her. Though she was rather proud of her work in *Tortilla Flat*, Hedy said,

> What I really want is to do certain things on the screen that will mean more to me personally, my inner feelings, my own ambitions. I want to play parts that are within my own natural limitations of feelings and understanding. . . . I would love to play a costumed character and, again a woman, say, like the one in "The Little Foxes." Those I feel, might be within my natural range.[13]

In October Hedy was the guest of George Burns and his wife, Gracie Allen, on their popular radio comedy *The Burns and Allen Show*. Hedy was now quite capable of playing comedy to rival that of her radio-show hosts. For some reason Metro just could never understand that beautiful women could be funny. With *The Heavenly Body* about to be previewed, Hedy was offered no further scripts by Metro.

On November 21 Hedy appeared yet again on *The Edgar Bergen / Charlie McCarthy Show*. (Also in the cast was fourteen-year-old songstress Jane Powell.) Hedy was also featured on two other radio talk shows in early December, *What's New* and *Soldiers with Wings*, both broadcast locally in Los Angeles.

For their first Christmas together, Hedy and John decorated their tree for Jamesie and exchanged gifts. Earlier that summer Hedy had entertained Madame Cartier, wife of the famous jeweler, and John's gift to Hedy that Christmas was a beautiful diamond ring. Hedy then told John she was giving him a Cadillac. When they handed their gifts over to each other on Christmas Day, Hedy gave John a small box. Inside, he recalled in his autobiography, was a small toy model Cadillac car.

During the early months of their marriage Hedy felt John did not assert himself enough. She told him he would make much more money if he would end his Warner Bros. contract and go out on his own as a freelance actor. Loder wrote that Hedy goaded him into charging into the front office and demanding more money from the studio chief Jack L. Warner. "Don't be an idiot, John," Warner allegedly told him. "When *Old Acquaintance* is released you'll be the Walter Pidgeon of Warners. You have a great future here."[14] Loder lost his Warner Bros. contract at any rate; however, he did make more money after he secured his release. But he proved to be a B star, no matter what.

Hedda Hopper informed her readers on December 29 in her *Los Angeles Times* column that Hedy would be cast opposite Cary Grant and Charles Laughton in *The Pirate,* to be directed by Henry Koster. Metro had other plans and considered William Powell for the male lead, with Vincente Minnelli as director. *The Pirate* would remain in limbo until the end of the decade, when the studio would dust it off, turn it into a musical for Judy Garland and Gene Kelly, and retain Garland's then-husband Minnelli to direct it. It got pummeled at the box office and lost a bundle.

To start off the new year, Hedy appeared on *The Lux Radio Theater* presentation of *Casablanca,* on January 24, starring Alan Ladd as Rick, John Loder as Victor, and Hedy in the role she was meant to play, Ilsa. Though she had a slight cold, Hedy would not have missed this opportunity for anything in the world. She would show Mayer what she could do with the role of Ilsa.

The radio play proceeded along briskly, though Ladd (as Rick) was more street savvy than world-weary, and Loder (as Victor) was a bit too crisp in his British delivery. Hedy's performance was assured, possibly a bit more coy than Bergman's interpretation but immensely convincing. When Sam (Ernest Whitman) plays "As Time Goes By," one visualizes what could have been captured on film with a Bogart-Lamarr-Henreid triumvirate.

Normally paid in cash, Hedy's compensation for these radio plays was sometimes unusual. "Once, for an appearance on *The Lux Radio Theater,*" she told one writer, "I got paid off in soap . . . cartons and cartons of it kept coming; I was swimming in it for years!"[15]

That spring *Look* magazine published a survey that asked readers who they thought was the most beautiful woman in Hollywood, and the tally ended in a four-way tie between Hedy Lamarr, Linda Darnell, Gene Tierney, and Ingrid Bergman.

For the complete eighteen months it was on the air, John hosted and occasionally starred on WABC radio's *Silver Theater.* In February Hedy appeared with him and Conrad Nagel in the thirty-minute drama "She Looked Like an

Angel." Hedda Hopper in her column then reported that Hedy was soon to star in the upcoming film *Salome Where She Danced* for Walter Wanger. Mayer would *not* allow Wanger to profit by Hedy again, and the picture was made by Universal in 1945 starring Yvonne De Carlo.

And then, quite inexplicably, Hedy was suddenly notified that she was being loaned out to both Warner Bros. and R-K-O for one picture each. Away from M-G-M, Hedy would hand in two of her better film performances. Production had already begun on *The Conspirators* over at Warner Bros., directed by Jean Negulesco.

On February 16, 1944, Warner producer Hal B. Wallis forwarded an inter-office memo to studio executive Roy Obringer advising him that a deal had been struck with M-G-M through Metro executive Benny Thau to secure the services of Hedy for the part of Irene for *The Conspirators* on an eight-week guarantee at her regular salary. Her starting date would begin the week of February 28. In return for Hedy's loan-out, Warner Bros. would lend M-G-M Garfield for two pictures, to be completed within two years.[16]

Two days later, Jack L. Warner copied Obringer, Steve Trilling, and Billy Wilder in a memo insisting that Warner Bros. get Hedy for *two* pictures in exchange for the two for Garfield, which paid the actor $33,000 and $36,000 respectively. Mayer did not approve, and the original deal went ahead.[17]

The Conspirators told a story of adventure, intrigue, and romance. In 1944 refugees from Nazi-occupied European countries flock into the safety of Lisbon, the last open port on the Continent and the center of departure and takeoff for the United States. Surrounded by soldiers of fortune, Nazis and anti-Nazis, and desperate refugees, is the Dutch underground agent Vincent van der Lyn (Paul Henreid), known by the Nazis as the Flying Dutchman, who is told to go to the Café Imperio, where he is to be given instructions from a fellow conspirator, Bernazsky (Peter Lorre).

Rushing up to Vincent's table that night at the club and seating herself down beside him is Irene (Hedy), a beautiful and mysterious Frenchwoman who is fleeing the police. When she leaves the café, Vincent follows her to the gambling casino Estoril, the Monte Carlo of Lisbon, where Irene tells him to forget about her. Bernazsky then tells Vincent to leave town for the night, and he journeys to the fishing village of Cascais and befriends Miguel (Vladimir Sokoloff) and his daughter (Carol Thurston). The following day Vincent secretly meets with the head of the conspirators, Ricardo Quintanilla (Sydney

Greenstreet), who tells Vincent he must give important information to another agent that evening.

Though she is married to Hugo von Mohr (Victor Francen), Irene agrees to spend the day with Vincent, and they drive to a roadside tavern, where the two fall in love. She tells Vincent she stays with Mohr because he rescued her from the concentration camp in Dachau. When Vincent returns to his hotel, he finds the agent he was to meet, Jennings (Monte Blue), dying from a gunshot wound. Vincent is arrested for murder and believes Irene set him up. He escapes jail dressed as a guard, locates Quintanilla, and discovers Irene is a fellow freedom fighter and not a Nazi. Quintanilla suggests that the murder was carried out by a traitor within their group. He and Vincent set a trap. Mohr turns out to be the guilty party and is shot outside the Estoril while trying to escape. In his pocket is evidence clearing Vincent of the murder. As Vincent leaves on another secret mission, he tells Irene he will return for her.

Warner Bros. purchased the Frederic Prokosch novel for $7,500 on April 16, 1943. Jack L. Warner announced on May 12 that reason behind the studio's decision to film it was essentially to "re-unite male members of the cast of *Casablanca*," Humphrey Bogart, Paul Henreid, and Sydney Greenstreet. The cast then was to also include Helmut Dantine, George Coulouris, and Ann Sheridan.[18]

The screenplay was left to Leo Rosten and Vladimir Pozner. Under its original title *City of Shadows*, the script was submitted on November 16, 1943, to the Breen Office, which approved it just seven days later.

Hedy was not the first choice for the role of Irene. On January 11, 1944, Signe Hasso had tested and was not cast. Producer Hal B. Wallis then considered Ida Lupino, another actress who had possibly less marquee value but nonetheless was a strong and commendable performer. She was not available. They then requested Hedy's services, and their timing could not have been better. Mayer still had nothing lined up for her, and he somewhat reluctantly agreed to the loan-out.

For *The Conspirators*, M-G-M was to be paid Hedy's salary of $2,000 a week beginning March 30 until April 9. Then, on April 10, Warner was to pay Metro $2,500 a week until the end of filming. (Hedy's contract with Metro required the pay increase.)

Hedy had requested that dialogue coach Ruth Roberts, called the Doctor of Dialects, be hired to help her in *The Conspirators*. Loder wrote in his autobiography:

When she was working on a script I used to go through it with her and
she was extremely good when she was natural and relaxed at home.
Then, suddenly she decided to get hold of a coach and employed the
same one as Ingrid Bergman. I was very much against the idea. By the
time she had finished being coached she had lost the slight Austrian accent I had found so attractive and she sounded exactly like hundreds of
other American movie actresses. I am convinced Hedy would have been
really great but for all that coaching.[19]

Nonetheless, Hedy was successfully tested as Irene on Wednesday, January
23, on stage 6 on the Warner lot. She then made three additional tests on stage 15.

Filming began on March 2, 1944. When Hedy arrived at Warner in Burbank, she was given the red-carpet treatment. While she attended a boardroom meeting before the film's commencement, Bette Davis rushed into the
room to greet her. Wrote one journalist, "Peter Lorre greeted Hedy with a kiss,
and said, 'But Hedy, you look so happy. You used to look so morose.' 'I was
never morose,' Hedy corrected him, 'I was just disappointed in things.'"[20]

In later years Lorre would tell the story of an incident that occurred during
the filming of a scene with Sydney Greenstreet. Hedy arrived on the set wearing a diaphanous dress. "Hey, Sydney," joked Lorre. "You're the only person on
the set with a pair of tits." Production was held up for over two hours as Lamarr
and Greenstreet chased Lorre about the set, said the diminutive actor, who
added that Jack L. Warner fined him $10,000 for the disruption.[21]

In a magazine piece, a journalist quoted Hedy: "I haven't been off the Metro
lot in over six years. I knew all the faces there—and they knew mine. When I
came to Warner Brothers it was like visiting a strange, friendly city. I like it
here. I am so happy with everything, I am dull. I am crazy about the picture."[22]

Metro, the press reported in March, had scheduled next for Hedy *Holiday in
Mexico,* a musical to be produced by Arthur Freed after he completed the studio's third installment of the Ziegfeld trilogy, *Ziegfeld Follies* (not released until
1946). When it was finally produced and released in 1946, *Holiday in Mexico*
starred Walter Pidgeon and Jane Powell, and it was produced by Joe Pasternak.

The Heavenly Body was previewed in Los Angeles on December 28, 1943.
The reviewer of *Harrison's Reports* commented, "Miss Lamarr and Powell
do their best with second-rate material."[23] The *PM* reviewer said, "As bores go,
The Heavenly Body is something rather special, in that it offers the ultra-luxury

of being bored by no less a personage than Hedy Lamarr."[24] Yet when it reached the screens, *The Heavenly Body* did brisk business with Powell and Lamarr fans.

The Heavenly Body is a delightfully fluffy and totally forgettable little film, though possibly the best comedy Hedy ever made. The picture surrounded her with comfortably talented people whom she liked and trusted. Her scenes with Powell absolutely sparkle.

With a crisp and amusing screenplay by Michael Arlen and Walter Reisch, the dialogue is funny and in keeping with the times. Hedy and James Craig sing one little song together, "I'm Dying for Someone to Love Me," and Hedy's voice was not dubbed. Irene outdid herself with Hedy's fashions in the film, thirteen in all.

Although *The Heavenly Body* was pure escapism, Hedy in this film, thanks to her ability to capably handle comedic timing and delivery, temporarily eradicated the memory of Tondelayo.

On March 31 Hedy was slapped with a lawsuit, named as a defendant along with agents of the Feldman-Blum Corporation in a $10,000 suit by William E. Barrett, a New York author, who claimed he was not paid for the film and radio rights to his story "Woman on Horseback." Hedy denied ever contracting with Barrett for the story. Responding to the charges, Hedy said she had found "the story was salacious, reflected unfavorably on certain South American nations and was unfit for the screen."[25] In the final outcome, Hedy was found not accountable.

Metro announced in May that Hedy would star in the upcoming film *Diamond Rock,* based on the British writer Alec Waugh's novel. A domestic love triangle set in the West Indies, the project was scheduled to begin shooting as soon as Hedy completed *The Conspirators.* When offered the role, Hedy declined in favor of a fairy tale called *Her Highness and the Bellboy,* another property Mayer had held in hock for her for the past three years.

At this point Louis B. Mayer was all but ignoring his studio, concentrating on his horses and his waning libido. Though all Hedy's pictures were turning tidy profits, the times were changing. On May 27, Mayer announced Metro was loaning Hedy to R-K-O for *Experiment Perilous,* a psychological mystery. Scheduled to star opposite her were Gregory Peck and Paul Lukas. (George Brent would replace Peck when production eventually began that summer.)

So far, *The Conspirators* was proving to be an interesting shoot. According to the production notes for the picture, it was called "Reunion in Vienna" by the cast and crew because of the large number of Austrian exiles involved in the project, including Hedy, Henreid, Lorre, and the editor Rudi Fehr, among others.

Many of the props used in *The Conspirators* were genuine antiques and worth untold thousands of dollars. For one particular scene in the German embassy, Negulesco used a genuine Gobelins tapestry valued at $75,000 that had hung in the Palace of Versailles before World War I and dated back to Louis XIV. In the casino sequence, Warner Bros. acquired the use of two magnificent matching crystal chandeliers valued at $35,000 apiece, which came to Hollywood via New York, where William Randolph Hearst had maintained them after purchasing them in Monte Carlo.

Using the same stamp of perfection and detail he had for Warner Bros.' forthcoming *The Mask of Dimitrios,* before the cameras rolled on *The Conspirators*, the director, Negulescu, prepared eighty-seven different set drawings and designs in which he envisioned the scenes and the action of the picture. "The result was one of the most lavish production mountings on the studio's current schedule," said a press release, "all of it contrived to point up the hothouse beauty of Hedy Lamarr and her courtship by Henreid."[26]

Unexpectedly, Hedda Hopper announced on April 22 that Jack Chertok was taking over the production from Hal B. Wallis on *The Conspirators* and reshooting most of the picture. (What went unreported was that Wallis had disagreed with Jack Warner, and was fired.) But Hedy, she said, was "loving every minute" of the filming. "She'll be glad when her Metro contract is over in October and she can freelance," said the columnist.[27]

Production wrapped on *The Conspirators* on June 9, 1944, with Hedy and Henreid filming on the exterior sets of the casino and on the beach for the finale. The picture had an original estimated end date of April 26. By its close the production had been running for eighty-two filming days and was thirty-four days behind schedule, in part because of Wallis's departure from the film and delay in reorganizing the shooting when Chertok came in. That transition, however, netted Hedy an additional $10,333 in overtime pay, for a total overtime compensation of $30,750. The picture's overall overtime costs came to approximately $335,864.08. (Its total cost was originally budgeted at close to $1.2 million.) The following Monday Hedy's portable dressing room was sent back to Metro-Goldwyn-Mayer.

Hedy was looking forward to cutting her ties with Metro. It was apparent not only to her but to fans and film critics alike that Mayer had squandered his chances of casting her in appropriate vehicles. The feeling Metro had was that Hedy was not making back their investments and that she was difficult to deal with.

After less than a month off to rest, Hedy stepped before the cameras for *Experiment Perilous* on the R-K-O Radio lot on July 12, 1944. Two weeks later, on July 23, she appeared with Walter Pidgeon in a radio play called "Romance" for *Stars and Their Stories* on CBS.

Experiment Perilous was based on Margaret Carpenter's 1943 suspense novel of the same name and was adapted for the screen by the producer Warren Duff. Originally slated as its producer was David Hempstead. Cary Grant was to star, but when Hempstead left the production so did Grant. Robert Fellows then was penciled in as producer, now with Gregory Peck as the star. But Peck had a previous commitment with David O. Selznick, and he too left the production. Léonide Moguy was then set to direct, and the studio considered both Maureen O'Hara and Laraine Day for the female lead. Eventually R-K-O got Hedy Lamarr. Her director for *Experiment Perilous* would eventually be Jacques Tourneur.

Hedy was pleased with the screenplay, writing, "*Experiment Perilous* . . . was a powerful script by Warren Duff . . . and I loved it. . . . It seems that he had finished two scripts and did not think of me for the one called *Lady in Danger* (the working title, which later became *Experiment Perilous*). I asked to look at it and from that moment on everything fell into place."[28] This could very well have happened, but Mayer still pulled the strings. What is true is that Hedy *did* like the script.

Experiment Perilous begins in 1903, when Dr. Huntington Bailey (George Brent) meets a talkative spinster, Cissie Bederaux (Olive Blakeney) aboard a train bound for New York. Cissie's brother Nick (Paul Lukas, fresh from his 1943 Best Actor Oscar win for Warner Bros.' *Watch on the Rhine*) is married to Allida (Hedy), and Cissie is making the trip to New York for her sister-in-law's birthday. At a party in New York that evening, Bailey hears that Cissie has died quite suddenly after arriving at the home of her brother and sister-in-law. Bailey becomes suspicious, and, with his friend "Clag" Claghorn (Albert Dekker), he pays a call on the Bederaux home.

Bailey meets Bederaux and his beautiful wife, Allida, who is obviously afraid of something. He is taken aside during the visit and told by Bederaux that his wife is unstable, and the following day the two men meet to discuss her condition. Bederaux's statements do not match with those Cissie had told Bailey on the train. Bailey becomes convinced that Allida fears her husband because of a past indiscretion with a young poet, Alec Gregory (George N. Niese), who was later found dead.

Fearing for the lives of Allida, whom he has fallen in love with, and her young son Alexander (William Ward), Bailey plans to move them to safety. His plan is found out by Bederaux. Bailey is told that the house is now filled with gas and will soon combust. Bederaux confesses to the murder of the young poet and his sister Cissie, who had discovered that it is he who is insane. Bailey attacks Bederaux and rescues Allida and her son before the house explodes and kills her husband.

Filming did not get off to a good start, and Hedy and the director Tourneur often did not see eye to eye. George Brent, who would give a lackluster performance in *Experiment Perilous,* was harshly critical of Hedy's work when they were filming. "Hedy was a lovely woman," he later said, "but her memory for remembering lines or set-ups was god-awful. The delays and cuts and retakes caused by this woman were unbearably exasperating."[29]

This was the first film in which Hedy portrayed a mother (apart from the brief ending in *Ecstasy,* and references made about Marvin's grown children in *H.M. Pulham, Esq.*), and she does so quite well. It is intriguing that in the film Allida's child, Alexander, is tormented by dreams of witches and evil monsters, and his mother fears for him. Much was made of Hedy's interpretation of her mother role, which somewhat paralleled her own concern for Jamesie.

As directed by the gifted Jacques Tourneur, *Experiment Perilous* was an A picture production awarded to him following his string of successful B suspense films produced by Val Lewton and that the studio had recently released (*Cat People* in 1942 and *The Leopard Man* and *I Walked With a Zombie*, both in 1943, all three considered classics today).

Tourneur, the son of the French film pioneer Maurice Tourneur, who had begun directing silent films in Fort Lee, New Jersey, in 1913 (he helmed *The Wishing Ring* for World Studios in 1914 and *The Poor Little Rich Girl,* with Mary Pickford, for Artcraft in 1917), never quite achieved the same historical prominence as his father. But the younger Tourneur's work on *Experiment Perilous* comes close to his father's style.

During the last days of filming *Experiment Perilous* in September, Hedy discovered she was pregnant. She and Loder advised the press on October 26 that the delivery date of the baby would be in June. Hedy, her husband, and her studio boss were not at all prepared.

13

Independence

The day after Hedy completed *Experiment Perilous,* she and John drove back to Big Bear to the very cabin that John's friend had turned over to them for their honeymoon. Loder had just completed *The Brighton Strangler* for R-K-O Radio, and the two looked forward to some much-needed rest. For several days, after loading the fireplace with logs, they would curl up on the couch and relax. Their trips to Big Bear in the first years of their marriage were frequent.

When he was old enough to understand, sometime in 1944 or 1945, Jamesie was taken into a courtroom, and the judge asked him if he would like to be adopted by John Loder. "He was always quite nice to me," James Loder recalled when he was an adult.[1] Now that he was James Lamarr Loder, called Jamie, Hedy saw to it that the boy had music in his life, and she would listen to classical music with him for hours. Hedy once told a reporter that she did not give Jamie many toys and made sure that he took care of those he had. However, Jamie was often left in the care of his new Canadian nanny, Frances "Frannie" Milner, as well as Hedy's friend and chauffeur from M-G-M, Marvin Neal, and Trude when the Loders made their sabbaticals to Big Bear.

"It is very secluded—no telephones, no visitors, not even servants," Hedy said to the columnist Edwin Schallert about their secret escape. "John and I spend our time there absolutely alone. It is sort of a shrine for us." According to Schallert, the two had pet names for each other; Hedy called Loder Pops and he called her Putzi. John had also compiled two scrapbooks for Hedy, something she had never done before for herself. As she told Schallert, "I have never been so happy about my own work that I wished to preserve any mementos. . . . John is very thoughtful. For see . . . he has kept two large memory books in which he has put everything that has been printed about our marriage." Including, noted Schallert, mementos of their wedding day.[2]

There was a famous story at the time about Hedy and John, as related by the actor Macdonald Carey: "A Hollywood tour bus passes her house as John is out front mowing the lawn," Carey wrote. "One of the tourists says, 'What the hell is he doing outside?' "[3]

Hedgerow Farm was built on a sloping mountainside high up in Benedict Canyon. The nine-room "farmhouse," which Hedy had purchased some four years before, was complete with an oddly shaped pool. The living room measured eighteen by twenty-seven feet and featured a fireplace with an exquisite antique hand-crafted mantel by the Dutch-born master wood-carver Grinling Gibbons (1648–1721). The walls of the room were a soft, ash-toned wood, and complementing the fireplace at the other end of the room was a huge custom-built sofa in front of wide blue draperies that opened to a vast panoramic view. Hedy's dining room was of early American influence, and in her French provincial sideboard she displayed pieces of her antique porcelain, copper, and pewter collections.[4]

Hedy's bedroom was paneled in dove-gray painted wood and carpeted in soft gray frieze. Her headboard and valance were of tufted material patterned in roses. Every night, Hedy would sleep with her windows wide open to the cleansing night air. John's bedroom was decorated in red buff plaid wallpaper, his carpet royal blue. The den featured wood paneling and a huge copper-covered chimney. The kitchen was white, and the walls were covered with hand-painted figures in red. Jamie's room had a patriotic red, white, and blue color scheme with plaid wallpaper. On a side table there was a large studio portrait of Hedy in braids from *Tortilla Flat*.[5]

Deploring the "glamour girl" image at home, Hedy would wear simple clothing at Big Bear. She did not own velvet negligés with feathers or any of the trappings associated with Hollywood screen sirens. She had a penchant for dime-store lipstick and wore little makeup in private or in public. She also wore very little jewelry, but those pieces she did wear were exquisite, some of which she designed herself. Frequently, she would wear a simple strand of pearls. Her more priceless and expensive gems she kept in a safe.

According to publicity, while at home Hedy generally had the radio playing, and she enjoyed listening to Bob Hope and Fred Allen. She liked jokes and enjoyed John's reading to her out loud, her favorite authors being John Steinbeck, Daphne du Maurier, and William Somerset Maugham. The Loders owned two cats and employed a cook, a nanny, and a maid, named Mary, who absolutely adored Hedy, to the point of frequently giving her mistress little hand-wrapped gifts.

But now arguments at home between Hedy and John became frequent. According to Loder, Hedy possessed a fierce temper. "Although she looked so ethereal and fragile she was really very tough," he wrote in his book. "But she was genuinely nervous in front of cameras and always worried that she wasn't good enough. Before starting a picture she was hell to live with as her nerves grew more and more ragged. She nagged me and when she lost her temper hurled anything she could lay her hands on at my head."[6] One bone of contention in their marriage was Hedy's intolerance of John's seven-year-old daughter Danielle, whom he would see every Saturday. The rows would start on Friday nights:

> One particular Friday while I was making *Abroad with Two Yanks* [United Artists, 1944] with William Bendix, I was lying on my bed learning a new scene which was to be shot the following morning. Hedy knew I would be taking Danielle out the next afternoon. She burst into the bedroom bristling with fury. Before I could stop her, she grabbed my new pages of script, tore them into small pieces and flung the shreds in my face. Unfortunately I burst out laughing. That did it. Hedy picked up the first thing she saw, which was a large pitcher of iced water on my bedside table and flung the contents smack in my face.[7]

The Allies invaded France on D-day in June 1944 as the war headed to a close. On August 19, the liberation of Paris was begun as troops marched into the French capital. In Hollywood the portly celebrity hostess Elsa Maxwell and Evalyn Walsh McLean (owner of the Hope diamond) hosted a celebration, about which the ageing playboy Jorge Guinle recalled in 1978: "Artur Rubenstein played the Marseilles . . . and singing along with him were Charles Boyer, Bing Crosby, Frank Sinatra, Judy Garland, and Hedy Lamarr."[8]

Hedy, now thirty years old and expectant, had mixed feelings when she was told the news. "I was pregnant," she remembered, "It kind of sneaked up on me and now I was to play out in real life a scene I had done twice before in pictures. I think I did it better in front of the camera." In her book she wrote, "At first I was delighted and then I was panic-stricken. . . . When I told John, he said, 'Ah-h-h.' I didn't know what that meant. Then he puffed his pipe. I suppose he was pleased. I think with me and thousands of women, as soon as you know you are pregnant or when a child is born, it is you and the child against the world. A husband takes a secondary position. I know that is wrong and unfair, but that's the way nature makes us."[9]

At least that was the way nature made Hedy Lamarr. Now John became, if anything, an annoyance to her. She acknowledged this, writing, "It was all unfair to John. . . . He began to hate me for building a wall between us. His faults appeared magnified a thousand times now. His falling asleep at the table, during movies, or sleeping upright after dinner infuriated me."[10]

On October 12, *The Conspirators* was previewed in Hollywood. When it opened nationally on October 21, Bosley Crowther of *The New York Times* did not enjoy it and wrote, "The faults are deep and extensive. The writers, in preparing the script from a novel by Frederic Prokosch, did nothing to bring it to life. . . . Furthermore, in his stilted direction, Jean Negulesco has pitched the whole thing in a mood of scowling solemnity. The players literally clench their fists and teeth."[11]

Critics as a whole panned the proceedings. *The Conspirators* was dismissed off-handedly by its film editor Rudi Fehr: "It was a mishmash of leftovers from *Casablanca* and *Passage to Marseille*. . . . Hal Wallis liked it; that was enough."[12] But when the studio head Jack L. Warner and the producer Hal B. Wallis had clashed, Warner fired Wallis and replaced him with the minor producer Jack Chertok. The footage already shot was scrapped and the script rewritten, changing the location and pace of the story. The two stars, Hedy and Henreid, took full advantage of the situation, according to the film's director, and started making demands.

What truly killed *The Conspirators* with the critics was the weak story line offered up by its two screenwriters, Vladimir Pozner and Leo Rosten, and *most* definitely the poor pacing and leaden direction of Jean Negulesco, who, like everyone else involved in the picture, pointed the finger of blame at someone else. Negulesco wrote in his autobiography, "Secretly the film became known as *The Constipators*, with 'Headache Lamarr' and 'Paul Hemorrhoid.' The professionals—Greenstreet, Lorre, and Victor Francen—gave me sympathy;

but the just valuation of the film was given by Max Steiner, who was called in to do the musical score. We saw the finished product together. After the show, the lights went on. Hopefully I waited for his comment. It was short, just one word: 'Ouch!' Brief and to the point."[13]

The Conspirators turned a profit—nearly $1.3 million—even after the critics crucified it. It is in some ways ahead of its time, predating the "007" James Bond spy films of the 1960s. Within the first three minutes of *The Conspirators,* Paul Henreid derails a train carrying Nazi officials, explodes a German-infiltrated warehouse, and tosses a hand grenade into a group of enemy soldiers. That was more action than *Casablanca* had in its complete one-hundred-plus minutes.

But what truly redeems *The Conspirators* are the competent acting of its cast, the luxurious sets, and the magnificent musical score by Max Steiner. Hedy simply does not *have* to act; she just has to be there. Alongside Paul Henreid at his romantic best (even more so than in *Casablanca*), Hedy is all allure and male fantasy.

In August 27, the sixty-year-old Louis B. Mayer was thrown from his horse and suffered a broken pelvis, his very first major physical injury. He was laid up for some time, and, after a brief scare over a blood clot in his lungs, it became obvious he would recover. Wrote Scott Eyman in Mayer's biography: "The stars at the studio competed to see who could bring him the largest supply of chicken soup as he recuperated."[14]

The past couple of years had been financially good ones for the studio chief. In 1941 his salary had been $704,425.60, and by 1943 it had risen to $1.139 million, making him once again the highest-paid corporate executive in the country.[15] Mayer and eight of his executives all agreed to wage cuts when Loew's, Inc., suggested a pension plan for all their employees. In 1944 Metro-Goldwyn-Mayer would show a net profit of $14.5 million and a gross profit of $166 million, making it the highest-earning studio in Hollywood.

"For the 1944–45 season," wrote Scott Eyman, "twenty-six of the studio's twenty-nine releases were profitable."[16] In 1944, Metro-Goldwyn-Mayer marked its twentieth anniversary and began a week of festivities around the country and Canada. Between June 22 and June 28, Metro pictures, newsreels, and film shorts were played in all but eight of Loew's, Inc.'s 16,493 movie houses in America and in 1,204 out of 1,285 movie houses in Canada—an unheard-of accomplishment. Metro-Goldwyn-Mayer was truly at its peak.

In the couple of years before its anniversary the studio began building up fresh talent. Gone now from Metro were Greta Garbo, Joan Crawford, Jeannette MacDonald, and Clark Gable—all the great stars of the 1930s either released from contract or serving in the war. In their places were newer, fresher faces like Lana Turner, the grown-up Judy Garland, June Allyson, and Van Johnson. And of those left behind, Hedy was perhaps the most bothersome.

Her salary for 1944 totaled $88,250. And when Hedy met with Mayer in his office at M-G-M, the two did not mince words expressing their frustrations with each other. According to Hedy's book, she and Mayer got off to a rocky start. He was just recovering from a bad cold and a miserable love affair and was not in a mood to humor her. And he had recently acquired a new "toy," a tape recorder, to utilize in his conferences.

Advising Mayer that she now planned to freelance and that she wanted out of her contract, his reaction was typical. Hedy would later write, "'Let me understand this,' Mr. Mayer said. 'Hedy Lamarr, a nothing in Austria, is discovered by an American producer. A lot of money is spent on her public relations. She becomes a famous actress and now . . . she wants to leave. Is that it?'"[17] The two stood there a few moments staring at each other, neither one saying a word. When they did, the final agreement was that Hedy would do her last picture under her original contract and also agree to do three more pictures for Metro within the coming five years, for which she would be paid $100,000 each.

Because of her dislike of Mayer and her continuing battles for more money, Hedy did not intend to renew a long-term Metro contract once *Experiment Perilous* completed production in early October. She had that one last commitment with the studio before the new three-picture agreement would come into effect, and she was determined to get it out of the way.

Hedy still possessed a marquee name in part because of her unique beauty and glamorous persona. According to *The Hollywood Reporter* on November 16, the novelist Niven Busch's lusty epic *Duel in the Sun* had been sold to R-K-O for Hedy to star in as the lusty Pearl Chavez opposite John Wayne. Busch originally wanted his wife, Teresa Wright, known for her portrayals of sweet young things, to play the part. But Wright felt that the role was out of her range, and then she became pregnant.

Busch then offered the role to Hedy, who announced she was also pregnant. ("I had nothing to do with that," chuckled Busch.)[18] Veronica Lake, with her blond hair dyed dark, was next considered, but her acting proved to be shallow. Busch eventually sold *Duel in the Sun* to David O. Selznick. Selznick then starred his paramour and later wife, Jennifer Jones, in the role in 1946, and her performance garnered Jones a Best Actress Oscar nomination.

On December 11, 1944, Hedy, now three months pregnant, reported to Metro for what would be the last picture she would do under her original contract, *Her Highness and the Bellboy.* It had been announced as a property for her back in March 1942. At that time Mayer was pairing Hedy with every major male star on the lot, trying to flush out another winning team. And in Mayer's way of thinking, why not match Metro's reigning glamour goddess with the studio's biggest male box-office star, Andy Hardy himself, Mickey Rooney?

Written by Gladys Lehman and Richard Connell and scheduled to be produced by Joe Pasternak, *Her Highness and the Bellboy* told the story of a New York bellboy (Rooney) and a European princess who teaches him Continental refinement in exchange for his instruction in "Americanisms." A fairy-tale romance. The script was still in development in January 1943, when the twenty-two-year-old Rooney was drafted. It then sat in limbo until it was dusted off for Hedy's last Metro picture. Production began on *Her Highness and the Bellboy* with Robert Walker now cast as the bellboy Jimmy Dobson and with June Allyson, third billed, as Leslie Odell, a girl who could not walk. Part fantasy, part musical comedy, *Her Highness and the Bellboy* was rushed into production because of Hedy's impending motherhood.

On December 18, *Experiment Perilous* opened to strong reviews and respectable houses. *The Hollywood Reporter* raved: "Nothing short of inspired casting brings Hedy Lamarr to play the role of a woman of such haunting beauty that every man who sees her falls in love with her. . . . Miss Lamarr might have been content merely to provide visual charms to her role of the lovely Mrs. Bederaux. Her advancement as an actress, however, matches her beauty and she gives a splendid performance. It is the most mature portrayal of her career."[19] And *Variety* felt the same: "Hedy Lamarr contributes a surprise performance with adroit shadings of terror, romantic interest, eerie characterization, and manages to separate the wife's young maidenhood and the distraught mother's fear about her son with a genuine span of maturity."[20]

When the picture opened in New York, *The New York Times* said of Hedy, "Miss Lamarr, to repeat, is every bit as fascinating as the script makes her out to be."[21] And the reviewer of *The New York Morning Telegraph* was in accord:

"*Experiment Perilous* holds attention from the opening shot and builds dramatically up to the sensational fade-out. Miss Lamarr brings dramatic brilliance to her role."[22]

The ninety-one-minute *Experiment Perilous* is an intriguing film to study today. It is sumptuously produced and expertly acted by its cast (even the often-wooden George Brent), and the top-billed Hedy never looked so vulnerable and lovely.

In Chris Fujiwara's definitive biography of director Jacques Tourneur, he writes: "The internal contradiction of Lamarr's casting perfectly suits the ambiguity of the film. Her strange, paradoxically triumphant performance is visibly a weird structure of compromises, required for the character simultaneously to seem insane' and be 'normal.' Lamarr's acting in this role (surely the most challenging she ever played) is hard to evaluate or even to describe: completely natural, she somehow suggests both fragile inadequacy (the character's and the performer's) and modest assurance."[23]

Experiment Perilous brought in over $2.7 million during its first U.S. run alone, and it was nominated for an Academy Award in 1945 for Best Black-and-White Art Direction (including set design). The picture would prove to be one of the finest films Hedy ever made, and some critics regard it as her best work. As for Hedy, it would always remain her favorite of all her films. But back at Metro, the nonsense of *Her Highness and the Bellboy* continued.

The plot of the picture tells of Princess Veronica (Hedy), who is visiting New York and staying at a plush Central Park hotel in Manhattan. She has come to America because she is in love with a New York reporter, Paul Mac-Millan (Warner Anderson), whom she met when he interviewed her in her country. One of the hotel's bellboys, Jimmy Dobson (Robert Walker), mistakes Veronica for a maid, and she, finding a chance to learn American customs and slang through Jimmy, plays along with the ruse. After Jimmy discovers Veronica is really a princess, she tells the hotel she wants Jimmy to be her personal attaché during her stay.

Through Jimmy, Veronica and Paul meet once more at a ball at the hotel. Paul tells Veronica that because of her royal status his love for her has waned. Jimmy mistakes Veronica's kindness toward him for love. Meanwhile, Leslie Odell (June Allyson), an attractive young invalid, lives with her Aunt Gertrude (Virginia Sale) above Jimmy and his friend Albert ("Rags" Ragland), a porter at the hotel. Aunt Gertrude works at night, and Leslie paints toy Santa Clauses to help support them. Leslie becomes upset at Jimmy's infatuation with a princess because she loves Jimmy and looks forward to his daily visits, when he reads her fairy tales and takes her "dancing at Melody Garden"—a fantasy since she cannot walk.

Veronica tells Jimmy that she had been married once before in her country and that it was when her husband had been shot and killed that she had stood Paul up. Veronica has Jimmy take her to Jake's Joint, where Paul hangs out. While there, they are involved in a brawl, and Veronica is jailed. Bailed out by Paul, she learns that the king, her uncle, has died, and she is now queen. As she prepares to leave for her country, Veronica tells Jimmy he can come with her. Mistaking this as a marriage proposal, Jimmy excitedly runs to Leslie to tell her his good news. Only then does he realize that he is in love with Leslie and not Veronica. When he tells Veronica he can not go with her and chooses not to be a king, she realizes that for her own chance at happiness as well, she will abdicate and hope to win Paul back.

Thin stuff. Hedy was sick of struggling with Mayer, and he with her, so they negotiated a new contract for this film, giving her $7,500 a week and the guarantee she would do the three other agreed-upon pictures. So production was rushed along, and Hedy's several scenes were completed by the end of January. Filming was then picked up on February 7 for a couple of weeks, the picture wrapping by mid-month. Metro's *Weekend at the Waldorf* was also in production at the same time, and the sets for the Waldorf-Astoria Hotel were used in *Her Highness and the Bellboy* after the other picture completed its filming.

Twenty-six-year-old Robert Walker was a very intense and terribly difficult young actor. Under contract with Metro, he had completed earlier in the year his role in David O. Selznick's *Since You Went Away,* which starred Claudette Colbert and Walker's wife, Jennifer Jones. It was by then no longer a Hollywood secret that Jennifer's career was in the hands of her lover, Selznick. When Robert and Jennifer separated, he began an emotional decline and turned to drink, which only accelerated his depression.[24]

A brilliant actor, Walker suffered throughout the filming of *Her Highness and the Bellboy.* His drinking and destructive lifestyle after losing Jennifer went unabated. June Allyson, who liked Walker personally, wrote in her autobiography, "Shooting a scene with Bob was a once-in-a-lifetime experience. No other actor I've worked with could make a scene more true—Bob could make you feel the scene with him as something urgent and surging with life. During the filming of *Her Highness and the Bellboy* he said to me, 'I'm absolutely miserable when I don't measure up to my own standards doing a scene.'"[25] Allyson concluded that "whenever I look back at my career and all my co-stars, I think of Robert Walker and I almost cry." Her memories of Hedy were succinct. "I would just stare, entranced, at her profile," Allyson wrote. "No doubt about it, she was stunning and she knew how to look at a man with an intimate little smile that turned him on."[26]

Mayer was making *Her Highness and the Bellboy* a showcase for June Allyson, and Hedy knew it. It was not a pleasant situation for the reigning queen of glamour on her last days on the Metro lot. Hedy was beginning to show her pregnancy as the film went on, and that, coupled with her vanity in front of the camera (and morning sickness), made it a difficult shoot. "There I am eight months [she was at the most five months] pregnant, being photographed behind potted palms and in full ball gowns, which fortunately fit the story," she told a reporter.[27] (Of the thirteen costumes she wore in the film, Hedy was also required to don a couple of woolen dresses, designed by Marion Herwood Keyes, which only made her scenes that much more uncomfortable.)

In February Hedy and George Brent repeated their roles in *Experiment Perilous* in an hour-long radio version for NBC's *Radio Hall of Fame*. It would be one of Hedy's last radio dramas for several years. After she completed her role in *Her Highness and the Bellboy*, effectively finishing her original Metro contract, she became a free agent, which enabled her to now pick, choose, and even finance her own film productions.

On one of her last days on the M-G-M lot, as she left the soundstage and entered the parking lot, Hedy saw a familiar red-haired actress sitting in her car crying. It was Lucille Ball, who had just been assigned a supporting part in Metro's *Without Love* (1946), starring Katharine Hepburn, as her last assignment for the studio. Metro was letting her go. "I'm never going to become a star," Ball told Hedy through her tears. "They're never going to make me a star. I'm a failure."[28] Hedy comforted her friend. Years later, Ball would reciprocate in kind.

When Hedy herself said farewell to Metro after eight years, her dressing room was handed over to the young girl who had once accompanied Hedy on a train trip—Ava Gardner, whom Mayer was now building up to replace her.

During her pregnancy, Hedy and John commissioned work on a new addition to the house for a nursery. Hedy continued to maintain her mother's Westwood apartment on Hollywood Boulevard, and every year she would send Trude on holiday. Little Jamie was now enrolled in Los Angeles's prestigious Page Military Academy, after having attended the Black Fox Military Kindergarten.

Victory in Europe and the fall of the Third Reich in early May marked the turning point and eventual end of World War II. Hedy had asked her mother to stay with her, John, and Jamie during the final months of her pregnancy, and she found her mother's presence comforting. Hedy spent her time reading books and scripts. On the evening of Monday, May 28, she went into labor.

Hedy, along with her mother and a nurse, and with John following in another car, was taken to the Cedars of Lebanon Hospital, where, at 7:40 A.M. on May 29, she gave birth to a seven-and-a-half-pound baby girl, twenty and one-half inches long, whom she and John named Denise Hedwig Loder.

The birth was difficult. Denise was a breech baby, and the labor was long. Hedy was administered one spinal tap, then another. There was a shortage of nurses at the hospital, which only added to Hedy's concern about proper care. Finally, the baby started to come, and, as Hedy wrote, "I was still in semi-consciousness. In the anesthetic fog I heard a squeak. My God, I thought, I gave birth to a mouse. But the doctor said, 'It's a beautiful baby girl. Another famous actress!' . . . that sweet baby girl that I held in my arms for the first time was never to cause me a whit of trouble."[29] Hedy's chauffeur and trusted friend Marvin Neal, a man who eventually would become a father figure in her children's lives, drove Hedy and Denise home from the hospital.

For Hedy, the birth proved to be emotionally traumatic, causing what is commonly understood today to be postpartum stress disorder. Hedy suffered physical pain, something she was never able to handle well, and apparently it triggered memories of emotional and physical abuse she had long suppressed. She still felt agonizing psychosomatic pains long after her baby's delivery. When long talks with John and the doctors at the hospital failed to alleviate her discomfort, the medical staff suggested she seek counseling.

Just weeks after the baby's birth, Hedy began seeing the first in a series of psychoanalysts. A recommended doctor lived in Boston, and Hedy would frequently fly to the East Coast to work with him, leaving her baby in the care of the nanny. Throughout most of the summer of 1945 Hedy spent time in Cape Cod conferring with her analyst, reliving her youth, and discovering herself.

Hedy, it seemed, felt that she had raised her mother. She had always shown concern about her mother's well-being, and, after she was able to ensure Trude's safe passage from Europe to Hollywood, she supplied Trude with a fine apartment, money, and travel. "My grandparents were really my parents," she wrote. "When they died and were buried my parents couldn't find me. They had the police looking for me. I was leaning against the tombstone of my grandfather. You see, my mother was like my daughter. I loved her but she didn't take care of me. I took care of her."[30]

Hedy also had repressed many serious personal issues that dealt with men and sex. She recalled an incident when she was still a schoolgirl, when a man jumped out from behind some lilac bushes and exposed himself to her. Years later she recalled that she had felt guilty over the fact that her curiosity compelled her to look. At the time, however, the incident had frightened her so much that she ran all the way to school and tried to forget what had happened.

As the summer of 1945 drew on, the doctor was able to relieve many of Hedy's inhibitions, which gave her confidence to speak and share her thoughts. She admitted in her book that she fell in love with her analyst, as some female patients do, but they remained platonically professional and personal friends for years.

Upon her return to California, Hedy became reacquainted with her new baby. She also found time for Jamie. As for her husband, Hedy was not talking to John. Hedy blamed John for her depressions and anxieties and confessed she no longer enjoyed his presence in her life.

In June the newspapers announced that the film producer Seymour Nebenzal, the producer of *M,* which was released in 1931 and starred Peter Lorre, and *Das Testament des Dr. Mabuse* (*The Testament of Dr. Mabuse*), which came out in 1933, and the uncle of Curt and Robert Siodmak, was now planning a remake of the French film *Mayerling,* based on the novel by Claude Anet about the tragic affair between Austria's Archduke Rudolf and his lover, Maria Vetsera. It had been filmed in 1936 by Nero-Film, directed by Anatole Litvak, and starred Charles Boyer and Danielle Darrieux. Nebenzal was contracting the writer Philip Yordan, who wrote *Anna Lucasta,* to do the screenplay and coproduce. Now that Hedy was freelancing, the ambitious Nebenzal was hoping to sign her to star opposite Cornel Wilde. He did not succeed.

This was a difficult period as Hedy searched for just the right property to begin a new creative phase in her career. John and Hedy were now fighting bit-

terly, and he would leave their home several times. They made numerous rec-
onciliations. John even took work on the East Coast to distance himself from
his wife. And Hedy took that as his turning his back on her and the children.

In September *Her Highness and the Bellboy* opened to mixed reviews. *The
Hollywood Reporter* commented, "Hedy Lamarr comes out a real winner. Now
why didn't anyone ever think of having her play gentle comedy before?"[31] *Photoplay* wrote, "Hedy for the first time since *Algiers* seems a woman of reality, of
emotional integrity and inner beauty."[32] *The Los Angeles Examiner* wrote, "As
the heavenly-faced princess, Hedy Lamarr contributes her best performance in
a long time."[33]

Some critics were not so kind. *Time* magazine wrote, "*Her Highness and the
Bellboy* was intended as a swatch of gossamer, but it seems to have been spun in
the innards of a Sherman tank and stitched together with a sledge hammer. . . .
Miss Lamarr, as usual, is one of the loveliest women alive—or even sleepwalk-
ing."[34] And *The New York Times* wrote, "A picture like 'Her Highness and the
Bellboy' just goes to show that even a producer with the enviable batting average of Joe Pasternak is likely to come a cropper once in a while."[35]

The script of *Her Highness and the Bellboy* gave the director Richard Thorpe
little to work with, though the performances of Robert Walker and Hedy
somewhat dragged it out of the mire. "I figured a way to overcome my negative
part [was] by making her human and sympathetic," Hedy told a journalist.[36]
And that she did, adding about the only sensibility of character in the whole
film. In particular, her realization sequence near the end of the picture, when
Veronica abdicates, would prove to be possibly her finest, albeit brief, scene in
any film she ever made for the studio. It is a beautiful and telling study, and one
of Hedy's best-acted moments.

The film is terribly dated today, and Walker and Ragland seem for the most
part weak talking cousins to Damon Runyon characters. Walker calls a newspaper column a "coll-yum," the comic Ragland is continuously obnoxious,
calling Leslie "Les-uh-lie," forget-me-nots "forgot-me-nets," and Santa Claus
"Santy Claus." Overused is a then-popular prank to confuse people: using the
names of cities in a rush of explanation, which after a few dozen repetitious
gags, even when done by Hedy's character, becomes simply annoying.

Worse still is the cloying, sugary sweetness of June Allyson, who was on her
way to becoming a big star for Metro.[37] Allyson delivers an overenthusiastic
and giggly, hiccupping cuteness when she plays make-believe—deadly for

most actresses her age. And her character suffers a bout of "old-movie disease"; no explanation is given for her sympathetic illness and her inability to walk, except that offered by a doctor, played by George Cleveland, who diagnoses that it is Leslie's spirit that is sick and that "when she was a little girl she didn't get enough love." (Awww . . .)

Hedy is top billed in *Her Highness and the Bellboy,* and she was carefully photographed because of her condition. She is either turned in a three-quarter position away from the camera and in long shots; shown in costumes that have long, full sleeves; or holds bouquets of flowers or packages to cover her expanding waistline. Thankfully, she is given many gorgeous close-ups. However, Hedy is most effective when she is allowed to play naturally, and in her scenes with Walker the two are remarkable together.

At the end of 1945, the 112-minute *Her Highness and the Bellboy* ranked among the "ten worst pictures of the year" according to *The New York Times.* Ironically, *Her Highness and the Bellboy* still turned a profit, though only marginally.[38]

The Loders remained friends with George and Boski Antheil, who now lived at 2711 Laurel Canyon Road. While composing his *Fourth Symphony,* Antheil and his wife "had several roundtable discussions . . . at these Hedy made numerous suggestions."[39] Antheil dedicated his overture "Heroes of Today" to Hedy, among others, and it was premiered as a surprise part of a performance under the direction of Leopold Stokowski at the Hollywood Bowl on July 15, 1945.

"I went home to Trenton to compose . . . 'Heroes of Today' and dedicated it to Hedy Lamarr and all the living heroes of all countries," wrote Antheil in his book. "I dedicated it to all the living heroes, but later, when I came back home to Hollywood, I additionally dedicated it to Hedy Lamarr, because I now suddenly remembered that I had promised to dedicate my very next piece to her, and now I had failed to do so. Hedy, however sweet, is not a person to take slights like this without squawking; so, saying a silent prayer to all the living heroes of this war, I slipped her name on the dedication page, hoping our heroes would please not too much mind sharing the dedication."[40]

Hedy had long known the Austro-Hungarian writer-director Edgar Georg Ulmer. He had been a set designer for Max Reinhardt in Vienna in the 1920s, then came to Hollywood with the director F. W. Murnau and worked on the director's stunning 1927 Fox film *Sunrise: A Song of Two Humans.* It won three

Academy Awards in the first year of the academy's existence, one for Cinematography (Charles Rusher and Karl Struss), one for Best Actress (Janet Gaynor), and one for Unique and Artistic Production.

Ulmer's third film in Hollywood was the 1934 art-deco horror classic *The Black Cat*. This picture demonstrated his striking visual style and was the season's biggest moneymaker for Universal. He next worked in various capacities around Hollywood, producing and directing a series of "race" films for independent film companies, including the Yiddish *Green Fields* (Collective Film Producers, 1937) and the all-black *Moon over Harlem* (Meteor Films, 1939).

Ulmer had recently completed *Detour* for Producers Releasing Corporation, and it would be recognized decades later as his one true masterpiece. He followed that by directing John Loder in *The Wife of Monte Cristo* for the same company. Hedy now wanted Ulmer for her first independent picture.

Hedy joined forces with Jack Chertok, *The Conspirators*' producer, and formed a production company in late summer of 1945—Mars Productions, Inc. They then selected Ben Ames Williams's sensational novel *The Strange Woman*, a story of an unrepentant adventuress named Jenny Hager that is set in nineteenth-century Bangor, Maine. When it was published, *The Strange Woman* was read by an estimated 500,000 readers and was considered a "hot" item in Hollywood. Two other properties were also purchased, *There's Always Love* and *The Immortal Smile*.[41]

Errol Flynn was planning to produce a film version in Europe of the William Tell fable and had just returned from Spain and was sharing an apartment in Hollywood with his pal, the British actor David Niven, when he finally met Hedy. "I think Hedy to be one of the most underestimated actresses, one who has not been lucky enough to get the most desirable roles," Flynn said in his 1959 posthumously published autobiography. "I have seen her do a few brilliant things. I always thought she had great talent, and as far as classical beauty is concerned, you could not then, nor perhaps even now, find anyone to top Lamarr. Probably one of the most beautiful women of our day. Naturally I wanted to meet her—and subsequently I would want her to play the female lead in my Italian fiasco *William Tell*."[42]

Invited to a dinner party at the home of the Loders, Niven and Flynn arrived in the company of Reggie Gardiner and his new Russian wife, among others. When Niven saw Hedy, he commented, "By God, she's beautiful, even without the jewels." Which of course only piqued Flynn's curiosity. What was the story? Niven explained the infamous evening in Vienna when Prince von Starhemberg came to call and Hedy had Fritz Mandl bring her all her jewels to wear at once. "Her jeweled entrance caused a sensation. . . . From her fingers to her shoulders in ice, red ice, blue ice, white ice, emeralds, rubies, diamonds. She must have weighed half as much as the late Aga Khan. As the dinner went on, Hedy developed a sick headache and excused herself, just for a moment, to go to the bathroom. But she never came back for coffee."[43]

As the evening with the Loders went on, Niven coerced Flynn to ask Hedy about the night she left Fritz and made her getaway. As Flynn recalled in his memoirs, "Hedy and I talked for awhile. I started leading up to it in a diplomatic way, and finally got out the words, 'Where is Mandl now?' At which, from this beautiful creature, came the growl, 'That son of a bitch!' She spat and walked off."[44]

Louella Parsons asked Hedy about her new role in Hollywood during this time. "It's so wonderful to have them [her producers] listen to my ideas," she told Parsons. "In the past, I just made pictures without really knowing anything about the story or the character I was to play until we were actually before the cameras."[45]

Continuing on, Parsons asked if she missed Metro, and Hedy replied, "Not at all. I miss my friends on the lot. . . . I was there for so many years and I have pleasant memories. If I could have my present setup and M.G.M., too, it would be perfect, but I don't like the idea of being told that I am to go into a picture four days before it starts and never given a chance to express an opinion of whether I like it or whether I don't like it."[46]

Getting around to *The Strange Woman,* Hedy said, "We are not going to make the picture . . . until we have a perfect script. . . . I have never been so excited over any picture, because, you see, I have a chance to do something other than merely be a clotheshorse or look pretty. I have always wanted to do character parts, and this gives me the chance I have been waiting for so long. At least . . . Jack Chertok thinks I have some intelligence, and it is up to me now to prove it to him."[47]

In Hollywood Hedy was being treated by the Beverly Hills psychiatrist Dr. Philip Solomon. In 2000 Solomon said that he "remembered Lamarr as vulnerable, troubled by the public focus on her beauty and suffering from emotional difficulties."[48] In later years Dr. Solomon would often fly to Acapulco and Houston to continue treating Hedy.

For *The Strange Woman,* Chertok and Hedy chose as executive producer

Hunt Stromberg, who for eighteen years had been with M-G-M and was responsible for some of the studio's most successful films. If there were troubles behind the scenes of such pictures as *Red Dust* (1932) with Clark Gable and Jean Harlow or *The Women* (1939) with Norma Shearer and Joan Crawford, Stromberg was right there to smooth them over. Unfortunately, Mayer let the producer go in 1942, three years before his contract ended, because Stromberg had developed a morphine addiction caused by treatment for a slipped disk. But Hedy still admired the producer's work.

On September 19 it was announced that, after *The Strange Woman*, Stromberg would star Hedy in United Artists' *Dishonored Lady,* based on a psychological play by Edward Sheldon and Margaret Ayer Barnes. Representing his own company—Foote, Cone, and Belding—Stromberg set about attempting to find additional properties for Hedy, including, by her request, a stage production.

Meanwhile, Jack Chertok was also set to coproduce *The Strange Woman*. At the same time, Hedy was somehow committed to the independent producer Arnold Pressburger for *Last Year's Snow.* Pressburger had produced *Mein braucht kein Geld* back in 1932 and was most anxious to begin his new project with Hedy as its star.

Stromberg had signed a producer's agreement with United Artists. His first picture under that deal was *Lady of Burlesque* (1943) with Barbara Stanwyck, and it made $650,000. His next film, *Guest in the House,* was made for just $50,000, and it too turned a hefty profit. After he did the same thing with the musical *Delightfully Dangerous* (1945) with Jane Powell, Stromberg agreed to finance *The Strange Woman* for release through UA. For the job of turning Williams's massive seven-hundred-page bestseller into a screenplay, Hedy chose Herb Meadow. For her leading men, she selected George Sanders and Louis Hayward. Filming of *The Strange Woman* began with great enthusiasm on December 10, 1945.

The plot of the steamy potboiler begins in 1824 Bangor, Maine, then a rough lumber town. When Jenny Hager (Hedy) reaches womanhood, her abusive alcoholic father (Tom Hoey) beats her, and she runs to the much-older shopkeeper Isaiah Poster (Gene Lockhart) for protection. His wife had run off with another man years before. He longs for Jenny, and eventually they marry. Jenny devotes herself to charitable causes and feigns kindness to become the center of the town's attention. She encourages Poster's son Ephraim (Louis Hayward) to return to college, at the same time teasing and taunting him into loving her. He too falls in love with Jenny, and instead of returning to school stays in Bangor.

Jenny then becomes infatuated with the boss of her husband's logging camp, John Evered (George Sanders), who is also the fiancé of her best friend Meg Saladine (Hillary Brooke). Scheming to rid herself of her husband and have Evered, Jenny promises to wed Ephraim if he will kill his father. Isaiah dies in a river accident, and the wealthy widow Jenny then scorns Ephraim. She eventually marries Evered, and Ephraim becomes a drunkard and hangs himself.

During a quarrel Jenny tells Evered all she has done to get him. Disgusted, Evered leaves Jenny, and Meg goes to the Indian Hill lumber camp to be with him. Jenny learns of the tryst and drives her horse-drawn rig to the camp. Seeing Evered and Meg together, Jenny becomes enraged with fury and attempts to run them down with her team of horses. The rig, however, hits a rock in the road, and Jenny, thrown from the buggy, dies.

Torrid romance and solid melodrama. Hedy's hopes for the future were riding on *The Strange Woman*. The picture, shot at the Samuel Goldwyn Studio, was given sumptuous and detailed sets designed by Nicolai Remisoff, and a whole logging community was constructed for the film. Hedy's gowns and costumes were created by Natalie Visart, and more than one critic wondered why the project was not shot in color.

Before the first week of production was completed, however, Hedy was felled by a severe case of influenza. On December 14 she was sent home by the studio's physician and confined to bed. Production was shut down on *The Strange Woman* until January 3, 1946. When it resumed, filming proceeded without much difficulty, and the picture was completed in mid-March.

Its outcome, and particularly Hedy's performance, would stun critics and audiences alike.

14

Producer

Throughout the filming of *The Strange Woman*, Hedy was deeply involved in every aspect of the story line and production. Her two producers advised her that she could either produce a sensible film that would look good for the town and lose money or make a money-making picture. Originally in accord with her director, Edgar Ulmer, Hedy soon felt that he was simply not getting it. She wrote, "Edgar was a bit afraid of me. . . . I would walk through a scene, step by step, and know there was something wrong with it. Yet the director was timid about suggesting changes. Once after playing a seduction scene through, I said to Edgar, 'I feel like it's a seduction by Hedy Lamarr instead of by Jenny Hager.'"[1]

Ulmer explained Jenny's motivations to Hedy and made a suggestion. "Your approach, Hedy, is too delicate and subtle," she related in her book. "'Jenny wouldn't be subtle. She goes after what she wants directly and quickly. Let's try it. Don't be Hedy Lamarr—be a tigress.' So with delicacy or dignity I crashed my way into the victim's shower, said a few words with directness, and ended the scene by slipping out of my robe. Edgar groaned. 'Like this,' he suggested. But he was too nice about it. I wasn't sure he was right. . . . I wasn't sure I was right. We did the bedroom scene over and over so often, I could do it now, twenty years later."[2]

Being her own producer brought challenges, Hedy found out. "It was odd making [*The*] *Strange Woman* with none of the luxuries of working for a studio," she wrote. "I was in business for myself now and had to hold down the pampering. When my mother called collect from the East Coast [during her annual holiday], I told her to drop some coins into the slots instead and I'd give the money back to her. I did not under any circumstances want to go over budget. Not that we stinted on production—but there was no waste."[3] Actually, the film ran over budget by $1 million.

While Hedy was still on bed rest with the flu, a near tragedy involving her seven-year-old son Jamie occurred. Frances Milner, who was the Loders' nanny, and the boy were involved in a car crash in Beverly Hills on Sunday, January 6. Jamie suffered minor cuts and bruises and a minor facial scar that would remain with him into adulthood. Taken to the Cedars of Lebanon Hospital for treatment, he was kept for a couple of weeks. Distraught, Hedy told the press, "I love little Jamesie so dearly."[4] She blamed John for allowing Jamie out of the house that day to accompany Frances.

On January 18, back on the set of *The Strange Woman,* Hedy told the press that she and her husband were separating. The couple had argued the day Jamie was injured, and Loder stormed out of the house. "I was very upset when my little son was hurt," Hedy said. "And I had hoped it was just a misunderstanding."[5] She had not talked with Loder since, though she did say he was stopping by the house while she was at the studio to see their baby daughter, Denise. Loder's only response to the press was, "No comment. You'll have to ask Hedy."[6]

Hedy's dressing room at the Samuel Goldwyn Studio was robbed during the filming of *The Strange Woman.* Advising the sheriff's deputies in Hollywood on February 11, Hedy said that she had lost a bowknot pin with a center band of five rubies. She told the police it was left in her dressing room off the set and that numerous people had access to the room. Like the flu symptoms she would experience throughout the remainder of the year, this mysterious robbery was only the beginning of a series of similar misfortunes that would revisit Hedy throughout her lifetime.

Hedy and John reconciled on March 18, and plans for divorce were set aside temporarily. But the quarrels continued, and the couple continued to periodically separate.

As Denise's christening approached, Hedy asked Bette Davis to be her baby's godmother. For Denise's godfather the Loders chose John's longtime family friend, the Honorable Max Aitken, the eldest son of Lord Beaverbrook. On April 6, at the All Saints Episcopal Church in Beverly Hills, ten-month-old Denise Hedwig Loder was christened, with John standing in as proxy for

Aitken, who was in England. Hedy wore a dark, high-collared outfit, accentuated by a double strand of pearls, a white-veiled hat, and white gloves. Bette Davis wore a large flouncy hat and a fur coat over her dress.

On the set of *The Strange Woman* Hedy's leading man was the forty-year-old British actor George Sanders, who was usually cast as a heavy. Sanders made a pleasant transition to leading man in a series of *The Saint* movies for R-K-O-Radio. He was then married to the beautiful Hungarian actress Zsa Zsa Gabor. During the filming of *The Strange Woman* Hedy and Sanders allegedly had an affair, and it was supposedly known to Gabor. "They had two dinner dates," Zsa Zsa told a reporter at the time. "That's all there was to it. In fact, he left Hedy in Hollywood to come to me in New York, without even saying good-bye to her."[7] Neither Hedy nor John ever acknowledged that an affair with Sanders took place. "Mercifully, things calmed down considerably for a time when our daughter Denise was born," John wrote in his book. "Hedy gave her full attention to her baby, proving herself a devoted mother."[8]

Hedy appeared on April 7 on NBC radio's *The Charlie McCarthy Show* (formerly *The Edgar Bergen/Charlie McCarthy Show*). On the evening of April 17, she and John attended a screening of a picture, leaving baby Denise in the care of her nanny, Frances. When they arrived home to 2707 North Benedict Drive at about 2:00 A.M., John noticed as he started to unlock the front door that it was already open. Rushing to the nursery to check on the baby, they found her safe and sound asleep. Waking up the nanny, John and Hedy were told that she had heard someone knocking on the front door around midnight, but she thought it was the Loders returning home. Upon further investigation, they discovered that they had been robbed.

According to the press, the burglar or burglars entered through the front door using a passkey and took furs and jewelry estimated at $19,000, including a $5,000 three-quarter-length chinchilla cape, an ermine wrap, a $12,000 nine-carat solitaire diamond engagement ring, three other rings valued at $2,000, five pairs of nylons, six bracelets, and, of all things, John's bottle of bourbon from Hedy's boudoir.

John told the police that, unfortunately, the items were uninsured. The following day photographers took pictures of John, kneeling down, looking about the ransacked room. Hedy offered a reward of 10 percent of the value of any items that might be found and returned to her. Then the worth of the stolen furs and jewelry was revalued by the Loders at $95,000 (the estimated value of chinchilla alone was in excess of $75,000, and the jewelry and the other items were upped to an approximate worth of $20,000). Hedy, shaken, was taken downtown by John to the Los Angeles City Hall and issued a gun permit. She said she feared for her baby's safety.

On May 18, the Los Angeles robbery-detail police recovered Hedy's chinchilla cape, ermine coat, and nine-carat diamond ring, along with other items stolen from neighboring Beverly Hills residents. Arrested in connection with the robberies were the nineteen-year-old radio technician William J. Stephany and thirty-five-year-old William Walden.

The following day, John and Hedy were called to city hall to confront the two men. Young Stephany stared Hedy down, and the older Walden shuffled uneasily. Suddenly Hedy burst into tears and fled the room, saying later, "I was so afraid something might have happened to the children." Later she told the press, "I feel sorry for the kid even if he did do the burglary."[9]

In June, the two men pleaded guilty to charges before Superior Court Judge William R. McKay. On July 2, they escaped extended prison terms when it was reported that the value of the items stolen was considerably less than had been originally claimed. Stephany was sentenced to ten years of probation with two years in jail if he violated probation, and the older Walden was given five years of probation with one year in jail if he violated the sentence. When Judge McKay was informed that the actual value of the items stolen totaled only $7,330, he commented, "Looks like the first report of a $90,000 burglary could have been upped for publicity purposes."[10]

With *The Strange Woman* finished, Hedy now prepared for her role in her second independent production, *Dishonored Lady,* for Mars Company. For her leading men she considered Herbert Marshall and George Brent but finally selected Dennis O'Keefe and William Lundigan; both signed on April 24. At Hedy's insistence, her husband John Loder was contracted for the film as well on April 30. *Dishonored Lady* was set to roll.

That year Alfred Hitchcock was gearing up to direct his long-awaited film version of *The Paradine Case* and wanted Hedy to star as Mrs. Paradine opposite Claude Rains. As far back as 1940 Hedy had been mentioned for the film, then to star opposite Leslie Howard. But by 1946 Hedy was her own producer and declined the role, which went to Alida Valli.[11]

The history of *Dishonored Lady,* from stage to screen, might be more interesting than the final film result. Staged by Guthrie McClintic on Broadway,

Dishonored Lady opened at the Empire Theatre on February 4, 1930, and it starred McClintic's wife, the talented Katharine Cornell. Written by Margaret Ayer Barnes and Edward Sheldon, the play ran 127 performances, closing in May of that year. The plot dealt with the murder of the lover of a woman who then refuses to take the stand at her own trial. The story had been inspired by an actual 1857 murder case involving a young Glasgow-born woman named Madeleine Smith who was accused of poisoning her lover but was later acquitted.

Metro-Goldwyn-Mayer obtained *Dishonored Lady* as the basis for their 1932 film *Letty Lynton,* which was produced by Hunt Stromberg and starred Joan Crawford. But complications arose with the Hays Office regarding the play's adaptation for the screen, and thus the source material for the movie was listed as coming from Marie Belloc Lowndes's 1931 novel *Letty Lynton,* which too had been inspired by the Smith case.[12] Upon the Metro picture's release, litigation arose between the studio and the play's two authors over ownership of the story.

An independent film version of *Dishonored Lady* was discussed in mid-1942, and both Bette Davis and Greta Garbo were announced in *The Holly-wood Reporter* in July of that year as being interested in playing the lead. Stromberg then acquired the property in 1944, announcing that André de Toth was set to direct and develop a screenplay. In March 1944 Hedy purchased a story called "Madeleine" by Paul Schiller, but it is not clear if any part of that was used in *Dishonored Lady*. (*Dishonored Lady* was later retitled *The Sins of Madeleine* in reissue.)

Problems with the Hays Office continued to plague the project. The moral character of Madeleine was controversial and even a rewrite by Ben Hecht failed to gain support. "This Ben Hecht script is thoroughly and completely unacceptable," wrote Joseph I. Breen in a memo dated February 23, 1946.[13]

When Edward H. North wrote *his* screenplay based on the Barnes and Sheldon play, he steered clear of the nymphomaniac issues that had kept the project from passing the censors. Such scenes as the one night of passion between Madeleine and one of her lovers, Felix Courtland, were not made graphic in the script. After the trial, Madeleine simply goes away and hopes her new love, David Cousins, will find her.

What resulted was a convoluted plot that insinuated that Madeleine was more psychopathic than nymphomaniacal. As directed by the British-born, Cambridge-educated Robert Stevenson, *Dishonored Lady* would have strong actors and fine production values.[14] But because its subject matter clashed with the censors, it would also have little substance.

The film's story tells of a successful New York magazine art editor, Madeleine Damien (Hedy), who is seeking meaning in her life. Depressed, she attempts suicide by crashing her car into a tree but is rescued by the psychiatrist Dr. Caleb (Morris Carnovsky), who suggests she quit her job and find a new life. (Ah, were it that simple.) Changing her identity to Madeleine Dixon, she moves downtown to Greenwich Village and starts life anew as a painter. She meets a penniless scientist named David Cousins (Dennis O'Keefe), whom she helps with his experiments. They become engaged. When Cousins is called out of town, Madeleine meets up at a nightclub with a former beau, the wealthy jeweler Felix Courtland (John Loder), and he takes her to his home. When his doorbell rings and Courtland excuses himself to answer it, Madeleine slips out the back door, not wanting to renew her relationship with him.

At the door is Jack Garet (William Lundigan), an associate of Courtland's who has stolen some jewels from his boss. He has come to plead with Courtland not to notify the police, and in an ensuing argument he murders Courtland by clubbing him over the head. Madeleine is known to have been the last person to have seen Courtland alive, and she is arrested. Because David is shocked about Madeleine's past, he will not see her, and thus she makes no attempt to defend herself. Through Dr. Caleb's intervention, David then stands by Madeleine, and she in turn fights for her life. Because of her testimony, the evidence is reexamined. When David sees Garet attempting to open Courtland's safe, Garet confesses, and Madeleine and David can now marry.

Hedy's leading man was the attractively affable thirty-six-year-old actor Dennis O'Keefe. O'Keefe had been around in movies using his real name, Bud Flanagan, since 1930. In 1937 he changed his moniker to Dennis O'Keefe, and his career took off. Tall and good-looking, O'Keefe's most memorable pictures up to this point were Jacques Tourneur's *The Leopard Man,* for R-K-O Radio (1943), and Cecil B. DeMille's *The Story of Dr. Wassell* (1944), for Paramount. With his fine appearance, masculine grace, and quiet demeanor, O'Keefe was visually an ideal match for Hedy on the screen.

On May 20 production began on *Dishonored Lady* on the soundstages of the Goldwyn Studio. Within weeks, just as had happened on the set of *The Strange Woman,* Hedy was struck down with intestinal flu, but soon she was back on the set completing her scenes.

On their third wedding anniversary, Hedy and John were working on the sequence where Madeleine tells Courtland they are through. "What a way to spend an anniversary," Loder told a journalist.[15] During the filming of *Dishonored Lady,* John and Hedy continued having problems and arguing in private. Regarding working with his wife, Loder wrote, "It was a really frightening experience while I was rehearsing my scenes with her. She would whisper in my ear, 'You're just awful. Come on now, you can do better than that,' just before a take, which hardly improved my performance."[16]

Filming of *Dishonored Lady* was tense for everyone involved. Stromberg sent constant memos to Hedy, and John showed cold indifference to her on and off the set. Mercifully, the picture wrapped production in the middle of July (it ran $1.2 million over budget), and Hedy had the unedited cut of the picture run for her at the studio.

"When *Dishonored Lady* was over and the lights went up I had seen one hundred and twenty-two minutes [it would be cut to eighty-five] of what I thought was an entertaining film," Hedy wrote. "I went to my severest critic, John Loder, who was in with his agent to collect the check. John always had an opinion. 'Well,' he said, 'you aren't my favorite actress but I see nothing wrong with the picture. Chances are it will make money and you'll make ten more. Of course I don't know if the film will give you any artistic satisfaction, but then a girl can't have everything, can she?' Then he grimaced. 'But what am I talking about? That's what you want, isn't it—everything.'"[17]

As *Last Year's Snow* approached its filming date, on July 20 Hedy sued Estate Management Corp., Ltd., which had been acting as her business manager, to recover stocks, war savings bonds, and other business documents she said were being withheld from her after her contract with them had expired. Filing in Superior Court, Hedy also named as codefendant her former business partner George A. Lovett. Her attorney, A. Ronald Button, represented her in the case.

Claiming $500 in damages, Hedy was requesting the handing over of property valued at $5,000, including additional promissory notes in the amounts of $1,900, $6,615, and $1,200; copies of state and federal income returns for 1944 and 1945; bank statements and deposit slips; a personal loose-leaf book of accounts; property-interest deeds; and conveyances of several rights for films. Most important, she was requesting "an executed agreement between Lovett and herself pertaining to picture, play and story rights for 'Last Year's Snow.'"[18]

The last issue in particular was important. On July 31, Hedy dropped the suit against George A. Lovett when her items were retrieved.

When *Dishonored Lady* ended, so did the Loder marriage. John would later write in his book: "After the film was finished our life together was becoming increasingly difficult. We were driving home one afternoon and she started nagging me. I would not rise to the scene she wanted so she grabbed my pipe from my mouth and hurled it through the car window. It was a nice pipe so I stopped the car and got out to retrieve it. Immediately Hedy moved over to the driver's seat and drove off. It took me over an hour to walk home."[19]

Then came an announcement on July 21. Hedy was pregnant, and the baby was due "sometime next spring."[20] She wrote in her book that since Jamie was away attending boarding school, she was determined to give Denise a baby brother or sister, as she didn't want her daughter to experience the loneliness she had felt as an only child. Yet at the same time Hedy wanted her freedom from Loder. She wrote the following account of what she did when she found out she was pregnant again:

> [I] marched into the den where John was reading and puffing on his pipe. I gained courage from the realization that nothing I did could surprise John any more. "John, I'd like to talk to you."
>
> "Certainly," he answered and put his book down.
>
> I blurted it out, "I am pregnant. And I want a divorce."
>
> John blinked. "Well, you hit the jackpot, didn't you? A regular Louella Parsons—two exclusives in one night."[21]

Calmly agreeing to grant her a divorce, Loder then told Hedy that she had never learned how to share, that she could have the children, and they would be *her* children, not "*our* children." He would not fight her.[22]

Now, instead of telling the press they were divorcing, the Loders announced that they were expecting and that the baby would be delivered on March 1 by caesarean. The divorce would wait. To compound John's woes, he had just lost an important part in another picture. So he decided to pack up and head out East to work.

Before his departure, though, Hedy allowed the journalist Kay Proctor to interview and photograph the family at their Benedict Canyon home. Proctor reported that when she arrived, the house was in chaos:

Downstairs a battery of three rug washers continued their ungodly racket. . . . In the next room an electrician pounded and sawed as he worked on the new house communication system. Across the hall a substitute nurse strove vainly to quiet 15-months old Denise 'Dee Dee' Loder. . . . Intermittently the bedside telephone jangled, 7-year old son Jamesie appeared in noisy complaint over the disappearance of a toy, and husband John popped in and out with progressive reports of an unsuccessful quest for meat for dinner that night. In addition, Hedy was uncomfortably *enceinte*; the new Lamarr-Loder baby is due in a few months. . . . [Hedy said], 'Poof! This is nothing! . . . After the nightmare of this last year I am immune to anything less than a bomb going off under my bed!"[23]

Despite all the recent renovations at Hedgerow, Hedy impulsively purchased a two-storey Spanish-style mansion for $75,000, located at 919 North Roxbury Drive. She then put Hedgerow up for sale on June 24, giving the Lawrence Block Company a ninety-day option to sell it. Hedy eventually sold Hedgerow to the newlyweds Humphrey Bogart and Lauren Bacall for $97,500. "It just suits us," Bacall told a news writer. "Hedy's house is such a warm, comfortable house. . . . I'm going to keep Hedy's carpeting."[24] (Two months after Hedy and John announced their final separation, Hedy was sued in Superior Court by Lawrence Block Company for a five percent commission on the recent sale of the house.)

When she moved into her new Beverly Hills home with her children, Hedy turned to her friends George and Boski Antheil and made them an offer. "Hedy . . . discovered that the so-called 'play' house in back of her swimming pool was fully equipped and furnished. She wanted us to move in free of charge. It was a pretty big house," Antheil wrote in his book.

"Why should you pay rent when you can live right here, next to me, for nothing? I wouldn't know what to do with that house anyway. Come on—move in."

"Do you go swimming every day?" asked Boski.

"Certainly," said Hedy, "but nobody else comes, excepting Ann Sothern."

Boski went into the house, saw that every window looked out on the swimming pool.

"No, thanks," she said.[25]

Now in second grade, Jamie was sent to a new school, Chadwick Military School, near Rolling Hills, and immediately problems began. By then Hedy was going through the preliminaries of divorce, headed her own film company, had just starred in two demanding film roles, and was pregnant yet again. The additional problems with Jamie were becoming stressful for her. His weekends home from boarding school were proving more and more uncomfortable for them both. Her energies exhausted, Hedy once again caught a severe case of the flu, her third that year, and had to be confined to bed by her physician.

Meanwhile, John, now on the East Coast, and Hedy did not officially announce their pending divorce to the press (they would wait until the following May), though speculation around Hollywood was rampant. More imminent, however, was the forthcoming release of *The Strange Woman*.

Hunt Stromberg had high hopes for the picture. For its advertising, a first of sorts was used. In the film's press book, a seductive close-up of Hedy's face was prominently displayed, the copy reading, "HEDY LAMARR is 'Jenny Hager,'" above the title and production notes for the film. It would become a fad reignited some sixteen years later upon the 1963 release of the Paramount film *Hud*, the taglines reading, "Paul Newman is HUD." For the masses, newspaper ads rang out with tauntingly sexy graphics and such lurid lines as "There are TWO Jenny Hagers . . . Innocent . . . Evil!", "Hotter than Tondelayo!", and "A woman whose beauty was as strong as sin—and twice as deadly!"

When the 101-minute *The Strange Woman* opened in previews on October 25, 1946, *Variety* cheered, "Miss Lamarr scores as the scheming Jenny Hager. . . . Her capacity of appearing as a tender, administering angel and of a mirroring sadistic violence bespeaks wide talent range."[26]

Philip K. Scheuer wrote in the *Los Angeles Times*, "Lightning plays around the pretty head of Jenny Hager throughout 'The Strange Woman' and at the end an abyss of fire and brimstone opens to receive her—figuratively at any rate. . . . As Jenny, Hedy Lamarr slips effortlessly back into the graceful recumbent position of the heroine in 'Ecstasy'—proving that lightning can strike twice in the same place."[27]

Jack D. Grant of *The Hollywood Reporter* spoke for most of the critics with the following comment:

Miss Lamarr, long celebrated for the exceptional beauty she presents to the camera, seemed determined to settle the question of her acting

abilities once and for all. There are those who have doubted that she is
an actress, others who don't care if she is or not, just so long as her image
appears in the movies for everyone to admire. Now Hedy establishes her
status in positive terms . . . she gives a performance that can rank with
the best of them. Don't be surprised to see her win an Academy nomination for her work here. . . . The star is the bewitching beauty she has
always been, but now she is an acting beauty.[28]

In *The Strange Woman* Hedy chews up the scenery—she goes all out and rel-
ishes every moment of it. What is amazing about her performance is that, no
matter what the viewer may think of Hedy or of her character, one simply cannot
take one's eyes off of her for a second. Hedy was proud of her work in *The Strange
Woman,* and the picture made $2.8 million upon its release in the United States.

In casting George Sanders, the producers were wise not to let the leading
man overshadow the star. Sanders would deservedly win an Oscar in 1951 for
his villainous work in Twentieth Century–Fox's *All About Eve.* As for Louis
Hayward, his performance was tragically perhaps a bit too close to home. After
his real-life experiences in the Pacific during World War II, Hayward suffered
extreme depressions and emotional problems. It is difficult knowing this and
watching his tormented performance.

Hedy, with John not in Hollywood, suffering the flu a third time that year,
and her delivery approaching, was emotionally and physically exhausted. By
the end of 1946 she appealed in Superior Court for relief from further film
work until the birth of her baby in March. In a suit against Arnold Pressburger
and director-producer Douglas Sirk and their concern, Marlborough Productions, Hedy requested release from her agreement for their upcoming film *Last
Year's Snow,* which she had signed on May 23.

On January 10, 1947, Hedy was thwarted in her attempt to renege on the
deal. Her attorney, Button, supplied the court with an affidavit signed by
Hedy's new physician, Dr. John Vruwink, stating that Hedy would be "prone to
worry and become highly nervous and emotionally upset" if her business affairs were not settled before the baby's birth. But that did not sway the court.[29]
Hedy and Pressburger eventually settled their litigation, freeing her from her
obligation to appear in *Last Year's Snow.* In lieu of appearing in the film, "Miss
Lamarr has paid him 'a substantial sum' in settlement, according to the producer," reported *The New York Times.*[30]

On February 28, Hedy was admitted to Los Angeles's Good Samaritan Hospital, where Dr. D. S. Mitchelson and Dr. John Vruwink planned to deliver her baby by caesarean on Saturday, March 1. Delayed by one day, on Sunday, March 2, they delivered a seven-pound, fifteen-ounce baby boy, whom Hedy named Anthony John Loder. Her room was filled with flowers, and she had her mother and friends stop by and see her and the new baby. John Loder was not around. He was still back East.

Later that month Edwin Schallert in the *Los Angeles Times* announced that Hedy was being sought by the producers Eugene Frenke and Philip Yordan for *Evangeline,* to be produced by United California Productions, another remake of the famous Longfellow poetic narrative, written by Anna Lee Stebbins. *Evangeline* never saw a new dawn.

Hedy was now sick with bronchial pneumonia, according to her new physician, Dr. Hans Schiff. She had been suffering during the last week in March, and her larynx was still infected. On April 4, she was taken to Cedars of Lebanon Hospital and given a blood transfusion, and by the next day was reported to be feeling much better. But she relapsed on April 14, entered the hospital for a second time, and was given yet another blood transfusion.

John Loder, meanwhile, was touring in the play *Laura,* based on the novel by Vera Caspary and on Jay Dratler's screenplay. John gave a telling and fanciful interview to Earl Wilson, a columnist for the *New York Post*, in April: "It's pretty tough being Mr. Hedy Lamarr," he complained to Wilson. "Since I've been Mr. Hedy Lamarr I've been sunk professionally. I'm married to the most beautiful girl in the world. She's the most perfect wife in the world. But I'm also married to a legend. . . . When I got married . . . I was playing opposite Bette Davis in a picture called 'Old Acquaintance.' I was doing well. But, because I married the most beautiful girl in the world—who doesn't even know how beautiful she is—film companies quit thinking of me as an actor. They say 'Loder? Oh, yes. The guy that married Lamarr!'"[31]

While John was bemoaning his fate, on May 16 *Dishonored Lady* opened to tepid reviews. Jack D. Grant of *The Hollywood Reporter* liked the film and Hedy's performance in particular: "It is immediately apparent that the role of Madeleine is a challenge, and Miss Lamarr is completely capable of meeting it. In stunning photography by Lucien Androit and beautiful gowns by Elois Jenssen, she makes the star part a fascinating study in dramatic overtones."[32]

Silver Screen wrote halfheartedly, "Miss Lamarr has bitten off quite a hunk of role here . . . but while she's no Cornell when it comes to acting, at least Hedy's a much better actress than she originally was."[33]

Dishonored Lady is *truly* a bad film. And its badness makes it entertaining. When Madeleine, who is suffering depression (she is a nymphomaniac plain and simple!), crashes her car into a tree and is thrown by the impact (a mortal would have been killed), it just so happens to take place at the home of a renowned psychiatrist. When the knowledgeable doctor informs the policeman who arrives on the scene, "I doubt it's serious," viewers can guess they are in for an enjoyable and sometimes ridiculous eighty-five minutes.

The script gets worse from there. After Madeleine is refreshed and rests a bit, her car, totaled, smoking, and wrapped around that tree just outside the good doctor's study window, is quickly forgotten about. It is definitely to the credit of the film's stars, Hedy, O'Keefe, and Lundigan, that *Dishonored Lady* holds up at all. Everything else about its production is bad, including the fifteen or so different outfits designed by Elois Jenssen, the fashions just pre-"new look" of the late 1940s.

But, lo and behold, there is in *Dishonored Lady* another one of the *best* scenes Hedy ever acted on film. When Madeleine becomes tipsy at the nightclub, the sequence is poised and stunning. Underplayed and handled carefully, Hedy's sense of humor is perfect. But later when Courtland asks Dr. Caleb where he can find Madeleine, Caleb replies, "She's busy growing a new soul." And we're back to the banal. When Courtland begins his romantic moves on Madeleine, his leading lines are, "You know you need relaxing—lots of relaxing. I can hear your nerves snapping like rubber bands." Edward Margulis reviewed *Dishonored Lady* for a film magazine in the 1990s and commented, "Could Lamarr be suicidal *because* men are forever hitting up on her with terrible pickup lines?"[34]

Dishonored Lady is a fun bad movie to watch today. Moviegoers and critics took it all very seriously, however, and *Dishonoured Lady* turned a marginal profit. High dramatics, no matter how realistically presented on-screen, were a great escape for audiences of the day. And *Dishonoured Lady* fit the bill.

After the birth of their son, the Loders announced their separation. In her *Los Angeles Times* column Hedda Hopper reported the break on May 31. Loder later stated in his book, "I always rushed home whenever possible when I was on tour and really thought, after our son Tony was born, that our marriage was going well." He reasoned, "As she adored her children I was convinced Hedy would settle down to a happy married life. We had an excellent nanny so she was able to carry on with her career as well as enjoy her family."[35]

However, John wasted little time in obtaining his own attorney to fight Hedy. Upon his return to Hollywood, John lamented that Hedy had him sign several papers that he claimed he did not read because he was just happy to be back with his family. Then Hedy told him he made her nervous, and he left the house. He advised the press he was determined to fight the divorce.

During their marriage, John told the press, when they were living at Hedge-row, the monthly bills amounted to about $800 a month, and John had contributed, so he said, $45,000 toward the upkeep of the home. Now that they lived in the new house in Beverly Hills, John complained to the press, "The monthly upkeep is $2,000, and I don't make that kind of money. Yet when I thought it would make her happy I signed a promissory note to pay off the $20,000 I was in arrears in meeting expenses. Then she came up with a demand that I pay my board at home when I wasn't working, even if I couldn't handle all the upkeep. I agreed to this, too. But I'm afraid I've just been playing the role of Chamberlain with the umbrella. As soon as I agree to one demand, there is another facing me."[36]

By July John was about to join the ranks of Fritz and Gene. In a brief complaint filed in Superior Court, Hedy charged cruelty, complaining her husband caused her mental anguish to the extent that he "defeated the legitimate ends of matrimony."[37] John, however, never raised a hand to Hedy. On July 17, Hedy was granted a decree of divorce by Judge Thurmond Clarke after a brief hearing, during which she reported that John used to fall asleep in the middle of conversations. Hedy, wearing a dress of silk shantung with red, white, and blue candy stripes; white sandals; no hat; and a white purse, fiddled with sunglasses she never wore while she was queried by her attorney, A. Ronald Button:

> "Is it true that he has been indifferent toward you and the children for the past two years?" began Button.
>
> "Yes, it is," Miss Lamarr replied. The actress then related that shortly before the birth of their son Anthony, when she was also facing the task of moving to another house, Loder insisted on accepting a radio engagement in New York and remained away for six weeks.
>
> "Was he in the habit of falling asleep about 9 o'clock in the evening

while conversing with you when both of you sat in the living room?" the lawyer continued.

"Yes, except that he was usually lying down," Miss Lamarr answered. "He would fall asleep even in picture shows."[38]

Hedy was awarded sole title of the Roxbury house and the "Wilshire Boulevard business properties, two automobiles, bank accounts, government bonds, shares in film enterprises, and real estate concerns, and four insurance policies of $30,000 each."[39] She was given custody of Denise and Anthony per an agreement signed by John on July 3, and he was ordered to pay $800 a month total child support for the couples' three children.

Money was an important issue with Hedy. She told one journalist, "I want my children to have security. . . . That's something I missed in my childhood. I never had security. I haven't got it now. I can't relax. I have so many people dependent on me. What if I should get sick and couldn't work? . . . I'm very tired. . . . I want to go away for a long rest."[40]

Hedy was now sailing without a compass. She was free of her third husband, and she had no studio contract. And, sadly, with no film offers pending, she was alone in dealing with her own personal fears. Both Hedy and John faced many issues for the future, the least of which was the truth. Responsibility for their individual actions was something neither was capable of addressing. "I must quit marrying men who feel inferior to me," Hedy would state somewhat indelicately later. "Somewhere there must be a man who could be my husband and not feel inferior. I need a superior inferior man."[41]

John's film career would never revive. As for Hedy's, hers would experience a major slump as her personal troubles and anxieties mounted. It would take the magic hand of a master film director to get her career back on track.

15

Delilah

The gossip columnist Louella Parsons wrote a magazine profile on the disintegration of the Loder marriage and made a very interesting remark in the piece: "with all the things in her past, and all she still holds of the material things of life, Hedy has been dangerously close to a nervous breakdown for the past year and she is still far from well."[1] Perhaps a breakdown of sorts had already occurred.

John Loder was in actuality a fine man, and his own ego certainly matched that of Hedy's. He would talk at length about the magnificent film projects in which he was speculatively involved, and he was quite good at giving all the proper, expected answers to the press. His repeated concern for his children and his love for his wife, in the ensuing years, never did bear out in his actions, however.[2]

As for Hedy, after the divorce she journeyed to Lake Tahoe, Nevada, taking along the children for a four-week vacation. They stayed at the Tahoe Tavern. Hedy was met there by the actor Mark Stevens, who flew up from Hollywood during a break in the filming of *The Snake Pit* at Twentieth Century–Fox. He had just recently separated from his wife, the actress Annelle Hayes. Hedy had met him at Warner Bros. on the set of *Passage to Marseille* when she was filming *The Conspirators*. "We had a delightful time together," she told the journalist Florabel Muir about the Tahoe vacation. "We both like to swim and go motorboating, and we love long walks in the mountains. And we found out that we both love to get away from the Hollywood hurly-burly."[3]

Hedy gushed, "Up at Lake Tahoe, Mark and I went dancing one night. It was the first time I had danced in five years. You can't imagine, Florabel, how it feels to be relaxed and carefree again. Up there at the lake we just lived for the day, from day to day. We made no plans. The time went by like a dream. Dances, plenty of laughs, long walks, and just quiet talks. I learned something about Mark that I like and admire. He is at heart kind. You wouldn't believe what a rare quality simple kindness is. He is tolerant and understanding. He loves the children and they love him. . . . Now we can laugh about the days that are behind us. . . . We find that we have a lot to talk about together, because our experiences getting a foothold were a good deal alike."[4] Obviously, Hedy wanted to believe she was falling in love.

Stevens flew with Hedy to Reno on August 21, and then together they came back to Los Angeles. When they disembarked from the plane, the thirty-year-old, six-foot-tall Stevens dramatically embraced Hedy for the waiting photographers. However, Stevens was still legally married and was the father of a new baby. The photographs embarrassed Hedy, and the whole affair was short-lived. By the end of September, Stevens had returned to his wife. (Hedy later remarked she knew the affair would not have lasted anyway, since Stevens had greeted her at the airport with the very distinctive smell of alcohol on his breath.)[5]

Bewildered and humiliated once again by a thwarted romance, Hedy told one journalist, "I just don't understand. . . . One week he says he loves me—and the next week, when I telephone him, his manager answers and says that Mark doesn't want me to call him and has gone back to his wife."[6]

Her affair with Stevens now history, Hedy turned her energies to her career. According to the actor and director Orson Welles, she approached him to direct her as Lady Macbeth. Welles avoided making any personal or professional commitments to Hedy. "Let me give you a rain check on that," he told her. She then suggested he direct her as Eustacia Vye in Thomas Hardy's *The Return of the Native,* to "cash in on that rain check."[7] Again he declined. Sadly, he felt she was a spent force.

As for Hedy, she was mentioned and actually slated for several projects during the waning months of 1947. In September Artists Alliance's producer, Lester Cowan, announced plans to star Hedy with Donald O'Connor, Dick Haymes, Dinah Shore, and Danny Thomas in a film adaptation of the musical play *One Touch of Venus.* Hedy would assume the role of Vienna, played by

Mary Martin on Broadway, and Dinah Shore, who had actually signed a contract for the film in November, would do the singing for her.

The following month Cowan attempted to coerce Fred Astaire into directing the picture, which was to commence filming in January 1948. Hedy and Astaire eventually declined, and Shore, O'Connor, and Thomas dropped out. In the final film version of *One Touch of Venus,* the stars were Robert Walker and Ava Gardner.

Hedy was then considered for *Gallows Hill,* described as a free adaptation of Nathaniel Hawthorne's *The Scarlet Letter.* It was supposed to be the first of three pictures for United Artists to be produced by Albert J. Cohen and Jack Goldberg. The deal went nowhere. And then in December Universal-International came up with a saga of love in the desert and the French Foreign Legion for Hedy, *Rogue's Regiment.* The producer-writer Robert Buckner was actively pursuing either Hedy or Marlene Dietrich for the female lead opposite Burt Lancaster and Edmond O'Brien. Buckner then discovered Märta Torén along the way. When the picture was made in 1948, she starred opposite Dick Powell.

At the end of the year, on the advice of Hedy's corporate lawyer, Harry E. Sokolov, but primarily for her peace of mind, Mars Productions, Inc., was dissolved. The five films Hunt Stromberg had contracted to produce for United Artists showed a total loss of $900,000. *The Strange Woman* and *Dishonored Lady* were breaking even at the box office, though, and still making some money. But Hedy wanted out because she felt that she had no control over the properties being considered for her, including the two she had rejected, *There's Always Love* and *The Immortal Smile.*

On December 1, 1947, she signed a SAG (Screen Actors Guild) contract with her new representative, the prestigious William Morris Agency. Hedy freely admitted that she did not always take her agents' advice, and when she was with the powerful MCA (Music Corporation of America, which packaged stars and pictures to film companies under the leadership of its newly assigned president, Lew Wasserman), "I had the reputation of being hard to handle. Only the most important men were allowed to negotiate for me, and yet I learned some years after this period that men assigned to 'the Hedy Lamarr case' considered it a punishment. . . . I was difficult."[8]

Hedy had cast around for a screen property to do, and Hedda Hopper, of course, broke the news about Hedy's return to the screen: "She is anxious to get back to work, and soon will [star] in 'Let's Live A Little.' An apt title, yes?"[9] On

January 6 a deal was signed for Eagle-Lion Films, Inc., to distribute the comedy. *Let's Live a Little* was to be produced by United California Productions, an organization headed by the actor Robert Cummings, the screenwriter Philip Yordan, and the film producer Eugene Frenke.

Primarily a distributor of B movies, new films produced by the British-owned Rank Organization, and rereleases of David O. Selznick productions, Eagle-Lion in 1948 alone distributed forty-eight recently made motion pictures, including *Tulsa,* with Susan Hayward; *Hollow Triumph,* with Joan Bennett; and, for its final picture of the year, *Let's Live a Little.*

Let's Live a Little, another film dealing with psychology, featured a plot that was a lighthearted attempt to ridicule the validity of the profession. The ad agent Duke Crawford (Robert Cummings) is being blackmailed by his former sweetheart, Michele Bennett (Anna Sten), who will renew a million-dollar contract for representation of her Michele Bennett Cosmetics line only if Duke agrees to renew their romance.

Duke is a nervous wreck and is taken off the Bennett account and given the promotion of a new book, *Let's Live a Little,* by Dr. J. O. "Jo" Loring (Hedy), a lady psychiatrist, whom he meets at her office to talk about her contract. Instead, they end up discussing his nervous condition. Dr. Loring, whose colleague is Dr. Richard Field (Robert Shayne), advises Duke that he should use reverse psychology with Michele by taking her out and drenching her with attention. At a nightclub where Duke has taken Michele, Dr. Loring and Dr. Field are there to observe Duke. They all meet.

After one look at Dr. Loring, Michele becomes jealous and starts a fight, and Duke's plan for her to sign the contract is thwarted. Now he is more distraught than ever. Dr. Loring, along with Dr. Field (who is in love with her), take Duke to Shady Lake Lodge for a rest, and Dr. Loring and Duke fall in love. But when Duke hears Dr. Loring say on the radio that he is just an experiment, a "guinea pig," he rushes back to Michele and agrees to marry her. Dr. Loring then becomes a nervous wreck. But before a marriage takes place, everything works out as it should, and Duke and Dr. Loring are in each other's arms.

Light and fluffy comedy fare, *Let's Live a Little* began filming in early February 1948, at the old Producers Releasing Corporation (PRC) studio, around the corner from the Goldwyn lot where Hedy had filmed her two dramas for United Artists. The film comedy's star and nominal producer, Robert Cummings, had enjoyed a so-so film career, making fifty-five pictures since his film debut in a 1933 Vitaphone musical short called *Seasoned Greetings,* with Lita Grey Chaplin and little Sammy Davis Jr. Cummings's best-known role in pictures had been that of Parris in the successful Warner Bros. 1942 drama *King's Row.* After making *Let's Live a Little,* Cummings would enter into the world of television and gain his more-famous celebrity.

Let's Live a Little marked the return to the screen of actress Anna Sten, once known as "Goldwyn's Folly." Sten had been a famous film actress in her native Russia before being coerced to Hollywood in the early 1930s by Samuel Goldwyn, who was hell-bent on making her a greater glamour star than Garbo or Dietrich combined. However, after several expensive film failures such as *Nana* (1934), *We Live Again* (1934), and *His Wedding Night* (1935), Sten failed to spark the public's attention. Filmgoers simply did not buy her, and Goldwyn eventually dropped his million-dollar discovery. Now she was making her only American film comedy. Sten was also the wife of the film's producer, Eugene Frenke.

Problems during filming arose almost immediately. The picture's original cinematographer was Stanley Cortez, who had dropped out of the production early on because of "illness." According to one reporter, Hedy had Cortez fired because she did not like his photography, and in another report it was stated that the cameraman was let go because Sten was appearing "too much to an advantage in the rushes."[10]

When telephoned at her home, Hedy's secretary told the press that Cortez had been fired by Frenke because "when we looked at the rushes we thought we were seeing Hedy's mother."[11] Hedy said of the incident, "This is what happened. I made a test with Stanley. It was not good. I made another. No one was satisfied. A meeting was held at my house. Mr. Frenke wanted to replace him. I said no. I phoned Stanley and told him exactly how I felt. He was sweet and appreciative. . . . It's a little discouraging."[12]

Whatever problems Hedy might have had on the set of *Let's Live a Little,* Frenke and Cummings were happy enough with her performance to offer her another teaming with Cummings in United California's next project, *Passport to Love,* based on a swashbuckling adventure by Alexandre Dumas. Another property they were considering was I. A. R. Wylie's novel *Ho, the Fair Wind,* which Frenke bought for $50,000 and also scheduled for Cummings and Hedy. In the meantime, *Let's Live a Little* was quickly completed at the end of March, coming in two days under schedule and $25,000 under budget. It had cost $1.3 million.

On the home front, Jamie's problems at school had come to a crisis. He was a difficult child. Hedy celebrated his ninth birthday with a chocolate cake on March 9. Hedy and Jamie were photographed with one-year-old Anthony and chubby five-year-old Denise. James, dressed in his school uniform, looked solemn. Hedy looked thin and drawn. It would be the last time they all were photographed together as a family.

As James related many years later, "What happened was when I was quite young, I think seven or eight years old, I went to Chadwick and I got into trouble . . . and they told me I couldn't go there anymore. But there was a teacher by the name of Ingrid Gray, who was also a German. Klopper was her maiden name. She said I could live with her and her husband, and go [to school during] the daytime . . . and since all my friends were there, everybody I knew, I agreed. And my mother was disenchanted with that, and she didn't want anything more to do with me. She was angry."[13]

Hedy agreed to let Jamie live with the Grays. By the time he was eleven years old, after years of telling the press her son was attending school in Europe or living with the Grays in Redondo Beach, Hedy stopped the façade and removed the boy from her life. (She did, however, set up a trust fund for him.)

By 1951, James Lamarr Loder was rarely reported in the press as part of the family. "The last time I saw my mother as a child would have been when I was about in fifth grade," he told a journalist in 2001. "I tried to write her, but the letters were returned. Effectively, she just said, 'You're no longer my son. Goodbye.'"[14]

Whatever demons haunted Hedy during this period of her life were probably not even understood by her. Her behavior was becoming erratic, and more than one insider saw major changes happening to Hedy as her career reeled out of control and her personal life became somewhat of an emotional shambles. Her behavior bordered on the frantic, the desperate, as she tried to maintain her lifestyle, her family, and her career without the benefits of a solid marriage or a studio to guide and support her decisions.

Financially Hedy took a beating by producing her two films. Her salary had been delayed until after production costs were made back. Still, her earnings for 1947 totaled $279,800, making her one of the top industry earners of the year. But Hedy still faced financial and emotional problems. Always she had relied on having a man in her life. First with George Montgomery and recently with Mark Stevens, Hedy had lovers who romanced her at the most sensitive and vulnerable times in her life. And both had, for whatever reasons, left her. In this nervous and anxious state of despair, Hedy possibly was also letting the happiness of a loving family slip right through her fingers.

In late 1947, Hedy was often seen publicly on the arm of the director-screenwriter Billy Wilder, whom she had once enjoyed a casual relationship with. Wilder was recently divorced from his wife of ten years, the mother of his two children. After he escorted Hedy to a premiere in Hollywood, they became the talk of the town. One columnist ran into Wilder at Romanoff's and bluntly said, "I hear that you and Hedy are getting married." To which Wilder smiled and replied, "Don't be ridiculous. . . . I've had one date with her."[15]

Louella Parsons asked Hedy about her relationship with Wilder, and her reply was frank: "He's fun, he's brilliant, and we have a good time together. I wish people wouldn't start trying to make a romance out of my friendship with him. We're just good friends. I do see him more than any other man. He gives me a mental stimulus, but I just couldn't imagine Billy ever settling down to marriage and really wanting a home life. . . . You know what a great director he is." When Parsons asked her why she did not do a picture with Wilder, Hedy's reply was, "I certainly hope to some day. . . . I've been waiting all my life for a great part."[16]

On April 15, 1948, Hedy filed a $200,000 lawsuit in the Superior Court of Santa Monica with her attorney Jerry Geisler against *Look* magazine, which had mentioned her in their April 13 issue in a piece entitled "A New Face Through Plastic Surgery," which she said used her face in a misleading way. "Look at my nose," Hedy fumed to a columnist. "Do you think I have ever had plastic surgery? Isn't that ridiculous for any magazine to say that I've had a nose operation?"[17]

Telling the press that the public had always accepted her as "a natural beauty," Hedy alleged in the complaint that the reputations of her children had been injured. It stated too that "it is untrue that the plaintiff had ever at any time or place whatsoever had performed on her during her entire lifetime any form of nasal or plastic surgery."[18] Hedy's beauty was her professional power, and she fiercely protected it. The case dragged on throughout the year.

With her life growing increasingly entangled, once again what Hedy really needed was a good picture. At one point she seriously considered moving to New York to star on Broadway for Alexander Ince and Joel Schenker in the Maurice Valency comedy *A Legend of Good Women*. But she soon dropped out of that project.

Then fate intervened, and Hedy's career was temporarily rescued. She met with an agent representing the Screen Actors Guild at Romanoff's for lunch one day in late spring. In her book, she called him Sidney. Sidney talked a blue streak, ordering martini after martini, all the while on the make for her, according to her account. Almost casually he mentioned the name of "C.B." Hedy's ears perked up. She wrote, "'Later, when I got through to C.B. myself,' said 'Sidney,'" 'he told me he was planning his all-time biggest spectacle, and asked if Betty Hutton was available for the part of Delilah. *Samson and Delilah.* . . . You mix muscles, tits, and sadism, and you got box office. You add genius like C.B. with all the money in the world, and you got significance. In fact, every picture the Old Man makes is significant.'"[19]

As soon as Sidney left the restaurant, Hedy asked for a telephone and called her agent to join her. She called him Robin in her book. That man was no doubt Robert Lantz, a German-born agent Hedy had met when she was sixteen years old in 1930 at the home of the Countess von Leipzig in Germany. Now established in Hollywood, Lantz was one of those aggressive agents who talked a great deal and usually landed terrific contracts for his clients.

When Lantz arrived, Hedy explained what had transpired, and from their booth he called DeMille's secretary. DeMille was unavailable, but Lantz was persistent, and within five minutes the great director was on the line. Lantz said, according to Hedy, "Mr. DeMille, this is . . . Miss Lamarr's agent. I just happened to be lunching at Mike's place [Mike Romanoff], and she was telling me how much she admired your pictures."[20] DeMille asked for a meeting the next day and sent a car for Hedy and Lantz to bring them to his office. After formalities, the master director got down to picture business. Hedy wrote:

The moment I heard it would be in Technicolor, I wanted to do it. I had never done a movie in color and my vanity succumbed under the very possibility. After two cups of coffee Mr. DeMille told us the story of Samson and Delilah, all his magnificent expensive plans. We could tell this was a labor of love. The Old Man sparkled with joy at this vast undertaking. He said then, "Hedy, I have followed your career. You have become an important personality. You will be bigger."[21]

Cecil Blount DeMille was born in August 1881 and originally entered show business as an actor, along with his older brother William C. de Mille (the rest of the family would all change the spelling of their last name to de Mille—C. B.'s was the actual spelling; William's daughter would become the legendary choreographer Agnes de Mille). Cecil B. DeMille is credited, along with Jesse Lasky, as being one of the founders of the American motion picture colony, one of the men who brought the fledgling American silent film industry from Fort Lee, New Jersey, to a sleepy little orange grove called Hollywood in 1913.

DeMille's debut picture was the first of his three film versions of *The Squaw Man* (1914) for Famous Players–Lasky Productions (which became Paramount Pictures). After a long string of early silent hits, in which he directed Mary Pickford, Wallace Reid, the opera diva Geraldine Ferrar, Gloria Swanson, and others, DeMille latched on to the perfect formula, for which he would forever be remembered. Beginning with the 1923 screen version of *The Ten Command-ments,* which was followed by *The King of Kings* in 1927, DeMille incorporated plenty of action, sin, sex, and debauchery before the wrath of God dealt His measure, giving the voyeuristic audience what they had come for *plus* moral retribution in the end to ease their consciences.

And, of course, all that added up to one thing—box office. Entering the sound era, DeMille signed a three-picture deal with M-G-M and made, in rapid succession, three dreadful films, the dull *Dynamite,* with Julia Faye, in 1929; the superlooney colossus musical *Madam Satan* in 1930; and his simply boring third remake of *The Squaw Man* in 1931—all starring Kay Johnson, the wife of Hedy's *Algiers* director John Cromwell. DeMille's first three talkies tanked at the box office; Metro let him go, and he signed back with Paramount.

By 1948, DeMille's best films, which made huge profits, were the super-spectaculars, employing big-name stars and extras by the thousands: *The Sign of the Cross* (1932), *Cleopatra* (1934), *The Crusades* (1935), *The Plainsman* (1937), *The Buccaneer* (1938), *Union Pacific* (1939), *Northwest Mounted Police* (1940), *Reap the Wild Wind* (1942), and *Unconquered* (1947).

One of the founding members of the Academy of Motion Picture Arts and Sciences, DeMille also was the director and host of *The Lux Radio Theater* from 1936 until January 1945, netting him an extra $100,000 a year. He left the show after a union dispute over a $1 union-contribution fee he refused to pay. And it was on *The Lux Radio Theater*'s 1941 presentation of *Algiers* that De-Mille originally met Hedy.

DeMille had wanted to do the story of Samson and Delilah as far back as 1934, with, over the years, Delores del Rio, Merle Oberon, Evelyn Brent, or Paulette Goddard as Delilah; Nick Foran, Ian Hunter, Donald Briggs, or Laird Cregar as Samson.

Various outlines and treatments of the biblical story were produced for De-Mille by the screenwriter Harold Lamb. DeMille commissioned Earl Bruce Powell to write a treatment based on the three books of Judges in the Bible and on the *Antiquities of the Jews* by Flavius Josephus, and a presentable screenplay was submitted to him in September 1935. The following year, he purchased the screen rights to the 1877 French opera *Samson et Dalila* by Camille Saint-Saëns (music) and F. Lemaire (libretto). DeMille then bought the rights to Vladimir Jabotinsky's 1930 novel *The Judge and the Fool*, as translated from German by Cyrus Brooks, just to cover all the bases.

He then assigned Jeanie MacPherson (who unapologetically wrote in silent-film style) and Sada Cowan to work on the script. Submitting a composite painting of his ideal Delilah to national newspapers and additional conceptual art by Dan Sayre Groesbeck to Paramount executives, DeMille began a publicity campaign to find just the right siren for his screen epic. It was a terrific publicity ploy, which drew national attention and thousands of responses, none of which DeMille ever intended to use. The director, who was now deep into completing *The Crusades* and about to begin *The Plainsman*, delayed the $5 million superproduction in 1935, and *Samson and Delilah* was shelved.

In 1946, in pitching his idea to the executives at Paramount for a revived film version of *Samson and Delilah*, DeMille was met with opposition. "Put millions of dollars into a Sunday-school story?" they asked him. DeMille then tried convincing them by "reducing the story elements to boy-meets-girl—and what a boy and what a girl!" Said DeMille, "I'm sometimes accused of gingering up the Bible with lavish infusions of sex and violence . . . but I wish that my accusers would read their Bibles more closely, for in those pages are more violence and sex than I could ever portray on screen."[22] That pitch worked, and he was given the go-ahead. DeMille told his executive assistant Phil Koury, "For Samson . . . I want a combination of Tarzan, Robin Hood and Superman. For Delilah . . . a sort of distilled Jean Simmons and Vivien Leigh, with a generous touch of Lana Turner."[23]

After completing his modern-day patriotic biopic *The Story of Dr. Wassell* (1944) and the adventure-drama *Unconquered*, DeMille was ready to "knock 'em dead" at the box office with a colossal biblical story. So out he dragged *Samson and Delilah* and its new screenplay, written by Jesse Lasky Jr. and Frederic M. Frank, which was based on Lamb's original treatment of the Samson and Delilah story and Jabotinsky's novel.

As production developed on the picture throughout the year, the director focused on whom he would cast as Samson. In a memo dated July 17, 1946, he jotted down the names of Jack Gifford, Clancy Ross, Bruce Kellogg, and Jim Davis (later Jock Ewing of TV's *Dallas* fame). Hedda Hopper had mentioned DeMille's newest sin-and-sex epic in her *Los Angeles Times* "Looking at Hollywood" column, in June of 1946. She had her ulterior motives. She literally campaigned for her son, William Hopper, to portray Samson.

Determined that her William land the virile role, Hopper ordered him to train with a coach at a local gym. On January 8, 1948, a test of the new, masculine, and renamed Bill Hopper was scheduled. But he did not make it to the studio. He was home, sick in bed with the flu. The test was finally filmed on January 26 with Hopper and the actress Ruth Roman. It consisted of two scenes from DeMille's screenplay of his 1934 picture *Cleopatra*, and Hopper promptly failed. He had not read the complete script of *Cleopatra*, obviously, and in DeMille's papers it was noted, "[he] did not know what was on Anthony's mind in either of the two scenes that he did. Mr. deMille [sic] noticed that he had a habit of pursing his lips. . . . If Hopper had known Anthony's intention he might have read it differently."[24]

A more likely list of possible Samsons was then drawn up, and it included Douglas Fairbanks Jr., Cary Grant (whom DeMille had actually spoken to about the role), Stewart Granger, James Mason (noted as "small"), Errol Flynn, Bruce Bennett, Burt Lancaster, Orson Welles, Robert Stack, Robert Ryan, and Robert Taylor.[25] Circled by DeMille was the one actor who stood out over the others—Victor Mature.

For the role of the Saran, the ruler of Gaza, DeMille was given a list that included Boris Karloff, Ray Milland, Michael Redgrave, John Lund, Macdonald Carey, Rex Harrison, Charles Boyer, and Cesar Romero (who wanted $50,000). DeMille wisely chose George Sanders.[26]

The director knew specifically what he was looking for in his screen Delilah: "The dark-eyed temptress . . . her beauty, her love and her greed on display," he told the press.[27] For Delilah, the tempestuous beauty who lures Samson to his doom, DeMille and his staff drew up an eclectic list of possible actresses to consider: Rhonda Fleming, Jeanne Crain, Lana Turner, Lucille Ball, Ava Gardner (someone wrote on the list "she 'whispers'"), Jennifer Jones, Vivien Leigh, Gail Russell, Alida Valli, Susan Hayward, Linda Darnell, Greer Garson, Rita Hayworth, Patricia Neal, and Jean Simmons. DeMille circled his choice—Hedy Lamarr—but only after he screened two reels of *Algiers*.[28] On May 24, Hedy's agent from William Morris sent recent photographs of her made for *Let's Live a Little* to DeMille's office. He had his Delilah.

For DeMille's Semadar, older sister to Delilah, it was an easier call. Despite the initial actresses listed, including Madeleine Carroll, Rhonda Fleming (again), Phyllis Calvert (who wanted $50,000), and Anna Sten, DeMille chose Angela Lansbury in September, after Phyllis Calvert, originally assigned the role in July, dropped out because of illness.[29]

With the cast in place, *Samson and Delilah* was set to begin production on October 4 and was scheduled for a ten-week shoot. DeMille signed Hedy on June 9. She received $25,000 upon signing and $7,500 a week, a total of $100,000 (with a $10,000 a week pro rata thereafter). Plus, Paramount paid for Hedy's own dialogue coach, which did not exceed $350 a week. Also, Hedy received her own hairdresser and wardrobe girl, at union scale. Her first scene as Delilah was set for October 8.[30]

Hedy's William Morris agent, Joe Schoenfeld (Lantz was her personal agent), made the deal, which included a chauffeured car (Marvin Neal was now paid by the studio) and the dressing room on the Paramount lot originally intended for Victor Mature (he was assigned another, less-posh space). Mature, borrowed from Twentieth Century–Fox, was signed for the role of Samson on June 12, 1948, for $75,000, his services to begin on September 16.

DeMille told the press, "What first impressed me about Miss Lamarr was her sincerity. . . . All of six years ago she was on a radio program of which I was the master of ceremonies. I remembered her from that when we decided to produce 'Samson and Delilah.' Actually she is one of the most unaffected persons that I have ever known in Hollywood. This is what gives great value to her work. She stands by what she believes."[31]

Hedy's comments about DeMille were equally gracious: "I was won over to appearing in the picture from the moment I entered his office and saw the extent of the research that he had done on the whole subject," she told the press. "You have no idea how thorough and comprehensive that research is. He has the first suggestion of a script and treatment down to the final shooting script. He has documents and evidence to support everything he does."[32]

As soon as contracts were signed, Hedy and her secretary left for a brief trip to Paris, leaving Denise and Anthony with their nanny and Trude. Hedy had been invited by Pierre Lazaress and the agent Felix "Fefe" Ferry to attend an all-star circus event for the United Nations Overseas Aid for Children. Flying into New York, Hedy stayed at John Loder's apartment for a couple of days. Loder had already flown to California to visit his son and daughter in Beverly Hills and told the press, "Hedy's done a wonderful job with the children."[33] Hedy then continued on to Paris for two weeks, arriving at Orly Airport on June 27. In an exchange of telegrams, Hedy advised DeMille on July 7:

> HAVING TIME OF MY LIFE STOP
> CAN I DO ANYTHING FOR YOU STOP
> STAYING GEORGE V
> LOVE=
> DELILAH=[34]

DeMille's reply in the form of a Western Union night letter the following day was:

> *My mind is much relieved. Stop. Reports here said Delilah was in hospital. Stop. The best thing for you to do for me is stay well have a good time and come home to*
>
> C.B. deM.[35]

At the circus, called *La grande nuit de Paris,* Hedy was photographed draped in mink in the company of her *Algiers* costar Charles Boyer and with Ingrid Bergman, handing out autographs. Hedy was again photographed on July 6 with Edward G. Robinson as the two turned over the proceeds from the circus, 16,000,000 French francs ($75,000).

On Bastille Day, July 14, Hedy arrived back at New York's Idlewild Airport and was the first one off the plane. She stayed again at Loder's apartment while he was on Cape Cod performing in the play *O Mistress Mine* with Gertrude Lawrence. At this time Hedy had four people managing her career—Jerry Geisler, her attorney; Joe Schoenfeld, her agent; Harry Friedman at MCA, her business manager; and her publicist, Jay Steele.

Hedy reported to Paramount for photographic makeup tests on July 29. Apparently there were problems before initial shooting on *Samson and Delilah* had even begun. Hedy had been advised her wardrobe was to be created by the legendary Paramount costume designer Edith Head. Hedy balked. She preferred the work of Elois Jenssen, who had designed her wardrobe in *Let's Live a Little*, to Head's designs, and said so. Jenssen was brought over to Paramount from Warner, but, according to one insider, "Edith didn't let her do anything."[36]

From the start, Head encountered difficulties with the headstrong Delilah. Wrote Hedy:

> The very first day Edith Head, the famous fashion expert at Paramount, came down on the set with the gown I was to wear in the first scene. I said, "It's beautiful but it does not fit the mood I have. This is too drab. I'm supposed to excite Samson."
>
> Mr. DeMille came over to referee. He looked at the dress on me and said, "I see nothing wrong with it."
>
> "I want a gown that says something positive—not one that just has nothing wrong with it."
>
> Mr. DeMille scowled. However, he ordered a camera test and looked at it on the screen. "It's not right," he told Edith Head. "Let's try the same thing in red." In red it was exciting and I wore that. Round one . . .[37]

Round two must have come quickly enough, for, shortly after filming began, Hedy made some comments that did not settle well with the director, and DeMille was heard to tell her, "I don't act, you don't direct."[38]

"There were easier stars to work with than Hedy Lamarr, too," Head remarked. She continued:

> Dressing her wasn't easy. It took a while for her to get a sense of the character she would be playing (I'm not sure she had acquired that sense before the cameras started rolling, either), so she didn't give me much trouble with regards to costumes. She did, however, have very specific demands about how things should fit. DeMille wanted her to look voluptuous, but she was small-busted and she wouldn't wear padding. She told me she couldn't act if she felt she had unnatural proportions. So I draped her and shaped her until I finally achieved DeMille's required sensuousness and Hedy's requested natural look.
>
> Often she would come into my salon for fittings, she'd float past my

secretary, one hand dramatically placed on her forehead, and immediately plop down on the floor, complaining that her back gave her constant pain, that she had never been the same since she had children. She'd get up to fit a dress but in between pinnings she'd plop down on the floor again, which gave me the impression that her back wasn't really aching; she was just lazy. We fitted a multitude of rather bare bras and skirts for her role as Delilah, but the real work came from helping her get up off the carpet. She never registered any enthusiasm at her fittings . . . it made it all the more difficult to enjoy working with her. . . .

If Hedy's navel was exposed it was censored. If I stuffed it with a pearl, we got by. I designed jewel belts to cover her belly button, but when I really wanted a sexy look, I used a jewel of some sort . . . if I showed too much of Hedy's cleavage or any protruding pelvic bones, the moral watchdogs were after us. . . . Since I was frequently called to the set during filming to make sure that Hedy was uncensorable, I wasn't finished with the film until the last day of shooting. . . . By working with Hedy carefully from 1946 to 1948, when we finally finished shooting, we ended up with a very sexy, but "morally acceptable" Delilah.[39]

The most important costume Head was required to design for Hedy was at DeMille's insistence—the magnificent peacock cape. For the last scene in the film, with Delilah on the throne beside Saran, DeMille wanted something memorable, a costume of feathers. Not having any idea what birds might have been around in Minoan days, Head sent her researchers out. She believed she might have been told peacocks had been about, so she sketched a long cape of feathers over an iridescent bra and skirt, obviously copied from a similar costume worn by Theda Bara in Fox's 1917 *Cleopatra*. When she presented it to the Old Man, he was impressed. "*That* I like," DeMille told her.[40]

Finding peacock feathers was a difficult task until DeMille advised Head and her staff to just wait until the molting season, since he had several peacocks on his ranch. When the time came, Head's staff collected over 2,000 peacock feathers, which were hand sewn or glued onto the cape's fabric. Head felt that this costume, as well as all the costumes for *Samson and Delilah,* was totally inappropriate. She never knew if it was historically authentic. Nevertheless, Head would be given an Oscar for her work on *Samson and Delilah.* (Hedy's peacock-feathered cape from *Samson and Delilah* and Kay Johnson's sequined masquerade outfit from *Madam Satan* were the only two costumes DeMille ever preserved in his own personal archives.)

In early August, Hedy planned to take a three-week vacation, and she had no intention to report at that time for costume fittings. Her body measurements were diligently made and logged down to the inch, but still she was requested to appear for fittings. In a Paramount interoffice memo dated August 6 (preserved in the Brigham Young University archives), William Meiklejohn advised DeMille about Hedy's imminent departure for Lake Tahoe.

Of course, Hedy was contractually free to take her vacation to Lake Tahoe, and during it she sent C. B. a message on his birthday (August 12), to which he replied on August 20 in a Western Union telegram:

> *Only Delilah would think of such a seductive thing to say on my*
> *sixty seventh birthday. As a reward I will tell you confidentially*
> *that George Barnes will be our cameraman. Greeting.*
> *Cecil B. deMille*[41]

Hedy's response was immediate, on August 22, in a telegram:

YOU ARE AN ANGEL TO GET BARNES.
YOU ARE AN ANGEL PERIOD.
DELILAH[42]

With a cameraman set, and Delilah happy, production of *Samson and Delilah* forged ahead. Budgeted at $2,995,000, Paramount soon raised the ante to $3.5 million. DeMille's version of *Samson and Delilah* is based on the Old Testament book of Judges, 13–16. From that brief passage, he built a motion picture of two hours in length. In 1100 BC, in the land of Dan, the Danites are held in slavery by the Philistines, and they look to the young, massively strong shepherd Samson (Victor Mature) to free them. In a feat of great strength and courage Samson kills a lion, and the leader of the Philistines, Saran of Gaza (George Sanders), allows Samson to choose a Philistine woman to marry. That woman is Semadar (Angela Lansbury), whose proud and beautiful younger sister Delilah (Hedy) longs for Samson herself.

Delilah betrays her sister, and Samson loses Semadar to Ahtur (Henry Wilcoxon) when she is given to him by her father (William Farnum). Delilah offers herself to Samson, but he scorns her. In an ensuing riot at the marriage feast, Semadar and her father are killed, Samson flees, and Delilah vows revenge. She soon becomes the favorite of Saran of Gaza. Delilah sets out to trap Samson, and she seduces him in the desert. He tells her he believes his great strength comes from his hair, and after Delilah drugs him, she shears his head. Samson is thus captured by the Philistines. Saran of Gaza promises Delilah no blade will touch his skin. Instead, unbeknownst to Delilah, Samson's eyes are burned, and he is blinded.

Tortured and chained, Samson is consigned to the gristmill, where Delilah for the first time realizes he cannot see. When Samson is brought into the Temple of Dagon to be publicly tortured, Delilah feigns to participate in his final humiliation and joins Samson alone in the arena. There she professes her love for him, and he asks her to take him to the massive stone columns that support the huge idol Dagon. Praying to his God, Samson's strength returns, and he brings the temple down on the pagans.

A handsomely muscular actor, thirty-five-year-old Victor Mature was an ideal choice for Samson. Born in Kentucky, he entered films in 1940 in the Hal Roach–produced, United Artists film *One Million B.C.,* opposite Carole Landis. He signed a contract with Twentieth Century–Fox before entering World War II, serving with the United States Coast Guard in the North Atlantic. Returning to his home lot after the war, Mature was featured in *My Darling Clementine* (1946) and in *Easy Living* (1949), with Lucille Ball, the latter under the direction of Jacques Tourneur at R-K-O Radio.

DeMille was advised that Hedy, Jerry Geisler (the super-Hollywood defense attorney), and the William Morris agent Abe Lasfogel were trying to iron out the *Look* lawsuit and that no payments were expected from him or Paramount to settle the issue. But DeMille did not want any problems with the national magazine in promoting his film. On October 4, just days before Hedy started her scenes in *Samson and Delilah,* Geisler told the press that Hedy had called off the lawsuit. Geisler then promptly billed Hedy $5,000 for his fee.

Hedy stepped before the camera on Paramount's stage 8 at 3:30 P.M. for one hour on October 9. Her first scene took place in Delilah's pavilion. DeMille was obviously looking for an actress to slink about and fill the latest Philistine fashions commendably. And Hedy did just that. Filming of *Samson and Delilah* proceeded on schedule, but there were some problems, prompting DeMille to state, "Many persons have given so much to bring it to life on the screen. Months of planning, worry, disappointment. But always perseverance. And always a willingness to keep at it."[43]

DeMille promoted the picture as "a story of power and prayer."[44] And he needed both when problems arose on the set. The director was none too pleased when Victor Mature refused to wrestle the lion in a sequence shot on stage 16, November 8–13. Said Mature to DeMille: "Look, C.B., there's only one Mature and I would hate to see him go this way."[45] For the scene on the closed set, Mature's stunt double, Mel Koontz, actually did the shot of the wrestle with a toothless, tamed lion named Brutus.

"She did not like Victor Mature," recalled Hedy's friend Robert Osborne.[46] And, indeed, Hedy lost respect for Mature for not doing the scene. For close-ups they used an obviously stuffed lion's head and paws to avoid scratching Mature's chiseled face. When a group of actors were hired for a fight scene, DeMille demanded complete dedication. "Mike Mazurki, Robert Barrat, Harry Woods, Ed Hinton—I assume they . . . will do their own fighting in the fight on the stairs where they throw things. If William Farnum [at 60] can take it at his age—they should be able to do so."[47]

Hedy recalled that she got along well enough with the no-nonsense DeMille. She took her work seriously and always appeared on the set knowing her lines. She allegedly did complain to DeMille, however, when she felt Mature was upstaging her in their scenes, to which the director replied, "Do you think there are any men in America who would rather look at his face than your ass?"[48]

Hedy was ill briefly during the filming, but she was back on the lot on November 16, to film the scene where coins are thrown at Delilah's feet for betraying Samson. "Well, Mr. DeMille . . . dragged me out of a sick bed for that one," she told a reporter. "And the dewy eyes are a direct result of a roaring 104 degree temperature."[49]

In a 2000 tribute to Hedy, Angela Lansbury recalled Lamarr's presence on the set of the picture, saying that Hedy surrounded herself in a cloak of intrigue. It made quite an impression on the young Lansbury, who watched and studied Hedy very carefully. Lansbury freely admitted to having been dazzled by Hedy's beauty.

An ever-indulgent and benevolent film pioneer, DeMille never forgot those whom he had met on his way up. Many former silent films stars who had been featured or starred in his pictures decades before were often employed by the Old Man in his later epics. Work as an extra or a bit player in *Samson and*

Delilah, sometimes with only a line or two of dialogue, was given to such former silent and early-talkie greats as William Farnum, Moroni Olsen, Victor Varconi, Nils Asther, Karen Morley, and Frank Mayo.[50]

Julia Faye, DeMille's one-time mistress, appeared in nearly every DeMille picture since 1917, sometimes as a star or as an extra, until his death.[51] DeMille was known to have a foot fetish, and he adored Faye's petite feet, giving them loving close-ups in a couple of his silent pictures. DeMille always made sure Faye was under contract with Paramount.

During the production of *Samson and Delilah,* a brief scene was filmed with the great director playing himself for inclusion in Billy Wilder's *Sunset Boulevard.* (It was released in 1950.) Starring DeMille's once-bright star Gloria Swanson, who in the scene wore a spare peacock feather from Delilah's cape in her hat for good luck, the sequence was of Norma Desmond (Swanson) coming onto the Paramount lot to talk with her former director, DeMille, about a script she had sent him. Wilder had hoped that Hedy would make a brief cameo offering her chair to Norma Desmond. But Hedy foolishly asked for $25,000 (the very use of her name would have cost him $10,000). Needless to say, Hedy did not appear in the picture. But Hedda Hopper did, heavily made up and portraying herself.

On December 13, Hedy completed her last scene in *Samson and Delilah*. She had been used a total of forty-six days. The following day DeMille himself took over the third camera unit, and *Samson and Delilah* officially wrapped on schedule. The biblical epic had cost a total of $3,097,563.05. DeMille had successfully brought it in just over $400,000 under budget.

Meanwhile, *Let's Live a Little* was reviewed in previews, and in November it opened nationwide. Thank goodness Hedy had *Samson and Delilah*.

16

Paramount

*I*n previews on October 21, the critics were kind to *Let's Live a Little*. *Daily Variety* said, "Lamarr is a knockout!"[1] The picture was released nationwide on November 9.

When the film was shown in Los Angeles, Philip K. Scheuer in the *Los Angeles Times* wrote, "Miss Lamarr is her customary self—vague, cool, and bewitching."[2] *Let's Live a Little* marked Hedy's return to a passively "feminine" role, and the eighty-five-minute picture clearly portrays the evolving post–World War II gender roles. As Robert Cummings makes his advances on the female doctor, she willingly forsakes her other patients to focus on him. In more than one way, *Let's Live a Little* is a very dated picture.

And it is really a very poor film. The plot is silly, almost pointless, and sadly Cummings is simply not Gable—actually, he is a very unconvincing leading man. In fact, none of the characters were "likable."

The film may have attempted to look glossy, but instead the whole affair appears phony: It features poor process shots and at times is almost claustrophobic in set design. Richard Wallace's direction is extremely weak, the pacing of the film and its rhythm uneasy. The costumes by Elois Jenssen, despite the fine work she would achieve in her later career, are hideous.

The totally unsleek glam gowns designed by Jenssen for Anna Sten are gaudy, extravagant, pre–World War II, Third Reich, and Euro-fashionable, and Sten looks preposterous. Her acting, glorious though it might have been in her native Russia, is liltingly "Zsa Zsa Gaborish" in its delivery, and her every scene looks lifted right out of 1934. It is a sad display.

Let's Live a Little made some money, but it was the only film that United California Productions ever produced. On April 22, 1952, the Bank of America National Trust and Savings Association foreclosed the first lien on the company. In the *Sunset Securities v. United California Productions, Inc.* suit in May 1952, Robert Cummings signed a disclaimer of default against the film, relinquishing any and all rights to *Let's Live a Little*.[3] The picture was later rereleased as *Hell Breaks Loose*.

In November Hedda Hopper revealed that Hedy was still in communication with Fritz Mandl. Hedda also asked Hedy if there was anything she wanted or wished for. Hedy replied, "To live in a period when people were gayer—say the Vienna of 50 years ago. I feel I was born in a wrong age. Something is different in this generation. The men and women don't seem to like each other."[4] Hedy's heart would always remain in Vienna.

On December 23 Hopper announced in her *Los Angeles Times* column that Hedy was dating the actor Edward Norris. The relationship came to a quick end when Hedy found out he was also seeing Joan Crawford. That same day, Cecil B. DeMille sent three copies of *Samson and Delilah* and two exquisite orchids to Hedy for Christmas. She graciously acknowledged his generosity by sending him a telegram on Christmas Day:

> TO THE GUIDING SPIRIT OF DELILAH MY WARMEST THANKS
> FOR YOUR THOUGHTFULNESS AND THE BEAUTIFUL
> GIFTS GOD BLESS YOU THIS NEW YEAR XXXX
> AND ALWAYS
> YOURS HEDY LAMARR[5]

DeMille and Hedy kept up contact with each other long after the completion of *Samson and Delilah*. His motive was simple. He was hoping possibly to secure her for his next extravaganza, whatever that might be.

With the coming of the baby-boom era, people were staying home more frequently and listening to the radio or watching the new medium of television. Theatres were beginning to feel the crunch after the war years, the boom years. Metro-Goldwyn-Mayer in 1947, for example, grossed $185 million through theatre attendance. Because of their extravagant production expenditures, however, their films netted the mother company Loew's, Inc., only $5 million. In effect, the studio system was dying. Also beginning in 1948, the film studios, which had marketed their pictures through their own movie theatres, were forced to liquidate their theatre holdings by order of the U.S. government. The demise of the Hollywood studio system was inevitable.

Though such pictures as Paramount's *Samson and Delilah* would still merit high production costs, the studios collectively were cleaning house. And with the onset of free home entertainment, they soon realized that change within the industry was unavoidable.

Meanwhile, Hedy was offered more roles. An intriguing piece of casting would have been Hedy as Margo Channing in Twentieth Century–Fox's *All About Eve* (1950). When the original list of actresses in consideration for the choice part was drawn up by the screenwriter-director Joseph L. Mankiewicz, it included Joan Crawford, Greer Garson, Norma Shearer, Katharine Hepburn, and Hedy Lamarr. Hedy was quickly dismissed from the group, and Claudette Colbert was cast instead. But Colbert suffered a back injury on the set of her Fox film *Three Came Home* (1950), and she was replaced by Bette Davis, who made the role her very own.

It was announced on February 19 that Hedy had signed a lucrative deal with Paramount Pictures, whose powers were very much impressed with her work in *Samson and Delilah*. She now agreed to star in *Copper Canyon,* another film in Technicolor, to be directed by John Farrow. Nominated for a Best Director Oscar in 1943 for Paramount's *Wake Island,* Farrow was a complicated man who was married to the actress Maureen O'Sullivan and the father of seven children, including the future actress Mia Farrow. As a director Farrow could be a hard, driven taskmaster. For the Western Hedy's leading men were Ray Milland, the recent Best Actor Oscar winner for Paramount's *The Lost Weekend,* and Macdonald Carey.

The forty-five-year-old Welsh-born Milland and his wife Malvina were longtime friends of Hedy's. Billed as Raymond Milland, the six-foot-two actor was brought to Hollywood in 1930 and appeared in several nondescript films. Eventually working his way up to leading man opposite the likes of Claudette Colbert, Carole Lombard, and Frances Farmer, he starred with John Wayne and Paulette Goddard in DeMille's 1942 Technicolor adventure yarn *Reap the Wild Wind* for Paramount. After his Oscar win in 1945, his popularity, for some unaccountable reason, began to decline.

The story of *Copper Canyon,* written by Richard English and turned into a screenplay by Jonathan Latimer, takes place in post–Civil War Coppertown, where former Confederates seek their fortune mining. They are thwarted by Northerners who will only buy the Southerners' ore on their own terms for the local Balfour Smelter factory. The Southerners seek out a trickster named Johnny Carter (Ray Milland) to help them. Carter immediately sets out to impress Lisa Roselle (Hedy), the French-born proprietor of the local Rainbow Saloon. He makes an enemy of the town's crooked sheriff's deputy, Lane Travis (Macdonald Carey), and joins the small-town miners when they send their ore thirty miles away to another smelter in Mesa City, which Travis previously had prevented.

Lisa has been a part of the conspiracy against the Southerners. Travis asks her to stop Johnny from helping the miners, and she tries but fails to get him drunk. Johnny becomes a masked rider and breaks up Travis's attempt to wreck the ore train, but Travis steals the Southerners' ore profits and frames him. Johnny goes to jail, and Lisa, who has fallen in love with him, bribes a jailer to free him. Johnny bands together the small-town miners and heads a brigade, with Lieutenant Ord (Harry Carey Jr.), that leads a second group to stop Travis. In the ensuing battle Travis is killed. Now the miners are sure to get a fair deal, and Lisa and Johnny leave Coppertown to begin a new life together in San Francisco.

For *Copper Canyon* Hedy was paid $100,000 for five weeks' work, pro rata at $12,500 a week. Milland was paid his contractual salary of $120,000 for six and one half weeks. Harry Carey Jr. received $1,000 a week. Budgeted at $1,654,000 for a forty-day shoot, *Copper Canyon* began filming on April 14. The following day, on stage 17, Hedy completed her first scene.

Production progressed without incidents; however, Hedy became ill and was not able to film on May 7, when Farrow moved the production from stage 17 to stage 4. She returned on May 9, but by then filming was falling slightly behind. *Copper Canyon* wrapped on June 7, four days over schedule. (Farrow reopened the production on September 27 to shoot additional scenes and retakes, which brought production costs up another $56,000. Hedy, who was used in those sequences, was paid an additional $8,000.) The final cost of *Copper Canyon* came to $1,722,000. By the end of the picture, her friendship with Milland had changed. Though they had socialized in public in years gone by, now "Hedy did *not* like Ray Milland," recalled her friend Robert Osborne.[6]

Macdonald Carey, who once sat at Hedy's feet years before in New York singing German love songs with her, noted his experiences working with her in *Copper Canyon* in his diary: "Hedy Lamarr, I find, is still extraordinarily beautiful, but she is also bizarre," he wrote. "She has an army cot on the set on which she lies resting until the assistant director calls the actors in for the shot. As soon as John Farrow says, 'Cut,' she goes back to the cot and lies down. . . . Hedy was always distant and cool, very much a European."[7]

Young Harry Carey Jr. was just twenty-eight years old when he appeared in *Copper Canyon.* Most of his scenes were with Mona Freeman and Ray Milland. But he does recall the square-dance sequence he did with Hedy:

> I don't think I had any dialogue with Hedy. She didn't come to rehearsals. There was Mona Freeman and myself, and the dance director, and Hedy's stand-in. So on the day they were shooting it, Hedy didn't know what to do. So, she turned to Farrow and said, "This young man doesn't know the dance." And he says, "It's not the young man. It's you, Hedy." Well, she got mad. She didn't get along well with Farrow. She never caused any more trouble after that.[8]

When her scenes were completed on the film, Hedy traveled to New York on her way to Europe for holiday. She brought along with her the script for *Vigilante* by Richard Sommers, a Barbary Coast story that the actor Joel McCrea and director Jacques Tourneur were hoping she would consider. Also in hand was another screenplay, *The Glittering Hill,* by Clyde Murphy, which the director Lloyd Bacon had given her to read. By the time she returned to the States, Hedy had declined both projects.

Hedy vacationed on the Riviera, in August renting a car and picking up the actor Burgess Meredith so the two could spend a week together in Deauville. Sailing from England aboard the Cunard liner, RMS *Queen Mary* later that month, she arrived in New York on August 25 for a few days. Flying on to Toronto on August 29 to be with the children, Hedy went unnoticed at the terminal when she arrived. Denise and Anthony had been vacationing in Canada since April, during which time Denise also had her tonsils removed.[9] The children were then sent on to California, and Hedy returned to New York and announced to the press that she wanted to do a play.

Paramount devoted almost a full year to postproduction and promotion for DeMille's *Samson and Delilah.* Magazine ads featured Hedy and Victor Mature advertising everything from cigarettes (Raleigh) to soda pop (RC Cola).

Kellogg's Corn Flakes even featured pictures of Victor Mature in Samson costume on the front of each box of cereal.

DeMille and Paramount both wanted Hedy to do promotion for the picture. On September 7, while she was staying at the Margery Hotel on Park Avenue, DeMille sent the following telegram:

> *If one tax collector is worth a thousand soldiers, then one Delilah is worth a thousand press agents. I cannot promise you that the air will be sweet with myrrh or that the flight of ibis will darken the sky, but the Council asks that you aid them in leading the great American public to worship at the feet of the woman who rules the ruler of the Five Cities.*[10]

But Hedy refused to participate, and actor Henry Wilcoxon became DeMille's official "ambassador" of promotion for *Samson and Delilah* and was sent out on a monthlong speaking tour during September to talk up the film. (After traveling to fourteen cities in twenty-eight days, the actor collapsed with pneumonia. The Paramount press agent Richard Condon finished the tour without him.)

When DeMille screened the picture, Harold Lamb, who had written the first treatment in 1935, told him, "This is a great picture, and the critics will slaughter you for it."[11] When the 120-minute film previewed in New York on October 17, Ivan Spear, the reviewer for *Boxoffice,* raved, "The lion's share of the acting honors undisputedly falls to Hedy Lamarr, who grows to unheralded and unexpected thespian stature as the seductive, sexy, scantily-clad and ravishingly beautiful siren. . . . It is Lamarr who gives the picture its Sex—with a capital quotient."[12] And the reviewer in *Showmen's Trade Review* agreed: "For the famous couple, Victor Mature and Hedy Lamarr are ideal choices. . . . Miss Lamarr is just about everyone's conception of the fair-skinned, dark-haired, beauteous Delilah, a role tailor-made for her, and her best acting chore to date."[13]

Samson and Delilah made its world premiere in New York at two theatres, the New York Paramount and the Rivoli, on Wednesday, December 21, 1949. Crowds were estimated at 3,500 for the Paramount opening, with lines stretching down both sides of the street for an entire block on 43rd Street between Broadway and Eighth Avenue; an estimated 2,000 lined up for the Rivoli premiere. Bosley Crowther of *The New York Times* wrote:

The first thing to be said about it, before the echoes have even died, is that, if ever there was a movie for DeMillions, here it is. . . . Victor Mature as Samson is a dashing and dauntless hunk of man whose hair is handsomely tonsured and whose face is as smooth as a baby's check. And Hedy Lamarr as Delilah is a sleek and bejeweled siren whose charms have a strictly occidental and twentieth-century grace and clarity.[14]

At the film's Los Angeles premiere on Thursday, February 2, 1950, DeMille asked Groucho Marx what he thought of the picture. Said one account, "Groucho replied, 'Well there's just one problem, C.B. No picture can hold my interest where the leading man's tits are bigger than the leading lady's.' DeMille was not amused, but Mature supposedly was."[15]

For all its hype and spectacle, good acting and bad, *Samson and Delilah* is what it is—pure escapism and fun to watch. With its sumptuous sets, magnificent Technicolor, and glorious music by Victor Young, *Samson and Delilah* is a prime example of the biblical cinema, a spectacle that truly marks it as a film of the 1950s.

Hedy's face graced the cover of *Newsweek* on November 28, 1949, and the magazine proclaimed her a "sex symbol unequalled for pure muzzle velocity in the Western World."[16] Throughout *Samson and Delilah* Hedy's acting is much better than the script called for. The director's penchant for assigning every crony bit player a line and dragging out a response shot for each ham actor to deliver his declamatory proclamation ("Look at Delilah!"; "Danites come ta woyship Dagon, heh?"; "Semadar is pretty as a poyle"; etc.) is actually part of the fun of watching DeMille's films. His antiquated screenplays were never masterpieces of literature, and it had to have been difficult for serious actors when they were required to utter such lines as, "Oh, Samson! What will come of you on the road you travel?" or "Bring in a woman and you bring in trouble" or "He was so strong . . . why did he have to die?"

What is always sad to witness (in all DeMille's pictures) is the performance of Julia Faye; here she plays Haisham, Delilah's servant. Faye never made it in talkies, try as DeMille earnestly did to make her a star. Her acting was always hopelessly amateurish, and her voice lacked character and inevitably seemed squeaky. In one scene she nasally warns Delilah in all somberness, "The trouble ya brew today, ya will drink tomorrah."

And the Old Man had a penchant for several other things that appear time and time again in his pictures. There is always at least one confrontational scene between the "good" woman and the "bad" wanton, just to keep the audience on its toes and to remind it what is going on. Also, in *Samson and Delilah,* there is constant reference to cats and lions: "Samson, you are rather like a lion"; and, when Delilah says, "Oh, Samson," his reply is, "One cat at a time." Then there are the references to cattle—the "milk-face girl with the cow eyes" and Samson's comment after Prince Ahtur has married Semadar (a line that somehow passed the censors), "If you had not plowed my heifer, you would not know the answer to my riddle."

One line in *Samson and Delilah* that is classic is "Where's your god now, Samson?" It echoes another line that the Brooklyn-born Edward G. Robinson allegedly uttered in DeMille's 1956 remake of *The Ten Commandments* (imagine his 1931 *Little Caesar* character speaking): "Where's your god now, Moses?" In truth, Robinson does not actually say the line in that picture. Yet these are the DeMillian touches that make his films so enjoyable.

When Samson and Delilah, chased by Ahtur's chariots, encounter the ferocious roaring lion in the desert (were there lions on the desert in the land of Minoa?), Delilah reaches for a spear and pleads with Samson, "Here . . . kill him before they get here." To which Samson casually replies, "I won't need that. He's a young lion." And every time there is a battle, Samson manages to pick up and pitch a struggling soldier, knocking down twenty others—amazing feats of strength coupled with bad acting. And, just to toss in a little questionable Hollywood history, DeMille has one merchant present some fabric and declare, "Here's a new weave from the looms of Gaza—they call it gauze." ("Aaahhh . . .")

Hedy is beautiful in this, her first, Technicolor film. DeMille's close-ups of her are gorgeous. The cost of her twelve costumes for the epic totaled $12,230. The famed peacock-feathered robe is only briefly seen, then casually tossed aside.

Of her final sequence with Mature, as Delilah leads Samson up the steps of the Temple of Dagon to the two pillars, Hedy recalled many years later,

> More stairs, only this time . . . I'm ascending them, dragging poor, blinded Victor Mature by the handle of a whip. The set is as gigantically faint-making as anything Mr. DeMille ever conceived, and every single extra within a 50 mile radius seems to be assembled as I slowly lead Samson to the top, where he is scheduled to pull the two enormous pillars of the

temple down around his ears and everyone else's. And do you know what I'm thinking as I watch this panoply on my television screen? Quite simply, it is "I can't take another step in those damned forties high heels!"[17]

DeMille, pleased with Hedy's performance, once said,

The casting was risky. If it turned out that my two leads had nothing to give to the story but the appearance of male strength and female beauty, however superlatively they shone in those qualities, the real point of the story would be lost. But when I saw the rushes of the scene in the grist mill, of Samson mocked in agony and Delilah discovering that the man she has loved and betrayed is now blind, I knew, if I had not known before, that the talents of Victor Mature and Hedy Lamarr are more than skin-deep.[18]

Hedy's definitive Delilah remains one of her best roles. Hedy's most memorable line in the picture perhaps best represents the woman and the character in one, as Delilah says to Samson after she betrays him, "No man leaves Delilah!"

Samson and Delilah would eventually bring in $5,564,825.17 upon its domestic release, the highest box-office earnings of any film in over three years (after Samuel Goldwyn's 1946 *The Best Years of Our Lives*). Eventually, it would earn $11.5 million for the Paramount coffers, surpassing the grosses of the reissued *Gone with the Wind* that year and becoming *the* highest-grossing picture of the decade and the highest-grossing Paramount picture up to that time.

In 1950 *Samson and Delilah* was nominated for five Academy Awards: for Best Score of a Dramatic or Comedy Picture (Victor Young); Best Special Effects (Paul K. Lerpae, Gordon Jennings, Devereaux Jennings); Best Cinematography, Color (George Barnes); and it would win two—Best Art Direction–Set Direction, Color (Hans Dreier, Walter H. Tyler, Sam Comer, Ray Moyer) and Best Costume Design, Color (Edith Head, Dorothy Jeakins, Elois Jenssen, Gile Steele, Gwen Wakeling).

Hedy was in New York, where *Samson and Delilah* was playing to packed houses. She had also been in talks with her former studio M-G-M regarding her first film of the three-picture commitment with them, *Visa*. Hedy was at the peak of her box-office popularity. And what Metro was offering Hedy for this picture deal was definitely *not* quality material.

Mayer had asked Hedy to attend a business meeting on the Metro lot before she left for New York. When she arrived, he introduced her to a gathered group of studio executives and producers. As he began his pitch for his projected film, Hedy recalled, "He was always careful with his wordage to *bend* the truth, not break it." Mayer began, according to Hedy, by telling the gathering how pleased he was that Hedy had returned to Metro and that the film he had for her would "out-gross *Samson and Delilah*." And, he said, its plot dealt with modern-day issues, which was perfect for her. Mayer then led her into his office, and the two old combatants hammered out the fine points of the agreement.[19]

After reminding Hedy that when she had left the studio she was being paid $7,500 a week, Mayer, wanting to renegotiate, now was willing to offer her $10,000 a week with a four-week guarantee, plus script approval. Hedy smiled and told Mayer, "So, now that you have presented your side, now let me present mine. . . . Yes, I do want to read the script but I will give you a fast answer. And as to price . . . I will do [the picture] for a flat fee of $100,000." Mayer, somewhat stunned, said simply as he rose from his desk, "Let's see . . . I offered you $40,000. You want $100,000. No deal. I wish you all the luck in the world. Maybe there is some studio that will give you $100,000. MGM just doesn't do those things."[20]

Without replying, Hedy carefully rose and began to walk out. But Mayer stopped her with, "Hedy, I'd really like you to do [this picture] for us. As an old friend, as your discoverer, what is your true bottom price you will do it for?" Hedy would not budge. Mayer then offered her a deal guaranteeing her $75,000, and at that point Hedy knew she could squeeze just a bit more out of her old boss. "You have offered me a $75,000 guarantee. I will waive reading the script, take a $90,000 guarantee and consider it a deal." Mayer agreed, and then opened his desk drawer to show her something. Pleased with himself as always, he said to her, "See, the tape machine still rolls."[21]

Hedy's agents were less than enthusiastic about her negotiation with Mayer. Proud of herself for getting that much money, Hedy had also made the fatal mistake of waiving script approval. The film Mayer had proposed to her, the picture that would outgross *Samson and Delilah,* was a minor-league potboiler dealing with immigration. Unfortunately, it would have very limited audience appeal. None of the characters in the story were sympathetic, especially her character, who is working against U.S. authority.

Still, Hedy was pleased that she had made such a financially secure deal. And she was confident that Metro would not have asked her to star in the picture unless they believed in its potential. Her agents explained to her that of the thirty to forty pictures M-G-M had slated for the year, they knew some would be programmers, designed to fill the demand for pictures at the theatres, and they all would need a big star to carry the film. They advised her at this point that she had to do the best work she could with the material.

The story line of *Visa* was set in Cuba. Pete Karczag (John Hodiak) is a U.S. immigration inspector who poses as a refugee, Josef Gombush, trying to gain acceptance into the United States, as he attempts to find evidence against a man named Palinov (George Macready), who heads an alien-smuggling ring. Karczag, as Gombush, contacts Palinov in Havana at Palinov's establishment the Gulf Stream Café and meets a beautiful Hungarian refugee, Marianne Lorress (Hedy), whom he falls in love with.

Marianne wants to emigrate to the United States. Her father, an illegal alien, is already there. Palinov becomes jealous of Marianne's feelings toward Gombush and soon finds out his true identity as Karczag. Palinov turns Marianne against Karczag by telling her he is using her for a dupe. Even though if she married Karczag she would automatically become an American citizen, Marianne feels betrayed and joins forces with Palinov in her illegal flight to the United States.

Karczag advises his immigration boss in Florida, Frank Westlake (James Craig), about the alien-smuggling plan, and Westlake sends navy aircraft out to begin a search. A plane starts tailing the smugglers' small aircraft. Palinov becomes aware of it and crash-lands his plane, with Marianne and others aboard, into the Florida Everglades to avoid capture. Karczag heads to the site, and he eventually catches up with Palinov and Marianne, who have escaped in a life raft to reach a motorboat that is waiting for them. Karczag outwits Palinov and rescues Marianne, who now realizes she was wrong to try to enter the country illegally. She is in love with Karczag and is ready to pay the penalty for her illegal actions.

Metro had changed considerably in the five years since Hedy had worked there. The pecking order of the stars was no longer in her favor. *Visa* (or *A Lady Without Passport* as it became known) was technically a throwaway picture for the studio. Hedy, unfortunately, had jumped at the money.

Though she may have had her doubts about her new film, Hedy was surrounded by many friends who cared about her. The beautiful red-haired actress Arlene Dahl, who had just signed with M-G-M, met Hedy in the studio hair designer Sydney Guilaroff's salon. "I gave her a compliment the first time I ever met her, and I told her she was the most beautiful woman I had ever seen," recalled Dahl in 2008. "Of course, she'd heard that many times before. But as a young girl, I thought it was something she'd like to hear again, and she did. . . . We chatted and she invited me to have lunch with her in the commissary. And, you know, we struck up a friendship. She told me she was very lonely, and I thought, how in the world could someone as beautiful as she be lonely?"[22]

Filming began in early January. John Hodiak was chosen for Hedy's leading man. Currently under contract with the studio, Hodiak came to films in 1943 and made quite an impression in such pictures as Alfred Hitchcock's *Lifeboat* (1944) and *A Bell for Adano* (1945), both for Twentieth Century–Fox; in Metro's *The Harvey Girls* (1946), with Judy Garland; and in *Homecoming* (1948), with Clark Gable. In 1946 Hodiak married the actress Anne Baxter.

Quite capable as an actor, Hodiak was not exactly the right choice for this film. Hodiak simply did not have the charisma to offset Lamarr's intense glamour. But Hedy and Hodiak became good friends, and during the filming Hedy helped him with his Hungarian, which he was required to speak in the film. When he and his wife met with Hedy one evening, she was most interested in a new camera that Anne had purchased the previous Christmas, a stereorealist. These unique cameras took stereo-optic images and were popular in the 1950s. Hodiak would later recall, "She wanted to know how I liked it, how the pictures were projected afterward, and whether there were any 'bugs' that might plague an amateur who undertook to operate such a camera."[23] Hedy's mind was at work, as always.

During the production of *A Lady Without Passport,* Hedy would arrive at the studio every day in a simple white blouse, casual flannel slacks, a camel-hair coat, and a bandanna around her head. Her costumes for the picture, designed by Helen Rose, were primarily white garments, and, if the situation called for it, they were wrinkled at Hedy's insistence.

In January, on one of her days off from Metro, Hedy met with DeMille for lunch. She wore a lovely, "new look" dark dress, its hemline nearly down to her ankles, and strands of pearls. DeMille wanted to discuss the possibility of her appearing as the high-wire walker in his upcoming production, *The Greatest Show on Earth*. It was just a pleasant little chat at a chic Hollywood restaurant, but DeMille saw to it that the press was in attendance. According to Hedda Hopper, "C.B. asked the lady if she'd reconsider and do some interviews. She replied, 'As soon as I get your check.'"[24] Hedy now had a new accountant, Owen Ward. Everybody, including Hedy's agents, talked to Ward first.

DeMille somehow had maneuvered Hedy into attending a performance of a circus with him just days before, to get her take. "'She amazed me in her reaction to this shock treatment,' said DeMille, 'but then Hedy always amazes me. She has that impenetrable calm of a Medusa. . . . She is a challenge. Her impassive air is one you want to break down.'"[25]

At the luncheon the two discussed the possibility of Hedy's also starring in another DeMille production, *Thais,* a tale about an Egyptian courtesan converted into penitence by a holy man who lusts after her, for which DeMille was trying to develop a workable script that would appease the censors. He also suggested they work together on a film about Salome called *The Queen of Queens.*

"I believe that the actor in a picture should be creative, and I am sure that Mr. DeMille also believes that," Hedy told the press. "His understanding of his people proves it, the manner in which he allows them to show what they have to offer on the picture set. Mr. DeMille has both knowledge and charm such as few people have. I respect and admire both these qualities in him. When he gets mad I do not listen." To which DeMille replied, "When I get mad I just look at her and that ends it."[26]

When *A Lady Without Passport* completed production in late February, Hedy flew back to New York, which was now becoming her second home. She made her television debut on March 4, 1950, when she was seen on the 1950 New York Heart Fund drive, broadcast over WPIX-TV live from New York. The four-hour telethon was hosted by Ed Sullivan; also appearing on the show were such stars as George Raft, Bob Hope, and Kirk Douglas.

After the telecast, Hedy traveled on to the Naples Beach Club in Florida, where she wired Cecil B. DeMille on March 14:

> DEAR C.B. HOPE YOURE FEELING WELL AND NOT WORKING
> TOO HARD. WOULD YOU BE SO KIND AS TO LET ME KNOW
> RIGHT AWAY TO NAPLES BEACH CLUB FLORIDA YOUR DECISION
> CONFIRMING MYSELF IN CONNECTION WITH CIRCUS PICTURE
> AND IF SO THE TIME SCHEDULE AS I HAVE
> A MOST ATTRACTIVE AND UNUSUAL STAGE OFFER FOR FALL
> AS ALWAYS YOUR EVER LOVING
> DELILAH[27]

DeMille's immediate response was sent on March 15:

> *Dear Hedy: I arrive in Sarasota Wednesday to make some photo-*
> *graphic tests. I haven't even started to cast as I do not have the*
> *story any where near set. I may not start shooting for a year.*
> *"SAMSON AND DELILAH" continue their triumphant progress*
> *through the world. As ever.*
>
>   *C.B.*[28]

If indeed there was a play offer, it apparently did not pan out. With time on her hands, Hedy spent April on holiday and returned to Hollywood at the end of the month in the company of her latest suitor, whom she had met in New York. Cholly Knickerbocker (aka Igor Cassini, the brother of Oleg) reported for *The Los Angeles Examiner* that Hedy was not only seeing wealthy playboy Herbert "Herbie" Klotz and the Texas oil-and-hotel magnate Glenn McCarthy but also the actor Bruce Cabot. But it was Klotz who had been Hedy's Manhattan beau for months. When he discovered Hedy was back in New York in April, reported Cassini, "Herbie, who was then down in Rio on business, dropped everything and flew up to meet his Hedy."[29] All New York speculated whether the two would marry. When she flew to California, Hedy told the press that she was in no hurry to wed. "My life is centered here in my home."[30]

Hedy was scheduled to take yet another holiday, to Palm Beach with former beau Woolworth "Wooly" Donahue, but she canceled it and flew off instead to Naples, Florida, with Herbie. His father, the Jewish millionaire Herbert Klotz Sr., had wisely moved his family and fortune to Switzerland when Hitler came to power. Arriving in New York at the outbreak of World War II, Herbie Jr., at six-foot-three and attractive with wavy blond hair, became somewhat of a debutante's delight. Society columns buzzed about him dating young Sari Gabor (before her name changed to Zsa Zsa). Herbie was in his midthirties when he met Hedy.

Over the years, Hedy had collected valuable pieces of art, and she now owned *The Homecoming* by Grandma Moses, a magnificent oil by Amedeo Modigliani, and priceless other pieces by Georges Rouault, Pierre Bonnard, and Maurice Utrillo. When she was home, Hedy actually did a lot of her own cooking, favoring Hungarian dishes. This was Hedy's "Hungarian phase," and at Christmastime she would make traditional Hungarian cookies for the children and for them to give as presents to their friends. Hedy always enjoyed music, and at the studio during the shooting of *A Lady Without Passport*, she brought her portable record player and listened to musical-comedy collections of *Brigadoon, Kiss Me Kate, South Pacific,* and *Finian's Rainbow.* John Hodiak recalled that Hedy favored Hungarian gypsy dances.

In interviews, Hedy referred to her son Jamie as being, more times than not, "off in Europe at school." Denise recalled that Marvin Neal had told her once that James was difficult, and Hedy just did not know what to do with him. However, she loved her children. Denise also would recall that some of her earliest clothes were made by her mother, little hand-knit dresses, booties, blankets, and hats.

Hedy's mother, Trude, had secured a job as a garment inspector with the renowned Lanz of Salzburg in Los Angeles, a clothing store, indirectly because of Hedy. She would remain with the company for thirty-six years. "Mom was very involved with Werner Scharf, the owner," Denise said of Hedy. "She would wear his clothing and bathing suits. It made him become a success. All his clothing had a kind of Austrian feel to it, and she loved it and would wear his clothing and kind of put him on the map. I mean, to this day, the little flannel nightgowns which are very Austrian with hearts and flowers are still selling even after his death. . . . Lanz was part of our life."[31] Hedy remained bound to her Austrian youth and culture. It made her feel at home. Every Christmas she would give Denise a flannel Lanz nightie.

Trude was an excellent seamstress and also made a lot of the clothing she, her daughter, and her grandchildren would wear. As a little girl, Denise called her grandmother Grangi. Denise recalled that Trude sometimes cooked for them and made wonderful sandwich fillings. Trude maintained her own apartment, living alone, though Hedy would still assist her with her monthly bills.

During the filming of *A Lady Without Passport*, both Anne Baxter and Hedy were invited to an important Sunday-afternoon soirée, an invitation that Hedy declined. She had promised Denise and Anthony to take them to a recreation center on La Cienega Boulevard. "So that's what I'm going to do," she told the Hodiaks. "It is important to keep a promise that one has made to a child. A broken promise is, to a child, simply a lie that one has told. I don't want my children to feel, ever, that I have misled them or that I have failed to live up to my promises."[32]

On the other hand, Hedy's habit of last-minute changes affected her friendship with Arlene Dahl. Dahl had just finished filming the musical *Watch the Birdie* (M-G-M, 1950) in Texas and had struck up a friendship with a wealthy Texan who lived in Mexico. (He had taken her shopping for a yellow diamond once at Neiman Marcus.)

"I knew he was single and a very nice man," Dahl recalled in 2008. "I just didn't connect with him. . . . I said, 'I have the perfect person for you to meet.' And he said, 'But I like you.' And I said, 'If you like me you'll like her better.' And he said, 'Who is it?' And I said, 'Hedy Lamarr . . . and she's wonderful and she's lonely, and you'll be the perfect person for her.'" Dahl explained, "So I set up a dinner in my house for eight to ten people. And of course I invited him alone, and I invited her." When Dahl called Hedy to tell her she was throwing the party just for her and that she wanted Hedy to meet the man, Dahl says, "Hedy asked, 'Is he handsome?' And I said, 'He's attractive. I won't say he's as handsome as John Loder or [Dahl's future husband] Fernando Lamas or any of the handsome men. But he's loaded and he wants to meet you.'"

Hedy accepted, and then telephoned one hour before the party complaining of a headache. Dahl was frantic, since the Texan had just called to get Hedy's address to pick her up. Dahl pleaded with her, "Hedy, this party is for you. All for you! You're the honored guest." Her reply was, "I know darling, but I just don't feel up to it." Dahl replaced Hedy with her young roommate Shirley Smith, the actress Constance Moore's stepsister, and she and the Texan hit it off. "So that was the end of my matchmaking for Hedy Lamarr," Dahl concluded. "And we weren't terribly friendly after that. . . . I liked her enormously but she did let me down when I tried to help her."[33] Hedy seldom took responsibility for her impulsive behavior.

In the coming years, many of Hedy's actions would contradict her motivations and cause irrevocable harm to her friends, her family, and herself.

17

Adrift

Hedy planned to spend the summer of 1950 in New York on Long Island. Robert Lantz of the Gale Agency, Inc., in New York, was her East Coast agent. On June 23 he forwarded C. B. DeMille a letter of inquiry regarding Hedy's future work with the director.

On July 11 Hedy sent DeMille a newspaper clipping on *Samson and Delilah* and a brief note advising him of her Long Island telephone number. His response was in a letter dated July 13:

> *Dear Hedy:*
> *Thank you for your note. I'll be at my grindstone all summer, envying you among the cool breezes of Easthampton—but hoping your summer will be completely delightful.*
> > *Sincerely,*
> > *Cecil B. DeMille.*[1]

Hedy and her two younger children flew to New York on July 14. Taking a cottage for the summer on the grounds of the fashionable Irving House in Southampton, she intended to make the social rounds out East. Meanwhile, on August 3, *A Lady Without Passport*, which Metro rushed through postproduction to capitalize on Hedy's sudden resurgence in popularity, opened to respectable reviews. It was nationally released on August 18.

After the picture's premiere in Los Angeles on September 14 at the Orpheum and Hawaii theaters, G. K. of the *Los Angeles Times* commented on Hedy's performance, stating, "To be sure the beauteous Lamarr is frequently an innocent bystander while the plot moves around her, but she does manage a few emotional sockos in some of the love scenes. . . . Incidentally, Miss Lamarr could do with a little stage experience so far as enunciation is concerned."[2] One film scholar, getting more to the point, wrote, "This was the type of film Columbia didn't make any better but somehow had greater success with, when they presented Rita Hayworth in *Gilda* and *An Affair in Trinidad*."[3] Still, *A Lady Without Passport* represents M-G-M's attempt at film noir, a new and exciting genre at the time, which was brought to this country by the cinema exiles of Europe and which postwar audiences found compelling and tantalizing.[4] Critics of the time just did not get it.

Perhaps it is unfair to dismiss the seventy-four-minute *A Lady Without Passport* as quickly as did reviewers of the day. After its original roadshow tour, it unfortunately ended up on the bottom of the bill on many double features. Today, *A Lady Without Passport* represents where motion-picture making in Hollywood was going in 1950. *A Lady Without Passport* is *not* the type of film Metro would have made during Hollywood's golden era of the 1930s and early 1940s. But the fact that it is an M-G-M production is noticeable because of the quality of the craftsmen who made it. (In the Gulf Stream Café sequence, look carefully on the wall as the characters talk about immigration— there is a large picture of the French Line's SS *Normandie,* the very ship on which the young Hedy Kiesler arrived in America in 1937.)

And, in fairness, Hedy's performance is quite good. Opposite Hodiak she becomes at times fleetingly brilliant, especially in the scene in her room after Karczag rescues her from the police in Havana. When Hedy is not posing, she does fine work. And she looked stunning. Helen Rose designed her five different outfits for the picture, all done in white, except for one gratuitous single-shoulder-strapped, sequined creation that no cigarette girl, even in Cuba, would have been caught dead wearing.

In retrospect, the director, Joseph H. Lewis, produced a minor noir classic. His direction is crisp, at times intense. His camera angles are stirring, and his atmospheric scenes mesmerizing. The set and art designs Lewis uses place the film apart from the average melodrama.

Unfortunately, and as usual, Metro was hoping for a bigger box-office re-

turn with *A Lady Without Passport*. When that did not happen, M-G-M canceled the final two films for which Hedy was contracted.

On Thursday, August 20, while in Manhattan and staying briefly at the
Hotel Sherry-Netherland, located at Fifth Avenue and 59th Street, Hedy was
robbed of $250,000 of uninsured gems. That evening she had attended the the-
atre, and when she returned to her suite around midnight, she noticed the
small bag in which she carried her jewels open and lying on a dresser table.

Hedy did not report the robbery immediately but waited until the following
week, thinking that the gems, which included a diamond necklace, an eleven-
and-a-half-carat diamond ring, a three-strand pearl necklace, a single-strand
pearl necklace with diamond clip, and various other pieces purchased in Europe, might have been left at her residence in Southampton. Checking out of the
Sherry-Netherland she returned to the Irving House, and a search there revealed nothing. On August 26, she reported the theft to the Sherry-Netherland
manager, John Hermance, who in turn reported it to the police.

The following morning, two New York City detectives, Paul Omark and
Rudy McLoughlin, traveled the one hundred miles to Southampton to talk
with Hedy. Arriving at 10:30 A.M. at her small cottage on the grounds of the
Irving House, they were told by Hedy's Chinese houseboy that she had attended a party given by the banker Frederick Lewisohn the night before and
was still in bed and not receiving visitors. The houseboy woke Hedy, and, taking the house phone in the kitchen, Officer Omark spoke with her for twenty
minutes. She told him that she had nothing to say, and, though she was sorry
for the officers' long trip, there was nothing she could do about it. Arriving back
in Manhattan, the detectives spoke with their superiors, who then made telephone calls to Southampton. Hedy agreed to meet with detectives the following day at noon.

On August 28, Hedy called her home in Hollywood for pictures of the
missing jewels. She told the detectives, when she did speak with them, that she
had gone to New York on Thursday to consult with her agent, Robert Lantz.
On the way into the city, she and a male companion stopped by a golf-driving
range, leaving the bag of jewelry unattended in the car. But she was sure they
were with her in her hotel suite the evening she was robbed. She did not name
her companion in order to avoid causing him embarrassment. The case was
not mentioned in the news again for many years, except in an item by Louella
Parsons the following January. Parsons said, "There has always been a question

whether or not the jewels were returned. This is one subject Hedy doesn't discuss even with her closest friends."[5]

Hedy's romance with Herbie Klotz ended around August, and like the theft of the jewels, next to nothing was made of it in the press. Hedy was soon seen in the company of multimillionaire Woolworth Donahue. On September 17, wearing a lace bodice and strapless evening gown and looking gorgeous, Hedy guest-starred on CBS's *The Toast of the Town,* hosted by Ed Sullivan. On the show she uncomfortably sang "Rock a Bye Baby."

Back in California Robert Lantz was staying at her Roxbury home while she remained in New York. Lantz set up a meeting with DeMille, and the two men met that following Friday.

For DeMille's circus picture, the part of Holly was eventually changed from that of a tightrope walker to a trapeze artist, and when DeMille advised Hedy of the change in early October she chose not do it. He then offered her the secondary female lead of the elephant girl, Angel. Hedy flatly turned this role down, and she was officially out of the running for the film.[6]

Paramount executives were still put out with Hedy after she had refused to promote *Samson and Delilah* and told her she would never make another picture with them again. When she returned to the Paramount lot after filming *Copper Canyon* to empty out her dressing room, she ran into Bob Hope. As Hedy remembered it, Hope approached her while she was filling her car and they had the following exchange:

"Say, Hedy," he asked. "Are you available for a picture?"

"Not here," I said. "They hate me here because I wouldn't do a personal appearance tour for them."

"That's crazy," he grinned. "No red-blooded American male could hate you. Do you have time in your schedule for a picture with me?"

"I have time, but Paramount would never let me do a picture here—with you or anyone."

"Do you mind of I talk to Frank [Freeman, a Paramount executive]?"

Hope did talk to Freeman and reported back to Hedy, "You were right . . . they hate you. But I'll fix that. Here's what we have."[7] Handing her the script for *My Favorite Spy,* Hope explained the plot and talked about her character.

Hedy had mentioned back in 1945 that she would love to do a picture with

Hope. Somehow, the comedian ironed things out with Paramount, and she signed the contract. Hope was to receive his usual per-picture salary of $150,000. Hedy was to be paid $125,000 for ten weeks, pro rata at $12,500 a week thereafter. *My Favorite Spy* was set to roll on November 8, 1950, and to wrap on January 2, 1951. It was based on an unpublished story called "Passage to Cairo," by Edmund Beloin and Lou Breslow. This film would complete a trilogy of Hope's *"My Favorite . . ."* pictures for Paramount, the other two being *My Favorite Blonde* (1942), with Madeleine Carroll, and *My Favorite Brunette* (1947), with Dorothy Lamour.

My Favorite Spy was a merry romp, a spoof of the current wave of espionage movies in fashion during the cold war. It tells the story of Eric Augustine (Hope), a foreign spy on the lookout for a German scientist who holds the link to Augustine's finding a piece of microfilm containing a shortcut to the making of an atomic bomb. Augustine is captured by the police on his way to Tangier but manages to escape. The police in turn pick up a look-alike comic named Peanuts White (also Hope), whose appearance is so similar to Augustine's that when they finally capture the real spy, they induce Peanuts to travel to Tangier, impersonate Augustine, contact the scientist, and buy the microfilm for $1 million.

In Tangier, Peanuts becomes involved with a nightclub singer, Lily Dalbray (Hedy), who is Augustine's girl. She performs at the Aigrette Room at the Hotel Imperio. She is also part of a spy ring headed by Karl Brubaker (Francis L. Sullivan). Peanuts meets the scientist, Rudolf Hoenig (Luis van Rooten), and gets the microfilm, but he is hampered by Brubaker, who is in love with Lily. Brubaker then steals the microfilm. The plot thickens when the real Augustine escapes again and journeys to Tangier. After several mishaps, Augustine is killed, and Peanuts confesses his true identity to Lily. She joins forces with him as they attempt to recover the stolen microfilm. When they do, Brubaker is arrested, and the government gives Peanuts $10,000 as he and Lily leave Tangier to open a haberdashery in New Jersey.

My Favorite Spy is Hope's film all the way. He mugs, tells one-liners, is the butt of all sorts of jokes, and basically plays a buffoon. Hope was forty-eight years old when he made the picture, not a young man. Yet his character is the very same type he had been playing in films for almost twenty years. In nearly every stunt, even a simple tumble, an obvious double was used, indicating that Hope was not as spry as he had once been.

Production of *My Favorite Spy*, directed by Norman McLeod, was delayed until January. In October, through her agent, Hedy optioned the screen rights to the late Antoine de Saint-Exupéry's fantasy novel *The Little Prince*. It was also announced in the press that Greshler Productions, Inc., had just acquired the Robert Baragrey novel *Miss Nancy*, about the riverboat days, for Hedy's consideration. She did not accept the offer.

Just as *My Favorite Spy* was preparing to begin, *Copper Canyon* was released. Advertisements promised, "Adventure! Romance! All You've Ever Looked For in a Motion Picture!" and "A Great Cast . . . A Thrilling Story . . . Brilliantly Filmed in Technicolor!" The public was guaranteed "sock-o" entertainment with *Copper Canyon*. The film, it was reported, had been postponed because Paramount wanted to coincide its premiere with the release of the pop song "Copper Canyon," by Jay Livingston and Ray Evans. Its words were dreadful, but the unforgettable melody has become a classic.

When the picture opened nationally on November 16, 1950, Edwin Schallert in the *Los Angeles Times* was generous: "Miss Lamarr switches to a new province, where she can seemingly wear just as attractive garb as in any other film. . . . She is well set off in the picture, and gives a pleasing performance."[8] But Bosley Crowther, in *The New York Times*, was ruthless: "Miss Lamarr's top-flight luxuriance in a typical frontier-charmer role—the lady who switches from the villains to the hero—is patently absurd. If the whole thing were done as a travesty, it might be something else again. But Jonathan Latimer has written it without humor and John Farrow has directed it that way."[9]

Copper Canyon is visually a gorgeous Western film. The glorious panoramas of Sedona Valley and its surrounding vistas rival anything captured on film by the director John Ford. And *Copper Canyon* had the added plus of Technicolor. Ray Milland and Macdonald Carey take their roles seriously, and both offer up convincing performances. Unfortunately, Hedy does not. She seems distracted. Surely she was out of her element in a Western—but beautiful just the same in glorious Technicolor.

Edith Head designed eight costumes for Hedy in *Copper Canyon*, and she wore them splendidly. The picture's score, by Daniele Amfitheatrof, is wonderfully integrated throughout. Despite the fact that Milland "confessed in a later interview that he 'hated working with Hedy Lamarr,'" together they made a convincing and handsome couple.[10] *Copper Canyon* brought in the fans, and the picture took in $2.6 million in domestic grosses.

The *Los Angeles Times* mentioned that Hedy was being considered for the role of the duchess in a love triangle in the proposed filming of *Goya*, based on Lady Eleanor Smith's biography of the artist, to be produced by British Lion Studios. It was scheduled to star Desi Arnaz and to be filmed sometime in the spring. But the project fell through.

For the Christmas holiday, Hedy was home with her children. Little Denise was sent to boarding school, having been enrolled in Years for Nursery Rhymes Kindergarten in Los Gatos, and Anthony was still being cared for at home by the nanny, Frances Milner. Hedy remained an identifiable box-office star, and at the end of January an international poll of film favorites listed her, Lana Turner, and Esther Williams as the top-three female motion picture stars in, of all unexpected places, Egypt.

When *My Favorite Spy* went into production, Hedy's chauffeur, Marvin Neal, was contracted by Paramount at $150 a week. On February 1, Hedy, Hope, and the actors Mike Mazurki and Arnold Moss all stepped before the cameras on a studio backlot for a scene at Tangier Airport and on the street, the first sequences photographed.

The following day, February 2, both Hope and Hedy were late to the set by thirty minutes. Hope would continually be delinquent after lunch throughout the filming of *My Favorite Spy*, since he had to rush to the NBC studios to do his radio show during the break, and then rush back to the Paramount lot afterward. Between February 19 and March 31 the production fell seven days behind schedule. Officially wrapping on March 23 after thirty-nine camera days, *My Favorite Spy* came in at a cost of $1,614,000, approximately $350,000 over budget.

Hedy later admitted she was tired of the grind of filmmaking. Now in her midthirties she could sense her body tiring sooner. She still looked good, "but I had to confess I wasn't a kid anymore. My ambitions were as strong as ever, but the strength to push them wasn't. . . . I resolved to do *My Favorite Spy*, and then concentrate on finding a husband and one good picture."[11] Rumors of her impending retirement began to circulate about town.

According to Louella Parsons's *Los Angeles Examiner* column on January 24, the columnist received an unsolicited telegram that read:

> *Dear Louella,*
>   *To straighten out all various statements about my retiring from the screen I want you to know it is true for the simple reason*

that I would like the privilege of a private life. As for marriage it is the normal desire of any woman, when I find the man I love enough to be my husband and father of my children.

Fond love to you,

Hedy Lamarr[12]

Meanwhile, Cusick International Films, Inc., was hoping to secure Hedy to star opposite Rex Harrison in Henry Kurnitz's adaptation of a 1928 William Somerset Maugham short story, "His Excellency," set to begin shooting in London in July. Hedy declined.

Seriously considering her children's financial position, she filed a petition on March 2, 1951, in Los Angeles Superior Court for their guardianship. The petition declared that Hedy's adopted eleven-year-old son Jamie owned $3,000 in a real estate corporation and her five-year-old daughter Denise had a $6,000 investment in the same firm. Hedy stated that she had been given custody of the two children and four-year-old Anthony by their father, who lived in London.

Hedy forwarded a telegram to C. B. DeMille on March 14, no doubt to feel him out about a project he had mentioned for her, *Helen of Troy*:

DEAR C.B.

HAVE JUST BEEN DRIVING A FIRE TRUCK, DRIVING
A CHARIOT WOULD BE DELIGHTFUL CHANGE
YOUR EVERLOVING DELILAH OF TROY[13]

DeMille had indeed announced to the press that he was researching the story of Helen of Troy, and Hedy's name had been mentioned. On August 9, script work was begun by Jack Garris on the project, which DeMille announced as definite in December. However, development bogged down, and *Helen of Troy* would have to wait until another filmmaker and studio would pick it up. (In 1955, Warner Bros. did just that.)

Meanwhile, to keep active, on April 10 Hedy appeared on the thirty-minute variety program *The Bob Hope Show,* broadcast over NBC radio, in a skit entitled "From Coronado Island."

Earlier on that same day in her gossip column, Hedda Hopper had announced, "Hedy's taking her children to Mexico for a rather lengthy stay."[14]

She was headed to Acapulco. Hedy later recalled how much she and the children had loved the tropical sunshine and fresh air. Hedy lounged around the resort pool, saw the cliff divers, and was rested within a week. And bored. She then met the proprietor of a restaurant, whose name was one she was somewhat familiar with. For some time he had been mentioned in the press in connection with Rita Hayworth. His name was Teddy Stauffer.

Teddy was born Ernest Heinrich Stauffer in Murten, Switzerland, on May 2, 1909. After schooling he became a band leader. His band, the Original Teddies, had their first engagement at the Café Chapel in Gliwice in 1929. By the next year the Original Teddies were playing around Berlin, specializing in Swiss swing music. Their greatest popularity came while playing gigs during the 1936 Olympic Games and, later, at the famous Delphi Dance Hall in Berlin. By 1937, the Original Teddies' recording of "Goody Goody" had sold over 700,000 copies.

After the Third Reich banned "negro music," Stauffer took the "Horst Wessel Lied," the German national anthem, and adapted it into a jazz number in 1938. He was not punished only because of the recording's success. At the outbreak of war in Europe he returned to Switzerland, where Teddy Stauffer and the Original Teddies performed at the 1939 Swiss World's Fair. Stauffer then emigrated to Canada and then to America, where he offered the young Lena Horne a contract. His immigration status was challenged by U.S. authorities, and he quietly crossed over into Mexico in 1941.

Upon arriving in Mexico City, Teddy opened the Casanova Club in 1942. He eventually landed in Acapulco in 1943 and opened the Casablanca Club. He managed various hotels, where he turned the boys who dove from the cliffs into the sea for coins into entertainers. After starting up the club Villa Vera, Stauffer obtained a commercial property that he called the La Perla Night Club in 1949, again promoting the cliff divers of La Quebrada. Nicknamed Mr. Acapulco by the governor of the state of Guerrero, Teddy was also Mexico's official Ambassador of Hospitality. He almost single-handedly changed Acapulco from a tiny fishing village of eight thousand into an international holiday resort within a decade by inviting international stars and celebrities to vacation and play there.

By early 1951, Stauffer and his first wife, the actress Faith Domergue, had been divorced for almost four years. Teddy knew and entertained such celebrities and stars as Gary Cooper and Cooper's longtime love, the actress Patricia Neal; President Dwight Eisenhower; and Errol Flynn. Everybody loved Stauffer, even Hedy.

Her daughter Denise recalled years later that as a little girl, the only thing she could remember about Stauffer was that he was a rakishly handsome man.

Teddy was already somewhat successful when he met Hedy. "When I started dating Teddy he was broke," Hedy wrote. "I take some credit for starting him on his way. Not that he wouldn't have made it anyway, but it would have been much harder."[15] Teddy enjoyed Hedy's sitting around the hotel or the restaurant. It was good for business. She would attract tourists, and when she would go down to the beach, they would follow her.

Hedy was attracted to Teddy because he was industrious and hardworking. What she did not care for was his jealousy. One night, as she recounted in her book, she ran into the actress Dolores del Rio, who asked her to dinner. When Hedy returned to Stauffer's hotel around midnight, she was told he was looking for her. Finding him on a secluded path, Teddy coldly asked her where she had been. She told him. When he did not believe her, he grabbed her wrist and demanded the truth. Incensed, Hedy went back to the hotel where her children were sleeping peacefully. There was a knock at the door, and Teddy, very remorseful, begged for her forgiveness. According to Hedy, this became a repeated ritual.

Teddy proposed marriage, and when she returned to Hollywood with the children, he was also in tow. On the morning of June 11, Hedda Hopper mentioned in her column, "Between dances with Ted Stauffer at the Mocambo, Hedy Lamarr told me she has no plans for future pictures—'I've made a lot of them and I'm tired. I want to rest and have fun.' She leaves for San Francisco with her children for a brief vacation."[16] A clever dodge. Hedy married Teddy Stauffer in West Los Angeles that evening.

After obtaining a marriage license earlier in the day, Hedy, dressed in a pale three-quarter-length-sleeved summer dress, and Teddy, tall and blond in a dark suit and tie, were wed at the home of Judge Stanley Mosk. Their witnesses were Mr. and Mrs. William I. Hollingsworth and Hedy's attorney, William G. Israel, and his wife. The couple planned on taking Hedy's children on their honeymoon upstate to the art colony in Carmel. Hedy told the press, "I may make a picture. . . . If I do, and it isn't decided yet, it will be my last one. I am going to devote my life to him."[17] Now set to commit herself to being domestic, Hedy shocked the Hollywood community by putting up her belongings for sale and moving to Acapulco.

On June 18 it was announced in the *Los Angeles Times* that the American

Art Galleries, Louis E. Wass and Arthur B. Goode auctioneers, in Beverly Hills were auctioning a million dollars' worth of furnishings and personal effects belonging to Hedy, including various paintings, $250,000 worth of jewelry, 480 dresses and gowns, furs, lingerie, and over seventy-five pairs of shoes. Also listed among the items being placed on the block were "four wedding rings."

Friends were stunned. Hedy was selling most of her magnificent collection of art, which she had taken such pride in. As Hedy, with her five-year-old daughter and her new husband, strung beads on the beach in Carmel, the auction house went to work itemizing her household belongings.

Because she was leaving Hollywood so quickly, according to the auctioneer, she had even left food in the icebox. Two huge moving vans pulled up to the house a day or so later, and it was emptied out. The press made a heyday out of the event.

The auction's first session began on June 25. Included were her fabulous paintings—the priceless Modigliani, an Utrillo, the Grandma Moses, a Chagall, a sculpted piece by Rodin, porcelains, china, a Steinway grand piano, crystal, and her diamond and precious-stone jewelry. Among the items were red-leather-bound copies of all her film scripts, a plaque that was given to her in 1942 for her work on behalf of the Motion Picture Relief Fund, and an autographed lobby card display from *Samson and Delilah* signed by DeMille himself. Her Steinway piano was purchased by the songwriter Jimmy McHugh for $2,400, and her bed sold for $250 to a Burbank aircraft-supply-company owner who bought it for his three-and-a-half-year-old daughter. And Hedy's "four" wedding rings (actually only three, one thick-banded ring had been cut in two so Hedy could add gems to it) went for $1,605 total—two for $25, and the gem-encrusted third one for $1,525 (the buyer found it matched her engagement ring). Going for $30 was the one plain gold-band ring, item number 660, inscribed inside, "Du Bist Mein Einzi' Leben" ("You Are My Only Life"). It was from Fritz.

As the auction proceeded, it was noted that the auctioneers were constantly being distracted as Hedy kept calling in to ask for various dresses and pieces of lingerie back. Also telling was a tin can the movers found when loading up belongings from Hedy's home. It rattled, and upon opening the tin, the auctioneers discovered gem-encrusted necklaces, lockets, bracelets, earrings, and other pieces of jewelry valued at over $2,500. Said Goode, "Only a woman would use a coffee can as a safety-deposit vault and then forget about it."[18] For the some 5,000 items on the block, the final take would be close to $1 million.

Hedy was burning bridges as fast as she could light the matches. Noble though her reasons may have appeared to her, in reality the move was desperately rash. When asked why she was leaving Hollywood and breaking with the past, her reply was long, somewhat bitter, rambling, and psychologically confounding:

> There are times when the past is dead and should be buried. . . . When my father died and I saw his empty chair, it reminded me of him, and that was bad. Now that I am married to a new husband, I don't want to have things around that will remind him of my old life when we are starting a fresh one. I don't think it is good if everything a husband sees reminds him of other lives that were not his. A man likes to feel a man. He expects to take care of a wife. His home should be his home, not hers. I want us to start out even, making a home like a young bride and groom. If we have an ashtray, it should be as much his as mine. There was a time when I never threw things away, but now I am through with all that. . . . I am through with Hollywood and the movies. . . . I am through with pictures, unless I make them where my husband is. . . . If someone offers me a picture where my husband will be, I may make it there.[19]

Hedy flew off to Acapulco with her children and new husband on July 12, as the auction continued. In fairness to Teddy, he had warned Hedy she would not like living permanently in Acapulco, even though his La Perla was beginning to thrive, thanks in no small part to her presence there. Yet he appreciated her desire to live there. When Hedy enrolled six-year-old Denise and five-year-old Anthony into school, they immediately disliked it, and for several reasons. Acapulco schools were dirty, and lizards ran across the floors. Worse, the Loder children knew no Spanish. Denise and Anthony lasted but one day in school. But Hedy was in love, and romance took priority.

Many famous celebrities would come to Acapulco, and they would stop by La Perla or stay at the El Mirador. Ava Gardner visited in early August with her lover Frank Sinatra (they would soon wed), and they stayed there. "I showed them how to enjoy the beaches and the bay," Hedy wrote.[20] They went out their first day at La Perla with their hosts, and Sinatra became incensed when Hedy focused her attention on him and totally ignored Ava. Stauffer had once courted Gardner himself, but Sinatra swore reprisals against Hedy for his imagined slight.

Film offers surprisingly continued to be offered to Hedy. American Pictures wanted her for *Sword of Venus* (1953), a decidedly B project; Universal wanted either Hedy, Ann Blyth, or Joanne Dru to replace Claudette Colbert in *The Korean Story;* and the Paramount producer Jerry Wald and the writer Norman Krasna sent the script of *Pilate's Wife* to Hedy in hopes of coaxing her to play Salome, as negotiations continued to secure Laurence Olivier and Vivien Leigh for the parts of Pilate and Claudia.

Hedy flew back to Hollywood briefly during her marriage to perform in "Samson and Delilah" with Victor Mature on *The Lux Radio Theater,* which was broadcast on November 19. With DeMille no longer associated with the program, it was just not the same. As television took a foothold on the industry, radio drama was becoming obsolete. Still, for her legions of fans, it was wonderful to hear Hedy's lilting voice once again as she portrayed Delilah.

As *My Favorite Spy* approached its release, Bob Hope kept telling Hedy that he would provide the laughs, and she would supply the sex appeal. He had brought her flowers, and literally courted her into accepting the role in the picture, and thus Hedy was never quite sure of Hope's intentions. She wrote that when the film wrapped, "my sigh of relief must have been heard in Vienna."[21] When Paramount asked Hedy to go on a promotional tour for the picture, her response, again, was to ask for full salary and all her expenses. They refused.

The ninety-three-minute *My Favorite Spy* was previewed in October. The critic of *The Hollywood Reporter* said, "Of course, as a sultry siren of international intrigue, Hedy Lamarr is a delight to the eye and just the foil Hope needs to enliven the romantics."[22] *Film Bulletin* wrote, "*My Favorite Spy* is a Bob Hope comedy that rides high from start to finish. . . . With Hedy Lamarr as his sultry vis-à-vis, the romantics are wildly insane, and both stars deliver in grand manner."[23]

By December 29, 1952, *My Favorite Spy* had racked up $1,726,502.53 of business, and eventually it would earn $2.6 million in the United States, primarily on the strength of Bob Hope's popularity.

When Hedy saw the film, she was shocked. Some of her best comedic moments in the picture were cut. Hedy never forgave Hope, and he never forgave her for not doing PR before the film's release. "I didn't think we made that great of a teaming," she would say later. "We didn't look right together."[24]

Paramount's Edith Head once again designed the costumes for Hedy, six of them. And they were lovely creations that showed off her still-impressive figure. Victor Young composed the score, even incorporating his theme from *Samson and Delilah*. All in all, *My Favorite Spy* is a fun comedy, nothing more. Hedy was splendid in her brief scenes, and it is obvious that there were extended sequences that did not make the final cut. But why they were edited, or whether Hope actually insisted they be, is unclear. As the character Brubaker (played by the actor Francis L. Sullivan) comments at one point in the picture, "A man's subconscious is a maudlin swamp."

Within months of settling into Acapulco, Hedy knew she was in trouble. For her and Stauffer, there were many long, romantic, moonlit tropical nights of passion and lovemaking. And then there were endless days of sunlight and nothing to do except socialize and stay up late. But all the sophisticated refinements and excitement of nightlife in a big American city were then missing in Acapulco. For a brief escape, it was restful. For a way of life, only a few could adapt.

There were far too many arguments and recriminations between the two. Teddy was always jealous, Hedy would later say. He questioned her when male friends would come over for a drink while he was not around, and this would lead to arguments. (Perhaps he knew Hedy better than she wanted him to.) These arguments were followed by flowers and gifts, tears and forgiveness, and more lovemaking. And the dangerous cycle repeated itself over and over.

After just seven months, Hedy had had enough. "I bundled up the kids and my things and got out of that sickening 'paradise,'" she wrote.[25] Once again in her life, humiliated by her reckless and rash actions, Hedy swallowed her pride and headed back to California.

18

Italy

rriving in Hollywood on January 21, 1952, Hedy told the awaiting press that her plans were to obtain an immediate divorce and resume her life exactly where she had left it off eight months before. In a prepared statement regarding the end of her marriage, Hedy blamed the climate of Mexico and said it was bad for her children. She also said that when they had wed, she and Teddy were both frightfully lonely and that it never was a real marriage.

Hedy also admitted she had made a mistake. Through her attorney, William G. Israel, who had been a witness at her wedding in June, she filed a petition for divorce, claiming that her husband had "inflicted grievous physical and mental suffering" on her without provocation. She claimed no community property in her holdings, and she asked to resume the use of her professional name.[1] Teddy did not contest the divorce, but he categorically denied the physical-and mental-cruelty charges.

He, meanwhile, had begun dating the actress Gene Tierney, who had recently separated from her husband, Oleg Cassini. Tierney told the press that she was soon flying off to Europe to divorce her husband.

Hedy quickly received screen offers. The actor Cesar Romero advised the press in February that he was planning to set up his own film company. The project he selected would give Romero the Humphrey Bogart–type, rugged-he-man role he had always longed to do. It was called *The Ming Lama*, an adventure drama written by Blake Edwards, about an airline pilot entrusted with the safe delivery of a rare Chinese idol. Romero was hoping to sign Hedy to star opposite him, and the film would start production for United Artists in August. Neither Romero's production company nor the film ever saw flight.

A much better prospect for Hedy would have been *The Story of Esther,* a biblical saga, purchased by United Artists' president Arthur Krim for $25,000. It was written by Frank and Doris Hursley. The producer was negotiating with Glenn Ford for the role of Xerxes and Hedy for the role of Esther. *The New York Times* later reported that Hedy owned the property. Whoever actually held the rights for *The Story of Esther,* she did not make the film.

Darryl F. Zanuck at Fox offered Hedy a strong role in *The Snows of Kiliman-jaro* (1953), which was based on a short story by Ernest Hemingway, starred Gregory Peck and Susan Hayward, and was directed by Henry King. Hedy originally had accepted the part but then realized hers was a supporting character, and she reneged at the last minute. Ava Gardner replaced her. Hayward was not happy with Gardner in the picture.

Delighted to be back in Hollywood, Hedy took a plush $1,500-a-month rented house in Benedict Canyon, and her agents told her to accept work right away since producers did not like waiting to hear no.

The actor Farley Granger attended a private party at the home of the M-G-M songwriter Saul Chaplin and his wife, Betty Levin, and recalled seeing Hedy there. "She was very shy, very quiet, and very retiring," he recalled. "She just kind of receded almost into the woodwork. She kept very much to herself, you know. Saul and his wife, their parties were always about music; they were always playing the piano together, four hands, singing and entertaining and carrying on. And, at this one particular party, at one point they started playing Kurt Weill's 'Three Penny Opera,' and [Hedy] sparked into life immediately and got up and joined them at the piano, and it was a complete transformation. She was enchanting."[2]

Hedy did as she pleased. And that included taking a trip to Europe once she saw Denise enrolled at Westland Elementary School and Anthony in preschool. Again, she had Frances Milner and Marvin Neal to watch over the children, and Trude was nearby. On that European trip, Hedy visited Gene Kelly's apartment in Paris, and Ginger Rogers and Judy Holliday showed up with some minor royals. Judy Garland appeared at the flat as well, and they all had a wonderful evening.

While in Europe she ran into her old friend Jean-Pierre Aumont. When

Aumont would call Hedy, he would always begin the conversation with "Will you marry me?" She states that it was indirectly through Aumont that she went back to work. He introduced her to the Italian film producer Francis Salvoli, who offered Hedy a "'staggering salary' to make a film of three stories."[3]

Hedy contacted her American agents, and they ironed out the details, warning her that Italian film producers were notorious for reneging on their money deals and for often backing out of their offers. Hedy heard none of that; instead, she focused on the stupendous salary they were willing to pay her.

During her absence, Hedy's agents secured a long-term advertising assignment using her image for a dietary candy that curbed the appetite called Ayds. One advertisement featured Hedy in the gorgeous Edith Head–designed white strapless gown from *My Favorite Spy,* and another showed her in a bathing suit on a beach. Residuals from Ayds would supply Hedy with a lucrative, if not totally sufficient, income for years.

Home on March 12, Hedy was seen at the Gourmet Beverly in Hollywood in the company of the forty-three-year-old French writer Pierre La Mure, author of a 1950 novel based on the life of the French impressionistic painter Henri de Toulouse-Lautrec called *Moulin Rouge.* La Mure was renting a quaint white stucco cottage in Beverly Hills during the filming of the 1952 screen adaptation of his book, directed by John Huston and starring José Ferrer and Zsa Zsa Gabor.

Within the week, on March 17, Hedy was in court with her attorney, Israel, to testify that her estranged husband, Teddy Stauffer, was a wife beater and had verbally abused her and even struck her on several occasions. Marvin Neal testified that he had witnessed Stauffer on the evening of November 22 in the suite where Hedy and the children were staying at the Beverly Hills Hotel. He said that as she attempted to close the door with the children present, Stauffer knocked it open "real hard" and pushed Hedy up against a wall and hit her in the face. Neal asked her, "Do you want me to do something about this?" And she said, "No." An interlocutory divorce decree was granted, the divorce to be final one year from that date. Teddy was not present but was represented by his attorney, Milton M. Golden. Hedy did not ask for alimony.[4]

Hedy's agents took stock of her public image and advised her that they were preparing to do damage control. She needed to be seen in a favorable light. And there was no better way to do that than to appear on television. For her first venture into the new medium as a television entertainer, Hedy was booked on *The Colgate Comedy Hour,* which starred the versatile Donald O'Connor.

A splashy, live-comedy revue, *The Colgate Comedy Hour* was NBC's first successful program to run opposite Ed Sullivan's Sunday night juggernaut, *The Toast of the Town*. On May 11, in the first of her three appearances on the program, Hedy was the featured guest star in a skit with O'Connor, where she portrayed Milady opposite his dueling cavalier. Next, on June 14, she guest-starred on NBC's *All Star Revue* (aka *Four Star Revue*), a summer show hosted by the ventriloquist Paul Winchell and his dummy, Jerry Mahoney.[5]

Louella Parsons a bit inaccurately announced in her column that Hedy was planning to film a television series of romance stories, entitled *The Great Loves of History*, in Acapulco, to be produced by Victor Pahlen, with Edgar G. Ulmer directing and based on works by Salka Viertel and Aeneas MacKenzie. Hedy would star as Madame Pompadour and Madame du Barry. "No actress could look the part better than Hedy who is 'lovely to look at,'" Parsons concluded.[6]

More exciting news was *Size 12,* the brainchild of the producer Jerry Wald, who was attempting to sign Hedy, Barbara Stanwyck (or Joan Crawford), Marilyn Monroe, and the young actress Ursula Thiess to star in a story about three fashion models making it in Manhattan. Ursula Thiess was the current love of actor Robert Taylor, now divorced from Stanwyck.

Size 12 was to have been a Jerry Wald–Norman Krasna Production, but it soon got bogged down, and negotiations fell apart. In 1953, Twentieth Century–Fox released *their* definitive Technicolor and CinemaScope production about three New York fashion models on the make. It was called *How to Marry a Millionaire,* directed by Nunnally Johnson, starring Betty Grable, Lauren Bacall, and Marilyn Monroe.

Though Hedy was still a relatively wealthy woman, that October she sold the Mayfair Apartments in Los Angeles, property she had long held as an investment. It brought her $300,000. In November she sued John Loder for $19,500 for back child support and maintenance. Loder was in arrears $300 a month for Denise and Anthony, which, when the suit was filed on November 25, totaled $23,500, of which Loder had only supplied $4,200. (The case would linger in the courts until 1958, when Loder was finally ordered to pay $19,500 in back alimony. It was never disclosed if he did.)

On December 28, Hedy made her second appearance on *The Colgate Comedy Hour* in a spy spoof with the guest host, the comedian Ben Blue. Hedy made her third and final guest appearance on the show on March 8. These television appearances made Hedy Lamarr a familiar face and name to a new generation of fans.

At the same time, Hedy was preparing to become a U.S. citizen. On April 10, she took the oath of allegiance, along with forty other individuals from thirty-four different countries. She had educated herself well on American history. "When I took my citizenship exam," Hedy recalled, "no one there [knew] how the White House came to be called the White House. I did. (When the original was burned, the red brick scorched, so they covered it with white paint.)"[7]

In early May, Hedy and Mrs. Shirley Ulmer, the wife of Edgar G. Ulmer, sailed from New York on the RMS *Queen Mary* to England for the filming of *The Great Love Stories* television series. The first sequence Hedy was to enact was about Queen Esther and would be shot in London. Hedy was financing 50 percent of the venture, along with Robert Clarke of Associated British Films. Ulmer was set to direct. The Queen Esther story, however, was not made, so on June 15, Hedy was scheduled to fly to Rome to begin filming one of the other six episodes. With its title changed to *The Great Loves of History,* the series was now being considered for theatrical release.

The following day Italy had its first demonstration for international film producers of its own version of the new 3-D process. So impressed with the method was Hedy's producer Victor Pahlen, who also financed the showing, that he considered using the process in the picture scheduled to begin filming in Rome as a "trio-style" feature film. Don Hyde was set to distribute it, and the producer Marcel Hellman was also involved in the project.

Neither 3-D nor CinemaScope were finally used for the 181-minute-long *L'Amante di Paride* (*The Lover of Paris*), but Technicolor was. The plot of the film is a bit convoluted. The narrative presents a compilation of various great love stories which all starred Hedy.

The problem with chronicling details of the making of *L'amante di Paride* is that its production history is often combined with that of Hedy's second Italian film, which she made the following year. Most archival sources are muddled, combining both productions into one, using the title of the unfinished second project, *L'eterna femmina,* as the sum of them both. Surprisingly, it is Hedy's questionable autobiography that clearly distinguishes the two separate cinema projects and best sheds light on their distinct separate histories.

Hedy's money was involved in both productions, and they both employed basically the same production crews, and even some of the same cast. In her book, Hedy confuses the issue by stating that the three episodes of *L'amante di Paride* were titled "The Face that Launched a Thousand Ships," "An Apple for Eve," and "The Love of Three Queens."[8] *The Loves of Three Queens* was the title eventually given to the truncated ninety-seven-minute, 1955 U.K. version of the film. It showcased Hedy as Saint Geneviève, Josephine, and Helen of Troy in stories (spoken in English), with an incongruous narration supplied by the character actor Hans Conried.

In Italy motion pictures with episodic dramas, or novellas, were popularized in 1946 with the release of *Paisà*, one of the founding films in the neorealist aesthetic, by Roberto Rossellini. This trend continued with *L'amore* in 1948, *Siamo donne* in 1953, Vittorio De Sica's *L'oro di Napoli* in 1954, and *Europa di notte* in 1959, culminating with *Boccaccio '70* in 1962.

Wrote the Italian film scholar Giovanni Secchi, "In Italy the genre was respected . . . very important stars such as Sophia Loren, Anna Magnani and Alida Valli willingly appeared in them."[9] Secchi also suggests that Warner Bros. bought the rights to *L'amante di Paride* to prevent it from appearing in America before the release of its own *Helen of Troy* in 1956.

Quite possibly this is the case. Edwin Schallert of the *Los Angeles Times* observed at the time, "A question about the release of the picture in this country seems to arise because it deals with 'Helen of Troy,' and Warner, of course, has a mammoth $6,000,000 spectacle based on the same chapter in history."[10] Still, twenty-foot-tall signs proclaimed the arrival of *An Apple for Venus* (yet *another* title for *L'amante di Paride*), at the Venice Film Festival in September 1954.

It was not an uncommon procedure to prevent a foreign film from being distributed in the United States, as Mayer had done with *Pépé le Moko* back in 1937. Twentieth Century–Fox also did the same when they were filming *Cleopatra* (1963), buying the American distribution rights to *Le legioni di Cleopatra* (Lyre, 1960); and when they lensed *The Sound of Music* (1965), they obtained the rights to *Die Von Trapp Familie* (Divina-Film, 1956), which also was never shown in the United States.

L'amante di Paride tells three different love stories and features two consecutively running prologues. The first story is of a modern-day gathering of two families at a Roman restaurant to celebrate the marriage of Paolo and Teresa. As the families rejoice and drink wine, they begin telling fanciful tales, and the women start challenging one another as to which one is the most beautiful. As the boasters become rowdy, the old Greek professor Lamberti speaks up and tells them the tale of Helen of Troy, at which point the action of the film's main plot unfolds: On Mount Olympus, the gods are holding a feast, and someone has forgotten to invite the goddess of discord, Eris. She appears and throws a golden apple onto the table, saying that whoever is the most beautiful of all the goddesses should pick it up. Chaos reigns, and it is decided that Paris (Massimo Serato), the son of Priam, King of Troy, will decide on earth who the most beautiful woman is.

His choice is Helen (Hedy), the wife of Menelaus (Robert Beatty), King of Sparta. Paris comes to Sparta and abducts Helen to Troy. She falls in love with him. King Priam also has a daughter, Cassandra (Serena Michelotti), who prophesies the coming war, in which the gods decide no side shall win. Yet when Sparta is defeated by the Trojan horse filled with soldiers, Paris is killed. Menelaus asks Helen to return with him to their homeland. She sadly agrees and mourns, "Then a bitterer punition does exist. . . . And may the gods impede that a mortal woman is again damned with as much beauty as I am."

The second part of *L'amante di Paride* is called *I cavalieri dell'illusione* (*The Knights of Illusion*) and begins with a traveling theatre troupe in Tuscany. Liala (Hedy) is the daughter of famed actor Romani (Luigi Pavese). Stopping one night to perform the story of Geneviève de Brabant, Liala's mysterious suitor sits in the audience and dreams the following: In troubled days Geneviève (Hedy), who is married to the Christian knight Count Sigfride (Cesare Danova), discovers she is with child as she awaits her husband's return from the holy wars. She is considered a saint in her land because of her generosity and goodness. Geneviève's thwarted suitor, Golo (Terence Morgan), is jealous of young Drago (John Fraser), who has returned from the wars to protect Geneviève until Sigfride's return. Golo accuses Geneviève of infidelity, and states that the unborn child is not Sigfride's. He makes advances on Geneviève and kills Drago. Upon his return Count Sigfride believes Golo's accusations, and Geneviève is condemned to die. The soldiers take pity on her, escort her to the woods, and release her. She bears a son, and many years later Sigfride finds them in the forest and they are reunited. The suitor's dream comes to an end.

The following evening, the theatre company performs "The Life and Loves of Josephine Bonaparte." Again, Liala's suitor imagines the story as the Teatro Romani troop performs its modest production: Josephine (Hedy) is traveling the country when she meets Napoleon (Gérard Oury), who falls in love with her. When Josephine cannot have a child, Napoleon divorces her. He takes up with a beautiful younger woman, Maria Luisa (Milly Vitale), who gives him a son. As the cannons blast one hundred bombardments, Josephine says, "A son . . . the Austrian has given him an heir. Now he'll learn to love." Thus ends the original three-hour *L'amante di Paride*.

Production began on the epic in Rome in mid-July, with some location shooting made in Monte Gelato. As filming progressed, Steve Cochran, currently working in Germany, was asked to appear in the picture. He declined.

In Rome Hedy began dating the Italian industrialist and Fiat scion Gianni (Giovanni) Agnelli. He never asked her to wed, but Hedy would always recall similarities between him and Fritz Mandl. "That's the one I should have married," she would tell people of Agnelli later in life.[11]

When filming started on an aborted Mary of Scotland sequence, Hedy disagreed so vehemently with Ulmer that she stormed off the set and simply disappeared. The episode was abandoned. The Teatro Romani segments, with Hedy as the theatre performer Liala, were slowly and successfully completed, but as the project stumbled through the late summer, things apparently did not improve.

As late as August 1953, Hedy and the producers were still casting the picture. It was announced that Richard Todd had been secured to portray Napoleon to Hedy's Josephine, and Jack Hawkins was signed for the Helen of Troy story. Actor Fred MacMurray was requested for the Geneviève de Brabant episode. Hedy was also attempting to secure Vittorio Gassman, and to convince the writer Sidney Sheldon, who was staying in Salzburg at the time, to come to Italy and help clean up the script. All declined the project.

But the handsome twenty-two-year-old British actor John Fraser did appear in the film, portraying Drago, the young suitor of Geneviève de Brabant, in what was originally called the "Lady Fair" episode. Ensconced in a modern hotel in the suburb of Parioli, outside Rome's historical district, the actors were transported daily to locations throughout Italy for their scenes. The interiors for *L'amante di Paride* were shot on sets at Rome's famed Cinecittà Studios. Fraser fell in love with Rome, but not with Hedy Lamarr. Working with her was a nightmare, he wrote in his memoirs.

Fraser recalled that every time he met Hedy before the shoot, she was talking a great deal, with no apparent train of thought. Once, while she was complaining about how her appearance would look in the production, Fraser abruptly raised his voice to reassure her she would look fine, stopping short her ramblings in midsentence. "She bent her lovely gaze on me without speaking for quite two minutes," Fraser wrote. "She then said in a gentle voice, extremely lucidly—'Who are you, you little flea, to tell me what to do?'" He later learned that she had attempted to have him fired.[12]

Filming had already begun on location for this segment, and when the actors were called for Drago's death scene in the arms of Geneviève, Fraser's treatment by Hedy was even harsher. He remembered she disliked Ulmer. "Their relationship was bitter and hate-filled and spectacularly stormy."[13]

According to Fraser, during the scene, filmed outdoors on grass artificially painted green, Geneviève bends down and cradles the dying youth in her arms as she exclaims, "Drago! Don't die!" Dressed in a priceless lilac velvet gown embroidered with seed pearls and semiprecious stones (a design she had insisted upon, according to Fraser), kneeling on a concealed stool, Hedy took Fraser's head to her bosom and wrenched Fraser's face away from the camera as she cried out her line.

Ulmer, recalled Fraser, stopped the scene and explained to Hedy in his broken, heavily accented English, that by turning Fraser's face away from the camera, the audience could only see the dying man's Prince Valiant wig. Not knowing if Drago was a boy or a girl, they would also not care at all if he expired. "Going again. . . . Action!" cried out the director. Once again, Hedy stooped to embrace Drago's head and repeated her line "Drago! Don't die!" And as Fraser painfully recalled, "The long fingers slowly tightening in my Prince Valiant hairdo, then SNAP! Defiant, Hedy rammed my face once more between her breasts."[14]

Ulmer yelled, "Cut!" from his stooping position behind the camera, approached Hedy to within inches of her face, and told her that *he* was the director. "Hedy dropped my head like a cabbage," continued Fraser, "and firmly putting one hand on the collar of the dress, with one savage wrench she ripped the priceless garment from neck to the naval."[15] For continuity purposes, the production was halted for a week until the exact material was located, and the heavily detailed embroidery replicated, before the sequence was completed.

By mid-October both Hedy and Ulmer had had enough. She fired him. It had taken Ulmer eight months to discover he could not cope with Hedy. It had reached a crisis point when she bought, for £50,000, an interest in the production and became the boss. Flying from London to New York on October 18,

Ulmer commented to the press that Terence Morgan, in a "honey" of a part, had given "one of the finest [performances] I have ever seen," but that "Miss Lamarr is no Academy Award winner."[16]

Arriving in Los Angeles on November 2, Ulmer said, "I had hoped she would approach these three classical parts with sincerity, if not actual humility. Instead, we got what I can only call the typical Hollywood cover girl attitude . . . Genevieve is a 12th century woman thrown into prison by her husband. Miss Lamarr wished to be dolled up like a fugitive from the *Ziegfeld Follies*. I just couldn't go on seeing the film being ruined by the caprice of one human being."[17]

Eventually production of *L'amante di Paride* came to a close in November. A severely edited version of the film extant in black-and-white today is called *The Love of Three Queens,* and it is terribly difficult to watch knowing what might have been—the over-three-hour-long version in glorious Technicolor. And, sadly, everything about the picture seems amateurish—the production, the direction, the special effects, and, worst of all, the acting.

Pacing is deadly, and line delivery staggeringly inept. All the participants, from the extras to the stars, seem to be performing on an amateur level of dramatics. And, jarringly, one is boggled to hear the familiar voice of the actor and comedian Hans Conried, the voice of Captain Hook in Walt Disney's animated cartoon *Peter Pan,* who was used to narrate the reedited mess.

Giovanni Secchi says in his evaluation of the story, "In *I cavalieri dell'illusione* the second part seems better than the extremely outdated first one (*L'amante di Paride*). . . . The story of the stock company to unite the two completely different episodes is weak. Of course *I cavalieri* is a classical Italian episodic movie of the '50s, probably not any worse than many of its kind."[18] There possibly were magnificent moments in *L'amante di Paride*, but not in its existing version. As Hedy stated pragmatically, "I made the picture and it didn't turn out very good. It was never released in America. But I did get the money."[19]

Hedy was now nearly forty years old, a difficult age for any actress. In her case, most everything she had always relied on was fading from her grasp—her career and her looks. Back in America, while visiting Houston to help raise money to open a new USO building, Hedy announced that she was in the market for backing for a film she wished to produce. She received many invitations to meet for dinner.

One was from the forty-five-year-old Texas oil millionaire W. Howard Lee.

He offered to put up collateral to finance her project, but he wanted her to come to his office to discuss the deal. She refused to go to any man's office, and Lee, finding Hedy impossible to deal with, dropped his offer. They did not meet. However, when he saw Hedy's picture in the paper, he was intrigued and called her Houston hotel, only to be told that she had returned to California.

Lee followed Hedy to Hollywood and contacted her. This time she agreed to meet him to discuss his backing her project. She estimated it would cost $500,000, and, after going over the figures, they were able to bring the budget down to $400,000. Though it was late at night, they called the film director Marc Allégret in Italy and advised him of their plans for Hedy's still-undetermined dream project. That evening, according to Hedy's account, Lee spent the night. Within days she announced their wedding plans.

Hedy was staying at the Beverly Hills Hotel. On December 21, accompanied by four friends, she applied for a marriage license at the Los Angeles Municipal Building. She gave her fiancé's address as the Shamrock Hotel in Houston, Texas. The following day, Tuesday, December 22, Hedy flew to New York and married Howard Lee in a brief double-ring ceremony in the Queens County Courthouse in Long Island City.

The presiding judge was Special Sessions Justice Doris I. Byrne, a friend of Hedy's. Her theatrical agent, Robert Lantz, and his wife stood witness for the couple. Hedy wore a simple black dress, with white hat and gloves and a double-strand necklace of matching pearls. They were wed at noon, and fifteen minutes later left in their rented Cadillac for Idlewild Airport to catch a flight to Los Angeles, where the children and Frances Milner met them at the airport. Hedy told the press that their new home would be in Houston.

Lee was a private man, austere and reserved, distantly related to the Civil War General Robert E. Lee of Virginia, born in Texas in 1908. His father founded a petroleum empire. Howard had two sisters, one named Faustine, who married Glenn McCarthy, the oilman who built the Shamrock Hotel. Howard's first marriage was to Helen Geraldine Torrance. Before they divorced in 1946, the couple had a daughter, Donna.

When Hedy and Lee arrived in Houston on January 12, they checked into a hotel apartment and immediately began shopping for a house. Marvin Neal drove the children by car from the West Coast. Denise recalled that they had a wonderful trip and that Neal, who liked to yodel, entertained them by doing so on their way to Texas. The children took to Howard Lee.

"I loved Howard," Denise recalled in 2009. "We were very close. That was the longest we ever lived with a dad. We called him Dad. And he adopted us."[20]

In January Lee found a large two-storey brick mansion in River Oaks, which he leased for $600 a month with an option to buy for $125,000. The family planned to move there in February. Enrolled into the River Oaks Elementary School, Denise was in third grade and Anthony in second. When Hedy settled into her new home, she remodeled the interior in French provincial and extensively landscaped the property, creating spacious grounds of cool and rich-looking greens.

Howard had no intention of buying the house. According to him, "I didn't intend to pick up the option . . . but the first thing she wanted was a swimming pool, then new carpets and drapes."[21] Hedy kept redecorating the home, until, Lee said, he was forced into buying it. Hedy even presented Howard with a $15,000 bill for the interior decorator. Lee gave Hedy an allowance of $1,000 a month for spending money, which she sent to her business manager, charging all her purchases instead to Lee.

When summer came, the children were sent to camp again, and afterward they spent time, with supervision, at Grand Lake, Colorado, where the two enjoyed boating until they returned to Houston and to school that fall. In Europe in mid-October, filming got under way on Hedy's new film, *L'eterna femmina*. The project was originally entitled *White Ermine* because an ermine wrap was featured prominently in the plot. It starred Hedy with, yet again, Massimo Serato, whom she now had under personal contract for six pictures. Serato was thirty-eight years old and had once had an affair with the Italian actress Anna Magnani, who had borne him a son.

L'eterna femmina was filmed by the same company that had produced Hedy's *L'amante di Paride*, Cine Del Duca Productions. The story told of romance in modern Roman society. It was being shot simultaneously in English and Italian. But from the start, Hedy faced obstacles. Rome was cold and miserable during the winter. Because the weather made location shooting impossible, Hedy tried to have the screenwriters alter the script, but they were in Paris on another project; when she hired two other screenwriters, they supplied "miserable work."[22] There were also new union hours to contend with, and Hedy said she simply could not get respect from the cast and crew. Then, a supporting actor broke his leg falling off a jeep, holding up production for several days.[23]

The project started to hemorrhage money. Hedy became sick, and no amount of blowing hot air onto the vast frigid Italian soundstages could warm the cast and crew. She missed her new husband tremendously and was ready to walk off the picture when, halfway through the production, with five cans of film completed, a fog machine broke down, and Hedy had to call in someone to fix it. When presented with the bill for the total costs so far incurred for *L'eterna femmina*, Hedy saw the writing on the wall. She had spent $398,999. She told the assistant director not to make a call for the cast and crew for the next day and advised Marc Allégret that she would see if her husband would advance more money. The production was shut down.

With Howard's financial support over the next few years, Hedy somehow managed to finish *L'eterna femmina*. "We finally did," she wrote in 1965. "But it was never released; and though law suits went back and forth through the years, I never could get my hands on it. The money is still tied up."[24]

Back in Houston, Hollywood came knocking, and briefly Hedy was considered for *Joseph and His Brethren*, to replace Rita Hayworth, who had just pulled out of the project. The picture, however, was shelved.

In the early years of her marriage to Lee, Hedy was happy and content living in Houston. Edwin Schallert of the *Los Angeles Times* made a personal visit to Texas to interview her that fall. He found Denise and Anthony playing in the backyard with their black-and-white cocker spaniel Cleo, which they had received for Christmas of 1951. Howard was away on a hunting trip, and Hedy welcomed the columnist into her home. Decorated with wall-to-wall carpet, it was furnished with New Orleans antiques, an Utrillo painting, and a tiny garden painting by Denise on the mantelpiece. Hedy's bedroom was in white and gold, with a huge king-size bed.

Hedy told Schallert of her still-unreleased film *L'eterna femmina*, in which "[I was] not only the star but also cut, edited, dubbed the film, supervised the production." She admitted she and Howard were waiting to share in the proceeds.[25]

Hedy was served a couple of lawsuits in early 1955. The first one was for $90,125 from the U.S. government in regards to her 1950 income tax. Requesting a redetermination of that amount, Hedy stated that she did not receive the full allowance for $147,000 worth of jewels taken from her at the Sherry-Netherland Hotel in August 1950. On April 24, 1958, a stipulation filed by Judge Allin H. Pierce was reached permitting a $60,000 settlement in her favor.

That May came another lawsuit, this one from Jerome B. Rosenthal and

Samuel P. Norton, two of Hedy's former lawyers, for $18,215.71, in a complaint made by their representing attorney, William Kraker. In response, Hedy said that she had actually overpaid them, alleging they were compensated a total of $35,171.96 when they were only entitled to $12,105.72. In a countersuit, Hedy demanded return of the difference. In September 1957, Hedy paid "a satisfactory settlement" to end the case before it was taken to court.[26]

On the evening of May 25, Hedy discovered she was missing some of her jewelry, valued at $50,000, from her plush River Oaks home. Joseph H. Rutledge, an insurance adjuster, advised the police that the gems were in a small green satin bag and included a 10.35–carat diamond ring, thirty-two pearl-shaped diamonds valued at $20,500, a $10,000 diamond bracelet, and a $9,000 watch bracelet. Hedy asked Howard if he had taken them, at which point he insisted on taking a lie-detector test.

Hedy was brought into police headquarters for questioning on May 27 and spent two hours answering their queries and failing three lie-detector tests. Detective B. M. Squyres told the press, "She is very emotional and she was quite excited. Ordinarily I would not have given the test to anyone who was so overwrought, but she wanted to take it. . . . She was too upset for the polygraph to function properly."[27] Howard passed his test, as did two house-staff employees, Ruby Lee Baker and Elizabeth Bradford.

As mysteriously as the jewels vanished, they suddenly reappeared on June 16. "You can say that the jewels were recovered on the premises at 5:30 P.M. yesterday," Howard advised the press. "Other than that we have nothing more to say at this time."[28] Apparently, Hedy's seamstress, Alberta Pears, found the missing bag of gems on a shelf in the upstairs sewing room.

To get away from Texas occasionally, Hedy and Howard (after vacationing at the historic Hotel Jerome) built a $300,000 ski lodge in Aspen, Colorado. They called it the Villa Lamarr. Both became avid skiers, and so did the children. That summer Denise and Anthony were sent to Camp Roosevelt in California. (One of Anthony's later camp counselors was the future American-born British writer, animator, and filmmaker Terry Gilliam of the Monty Python troupe, who worked there during the summer to put himself through college.)

With the children away, Howard sensed Hedy withdrawing from him. To please her he flew her to Austria, somewhere she had wanted to go for some time. When she arrived in Vienna on August 19, she emotionally recalled, "It was like caressing an old friend. I loved my home and I hadn't realized how much I missed it."[29] It was her first visit to her beloved country since leaving in 1937. "I cried like a little schoolgirl when I arrived here," she told the awaiting press. She was back in her homeland. So much had happened, so little had changed.

Two weeks later Hedy arrived in Italy, to attend the sixteenth annual Venice Film Festival. *L'amante di paride* was an entry in the festival, but it won no awards.

When she finally returned to Houston, Hedy was offered *Tonight with Ernest Hemingway,* a staged reading of selections from the author's novels and short stories that was set to be produced on Broadway in the spring of 1956. The sponsors were Alfred Rice, Hemingway's attorney, and A. E. Hotchner, who compiled the readings. Hedy did not accept the offer.

Nor did she take the starring role in *Passion Is the Gale,* a story about adventure in the Virgin Islands, offered to her by the actor Richard Denning and his agent, Milton Hamilburg, who had created their own independent film company, Hamden Productions, in May 1956.

What she *was* considering was a role in *The Story of Mankind* for Warner Bros. Based on the bestselling six-hundred-page nonfiction book written by Hendrik van Loon, the picture was to be a sort of star-studded epic along the lines of Michael Todd's *Around the World in 80 Days* (UA, 1956), which would win the Best Picture Oscar.

Scheduled to produce and direct *The Story of Mankind* was Irwin Allen, a self-promoter of the highest order. Allen would later achieve major success in the 1970s, when he hit his stride as creator of the "disaster" genre with Twentieth Century–Fox's star-studded *The Poseidon Adventure. The Story of Mankind,* though there was little adventure, lesser stars, and even less excitement, would subsequently prove to be a sort of "disaster" film in its own right.

Unfortunately, Allen was *not* Cecil B. DeMille, and if any research was done in the preparation for *The Story of Mankind,* it was not evident. Cast in the picture were the distinguished Ronald Colman as The Spirit of Man, Vincent Price as Mr. Scratch (the Devil), Sir Cedric Hardwicke as the High Judge, Agnes Moorehead as Queen Elizabeth I, and others—including the Marx Brothers, Groucho as Peter Minuit, Harpo as Isaac Newton, and Chico as a monk.

Hedy was to portray Joan of Arc in one segment of the multiepisodic picture. It was another nod to her vanity and ego, and Warner Bros. was willing to pay her $2,500 a week to portray the doomed saint. Through Hedy's own company, Lamarr Productions, and Irwin Allen's Cambridge Productions, Inc., an agreement was signed in November, guaranteeing her the said amount, with two days' additional work. A check was cut to her for a total of $5,000 on May 17. That fall, Hedy flew to Hollywood. Her representation at this time was through the Lester Salkov Agency, and they immediately began promoting her to other film studios and television networks in a grand assault to get her name before the public eye.

Filming commenced on the Warner Bros. soundstages on November 12. It was a quick shoot: Only sixteen shooting days were allotted for the picture. Hedy's sequences were filmed on stage 12A on November 26. By then, the picture was already five days behind schedule.

Hedy was extremely anxious doing her brief role. When Allen asked her why, she replied, "Listen, I don't get to save France every day!"[30] William Schallert, son of the *Los Angeles Times* drama critic Edwin Schallert, appeared in one sequence with Hedy. "I was a day player in 'The Story of Mankind,' which was, you know, the usual schlock. I wore a bald cap and a cereal bowl haircut and worked only one day," Schallert recalled in 2007. "I think the reason Hedy Lamarr was cast was because she had appeared in *Ecstasy,* and that casting was Allen's ironic choice."[31]

Vincent Price recalled working with the elegant Ronald Colman, in what would be Colman's last film. (He died in 1958.) Said Price about the actor, "He was a marvelous gentleman, quiet and charming, and with a delicious humor. We knew during the filming that the picture was heading downward; the script was bad to begin with and it worsened with daily changes. I remember one puzzled visitor asking Ronnie: 'Is this picture based on a book?' and he replied in that beautiful, soft diction of his, 'Yes, it is. But they are using only the notes on the dust jacket.'"[32]

Filming concluded on *The Story of Mankind* on Friday, January 25, 1957, six days behind schedule. After spending years in Houston and working on her marriage with Howard, which at best was dull, Hedy knew she needed her career to make her feel alive. The year 1957 would be her most productive in over a decade.

19

Television

edy's first television appearance of 1957 was on the hour-long variety show *Shower of Stars* on March 14. The show also featured Jack Benny, Gale Storm, the dancer Jacques d'Amboise, the puppeteer Sid Krofft, and Lawrence Welk. The second half of the show was an intrigue spoof, apparently one of the only motifs television writers managed think of to use Hedy in, at a Lisbon café with Benny, and the other guest stars making brief appearances.

Rehearsals began on Monday, March 11. Krofft remembered meeting Hedy. "We were all waiting for the great beauty to arrive for rehearsal," he recalled. "And in she came with a scarf on her head and she looked like the charwoman or something, you know. And they escorted her into makeup, even then, for rehearsals. . . . We all went into shock. After makeup she came out and she looked like someone else."[1]

After the show aired, Helm in *Daily Variety* remarked, "Miss Lamarr, more glamorously decorative than functional, was used only sparingly in the spoof on foreign intrigues. She was more posed than practiced in her lines."[2]

Hedy was interviewed by Aline Mosby in Hollywood. She spoke about her life in Houston and of her marriage. "I'm just an old-fashioned housewife who has to do these TV things [so as] not to get into a rut," she said. "Now the children are in school and I'd love to work again. Otherwise it's a monotonous life. I can't be what people expect me to be and build homes, run them, bring up children, be a tool, and have everybody lean on me."[3]

Asked if she and her husband Howard Lee were separated, Hedy replied, "I am here in Hollywood and he is not here so we are not together." Did she not like living in Houston? Her response was telling. "Texas is very humid and I'm from the Alps. . . . It's difficult to live without roots. But my roots are in Austria! My second home is in California and to have made this change to Texas under most awkward circumstances . . . some day I want to get a house and a boat and live on a lake near Salzburg."[4]

Hedy then flew to New York for *The Perry Como Show,* broadcast on March 30. Como sang several songs, including "Hi Neighbor" (backed by a line of dancing outer-space girls, one of whom is Hedy); "April in Paris"; another musical number with Hedy and Julius LaRosa; and an "I Love You, I Love You / Love Letters" medley with Hedy dressed as an old woman. The following evening she was the "mystery guest" on *What's My Line?,* and she appeared on yet another New York–based game show, *I've Got a Secret,* on April 10.

The producer Albert Zugsmith at Universal-International Studios in Hollywood had approached Hedy for the starring role in a project called *Hideaway House.* Hedy showed interest, and to sweeten the deal, Zugsmith promised her everything—star treatment, big Hollywood press parties, and her choice of Universal's stable of good-looking, beefy young actors for her leading man. Hedy liked the idea and agreed to meet with Zugsmith after her flurry of New York commitments. Returning to California in late April, Hedy was fêted by the producer, and on May 3 she signed for *The Female Animal,* as *Hideaway House* was now called.

Cast in the picture to portray Hedy's troubled nineteen-year-old daughter was twenty-eight-year-old former M-G-M star Jane Powell, and John Gavin was selected as her leading man, Chris Farley.

But before production commenced, Hedy filmed a brief cameo in the studio's *Slaughter on Tenth Avenue,* starring Richard Egan, Jan Sterling, Walter Matthau, and Julie Adams. Hedy played the role of Mona, a fashion-house designer.

Zsa Zsa Gabor had actually begun filming the brief role on May 10 (she was paid $1,000 for the day), but it immediately became apparent, according to company files, that Gabor could not comprehend being a fashion-house employee. She did not complete the scene. Zugsmith then asked Hedy to step in and repeat the part for the cameras.

Hedy was scheduled for three days' work on the picture, one day of tests (Saturday, May 11), one day of filming her brief scene with actress Julie Adams (the following Wednesday), and one day for pickup shots and close-ups. *Slaughter on Tenth Avenue* was a crime drama along the lines of Columbia's 1954 film *On the Waterfront*, but instead of dealing with the corruption of long-shoremen's unions, *Slaughter on Tenth Avenue* focused on the attorneys and justice system set to defend those unions.

In an obviously gratuitous scene that allowed Adams a moment of feminity in what was quite frankly a brutal picture, Hedy completed her part efficiently and professionally. Unfortunately, when *Slaughter on Tenth Avenue* was re-leased on November 5, 1957, the scene was cut, no doubt because it had little to do with the story.

Harry Keller was assigned to direct *The Female Animal*, in which a hand-some hunk, Chris Farley, a Hollywood film extra, saves the fading movie queen Vanessa Windsor (Hedy) from a serious on-set accident, and she takes a liking to him. Suggesting he might be perfect as the caretaker of her beach house, called Windsor Castle, Vanessa foolishly falls in love with the younger man. One evening at a bar Chris rescues a very drunk and pretty young blonde named Penny (Jane Powell) from the clutches of an equally drunk brawler named Piggy (Gregg Palmer). Taking her to the beach house, Chris has no idea that Penny is actually Vanessa's adopted daughter.

When Vanessa runs into her friend and fellow aging sexpot Lily Frayne (Jan Sterling) and her young "escort" Pepe (Richard Avonde), Lily tells Vanessa that Chris is the same type of man as Pepe—a gigolo. Upset that his character is in question, Chris leaves Vanessa, but she manages to tell him of her feelings for him. Then, after Penny confesses to Chris that she is Vanessa's daughter, Chris and Penny fall in love. Penny tells her mother that she loves Chris, and Vanessa tells a gossip columnist that *she* and Chris will wed. Furious, Chris returns to his old apartment, and Vanessa begs him to marry her. Drunk and forlorn while on the set of her new movie, Vanessa falls doing a stunt, and Chris rescues her again. Only then does Vanessa relinquish Chris to the love of her daughter.

Although she was expected to report on May 9 to stage 21 at 11:00 A.M. for silent CinemaScope, black-and-white wardrobe, makeup, and hair tests, Hedy showed up on the lot at 12:15 P.M. Not a good sign. Her costar John Gavin had been kept waiting with the crew, all of whom were on salary. At 1:00 P.M. the film tests began, directed by Keller and ending at 2:15 P.M. For the picture, Hedy was paid $50,000 for six weeks work (May 23–June 25), plus twelve days free, for an additional $8,333. Jane Powell was given the same deal.[5]

For the devastatingly handsome twenty-six-year-old Gavin, who had been placed under contract with Universal as a threat to the studio's biggest box-office draw Rock Hudson, *The Female Animal* would have been his fourth screen venture. He had yet to prove his merit in his three most memorable studio blockbusters, *Imitation of Life* (1959), with Lana Turner, Alfred Hitchcock's *Psycho* (1960), and *Spartacus* (1960). In all three he would hand in respectable performances.

In the late 1990s, Hedy confided to her friend Madeleine Merrill that when Gavin walked onto the set for the first time, she fell for him. "He was her secret love," Merrill recalled.[6] In a 2008 interview, Gavin seemed unaware of this, stating he recalled very little about his work in the film, "I can't help much . . . I didn't get that far [into the project]." The actor did remember Hedy was "very nice."[7] But other than maybe meeting her off-set at a dinner or a party, he could not recall anything else about her.

Gavin may have been acting the gentleman. Other sources say that Hedy had handpicked him for the part. But during the second week of film tests, something occurred that ended his participation in *The Female Animal*. Hedy told the actor John Carlyle in 1961 that she had Gavin fired because he could not act.[8] (It was hardly necessary that he could; Gavin's own male beauty rivaled that of Hedy's at her peak.) Possibly he did not succumb to her desires to rehearse their scenes in their off-hours.

At any rate, on May 16 Gavin was removed from the picture, and in an empty studio, a fifteen-minute stage rehearsal (an audition actually) was held with thirty-six-year-old Universal contract player George Nader. Hedy approved of him, and the manly, muscular Nader was assigned the part of Farley at his flat contract salary of $20,000. (Off-the-set rehearsals with Nader truly did not take place, since the rugged actor was gay.)

Nader had made his film debut in 1950 and contracted with Universal-International, finding himself competing for roles with other beefcake stars on the lot at that time—Tony Curtis, Jeff Chandler, and Rock Hudson, who became his great friend.[9]

For the role of Penny, Jane Powell somehow was thrown into the mix. Powell's kind of sugarcoated, cute musical persona, established after starring at Metro in over a dozen Technicolor films, just did not fit into the newly popular film genres. About her last two pictures, *The Female Animal*, and R-K-O Radio's *The Girl Most Likely* (1958), Powell sorely complained in her autobiography, "I did do a couple of B movies—not knowing they were going to be 'B.' I'd hoped that they might be a foot in the door to bigger things. I didn't do them for the money; I just wanted to work, and to be wanted."[10]

For *The Female Animal,* Universal's resident fashion designer, Bill Thomas, created a $6,870.44 wardrobe for Hedy. Her living expenses, which included luggage transfers, roundtrip airfare to and from Houston, medical expenses, a nurse, and a masseuse, cost the studio an extra $6,025.

Filming began, but by the end of May it was obvious the picture was running into trouble. Hedy was continually late, if she showed up at all. She called in sick several times and had doctors on the set. And, worst of all, she argued continuously with Harry Keller, usually in the privacy of her dressing room.

Nevertheless, *The Female Animal* was a quick shoot, wrapping up on June 21. The original cost had been set at $687,180 but was now increased to $697,800. Hedy was "too ill" to perform on the last day of filming. She was called back, though, on October 10 to film a sequence where Vanessa falls against a fence in a dolly shot.

Back in Houston that late summer, the Lees' beautiful mansion "was swept by fire."[11] Damages were high, and Hedy set about restoring and refurnishing the house. But by mid-August she had accepted a role on the television Western-drama anthology, *Dick Powell's Zane Grey Theater,* which aired on CBS. The title of her thirty-minute episode was "The Proud Woman," and Hedy starred as Consuela "Connie" Bowers, a South American ranch owner who tangles with the wranglers Carson (Val Avery) and Laredo (Donald Buka) over her father's valuable palomino stallion Chuparo. The wranglers hire Frank Fayne (Paul Richards) to help them abduct the horse, and of course Consuela and Fayne fall in love. Fayne eventually saves the horse and wins Connie. Filming began on the show on August 15 and concluded two days later.

On August 25, Hedy appeared on *The Steve Allen Show* for NBC. In one skit Steve and Hedy portrayed a married couple, and she once again showed that she was inept at improvising, or "going with the moment." Hedy was beautiful to behold, but her performance was stilted.

Back in Houston things had not improved between her and Howard, and within two months she returned to Hollywood to guest-star with the singer Eddie Fisher on *The George Gobel Show,* broadcast on October 22.[12] Three days later *Dick Powell's Zane Grey Theater* aired "The Proud Woman." Kove of *Daily Variety* reported, "In perhaps the most spectacular miscasting yet this season, Hedy Lamarr, a Middle-European schnitzel more accustomed to boudoir dramas, portrays a fiery Spanish-American ranchero in the old west."[13]

The thirty-minute "Proud Woman" is dreadful. Everything—the sets, the costumes, the script, the acting, the direction, even the casting—is awful. Nothing gels, and Hedy's performance is especially bad. Her makeup is bizarre, she sports the same wig she wore in *The Female Animal,* and she is unflatteringly photographed. Obviously, she had no dialogue director on this quickly-tossed-together mishmash, and her line delivery lilts to the extreme. One wonders, as perhaps Charles Boyer and Spencer Tracy had, if she even comprehended what she was saying.

On October 29, 1957, Louis B. Mayer died. He had reigned for seven consecutive years (the same years Hedy had starred at Metro) as the highest-paid executive in the country. Mayer's forte had been building pictures around stars, but with the beautiful and headstrong Hedy, he had been at a total loss concerning what properties would work for her. She was perhaps his one big failure. Mayer had been besieged with personal problems in the late 1940s. He divorced his wife, and then began breeding and racing Thoroughbred horses instead of attending to studio matters. He eventually remarried. By 1947 questions pertaining to Mayer's capability and reputation reached a crisis with his bosses at New York–based Loew's, Inc.

After the elimination of the studio-owned theatre chains in 1949, by 1951 M-G-M had gone three years without winning a single Academy Award, and again Mayer and his Loew's, Inc. boss, Nicholas Schenck, were at each others' throats. Under orders, Mayer hired Dore Schary as production chief for the studio. Schary was au courant with the public tastes, and he produced "message pictures," in direct contrast with Mayer's favored family-pictures formula.

Waging yet another of his battles with Schenck over Schary in New York in 1951, Mayer made a grievous mistake. He told Schenck it was either him or Schary. Mayer, who had been given an honorary lifetime-achievement Oscar earlier that year and had successfully run M-G-M for over thirty years, was fired. His health began to decline; he suffered from leukemia; and, though he did attempt to stage a boardroom coup to regain his position, he failed, and then he retired from public view. He died of kidney failure. Hedy did not attend the funeral.

Meanwhile, *The Story of Mankind* was limping into theatres that fall. It had premiered in Philadelphia on October 23, 1957, to dismal box-office returns and fatal reviews. The cast contained all familiar names, for certain. But none of them were current stars. After preview screenings, *Films and Filming* said, "The film is . . . a collector's piece for those who like spotting the great with their hair down."[14]

Newsweek wrote, "Unearthly . . . a poor excuse to use a bunch of available actors in some of the weirdest casting ever committed."[15] Philip K. Scheuer of the *Los Angeles Times* was appalled: "Amateurishly conceived and acted . . . in *The Story of Mankind* a High Tribunal is called into session somewhere in heaven to decide whether or not we folks down here have done anything to make us worth saving. It is my personal observation that if the High Tribunal ever catches this picture, we're goners."[16]

The film runs a long and monotonous one hundred minutes, and, though glorious to behold in Technicolor, it lacks anything vital (like an intelligent script) to make good entertainment. Indeed, it is simply a series of vignettes, some sequences with big-name stars lasting less than thirty seconds, tied together with a tediously dull debate between Colman and Price, as The Spirit of Man versus The Devil, with an overly abundant amount of stock footage from other Warner Bros. historical films.

Today *The Story of Mankind* is considered one of the "50 worst films of all time," and it rightfully deserves that definitive honor. What a sad disappointment to see the great Ronald Colman at age sixty-six in his final role. He was greatly disappointed with the whole affair. Hedy's sequence as Joan of Arc is the eighth of two dozen episodes in the film, and testifying to the reviews of the day is the statement the young William Schallert exclaims in his ten-second scene: "Get on with the burning. Put an end to this trial!" When Chico Marx, as a monk, advises Christopher Columbus (Anthony Dexter) that when he decides to sail around the world, "Ya'll fall off de end of de eoyt!" one ponders, Were they serious?

As Joan of Arc, Hedy has a quick costume change once voices speak to her, and, suddenly decked out in a white tunic under gray chain-mail battle armor, she is shown giving orders to her men while sitting on a stationary white steed. When brought to trial, the inevitable worst line in epic pictures (better used by DeMille) is declaimed by yet another bit actor relishing his fleeting moment on the screen: "Where is your Saint Michael now, maid of Orleans?" In her final sequence, Hedy, in a white robe, burns at the stake. Were it but the film that had gone up in flames!

Hedy was a guest on the hour-long *Arthur Murray Party* on December 28, broadcast in color on NBC. On January 5, 1958, she was once more on the half-hour *What's My Line?*, this time as a guest panelist with the publisher Bennett Cerf, the columnist Dorothy Kilgallen, and the actor Martin Gabel. (The mystery guest that evening was the pop singer Pat Boone.)

Back in Houston, Hedy was hit with yet another lawsuit at the end of the month, this one from her lawyers, William G. Israel and Morton B. Harper. The two claimed that Hedy had failed to pay them $8,557 in expenses incurred over the past four years. They were also asking for an additional $25,000 for special services they provided her in connection with *The Love of Three Queens,* of which they claimed they had only been paid $9,000. The suit was dismissed in February 1959.

On January 22, 1958, Hedy's final film, *The Female Animal,* opened to bland reviews. In advertisements the taglines read, "It is said that when a woman fights for a man she is like an ANIMAL . . . This is the motion picture that proves it!" But one reviewer observed, "The houses are in better taste than the occupants."[17] Another critic commented, "Mr. Nader looks, on the whole, much too intelligent for the dumb ox-head role he is called upon to play; and Miss Lamarr never convinces you that she cannot tell the difference between a sweetheart and a kept male lover."[18]

When the film was shown on the lower half of a double bill in New York, H. H. T. of *The New York Times* wrote, "After the showdown, Miss Lamarr nobly tries suicide, then smilingly waves the two younger people off into the future. . . . The real trouble is nobody matters—none of them."[19]

Compared with the pictures both Bette Davis and Joan Crawford were turning out during the 1950s, *The Female Animal* is certainly no worse and is possibly even more interesting. Shot in CinemaScope and promising torrid clichés and insinuating, sexual dialogue, as written by the screenwriter Robert Hill the film just sadly disintegrates from the start.

In the picture Hedy is garbed in ten gorgeous outfits, and her figure is still quite impressive. However, one soon begins to lose count of her costume changes and starts adding up how many times Nader strips down (four to be exact) to show off his muscular torso and biceps and display himself in form-fitting, open-to-the-waist cotton shirts with rolled-up sleeves and snug dark jeans. (In actuality, this was the "gay" look of the 1950s.)

There is something different in Hedy's appearance in *The Female Animal*. Her hairstyle is wrong for her (she wore a wig), and she sports the then-fashionable Italian upsweep eye makeup so popular during the decade. It worked for young starlets with short pixie cuts and cherubic faces, but not on more mature actresses with the classical beauty on which Hedy had based her fortune. She simply looks hard. Her performance in the picture veers from bad to distracted, yet at times it is actually quite sensitive.

Hedy is light-years ahead of Jane Powell in acting ability in their scenes together. "Hedy did not like Jane Powell," Robert Osborne said in 2007. "And for both of them it was a Universal picture, not a major production. Hedy was playing a mother [of a grown child] for the first time. Hedy wasn't [keen on] Jane or playing a mom."[20] To be generous, Powell's performance is dreadful and over the top. She had no idea how to *underplay* being drunk, and her first scenes in the picture are embarrassingly amateurish. Petite and wholesomely attractive, Powell was simply out of her element.

As *The Female Animal* slowly faded away, so did Hedy's Hollywood career. More and more she was flying to New York, to California, to Jamaica, anywhere to escape being with her husband. When Denise and Anthony finished their school terms, once again Hedy saw that they summered at a new camp, Southland, in California.

By June, she had begun living permanently in Hollywood, her new address 614 North Beverly Drive in Beverly Hills. She was interviewed by Hedda Hopper in July, telling the columnist that she was in the process of cutting *L'eterna femmina,* which she had shot abroad, and working on her autobiography: "I'll tell the whole truth." When Hopper asked her what the status of her marriage was, Hedy replied vaguely, "How is any marriage? You do your best and hope. My husband calls me several times a week, but I can't believe he'll be here."[21]

Hedy had recently told another reporter, "I feel sure that Howard and I will never get a divorce. Basically, we are very fond of each other. Howard loves me in his own fashion, I know. It's not quite my idea of love, but it is sincere."[22]

On August 8, Hedy announced her separation from Howard Lee. At the end of the summer, the children came to live with their mother in California.

When they asked her when they were returning to Houston, she told them they were instead settling in Hollywood, since she was divorcing Howard.

Denise suddenly had lost her stepfather, her best girlfriends, and her boyfriend and would only be allowed to see them again when she returned to Houston to visit. Now a teenager, that summer she obtained her first job filing in a warehouse at Lanz of Salzburg, where her "Grangi" Trude worked. At thirteen, Denise had already attended one year at Lanier Junior High School in Houston. Her two very best friends there were Lucy Holmes, her next-door neighbor, and Joanne Levy. Denise and Anthony were then enrolled in the Hawthorne School in Hawthorne, California, that fall.

When she was a little girl, Denise collected small glass and stuffed animals and took ballet and ballroom dancing. Since her mother was away a good deal of the time, Denise naturally missed her and would recall that as a child she often cried out of loneliness when she played with her Hedy Lamarr paper dolls. In the sixth grade, Denise won an art contest, and that sparked a desire in her to paint. She loved and admired her mother immensely, and she wanted to go to the International School in Geneva and try her hand at acting. She also decided at an early age that she wanted to be married by the time she was twenty-two and to have two children.

As a youth, Anthony occupied his time playing with his H.O. scale model trains and reading war comics, like so many boys did in the 1950s. On Tuesday, December 9, the eleven-year-old was seriously injured in an accident. He had been riding his bike on the street in the same direction as traffic when he suddenly collided with an automobile driven by sixty-five-year-old Frank Burnell. Taken to the Beverly Hills Receiving Hospital first-aid station for emergency treatment, he was then rushed to the Cedars of Lebanon Hospital, where it was discovered he was suffering from a small skull fracture and a cerebral concussion. His condition was pronounced serious, and Hedy rushed to his side. The following day Anthony was taken off the critical list.

Hedy was traumatized by her son's accident. She was "in shock" the day after, the papers reported, and not giving interviews. According to a later report, she said the following about the extent of her shock from the incident: "I lost all my hair. . . . I just don't dare let people see me like this."[23]

But it wasn't just this crisis that had Hedy in turmoil and despair. Her estranged husband Howard was preparing to play hardball with her. His oil investments were huge, and his holdings complicated. In her past divorce proceedings, her husbands realized she was headstrong and determined, but perhaps their hands were not so clean. Up to then none of Hedy's other husbands had ever put up a battle for their assets as did Lee. And Hedy was equally stunned and furious.

On January 21, 1959, after a conference with her trustees; her accountant, William Kraker; and her business manager, William Stein, Hedy announced to the press that she was suing Howard for financial aid to the tune of $51,000, half the amount of the sale of the house. She claimed that Howard had violated their separation agreement, signed on August 6 when they decided to live separate lives. Hedy's prepared statement read, "As a direct consequence of the defendant's utter failure and refusal to recognize, perform or fulfill his obligations under said agreement, plaintiff Hedy Lamarr Lee has been catapulted into desperate financial straits, becoming seriously ill."[24]

Hedy further claimed that because of Anthony's medical bills, she was required to sell off her assets and that she was now nearly penniless. The suit demanded immediate payment from Lee, plus Hedy wanted the court to appoint a receiver to make sure she received half the assets from the sale of their Houston home. Lee was unavailable for comment, supposedly in Aspen at the Villa Lamarr.

"He was the only man I ever really loved," Hedy told the *Houston Chronicle* in a statement aimed at garnering emotional support. "I loved Houston, but, it was a miserable mistake. . . . I made many friends in Houston. . . . I tried so hard but they wouldn't accept me. Howard is now three months behind in his payments and he didn't even send me a Christmas card." She said she had just recovered from a recent bout with pneumonia, which had kept her from accepting acting roles. "I've been too ill to take them," she complained. "At present my only means of support is from Howard."[25] Hedy said Howard was behind in his monthly separation payments, which amounted to $9,000.

Lee countersued Hedy on February 3 for divorce. The petition, filed in the District Court of Houston, alleged that the couple's extremely large living expenses prevented them from accumulating a community estate. "For a period of many months prior to the time that defendant separated from plaintiff she was guilty of such excesses, cruel treatment and outrages as to seriously affect and endanger plaintiff's health and to render living together insupportable," the petition read. Lee also asked that all separate property owned by him before the marriage be awarded to him, "and that the courts determine what equity Miss Lamarr may have in other holdings."[26]

As spring approached, Hedy was involved in even more lawsuits. On March 3, she was named a defendant in two separate cases initiated by accountants in Los Angeles. The first was by Jack A. Sain, who claimed that Hedy owed him $8,997 for 1950 income-tax deductions he was able to secure for her, amounting to $89,970.

The second was by the accountant Robert J. Mason, who sued for $7,000 that he said Hedy had failed to pay him and his partner, Eli G. Gold, for services they rendered her between 1950 and 1952. A settlement for that lawsuit was reached in 1960, but only after Hedy failed to appear for trial.

On March 7, Hedy filed a countersuit to Lee's divorce action. She was now demanding $7,500 a month in support payments pending the settlement of the case. She also insisted that Howard desist from disposing of their community estate, which remained under his control. A hearing was set by Judge Wilmer Hunt for March 23.

Hedy then sued Frank J. Burnell, the driver of the automobile that struck Anthony in December, demanding $100,000 for negligence. The complaint was filed in Los Angeles Superior Court. Hedy, sporting a sable coat, accepted only $3,500 from Burnell, the manager of a golf-driving range, when the verdict was made by Judge Clarke E. Stephens in March 1961.

She sorely complained that she would be receiving nothing under the compromise in the settlement. Her attorneys' expenses totaled $875, and the rest was used to pay medical bills.

Hedy once said, "After a taste of stardom, everything else is poverty."[27] What had begun with so much promise in 1957, Hedy's return to films and television, had ended in disappointment and despair. However, as dark as the 1950s were both professionally and personally, the next fifteen years for Hedy would prove to be a nightmare.

20

Purgatory

Hedy and George Antheil had remained in touch with each other over the years, and his life had nearly been as complicated as hers. He continued writing music throughout the 1940s and 1950s, somewhat unsuccessfully. With another woman, he fathered another son toward the end of his life, though he stayed married to Boski. On February 12, 1959, Antheil died of a heart attack at his home at 610 West End Avenue in New York. He was just fifty-eight years old. Hedy did not attend his memorial service.

In the endless divorce proceedings, a hearing for monthly support was held on April 14, topping off three months of bitter disputes between Hedy and Howard. The Lees' bookkeeper said Hedy's monthly household expenses came to $5,527, her medical expenses averaged $1,000, and her monthly telephone expenses amounted to $500. According to her business manager, Hedy was currently overdrawn at her bank by $2,000 and was in debt for over $45,000.

Besides her rent on the Beverly Hills house, each month Hedy had to pay domestic help, $600; her personal wardrobe expenses, $500; her spending money, $100; entertainment, $150; automobile expenses, $40; allowances for her mother Trude and her two children, $262; food and supplies, $600; and cosmetics and beauty-salon costs, $100. These were not excessive or extravagant amounts for film stars of the day.

Under cross-examination, Hedy's business manager, William Stein, conceded that some of her monthly expenditures could possibly be eliminated, including the $850 a month spent for rent on her unfurnished North Beverly Drive house in Beverly Hills. Judge Hunt's decision was to award Hedy a temporary settlement of $3,000 a month. She told the press, "This is what I get for putting up with Mr. Lee."[1]

For months Hedy secluded herself in Beverly Hills. Wrote Helena Kane of *The Newark Evening News*: "Her heart is heavy. Her beauty is gone. . . . The former Viennese temptress is unwanted, unloved, unhappy. She . . . does not work and has no immediate prospects in view." Hedy did tell Kane she was working on her autobiography in collaboration with "a West Coast writer." She called it *Ecstasy and Me*. "The title of the book is meant to be ironic," Hedy explained.[2]

Hedy vowed never to return to the state of Texas. When she failed twice to answer a summons to appear in court for pretrial hearings, Houston Domestic Relations Judge Benjamin Woodall slashed her alimony from $3,000 to $250.[3] She told the press pathetically, "We've been eating TV dinners for the last three months."[4]

On April 19, Hedy failed to appear in court in Houston once again. She instead sent her former stand-in Sylvia Hollis (also known as Sylvia Lamarr) to testify with a letter of explanation. Hedy had also fired her three attorneys, Jack Okin, Frederick Robinson, and J. Edwin Smith, by mail, stating, "You told me that the judge said that I would not have to come to Houston. Since you have refused to answer my questions pertaining to the lawsuit Lee vs. Lee, and for other reasons, you give me no choice but fire you herewith."[5]

When Hollis arrived dressed as Hedy in court, even Hedy's attorney Smith, who had just been advised of his dismissal but still appeared, was shocked. Howard Lee simply smiled in amusement. "I cannot swear to this," Smith told the court. "But I believe my client is being mis-advised by someone in California or Colorado." Hollis, her auburn-colored hair covered by a straw hat with dark ties under her chin, exactly as Hedy had appeared last in court, told the judge, "In my own foolish way I thought I could help."[6]

Smith asked that Judge Woodall rule if he was still attorney for Hedy or not, and the judge bypassed a ruling. Instead, he sent a wire to Hedy demanding her appearance the following morning at 10:30 A.M. for the trial, stating that if she did not appear, he would rule an uncontested divorce in Howard's favor, meaning Lee would not owe her a dime. In Hollywood, Hedy's business manager William Stein told the press she was too upset to discuss the case.

"Why should I go?" she said. "Howard couldn't hurt me any more than he

already had in the years of our married life. I had nothing to gain."[7] The following day, Hedy still did not appear but sent her new attorney, Seymour
Lieberman, instead, and Judge Woodall allowed her former attorney, Smith,
to intervene when he found it necessary.

It was eventually revealed that Hedy had been working with the Denver attorney James B. Radetsky by telephone to discuss some sort of agreement regarding a settlement with Howard's two attorneys, Frank Knapp and Willard
Scheurer. It was also explained that Hedy's Lincoln Continental had been attached to her debts because she was unable to pay Cedars of Lebanon Hospital
an $800 bill accrued from Anthony's treatment after his accident.

Hedy saw herself as the victim. She told the press, "For many months I was
in a coma as a result of my life with Howard. . . . I guess I took too much upon
myself. I always had to make excuses for him when we were invited out to parties. I could never tell the truth."[8]

On April 22, Hedy was awarded a settlement of approximately $500,000 in
Howard's uncontested divorce from her. The news was brought to Hedy at her
Beverly Hills home by Radetsky. (He could not call her with the news since her
telephone had been shut off because of a $1,000 overdue bill.) In the settlement
she was to receive interests in some of Howard's oil-well investments, which
would bring her a steady income of $3,600 a month; she would receive $73,000
in cash to clean up her debts and $50,000 in negotiable notes. She was allowed
to keep her furs, jewelry, and furniture then in her possession.

Hedy was required to pay, from her settlement, $50,000 each to her two
attorneys, J. Edwin Smith and Jack Okin, and $25,000 to Frederick Robinson.
Seymour Lieberman and James Radetsky were each given $50,000.

Regarding the fate of the Tyrolean chalet in Aspen, Colorado, Hedy insinuated
to the press that she had built it for Howard as a getaway from Houston. She
suggested he did not now need it. Apparently, however, Howard *did* need it
now that he was single again. He had met the actress Gene Tierney in Aspen
before the divorce, and they would marry at the Aspen Methodist Church on
July 11, 1960. Tierney gave up her career and retired to Houston. Howard
passed away there on February 17, 1981. Tierney, who never remarried, died of
emphysema ten years later. W. Howard Lee and Gene Tierney are buried side
by side in a Houston cemetery.

In 1961, Denise turned sixteen and was an attractive girl with a strong
resemblance to her mother. Anthony was a fifteen-year-old teenage lad and

growing good-looking and tall like his father. As her children matured, Hedy concentrated much of her desperation on their well-being.

Hedy focused herself on reorganizing her complicated life. She traveled, and she made a brief television appearance before Thanksgiving on a live Los Angeles broadcast of the annual *Santa's Wonderland,* on behalf of Saints and Sinners, a benevolent organization.

Hedy needed immediate money and contacted the Plaza Art Galleries in Manhattan to conduct a sale, held on May 3, of some of her remaining collection of paintings, watercolors, and bronzes. Among the pieces she put up for auction were the watercolors *St. Mark's Square, Venice,* by Raoul Dufy, and *Summer Landscape with Poplar Trees,* by Maurice de Vlaminck; the oil paintings *Three Wise Men,* by Georges Rouault; *Italian Peasants,* by Maurice Utrillo; plus other paintings by Pierre-Auguste Renoir, Armand Guillaumin, and Alexej von Kawlensky and sculptures by Auguste Rodin, Honoré Daumier, and Antoine Louis Barye.[9] The profits Hedy made from the sale of her art treasures kept the children in private school and her payments up on her home in Beverly Hills.

Hedy traveled to New York, and before the auction she appeared on *The Tonight Show* at NBC's Rockefeller Center studios, on April 23. At a party one night, Hedy told the Random House publisher Bennett Cerf that she was writing her memoirs. "I've always thought I had quite an exciting life," she later told a newspaper writer, "but he told me I had only enough to fill one magazine issue." She replied to Cerf with a giggle, "Why, my lawsuits alone would fill two chapters."[10]

Catching up with her in September was the lawsuit field by her two former lawyers, Morton B. Harper and William G. Israel. Hedy testified to the attorney M. C. Inman Jr. that she could not pay the balance of her agreement to the two men since it was based on profits made from *The Love of Three Queens,* which played briefly in Europe and not in the United States. Hedy claimed that she could not even buy a postage stamp if she wanted to—an exaggeration, but on December 17 Superior Court Judge Brodie Ahlports ruled against Harper and Israel.

On November 19, Hedy guest starred as a panelist on CBS's popular nighttime game show *Stump the Stars,* where two teams of four celebrities each pantomimed a secret phrase in a limited amount of time. Hedy's team lost. But, nevertheless, she looked attractive in a sleeveless black dress and with her shoulder-length hair stylishly coiffed.

Another lawsuit Hedy dealt with during this time was brought on by her former friend Lois Ross, who fell down a flight of stairs at Hedy's home on North Beverly Drive on May 19, 1962. Ross claimed she suffered a spinal fracture and sued Hedy and the owner of the property, Beatrice A. Sedway, for $150,000. On Monday, December 17, the same day Hedy won the suit filed by her two former attorneys, the court ruled against Ross's claim and in Hedy's favor.

Hedy was in the news in January 1963, when it was announced that the cameras were set to roll within weeks on *Hotel Paradise,* a television play to be directed by Ralph Nelson for CBS, starring Robert Horton, Hedy, and Angie Dickinson. But the project was delayed and then abandoned.

In February, Hedy moved into an apartment located at 1802 Angelo Drive in Beverly Hills. She had been looking for a new lawyer, and her friend Jerry Geisler suggested she confer with a colleague of his in his law firm, Lewis W. Boies Jr. Born in 1921, Boies was a Stanford law graduate who had once been a deputy district attorney. He had been married and divorced and had two children, a boy and a girl. Boies apparently advised Hedy on several issues, and eventually he fell in love with her, courting her with flowers and taking her to dinner. Soon the two were living together.

On March 4, 1963, Hedy married for the sixth time. Planning a business trip to Fresno earlier that day, Boies asked Hedy to come along. After driving to Turlock to see his parents in the morning, the couple then drove on to Fresno. Around 5:45 P.M., after arriving at the home of Boies's friend and former law partner, L. Kenneth Say, the couple announced they wanted to marry. Say asked his friend Judge Joseph L. Joy to officiate at the wedding.

Obtaining a marriage license from another of Say's friends, County Clerk J. Les Brown shortly after 7 P.M., Hedy and Lewis were wed. Present at the brief ceremony were Say's wife and stepdaughter and Judge Joy's wife and son. After splitting a bottle of champagne, the newlyweds stayed briefly to visit before departing.

There were several reasons why Hedy wed a sixth time. According to her, Lewis promised she would never have to worry about money again. She once wrote that she felt almost pressured into marrying because she worried for her children. But, more telling than that, Hedy confided that she was impressed with Lewis's masculinity and "his insatiable need for me."[11] The couple took a two-year lease on a house in Beverly Hills, located at 9550 Hidden Valley Road, right across the street from Jack L. and Ann Warner. Hedy signed for it.

On Sunday, May 3, 1964, Hedy appeared on yet another nighttime game show, CBS's *The Celebrity Game,* hosted by Carl Reiner. The premise of the show was for the guest panelists to answer set questions and for contestants to guess what their answers might be.

In 2008 Reiner recalled of Hedy:

> Her beauty was breathtaking. . . . You were very aware you were sitting next to an icon. . . . After the show my wife [Estelle] and I drove her home. . . . I was very taken with her high intelligence. When we got to her home, she asked if we wanted to come in for a cup of coffee. And then there was the shocking surprise of the knowledge and the collection of good art that she had in the house. She never talked about it, you know, her art collection. My wife was an artist, and she was stunned by the quality and the depth of her understanding of fine art. Her collection was probably one of the best private collections she had ever seen.[12]

On August 15 the press announced that the director Mitchell Leisen was planning to film *The Spring of the Tiger,* a modern version of *Don Juan* taken from the poem by Lord Byron. The picture was scheduled to start shooting in Madrid that November, with Hedy to appear opposite one of Spain's biggest stars, the thirty-two-year-old Venezuelan-born actor Espartaco B. Santoni, who was also coproducing the film. Also to be in the cast were Tab Hunter, Ramon Novarro, and Pier Angeli. Like so many other projects, the production ran into troubles.

By the end of the year it was history. Hedy filed a $700,000 breach-of-contract suit on December 20 against Santoni and the film's backers, claiming she was scheduled to begin work no later than November 9 and had never been called. And, more to the point, she was never paid. She was seeking her contracted salary of $50,000 plus $650,000 in damages. The outcome of the suit was never made public.

Hedy realized early on in her marriage to Boies it was a mistake. They had begun to quarrel frequently. Married just a year and a half, she and Lewis separated on October 15, 1964.

By now Hedy's children were on their own. Hedy's elder son, James Lamarr Loder, who had not heard from his mother for over ten years, left the Gray

Hedy selling War Bonds on tour, 1942 (AUTHOR COLLECTION)

Hedy and James Lamarr Markey
(later Loder), c. 1945 (COURTESY OF
THE ARLENE ROXBURY COLLECTION)

John Loder and Hedy Lamarr wed, May 27, 1943 (Denise Loder-DeLuca Collection)

Hedy Lamarr, *The Heavenly Body*, 1943 (Denise Loder-DeLuca Collection)

With Peter Lorre in *The Conspirators*, 1944 (Author Collection)

With Paul Lukas in *Experiment Perilous*, 1944 (Denise Loder-DeLuca Collection)

With Robert Walker in *Her Highness and the Bellboy*, 1945 (Denise Loder-DeLuca Collection)

With John and their baby, Denise Hedwig Loder, 1945 (Denise Loder-DeLuca Collection)

With George Sanders in *The Strange Woman*, 1946 (Author Collection)

On the set of *The Strange Woman*, 1946 (Author Collection)

With soon-to-be ex-husband John Loder in *Dishonored Lady*, 1946 (AUTHOR COLLECTION)

The last family photo with James Lamarr Loder: his ninth-birthday celebration with his mother, Denise, and Anthony, March 1948 (AUTHOR COLLECTION)

TOP: With Robert Cummings in *Let's Live a Little*, 1948 (AUTHOR COLLECTION)

BOTTOM: As Delilah in the Edith Head–designed peacock-feathered robe in *Samson and Delilah*, 1949 (AUTHOR COLLECTION)

With Victor Mature in *Samson and Delilah*, 1949 (Denise Loder-DeLuca Collection)

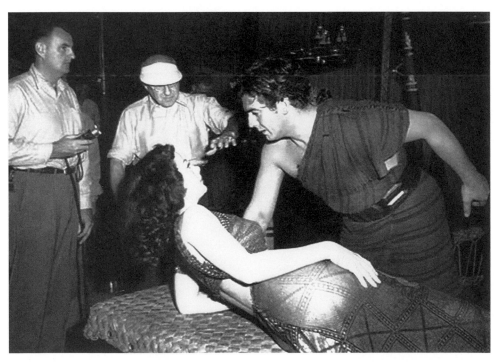

On the set of *Samson and Delilah* as director Cecil B. DeMille (wearing visor) gives direction, 1948 (Author Collection)

With John Hodiak in the film noir, *A Lady Without Passport*, 1950 (AUTHOR COLLECTION)

In *A Lady Without Passport*, 1950 (AUTHOR COLLECTION)

In *Copper Canyon*, 1950 (COURTESY OF THE ARLENE ROXBURY COLLECTION)

With Bob Hope in *My Favorite Spy*, 1951 (Denise Loder-DeLuca Collection)

Hedy weds Teddy Stauffer, June 11, 1951; Superior Judge Stanley Mosk, left (Photofest)

As Helen of Troy in *L'Amante di Paride*, 1953 (Denise Loder-DeLuca Collection)

Hedy weds W. Howard Lee, New York,
1953 (Photofest)

Hedy on holiday in Europe, c. 1954

(Denise Loder-DeLuca Collection)

Top: The real Hedy Lamarr, early 1950s (DENISE LODER-DELUCA COLLECTION)

Bottom: Hedy painting on the beach (her daughter's favorite picture of her mother), early 1950s (DENISE LODER-DELUCA COLLECTION)

With Julie Adams in a deleted scene from *Slaughter on Tenth Avenue*, 1958
(AUTHOR COLLECTION)

As Joan of Arc in *The Story of Mankind*, 1958 (AUTHOR COLLECTION)

In "The Proud Woman," an episode of *Dick Powell's Zane Grey Theater*, 1957 (AUTHOR COLLECTION)

Denise, Hedy, and Anthony during the filming of *The Female Animal*, 1958 (DENISE LODER-DeLUCA COLLECTION)

Hedy with Lewis Boies Jr., Christmas Day,
1963 (ANTHONY LODER COLLECTION)

Costume test for *Picture Mommy Dead*,
January 1966 (AUTHOR COLLECTION)

With Anthony Loder, Los Angeles shoplifting trial victory, April 1966
(PHOTOFEST)

Hedy with Denise, holding granddaughter Wendy Colton, c. 1970 (Denise Loder-DeLuca Collection)

On holiday, 1969 (Denise Loder-DeLuca Collection)

Hedy in repose during the Christmas holidays, 1980. On the back Hedy wrote to Wendy, "Now and always with love Mom and Granny" (Denise Loder-DeLuca Collection)

Hedy Lamarr toward the end of her life, 1997 (Courtesy of the Arlene Roxbury Collection)

home after completing his education. At age eighteen he joined the United States Air Force, serving his country approximately eight years. In 1965 he was living in Omaha, Nebraska, and training for the police force.

Both Denise and Anthony were now enrolled at the prestigious Stockbridge School in Interlaken, Massachusetts. Hans K. Maeder and his wife Ruth opened the small, elite institution in 1949. It was considered one of the most advanced, progressive private boarding schools in New England, stressing interracial understanding and international education. Its students were required to read *The New York Times* and listen to a minimum of twenty minutes of classical music daily.

The Stockbridge School also graduated many illustrious alumni, including the singer Arlo Guthrie, the future actress Rosemary Forsyth, Jackie Robinson Jr., and Denise's best friend, Steve Rivers, the son of the artist Larry Rivers. While attending Stockbridge, Denise briefly dated fellow student and future comic Chevy Chase.

For the last half of her junior year, Denise was schooled in Paris. She recalled in 2009, "Each class would go to a different place. . . . We attended outside Paris a regular school, and we had teachers there. But I was so interested in art. I would go into the city, taking it all in myself. I was reprimanded, 'Denise needs to quit looking at all the art,' and needs to get back, you know, to reading, writing, and arithmetic."[13] Hedy proudly told the press, "She's really a fine painter and wrote me the most wonderful letter about conditions over there. She's a beautiful girl, and I'm glad she doesn't want to be an actress."[14] Denise graduated from Stockbridge in 1963.

She then enrolled at the University of California-Berkeley. Now a beautiful young woman with her mother's eyes and coloring, in April 1965, when she was a sophomore, Denise became engaged to the minor-league Philadelphia Phillies' baseball player, twenty-three-year-old Lawrence "Larry" Colton, a 1964 graduate of the university, whom she had met on campus. Colton was then pitching in Eugene, Oregon.

After his graduation in 1964, Anthony attended the University of California-Los Angeles. At the age of seventeen, he could not remember ever having met his father. He wrote John Loder, who was at the time retired from acting and living in Buenos Aires with his South American wife, and told his father that he wanted to meet him. Loder wrote back to his son and suggested that he learn Spanish, get a job on a tramp steamer, and sail down to South America.[15]

It took Anthony a year and a half to do so, but sail to South America he did, only to find that Loder had returned to England.

On May 10, 1965, Hedy sued Lewis W. Boies Jr. for divorce in superior court, charging extreme mental cruelty and grievous mental suffering. She asked for $3,510 in monthly alimony and all community property, and, as she had done in the Lee divorce, she again advised the court she was broke and could not pay court costs. According to Hedy, Lewis liked vodka, though he said she drove him to it. He also liked to talk in bed, which Hedy did not. His favorite subjects were usually baseball and law. Hedy complained she had little sleep during their marriage. Boies did not contest the divorce. Despite the divorce, Lewis still cared for her.

Hedy would always believe that Lewis loved her. Shortly after she began the divorce proceedings, she received a note from him. "Hedy, Darling, I had a long talk with Mike [Inman, the lawyer]—you've apparently given up on me," he wrote. "Although I've hurt you, I love you. I can't seem to organize myself to give you what you want and need. I'm very humble, but I will not contest anything you want. I can't see my life without you."[16]

Testifying in court on June 2 to Judge Roger Alton Pfaff, Hedy said that Lewis was locked out of the house one night and came crashing through the window with a baseball bat in his hands, threatening to kill somebody. Hedy also testified that another time, at a party, Lewis, without provocation, picked up a card table and threw it across the room in front of guests. Through her two attorneys, Alfred E. Paonessa, a retired superior court judge, and Bruce A. Thabit, Hedy told the court that in the two and a half years they were together, Lewis, who had promised her financial security, had actually run into debt and that, because of the sale of some of her valuable French paintings, for which she took a huge loss, she had spent some $500,000 of her own money during the nineteen months of their union.

Hedy received little sympathy in the press during these proceedings. The public had heard it all before. Still, she was defensive about public criticism. "My problem is, I'm a hell of a nice dame," she said. "The most horrible whores are famous. I did what I did for love. The others did it for money."[17]

Nineteen-year-old Anthony was with his mother throughout her divorce trial, and he testified that he felt the marriage was a destructive relationship. He also stated that he was forced to intercede for his mother and push Lewis away from her on occasion. Hedy was granted $1,250 a month in alimony for two years and half of Lewis's gross income over $15,000, again for two years, plus interest in a company he owned, Jamsco Corp., a manufacturer of message machines.

On August 10, Hedy, with her attorney Fred DeLuca, took Lewis back to the county courthouse, charging him with contempt. Hedy portrayed herself as so broke she could not buy food. She said she had not received any of the alimony Lewis had been ordered to pay. Boies had resigned "by mutual agreement" from the law offices of Jerry Geisler and claimed in court that he had only earned $1,250 since May. Superior Court Commissioner Frank H. Stoddard ruled in Boies's favor, concluding his failure to make payment was not willful.[18]

Boies was actually a good and very decent man, despite what was charged in court. As an adult, Denise would say that she loved Lewis dearly, and he was always very good to her and her brother. Hedy never completely morally crucified her husbands in court, though there were times she possibly could have. A couple of her former husbands had serious drinking problems, a problem barely touched on in her complaints. She stuck to propriety as much as she could (or her lawyers would allow), only venting her frustrations and anger with her spouses' reluctance to pay her alimony.

On Saturday, July 10, 1965, Denise Hedwig Loder Lee married Lawrence Robert Colton at 4:00 P.M. at the All Saints' Episcopal Church in Beverly Hills, with a reception following at the Santa Ynez Inn in the Pacific Palisades. The bride, her lush dark hair coiffed fashionably under a waist-length veil, wore a form-fitting white wedding dress with a long-sleeved lace bodice. She carried a bouquet of pale flowers. Her groom wore a white jacket, dark pants, and a bow tie. Dressed in a colorful print outfit and sporting a sun hat and a simple strand of pearls, Hedy looked tired but happy for her daughter. John Loder was not present, and Marvin Neal walked Denise down the aisle.

The film historian and television personality Robert Osborne, the future host of Turner Classic Movies, met Hedy Lamarr in late July 1965, and the two become close friends. As Osborne recalled in 2007, "I was living in Hollywood at a very exciting time, working as a model at the May Co. in Los Angeles." His boss, Jean Raines, wanted him to attend a party one Saturday night and told him, "I want you to pick up this old movie star. You might enjoy meeting her." Osborne said, "Well, sure. Who is it?" When she said it was Hedy Lamarr, he thought, "Oh, my God!" After he picked Hedy up, "Right off the bat we clicked. She was so down-to-earth. That was so surprising. She looked wonderful. She didn't look exactly like Hedy Lamarr as people would recognize her with jet-black hair parted down the middle. But she was beautiful. And she had kind of champagne-colored hair. And she was so much fun—that was the thing that was so amazing!"[19]

As he got to know her, Osborne recalled thinking, "This is a peasant girl who likes to have fun. . . . She liked to go on picnics; we'd go on picnics all the time. She'd like to get in the car and go. I never could figure out how I got into her life so easily. She didn't have a lot of pals to do things with. She had great energy."

He described the time they spent together: "She would call me and I'd call her. I wasn't regularly employed. I was trying to write . . . and I was doing modeling, and I was trying to be an actor, all these things. But I wasn't that busy. . . . We'd go on adventures. She loved to go and park the car and climb over walls . . . and fences and go into fields and stuff we weren't really supposed to be in. Just to investigate things. There was a group [of us] that included Rafer Johnson [the 1960 Olympic decathlon gold medalist] and [the actor] Jack and Camille De Mave," Osborne said. "I remember going to John Carlyle's house one time, and Judy Garland gave a party at his house, and Hedy was there," recalled Osborne. "All evening she and Judy were giggling and laughing, and Hedy didn't drink, maybe a little wine or so, but did not drink. Judy did and was taking her pills. They would be giggling and laughing and they'd go into the bathroom and come out and they would have changed clothes. Then they'd be laughing and giggling, and go back into the bathroom and they'd come out in a different change of clothes again."[20]

Hedy was beginning to enjoy her life in the company of handsome, single young men who did not pose a threat to her yet kept her company, made her laugh, and cared for her well-being. After her divorce, despite living alone in a small unfurnished house, this brief moment in time may have been one of the happiest in Hedy's life.

On October 21, 1965, Hedy made a startling appearance on the teenage-focused television program on ABC, *Shindig*. She looked stunningly youthful, with a new and stylishly shorter hairdo, wearing a sleeveless blouse, dark pants, and go-go boots. One would never guess Hedy was then fifty years old.

Ed Rambeau, who was on the show and sang two of his hit songs ("Concrete and Clay" and "The Train"), remembered meeting her. "The ratings were dropping and they threw in celebrity stars to pick up the ratings," he said.

"They weren't using anybody in the record industry, just celebrities." The show was rehearsed in full during the afternoon, then performed live and recorded on kinescope. "I remember at the end of the show, because it was all done in one take, and all of a sudden we all had to go on and dance. She came to me and said, 'What do I do?' And I said, 'Go out and shake it and move it, Hedy.' And she went out and did it."[21]

Judy Garland's daughter by Vincente Minnelli, Liza Minnelli, fresh from her breakthrough performance off-Broadway in *Best Foot Forward,* opened at Hollywood's Cocoanut Grove in early November 1965. Judy, who had just married that week, chose not to attend the opening night to avoid attracting attention away from Liza. Robert Osborne recalled that Judy's new husband,

> Mark Herron . . . was a good friend of mine . . . and he said [to Judy on the second night] why don't we get Robert and Hedy, because they knew we were doing a lot of stuff together, and get Lana Turner and her husband, she'd just married Bob Eaton, and get the three Ziegfeld girls together. . . . So Mark called me, and it was fine with Hedy. And Judy got on the phone and called Lana and had a long, long giggly talk, but Lana couldn't go, so instead they invited Mickey Rooney and his [then] wife [Barbara].
>
> So we went to this thing . . . we were all at this table and I remember Hedy looked wonderful, just looked beautiful. And Frank Sinatra came to the second night and Dean Martin was there and they came over to the table to greet Judy. And we're chatting and everything, and Judy said, "Oh, Frank. You know Hedy Lamarr." And he kind of turned and said, "Uh, I beg your pardon?" And he didn't recognize her. And she just went white. And she said, "Frank, it's Hedy." And he kind of looked, and then went, "Oh!" And then he was very charming.[22]

Perhaps Sinatra had not recognized her. Or maybe perhaps he remembered Acapulco.

Osborne's friend the late John Carlyle had also had a *Ziegfeld Girl* reunion of sorts at a small party in his home some time before Garland and Herron wed. Judy, dressed in pearls and a floor-length black dress, showed up with Paul Millard. Hedy came dressed in a trendy fur jacket and slacks on the arm of a casting director, and Lana Turner's daughter, Cheryl Crane, came with a girlfriend. When Hedy saw Judy she told her "how zilly you look." Wrote one observer, "Judy Garland and Hedy Lamarr spent a long time huddled on his bed talking about what better mothers to Cheryl they would have been than Lana." Later that evening, Hedy asked Judy to sing "Over the Rainbow," and Judy said, "You sing it." And Hedy did, with a Viennese accent.[23]

Shortly before Thanksgiving, Hedy contracted Charles Stern as her agent. *Variety* reported on January 19, 1966, that Hedy was then signed for a cameo role by the independent film director Bert I. Gordon for *Picture Mommy Dead,* written by Robert Sherman and to be produced by Joseph E. Levine's Embassy Pictures. Hedy was to share top billing with Don Ameche and Martha Hyer. She was to be paid $10,000 for her role. (Ironically, unbeknownst to Hedy, the part had first been offered to Gene Tierney, who had declined.) Filming was scheduled to begin the last week of January 1966, location shooting to take place at the historic Greystone Mansion.

Still photography of Hedy wearing a $165 strapless, ermine-trimmed bodiced evening gown was made by Gordon himself at the home of the actor George Hamilton. That evening the M-G-M makeup man Bill Tuttle, and the hairstylist Joel Israel arrived to do Hedy up for the session. (A portrait of Hedy from these stills was also painted for the film.) Israel created a chic hairstyle for her. His devotion to Hedy was limitless, since he had been doing her hair for the past six months without charge.

"After the pictures had been taken that night," wrote one journalist, "the whole group from the Hamiltons had gone out to dinner and Hedy had been so excited . . . her friends had never seen her so excited or so beautiful, wearing the mink coat that had just been released from some legal entanglement in Texas, and excited because she was going back to work."[24] The future looked bright for Hedy.

But something happened that no one could have foreseen, much less have anticipated. In April 1961, Hedy had told Hedda Hopper that she had been offered a chance to do a stage production of *Black Chiffon,* a play in two acts by Lesley Storm. It had been produced in London's West End in 1949 and on Broadway in 1950. The plot dealt with a society woman's desperate attempts to cope with her demanding family. It was a deeply psychological study of a normally sane woman driven to the edge by cumulative stress. In a final defiant gesture, actually a cry for help, the woman steals a black chiffon nightdress from a famous department store on the eve of her son's society wedding. Hedy refused to do the play, but *Black Chiffon* foreshadowed a very real tragedy in her life. Hedy was arrested for shoplifting.

While leaving the May Company department store in Los Angeles on Thursday, January 27, accompanied by her business manager, Earl Mills, Hedy was stopped on her way out of the store wearing a pair of unpaid-for gold slippers and allegedly concealing in her purse and a shopping bag "various sundries." Also inside her purse were $13 and two crumpled checks written out to her that totaled $14,000.

The nation's newspapers blazed with headlines: "HEDY LAMARR JAILED" and "HEDY LAMARR HELD."[25] She was arrested at 9:15 P.M. by a store detective, Helen McGarry, who said she had observed the actress lifting items before. When she was taken into custody, Hedy had told McGarry that she would pay for the merchandise, because "some of the other [stores] let me do it."[26] She and Mills were taken to the Sybil Brand detention facility. Mills was not charged. Hedy was booked under the name Hedy Boies and charged.

Released on $550 bond at 2:00 A.M., Hedy faced arraignment at 1:00 P.M. on Wednesday, February 2, in Los Angeles municipal court. Her attorneys Arthur G. Lawrence and Irwin Franklyn said they would arrange a press conference to let Hedy explain her side of the story. A city attorney later announced that Hedy was being charged with one count of petty theft, a misdemeanor. The items in question were a $40 two-piece knit suit, a $3 pen, a $2 necklace, eight greeting cards, and a 50¢ makeup compact.

Friends rushed to Hedy's side. Osborne remembered when he heard the news that Hedy had been taken in custody: "When I first came to Hollywood, Lucille Ball had been my boss. I was under contract with Desilu," Osborne said. "I called her [Hedy's] house. Who answered the phone but Lucille Ball! And I know they weren't great friends, but Lucy made a beeline over there. You know, helping out a friend, another star who was in trouble."[27] Indeed, Lucy was the very first of several of Hedy's colleagues to offer their support.

Denise recalled discovering her mother's arrest while she was walking across campus and glanced at a newsstand and saw a picture with her mother's face behind bars on the front page. Anthony, just nineteen years old, came to his mother's defense and spoke to Harry Tessel and Dick Horning of *The Los Angeles Herald-Examiner*: "For the past 30 years my mother has been doing a great deal for the United States and the people in it and in return she has received a slap in the face."[28]

At a press conference held the following day at the fashionable restaurant, the Bistro, in Beverly Hills, Hedy, dressed casually in a soft gray jersey dress and a veiled hat, with her press agent Marvin Paige by her side, attempted to tell her side of the story. Producing the two checks made out to her and in her possession when she was arrested, she said she was "mystified and surprised. I don't know what happened."[29] Her attorney ended the conference abruptly and oddly, by standing up and saying, "My client has paid you the courtesy of meeting you. Now she will leave."[30]

One matron loitering outside the Bistro hoping to get a look at the actress told the press, "Why don't you leave her alone? Let her be a star."[31] Just days later, Hedy checked into the Westwood Hospital for a rest. "I was so tired from sleeping only one hour in four days," she told a journalist. "I just sort of collapsed for a day. That's human, isn't it? . . . I just needed a good night's sleep. Should one day's sleep upset that much? I could have worked today. I am ready today."[32] Regarding her appearance in *Picture Mommy Dead,* the film's director, Bert I. Gordon, expressed his support to the media: "This unfortunate happening will make no difference with our plans. . . . I'm behind her 100%."[33]

Apparently the picture's producer, Levine, was not, and Hedy was replaced in the film on February 3 by Zsa Zsa Gabor, who would squeeze tightly into Hedy's strapless gown and smirk her way through her scenes as only Zsa Zsa was ever able to do.

Friends continued their support. *The Hollywood Reporter* announced on February 16 that actress Viveca Lindfors planned to coach Hedy for her New York stage debut in Norman Krasna's revival of *Kind Sir,* a production to be directed by Lindfors's husband, George Tabori. The play was not done. That same day, Hedy pleaded not guilty to charges of petty theft, and a trial was set to commence on April 13. Shortly before it began *Variety* announced that Hedy was scheduled to star in an independent film beginning in July for Playmates Productions called *Playgirl,* with a script by John McCarthy and with George Cutner listed as executive producer. That project too never saw the light of day.

With her trial about to start, Hedy was finding her life and now her career in shambles. Sadly, both would only become worse.

21

Scandal

*H*edy did not appear in municipal court, but through her lawyers she pleaded not guilty of misdemeanor charges filed against her, and she asked for a trial by jury. She repeatedly claimed the whole thing was "just a big misunderstanding."[1] She could not understand why they would think she was shoplifting when she had $14,000 in checks in her purse.

Escorted into court for the trial by her attorney, Jordan M. Wank, Hedy was dressed in a beige suit, a broad-brimmed straw hat, and black stockings and suede pumps. She looked drained and tired. A five-woman, seven-man jury was selected, and Judge Erich Auerbach was assigned to preside over the trial.

Hedy's friends and fans were among the well-wishers in the courtroom. Robert Osborne was with Hedy every moment, as were Bill Tuttle and Sydney Guilaroff from Metro. "I went to court with her every day, which maybe wasn't a great idea because I was a beginning actor, and it was in the papers a lot, pictures of us together in court," Osborne recalled in 2007. "It was interesting because so many people came to her defense."[2] When the trial began on April 20, Hedy's business manager, Earl Mills, also sat in court with her.

In his opening remarks, Deputy City Attorney Ira K. Reiner stated that Hedy had on January 27 "systematically and methodically" stolen $86 of merchandise, including a ten-cent shopping bag, from the May Company department store. He further alleged that Hedy had done this two additional times in the past. Nedra Thomas, the handbag department manager, was called to the stand, and under oath testified she had observed Hedy on November 18 slip a sweater off a counter as she boarded an escalator, slide it down the handrail, and then drop it into her bag. Thomas confronted Hedy at that time, she said, and told her, "If I were you, I would take that sweater back." To which Hedy replied, "You do it yourself, if you want to," and then shoved the merchandise over to Thomas. However, Judge Auerbach ordered Thomas's testimony stricken from the record as prejudicial.[3]

The next witness called was the arresting security officer, Helen McGarry, who under oath said she had been contacted by Thomas in January to observe Hedy, after Thomas had seen her place a pair of slippers on the edge of a counter and casually drop them into a large handbag. She also testified that on December 30 Hedy had placed a sweater in her purse. McGarry did not actually witness the first two alleged thefts, but she did watch Hedy the day of the arrest by following her from department to department. She claimed she saw Hedy trying on a plastic headband, then pulling her scarf over it to hide it. She then saw Hedy slip two other headbands into her handbag and later transfer them into a shopping bag. Then, said McGarry, Hedy moved over to the cosmetic counter.

McGarry said that Hedy took "a jar of facial cream, 'palmed' a lipstick and took a box of eye shadow and a lipstick brush." She then was observed taking birthday cards, a bottle of men's cologne, and the shopping bag. Going to another floor, McGarry testified she saw Hedy place the shopping bag beneath a rack of clothing and "casually drop a beige suit into the open bag." McGarry, a slight, blond store detective, said that Hedy's business manager Mills did not see her take any of the items and that she knew it was Hedy Lamarr the actress "when I first started to follow her."[4]

McGarry approached Hedy as she was leaving the store and confronted her, saying, "You have items that you have not paid for." Hedy's reply was, "I want to sit down." McGarry then led Hedy back into the store, when she suddenly realized that Hedy was not carrying the bag she had stepped out of the store with. "I looked back and saw the shopping bag on a chair in the glove department," she testified.[5]

The third witness of the day was the store's night-service manager, Howard W. Palmer, who had called the police. He testified that Hedy attempted to bargain with him: "I'll pay for these things and that will settle everything." She told him that she had "always shopped this way at I. Magnin's and Neiman-Marcus."[6] The court was told that Hedy was observed taking only eighteen

items, but when they searched her shopping bag they found twenty-five objects that had not yet been purchased.

The following day, April 21, the psychiatrist Dr. Henry Hamilton testified that,
to date, he had treated Hedy two or three times a week from May 1964 and that
he had seen her the Tuesday before the trial began. In his estimation Hedy
needed further treatment since she was "tense, upset and confused" and she had
a "very low threshold of emotional resistance." She would sometimes ramble in
conversation and become forgetful, not knowing what she was doing.[7]

Hamilton stated that her problems were "rooted in a very unhappy marriage," referring to Lewis W. Boies Jr., and, he added, "She faced eviction from
her new house. Her general health was not good. . . . She is a sick person." He
also stated that "in her normal behavior she would not want to take any property to deprive the owner of it permanently." Most important, Hamilton said
he did not consider Hedy a kleptomaniac.[8]

It was true that Hedy faced eviction from her home by the Arrowhead Savings and Loan Association, who said Hedy had moved into the premises with
the promise to purchase the house, and she had not. She had been served
papers at her daughter's wedding regarding the matter. Reporters had been to
her home in Hidden Valley and had seen what looked like "signs of disrepair
unusual in a wealthy neighborhood."[9] There were broken windows, no draperies, and an unfinished swimming pool containing muddy rainwater and a
discarded Christmas tree. When questioned about the eviction, Hedy told
the press, "I have never experienced anything like that before. . . . I have always
been forgetful, but I was more so this time. I had so much on my mind."[10]

Publicly, Hedy's behavior also came into question. The actor Len Lesser recalled seeing her at a Little Theater production in Los Angeles on the arm of
her publicist, Marvin Paige, soon after her trial. Said Lesser, "The one thing I
remember was that she was wearing soiled long white gloves. That surprised
me."[11] Truly, something was severely wrong.

On April 22, Hedy's son Anthony took the stand in his mother's defense.
Under oath the young man responded to questions regarding his mother's
state of mind in the days leading up to her arrest. There were several reasons,
Anthony believed, that led to his mother's irrational behavior. She was upset
because she had been ordered out of her home; she was suffering from an infected tooth, and her jaw was swollen; and she was nervous about starting her
new film. Anthony remembered, "She didn't think she looked very good."

Anthony told of his leaving his dormitory to take care of his mother two months before. When he came home he found her thin and nervous. He also related an incident that had happened just days before the arrest, when Hedy had been pulled over by a policeman who thought she was drunk. She had just had a vitamin injection administered by her doctor that afternoon, and she was feeling woozy. Hedy had never been drunk in her life. She was not fined, but the incident nevertheless rattled her.[12]

Earl Mills then took the stand, testifying that he had indeed seen Hedy take two objects and place them in her bag but that in the past she would always collect up items before paying for them. He was told by Hedy to meet her in the parking lot, and the next thing he knew she was calling for him. He turned and saw her being arrested.

The third witness that day was Dr. Howard Ross, a Beverly Hills psychiatrist who had examined Hedy on February 2. Dressed in a rust-colored alpaca dress with black trim, and wearing kid gloves on that day, Hedy sat quietly as he testified. Dr. Ross said that Hedy's behavior seemed to "indicate frenetic and frantic activity . . . one situation after another and a disregard for anyone who might be observing." That led to the only instance when Hedy lost her composure during the trial. After Dr. Ross said under cross-examination, "This is indicative of disturbance and stress and a separation from reality," she slammed her gloved hand down on the table and started to rise from her chair. Dr. Ross concluded, "I do not think she could formulate any intent to deprive anyone of property because of the great emotional stress she was under at the time."[13] Then the court recessed for the weekend.

On Monday, April 25, Hedy testified on her own behalf. Dressed in a dark, one-piece knit suit and wearing black heels and tiny pearl earrings, Hedy took the stand looking composed and glamorous. Under oath she said that one of the checks in her purse was for an advance from her publisher of $5,000 and the other was a $9,000 payment for a cosmetic endorsement. Telling the jury she had been under extreme financial and emotional stress at the time of her arrest, she confirmed she was also suffering from bad health, "indigestion," and the repercussions from her failed marriage. She recapped the abuse she had suffered from Boies and the fact that she "didn't want to act," which had only added to her financial woes.[14]

Hedy then stated that she had seen, about two weeks before the incident, the motion picture The Pawnbroker (Allied Artists, 1964), which was about a refugee from Nazi Germany, and it had reminded her of her own flight from Europe in 1937. "Our president was killed. I knew him very well," Hedy said quietly, referring to the assassination of Austria's Engelbert Dollfuss in 1934. She testified for an hour and a half without a break, questioned by her attorney. Under cross-examination by the prosecutor Reiner, Hedy gave her side of the previous incidents, explaining away her acts as accidents. "I never did intend to steal," she concluded in her testimony.[15]

In closing arguments, Reiner said that Hedy had contradicted herself in her testimony and that she had deliberately "tailored" her story to fit the facts of her arrest. "Her explanations are a recent contrivance," he said in his summation, adding that she should not be found innocent just because she was Hedy Lamarr.[16] Stated Reiner, "The overwhelming inference to be drawn from the evidence is that she was doing just what she appeared to be doing: shoplifting."[17]

The defense attorney, Jordan Wank, argued that Hedy had every intention of paying for the items and that her manner of shopping was just different. "I don't shop that way. You don't shop that way, but Miss Lamarr does," he told the jury. Judge Auerbach instructed the jurors they should find Hedy guilty if they felt she had "intent" to take the merchandise and that they "presume" that she was sane at the time of the arrest.[18]

Wank reminded the jury in his closing statement that Hedy was held three hours without being allowed to contact a lawyer, to go to the bathroom, to have a glass of water, or to see anyone. "This is Gestapo tactics," the attorney declared. "You don't treat people in that manner."[19]

The following day, April 26, Hedy was acquitted of all charges by the jury after nearly five hours of deliberations. The jury had met that morning, but by midafternoon they had reached a deadlock of 6 to 6. They were then ordered to resume deliberations by Judge Auerbach, and the foreman, Robert W. Thompson, said Auerbach's intervention helped resolve the impasse, which then became 10 to 2. Two hours later, at 5:28 P.M., they reached a unanimous decision of acquittal.

When the verdict was returned and read, the forty-five spectators in the courtroom burst into applause and were quickly reprimanded by the judge. Hedy smiled broadly and took hold of her attorney's arm. She went to each of the jurors afterward and shook their hands, telling each either "thank you very much" or "I knew I would get fair treatment." She then kissed on the cheek the three people who had been with her throughout the ordeal: her lawyer, Jordan Wank; her dear friend Robert Osborne; and her business manager, Earl Mills.

Hedy then told the reporters, "Everyone's been very kind. These have been try-ing days, in fact, trying months. I will finally get a good night's sleep." When asked by the press if she had expected to be exonerated, Hedy replied, "I ex-pected it. I really did, but you never can tell." She then lingered in the court-room signing autographs for thirty minutes.[20]

Prosecuting attorney Ira Reiner recalled in 2002,

I was just two years out of law school and I bent over backwards, all but apologized to be fair to her. . . . During the trial, when the jurors were out to lunch, I walked into the jury assembly room and found her lying flat on the table, resting. Not wanting to disturb her, I quickly walked out. When the trial was over, about half the jurors approached me and said they knew she was guilty, but it was so clear that I didn't want them to convict her. That was the last time I was Mr. Nice Guy in the courtroom.[21]

There were a couple of telling facts about Hedy brought out during the trial that bear some explanation. One was that Hedy possessed a very imaginative mind. "The one thing about her was her mind worked so fast sometimes her mouth couldn't keep up with her talking," Robert Osborne recalled. "Some-times when she would start telling you a story, by the time she got out the first part . . . her mind had jumped to the latter part of the story, so she would talk about that and leave out the middle sections, and you'd think, 'What the hell is she talking about?'"[22]

The other fact was Hedy's preoccupation with money. Said Osborne, "Hedy was complicated. . . . She was also so dedicated to money. I mean money was such an important thing. . . . She was very money conscious."[23] In concurrence with that, John Carlyle wrote in his posthumously published autobiography, "She was preoccupied with cash, light-fingered, chattered like a child, and un-like her peers, never said a cruel word to anyone. She was a treat to look at and to have on my arm—in small doses."[24]

When Osborne was sick, Hedy brought him soup, and on his birthday in May of that year, she threw a party for him at a friend's house. Osborne came in the door with Mark Herron right behind him and saw that everyone had store price tags on their clothing. He found that hilarious since he totally under-stood Hedy's humor.

Both major and minor lawsuits would plague Hedy for the rest of her life.

During her divorce from Lewis W. Boies Jr., Hedy had hired a private investigator, William V. Lowe, and she had failed to pay for his services. He sued her. Hedy failed to appear in small-claims court to contest the suit on the same day her May Company trial had begun on April 21, and on May 4, the judge made a default ruling against her for payment to Lowe, for the amount of $200.

A week after her acquittal, on May 12, Hedy sued the May Company for $5 million over her arrest and prosecution on shoplifting charges. Filed by her attorney Jordan M. Wank, the suit named the department store and ten other "John Does" as defendants. "She asked $3 million actual damages and $2 million punitive damages charging false arrest, assault and battery, false imprisonment and malicious prosecution."[25]

The columnist Sheilah Graham conducted an in-depth interview with Hedy. Hedy told Graham that she was going to be on a new Bob Hope television special and that she was planning to do a film entitled *Olivia*, beginning in October. Graham brought up Hedy's trial and her recent lawsuit against the May Company and asked, "You were acquitted. Why don't you drop it?" Hedy's reply was firm: "Oh, no. I was acquitted, but I have not acquitted them."[26]

She should have left well enough alone. "There's a saying," Hedy was fond of repeating, "if you go into a back yard and a dog bites you, it's an accident. If you go again, it's your own damned fault." It was a shame she did not heed her own advice.[27] In September her claim was rejected by the city council's finance committee, citing the opinion of the city attorney's office that the claim was not filed in accordance with provisions of the government code. It then went to full council deliberation. On January 30, 1970, the suit was dismissed in superior court.

In June 1966, Hedy's business manager planted an item in the papers announcing her return to films, in a suspense thriller called *Circle*, with a screenplay by David Durstin, scheduled to begin shooting on August 15 in Georgetown, in the nation's capital, Washington, D.C. Hedy had agreed to do the picture for the producer Barnard L. Sackett.

But she would not sign for the picture until she first met Sackett in person. So he flew to the West Coast, met Hedy, and stayed a week. Now the film was called *The Handsome Young Savages*, but, according to *Philadelphia Magazine* (January 1968), it was never made because Sackett lost the only copy of the script and did not feel like having it rewritten.

What was still definite was the forthcoming publication of Hedy's memoirs, *Ecstasy and Me: My Life as a Woman*, on October 3. The hardcover edition was to be published by Bartholomew House. Paperback rights were sold in July to Fawcett Publications for a $200,000 advance against royalties to the authors, Leo Guild and Cy Rice.

Hedy had made tape recordings of her life story, and the book was ghost-written by Leo Guild. Her recorded interviews were conducted by Cy Rice. On April 17, she signed her name to the agreement contract stating that she had read the final manuscript, and then she initialed the first and last pages of the statement. All told, Hedy would see just $80,000 for selling her life story.

But when she finally read the manuscript of *Ecstasy and Me,* Hedy knew its release would kill her in Hollywood. In the book there are numerous passages of sexual escapades with both men and women. These episodes were clearly pandering to a tabloid mentality and, according to most sources close to Hedy, complete lies. Yet it is surprising that several facets of the book, especially those dealing with Hedy's nonsexual encounters, *are* accurate, though many are chronologically out of sequence. Hedy's voice can be heard distantly in the pages, though it is suffocated by the obvious sexual padding. Until the end of her days Hedy claimed she did not write *Ecstasy and Me.* But sign the contract she did.

"I was there when she read *Ecstasy and Me* for the first time," Robert Osborne recalled. "She was shocked by it. But that was the foolish side of her. She wanted money. They simply made up passages in that book and she allowed them to. It was her own fault she let them do that. She wanted money. . . . It was part of her capriciousness, giving away parts of her life for a book and not worrying about the consequences."[28]

Hedy became a grandmother on July 26, 1966, when twenty-year-old Denise gave birth to a baby girl, whom she and Larry Colton named Wendy. Anthony was married that year to Roxanne Chase (they would divorce in 1968). Hedy should have taken pleasure in the events of her family. Instead she focused on defending her irrational behavior.

On September 26, she appeared in Los Angeles Superior Court in regard to her lawsuit against Macfadden-Bartell Corp., owners of Bartholomew House, a suit requesting $9.6 million in an effort to prevent publication of *Ecstasy and Me: My Life as a Woman.* Addressing Judge Ralph H. Nutter, who had reviewed the book and found it "filthy, nauseating and revolting,"[29] Hedy claimed she herself did not write it and she found the contents "fictional, false, vulgar, scandalous, libelous, and obscene."[30]

In court, the attorney Isaac Pacht, representing the publisher, spoke: "We are dealing with the experiences, mostly sexual, of a woman out of pictures for 15 years," he told the judge. "She was in the doldrums as far as the picture business is concerned, and she was desperate to revive her name in the public mind." As for the book damaging her career, Pacht concluded that Hedy's "reputation for morality, integrity and honest dealing was and is notoriously bad."[31]

Hedy appeared in court with her two lawyers, Jordan Wank and Leo Burgard, and provided fifty hours of interviews recorded on twenty-two audiotapes, apparently now lost, from which the book was supposed to have been transcribed. However, the court did not listen to those tapes, and transcriptions of them were not used in evidence. Burgard addressed the judge, stating that the two ghostwriters, Guild and Rice, went "far beyond the bounds of reality and propriety. In some parts I was shocked if not nauseated . . . and I thought it was a filthy thing."[32]

Judge Nutter said, "This is a court of equity, and whether or not to permit this book to be spread around the world is not the question." Hedy had approved the 393-page manuscript and signed the papers. She claimed she had only been paid $30,000, and the publisher corrected that statement. The judge denied Hedy's claim.[33]

Leo Guild spoke to the press on September 28 and accurately told them that Hedy had received $5,000 upon agreement to do the project and $25,000 upon initialing the completed manuscript. Hedy would then receive a flat 15 percent royalty from the sale of each book. Cy Rice had begun conducting the interviews in January, and eventually he handed just twenty tapes over to Guild, which Rice said he got from Hedy. Guild said there were fifty hours of tapes from which he wrote, of which eleven hours, he said, contained "the sexy material."[34]

A *Bob Hope Special,* taped a couple a few weeks before, was broadcast in color over NBC television the night of the verdict. An all-star, sixty-minute comedy, the show featured a dozen or so of Hope's leading ladies from his movies, including Hedy, Lucille Ball, Phyllis Diller, Arlene Dahl, Rhonda Fleming, Virginia Mayo, and Janis Paige.

On October 3, 1966, *Ecstasy and Me: My Life as a Woman* hit the book stores, and it instantly became a bestseller. The damage it did to Hedy's career and reputation was irreversible. For a great deal of the read, it is apparent that the narrator is *not* Hedy Lamarr but someone else. Some chapters contain narratives by presumed psychiatrists. The introduction of the 318-page tome is credited to a physician named J. Lewis Bruce, M.D., who offers up his opinions about the woman. It is then followed by a preface by the University of

Wisconsin's Dr. Philip Lambert, psychologist, who explains why he believes Hedy is oversexed. Not a positive beginning.

It would be odd *not* to think Hedy would have had many lovers and husbands. However, the book makes Hedy out to be an insatiable nymphomaniac. The fact was that, although she appeared nude in a European film and had many love affairs, she was not immoral. Hedy never discussed her private sexual rendezvous, let alone spelled them out for the general masses.

Most damaging of all were the lewd passages that graphically explored lesbian activities. Not a single lesbian encounter mentioned in the book has ever been corroborated. Those particular passages are exploitive, pandering, and most important, based on all existing evidence, imagined.

One of those encounters supposedly occurred in her dressing room. "My dressing room door was always open," Hedy argued later. "[The music composer] Bronnie Kaper . . . and [the studio makeup artist] Bill Tuttle . . . and [the Metro hairstylist] Sydney Guilaroff . . . *these* were the people who were in my dressing room, not those revolting characters in the book."[35]

But the hard truth was that she had wanted the money and perhaps trusted the writers and the publisher to do a respectable job. Without reading the manuscript she signed her name on the dotted line. *Ecstasy and Me* would haunt Hedy for the remainder of her life.

By the end of 1966, there were three more lawsuits. The first was an amendment of her original suit against Macfadden-Bartell from $9.6 to $17 million, filed on October 7. The second was a breach-of-contract suit filed on December 16 against Berkeley Productions, Inc., and Bert I. Gordon for her lost role in *Picture Mommy Dead*. Hedy claimed $499,000 in damages, having been promised $4,000 a week for her work (a total of $8,000 for at least two weeks); $1,000 for clothes and cosmetics she claimed she purchased for the role; an additional $10,000 for indebtedness she felt owed her by the company; and the balance of the suit for damages to her career. Hedy said she had agreed to take the part "for the expectation of consequential benefits . . . in future employment."[36]

The third lawsuit Hedy filed was against the cosmetics firm of Eileen Feathers Enterprises, which had hired her as a consultant. The day after she signed the contract, payment on the check was stopped and Hedy's contract canceled, possibly because the firm believed the shoplifting scandal would damage their reputation. The final outcome of that suit was not made public. Over New

Year's Day, Hedy told friends that the May Company had offered her $250,000 in a settlement, which she was refusing to accept.

By 1967 James Lamarr Loder was married to Ona Minor, and they would have four children, Timothy, Ronald, Nadine, and Susan, all given the middle name of Lamarr. James was a policeman living in Milwaukee. Denise was happily married to Larry Colton and residing in Seattle, contentedly raising her baby daughter. Anthony, now twenty years old, made his acting debut in the play *The Warm Body*, which opened in Palm Beach in March. He received "warm notices."[37] Anthony would continue to pursue his acting career, and, according to his sister, he was almost cast in the role of Ryan O'Neal's college roommate, Hank Simpson, in the 1970 Paramount film *Love Story*, which costarred Ray Milland. (Tommy Lee Jones won the role.)

For the rest of year, Hedy appeared in a variety of follow-up court appearances pertaining to her various lawsuits. As the summer came to a close additional distressing events occurred. Hedy for some time had been dating the forty-year-old Donald Ross Blyth, a business-machine repairman employed in the Los Angeles school system.

On the weekend of August 19–20, Blyth stayed with Hedy at her home in West Los Angeles. According to Hedy, he drew a gun on her when she refused his sexual advances, and then he attacked her in her bedroom. On Monday morning Blyth called Hedy and told her he was coming over that evening, and Hedy notified the police. Two detectives were waiting in her house and took Blyth into custody around 7:00 P.M., booking him on suspicion of rape.

Blyth denied the charges, and Hedy was questioned at length in Santa Monica by District Attorney Mark T. McDonald on Tuesday, August 22. Advised by her attorney of the seriousness of her accusations, Hedy changed her mind and dropped the charges. "In an interview with Miss Lamarr, she indicated after going over all the facts that she did not wish to go further with this matter . . . to pursue the case would be detrimental to her health and well-being." Blyth was released the following evening.[38]

A month later Blyth filed for damages in a suit against Hedy in superior court for $1 million for misrepresentation causing him false imprisonment, loss of reputation, and emotional and physical suffering. Blyth had never been arrested before. His attorney stated that his client was suing for $500,000 for the damage to his reputation, and another $500,000 for punitive damages for

Blyth's "loss of liberty, degradation in the eyes of his mother and . . . mental and physical injury."[39] The case would drag on for years.

Just days before that lawsuit, Hedy's now-former business manager, Earl Mills, filed a $303,900 complaint against her in superior court for what he charged was her breach of contract with him for 10 percent of her royalties on the paperback sales of *Ecstasy and Me*. That case too would linger in the courts.

In October, in responding to a suit filed by Leo Guild and Cy Rice, Hedy's new council, Sandy Sapin, of Sapin & Woldman, countersued the two writers for $2,250,000. Hedy claimed she never approved Leo Guild to write her story. And, just like the others, that case continued on as well.[40]

By now Hedy's professional reputation was shot in Hollywood. It was impossible at this point for her to think she could find work in California. Her never-ending litany of lawsuits was more than out of hand. Hedy was financially strapped, and she was emotionally falling apart. She knew she was through in Hollywood and she was ready to leave town. "I'm too particular to stay here in this aggressive place," she reasoned.[41] In October 1967, Hedy moved away from Hollywood and took up a new life in New York.

There were many close friends who had watched Hedy destroy herself in the courtrooms of California, and they shared mixed feelings about her leaving. "We were really close for three or four years," Robert Osborne reflected,

> And then, it was one of those things where . . . she [had] a lot of free time, and I got busy with work. She was so demanding upon my time that I had to kind of cut it off. We stayed in touch, but when she moved to New York, it was really great for me because she wasn't in California anymore. And I used to go to New York and call her and see her occasionally. And when I would see her she would start going on and on and on. I was just sort of grateful that wasn't a part of my life anymore. Hedy was a handful.[42]

In New York, Hedy settled into the Blackstone Hotel, located between 57th and 58th Streets between Park and Madison in Midtown Manhattan. (The Blackstone has long since been torn down, and the Four Seasons Restaurant was built on its site.) Hedy promptly entered into an unhealthy affair with Barnard L. Sackett, the would-be producer. An aggressive, fast-talking hustler from Germantown, Pennsylvania, he had big dreams of making Philadelphia a major film town.

Born in the early 1920s, and having served in the war, Sackett then performed as an actor for some years in summer stock before entering the film industry. He had written and produced a documentary about silent films in 1962 called *Nickelodeon Days* for his Adelphia Pictures and followed that with a few rather sleazy pictures such as *Sweet Smell of Sex* (1965, directed by Robert Downey Sr.), *All Men Are Apes* (1965), and, eventually, *Eroticon* (1971, starring the porn star Harry Reems). All three contained sexually explicit story lines.

Boasting to the press that he could not believe Hedy was going to marry him, making him her seventh husband, Sackett gushed about his good fortune. Hedy most likely promised Sackett nothing. His C-list films had made him money, though, and he bought an expensive Upper East Side apartment in Manhattan. It was there shortly after Hedy's arrival in the Big Apple that the journalist Gaeton Fonzi met up with her and Sackett.

Fonzi described Sackett as a big talker with lofty ambitions. In a disturbing magazine article about Sackett, Fonzi painfully etched a haunting picture of how sadly and desperately lost Hedy was at this time. Still a remarkably attractive woman in her early fifties, Hedy had tirelessly maintained her figure. Fonzi tells in almost surrealistic imagery of Sackett's using Hedy Lamarr as his calling card and planning his next big project, which was called *Sugar, Sex and Savages*. ("It was Hedy's idea.")[43]

The writer observed Hedy wandering about the apartment in a Day-Glo miniskirt and go-go boots. The stereo speakers were blaring "a crazy rock beat" as Hedy entered the room doing a dance. "Do you know what I am doing?" she asked the writer. "'It is called the Frog [sic],'" she explained, moving her hips and snapping her wrists. 'I am not too bad for a grandmother, am I?'"[44]

Sackett told the writer, "The funny thing is nobody believes it's really her." And Sackett then related how he had taken Hedy to the Warwick Hotel for dinner the night before and introduced her to some friends and "a big attorney" who did not believe the attractive woman with Sackett was *the* Hedy Lamarr. The attorney then proceeded to insult Hedy to her face, in the public venue, laughing all the way back to his table.[45]

When it was explained to him that she truly *was* Hedy Lamarr, the attorney came back to her with his abject apologies. Sackett loved it. He boasted, "A buzz went through the theatre the other night when we came in and during intermission people were just craning their heads like, you know, they weren't sure. 'Why, that can't be . . .' 'Why, she seems so youthful.'"[46]

The article is painful to read. "Isn't she wild?" Sackett continued, telling Fonzi of another incident that took place at Mount Vernon, the historic home of President George Washington, in Virginia. "This guy was trying to pull a deal on her. He had this club with all these crazy lights and he wanted to plaster huge photographs of her all over the place and have her come in and dance a couple of nights a week. . . . You should have seen her. It was beautiful. She really put on an act for him. She came on like a real hippie, swinging her backside, sitting down on his desk and letting her dress go up to here. The guy practically dropped his glasses."[47]

As Sackett gleefully told his story to the writer, Hedy lit a cigarette and said, "'Just because I'm human they think I can't put them on.' . . . Suddenly, in her seriousness, Hedy looked her age for a moment. Her mouth, heavy with lipstick—those same sensuous lips once devoured by Clark Gable and Charles Boyer—became tight and her face seemed to harden beneath her pale crust of makeup."[48] Hedy's time with Sackett was mercifully brief, and they did not marry. But in this one sad account, it was obvious Hedy's life had spun out of control.

Hedy's belongings, left in California, were put up for auction in January of 1968. Once again the sale was handled by Arthur B. Goode. Gloria Geale, a British press representative and friend of Hedy's, had been looking after the belongings when Hedy moved to New York. She told the press, "Miss Lamarr is living in an apartment and has no room for all these things. Miss Lamarr is not abandoning Hollywood, but she wants to live nearer her children in the East."[49]

Included in the auction were such items as Louis XV and XVI pieces of marble-topped furniture, "A Rare Collection of Early 18th and 19th Century Judaica," "A Superb Collection of Unusual Antique Orientalia," bronze art pieces, china, clothing and worn furs, hand-painted pictures, and sixteen used mattresses.[50]

The crowds consisted of many curiosity seekers not intending to buy anything. But some did, including a woman who wanted anything that Hedy might have worn to bed or slept in. It was a morbid affair. But it brought in a much-needed $300,000, of which 25 percent went to the auction house.

During the three years Hedy lived at the Blackstone Hotel, she acclimated to life in New York. She kept busy by attending the theatre and going to movies and enjoying the newfound friendship of several of New York's more upwardly mobile young artists and professionals, many of whom were gay men. She would socialize in the city and vacation at Sag Harbor or on Fire Island.

During her early days in Manhattan, Hedy resumed an old friendship. The actress Mamie Van Doren recalled in 2008 that she and Reginald Gardiner were "doing a play" out East, and he would frequently stop by Hedy's apartment.[51] Until his death in 1980, Reggie would remain a stalwart friend of and ally to Hedy. He was always able to make her laugh.

Not able to let go of her resentment regarding the publication of *Ecstasy and Me,* on February 17, Hedy filed a $21 million lawsuit in Manhattan's New York Supreme Court against nine defendants, including Leo Guild, Cy Rice, Earl Mills, and Dr. Irving Taylor. Hedy charged that the said defendants "conspired and conceived a plan to defraud and exploit" her and to "deprive her valuable literary, motion picture and other property rights to her life story, at the expense of her good name, fame, and fortune."[52] She would not let it go.

It was Dr. Taylor with whom Hedy was particularly incensed because he had allegedly relinquished her confidential tapes to the ghostwriters. Hedy's suit held some validity since those tapes were made by Taylor as her psychiatrist and were never meant to be made public. They may have held some private details that the ghostwriters in turn elaborated on to titillate readers. She was asking for $1 million for loss of film rights; $10 million for loss of earnings, her good name, and her reputation; and $10 million in punitive damages.[53] Had Hedy been able to prove Dr. Taylor turned over confidential tapes to the ghost writers, without her consent, it is likely she could have won her lawsuit had it not been for one technicality. She had failed to prove that actions leading to the publication of the book occurred in New York State. Eventually, on May 4, 1972, the suit was dismissed in Albany by the New York State Court of Appeals.

On June 2, 1969, Hedy returned to television as a guest on ABC's *The Dick Cavett Show.* She looked spectacular, with long dark hair. But she was unhappy with Cavett, who asked her about the book.

James Lamarr Loder and his family were now living in Omaha, Nebraska, in the summer of 1969. On the evening of June 24 in North Omaha, the thirty-year-old patrolman Loder allegedly shot and killed a fourteen-year-old African-American girl, Vivian Strong, who was running through a public housing project during a gang-related disturbance.

Loder was charged with manslaughter in the girl's death, and he pleaded not guilty. Released on $500 bond, he was suspended from the police force for fifteen days. In September he was ordered to a Douglas County, Nebraska, district court to face manslaughter charges. In March of 1970 he was found innocent and released. Hedy surely was made aware of the tragedy. But she apparently remained incommunicado with her son throughout his ordeal. Meanwhile, she continued making television appearances.

Hedy followed *The Dick Cavett Show* two months later with an appearance on *The Mike Douglas Show*. Just two nights later she appeared on *The David Frost Show*. She was exceptionally happy that evening, since, just the previous day, she was awarded by the Los Angeles Superior Court a $12,500 judgment against the automobile dealer Henry Finer, in another minor lawsuit that had lingered in the courts for five years.

On August 15, Hedy was seen on the NBC panel show *Personality*. Three days later she was a guest on CBS's *The Merv Griffin Show*. For that appearance Hedy wore a long-sleeved, form-fitting, white-beaded floor-length gown, and she looked remarkable. Her television appearances restored her confidence and showed the public that she was still a stunning woman.

In late 1969 Hedy agreed to talk to a film crew in her apartment for a European documentary. Speaking in German, she was guarded yet honest about her life and career. At fifty-four she looked twenty years younger, her hair down to her shoulders, her clothing youthful and fashionable. She made an observation about her life in the United States, and viewers could tell she longed for some kind of personal peace: "To live in a hotel means that I don't live here, it's like a bridge," Hedy stated matter-of-factly. "My home is Vienna and Austria . . . never America. . . . I am longing for Vienna. I want to make a film about it—the opera, the Spanish riding school, Schonbrunn, my school in Doebling."[54] There was a time Hedy could recall when her life was filled with love and the wonder of youth. Her heart would always return to Austria.

In 1970, Hedy moved into an apartment building on Manhattan's fashionable Upper East Side, the Renoir Arms. She maintained an orderly life, continuing her regimen of taking vitamins and usually eating just one meal a day, which often was steak tartare. She still maintained a size 10 and believed in lots of rest. She slept in late, not turning her telephone on until the afternoon.

Yet still Hedy suffered from her demons. When entertaining at her home, Hedy's friends would often have to listen to her talk for hours about Gene Tierney and her troubles with Howard. And once, after attending a nightclub performance by her former M-G-M stablemate, Lena Horne, Hedy reminisced with the songstress, "Wasn't it wonderful at MGM? Our clothes were chosen, we didn't have to think for ourselves, Howard Strickling took care of every-thing we had to say."[55] Lena was a bit taken back by that, since she recalled that as an African-American performer it was for her only half as wonderful as Hedy remembered.

Hedy's former psychiatrist admitted in 2001 that Hedy had an apparent tendency to fantasize. After her move to New York she told people she had re-located from Los Angeles to New York out of fear for her life because of the Tate-LaBianca murders at the hands of Charles Manson and his tribe of mur-derous hippies in 1969.

Her imagination notwithstanding, Hedy was still offered acting opportuni-ties. One thing she could not see herself doing was the leading role in a stage production of *The Killing of Sister George,* a bleak drama about an aging les-bian, being presented at the Tappan Zee Playhouse in the spring of 1970. They had offered her $5,000 to appear in the play. Instead, on June 2, Hedy made her last network television appearance on *The Merv Griffin Show.*

Another lawsuit came to a conclusion on November 12, when Hedy was ordered to pay $15,000 in damages to Donald Ross Blyth, whom she had ac-cused of assaulting her four years before. Hedy once again failed to show up in court, and she was not represented by a lawyer. Blyth was awarded $5,000 in general and $10,000 in punitive damages.

For the documentary film producer Irwin Rosten, on January 5, 1972, Hedy allowed herself to be photographed descending the stairs, à la *Ziegfeld Girl,* at Nathan's Restaurant in Times Square as a publicity stunt promoting the up-coming M-G-M documentary *Hollywood: The Dream Factory* (1972). Dressed in tartan slacks and looking youthful and glamorous, Hedy was lovely to be-hold, though most of the onlookers had no idea who she was.

Before the year was out, Hedy was hit with a $26,000 lawsuit from the state of California for back taxes, penalties, and interest accrued from her last auction in Los Angeles. According to the suit, Hedy was still a legal resi-dent of California from January 1, 1966, until December 31, 1969. The Black-stone Hotel said that at the time of the auction Hedy had only lived there eighteen months. The outcome of the lawsuit was not made public.

And, sadly, as the decade wore on, Hedy's life in New York would eventu-ally become a world of seclusion and remorse, her own reality clouded by im-pending gloom and increasing darkness.

22

Seclusion

For Hedy the 1970s were a period of introspection and gradual seclusion as she faced the eventual maladies of ageing. Most noticeable was her increasing blindness. Kenneth Anger, an underground filmmaker and a pal of Hedy's masseuse, befriended her in the early 1970s, at a time when her private life had become reclusive because of her clouded vision from macular degeneration, a loss of vision caused by damage to the retina.

Anger recalled visiting Hedy's three-room apartment at 225 East 63rd Street. "She didn't see how dirty it was, and she wouldn't let any maid come in to clean it," he recalled. Hedy feared robbery. There was a dirt ring around her bathtub, Anger noticed. He would walk with her, "she loved to walk in those days," around Third Avenue and Park Avenue, and then they would dine at a nearby restaurant.[1] Anger recalled that she was too proud to wear glasses, and so remained living in "a dreamland of her own."[2]

Hedy traveled often and would fly to Seattle to visit her daughter and granddaughter. She would also occasionally take Denise with her on trips to Aruba, where she rented a condo for two or three months each year. In 1972 Hedy started dating Dr. Henry Ross, a noted New York surgeon who was the widower of the actress Glenda Farrell. With Ross Hedy found some much-needed contentment and tranquility.

Hedy was offered scripts, television commercials, and stage projects through-out the decade, but most were uninteresting or simply terrible. "You know, acting is believing in your role," she told one magazine journalist in 1973. "About getting scripts—some of them are really bad. Most, in fact. I don't think there is anything wrong with horror films, but I'm just not the type. There are times when I would enjoy working very much, and when I read a new script, I'm always open. In fact, sometimes I actually hope that the script I'm reading will be the right one—the one that is so marvelous I just can't turn it down."[3]

In 1970, Denise divorced Larry Colton.[4] After a brief second marriage in 1972 to Thomas Kavanaugh, which ended in divorce two years later, Denise signed with the Lola Hallowell Model and Talent Agency in Seattle. Her print portfolio was reminiscent of her mother's early portraits taken in Hollywood. At five foot eight and 125 pounds, Denise was classically attractive. She was modestly successful as a model too, working at times with Candice Bergen and Mia Farrow. Denise was content in Seattle and would often have her grandmother and brother and his family for guests.

Anthony lived briefly in New York, became an artist, and once set up a street gallery on the corner of Park Avenue and 53rd Street. He met a Frenchwoman named Dominique "Oni" Rongier, who became his second wife and with whom he made lamps out of antique gumball machines. The couple married in 1970 and had three children, a daughter named Lodi in 1971, and a son they called Sime-Raju (later Andrew) in 1975. Their third child, Thomas, was born two years before they divorced in 1982.

In 1972 Anthony completed an art film called *Images of France* for his own company, Filmograph. He made "still movies," as he called them, which were projected slide images put to film. That year too he was finally able to meet his father, John Loder, in England; to introduce John to his granddaughter Lodi; and to spend a few days getting to know him. Later Anthony attempted to establish himself as a film director and a photographer, among other trades. "I even worked as a cowboy on a Californian ranch for a couple of years," Anthony said. He eventually found his niche in electronics in the early 1980s.[5]

Trude was nearly eighty years old when she came to stay with Anthony's family because she had become unable to live alone. Anthony and Denise loved their grandmother, who had been a great constant for both of them. Said Anthony, "I learned from Trude patience and steadfastness and the meaning of family."[6]

In the summer of 1974 the writer-producer Mel Brooks's Warner Bros.

Western satire, *Blazing Saddles,* was released, and it became a huge hit. One of the characters in the film, portrayed by the comedian Harvey Korman, was called Hedley Lamarr. Throughout the film, his name is repeatedly mispronounced "Hedy" Lamarr. One despicable character, portrayed by Brooks himself, actually says to Lamarr, after Lamarr corrects Brooks's character on the pronunciation of his first name, "What the hell you worried about? This is 1874. You'll be able to sue her."[7] Hedy did not find the film amusing.

In June she filed an invasion-of-privacy lawsuit for $10 million in New York City supreme court against Brooks and Warner Communications, Inc., the producer and distributor, stating her name was "entirely unauthorized" for use in the picture. Just two years before, in 1972, she had filed a $1 million lawsuit against a New York department store and a cosmetic firm for using her image in their advertising.[8]

The case was eventually settled out of court. For the commentary on the 2006 DVD release of *Blazing Saddles,* Brooks said that the settlement was "a couple of thousand dollars" and that he apologized to Hedy for "almost using" her name. But the damage was done.

In the aftermath of that running gag in *Blazing Saddles,* Hedy became something of a joke—the punch lines were her ability as an actress and her credibility. Suddenly, it was assumed by pop-culture sensibility that the very name *Hedy Lamarr* was something to laugh at.

On September 28, 1982, Lana Turner appeared on NBC's *The Tonight Show Starring Johnny Carson.* The guest host that evening was the comedienne Joan Rivers. Lana had just landed a recurring role on the primetime soap opera *Falcon Crest* (CBS), and she was out promoting it as well as her autobiography. During the interview Rivers asked Lana what actress she thought was the most glamorous woman in Hollywood in her heyday.

Turner unhesitatingly answered that the most beautiful and stunning woman *ever,* when she walked onto a set, was Hedy Lamarr. "She was absolutely breathtaking," said Lana in awe. Then with a sly smile she added, "She couldn't act . . . but she was definitely *the* most beautiful woman." With that casual jibe, said with a smirk and tossed off as if it were common knowledge, Turner perpetuated the myth that Hedy Lamarr was worthy of a bit of derision.

In April 1975 Hedy filed for Social Security disability benefits because her cataracts had robbed her of most of her vision. She told the press that she was living "like in a London fog." Because of her near blindness, Hedy claimed she was unable to work, and she said, "When you can't see, you can't do anything."[9] Her attorney, Richard H. Wels, made a point of telling the press, "She made millions over the years. . . . It wasn't all in good hands. But she gets by."[10] In early March Hedy had an operation on her right eye and awaited surgery on the left.

After surgery some of her sight was restored, and in June she was stopped on the street and photographed wearing protective sunglasses as she was leaving a late-night private party held at Club Cecil in Manhattan for the benefit of an organization for artists' rights. Hedy sported an array of large and flashy pieces of jewelry, which she told the press she planned to offer at boutiques she was hoping to open in New York and London. She also planned a line of clothing carrying the Hedy Lamarr label.

That fall of 1976 Hedy underwent her first plastic surgery. In Manhattan in December for the Dupont Fashion Show held at the Waldorf-Astoria grand ballroom, which featured "living legends" (Hedy, Alexis Smith, Raquel Welch, Ethel Merman, and Ruby Keeler), Hedy unveiled her new look. Draped in a long-sleeved, high-neck clinging gown with boa cuffs, she was photographed extensively alongside the singer Paul Anka. Her cheeks were still swollen and her face in the photographs looked masklike.

Sadly, just weeks later, her mother quietly passed away in California. Gertrud "Trude" Kiesler died on February 27, 1977, at eighty-three. Her last years had been quiet and peaceful, thanks in part to Anthony and his family. Trude had not seen her daughter as frequently as Anthony because Hedy lived mostly in New York. After her mother's death, Hedy would tell friends that her mother did not like her, that she had wanted a boy, and that she had been cold and distant. Hedy did not journey to California for the funeral. Trude was laid to rest at Woodlawn Cemetery in Los Angeles. On her headstone are these words:

> DEW EVAPORATES
> AND ALL OUR WORLD
> IS DEW . . . SO DEAR,
> SO FRESH, SO FLEETING.

Despite her unwillingness to stay in regular touch with her mother, Hedy did keep in contact with many of her former lovers and husbands. In September

1977, Fritz Mandl died in Austria after remarrying several times and fathering three children. Until his death he had kept in touch with Hedy either by telephone or correspondence, always affectionately signing his letters to her, "Bunny." On May 1, 1980, Hedy's second husband, Gene Markey, passed away, and in July of that same year so too did her beloved Reggie Gardiner. Both were men she had once loved, and now they were gone. The following year, in February, W. Howard Lee, still married to Gene Tierney, died. There were few people from Hedy's past now living whom she could call to talk.

Hedy Lamarr, however, was still news. *The Hollywood Reporter* reported she was planning to open a spa bearing her name on the Dutch island of Aruba. And the columnist James Bacon wrote a disturbing piece telling readers that Hedy had given her son Anthony a couple of furs to help him out financially. Friends Abe and Muriel Lipsey, furriers, who were trying to help Anthony out, said the children's father, John Loder, simply would not have anything to do with them. Bacon also recalled once visiting Hedy in Hollywood and her removing a valuable Picasso from off her walls to sell to keep her two children in Stockbridge.[11]

In May Hedy attended a Friar's Club event in New York honoring the ophthalmologist Dr. Charles Kelman, who had, the previous October, operated on Hedy's eyes, restoring her vision. "I was blind for seven years," she told the New York *Daily News*. "But I'm fine now. Dr. Kelman gave me my sight back. He gave me my eyes."[12]

In September 1981, Hedy flew to her rented condo in Aruba. There she met a woman who would become her closest and dearest friend and confidante.

Arlene Roxbury, a married businesswoman from Long Island; her husband, Lawrence; and another couple they knew in New York had all flown to Aruba on holiday. The night before they left New York, as she was packing, a Hedy Lamarr movie came on television, and for some reason Arlene watched it. When they arrived in Aruba the following day, Arlene and her friend were lying in the sun when, as Arlene recounts,

> this woman in a beautiful pink bikini walked onto the beach . . . [and by] just the way she walked, she was very tall and statuesque, when she came onto the beach she was just very elegant. You could tell she was somebody, but I didn't know who. She sat down beside us, and after about twenty minutes, she asked us, "Do you know what time it is?" I

detected an accent, though I never thought of Hedy Lamarr having one. Eventually she started talking to us, and as we were leaving the beach, a stranger came up to us and said, "Do you know who you were talking to? Hedy Lamarr. If you let on you know, she won't be friendly."[13]

Arlene continued: "As we left, Hedy came up and started talking to me as if I knew who she was. 'I really like you,' she said to me. 'What's your sign? You're either a Taurus or a Scorpio.' I said, 'I'm a Taurus.' And she said, 'I think we're going to be friends for a long time.' She was a little psychic, you know. And I was so naïve. She started talking about Clark Gable, Spencer Tracy, M-G-M people. And then she said, 'I want to give you my card.' She knew I was a travel agent and living in New York. We invited her to dinner with us and the other couple, and we had a lovely evening."[14] They flew to New York together, and during the trip back Hedy never left Arlene's side.

Hedy's friendship with the Roxburys would become closer as the years went by. From 1981 until Hedy moved to Miami Beach in 1987 and even after that, Arlene and Hedy would share intimacies with each other. When Hedy came to stay at the Roxbury home on Long Island, they had prepared an upstairs suite for her, and she would stay for months at a time, relishing their hospitality. "She felt very safe with me, very secure with me. And here she had a safe haven. . . . I did a lot for Hedy, and never expected anything in return. I just loved her. She spent months at my home. She had not many friends because she was pretty selective. But she had the ones she was close to. And she was a wonderful, wonderful person."[15]

Hedy loved to shop and enjoyed a flea market the two women would frequent. Once a woman approached Hedy "and got in her face saying, 'You're Hedy Lamarr!' And she panicked. She just didn't want to be around people. She was very, very vain, and she didn't *look* like 'Hedy Lamarr,'" Arlene recalled. "I went shopping with Hedy many, many times. She would relate to me that in Texas, Neiman Marcus came to her home, or she would simply pick up things and they would charge it to her."[16]

Hedy would dress casually when she stayed with the Roxburys. She wore a cross around her neck, though "she did not practice her faith," Arlene recalled. Once when Hedy was visiting, *White Cargo* came on television. Hedy's favorite position when she watched television was lying on her stomach on the floor of the family room. As the film progressed, she told Arlene about the colors of her costumes. While making those movies, she said, she did not even know what she was saying half the time and did many scenes phonetically. And she told Arlene that Bob Hope, during the making of *My Favorite Spy,* would often make her flub her lines.

Hedy told Arlene that her favorite film was *Samson and Delilah*. For years she had wanted to develop her own fragrance, as Elizabeth Taylor had done, and Hedy would have called hers Delilah. Of all her leading men, she told Arlene, James Stewart was her favorite. (Clark Gable was "OK.") Hedy reluctantly would talk about her son James but would always elaborate on Denise, Anthony, and her grandchildren. When Hedy was at her apartment in Manhattan, and even when she later moved to Florida, she would talk endlessly with Arlene on the telephone two or three times a day.

Hedy loved to play the stock market, Lawrence Roxbury recalled, and would call him at odd hours to ask, "What do you think about such and such stock?"[17] She invested fairly well, too, and made some money, he said. According to Arlene, Hedy admitted to having had two face-lifts, plus her legs and knees, and even her hands, "lifted" before 1981.

Arlene was quick to point out that Hedy had a charming sense of humor. Once Arlene took her to a pharmacy, and Hedy stayed in the car while she went inside to refill a prescription. The druggist said to Arlene, "Is this *the* Hedy Lamarr? Would she give me an autograph?" Arlene said she could ask, and the druggist handed her a plain brown bag to have Hedy sign. When Arlene came out to the car and asked Hedy if she would sign the bag, she complied and jokingly remarked, "Well—from one old bag to another." Arlene is convinced Hedy was happy with her life at this time, concluding, "She really liked the simple life, and I think she liked coming out here [to Long Island]."[18]

In 1986, Hedy threatened to sue the Florida-based tabloid the *Globe* for pictures they were planning to publish of her taken by her plastic surgeon, which she claimed had been stolen from her purse. The pictures were apparently never published, but Hedy knew that her every move created publicity. She wanted out of the limelight, and she had tired of New York.

A longtime friendship Hedy maintained was with a prominent Manhattan doctor (not Henry Ross), who lived on Park Avenue. It had ended before 1981. And a six-year relationship with a man Hedy referred to as The Captain, whom she never really talked about with the Roxburys, also came to a close. Hedy had always enjoyed warmth and sunshine, and so she chose to move to

Miami Beach. Now there would be no auctions or misleading stories for the public to digest. There would be no speculation or publicity. Hedy was simply tired of celebrity. And, as always when life handed her disappointments, she just wanted to go away.

Her decision to move brought her a newfound peace. Hedy's son James reconnected with her and they would talk on the telephone occasionally; he recalled, "She sounded like she was 38. She was totally hip and chic."[19] In 1987, Denise married Vincent DeLuca, a commercial real estate investor in Seattle, whom she had met in 1979. She became a Borghese cosmetic consultant at Nordstrom in Seattle, and, through her enthusiastic and knowledgeable efforts and work, she befriended Princess Marcella (née Fazi) Borghese, who marketed the line of fine cosmetics. Princess Marcella was the wife of Italian nobleman Paolo Borghese.

The two women would remain very close until the princess's death in 2002. When Denise and her husband Vincent were in Europe, the princess entertained them in Switzerland and at her home, the Villa Borghese in Rome, Italy. It was through Denise's association with Princess Borghese that a new career opened up for her in Seattle.

She eventually became the regional training artist for the Borghese cosmetics line at Nordstrom, remaining with the company for twenty-eight years. Like her mother, Denise enjoyed painting. After her departure from Nordstrom, she became an accomplished and respected artist. Over the ensuing years, her portraits would grace several important art galleries.

In 1982 Anthony founded PhonesUSA, a business specializing in information technology, and he eventually became its CEO. After his second divorce, in 1982, Anthony married Lisa Marie Verzotti in 1987, a mother of three children. The next year the couple had a son, whom they named Nikola Max Anthony.

After she settled into a small $500-a-month, third-floor condo in Miami Beach's North Bay Village in 1987, Hedy gave an interview to Cindy Adams of the *New York Post*. Talking about her life then, Hedy told Adams, "I swim. I look much the same. I don't go in the sun, no matter what. And I exercise in the pool. . . . I haven't even made out a will yet. I paint, play gin rummy, write poetry, invent things. . . . I don't need much. . . . I do my own housework."[20]

"Before, I never had any toys," she continued. "Never saw daylight! All I knew was to get up at 4:40 every morning. That's not my idea of heaven. . . . I'd like to play George Sand, or do 'The Little Foxes,' but I am not ambitious now, unless there was a Cecil B. DeMille whom I could respect." She told Adams that she did not like to be interviewed, "until I have something special to say." And about re-marriage, Hedy concluded, "I'd like to belong, but I really want to live alone."[21]

In 1988, Hedy reported the theft of $250,000 worth of jewelry from her home, saying she had last seen the gems two or three months before. She had kept them in a bag in the hall closet and noticed them gone on Tuesday, September 4. The investigators appeared none too eager to pursue the case. Detective Frank DeAlimi contacted Tiffany & Company in New York to verify that Hedy had purchased the costly jewels and indeed had them in her possession. There had been no signs of forced entry into her home, and DeAlimi told the press, "Until I have proof that she had it, I'll have to play all the ropes."[22]

Arlene and Lawrence Roxbury recalled that when Hedy would stay with them she would leave her jewels in their care while she would go to Aruba. Hedy called them her "hidden iron reserve." "Mounds and mounds of jewelry she'd keep in a plastic bag—diamonds, emeralds, sapphires, rubies," the Roxburys recalled.[23] According to Arlene, Hedy apparently had befriended a man who, Hedy claimed, simply found the jewelry in the hall closet, and he had stolen them. The jewels were never recovered.

Now in her seventies, Hedy was not in the best of health. According to her North Miami Beach physician, she suffered from hypertensive vascular disease, allergic rhinitis, and Taiwan flu, an influenza virus whose reported cases in the United States had begun in 1986.[24]

Hedy was living off her Social Security checks and a small Screen Actors Guild pension. In 1989 she planned to move again but was advised by her heart doctor that because she was now suffering from congestive heart failure as well it would be advisable for her not to move from Miami Beach for a couple months. In February 1991 Hedy made the move.

She took a second-floor, two-bedroom apartment in the Sandy Cove Condominium complex, in Altamonte Springs, Florida, just north of Orlando. Her apartment overlooked a pool, and her neighbor Peter Giglio recalled her swimming late at night by herself after the other residents had turned in. Her home was tastefully appointed with a wooden armoire and a white satin couch in the living room. Her bedroom contained beautiful, fine-quality furniture. Other than having a housekeeper, Hedy only had a girl who helped her with her paperwork. She kept to herself, Giglio said, and most people at the complex did not know who she was.

One person who *did* know she was Hedy Lamarr was her adopted son, James. He had informed Hedy that his adult son Tim lived in Ocala, Florida, raising exotic animals. Hedy would allow Tim to visit often. She liked him. When James and his wife came to see her for two hours, his first reunion with Hedy in forty-one years, the meeting was cool. James said Hedy acted "like a queen" and "reminded me of what I could have had. . . . I just feel that I made my own way. I'm not a rich man, but I have enough."[25]

"I think she did the best job she could as a mother with her schedule, and I know she loved me," he said in a 2005 documentary. "I have always called her mother. She's still my mother as far as I'm concerned, my stepmother. . . . And that's how I feel about it."[26] But when James came to Florida to see his son and mother on another visit, he was turned away from Hedy's door.

On Tuesday, August 1, 1991, around 4:40 P.M., Hedy, now seventy-six years old, was arrested as she left a Casselberry, Florida, drugstore without paying for $21.48 of personal-care items she had concealed in her purse (laxative tablets and eyedrops). Wearing jewels, a hat, and dark sunglasses, Hedy had been accompanied by a lady companion who had driven her to the store.

The store manager reported the theft. Hedy's friend (whom she would later identify as a woman named Julie) left before the police could get her name (one report stated that Julie was really a he, a transvestite, who did not want to get involved), leaving Hedy stranded at the police station, where she was charged with shoplifting. Hedy was told she had to appear in Seminole County Courthouse on August 20. Signing a statement, Hedy was released and taken by Officer Baldwin back to her apartment.

Unfortunately, the arrest made national headlines. Hedy denied that it was theft. She did say, "I went into the drugstore to buy Lanacane and stuff you need, and I paid all of that in cash, and I have the [receipt]. . . . I'm sick and tired of being in the limelight. . . . I have children and I don't want to upset them."[27]

Denise was notified in Seattle and was stunned. "She was living her final years out in a decent and quiet life, but now this happened," Denise told the press. "I do not think she has a shoplifting problem. She simply forgot to hand [her shopping companion] the last two items for checkout. . . . My mother used to go to Neiman Marcus and Saks, and they used to say, 'Miss Lamarr, take anything you want.' . . . She has friends, she has money. She has her life in order."[28]

Arlene Roxbury was contacted and was equally shocked, advising the press that since Hedy had been out of the limelight for so long she was surprised by all the attention. "She doesn't even realize that she's Hedy Lamarr," Arlene said.[29]

Hedy's arraignment was postponed until September 17 so that the state attorney's office could further review the case. It was then postponed a second time until October 15. Hedy filed a plea of not-guilty through her attorney, Joerg Jaeger. Mercifully, the case was quickly resolved.

Hedy's attorney told *The Washington Post,* "I just don't think the state can prove this woman had any intent. . . . She just wants to get this thing behind her and get on with her life."[30]

On October 25, the *Los Angeles Times* reported, "Prosecutors in Florida have decided not to charge former screen siren Hedy Lamarr with shoplifting from a drugstore because of her age, poor eyesight and circumstances of the case. Lamarr, 76, signed an agreement promising not to break any laws for a year. If she does, theft charges will be filed."[31]

As Hedy's life settled back into routine, only occasionally would her name appear in the news. She was once asked to attend the Telluride Film Festival to receive an honor and a tribute, but she made exorbitant demands such as requiring a makeup artist to accompany her and a costume allowance, and the offer was retracted. There appeared in 1996 yet another tabloid article entitled "Hedy Lamarr's Sad and Lonely Last Days." Aside from there not being anything scandalous to expose, the piece related a story about an elderly lady who kept to herself, watched television, and handled her voluminous fan mail. Hedy was not interested in suing. At the age of eighty-one, she simply did not care.[32]

James Loder, at the time a security guard working a riverboat casino and living with his wife in Omaha, Nebraska, had received a surprise envelope from his mother the year before. When he opened it, he found a photograph of himself as a little boy, his arm draped lovingly around his mother. Hedy had inscribed on it:

> *Dear Jim,*
> *I thought you would want a photo of us.*
> *Much love to you and your family.*
>
> > *From*
> > *Mom*[33]

In February 1996, Larry and Arlene flew to Florida to visit Hedy, and Arlene videotaped Hedy. This video was used in part in *Calling Hedy Lamarr,* a documentary that Anthony Loder spearheaded after his mother's death.

As she waves to the camera inside her apartment, Hedy says, "That'll be two thousand dollars." Her delicious sense of humor in play, Hedy continued talking for the camera. "Mr. DeMille, I'm ready for my close-up," she says, striking a Norma Desmond pose and falling back on her bed, sighing with exhaustion, "Finally, at rest." The complete videotape, which includes Hedy swimming and laughing and singing, presents a still-vital yet elderly lady enjoying her life with dear, trusted friends.

Hedy always kept herself made up and glamorous, even in her eighties. She did not look like the aloof and mysterious Hedy Lamarr of 1937 but more like an elegant and charming grandmother. In video sequences taken inside her tastefully furnished apartment, Hedy points out pictures of her children and her grandchildren with loving pride. The video is a touching tribute and documentation of her later years. There is more truth in that film footage than in anything on celluloid Hedy Lamarr ever made in Hollywood.[34]

Hedy had once gone shopping at a store where a young high school student, Jessica Merrill, was employed. When Hedy met the girl, the two sat outside on a bench, and Hedy asked Jessica if there was some way she could obtain a card so that she could cash her checks. Jessica saw to it that she could, and she became Hedy's friend and secretary. When Jessica went off to college, she introduced Hedy to her mother, Madeleine Merrill, who took over her daughter's job, coming over to help Hedy after her own work and on Saturdays and Sundays.

"I went through all her mail," Madeleine recalled in 2008. "I paid her bills. I was her bookkeeper as well as her personal secretary. I answered all of her fan mail, read her bank statements to her. Her stocks—so noted on the forms that those were the ones she really wanted. Just everything in general."[35]

On weekends Madeleine would also prepare meals for Hedy, which she could dine on throughout the week, foods like fettuccini with a cream sauce, steaks, and hamburgers, which were placed in Tupperware containers and stored in the refrigerator. Madeleine said she introduced Hedy to croissants, and she would make sure that Hedy had plenty of fruits, which she loved. Madeleine would also see that the freezer was stocked with ice cream bars, something else Hedy was always fond of.

To occupy her time Hedy would sketch a great deal, using colored pencils, and create beautiful abstract drawings. She was once invited to display her work at an art exhibition in Las Vegas but declined. As she aged Hedy suffered such common maladies as nervousness, low resistance to stress, and difficulty in sleeping. "She did stay up all night," Merrill said, "just because during the day she slept. At night is when she did her best thinking."[36]

Hedy was quite successful investing in such stocks as Microsoft. "She was highly intelligent," Madeleine recalled. "When she got to Florida, she took hold of herself, control of her life, put her feet down. Before, people were always telling her what to do. With the stock market she told them what to buy. She told them when to sell. And when they would give her a bad time, I would get a call, 'They're not listening to me. Do something!' "[37]

"I would have to call the stockbroker and remind him, 'You need to do what she wants. It's her money; it's her decision. Please don't fight her on this.' I don't know how many times I had to do this. But that's the way she wanted it. . . . She did her research on what she wanted. And it paid. She sure built up her bank account."[38]

As the twentieth century was coming to an end, so was the life of Hedy Lamarr. There were no more motion pictures to be made, millionaires to wed, or lovers at her beck and call. There was just a full life winding down. But a startling revelation was about to be made. The announcement would not alter the last years of Hedy's life either personally or financially, though the importance of its content had already changed the world.

23

Legacy

Hedy once told a documentary film company, "My life was full of colors, full of life, and above and below and over and under. But I don't regret any thing. . . . I learned a lot."[1] And just when Hedy was finally finding peace and serenity, another facet of her life was announced around the world.

The patent that she and George Antheil had placed their energies and hopes on in 1941 lay in limbo throughout the war, as the navy considered the device too unwieldy. In 1959 the patent rights expired. Neither Antheil nor Hedy had made further inquiries about its development in all those years after the war. A patent lawyer could have suggested to them improvements on their patent to extend its rights, but they had simply chalked their invention up as their contribution to the war effort.

It remained virtually untouched until 1957, when engineers at the Sylvania Electronics Systems Division in Buffalo, New York, revisited their concept, substituting electronic circuitry for Antheil's paper rolls. Wireless communication technology had advanced considerably in Germany and Japan by then with the advent of transistors, which were not truly perfected until the 1960s. America in the late 1950s jumped into the field of electronic and wireless technology as well.

In 1962, the United States was threatened with another possible war. After the Bay of Pigs fiasco in April 1961, in which CIA-trained Cuban militants unsuccessfully invaded Cuba, it was discovered that the United States had backed the failed brigade. The Cuban Communist dictator Fidel Castro implored Premier Nikita Khrushchev and the Soviet Union for intervention and military support. By supplying the island with armaments in direct defiance of the United States, the Soviet Union and Cuba were in fact threatening war.

Spy photographs and U-2 aerial shots of the military buildup in Cuba were shown to President Kennedy on October 16, and security and military staffs hurriedly gathered in Washington, D.C. Pictures showed Soviet cargo ships at sea loaded with soldiers and armaments, and, on land, 170 warheads and intermediate-range ballistic missiles on the beaches of Cuba, aimed at the United States. A U.S. naval blockade was deployed to the Caribbean.

Kennedy took to national television on October 22 and warned that unless the Soviet Union and Cuba desisted and halted the buildup and immediately dismantled Cuba's armament sites, a state of war would be declared. Khrushchev laughed at the young president's stand, but eventually he backed down from his support of Cuba.

The Cuban Missile Crisis was averted, in no small part because of the advancement of technology and the use of the idea behind the original Hedy Kiesler Markey–George Antheil patent. Three years after its expiration date, the navy was able to develop Hedy's frequency-hopping into a secure-communications method by using sonobuoys and surveillance drones. The government then improved on the patent to avoid directing torpedoes and to provide secure communications between ships deployed in the naval blockade of Cuba. Only then did research by the Defense Department begin in earnest as scientists further developed the device.

By the time the Vietnam conflict was raging in the late 1960s, the Markey-Antheil patent had been further looked at and used in several secret military communication devices, and it was more commonly referred to as FHSS (frequency-hopping spread spectrum), which used a narrowband carrier that changed frequency in patterns known only by the transmitter and the receiver.

Was Hedy ever made aware of the developments and use of her and Antheil's invention? Probably not. The government had no real cause to advise her now that her rights had expired.

In February 1974, the *Los Angeles Times* ran a short article entitled "Salute to Inventors" for Inventors' Day (Thomas A. Edison's birthday, February 11). The piece was a profile featuring a brief synopsis of a handful of celebrity inventors, including Abraham Lincoln, who long before he was president patented a device "to buoy vessels over shoals"; the actress Lillian Russell, who patented a dresser trunk in 1912; Dorothy Rodgers, the wife of the composer Richard Rodgers, who invented the Johnny mop, a tool to clean toilets; and Hedy Lamarr.[2]

"Concerning Miss Lamarr's invention," read the brief overview, "she and officials of the patent office told them they are unaware whether the invention was ever used. The coinventor, they said, was George Antheil of Manhattan Beach, Calif. They said the system was patented in 1942 and that Miss Lamarr filed for the patent under her legal name, Hedwig Kiesler [sic]."[3] Knowledge of advancements on the patent was not made public then, and little was made of the article.

By 1981 the Markey-Antheil invention had taken on new importance. For years it had been considered classified technology. That year it was declassified for commercial use. The FCC (Federal Communications Commission) further developed frequency-hopping into spread spectrum, which allowed for a special section of the radio spectrum to be used to make cellular telephone calls even more secure. Such scientific communications as CDMA (code-division multiple access) as well as RFID (radio-frequency identification) use spread-spectrum technology. Millions of corporate dollars were invested in the program, now an important component of modern-day cell phones. In 1985 the technology was also integrated into radios.

In 1989 there was yet again mention of Hedy and Antheil's contribution to the war effort. "Hedy was a war hero," read the headline of a piece in the *Orlando Sentinel.* The article states, "A patent was awarded jointly to Hedy and Antheil in 1942 and the concept was incorporated into a whole new generation of torpedoes—weapons far more accurate and deadly than those used in the past."[4] Again, little attention was paid to the piece.

But major interest finally was generated when *Forbes* magazine interviewed Hedy by telephone in early 1990 about her invention. She told the magazine, "I can't understand why there's no acknowledgment when it's used all over the world. . . . Never a letter, never a thank you, never money. I don't know. I guess they just take and forget about a person."[5] By the end of the decade, the international scientific community finally remembered.

In February 1997 *The Wall Street Journal* reported that electronic engineers were looking at Hedy Lamarr as more than just a pretty face. Hedy was, said David C. King, chief executive of the Wi-Fi manufacturer Proxim Wireless, a "huge part of the history of this industry. . . . We thank Hedy Lamarr for a lot of things." Qualcomm vice chairman Andrew J. Viterbi stated that his company's cellular phones used a variation of spread spectrum originally developed by Hedy and George Antheil and that the "fundamental concept is the same" today.[6]

The Markey-Antheil invention, outdated as it may have been, was now used in the vast new technology of cordless cellular telephones, alarm systems, and military radios, even global-positioning satellites and the wireless linking of portable desktop computers to corporate networks.

By 1997 the Markey-Antheil invention had become the basis of modern antijamming applications, such as the $25 billion U.S. Milstar defense-communications satellite system. "Hedy didn't suffer fools gladly," said the Colorado researcher-scholar David Hughes, whose work for the National Science Foundation on wireless communication was partly based on the technology Hedy had envisioned over a half century before. "George Antheil was not only a musician, but a formidable enough intellect that she could hold an intelligent conversation with him." Franklin Antonio, the technical officer of Qualcomm, remarked, "I read the patent. You don't usually think of movie stars having brains, but she sure did."[7]

On March 20, 1997, Hedy and Antheil were officially recognized for their invention with honors and an award, the sixth annual Electronic Frontier Foundation's Pioneer Award, presented at the Computers, Freedom and Privacy conference in Burlingame, near San Francisco. Said Mike Goodwin, the staff counsel for the Electronic Frontier Foundation, "Ironically this tool they developed to defend democracy half a century ago promises to extend democracy in the 21st century."[8] The music composer Charles Amirkhanian, who maintained the George Antheil Archive, accepted for the late composer.

Hedy did not attend because of her declining health, but Anthony accepted the bronze statue inscribed "To Hedy Lamarr for Her Contribution in Pioneering Electronics" on his mother's behalf. Said Anthony, "She's happy for all that grew from the seeds she planted; that it was not conceived in vain."[9] He then played an audiotape recording from Hedy: "This is in acknowledgement of your honoring me. I hope it'll do you good as well. I think about it and it was not done in vain. Thank you."[10]

The recognition continued. Hedy next was granted a BULBIE Gnass Spirit of Achievement Bronze Award, which some call the Oscar of inventing, in 1997.

She was the first woman ever given the award, in a ceremony held at a national convention in Pasadena, California. Again, Hedy was unable to attend.

Equally impressive was the award bestowed on her in her beloved Austria in October 1998. Hedy was given the Viktor Kaplan Medal from the Austrian Association of Patent Holders (the Austrian Academy of Science.) The Kaplan medal is the highest award an inventor in Austria can receive. Anthony traveled to his mother's homeland to receive the award for her. In honor of her eighty-fourth birthday that year, a distinct and artful exhibit called "Hommage à Hedy Lamarr" toured the country, containing photographs, film clips, and memorabilia.

The Wi-LAN company, creators of high-speed Wi-Fi communications, bought into some of the rights of the technology that was built from the patent and generously afforded Hedy a small residual for her participation in its development. At the close of the 1990s, after long being labeled a beautiful and troubled film actress, Hedy was effectively and at long last acknowledged as having originally copatented an idea that became one of the most important technologies of the twentieth century.

But with that recognition problems followed. Within a year the Canadian-based Corel Corporation held an art contest for the packaging of their new software, Corel Draw. The winner submitted a vector illustration of Hedy, which the company printed on the outside of the software boxes. Corel also used Hedy's image in their advertising. In 1998, protecting her image as always, Hedy notified her attorney, Michael McDonnell, who was based in Naples, Florida.

She sued Corel for $15 million for the unauthorized use of her face. "She doesn't endorse things," McDonnell told the press. "A great lady of the screen touting some software from a Canadian company? That's not her style.[11]

"Some people might be flattered by their 15 minutes of fame," McDonnell said about this latest public interest in Hedy. "But she's had it and wants her privacy."[12] The case was eventually settled out of court in 1999 for almost $5 million, with the agreement that Corel would have exclusive rights to use Hedy's image for five years. "The image of Hedy Lamarr is a unique combination of grace, beauty, and incredible artistry," said a Corel spokesperson when officially announcing the license.[13]

Hedy became a great-grandmother in February 1997, when Denise's daughter Wendy, a mediator for a nonprofit organization, gave birth to a son, whom she named Robert Colton "Cole" Boyd. Hedy gave another lively interview over the telephone to Cindy Adams of the *New York Post* on June 18, 1998: "I'm recovering from a fall. I fell on a step going into the pool," she told Adams. "But I'm fine, coming along nicely.... I'm ... a great-grandmother. Everybody I knew is dead but me. Somebody upstairs must have made a mistake, because I definitely only feel like I'm 40."[14]

In June, she sued the E. & J. Gallo Winery for using her image in a television ad for Gallo's Gossamer Bay Wines. It appeared in a two-second snippet where a husband and wife are battling over the television channel. There is a brief flash of Hedy and Charles Boyer in a scene from *Algiers*. Hedy considered it an invasion of privacy and an insinuation that she was connected with the winery. She asked for $17.5 million. Again, McDonnell was summoned, and a suit was filed in federal court in Orlando on June 19.

Vanity Fair magazine did a "Proust Questionnaire" with Hedy for their April 1999 issue and asked her twenty-three questions, which she answered rather candidly. What do you consider your greatest achievement? "Having been a parent." When and where were you happiest? "Between marriages." Which historical figure do you most identify with? "Elisabeth of Austria." If you could change one thing about yourself, what would it be? "My nail polish." What or who is the greatest love of your life? "My father."[15]

Hedy lived in Altamonte Springs for eight years, until the owners she rented from wanted to give the condo to relatives and asked Hedy to leave. "She was distraught," said Madeleine Merrill. "I wanted to give her some peace of mind, so I went over to the manager of the complex and asked if he could write her and tell her how happy they were she had lived there, and that they were sorry she had to leave, and how much they were all going to miss her, so she wouldn't feel so bad."[16] They obliged.

Now, financially solvent for the first time in decades, in October of 1999, Hedy purchased a four-bedroom house in Casselberry, Florida, located at 968 Wesson Drive, for which she paid $130,000. The day she moved in, she hid in the car when driven to her new home. Change had become difficult for her.

Immediately after settling in, Hedy befriended police lieutenant Chuck Stansel; his wife, Edie; and their eight-year-old daughter, Caitlin. The Stansels took a liking to Hedy, and Chuck would check in with her a couple of times a week, running errands and shopping for her.

Hedy's new home had a heated pool, one of the reasons she took the place. "She was starting to get a little feeble, and I got her an exercise bicycle; she wouldn't use it," Merrill recalled. "But swimming was the only exercise she'd do. She loved to swim."[17]

Hedy's new home had a step-down living room with two large French provincial white-brocade couches facing each other, a huge gilt-framed mirror hanging above them on the wall, and a big-screen television. All about were pictures of her three children, her eight grandchildren, and her great-grandson.

Both her living room and kitchen had large glass doors that opened onto the pool, which had a fountain that lit up at night. Hedy loved to spend time out by her pool listening to the fountain, which she ran twenty-four hours a day. "Unless I sat down to eat with her, Hedy wouldn't sit down at the dining room table," Merrill said. "I'd bring her tray to her room and she would be there on her comforter and watching her old movies on TV."[18] However, Hedy preferred living in the present, Merrill was quick to add. She was hesitant to let Madeleine know of the bad things that had happened in her past, changing the subject if they came up in conversation.

"Hedy either liked you or she didn't," Merrill said. "It was so hard for her to trust people." For a while, she had not wanted to meet Madeleine's husband, Raymond, "because he was a Gemini."[19] When the two women were having difficulties putting up pictures in the new house, Hedy said, "Well, Raymond's probably good at hanging pictures up . . . call him and ask him to help me." When he came over he embraced Hedy and the two sat down like old friends, leaving Madeleine to finish the work. After that, whenever Hedy needed something done, she would say to Madeleine, "See if Raymond can come over."[20]

Hedy did not want to celebrate her eighty-fifth birthday in November 1999. But Madeleine told her they would, just the two of them. She blew up some balloons, bought Hedy a birthday cake, and placed candles on it. When she arrived at Hedy's house, Madeleine lit the candles and sang "Happy Birthday" to her. "She had never had something like that," Madeleine said.[21]

The two women then spent a "wonderful" evening together watching television. (Hedy's favorite TV shows were *Judge Judy* and *Who Wants to Be a Millionaire?*) Hedy spoke highly of her leading men James Stewart and John Garfield, of whom she had autographed, framed photographs prominently displayed in her living room.

Hedy did little traveling during these later Florida years. "She was a recluse," said Denise. "And she had tired of the effort of looking like the person she was when she was young."[22] When her children and grandchildren would call and ask to visit, Hedy would put them off with, "I just want to feel better. Wait until I feel better."[23] Aside from those immediately around her like the Stansels, Madeleine, and the housekeeper, Robin Pettis, Hedy saw no one and would remain inside her home and seldom venture out.

Hedy drew up her last will and testament on November 3, 1999. In it she bequeathed everything to her two children, Denise (or, if she did not survive her mother, her granddaughter, Wendy Colton), and Anthony. Hedy had no intentions of departing right away, but she felt it necessary to get her house in order. In hindsight, there were signs that she may have felt her final curtain was at hand.

Hedy owned a portable Sony stereo radio/tape/DVD player. Because her eyesight was so poor, she had marked the "play" control knob with red finger-nail polish so that she could see it. "Hedy loved this particular song, and was constantly playing it—four, five, to ten times a day," Arlene said about that last year, 1999. It was Andrea Bocelli's recording of the haunting "Time to Say Goodbye," the lyrics in Italian.[24] It is a mesmerizing and passionate piece, and Hedy would play it continuously in her home for Chuck Stansel and his wife.

Hedy was very reclusive the last part of 1999. Her housekeeper, Robin Pettis, said, "She wouldn't let anybody see her."[25] Robin took care of and watched over Hedy throughout the day. As the new millennium approached, Hedy was as excited by its prospects as everyone else. She had purchased a bottle of Dom Perignon champagne to celebrate the Corel decision, but it had gone uncorked. So, it was decided the champagne would be opened on New Year's Eve. But when New Year's came, for some reason it remained sealed.

Robin recalled that some days Hedy's mood would be happy and giddy, and she would dress up. But, because of her sensitive eyes, she would sit in the dark. In early January, Hedy called Arlene and Lawrence Roxbury. Arlene agreed to come down for a visit so they could go shopping for furnishings for the new house. "I have everything ready," Hedy excitedly told her.[26] When she found she could not make the trip, around January 12, Arlene called Hedy, who was sad to hear she was not coming. According to Lawrence Roxbury, Hedy loved Arlene so much that she once told her on the telephone, "You and Larry move down here. I'll buy you a house."[27] They thanked her for her generous offer but declined.

On Sunday, January 9, Madeleine spent the day with Hedy, making her a breakfast of scrambled eggs and a warmed croissant with strawberries. She stayed with Hedy throughout the day, and that afternoon they watched John

Huston's 1952 picture *Moulin Rouge* on television. At some point while watching the film, Madeleine recalled, Hedy casually said, "You know I was instrumental in getting Joe [José] Ferrer that part." Apparently, Hedy had attended a party at Huston's house (possibly with Pierre La Mure, the writer), and, when the director mentioned he was having trouble finding the right star for the film, Hedy noticed Ferrer standing across the room and brought him over to Huston, saying, "This is who I recommend."[28]

When the movie was over that evening, Madeleine prepared to leave. "When she'd walk me to the door, I'd always embrace her and say, 'Good night, Hedy,'" Madeleine said. "And you know she'd never come to you, but you know she'd stand there waiting for you to hug her good night. I'll tell you this . . . the last time I saw her . . . I said, 'You know, you're looking a little tired, Hedy. I'm going to go home now, and if you need me, you call me.' And she said, 'OK, all right.' Well, she walked me to the door, and she embraced me and said, 'Thank you, sweetie.' And that was the last time I ever saw her."[29]

The following Sunday, January 16, Chuck and Edie Stansel stopped by Hedy's home, and Madeleine said that Hedy called her that day. "The next [weekend] I was supposed to come and see her," Madeleine recalled. "But she could never visit with more than one person. The police officer Chuck and his wife were there, and she called me and said, 'Chuck and his wife are here. Can you come over tomorrow night?' So I missed seeing her that night."[30]

For some reason, Hedy was reluctant to let Chuck, whom she always called Charles, and Edie say good night. She wanted to show them pictures of her granddaughter Lodi, and she insisted they come into her bedroom, where she had Chuck remove a framed drawing of the Lamarr face off the wall, which she then signed and gave to them saying, "My signature will be worth millions." Hedy then showed them that underneath the sweater of a stuffed bunny was the key to her lockbox. "Just in case," Hedy whispered.[31] The Stansels had an engagement later that evening and told Hedy they would see her the next day and finally left. Sometime on that following Tuesday evening Hedy did her makeup, lightly applied her favorite perfume Fendi to her wrists and the nape of her neck, tastefully dressed, and lay down on her bed.

On Wednesday, January 19, Chuck stopped by Hedy's home around noon after she did not answer telephone calls. When he could get no response by knocking at her front door, he entered with his key. The living room was dark and stuffy, and he heard the television playing in Hedy's bedroom. "Hedy was a little hard of hearing," Arlene said.[32] Stansel always referred to Hedy as "Miss Lamarr," and, upon calling out her name, he still had no response. When he entered Hedy's bedroom he found her lying on her side on the bed, dressed and made up, the television playing. He took her pulse, and her hand was cold. Hedy Lamarr was dead. Underneath her body was her will.

"It struck me . . . that she was all made up," Arlene later said, "because she never went to bed with her makeup on. Maybe she had this little inkling that something was happening."[33] The coroner announced Hedy had died of natural causes—her death certificate lists three: heart failure, chronic valvular heart disease, and arteriosclerotic heart disease. When the ambulance arrived and the paramedics removed her from the bed, they also discovered underneath her body a note to Edie Stansel (which Hedy had addressed to "Idie"— briefly it was mistaken for a suicide note) and a list of daily things to do made out for Madeleine.

The international news media picked up the story, and reams of obituaries rehashed Hedy's life and career, her nude appearance in the notorious *Ecstasy,* her "discovery" by Louis B. Mayer, her films, her lawsuits, her marriages, her book, the shoplifting charges, and so on. Several pieces even mentioned Hedy's recent recognition for her contribution to science. It was a "last hurrah!" of sorts for the lady who was once called "the most beautiful girl in the world." To the press, her attorney, Michael McDonnell, said simply, "She had the burdens of old age, but she was sharp as a tack and always able to care for herself."[34]

Madeleine Merrill handled the funeral arrangements after conferring with Denise in Seattle. When Denise arrived in Florida with Anthony, she chose for her mother a simple pair of khaki slacks, a white shirt, and a navy blue jacket. For her head, Denise chose a velvet riding hat, which Hedy always liked to wear.

"As much as I loved the dear lady, I fixed her all up in her coffin," Madeleine said. "She looked really nice. I wanted to make her done up because [the children] hadn't seen her in all those years. I made the arrangements with the funeral home. . . . So I brought all of her makeup and all the things I wanted to put on her."[35]

After she applied makeup on Hedy's face with a tissue, Madeleine added a little rouge and pink lipstick and tucked Hedy's hair behind her ears. She then placed a scarf around Hedy's neck. "The first time I met her," Madeleine recalled, "she had pink sunglasses on. It was about fifteen minutes into our visit and she took her glasses off and I knew she had accepted me as her friend. So I put those pink glasses on her. It was like my little farewell to her. She looked lovely, just looked so nice . . . I wanted everything to be perfect."[36]

The services were private. The Baldwin-Fairchild Cemeteries and Funeral Home had two locations, one in Altamonte Springs and the other in Orlando, and they kept moving the casket with Hedy's remains about. They eventually had to tie ropes around the coffin for fear that it might be opened and pictures taken by some tabloid. Anthony, not mincing words, firmly told the funeral-home director, "If I find that somebody opened up this casket, I'll sue you."[37]

There were only a dozen people who attended the funeral: Hedy's family (Anthony and his daughter, Lodi, and Denise); her friends Lawrence and Arlene Roxbury, Chuck and Edie Stansel, and Madeleine Merrill; personal friend Don Nardone; and her attorney, Michael McDonnell, and his wife.

Arlene recalled that the funeral home was closed except for Hedy's service and that, when her friends and family entered, Denise said, "Nobody's going to view my mother."[38] Hedy had been on display her whole life. At the service, eulogies were read by Nardone, Arlene, and both Denise and Anthony.

Afterward, the cork was finally popped on the bottle of Dom Perignon that Hedy had purchased for the Corel victory, and family and friends toasted "Miss Hedelweiss." Arlene Roxbury was made executrix of Hedy's will, something she had never been advised of by Hedy during her lifetime, and she received a generous bequest of some of Hedy's beautifully beaded and brocaded gowns, her old passports, and other items.

When Hedy's will was read on March 10, 2000, it was estimated that she had left behind some $3.3 million, mainly in stocks. To her closest and dearest friends, Arlene, Madeleine, Don Nardone, and Chuck Stansel, Hedy bequeathed $83,000 each. She left her valuable stamp collection to her eleven-year-old grandson, Max. The bulk of her estate was given to Anthony ($1.8 million) and Denise ($1.2 million). Not mentioned in the will at all was James Lamarr Loder.

Denise recalled that she and Anthony had discussed this oversight and were prepared to offer James a specific amount from their individual bequests, when they were suddenly petitioned with a lawsuit. Lawyers representing James claimed that he had been neglectfully written out.

One unscrupulous British journalist interviewed family members and friends under the guise of writing a positive profile on Hedy. He then produced a scathing magazine piece about the disagreements regarding the will. Feelings on both sides were hurt.

Ultimately, from the estate, a settlement of $50,000 was given to James by Hedy's two natural children. James called Denise and explained his side of the story, telling her the issue was pushed by his attorneys, and he was sorry that it had created problems. Denise and James today keep in touch, and she understands his feelings. His life had not been easy. "I have much empathy for Jimmy," Denise said in 2009.[39]

When the funeral service for Hedy was held that day in late January, as the mourners moved slowly into the lobby, over the sound system softly played "Time to Say Goodbye" with the sound of Bocelli's magnificent voice filling and caressing the rooms. Arlene and Madeleine began to weep. Officer Chuck Stansel, who was always so in control, hurriedly left the building. They had been given the gift of Hedy's favorite song. As the mourners listened, their hearts were breaking. It was time to say good-bye.

Epilogue

On Wednesday, June 28, 2000, U.S. District Judge Anne Conway settled Hedy's final pending lawsuit against E. & J. Gallo Winery in favor of Gallo, since no damages to Hedy's life and career were likely to then occur. Hedy's estate, represented by her lawyers Gary Green and James Nici, was ordered to pay the court restitution costs of $263,000.

In the aftermath of Hedy Lamarr's death, there have been various independent documentaries, including two, *Calling Hedy Lamarr* and *Hedy Lamarr: Secrets of a Hollywood Star,* that have described in part the Hedy Kiesler Markey–George Antheil patent. In most instances these pictures have contained inaccuracies. In addition to *Ecstasy and Me,* books published about her include two coffee-table books of photographs; a book about her films; a couple of clinical, social, and technical evaluations of her patent; a recent tome speculating on Hedy's imagined involvement with Adolf Hitler; and even three children's books dealing with Hedy and her invention.

There have also been staged theatrical plays that have dealt with Hedy and George Antheil. The first was a one-woman show called *Hedy Kiesler Lamarr,* presented at the Donau-Universität Krems (Danube University Krems) in Krems, Austria, near Vienna, in 2006. The second, and more significant play, was *Frequency Hopping,* which opened off Broadway in New York in late May 2008 at the Three Legged Dog Art and Technology Center in Greenwich Village. It was written and staged by Elyse Singer and starred Erica Newhouse as

Hedy and Joseph Urla as Antheil. This production also incorporated a musical presentation of Antheil's *Ballet mécanique*.

Even in the field of fashion, Lamarr's influence is felt. In the 2009 documentary *Valentino: The Last Emperor*, the legendary couture tenderly acknowledged Hedy Lamarr's appearance in the film *Ziegfeld Girl* as being a great influence on his life and career.

At the time of her death Hedy was still inventing—a device to attach pockets to Kleenex boxes for used tissue, and she was also drawing up designs for a traffic signal that would warn drivers when the light was about to change. Though age had faded her beauty, Hedy's mind remained fertile, and her soul continued to thrive. What was Hedy trying to accomplish when death finally took her? Perhaps she was yearning to contribute still, to justify all that had been given her and all that she had lost.

So what is her legacy? Motion pictures are tangible, and the celluloid image of Hedy Lamarr remains unforgettable. But Hedy perhaps encapsulated the final word: "Films have a certain place in a certain time period. Technology is forever."[1] Hedy's daughter has always insisted that she would like her mother to be remembered for her contribution to science, though she acknowledges that modern technology had outpaced her mother. "She was totally untechnical; in her later life she even hated the Internet."[2]

In 2003 the Boeing Corporation ran a series of recruitment advertisements featuring the image of Hedy Lamarr as a woman of science. "Don't Let History Happen Without You," read the ad campaign. "We're trying to remind people that the horizon is limitless," said Dan Ivanis, spokesman for Boeing's global staffing.[3] No mention of Hedy Lamarr's being a film star was made. On November 9, 2005, on what would have been Hedy's ninety-first birthday, Austria, Germany, and Switzerland inaugurated the very first Inventors' Day in honor of Hedy Lamarr. Today, November 9 is internationally celebrated as Hedy Lamarr Day or Inventors' Day in her honor.

The film historian Jeanine Basinger once wrote, "When I was a little girl going to the movies, Hedy Lamarr represented the concept of movie star. The movies presented her in magnificent close-up. . . . Any woman, movie star or not, born with the exceptional beauty that was Hedy Lamarr's is not in for an easy time of it. . . . She found her way out of it. She survived. . . . Anyone who survives Hollywood in that era had to be a very strong person. . . . It was crushing for some."[4] Icons like Dietrich, Gable, Garbo, Dean, Harlow, Shearer, and Crawford, for instance, will always be remembered as movie stars, their work forever captured on film. But few film stars, if any, have left scientific contributions impacting future generations.

Brilliance and beauty, however, are not without their costs. Hedy was idolized and adored by her millions of fans worldwide, but she was misunderstood by many close to her. Lamarr possessed physical and mental attributes not often found in one person. And, accordingly, she failed the many normal expectations of others.

Her former costar John Fraser later reflected on Lamarr, writing quite elegantly and compassionately:

> She had been fawned upon, indulged and exploited ever since she had reached the age of puberty. Her extraordinary intelligence did not encompass wisdom. How could she have learnt about the values that matter, about kindness and acceptance and laughter, in the Dream Factory that is Hollywood? She had been thrust into the limelight at a pitilessly early age, been devoured by rapacious lovers and producers who saw her ravishing beauty as a ticket to success, and who looked elsewhere when she began to grow older. Beauty and money in moderation are undoubtedly a blessing. In excess, they are surely a curse.[5]

Lamarr is underrated as an actress, most certainly. Today her motion pictures are being reevaluated by film scholars and historians, and certain qualifications are coming to light in a more accepting and objective society. "Hedy Lamarr was a huge star," the TCM host and her old friend Robert Osborne comments,

> and she was also a better actress than she was ever given credit for. But she had that curse that all those beautiful women had—nobody could see beyond that. . . . I think she did many interesting things, and for anyone to think that's easy what she did has never been in front of a camera and a whole crew and all that. And she's very, very good, and was always good. She particularly was wonderful because she did what was needed for the women she portrayed.[6]

"She wasn't often given complex moments to play," he concluded. He adds:

> You take something like *Ziegfeld Girl*. I mean, she wasn't really required to do anything but be beautiful. That's her purpose in the film and she does what she's supposed to do just wonderfully. There are a lot of actresses that give terrible performances in movies, and she was never one of those. She never had line readings . . . that were not good . . . [and] she was the most beautiful woman ever in film, without question.[7]

Hedy's legacy might very well be twofold. Her contribution to the scientific community during the last century is unquestionable. Her body of film work remains for us to ponder, appreciate, and we yearn for an era that once was. In January 1999, two years after Hedy's acknowledgment in science was announced, *Playboy* magazine listed her as one of the top 100 sexiest film stars of the twentieth century. Scientist or film goddess—which was Hedy Lamarr?

Perhaps she was in actual fact just a simple, shy, pretty Viennese schoolgirl who was swept up by the cataclysmic events of the twentieth century. As a child full of dreams and ambitions Hedy had played in the Wienerwald, the Vienna Woods. Her imagination and ambitions ran free. And throughout all the years of her tumultuous life she longed for the romance and the serenity of her charmed childhood in old Vienna.

"Well, of course my hometown is Austria," she once wrote. "I lived a great deal in the lake and mountain areas and around me were happy and jolly people who were trying to please. . . . I was happy with my first love."[8] Denise confirmed her mother's love of her homeland, recalling, "Anytime anything about Vienna was on television, she would call me. She was totally homesick for Vienna and [she] was totally Austrian."[9]

During the filming of the documentary *Calling Hedy Lamarr*, Denise and Anthony flew to Vienna to distribute their mother's remains in the Wienerwald. In the film they are shown doing just that. But it is a reenactment. "We did it privately," Denise said.[10] On a warm and sunny Monday afternoon, September 15, 2003, Denise and Anthony quietly spread their mother's ashes where she had always longed to be—among the lush undergrowth of sweet-smelling oaks, hornbeams, beeches, firs, and pines of her beloved Vienna Woods. Hedy had been so happy there as a child. Now, finally, she was at peace. She was home.

Appendix

Theatrical Appearances

Das schwächere Geschlecht (The Weaker Sex), The Deutsches Theater, Berlin, December 1930. Staged by Max Reinhardt; assistant director, Otto Preminger; written by Edouard Boudet.

CAST: Hedy Kiesler (2nd American Girl).

Das schwächere Geschlect (The Weaker Sex), The Theater in der Josefstadt, Vienna, 1931. Staged by Max Reinhardt; assistant director, Otto Preminger; written by Eduoard Boudet.

CAST: Joseph Schildkraut, George Weller (An American Man), Hedy Kiesler (2nd American Girl).

Private Lives, The Theater in der Josefstadt, Vienna, 1931. Staged by Max Reinhardt; assistant director, Otto Preminger; written by Noël Coward.

CAST: George Weller (Victor Prynne), Hedy Kiesler (Sibyl Chase).

Intimitaten (Intimacies), Vienna, 1932.

CAST: Hedy Kiesler.

Sissy, The Theater an der Wien, Vienna, December 1932. Staged by Otto Langer; producer, Hubert Marischka; written by Ernest and Hubert Marischka, based on the comedy by Ernst Decsey and Gustav Holm; music by Fritz Kreisler; musical director, Anton Paulik; women's costumes by Lillian; ballet under the direction of Hedy Pfundmayr from the state opera; set decorator, Ferdinand Moser; choreography, Camillo Feleky; dance master, Budapest; film sequence between acts painted and animated by Lotte Reiniger; stage manager, Hubert Marischka-Karezag.

CAST: Hans Jaray (Franz Joseph, Emperor of Austria), Paula Fiedler (Archduchess Sophie, Empress of Austria), Hubert Marischka (Duke Max of Bavaria), Traute Carlson (Ludovika "Luise," his wife), Maria Tauber (Helene "Rene"), Hedy Kysler [Kiesler] (Elisabeth "Sissy").

Film Appearances

Geld auf der Strasse [Money on the Street], Sascha Films, 85 minutes, released December 29, 1930. Producer, Nicolas Deutsch; director, George Jacoby; screenplay, Rudolf Österreicher, Friedrich Raff, Julius Urgiss; based on a play by Rudolph Bernauer and Rudolf Österreicher; art directors, Hans Jacoby, Emil Stepanek; musical score, Stefan Weiss; cinematography, Nicolas Farkas; sound, Alfred Norkus.

SONG: "Lach mich nicht, weil ich Dir so true bin!", "Mir ist alles einerlei ganz einerlei" (sung by Harry Payer) by Peter Herz and Stephen Weiss.

CAST: Lydia Pollman (Dodo), Georg Alexander (Peter Paul Lutz), Franz Schafheitlin (Bornhausen), Leopold Kramer (Emil Reimbacher), Rosa Albach-Retty (Lona Reimnacher), Hans Moser (Albin Jensch), Hugo "Hans" Thimig (Max Kesselberg), Hedwig Kiesler (Young Girl at nightclub table).

Sturm im Wasserglas [Storm in a Water Glass], Sascha-Felsom Film Production, 70 minutes, released April 21, 1931. Producer-director, Georg Jacoby; screenplay, Walter Wassermann, W. Schlee, Felix Salten; based on a play by Bruno Frank; set director, Hans Jacoby; cinematography, Guido Seeber, Bruno Timm; sound, Alfred Norkus; song lyrics, Peter Herz.

CAST: Hansi Niese (Frau Vogel), Renate Müller (Viktoria), Paul Otto (Dr. Thoss), Harald Paulsen (Burdach), Herbert Hübner (Quilling), Grete Maren (Lisa), Oscar Sabo (Dog Catcher), Otto Tressler (Judge), Franz Schafheitlin (Prosecutor), Hedy Kiesler (Burdach's secretary), Grete Maren, and Fritz Mueller.

Die Koffer des Herrn O.F. [The Trunks of Mr. O.F.], Tobis-Film Production, 80 minutes, released December 2, 1931. Producers, Hans Conradi, Mark Asarow; director, Alexis Granowsky; screenplay, Léo Lania, Alexis Granowsky; based on a story by Hans Hömberg; set director, Erich Czerwonskï; musical conductor, Kurt Schröder; costumes, Edward Suhr; cinematography, Reimar Kuntze, Heinrich Balasch; editors, Paul Falkenberg, Curt von Molo; sound, Hans Grimm.

SONGS: "Hausse-Song," "Cabaretsong," "Barcarole," "Die Kleine Ansprache," and "Schluss-song," music by Dr. Karl Rathaus, lyrics by Erich Kastner.

CAST: Alfred Abel (The Mayor), Peter Lorre (Stix), Harald Paulsen (Stark), Hedy Kiesler (Helene, the Mayor's daughter), Ludwig Stössel (Brunn), Margo Lion (Viola Volant), Ilse Korseck (Mayor's wife), Liska March (Eve Lune), Aribert Mog (Stark's assistant), Alfred Döderlein (Alexander, Helene's brother).

Wir brauchen kein Geld [We Need No Money], Allianz-Tonfilm Productions, 92 minutes, released February 2, 1932. Producers, Arnold Pressburger, Dr. Wilhelm Szekely; director, Karl Boese; screenplay, Károly Nóti, Hans Wilhelm; based on a play by F. Altenkirch; art director, Julius von Borsody; cinematography, Willy Goldberger; cinematography director, Karl Sander; musical arranger, Arthur Guttmann; editor, G. Pollatschik; sound, Erich Lange.

CAST: Heinz Rühmann (Heinz Schmidt), Hedy Kiesler (Käthe Brandt), Hans Moser (Thomas Hoffmann), Ida Wüst (Frau Brandt), Hans Junkermann (Herr Brandt), Kurt Gerron (Bank President), Paul Henckels (The Mayor), Lisl Isa Steffi (Hedy Kiesler's stand-in), Ludwig Stössel, and Lilia Skala.

Extaze [Symphonie der Liebe; Symphony of Love], Elekta Film Production, 85 minutes, released January 20, 1933. Executive producers, Frantisek Horký, Moriz Grunhut; producer, Gustav Machatý for Elekta Film AG; executive producer, Otto Sonnenfeld; director, Gustav Machatý; screenplay, Gustav Machatý, Frantisek "Franz" Horký, Vitezslav Nezval; based on a book by Robert Horky, Jacques A. Koerpel; dialogue, Jacques A. Koerpel; art director, Bohumil Hes, Stepan Kopecky; set director, Hosch; musical score, Dr. Josef "Guiseppe" Becce; musical directors, Kopf and Herz; musical arrangements, Franz Schimak, Walter Kiesow; song lyrics, Hedy Knorr; song arrangement, Walter Kiesow; cinematography, Jan Stallich, Hans Androschin; scene designer, Alexander Hackenschmied [Hammid]; sound, Joseph Zora; editor, Antonin Selenka; production supervisor, Otto Sonnenfeld.

CAST: Hedy Kielser (Eva Hermann), Zvonimir Rogoz (Emile), Aribert Mog (Adam), Leopold Kramer (Eva's father), Emil Jerman (Eva's husband's—voice), Bedrich Vrbský (Eva's father—voice), Jirina Stepnicková (Eva—voice), Antonin Kibový, Eduard Slégl (roadworker), Karel Macha-Kuca (the lawyer), Pierre Nay (young man), André Nox (the father), Jirina Steimarová (stenotypist), Jan Sviták (dancer on the terrace of Barandov), Ladislav Bohác (Adam, uncredited), and the Comedian Harmonists (Themselves, uncredited, in the outdoor café sequence).

Algiers, United Artists release of a Walter Wanger Production, 95 minutes, released May 23, 1938. Producer, Walter Wanger; director, John Cromwell; screenplay, John Howard Lawson and James M. Cain, based on the French screenplay *Pépé le Moko*, by Julien Duvivier and Detective Roger D'Ashelbe from a novel by D'Ashelbe; art director, Alexander Toluboff; associate art director, Wade B. Rubottom; musical score by Vincent Scotto and Muhammed Ygner Buchen; lyricist, Ann Ronell; costumes, Omar Kiam and Irene (for Ms. Lamarr); hair stylist, Nina Roberts; cinematography, James Wong Howe; editors, Otho Lovering and William Reynolds; sound, Paul Neal.

CAST: Charles Boyer (Pepe le Moko), Hedy Lamarr (Gaby), Sigrid Gurie (Ines), Joseph Calleia (Slimane), Gene Lockhart (Regis), Johnny Downs (Pierrot), Alan Hale (Grandpere), Mme. Nina Koshetz (Tania), Joan Woodbury (Aicha), Claudia Dell (Marie), Robert Greig (Giroux), Stanley Fields (Carlos), Charles D. Brown (Max), Ben Hall (Gil), Leonid Kinsky (L'Arbi), Walter Kingsford (Louvain).

Polo Match Santa Monica, "California—Santa Monica Polo Match," British-Pathe newsreel short, 1:36 minutes, released July 28, 1938. Produced by British-Pathe.

CAST: Joan Crawford, Ginger Rogers, Joan Bennett, Spencer Tracy, Frank Borzage, Charles Farrell, Hedy Lamarr, Jack Benny (Themselves).

Hollywood Goes to Town, Metro-Goldwyn-Mayer, 9 minutes, released July 1938. Director, Herman Hoffman; original music, David Snell.

CAST: Frank Whitbeck (Narrator), Judy Garland, Freddie Bartholomew, Una Merkel, Fernand Gravet, John Barrymore, Elaine Barrie (Mrs. Barrymore), Gilbert Adrian, Norma Shearer, Tyrone Power, Spencer Tracy, Fanny Brice, Robert Young, James Stewart, Jeanette MacDonald, Helen Hayes, Louis B. Mayer, Hedy Lamarr, Reginald Gardiner, Douglas Fairbanks Jr., Merle Oberon, Paul Muni, Bella Muni (Mrs. Muni), Charles Boyer, Pat Paterson

(Mrs. Boyer), Clarence Brown, Jack Benny, Claudette Colbert, J. Walter Ruben, Virginia Bruce (Mrs. Ruben), Clark Gable, Carole Lombard (Mrs. Gable), Robert Taylor, Barbara Stanwyck (Mrs. Taylor), Elsa Maxwell, Ed Sullivan, etc. (Themselves)

Screen Snapshots Series 18, No. 10, Columbia Pictures, 10 minutes, released May 26, 1939. Executive producer, Harriet Parsons; producer, Ralph Staub; director, Ralph Staub; writer, Ralph Staub; cinematography, Robert Tobey.

CAST: Basil Rathbone (Host), Ouida Bergere (Mrs. Rathbone, Hostess), Dolores del Rio, Hedy Lamarr, Rosalind Russell, Claire Trevor (Themselves).

Lady of the Tropics, Metro-Goldwyn-Mayer, 91 minutes, released August 11, 1939. Producer, Sam Zimbalist; director, Jack Conway, Leslie Fenton (uncredited); screenplay, Ben Hecht; art directors, Cedric Gibbons, Paul Groesse; set director, Edwin B. Willis; costumes and gowns, Adrian; men's costumes, Valles; musical score, Franz Waxman; orchestrators, Leo Arnaud, Paul Marquardt, and Leonid Raab; composer, additional music, George Bassman; opera staging, William von Wymetal; cinematography, George Folsey, Norbert Brodine (uncredited); editor, Elmo Vernon; sound, Douglas Shearer.

SONG: "Each Time You Say Goodbye (I Die a Little)" by Phil Ohlman and Foster Carlin.

CAST: Robert Taylor (Bill Carey), Hedy Lamarr (Manon de Vargnes), Joseph Schildkraut (Pierre Delaroch), Gloria Franklin (Nina), Ernest Cossart (Father Antoine), Mary Taylor [Zimbalist] (Dolly Harrison), Charles Trowbridge (Alfred Z. Harrison), Frederick Worlock (Colonel Demassey), Paul Porcasi (Lamartine), Margaret [Marguerita] Padula (Madame Kya), Cecil Cunningham (Countess Berichi), Natalie Moorhead (Mrs. Hazlitt), Leon Belasco (assistant manager of rubber company), Abner Biberman (wardrobe buyer), Zeffie Tilbury (woman congratulating Manon).

I Take This Woman, Metro-Goldwyn-Mayer, 96 minutes, released January 26, 1940. Producers, Lawrence Weingarten, Louis B. Mayer, James K. McGuinness, Bernard H. Hyman; director, W. S. (Woodbridge Strong) Van Dyke II, Josef von Sternberg, Frank Borzage; screenplay, James Kevin McGuinness, Charles MacArthur, Ben Hecht; based on a story by Charles MacArthur; musical score, Bronislau Kaper, Arthur Guttmann (Artur Guttmann); orchestrators, Leo Arnaud, George Bassman, Paul Marquardt; art directors, Cedric Gibbons; associate art director, Paul Groesse; set director, Edwin B. Wallis; costumes and gowns, Adrian; cinematography, Harold Rosson, Bud Lawton Jr.; sound, Douglas Shearer; editor, George Boemler; still photographer, Clarence Sinclair Bull.

CAST: Spencer Tracy (Dr. Karl Decker), Hedy Lamarr (Georgi Gragore), Verree Teasdale (Madame Marecsca), Kent Taylor (Phil Mayberry), Mona Barrie (Sandra Mayberry), Paul Cavanaugh (Bill Rodgers), Jack Carson (Joe), Louis Calhern (Dr. Martin Sumner Duveen), Laraine Day (Linda Rodgers), Reed Hadley (Bob Hampton), Frances Drake (Lola Estermont), Marjorie Main (Gertie), Dalies Frantz (Dr. Joe Barnes); George E. Stone (Sid, the taxi driver), Willie Best (Sambo), Leon Belasco (Pancho).

Starring cast deleted [for Josef von Sternberg (1938)]: Fanny Brice (Madame Marcesca), Walter Pidgeon (Phil Mayberry).

Starring cast deleted [for Frank Borzage (1938/1939)]: Ina Claire (Madame Marcesca),

Walter Pidgeon (Phil Mayberry), Adrienne Ames (Linda Rodgers), Leonard Penn (Bob Hampton).

Hearst Metronome News, "News of the Day—Here and There," "Producers Beat Actors in Polo Match 2–1—Los Angeles," distributed by Metro-Goldwyn-Mayer, approximately 10 minutes, released July 1, 1940.

CAST: Frank Capra, Loretta Young, Hedy Lamarr (Themselves).

Boom Town, Metro-Goldwyn-Mayer, 119 minutes, released August 30, 1940. Producer, Sam Zimbalist; director, Jack Conway; screenplay, John Lee Mahin, based on the short story "A Lady Comes to Burkburnett," by James Edward Grant; art directors, Cedric Gibbons, Eddie Imazu; set decorators, Edwin B. Willis, Henry Grace, Hugh Hunt, Jack D. Moore; costumes and gowns, Adrian, Gile Steele; hair stylist, Sydney Guilaroff; makeup artist, Robert J. Schiffer; musical score, Franz Waxman; cinematographer, Harold Rosson, Elwood Bredell; sound, Douglas Shearer; editors, Blanche Sewell, Paul Landres.

CAST: Clark Gable (Big John McMasters), Spencer Tracy (Square John Sand), Claudette Colbert (Betsy Bartlett), Hedy Lamarr (Karen Vanmeer), Frank Morgan (Luther Aldrich), Lionel Atwill (Harry Compton), Chill Wills (Harmony Jones), Marion Martin (Whitey), Minna Gombell (Spanish Eva "Evie"), Joe Yule (Ed Murphy), Horace Murphy (Tom Murphy), Ray Gordon (McCreery), Richard Lane (Assistant District Attorney), Casey Johnson (Little Jack), Baby Quintanilla (Baby Jack), Sara Haden (Miss Barnes), Frank Orth (Barber), Frank McGlynn Sr. (Deacon), Curt Bois (Ferdie), Dick Curtis (Hiring Boss), Barbara Bedford (Nurse), Bess Flowers (Worker in McMaster's office), Byron Foulger (Geologist), Yakima Canutt, Herbert Holcombe, Frank Hagney (stuntmen), George DeNormand (Spencer Tracy fight double), Joe Hickey (Clark Gable fight double).

Comrade X, Metro-Goldwyn-Mayer, 87 minutes, released December 3, 1940. Producer, Gottfried Reinhardt; director, King Vidor; screenplay, Ben Hecht, Charles Lederer, Herman J. Mankiewicz (uncredited); based on a story by Walter Reisch; art director, Cedric Gibbons; associate art director, Malcolm Brown; set director, Edwin B. Willis; women's costumes and gowns, Adrian; men's costumes, Gile Steele; makeup, Jack Dawn; musical score, Bronislau Kaper; cinematographer, Joseph Ruttenberg; special night photography, Karl Freund (uncredited); special effects, A. Arnold Gillespie; sound, Douglas Shearer; editor, Harold F. Kress.

SONGS: "Funiculi Funicula," lyrics by Peppino Turco and Luigi Denza; "To Vania," arranged by Bronsilau Kaper; "Burial Chant," music by Bronislau Kaper, lyrics by Andrei Tolstoy; "We Are Free," music by Bronislau Kaper, lyrics by Andrei Tolstoy.

CAST: Clark Gable (McKinley B. "Mac" Thompson), Hedy Lamarr (Theodora Yahupitz "Lizzie"), Oscar Homolka (Commissar Vasiliev), Felix Bressart (Igor Yahupitz "Vanya"), Eve Arden (Jane Wilson), Sig Rumann (Emil von Hofer), Natasha Lytess (Olga Milanava), Vladimir Sokoloff (Michael Bastakoff), Edgar Barrier (Rubick), George Renavent (Laszlo), Mikhail Rasumny (Russian Officer).

A New Romance of Celluloid: The Miracle of Sound, Metro-Goldwyn-Mayer, 11 minutes, released 1940. Director, Douglas Shearer; original music, Daniele Amfitheatrof; cinematography, Lester White; editor, Jack Ruggiero.

CAST: Frank Whitbeck (Narrator), Jeanette MacDonald, Nelson Eddy, Clark Gable, Hedy Lamarr, Spencer Tracy, Norma Shearer, Robert Taylor, Conrad Veidt, Alla Nazimova, The Marx Brothers (Groucho, Harpo, Chico), Ann Sothern, Ruth Hussey, Walter Pidgeon, Robert Young, Lew Ayres, Lionel Barrymore, Laraine Day, Judy Garland, Lana Turner, Joan Crawford, Cary Grant, Katharine Hepburn, James Stewart, George Murphy, Greer Garson, Douglas Shearer, W. S. Van Dyke, etc. (Themselves).

Come Live with Me, Metro-Goldwyn-Mayer, 86 minutes, released January 29, 1941. Producer-director, Clarence Brown; screenplay, Patterson McNutt; based on a story by Virginia van Upp; musical score, Herbert Stothart; art director, Cedric Gibbons; associate art director, Randall Duell; set director, Edwin B. Willis; gowns and costumes, Adrian; cinematography, George J. Folsey; editor, Frank E. Hull; sound, Douglas Shearer.

SONGS: "Come Live with Me," music by Herbert Stothart, lyrics by Christopher Marlowe; "Oh Johnny, Oh Johnny," music by Herbert Stothart, lyrics by Ed Rose.

CAST: James Stewart (Bill Smith), Hedy Lamarr (Johanna Janns [Johnny Jones]), Ian Hunter (Barton Kendrick), Verree Teasdale (Diane Kendrick), Donald Meek (Joe Darsie), Barton MacLane (Barney Grogan), Edward Ashley (Arnold Stafford), Ann Codee (Yvonne), King Baggott (Doorman), Adeline de Walt Reynolds (Grandma), Frank Orth (Jerry), Si Jenks (Man in café), Fritz Feld (Headwaiter), Frank Faylen (Waiter), Joe Yule (Sleeping Neighbor), Alan Curtis (Bit).

Ziegfeld Girl, Metro-Goldwyn-Mayer, 133 minutes, released April 17, 1941. Producer, Pandro S. Berman; director, Robert Z. Leonard; musical numbers staged by Busby Berkeley; specialty dance sequence and ensemble dance direction, Danny Darel; screenplay, Marguerite Roberts, Sonya Levien, Annalee Whitmore, based on a story by William Anthony McGuire; musical score, Herbert Stothart; musical director, George E. Stoll, vocals and orchestrations, Leo Arnaud, George Bassman, Conrad Salinger; musical presentation, Merrill Pye; musical arranger, Roger Edens; art director, Cedric Gibbons; art associate, Daniel B. Cathcart; set director, Edwin B. Willis; costumes and gowns, Adrian; makeup, Jack Dawn; hair stylist, Larry Germain; cinematography, Ray June, Joseph Ruttenberg; sound, Douglas Shearer; editor, Blanche Sewell.

SONGS: "You Stepped Out of a Dream," music and lyrics by Gus Kahn and Nacio Herb Brown; "Whispering," music and lyrics by John Schonberger, Richard Coburn, and Vincent Rose; "Mr. Gallagher and Mr. Shean," music and lyrics by Edward Gallagher and Al Shean; "I'm Always Chasing Rainbows," music and lyrics by Joseph McCarthy and Harry Carroll; "Caribbean Love Song," lyrics by Ralph Freed and music by Roger Edens; "The Kids from Seville," music and lyrics by Antonio and Rosario; "You Never Looked So Beautiful Before," music and lyrics by Walter Donaldson (from M-G-M's *The Great Ziegfeld*, 1936); "Minnie from Trinidad," "Ziegfeld Girls," and "Laugh? I Thought I'd Split My Sides," music and lyrics by Roger Edens; "You Gotta Pull Strings," music and lyrics by Harold Adamson and Walter Donaldson (from M-G-M's *The Great Ziegfeld*, 1936), "Too Beautiful to Last" and "We Must Have Music," both cut from final film. Filmed in Sepia.

CAST: James Stewart (Gilbert "Gil" Young), Judy Garland (Susan Gallagher), Hedy Lamarr (Sandra Kolter), Lana Turner (Sheila "Red" Regan, later Hale), Tony Martin (Frank Merton), Jackie Cooper (Jerry Regan), Ian Hunter (Geoffrey Collis), Charles Winninger (Ed "Pop" Gallagher), Edward Everett Horton (Noble Sage), Philip Dorn (Franz Kolter), Paul Kelly (John Slayton), Eve Arden (Patsy Dixon), Dan Dailey Jr. (Jimmy Walters), Al Shean (Himself), Fay Holden (Mrs. Regan), Felix Bressart (Mischa), Rose Hobart (Mrs. Merton), Bernard Nedell (Nick Capalini), Ed McNamara (Mr. Regan), Mae Busch (Jenny), Renie Riano (Annie), Joyce Compton (Miss Sawyer), Josephine Whittell (Perkins), Sergio Orta (Native Dancer), Six Hits and a Miss (Singers), Music Maids (Auditioning Singers), Joan Barclay (Actress in Slayton's Office), Ruth Tobey (Betty Regan), Bess Flowers (Palm Beach Casino Player), Antonio and Rosario (The Kids from Seville, Specialty Dancers), Jean Wallace, Myrna Dell, Lorraine Gettman [aka Leslie Brooks], Louise La Planche, Georgia Carroll, Frances Gladwin, Dorothy Tuttle, Madeline Martin, etc. (Ziegfeld Girls).

H.M. Pulham, Esq., Metro-Goldwyn-Mayer, 119 minutes, released December 3, 1941. Producer-director, King Vidor; screenplay, Elizabeth Hill, King Vidor; based on the novel *H.M. Pulham, Esquire*, by John P. Marquand; art director, Cedric Gibbons; associate art director, Malcolm Brown; set director, Edwin B. Willis; musical score, Bronislau Kaper; musical director, Lennie Hayton; costumes and gowns, Robert Kalloch; men's costumes, Gile Steele; makeup, Jack Dawn; makeup man, Jack Young; hairstylist, Edith Keon; cinematography, Ray June; sound, Douglas Shearer; editors, Harold F. Kress, Frank Sullivan; still photographer, Jimmy Manatt.

SONGS: "Three O'Clock in the Morning," music by Julian Robledo, lyrics by Dorothy Terriss; "The Wedding March," from *A Midsummer Night's Dream*, by Felix Mendelssohn-Bartholdy; "The Bridal Chorus," by Richard Wagner; "The Band Played On," by John E. Palmer.

CAST: Robert Young (Harry Pulham Jr.), Hedy Lamarr (Marvin Myles Ransome), Ruth Hussey (Kay Motford Pulham), Charles Coburn (Mr. Harry Pulham Sr.), Van Heflin (Bill King), Fay Holden (Mrs. Pulham), Bonita Granville (Mary Pulham), Leif Erickson (Rodney "Bo-Jo" Brown), Phil Brown (Joe Bingham), Douglas Wood (Mr. Bullard), Sara Haden (Miss Rollo), Walter Kingsford (Skipper), Bobby Cooper (Harry, as a boy), Brenda Henderson (Kay, as a child); David Wilmot (Joe, as a child); Bobby Cooper (Harry, age 12); Clare Verdera (Ellen); Billy Engle (Newsman); Earle Dewey (Chris Evans), Byron Foulger [replaced Philip Coolidge] (Curtis Cole), Harry Crocker [replaced Byron Shores] (Bob Ridge), Harry Brown (Charley Roberts), Douglass Newland (Sam Green), Grant Withers (Sammy Lee, Harvard Coach), Connie Gilchrist (Tillie), Ava Gardner (young socialite at the wedding, back row), Sarah Edwards (Mrs. Motford, Kay's mother), Frank Faylen (Sergeant), Anne Revere (Miss Redfern).

Tortilla Flat, Metro-Goldwyn-Mayer, 105 minutes, released April 21, 1942. Producer, Sam Zimbalist; director, Victor Fleming; fill-in director, Sam Zimbalist; screenplay, John Lee Mahin, Benjamin Glazer; based on the novel *Tortilla Flat*, by John Steinbeck; musical score, Franz Waxman; choir director, Robert Mitchell; "Varsoviana" dance director, Ramon Ros; dialogue coach, Dr. Simon Mitchneck; art director, Cedric Gibbons; associate art director, Paul Groesse; set directors, Edwin B. Willis, F. Keogh Gleason; gowns and costumes, Robert Kalloch; men's costumes, Gile Steele; makeup, Jack Dawn; cinematography, Karl Freund,

Harold Rosson, Sidney Wagner; Monterey exteriors cinematography, Jack Smith; editors, James E. Newcom, Robert J. Kern.

SONG: "Ay, Paisano!" music by Franz Waxman, lyrics by Frank Loesser.

CAST: Spencer Tracy (Pilon); Hedy Lamarr (Dolores "Sweets" Ramirez); John Garfield (Danny Alvarez); Frank Morgan ("The Pirate"), Akim Tamiroff (Pablo); Sheldon Leonard (Tito Ralph), John Qualen (Jose Maria Corcoran), Donald Meek (Paul D. Cummings), Connie Gilchrist (Mrs. Torrelli), Allen Jenkins (Portagee Joe), Henry O'Neill (Father Juan Ramon), Arthur Space (Mr. Brown), Tim Ryan (Rupert Hogan), Charles Judels (Joe Machado), Yvette Duguay (Little Girl), Louis Jean Heydt (Young Doctor), Barbara Bedford (Nun), The Robert Mitchell Boy Choir (The Saint Brendan's Boys Choir).

Crossroads, Metro-Goldwyn-Mayer, 83 minutes, released July 23, 1942. Producer, Edwin Knopf; director, Jack Conway; screenplay, Guy Trosper and Frederick Kohner; based on a story by John H. Kafka and Howard Emmett Rogers; art director, Cedric Gibbons; associate art director, John S. Detlie; set director, Edwin B. Willis; gowns and costumes, Robert Kalloch; makeup, Jack Dawn; musical score, Bronislau Kaper; cinematography, Joseph Ruttenberg; editor, George Boemler; sound, Douglas Shearer.

SONG: "Till You Return," music by Arthur Schwartz, lyrics by Howard Dietz.

CAST: William Powell (David Talbot), Hedy Lamarr (Lucienne Talbot), Claire Trevor (Michelle Allaine), Basil Rathbone (Henri Sarrou), Felix Bressart (Dr. Andre Tessier), Margaret Wycherly (Madame Pelletier), Reginald Owen (Concierge), Philip Merivale (Commissioner of Police), Sig Rumann (Dr. Alex Dubroc), Vladimir Sokoloff (Carlos Le Duc), H. B. Warner (Prosecuting Attorney), Guy Bates Post (President of Court), Fritz Leiber (Deval), John Mylong (Baron De Lorraine), Anna Q. Nilsson (Madame Deval).

Hearst Metronome News, "News of the Day—Here and There," "Movie Stars Leave for Washington Command Performance and War Bond Tour," distributed by Metro-Goldwyn-Mayer, approximately 10 minutes, released August 27, 1942.

CAST: Greer Garson, Ronald Colman, Irene Dunne, Hedy Lamarr, Joan Leslie, Virginia Gilmore, Lynn Bari, Ann Rutherford (Themselves).

Hearst Metronome News, "News of the Day—Here and There," "Stars over America! Film Caravan Tours Nation in War Bond Drive!" distributed by Metro-Goldwyn-Mayer, approximately 10 minutes, released August 31, 1942.

SONG: "This Is What Fighting's For," sung by Bing Crosby.

CAST: Secretary of the Treasury, Senator Henry Morgenthau (Host), Hedy Lamarr, Bing Crosby, Dinah Shore, Bud Abbott and Lou Costello, Kay Kyser, James Cagney, Irene Dunne, Ronald Colman, Greer Garson, Herbert Marshall, Lynn Bari, Gene Tierney, Bob Hope, Martha Scott, George Brent, Joan Leslie, Virginia Gilmore, Edward Arnold, Ann Rutherford, Charles Laughton, and Walter Able.

A New Romance of Celluloid: We Must Have Music, Metro-Goldwyn-Mayer, 11 minutes, released 1942.

SONG: "America the Beautiful," music by Samuel A. Ward, lyrics by Katherine Lee Bates, sung by Rise Stevens.

CAST: Frank Whitbeck (Narrator), Judy Garland, Tony Martin, Rise Stevens, Six Hits and a Miss, Herbert Stothart, Bronislau Kaper, Busby Berkeley, Hedy Lamarr, Lana Turner, Robert Taylor, Greta Garbo, Ruth Hussey, Spencer Tracy, Clark Gable, Mickey Rooney, Virginia Weidler, Wallace Beery, Marjorie Main, Lionel Barrymore, Lew Ayres, Walter Pidgeon, Joan Crawford, Robert Young, Nelson Eddy, Greer Garson, Van Heflin, Red Skelton, Ann Sothern, James Stewart, Norma Shearer, James Craig, Melvyn Douglas, Philip Dorn, Myrna Loy, Frank Morgan, Eleanor Powell, William Powell, Conrad Veidt, etc. (Themselves), Charles King, Anita Page, Bessie Love (archival footage).

A New Romance of Celluloid: Personalities, Metro-Goldwyn-Mayer, 10 minutes, released 1942.

Song: "Tulip Time," lyrics and music by Franz Waxman (sung by Kathryn Grayson); "'Til We Meet Again," music by Richard A. Whiting, lyrics by Raymond B. Egan (sung by Lucille Norman). Original music by Lennie Hayton; editor, Ira Heymann.

CAST: Frank Whitbeck (Narrator), Robert Sterling, Patricia Dane, Lana Turner, Clark Gable (*Somewhere I'll Find You*), Richard Ney, Van Johnson, Fay Bainter, Edward Arnold, Jean Rogers, Spring Byington (*The War Against Mrs. Hadley*), Kathryn Grayson, Marsha Hunt, Cecilia Parker, Frances Raeburn, Peggy Moran, Dorothy Morris (*Seven Sweethearts*), Susan Peters, Ronald Colman (*Random Harvest*), Donna Reed, Edward Arnold, Ann Harding (*Eyes in the Night*), Lucille Norman, Judy Garland, Gene Kelly, Ben Blue, George Murphy (*For Me and My Gal*), Hedy Lamarr (*White Cargo, Crossroads*), Spencer Tracy, John Garfield, Sheldon Leonard, Hedy Lamarr (*Tortilla Flat*), Mickey Rooney, Carole Gallagher, Esther Williams, Frances Rafferty, Greta Garbo, Greer Garson, Robert Taylor, Robert Young, Lionel Barrymore, Ann Sothern, James Stewart, Laraine Day, Virginia Weidler, Eleanor Powell, William Powell (archival footage).

Hearst Metronome News, "News of the Day—Here and There," "Hedy Lamarr Spurs War Bond Sales," distributed by Metro-Goldwyn-Mayer, approximately 10 minutes, released September 4, 1942.

CAST: Hedy Lamarr (Herself).

White Cargo, Metro-Goldwyn-Mayer, 89 minutes, released September 20, 1942. Producer, Victor Saville; director, Richard Thorpe; screenplay, Leon Gordon, based on his play *White Cargo*, based on the novel *Hell's Playground,* by Ida Vera Simonton; art director, Cedric Gibbons; associate art director, Daniel B. Cathcart; set director, Edwin B. Willis; associate set director, F. Keogh Gleason; musical score, Bronislau Kaper; makeup, Jack Dawn; native costumes, Robert Kalloch; dance directors, Ernest Matray and Maria Matray; cinematography, Harry Stradling Sr.; sound, Douglas Shearer; editor, Frederick Y. Smith.

SONG: "Tondelayo," music by Vernon Duke, lyrics by Howard Dietz.

CAST: Hedy Lamarr (Tondelayo), Walter Pidgeon (Harry Witzell), Frank Morgan (Doctor), Richard Carlson (Langford), Reginald Owen (Skipper), Henry O'Neill (Reverend Roberts), Bramwell Fletcher (Wilbur Ashley), Clyde Cook (Ted), Leigh Whipper (Jim Fish), Oscar Polk (Umeela).

British-Pathe News, "Calling All Stars—(Dublin edition)," British-Pathe newsreel short, 1:24 minutes, released September 24, 1942.

Produced by British-Pathe.

CAST: Secretary of State Henry Morgenthau, Greer Garson, James Cagney, Hedy Lamarr, Ann Rutherford, Irene Dunne, Kay Kyser, Ann Sothern, Ginny Simms, Larry Adler, Bud Abbott, Lou Costello, Spring Byington (Themselves).

The March of Time Vol. IX, Issue 10: Show Business at War, Twentieth Century–Fox, 17 minutes, released May 21, 1943. Producer, Louis de Rochemont; director, Louis de Rochemont.

CAST: Jackson Beck (Narrator), Ethel Barrymore, Robert Benchley, Jack Benny, Edgar Bergen, Irving Berlin, James Cagney, Bing Crosby, Michael Curtiz, Linda Darnell, Bette Davis, Olivia de Havilland, Marlene Dietrich, Walt Disney, Irene Dunne, Deanna Durbin, W. C. Fields, Errol Flynn, Kay Francis, Clark Gable, John Garfield, Rita Hayworth, Alfred Hitchcock, Bob Hope, Hedy Lamarr, Dorothy Lamour, Carole Landis, Gertrude Lawrence, Anatole Litvak, Carole Lombard, Myrna Loy, Eugene Ormandy, Tyrone Power, Ginger Rogers, Mickey Rooney, Frank Sinatra, Lana Turner, Hal. B. Wallis, Jack L. Warner, Orson Welles, Loretta Young, Darryl F. Zanuck, etc. (Themselves).

Hearst Metronome News, "News of the Day—Here and There," "Shangri-La War Stamp Campaign," distributed by Metro-Goldwyn-Mayer, approximately 10 minutes, released June 25, 1943.

CAST: Ted Lawson (Narrator), Hedy Lamarr (Herself).

Hearst Metronome News, "News of the Day—Here and There," "Mexico Honors American Film Notables—Louis B. Mayer Honored for Service to Mexico!" distributed by Metro-Goldwyn-Mayer, approximately 10 minutes, released June 25, 1943.

CAST: Louis B. Mayer, Hedy Lamarr, Walt Disney, John Loder (Themselves).

The Heavenly Body, Metro-Goldwyn-Mayer, 93 minutes, released March 23, 1944. Producer, Arthur Hornblow Jr.; director, Alexander Hall; fill-in director, Vincente Minnelli; dialogue director, Joan Hathaway; screenplay, Michael Arlen, Walter Reisch; based on a story by Jacques Théry, adapted by Harry Kurnitz; art director, Cedric Gibbons; associate art director, William Ferrari; set director, Edwin B. Willis; associate set director, McLean Nisbet; musical score, Bronislau Kaper; costumes, Irene; cinematography, Robert H. Planck, William H. Daniels; matte paintings, Warren Newcombe; matte paintings camera, Mark Davis; miniatures, Danny Hall; editor, Blanche Sewell; sound, Douglas Shearer.

SONGS: "Happiness Is Just a Thing Called Joe," music by Harold Arlen, lyrics by E. Y. Harburg; "Hungarian Dance No. 1 in G Minor," by Johannes Brahms; "I'm Dying for Someone to Love Me," unknown; "The Volga Boatman," unknown; "The Merry Widow Waltz," by Franz Lehar.

CAST: William Powell (Prof. William Stewart Whitley), Hedy Lamarr (Vicky Whitley), James Craig (Lloyd X. Hunter), Fay Bainter (Margaret Sibyll), Henry O'Neill (Professor Stowe), Spring Byington (Nancy Potter), Robert Sully (Strand), Morris Ankrum (Dr. Green), Connie Gilchrist (Beulah [Delia Murphy]), Arthur Space (Pierson), Marietta Canty (Pearl Harrison), Nicodemus (Willie), Sylvia Hollis (Hedy Lamarr's stand-in).

Scenes deleted: Phillip Terry (Whitley's assistant), Bobby Watson (Adolf Hitler, photo insert), Rex Evans (Hermann Göring, photo insert).

The Conspirators, Warner Brothers, 101 minutes, released October 21, 1944. Executive producer, Jack L. Warner; producer, Jack Chertok; director, Jean Negulesco; screenplay, Vladimir Pozner, Leo Rosten; additional dialogue, Jack Moffit; based on a novel by Fredric [Frederic] Prokosch; dialogue director, Herschel Daugherty; art director, Anton Grot; set director, Walter F. Tilford; gowns and costumes, Leah Rhodes; wardrobe, Mildred Duncan, Marie Pickering, Leon Roberts; makeup, Perc Westmore, Bill Cooley, Al Greenway, John Wallace; hair stylist, Jean Burt Reilly; musical score, Max Steiner, Hugo Friedhofer; musical director, Leo Forbstein; orchestral arrangements, Leonid Raab; cinematography, Arthur Edeson; sound, Robert B. Lee; editor, Rudi Fehr; still photographer, Milton Gould; dialogue coach for Miss Lamarr, Ruth Roberts; singer of "Maringa," Aloysio De Oliveira.

SONGS: "The Blue Danube Waltz, Opus 314," by Johann Strauss; "Maringa," music by Joubert de Carvalho; "Orchid Moon," music by Max Steiner, lyrics by Albert Stillman.

CAST: Hedy Lamarr (Irene von Mohr), Paul Henreid (Vincent van der Lyn), Sydney Greenstreet (Ricardo Quintanilla), Peter Lorre (Jan Bernazsky), Victor Francen (Hugo von Mohr), Joseph Calleia (Captain Pereira), Carol Thurston (Rosa), Vladimir Sokoloff (Miguel), Edward [Eduardo] Cianelli (Captain Almeida), Steven Geray (Dr. Schmitt), George Macready (Schmitt's Special Agent), Doris Lloyd (Mrs. Benson), Monte Blue (Jennings), Luis Alberni (Prison Guard), Hal Kelly, Philip van Zandt (Customs Officers), Jay Novello (Detective), Doris Lloyd (Mrs. Benson), Bess Flowers (Diner at Café Imperio), Marcel Dalio (Croupier), Aurora Miranda (Fado Singer), Carmel Myers (Baroness von Kluge), Sylvia Hollis (Hedy Lamarr's stand-in).

Experiment Perilous, R-K-O Radio, 91 minutes, released December 18, 1944. Executive producer, Robert Fellows; producer, Warren Duff; director, Jacques Tourneur; screenplay, Warren Duff; based on the novel *Experiment Perilous* by Margaret Carpenter; art directors, Albert S. D'Agostino, Jack Okey; set decorators, Darrell Silvera, Claude E. Carpenter; costumes, Leah Rhodes (gowns for Ms. Lamarr), Edward Stevenson (other gowns); musical score, Roy Webb; musical director, C. Bakaleinikoff; sound, John E. Tribby; cinematography, Tony Gaudio; editor, Ralph Dawson.

CAST: Hedy Lamarr (Allida Bedereaux), George Brent (Dr. Huntington Bailey), Paul Lukas (Nick Bedereaux), Albert Dekker ("Clag" Claghorn), Carl Esmond (John Maitland), Olive Blakeney (Clarissa "Cissie" Bedereaux), George N. Neise (Alec Gregory), Margaret Wycherly (Maggie), Stephanie Bachelor (Elaine), Mary Servoss (Miss Wilson), Julia Dean (Deria), William Post Jr. (District Attorney MacDonald), Billy (Perry William), Ward (Alec, age 5), Sam McDaniel (Porter), Michael Orr (Nick, age 3), Peggy Miller (Cissie, age 8), Evelyn Falke (Cissie, age 5), Janet Clark (Deria as a girl), Paula Raymond (singing voice for Hedy Lamarr).

Her Highness and the Bellboy, Metro-Goldwyn-Mayer, 112 minutes, released September 11, 1945. Producer, Joe Pasternak; director, Richard Thorpe; screenplay, Richard Connell, Gladys Lehman; musical score, George (Georgie) E. Stoll; musical director, George (Georgie) E. Stoll; orchestrations, Calvin Jackson; choreography, Charles Walters; art director, Cedric Gibbons, Urie McCleary, Hugh Hobson; set director, Edwin B. Willis; associate set decorator, McLean Nisbet; costumes, Irene; associate costumes, Marion Herwood Keyes; men's costumes, Valles; makeup, Jack Dawn; cinematography, Harry Stradling Sr.; matte paintings director, Mark Davis; sound, Douglas Shearer; editor, George Boemler.

SONGS: "Honey," music and lyrics by Seymour Simons, Haven Gillespie, and Richard A. Whiting; "Wait 'Til the Sun Shines, Nellie," music by Harry von Tilzer, lyrics by Andrew B. Sterling; "The Fountain in the Park" ("Strolling Through the Park One Day"), music and lyrics by Ed Hailey; "Dream," music and lyrics by Georgie Stoll and Calvin Jackson.

CAST: Hedy Lamarr (Princess Veronica), Robert Walker (Jimmy Dobson), June Allyson (Leslie Odell), Rags Ragland (Albert Weever), Agnes Moorehead (Countess Zoe), Carl Esmond (Baron Zoltan Faludi), Warner Anderson (Paul MacMillan), Ludwig Stössel (Mr. Puft), Konstantin Shayne (Count Yanos von Lankofitz), Ann Codee (Countess Tradiska), Gladys Blake (Pearl), George Cleveland (Dr. Elfson), Olga Fabian (Mrs. Korb), Edward Gargan (First Cop), Audrey Totter (Mildred), Virginia Sale (Aunt Gertrude Odell), Jack Norton (Mr. Pook, drunk at Jake's Joint), Constance Weiler (Gladys, newsstand girl), Betty Blythe, Greta Gould, Ottola Nesmith (Diplomat Wives), Michael Visaroff (Diplomat), Richard Hall, Sharon McManus (Children), Bess Flowers (Woman), Symona Boniface, Wanda Perry, Franz Dorfler (Maids).

The Strange Woman, United Artists' release of a Hunt Stromberg Production, 101 minutes, released October 25, 1946. Executive producers, Hedy Lamarr, Hunt Stromberg; producers, Jack Chertok, Eugene Schufftan; director, Edgar G. Ulmer; screenplay, Herb Meadow, Hunt Stromberg, Edgar G. Ulmer; based on the novel *The Strange Woman*, by Ben Ames Williams; production design and art director, Nicolai Remisoff; assistant art director, Victor Greene; costumes, Natalie Visart; hair stylist, Blanche Smith; makeup, Joseph Stinton; musical score, Carmen Dragon; cinematography, Lucien N. Andriot; sound, Corson Jowett; supervising editor, James E. Newcom; editor, John M. Foley, Richard G. Wray; script supervisor, Shirley Ulmer.

CAST: Hedy Lamarr (Jenny Hager), George Sanders (John Evered), Louis Hayward (Ephraim Poster), Gene Lockhart (Isaiah Poster), Hillary Brooke (Meg Saladine), Rhys Williams (Deacon Adams), June Storey (Lena Tempest), Moroni Olsen (Reverend Thatcher), Olive Blakeney (Mrs. Hollis), Dennis Hoey (Tim Hager), Alan Napier (Judge Henry Saladine), Ian Keith (Lincoln Pittridge), Katherine Lockhart (Mrs. Partridge), Billy Gray, Teddy Infuhr (Boys on the Bridge), Jo Ann Marlowe (Jenny, as a girl), Helen McLeod (Hedy Lamarr's stand-in), Arianne Castle [Ulmer] (Bit).

Dishonored Lady, United Artists' release of a Hunt Stromberg Production, 86 minutes, released May 16, 1947. President, Hunt Stromberg; producer, Jack Chertok; director, Robert Stevenson; screenplay, Edmund H. North; contributing screenwriters, André De Toth, Ben Hecht; based on the stage play *Dishonored Lady*, by Edward Sheldon and Margaret Ayer Barnes; dialogue director, Frances Dawson; production design and art director, Nicolai Remisoff; assistant art director, Victor Green; interior decorator, Robert Priestly (Priestley); gowns, Elois (Eloise) Jenssen; makeup, Joseph Stinton; hair stylist, Ruth Pursley; musical score, Carmen Dragon; cinematography, Lucien Andriot; supervising film editor, James E. Newcom; editor, John M. Foley; sound, John Carter, Joseph I. Kane. Stage producer, Guthrie McClintic. Special thanks for the use of Robert Stevenson to David O. Selznick.

CAST: Hedy Lamarr (Madeleine Damien), Dennis O'Keefe (Dr. David Cousins), John Loder (Felix Courtland), William Lundigan (Jack Garet), Morris Carnovsky (Dr. Caleb), Paul Cavanaugh (Victor Kranish), Natalie Schafer (Ethel Royce), Douglas Dumbrille (District Attorney), Margaret Hamilton (Mrs. Geiger, landlady), James Flavin (Police Sergeant Patella), Dewey Robinson (Jim), Helen McLeod (Hedy Lamarr's stand-in).

Screen Snapshots: Hollywood Party, Columbia Pictures, 9 minutes, released June 10, 1948. Producer, Ralph Staub; director, Ralph Staub.

CAST: Ralph Staub (Himself), Joan Bennett, Dane Clark, Marie Dressler, James Gleason, Lucille Gleason, Hedy Lamarr, Zasu Pitts, May Robson, Roy Rogers, James Stewart, Lana Turner (archival footage).

Hearst Metronome News, "News of the Day—Here and There," "Movie Stars' Night in Paris!" distributed by Metro-Goldwyn-Mayer, approximately 10 minutes, released July 30, 1948.

Arias: "Rigoletto," Giuseppe Verdi.

CAST: Charles Boyer, Rita Hayworth, Hedy Lamarr, Vincent Auriol, Ingrid Bergman, Edward G. Robinson, Lily Pons (Themselves).

Camera Angles, Warner Bros., 8 minutes, released 1948. Producer, Gordon Hollingshead; director, Gene Lester.

CAST: Art Gilmore (Narrator), Hedy Lamarr, Jack Carson, Sonja Henie, Alexis Smith, Barbara Bates (cameos).

Let's Live a Little, Eagle-Lion, 85 minutes, released December 9, 1948. Producers, Eugene Frenke, Robert Cummings; associate producer, Joe Gottesman; director Richard Wallace; screenplay, Howard Irving Young, Edmund L. Hartmann, Albert J. Cohen, Jack Harvey; based on an original story by Albert J. Cohen, Jack Harvey; dialogue director, Frances Dawson; art director, Edward L. Ilou; set directors, Armor Marlowe, Robert P. Fox; costumes, Elois [Eloise] Jenssen; makeup, Ern Westmore, Joe Stinton; hair stylist, Joan St. Oegger, Helen Turpin; musical score, Werner R. Heymann; musical director, Irving Friedman; theremin musician, Dr. Samuel Hoffman; cinematography, Ernest Laszlo; editor, Arthur Hilton; sound, Leon S. Becker, Howard J. Fogetti; E. Truman Joiner; still photographer, George Hommel; production supervisor, James T. Vaughn.

CAST: Robert Cummings (Duke Crawford), Hedy Lamarr (Dr. J. O. Loring), Anna Sten (Michele Bennett), Robert Shayne (Dr. Richard Field), Mary Treen (Miss Adams), Harry Antrim (James Montgomery), Hal K. Dawson (M.C.), Billy Bevan (Morton), Curt Bois (Chemist), John Newland (Newcomb), Oliver Blake (Herbie, photographer), John Dehner (Dempster), Frank Wilcox (Salesman), Eve Whitney (Miss O'Reilly), Norma Varden (Nurse Brady), Lillian Randolph (Sarah), Lucien Littlefield (Mr. Tinker), Byron Foulger (Mr. Hopkins).

Samson and Delilah, Paramount, 121 minutes, released December 21, 1949. Producer-director, Cecil B. DeMille; screenplay, Jesse L. Lasky Jr., Frederic M. Frank; based on the story of Samson and Delilah in the Holy Bible, Judges 13–16, and *Judge and Fool,* by Vladimir Jabotinsky; screen treatment by Harold Lamb and Vladimir Jabotinsky; research, Henry Noerdlinger, Gladys Percey; dialogue director, Francis [Frances] Dawson; musical score and director, Victor Young; art directors, Hans Dreier, Walter Tyler, John Meehan; set decorators,

Sam Comer, Ray Moyer, Maurice Goodman; women's costumes, Edith Head, Gus Peters, Gile Steele, Gwen Wakeling; men's costumes, Dorothy Jeakins; Miss Lamarr's costumes, Elois [Eloise] W. Jenssen [Jensson]; makeup, Wally Westmore, Hal [Harold] Lierly, William Woods; hair stylist, Nellie Manley, Elaine Ramsey, Doris Clifford; hair stylist for Hedy Lamarr, Lenore Weaver; musical score, Victor Young; musical director, Victor Young; cinematography, George Barnes; process camera, Farciot Edouart, W. Wallace Kelley; matte artist, Jan Domela; sound, Harry Lindgren, John Cope; Holy Land location cinematographer, Dewey Wrigley; editor, Anne Bauchens; choreography, Theodore Kosloff; publicist, Phil Koury; physical trainer for Victor Mature, Joseph Davies; Technicolor director, Natalie Kalmus; assistant Technicolor director, Robert Brower. Filmed in Technicolor.

SONG: "Song of Delilah," music by Victor Young, lyrics by Ray Evans and Jay Livingston.

CAST: Hedy Lamarr (Delilah), Victor Mature (Samson), George Sanders (The Saran of Gaza), Angela Lansbury (Semadar), Henry Wilcoxon (Ahtur, military governor of Dan), Olive Deering (Miriam), Fay Holden (Hazel), Julia Faye (Haisham), Rusty [Russ] Tamblyn (Saul), William Farnum (Tubal), Lane Chandler (Teresh), Moroni Olsen (Targil), Francis J. McDonald (Story Teller), William Davis (Garmiskar), John Miljan (Lesh Lakish), Arthur Q. Bryan (Fat Philistine Merchant/bit), Victor Varconi (Lord of Ashdad), Frank Wilcox (Lord of Ekron), John "Skins" Miller (Man with Burro), Mike Mazurki (Leader of the Philistine Soldiers), Davison Clark (merchant priest), George Reeves (Wounded soldier), Pedro de Cordoba (Bar Simon), Rosemary Dvorak (Lady), Lester Dorr, Wheaton Chambers (Victims), Ted Mapes (Captain killed by jawbone/stunts), Colin Tapley, Nils Asther, James Craven (Princes), Frank Mayo (Master Architect), Phyllis Kennedy (Wide-Eyed Girl), Byron Foulger, Stanley Blythstone (Men), Karen Morley, Gertrude Messinger, Betty Boyd, Claire DuBrey, Miriam Jaye, Greta Granstedt (Women), Charles Judels (Danite Merchant), Harry Woods (Soldier), Philo McCullough (Merchant), Leota Lorraine (Merchant's Wife), Crauford Kent (Court Astrologer), Harry Woods (Gammad), Tom Tyler (Gristmill Captain), Laura Elliott, Sarah Edwards, Ottola Nesmith, Margaret Field, John Kellogg, Dorothy Adams (Spectators), Fairy Cunningham, Arthur Q. Bryan, Weldon Heyburn, Ynes Seabury, Fred Datig Jr., Kathleen Key, Crissy Ellen Pickup (Bits), Ed Hinton (Victor Mature's double in fight sequences), Mel Koontz (Victor Mature's double in lion-fighting sequence), Leo Frie, Louis Friedman (First midget men), Jerry Marin (Torch-bearing midget in the arena), Billy Curtis, John George, Nels Nelson, George Spotts, Edward Aquilor, Eugene Henderson, Charles Dayton, Angelo Rossitto, Arthur Irvin ("Monkeymen" in arena with Samson), John Bamber (Midget stand-in), Kay Bell, Frank Cordell (Victor Mature's doubles), Sylvia Hollis (Hedy Lamarr's double/bit), Carl Andre (spectator/stunts), Brutus (lion).

A Lady Without Passport, Metro-Goldwyn-Mayer, 74 minutes, released August 18, 1950. Producer, Samuel Marx; director Joseph H. Lewis; screenplay, Howard Dimsdale; adapted by Cyril Hume; suggested by a story by Lawrence Taylor; art directors, Cedric Gibbons, Edward C. Carfagno; set designer, Edwin B. Willis; musical score, David Raksin; costumes, Helen Rose; makeup creator, Jack Dawn; makeup, Gene Hibbs; hairstyle designs, Sydney Guilaroff; hair stylist, Jane Roberts; dialogue director, Francis [Frances] Dawson; cinematography, Paul

C. Vogel; editor, Frederick Y. Smith; still photographer, Sam C. Manatt; sound, Douglas Shearer.

CAST: Hedy Lamarr (Marianne Lorress), John Hodiak (Pete Karczag, "Joseph Gombush"), James Craig (Frank Westlake), George Macready (Palinov), Stephen Geray (Frenchman), Bruce Cowling (Archer Delby James), Nederick Young (Henry Nordell), Steven Hill (Jack), Robert Osterloh (Lieutenant Lannahan), Charles Wagenheim (Ramon Santez), Renzo Cesana (Asa Sestina), Nita Bieber (Cuban dancer), King Donovan (Surgeon), Paula Drew (Stewardess), Jay Barney (Chemist), Paul Picerni (Italian), Angela Carabella (Italian wife), Ann Codee (Maria), Lillian Molieri (girl), Movita (Lorena), Arthur Loew Jr. (Sam), Nina Bara (young Cuban girl).

Deleted scenes: James Whitmore and Peter Coe.

Copper Canyon, Paramount, 83 minutes, released November 15, 1950. Producer, Mel Epstein; director, John Farrow; screenplay, Jonathan Latimer [Marquis Warren]; based on a story by Richard English; dialogue director, Frances Dawson; set directors, Sam Comer, Ross Dowd; art directors, Hans Dreier, Franz Bachelin; women's costumes, Edith Head; men's costumes, Gile Steele; makeup supervisor, Wally Westmore; makeup, Harold Lierly, Carl Silvera; hair stylist, Lenore Weaver; musical score, Daniele Amfitheatrof; choreography, Josephine Earl; cinematography, Charles B. Lang Jr.; sound, Harold Lewis, Gene Garvin, James Miller; editor, Eda Warren; Technicolor color consultant, Monroe W. Burbank; Technicolor technicians, John Hamilton, Phil Eastman. Filmed in Technicolor.

SONGS: "Copper Canyon," music by Ray Evans, lyrics Jay Livingston; "Square Dance Calls," music by Phil Boutelje, lyrics by Les Gotcher.

CAST: Ray Milland (Johnny Carter), Hedy Lamarr (Lisa Roselle), Macdonald Carey (Lane Travis), Mona Freeman (Caroline Desmond), Harry Carey Jr. (Lieutenant Ord), Frank Faylen (Mullins), Hope Emerson (Ma Tarbet), Taylor Holmes (Theodosius Roberts), Peggy Knudsen (Cora), James Burke (Jeb Bassett), Percy Helton (Scamper Joad), Philip van Zandt (Sheriff Wattling), Paul Lees (Bat Laverne), Robert Watson (Bixby), Georgia Backus (Martha Bassett), Ian Wolfe (Mr. Henderson), Bob Kortman (Bill Newton), Nina Mae McKinney (Theresa), Shep Houghton (Specialty Dancer), Betty Hannon, Joanne Linville, Dorothy Abbott, Mary Brewer, Marguerite Campbell, Marion Colby, Maxine Gates (Showgirls), Stanley Andrews (Bartenders), Earl Hodgins (Joseph Sand, miner), Robert Stephenson (William Barton, miner), Buddy Roosevelt (Lew Partridge), Julia Faye (Proprietor's Wife), Ann Cavendish (Girl), Stanley Andrews (Bartender), Hank Bell (Man), Ethan Laidlaw (Deputies), John Marchek, Johnny Michaels, Alan Dinehart III (Bassett Boys) Rex Lease, Ray Bennett, Don House, (Southerners).

My Favorite Spy, Paramount, 93 minutes, released December 25, 1951. Producer, Paul Jones; director, Norman Z. McLeod; screenplay, Edmund L. Hartmann, Jack Sher; adapted from a story by Edmund Beloin, Lou Breslow; additional dialogue, Hal Kanter; art directors, Roland Anderson, Hal Pereira; set designers, Sam Comer, Grace Gregory; costumes, Edith Head; makeup, Wally Westmore; musical score, Victor Young; cinematography, Victor Milner; process photography, Farciot Edouart; sound, Gene Garvin, Gene Merritt; editor, Frank Bracht.

SONGS: "I Wind Up Taking a Fall," music by Robert Emmett Dolan, lyrics by Johnny Mercer; "Just a Moment More," music by Jay Livingston, lyrics by Ray Evans.

CAST: Bob Hope (Peanuts White/Eric Augustine), Hedy Lamarr (Lily Dalbray), Francis L. Sullivan (Karl Brubaker), Arnold Moss (Tasso), Tonio Selwart (Harry Crock), [Alden] Stephen Chase (Donald Bailey), John Archer (Henderson), Morris Ankrum (General Fraser), Angela Clarke (Gypsy Fortune Teller), Frank Faylen (Oliver Newton), Marc Lawrence (Ben Ali), Iris Adrian (Lola), Luis van Rooten (Rudolf Hoenig), Mike Mazurki (Monkara), Ralph Smiley (El Sarif), Nestor Paiva (Fire Chief), Joseph Vitale (Fireman), Dorothy Abbott, Sue Casey, Lillian Molieri (Girls), Michael Ansara, Don Dunning (House Servants), Roy Roberts (Johnson, FBI Man), Casey Rogers (Maria), Jack Pepper (FBI Man), Chester Conklin, Billy Engle, Hank Marr (Short Comics), Delmar Costello, Loyal Underwood (Beggars), Suzanne Dalbart (Barefoot Maiden), Steven Geray (Croupier), Crane Whitley (Willie, Hoenig's Second Gunman), Joan Whitley (Blonde in Bathtub), Martha Mears (voice double for Hedy Lamarr).

L'amante di Paride (*The Lovers of Paris*), Cino Del Luca–P.C.E. Productions, 181 minutes, released 1953. Producer, Victor Phalen; associate director Edgar G. Ulmer; director, Marc Allégret; story and screenplay, Salka Viertel, Vadim Plemiennikov [Roger Vadim], Aeneas MacKenzie; art director, Virgilio Marchi; costumes, Vittorio Nino Novarese; cinematography, Desmond Dickinson; special effects, O. Natanzini; editors, Thomas Pratt, Manuel del Campo; sound, K. Dubrowsky. Filmed in Technicolor. A Hedy Lamarr Production.

CAST ("The Face That Launched a Thousand Ships"): Hedy Lamarr (Helen of Troy), Massimo Serato (Paris), Sunrise Arnova (Venus), Elli Parvo (Juno), Cathy O'Donnell (Enone), Piero Pastore (Sinon), Enrico Glori (Priam), Robert Beatty (Menelaus), Anna Amendola (Minerva), Guido Celano (Jupiter), Serena Michelotti (Cassandra), with Niero Bernardi, Enzo Fiermonte, Piero Palermino, Luigi Tosi, Rosy Mazzacurati, Valeria Moriconi, Aldo Nicodemi, and Mimo Billi.

CAST (Teatro Romani): Hedy Lamarr (Liala), Luigi Pavese (Romani), Gérard Oury.

CAST ("I Cavalieri dell'illusione"): Hedy Lamarr (Geneviève de Brabant), Cesare Danova (Count Sigfride), Terence Morgan (Golo), Richard O'Sullivan (Benoni), John Fraser (Drago).

CAST ("Napoleon and Josephine"): Hedy Lamarr (Empress Josephine), Gérard Oury (Napoleon), Milly Vitale (Maria Luisa).

Released in Great Britain as *The Loves of Three Queens*. Edited to 97 minutes in 1955.

Narration: Hans Conried.

L'eterna femmina (Eternal Woman), Cino Del Luca–P.C.E. Productions, 1955. Producer, Victor Pahlen; director, Marc Allégret; assistant director, Leonardo Scavino; screenplay, Nino Novarese, Marc Allégret; dialogue, Aeneas MacKenzie, Hugh Gray; art director, Virgilio Marchi, Mario Chiari; original music, Nino Roti; cinematography, Desmond Dickinson, Ferdinand Risi; editor, Manuel del Campo; sound, K. Dubrowsky. Filmed in Technicolor.

CAST: Hedy Lamarr, Massimo Serato, (Undetermined roles): Franco Coop, Mino Doro, Lia Nitali, Andre Hildebrand, Anna Arena, Augusto Di Giovanni, Remington Olmstead, Luigi Pavese, Liliana Rondoni, Rosanna Rory, Rita Rosa, Faustone Signoretti, Narida Vanni.

Film shut down in December 1954. *L'eterna femmina* was eventually completed but never released.

The Story of Mankind, Warner Bros., 100 minutes, released October 23, 1957. Associate producer, George E. Swink; producer, Irwin Allen; director, Irwin Allen; screenplay, Irwin Allen, Charles Bennett; based on the book *The Story of Mankind*, by Hendrik van Loon; art director, Art Loel; set director, Arthur Krams; costumes, Marjorie Best; men's wardrobe, Ted Schultz; women's wardrobe, Florence Hackett; makeup, Ray Romero, Emile Lavigne; hairstylist, Margret Donovan; original music and musical director, Paul Sawtell; music editors, Leon Birnbaum, Robert Tracy; cinematography, Nick Musuraca; editor, Roland Gross. Filmed in Technicolor.

CAST: Ronald Colman (Spirit of Man), Hedy Lamarr (Joan of Arc), Groucho Marx (Peter Minuit), Harpo Marx (Sir Isaac Newton), Chico Marx (Monk), Virginia Mayo (Cleopatra), Agnes Moorehead (Queen Elizabeth), Vincent Price (Mr. Scratch, the Devil), Peter Lorre (Nero), Charles Coburn (Hippocrates), Cedric Hardwicke (High Judge), Cesar Romero (Spanish Envoy), John Carradine (Khufu), Dennis Hopper (Napoleon Bonaparte), Marie Wilson (Marie Antoinette), Edward Everett Horton (Sir Walter Raleigh), Helmut Dantine (Marc Antony), Reginald Gardiner (William Shakespeare), Marie Windsor (Josephine), Cathy O'Donnell (Early Christian Woman), Franklin Pangborn (Marquis de Varennes), Melville Cooper (Major Domo), Henry Daniell (Pierre Cauchon, Bishop of Beauvais), Francis X. Bushman (Moses), Jim Ameche (Alexander Graham Bell), Dani Crayne (Helen of Troy), Anthony Dexter (Christopher Columbus), Austin Green (Abraham Lincoln), Bobby Watson (Adolf Hitler), Reginald Sheffield (Julius Caesar), Nick Cravat (Apprentice), George E. Stone (Waiter), Ziva Sabra [Rodann] (Egyptian Concubine), Melinda Marx (Early Christian Child), Marvin Miller (Armana), Major Sam Harris (Nobleman in Queen Elizabeth's Court), Abraham Sofaer (Indian Chief), Harry Ruby (Indian Brave), William Schallert (Earl of Warwick), Joe Rudin (Soldier, Joan of Arc sequence).

Slaughter on Tenth Avenue, Universal-International Pictures, 103 minutes, released November 5, 1957. Producer, Albert Zugsmith; director, Arnold Laven; screenplay, Lawrence Roman; based on the book *The Man Who Rocked the Boat*, by William J. Keating and Richard Carter; art directors, Alexander Golitzen, Robert Emmet Smith; set directors, Russell A. Gausman, Julia Heron; musical score, Herschel Burke Gilbert, Richard Rodgers, Henry Mancini; musical director, Joseph Gershenson; costumes, Bill Thomas; cinematography, Fred Jackman Jr.; editor, Russell F. Schoengarth; sound, Leslie I. Carey, Frank H. Wilkinson; stunt coordinator, David Sharpe.

Musical Theme, "Slaughter on Tenth Avenue," by Richard Rodgers.

CAST: Richard Egan (William "Bill" Keating), Jan Sterling (Madge Pitts), Dan Duryea (John Jacob Masters), Julie (Julia) Adams (Dee Pauley), Walter Matthau (Al Dahlke), Charles McGraw (Lieutenant Anthony Vosnick), Sam Levene (Howard Rysdale), Mickey Shaughnessy (Solly Pitts), Nick Dennis (Midget Dock Worker), Joe Downing (Eddie "Cockeye" Cook), Mickey Hargitay (Big John), Franklyn Farnum (Juror), Gil Frye (Court Bailiff), Tom Greenway (Stu), Jack Perry (Dock Worker), Tom Kennedy (Dock Guard), Ethan Laidlaw (Courtroom Spectator), Jack La Rue (Father Paul), Len Lesser (Sam), Sammee Tong (Sam), Paul Weber (Norm, District Attorney's staffer), Isabel Withers (Landlady), Morgan Woodward (Tilly Moore), Hedy Lamarr (Mona, scene deleted), Isabel Withers, Carey Loftin (Bits, scenes deleted).

The Female Animal, Universal-International Pictures, 82 minutes, released January 22, 1958. Producer, Albert Zugsmith; director, Harry Keller; screenplay, Robert Hill; based on a story by Albert Zugsmith; dialogue coach, Francis [Frances] Dawson; art directors, Alexander Golitzen, Robert Clatworthy; set directors, Russell A. Gausman, Ruby R. Levitt, Julia Heron; costumes, Bill Thomas; wardrobe, Rose Brandi, Truman Eli; makeup, Bud Westmore, Vince Romain, Nick Marcellino; hair stylists, Lillian Burkhart, Virginia Jones; musical score, Hans J. Salter; musical supervisor, Joseph Gershenson; cinematography, Russell Metty; editor, Milton Carruth; sound, Leslie I. Carey, Frank Wilkinson; editors, Ed Curtis, Milton Carruth. Filmed in Cinemascope.

CAST: Hedy Lamarr (Vanessa Windsor), Jane Powell (Penny Windsor), George Nader (Chris Farley), Jan Sterling (Lily Frayne), Jerry Paris (Hank Galvez), Gregg Palmer (Piggy), Mabel Albertson (Irma Jones), James Gleason (Tom Maloney), Casey Adams [Max Showalter] (Charlie Grant), Ann Doran (Nurse), Almira Sessions (Mabel, landlady), Isabel Dawn (Masseuse), Richard Avonde (Pepe, Lily's gigolo), Frank Sully (Taxi driver), Steve Ellis, Gertrude Astor (Bits), Bob Morgan (Hedy Lamarr stunt double), John Gavin (originally cast as Chris Farley).

The Love Goddesses, Janus Films, 87 minutes, released March 3, 1965. Producers, Graeme Ferguson, Saul J. Turell; director, Saul J. Turell; screenplay, Graeme Ferguson, Saul J. Turell; original music, Percy Faith; editors, Nat Greene, Howard Kuperman; technical supervisor, Ray Angus.

CAST: Carl King (Narrator). Hedy Lamarr (archival footage).

Selected Feature Films and Documentaries

Hollywood: The Dream Factory, Metro-Goldwyn-Mayer, 51 minutes, released 1972. Executive producer, Nicholas L. Noxon; producers, Bud Friedgen, Irwin Rosten; original music, George Romanis; music supervisor, Harry V. Lojewski; music conductor, George Romanis; cinematography, John A. Alonzo, James Wilson; editors, Bud Friedgen, Pieter S. Hubbard.

CAST: Dick Cavett (Narrator), All-star cast in archival footage. Hedy Lamarr (footage deleted).

Brother, Can You Spare a Dime? Dimension Films, 103 minutes, television broadcast August 6, 1975. Executive producer, Sanford Lieberson; producer, David Puttnam; director, Philippe Mora; editor, Jeremy Thomas; sound rerecording mixer, Bill Rowe; research, Michael Barlow, Jennifer E. Ryan, Susan Winslow.

CAST: All-star cast (archival footage).

That's Entertainment II! Metro-Goldwyn-Mayer, 133 minutes, released May 17, 1976. Producers, Saul Chaplin, Daniel Melnick; executive producers animation, Joseph Barbera, William Hanna; director, Gene Kelly; writer, Leonard Gershe; music supervisor, Harry V. Lojewski; music arranger, Nelson Riddle; music editor, William Saracino; music conductor, Nelson Riddle; music composer, new sequences, Nelson Riddle; composer, "For Me and My Gal," E. Ray Goetz; production design, John DeCuir; cinematographer, George J. Folsey; editors, David E. Blewitt, David Bretherton, Bud Friedgen, Peter C. Johnson; sound, William Edmondson.

CAST: Leonard Gershe, Fred Astaire, Gene Kelly (Narrators). All-star cast (archival footage). Hedy Lamarr (clip from *White Cargo*).

That's Action, Epic Productions, 60 minutes, released 1977.

CAST: Art Linkletter (Narrator). Hedy Lamarr in archival footage.

Texaco Presents Bob Hope in a Very Special Special: On the Road with Bing, Hope Enterprises, 120 minutes, television broadcast October 28, 1977. Executive producer, Bob Hope; producer, Howard W. Koch; director, Howard W. Koch; screenwriters, Charles Lee, Gig Henry, Robert L. Mills; editors, Chip Brools, Hal Collins; makeup, Don Marando.

CAST: Bob Hope (Himself), Bing Crosby, Dorothy Lamour, Hedy Lamarr (archival footage).

Showbiz Goes to War, The Video Late Show, 90 minutes, released 1982. Producers, Norman Sedawie, Gayle Gibson Sedawie; writers, Norman Sedawie, Gayle Gibson Sedawie; editor, Gary Smith. Produced by T.A.D. Productions. In association with Glen-Warren Productions. A Bill Green Production.

CAST: David Steinberg (Host). All-star cast (archival footage).

Going Hollywood: The War Years, Warner Home Video, 106 minutes, released 1988. Associate producers, Jonathan Kaplan, Anthony Pittinza; producer, Julian Schlossberg; director, Julian Schlossberg; teleplay, Charles Badaracio; editor, Ken Brady; cinematographer (New York), Ron Myrvik; cinematographer (Los Angeles), Paul Savage; sound, Charles "Skip" Newman, David Sperling, Pawel Wdowczak.

CAST: Van Johnson, Tony Randall, Vivian Blaine, Jackie Cooper, Dane Clark, Gloria DeHaven, Douglas Fairbanks Jr., Evelyn Keyes, Joan Leslie, Roddy McDowall, Sylvia Sidney (Themselves), Joan Crawford, Hedy Lamarr, Humphrey Bogart, Farley Granger (archival footage).

Instant Karma, Metro-Goldwyn-Mayer, 102 minutes, released April 27, 1990. Executive producer, Steven Bratter; producers, Dale Rosenbloom, Craig Sheffer, Bruce A. Taylor; director, Roderick Taylor; screenplay, Bruce A. Taylor, Dale Rosenbloom; cinematography, Tom Jewett.

CAST: Craig Shaffer (Zane), Annette Sinclair (Amy), Orson Bean (Dr. Berlin), Hedy Lamarr (archival footage, *Algiers*), Chelsea Noble (Penelope), Marty Ingles (Jon Clark).

O spectator queue o cinema esqueceu, Formos do Olhar Cinema a Video (Brazil), 20 minutes, released 1991. Executive producers, Robson de Azevedo, Joel Yamaji; producers, Robson de Azevedo, Joel Yamji; cinematography, Robson de Azevedo.

CAST: Waldemar Iglesias Fernandes (Himself), Luiz Rosemberg Filho (Interviewer), Ana Bach (Young woman in the cinema), Luis Emilio Strassburguer (Young man in the cinema), Ingrid Bergman, Charles Boyer, Bette Davis, Greta Garbo, Hedy Lamarr, Anna Magnani, (archival footage).

That's Entertainment III! Metro-Goldwyn-Mayer, 113 minutes, released July 1994. Executive producers, Peter Fitzgerald, George Feltenstein; producers, Bud Friedgen, Michael J. Sheridan; Turner Entertainment Co. executive, Roger Mayer; directors, Bud Friedgen, Michael J. Sheridan; writers, Bud Friedgen, Michael J. Sheridan; music supervisor, Marilee Bradford; cinematography, Howard A. Anderson III; editors, Bud Friedgen, Michael J. Sheridan.

CAST: Granville van Dusen (opening narration), Gene Kelly, June Allyson, Cyd Charisse, Ann Miller, Mickey Rooney, Howard Keel, Lena Horne, Esther Williams, Debbie Reynolds (Hosts). All-star cast (archival footage); Hedy Lamarr (clip from *Ziegfeld Girl*).

The Casting Couch, Lumiere Video, 57 minutes, released 1995. Associate producer, Alan Selwyn; producer, John Sealey; screenplay, Derek Ford (Selwyn Ford), based on his book *The Casting Couch: Making It in Hollywood*; original music, The Leatherbridge Parker Ellis Trio; cinematography, Freddie Besch; editor, Marc Corrance.

CAST: All-star cast (archival footage).

Calling Hedy Lamarr, Mischief Films, 71 minutes, released August 10, 2004 (Austria). Producers, Gunter Hanfgarn, Anthony Loder, Georg Misch, Martin Rosenbaum, Ralph Weiser; director, Georg Misch; writer, Georg Misch; original score, Jim Howard; cinematography, Jon Sayers; editor, Michael Palm; production manager, Dagmar Hovestadt.

CAST: Anthony Loder, Denise Loder-DeLuca, Charles Stansel, Edie Stansel, Caitlin Stansel, Hans Janitschek, Peter Shen, Sergeant Major Roy Dunnegan, Arlene Roxbury, David Hughes, Marc Levin, Peter Gardiner, Arianne Ulmer-Cipes, John Pohan, Patricia Place, Lilyan Chauvin, Claudia Genah, Stephanie Khalighi, Sara Rinde, Lyn Segerblom, Nancy Greco, Jorie Lodes, Kate Clarke (Themselves), Heidi Scholler (Hedy Lamarr), Hedy Lamarr (archival footage).

Shown on BBC2 (UK) *Arena* as "Queen of the Screen: Hedy Lamarr," February 12, 2005.

Edgar G. Ulmer—The Man Off-Screen, 77 minutes, Mischief Films, released September 4, 2004. Producers, Georg Misch, Arianne Ulmer-Cipes, Ralph Wieser; line producers, Georg Misch, Ralph Wieser; cinematographer, Jeorg Burger; editors, Marek Kralovsky, Michael Palm.

CAST: Edgar G. Ulmer (Voice), Peter Bogdanovich, Christian Cargnelli, Roger Corman, Joe Dante, Stefan Grissemann, Alexander Horwath, Noah Isenberg, John Landis, Jimmy Lydon, Gregory W. Mank, Peter Marshall, Michael Omasta, Michael Palm, Ann Savage, John Saxon, William Schallert, Arianne Ulmer-Cipes, Tom Weaver, Wim Wenders (Themselves), John Carradine, Robert Clarke, Margaret Field, Boris Karloff, Hedy Lamarr, Tom Neal, Jean Parker, George Sanders, Betta St. John (archival footage).

Hedy Lamarr: Secrets of a Hollywood Star, Dubini Filmproduction, 80 minutes, released September 7, 2006 (Germany). Producers, Cardo Dubini, Donatello Dubini, Fosco Dubini, Monique Indra, Barbara Obermaier; directors, Donatello Dubini, Fosco Dubini; writers, Fosco Dubini, Barbara Obermaier; cinematography, Donatello Dubini; editors, Donatello Dubini, Fosco Dubini; sound, Mischa Marx.

CAST: Jan-Christopher Horak, Lupita Tovar, Hans Janitschek, Marvin Paige, Jan Rooney, Mickey Rooney, Maria Wrigley, James Lamarr Loder, Robin Pettis, Arlene Roxbury, Robert Rodenburg, Robert Lantz, Peter Shen, Kenneth Anger, Pete Giglio, Eric Root (Themselves), Hedy Lamarr (archival footage).

Valentino: The Last Emperor, Acolyte Films, 96 minutes, March 18, 2009 (USA). Executive producers, Carter Burden, Adam Leff; producers, Matt Kapp, Frederic Tcheng; assistant producer, Justin Morris; consulting producers, Ted Alexandre, Aimee Bell; director, Matt Trynauer; original music, Joel Goodman; composer (additional music), David Bramfitt; cinematography, Tom Hurwitz; additional camera, Matt Kemp; second camera, Frederic

Tcheng; editors, Bob Eisenhardt, Frederic Tcheng; sound, Peter Miller; sound editor, John Moros; assistant sound editors, Jeff Seelye; title design, Patrick Li; graphics, Dan Schrecker.

CAST: Valentino (Garavani), Giancarlo Giametti, Giorgio Armani, Jeannie Becker, Alessandra Facchinetti, Tom Ford, Karl Lagerfeld, Matteo Marzotto, Gwyneth Paltrow, Claudia Schiffer, Andre Leon Talley, Donatella Versace, Diane von Furstenberg, Alek Wek, Anna Wintour (Themselves), Hedy Lamarr (archival footage from *Ziegfeld Girl*).

Television Appearances

The 1950 New York Heart Fund Drive, WPIX, 240 minutes, March 4, 1950. 10:30 P.M. EST.

CAST: Ed Sullivan (Host), Hedy Lamarr, Bob Hope, George Raft, Kirk Douglas, Juanita Hall, etc. (Guest Stars).

Toast of the Town, CBS, 60 minutes, September 17, 1950. 8:00–9:00 P.M. EST. Producer, Chester Feldman; coexecutive producer, Mario Lewis; directors, Kenneth Whelan, John Wray; original music, Buddy Arnold; orchestrator, Will Schaefer; music, Ray Bloch and His Orchestra; writers, Jerry Bresler, Lyn Duddy; art director, Bill Bohnert; camera, Pat McBride, George Moses; choreographer, David Winters; stage manager, Eddie Brinkman.

CAST: Ed Sullivan (Host), Hedy Lamarr, Al Kelly, The Blackburn Twins, Jean Carroll, Pat O'Brien, Mimi Benzell, The Ivanoffs Acrobats, Eddie and Tony (Guest Stars), Art Hannes (Announcer), the June Taylor Dancers.

The Colgate Comedy Hour, NBC, 60 minutes, May 11, 1952. 8:00–9:00 P.M. PST. Producer, Ernest D. Glucksman; directors, William Asher, James V. Kern; original music, Ronnie Graham; composer (title theme), Lester Lee; creator, Fred Hamilton; staff writer, Larry Rhine; writers, Sid Kuller, Sidney Miller; art director, Paul Barnes; choreographers, Louis Da Pron, Wiletta Smith; costumes, John Derro; gowns, Beaumelle, Pauline Trigere; production assistant, Samuel Fuller; floor manager, Arthur Penn.

CAST: Donald O'Connor (Host), Hedy Lamarr (Guest Star), Anthony Dexter, Tom D'Andrea and Hal March, Scatman Crothers, Sidney Miller, Martha Tilton, Al Goodman (Orchestra Leader).

Four Star Revue, "All-Star Review," NBC, 60 minutes, June 14, 1952. 8:00–9:00 P.M. PST. Producer, Dee Englebach; coproducer, Dean Elliott; directors, Dick Berger, Dee Englebach, Buzz Kulik; writers, Charles Isaacs, Bob Schiller; original music, Dean Elliott, Jack Mason.

CAST: Paul Winchell, Jerry Mahoney, Hot Lips Page (Hosts), Hedy Lamarr (Guest Star), De Marco Sisters.

The Colgate Comedy Hour, NBC, 60 minutes, December 28, 1952. 8:00–9:00 P.M. PST. Producer, Ernest D. Glucksman; directors, William Asher, James V. Kern; original music, Ronnie Graham; composer (title theme), Lester Lee; creator, Fred Hamilton; staff writer, Larry Rhine; writers, Snag Werris, Ben Blue, Ernest D. Glucksman; choreographer, Fred Kelly; costumes, John Derro; gowns, Beaumelle, Pauline Trigere; production assistant, Samuel Fuller; floor manager, Arthur Penn.

CAST: Ben Blue (Host), Hedy Lamarr (Guest Star), Peggy Lee, Phil Harris, The Sportsmen, Tom D'Andrea, Hal March, Donald O'Connor, Al Goodman (Orchestra Leader).

The Colgate Comedy Hour, NBC, 60 minutes, March 8, 1953. 8:00–9:00 P.M. PST. Producer, Ernest D. Glucksman; directors, William Asher, James V. Kern; original music, Ronnie Graham; composer (title theme), Lester Lee; creator, Fred Hamilton; staff writer, Larry Rhine; writers, Woody Allen, William A. Attaway, Pat Costello, Eddie Foreman, Charles Isaacs, Danny Simon; art director, Paul Barnes; choreographer, Fred Kelly; costumes, John Derro; gowns, Beaumelle, Pauline Trigere; production assistant, Samuel Fuller; floor manager, Arthur Penn.

CAST: Donald O'Connor (Host), Hedy Lamarr (Guest Star), Cecil Kellaway, Sid Miller, Tom D'Andrea, Hal March, Marilyn Maxwell, Scatman Crothers, Sidney Miller, Al Goodman (Orchestra Leader).

The Shower of Stars, "Cloak and Dagger," CBS, 60 minutes, March 14, 1957. 8:30–9:30 P.M. PST. Producer, Ralph Levy; director Ralph Levy; writers, Hugh Wedlock, Howard Snyder; music, Mahlon Merrick. Sponsored by the Chrysler Corporation. In color.

CAST: William Lundigan (Host), Jack Benny, Hedy Lamarr, Gale Storm, Jacques d'Ambroise, Lawrence Welk, Sid Krofft (Guest Stars), Dick Winslow.

The Perry Como Show, NBC, 60 minutes, March 30, 1957. 8:00–9:00 P.M. PST. Associate producer, Henry Howard; producer, Robert S. Finkel; directors, Grey Lockwood, Robert S. Finkel; writers, Goodman Ace, Mort Green, George Foster, Jay Burton; original music, Danny Hurd; music arranger, Danny Hurd; musical director, Mitchell Ayres; choral director, Ray Charles; fashions by Orbach; jewelry by Marbella; men's formal wear, After 6; costumes, Michi; hair stylist, Ernest Adler; dances staged by Louis Da Pron; set designer, Don Shirley Jr.; graphic arts, James Glenn; technical director, Hank Bomberger; arrangements, Joe Lipman, Jack Andrews; lighting, Dick Feldman; sound, Neal Smith; video, Warren Deem. Supervisor for NBC, Leonard Hole. A Roncom Production.

CAST: Perry Como (Host), Hedy Lamarr, Julius LaRosa, Dan Rowan, and Dick Martin (Guest Stars), Donna Douglas (Letters Girl).

What's My Line?, CBS, 30 minutes, March 31, 1957. 10:30–11:00 P.M. EST. Producers, Mark Goodson, Bill Todman; production coordinator, Bob Bach; technical directors, William Guyon, Walter Pile, Hal Warner; lighting director, Stanley Alper.

CAST: John Charles Daly (Host), Hedy Lamarr (Mystery Guest), Bennett Cerf, Dorothy Kilgallen, Arlene Francis (Panelists).

I've Got a Secret, CBS, 30 minutes, April 10, 1957. 9:30–10:00 P.M. EST. Creators, Howard Merrill, Allan Sherman; directors, Alan Mifelow, Ira Skutch; composer (theme music, "Plink, Plank, Plunk"), Leroy Anderson; musical director, Norman Paris; stage manager, Joseph Papp.

CAST: Garry Moore (Host), Hedy Lamarr (Guest Star), Faye Emerson, Jayne Meadows, Henry Morgan, Bill Cullen (Panelists).

The Steve Allen Show, NBC, 60 minutes, August 25, 1957. 8:00–9:00 P.M. PST. Producer, Nick Vanoff; executive producer, Jules L. Green; director, Dwight A. Hemion; comedy producer and writing supervisor, Leonard Stern; writers, Stan Burns, Herb Sargent, Bill Dana, Don Hinkley; feature writer, Claire Rosenstein; costumes, Hazel Ray; makeup, Ray Voege; musical director, Skitch Henderson; talent coordinator, Henry Frankel; choreographer, John

Butler; set director, Don Swanagan; lighting, Fred McKinnon; audio, Scott Schachter; video, Bill Little; film technical director, John Canevari; NBC program director, Alan D. Courtney; production stage manager, Dick Lerner; unit manager, Jim Reina. A Bellmeadows Entertainments Production.

SONG: "Searchin'," The Coasters.

CAST: Steve Allen (Host), Hedy Lamarr, The Coasters, Irish McCalla (Sheena, Queen of the Jungle), Joe E. Brown (Guest Stars), Gene Rayburn, Pat Kirby, Val Philips, Don Knotts, Tom Poston, Louis Nye (Regulars), Gabriel Dell (Count Dracula), John Cameron Swayze (Himself).

Sponsored by Mr. Fresh, Greyhound ("It's such a comfort to take the bus and leave the driving to us").

The George Gobel Show, NBC, 60 minutes, October 22, 1957. PST. In black and white and in color. 8:00–9:00 P.M. Producer, Alan Handley, Al Lewis, William Rowland; directors, Alan Handley; writers, Harry Winkler, Jack Brooks, Milton Rosen, Elon Packard; original music, Ronny Graham; musical conductor, John Scott Trotter; musical arranger, John Scott Trotter; choreography, Lee Scott.

CAST: George Gobel (Host), Hedy Lamarr, Eddie Fisher, Shirley Harmer, Barbara Bostock, Howard McNear (Guest Stars), John Scott Trotter (Orchestra Leader), the Johnny Mann Singers.

Sponsored by RCA Whirlpool and Ligget & Myers.

Dick Powell's Zane Gray Theatre, CBS, "Proud Woman," 30 minutes, October 25, 1957. 8:30–9:00 P.M. PST. Creator, Charles A. Wallace; producer, Hal Hudson; director, Louis King; teleplay, Clarke E. Reynolds, John McGreevey; from a story by Harold Shumate; story supervisor, Aaron Spelling; story editor, Nina Laemmle; cinematography, Guy Roe; original music, Harry Lubin; art director, Frank Smith; set decorator, Clarence Steensen; wardrobe, Robert B. Harris; makeup, Karl Herlinger; editor, Chandler House; editorial supervisor, Bernard Burton; production manager, Glenn Cook; sound, Don Rush; sound effects, Norvel D. Crutcher Jr.; production executive, Bill Bauer; casting, Lynn Stalmaster.

CAST: Dick Powell (Host), Hedy Lamarr (Consuela Bowers), Paul Richards (Frank Fayne), Roy Roberts (Don Miguel Bowers), Donald Buka (Laredo), Edward Colmans (Esteben), Iphigenie Castiglioni (Maria Delgado).

Sponsored by Maxwell House Coffee.

The Arthur Murray Party, NBC, 60 minutes, December 28, 1957. In color. 9:00–10:00 P.M. PST. Choreography, Rod Alexander, June Taylor.

CAST: Arthur Murray, Kathryn Murray (Hosts), Bill and Cora Baird, Tallulah Bankhead, Gertrude Berg, Hedy Lamarr, Paul Hartman, June Havoc, Larry Parks, Betty Garrett, Walter Slezak, Sarah Vaughn, Paul Winchell, Buddy Holly and the Cricketts (Guest Stars), the Arthur Murray Dancers.

What's My Line?, CBS, 30 minutes, January 5, 1958. 10:30–11:00 P.M. EST. Producers, Mark Goodson, Bill Todman; production cocoordinator, Bob Bach; technical directors, William Guyon, Walter Pile, Hal Warner; lighting director, Stanley Alper.

CAST: John Charles Daly (Host), Pat Boone (Mystery Guest), Bennett Cerf, Dorothy Kilgallen, Martin Gabel (Panelists), Hedy Lamarr (Guest Panelist).

The Santa Claus Lane Parade, KTTV, 90 minutes, November 26, 1958. 7:30–9:00 P.M. PST.

CAST: Sheriff John, George Putnam, Paul Coates, Jackson Wheeler, Steve Martin (Hosts), John Bromfield, Art Linkletter, Alan Hale Jr., Minerva Urecal, Peter Potter, Richard Carlson, Adolph Menjou, Beverly Garland, James Stewart, Jerry Lewis, Jayne Mansfield, Hedy Lamarr, Joan Davis, Bob Cummings. Gene Autry, etc. (Guest Stars).

Premiere Telecast, "Santa's Wonderland," KCOP, 60 minutes, November 23, 1961. 7:30–8:30 P.M. PST.

CAST: Gene Barry, Jayne Mansfield, Hedy Lamarr, Louis Prima, Madelyn Rhue, Broderick Crawford, Wendell Corey, George Raft, Stuart Whitman, Vincent Edwards, Wade Preston, John Carroll, Mitzi Gaynor, Molly Bee, Ann-Margret, Donald O'Connor, Dan Dailey, George Hamilton, Macdonald Carey, "Slapsie" Maxie Rosenbloom, Maria Casper, Herb Jeffries, Jackie Coogan, June Lockhart, Jeanne Crain, Steve Forrest, etc. (Guest Stars).

The Tonight Show, NBC, 95 minutes, April 23, 1962.

CAST: Robert Cummings (Host), Hedy Lamarr, Jayne Mansfield, Vincent Price, Patricia Morison, Moulton Taylor (Guests).

Stump the Stars, "Pantomime Quiz," CBS, 30 minutes, November 19, 1962. Creator, Mike Storey; coproducer, Ethelyn Davis; musical director, Frank De Vol.

CAST: Pat Harrington Jr. (Host), Hedy Lamarr, Jan Clayton, Sebastian Cabot, Ross Martin (Guest Team 1), Barbara Nichols, Ricardo Montalban, Beverly Garland, Mickey Manners (Guest Team 2).

Hedy's pantomime: "Executioner wishes to meet manicurist: Object—hangnail."

Celebrity Game, CBS, 30 minutes, May 3, 1964. 9:00–9:30 P.M. PST. Producers, Merrill Heather, Bob Quigley; director, Seymour Robbie; art director, Robert Tyler Lee; music, Arlo; set director, Anthony Mondello; lighting, Dick Holbrook; sound, Marshall King; technical director, A.J. Cunningham; talent cocoordinator, Mary Markham; production staff, Keith Quigley, Art Alisi; production supervisor, Andrew J. Selig; consultant, Dr. Joyce Brothers. In association with Four Star Productions.

CAST: Carl Reiner (Host), Hedy Lamarr, Walter Brennan, Joseph Cotton, Betty Hutton, Edd Byrnes, Eartha Kitt, Paul Lynde, Cliff Arquette "Charley Weaver," Shari Lewis (Guest Panelists), Sally Nichols, Ken Madden, Sue Grieb (Contestants), Kenny Williams (Announcer).

Sponsored by The American Tobacco Company (Pall Mall, Tareyton cigarettes), Maxwell House Coffee (Barbara Stanwyck), Gravy Train Dog Food.

Shindig, ABC, 30 minutes, October 21, 1965. 7:30–8:00 P.M. PST. Creators, Jimmy O'Neill, Sharon Sheeley; executive producer, Leon I. Mirell; producer, Dean Whitmore; director, Richard Thorpe; art director, Lawrence Klein; original music, Harry Robinson (Robertson); musical director, Ray Pohlman; choreographer, Andre Tayiv; technical director, Ted Hurley; lighting director, Vincenzo Cilurzo; costumes, Dorothy Saunders; hair stylist, Donna Barrett Gilbert. Selmur Productions in association with the American Broadcasting Company. Selig J. Seligman in charge of production.

CAST: Jimmy O'Neil (Host), Hedy Lamarr, Brenda Holloway, The Dave Clark Five (Dave Clark, Lenny Davidson, Mike Smith, Denis West Payton, Rick Huxley), The Kingsmen, Joe Tex, The Blossoms (Darlene Love, etc.), The Eligibles, Eddie Rambeau (Guest Stars), The Shindig Band (Glen D. Hardin, Jerry Scheff, etc.), The Shindig Singers, The Shindig Girls (Pam Freeman, Brenda Benet, etc.).

A Bob Hope Comedy Special, NBC, 60 minutes, September 28, 1966. Producer, George Hope; director, Jack Shea; writers, Mort Lachman, Bill Larkin, John Rapp, Lester White, Charles Lee, Gig Henry; musical director, Les Brown.

CAST: Bob Hope (Host), Hedy Lamarr, Lucille Ball, Madeleine Carroll, Anita Ekberg, Virginia Mayo, Rhonda Fleming, Signe Hasso, Dorothy Lamour, Joan Collins, Joan Fontaine, Marilyn Maxwell, Vera Miles, Joan Caulfield, Arlene Dahl, Dina Merrill, Janis Paige, Phyllis Diller, Peter Leeds, Jane Russell, Jerry Colonna, Paul Lynde, Ken Murray, Les Brown and His Band of Renown (Guest Stars).

To Tell the Truth, CBS, 30 minutes, 1967. 10:00–10:30 P.M. EST.

CAST: Bud Collyer (Host), Hedy Lamarr, Denise Loder, Anthony Loder (Guest Stars), Kitty Carlisle, Tom Posten, Orson Bean, Peggy Cass (Panelists).

The Dick Cavett Show, ABC, 60 minutes, June 2, 1969. 10:00–11:00 P.M. PST. Producer, Tony Converse; writer, Raymond Siller.

CAST: Dick Cavett (Host), Hedy Lamarr, Rex Reed, Nicol Williamson (Guest Stars).

The Mike Douglas Show, CBS, 90 minutes, August 12, 1969. Executive producer, Woody Fraser; makeup, Curry Bushnell.

CAST: Mike Douglas (Host), Hedy Lamarr, Rex Reed, Frankie Valli, Tiny Tim, Norm Crosby (Guest Stars), Jay Stewart, Charlie Tuna (Announcers).

The David Frost Show, Westinghouse, 90 minutes, August 14, 1969. Musical director, Billy Taylor Orchestra.

CAST: David Frost (Host), Hedy Lamarr, Pat Henry, The Primo Family (Guest Stars).

Personality, NBC, 30 minutes, August 15, 1969. Executive producer, Bob Stewart; original music, Bob Colbert.

CAST: Larry Blyden (Host), Tom Kennedy, Rita Moreno, Rocky Graziano, Hedy Lamarr on film (Guest Stars), Jack Clark (Announcer), Bill Wendell (Subannouncer).

The Merv Griffin Show, CBS, 90 minutes, August 18, 1969. 11:30 P.M.–1:00 A.M. PST. Executive producers, Merv Griffin, Bob Murphy; producer, Bob Shanks; director, Kirk Alexander; first assistant director, Kevin McCarthy Jr.; writers, Bob Howard, Noel Killgan, Norman Stiles; musical conductor, Mort Lindsey; trumpet musician, Bill Berry; research director, Reva Solomon; talent cocoordinator, Ray Vurry; stunt cocoordinator, Dan Koko.

CAST: Merv Griffin (Host), Hedy Lamarr, Woody Allen, Leslie Uggams, Ted Sorenson, Jackie "Moms" Mabley (Guest Stars), Arthur Treacher (Announcer).

The Merv Griffin Show, CBS, 90 minutes, June 2, 1970. 11:30 P.M.–1:00 A.M. PST. Executive producers, Merv Griffin, Bob Murphy; producer, Ernest Chambers; director, Dick Carson; first assistant director, Kevin McCarthy Jr.; writers, Jerry Bresler, Ernest Chambers, Lyn

Duddy; musical conductor, Mort Lindsey; trumpet musician, Bill Berry; talent cocoordinator, Ray Vurry; stunt cocoordinator, Dan Koko.

CAST: Merv Griffin (Host), Hedy Lamarr, Soupy Sales (Guest Stars), Bill Berry, Robert V. Greene, Jack Sheldon (Themselves), Arthur Treacher (Announcer).

The World at War, BBC, 26 episodes, 52 minutes each, 1973. Producers, Peter Batty, John Pett, David Elstein, Ted Childs, Michael Darlow, Martin Smith, Phillip Whitehead; directors, Hugh Raggett, John Pett, David Elstein, Ted Childs, Michael Darlow, Martin Smith; writers, Peter Batty, Neal Ascherson, Laurence Thompson, Charles Bloomberg, Jerome Kuehl, David Wheeler, John Williams; original music, Carl Davis; cinematography contribution, Eva Braun.

CAST: Sir Laurence Olivier (Narrator), Hedy Lamarr (archival footage).

LIFE Goes to War, NBC, 120 minutes, broadcast September 18, 1977. Producers, Jack Haley Jr., Malcom Leo; director, Jack Haley Jr.; editors, David E. Blewitt, John Wright.

CAST: Johnny Carson (Host). Hedy Lamarr (archival footage).

NBC: The First 50 Years—A Closer Look, NBC, 150 minutes, October 23, 1977.

CAST: Orson Welles (Narrator), Chevy Chase, George Burns, Burt Reynolds, Dan Haggerty, Don Rickles (Guest Hosts), Hedy Lamarr in filmed segment.

Entertaining the Troops, PBS, 90 minutes, June 22, 1994. Producer, Robert Mugge; coproducer, Desmond McElroy; director, Robert Mugge; screenwriter, Robert Mugge; research, Bob Summers.

CAST: All-star cast (archival footage).

Masters and Madmen, "Mystery of Genius," A&E, 100 minutes, 1998. A&E executive producer, Michael E. Katz; A&E supervising producer, Amy Briamonte; A&E vice president, Richard K. Rosenberg; executive producer, Glenn R. Jones; executive in charge of production for Jones Entertainment Group, Robert Fiveson; producer, John Methrell; writer, Lorraine B. Markus; musical composer, David Rackley; editor, Gary J. Westphalen.

CAST: Joseph Campanella (Narration), Hedy Lamarr, Albert Einstein, Howard Hughes, others.

Sharon Stone—Una mujer de 100 caras, Canal + Espana (Spain), 25 minutes, 1998. Writer, Guillermo Cabrera Infante.

CAST: Guillermo Cabrera Infante (Narrator), all-star cast (archival footage).

E! Mysteries and Scandals, "Hedy Lamarr," E! 30 minutes, August 6, 2001. Producer, Lynne Morgan; writer, Michael Seligman; production cocoordinator, Samantha Apley; production supervisor, Joanne Bernstein; research producer, Jenna Girard; Avid editor, Conrad Stanley; camera, Harold Henderson; sound, Gary Wright; online editor, Bernie Espinoza; musical cocoordinator, Carmen Jans; additional stills courtesy of Photofest, Ray Windham, Anthony Loder.

CAST: Anthony Loder, Denise Loder-DeLuca, Ray Windham, Jay Bernstein, Madeleine Merrill, Michael McDonnell, Charles Stansel, James Loder (Themselves).

American Masters: Judy Garland—By Myself, PBS, 114 minutes, February 25, 2004. Executive producers, George Feltenstein, Susan Lacy, Roger Mayer; producers, Susan Lacy,

John Fricke; director, Susan Lacy; writers, Susan Lacy, Stephen Stept; original music, Michael Whalen; editors, Kate Hirson, Kristen Huntley, Deborah Peretz.

CAST: Harris Yulin (Narrator), Voice-overs re-creating the life of Judy Garland. Hedy Lamarr (archival footage).

Celebrity Naked Ambition, Channel 5 (UK), 105 minutes, September 1, 2004. Producer, Bruce Hepton; writers, Chuck Cartmel, Harry Harrold, Bruce Hepton; cinematography, Ben Frewin; archive consultant, Sam Dwyer; research, Julia Raeside, Robin Block.

CAST: Nick Frost (Host), all-star cast (archival footage).

War Stories with Oliver North, syndicated series, episode, "The Women of World War II," 60 minutes, June 19, 2005. Executive producer, Pamela K. Browne; associate producer, Kelly Guernica; producers, Cyd Upson, Ayse Wieting, Gregory M. Johnson; writers, Cyd Upson, Ayse Wieting, Gregory M. Johnson; cinematographer, Brandon W. Ziegenhfuss; editors, Chris Carter, Chris Scolaro; sound mixers, Graham Gardner, Jeremy Settles.

CAST: Oliver North (Himself), Clark Gable, Winston Churchill, Hedy Lamarr, Amelia Earhart, Franklin Delano Roosevelt, Eleanor Roosevelt, Katharine Hepburn, Betty Grable, Carole Lombard, George Marshall, etc. (archival footage).

Cinema's Exiles, PBS, 115 minutes, January 1, 2009. Producer, Karen Thomas; coproducer, Sophia Maroon; executive producers, Margaret Smilow, Karen Thomas; supervising producers, Junko Tsunashima, Kristin Lovejoy; director, Karen Thomas; written by Karen Thomas; musical composer, Peter Melnick; cinematography, Joan Churchill, Emil Fischaber; sound, Alan Barker, Armin Erzinger; editor, Anny Lowery Meza; project manager, Jane Buckwalter.

CAST: Sigourney Weaver (Narrator).

Radio Appearances

Lux Radio Theatre, CBS, "Algiers." July 7, 1941. 60 minutes. Monday, 9:00–10:00 P.M., from Hollywood. Seventh Season.

Presented by Lever Brothers–Lux Toilet Soap (Kathleen Fritz as "Libby Collins" in Lux commercials).

Producer, Cecil B. DeMille; director, Sanford Barnett; music, Louis Silver; writers, George Wells, Sanford Barnett, based on the screenplay by John Howard Lawson from the novel *Pépé le Moko* by Henri La Barthe (Roger Ashelbé); set decorator, George Sawley; special effects, Max Uhlig, David Light, Walter Person, Charlie Forsyth.

CAST: Charles Boyer (Pepe le Moko), Hedy Lamarr (Gabrielle "Gaby"), Alan Napier (Inspector Slimane), Bea Benaderet (Ines), Hans Conrad (Regis/Gendarme), Jeff Corey (L'Arbi), Virginia Gordon (Marie/Girl), Howard McNear (Max), Cecil B. DeMille (Host). Melville Ruick (announcer).

Lux broadcast another version of *Algiers* on December 14, 1942, with Boyer and Loretta Young.

The Edgar Bergen / Charlie McCarthy Show, NBC, November 30, 1941. 30 minutes. Sunday, 8:00–8:30 P.M., from Hollywood.

Director, Earl Ebi; music, Ray Noble and His Orchestra; writers, Carroll Carroll, Dick Mack, Shirley Ward, Stanley Quinn, Joe Bigelow, Joe Connelly, Bob Mosher, Alan Smith, Zeno Klinker, Royal Foster, Roland MacLane, etc.; sound effects, John Glennon, etc.

CAST: Edgar Bergen, Charlie McCarthy, Bud Abbott, Lou Costello, Hedy Lamarr (Guest Star), Buddy Twiss (Announcer).

Presented by Chase and Sanborn Coffee.

Lux Radio Theatre, CBS, "The Bride Came C.O.D.," December 29, 1941. 60 minutes. Monday, 9:00–10:00 P.M., from Hollywood. Eighth Season.

Presented by Lever Brothers–Lux Toilet Soap (Kathleen Fritz as "Libby Collins" in Lux commercials).

Producer, Cecil B. DeMille; director, Sanford Barnett; music, Louis Silver; writers, George Wells, Sanford Barnett, based on the screenplay by Julius J. and Philip G. Epstein, story by M.M. Musselman and Kenneth Earl; set decorator, George Sawley; special effects, Max Uhlig, David Light, Walter Person, Charlie Forsyth; announcer, Melville Ruick.

CAST: Bob Hope (Steve Collins), Hedy Lamarr (Joan Winfield), Gene O'Donnell (Alan Brice), Wally Maher (Tommy Keenan), Ferdinand Munier (Jones's uncle), Eddie Marr (Pee Wee Defoe/Pilot), Warren Ashe (Man/Reporter), Cecil B. DeMille (Host).

Based on the 1941 Warner Bros. film *The Bride Came C.O.D.*, which starred James Cagney and Bette Davis.

The Edgar Bergen / Charlie McCarthy Show, NBC, February 22, 1942. 30 minutes. Sunday, 8:00–8:30 P.M., from Hollywood.

Director, Earl Ebi; music, Ray Noble and His Orchestra; writers, Carroll Carroll, Dick Mack, Shirley Ward, Stanley Quinn, Joe Bigelow, Joe Connelly, Bob Mosher, Alan Smith, Zeno Klinker, Royal Foster, Roland MacLane, etc.; sound effects, John Glennon, etc.

SONG: Rose O'Day," sung by The Mellowaires.

CAST: Edgar Bergen, Charlie McCarthy, Mortimer Snerd, Bud Abbott, Lou Costello, The Mellowaires, Hedy Lamarr (Guest Star), Buddy Twiss (Announcer).

Presented by Chase and Sanborn Coffee.

The Gulf Screen Guild Theater, WABC, "Too Many Husbands," March 8, 1942. 30 minutes. Sunday, 7:30–8:00 P.M., from Hollywood.

Producer, Bill Lawrence; director, Bill Lawrence; writers, Bill Hampton, Harry Kronman; based on the comedy "Too Many Husbands," by William Somerset Maugham, and screenplay by Claude Binyon. Music by The Oscar Bradley Orchestra.

CAST: Roger Pryor (Host), Bob Hope (Bill Cardew), Bing Crosby (Henry Lowndes), Hedy Lamarr (Vicky Lowndes).

Presented by Gulf Oil.

Three Ring Time, WJZ, April 14, 1942. 30 minutes. Tuesday, 8:30–9:00 P.M., from Hollywood.

CAST: Milton Berle (Host), Hedy Lamarr (Guest).

Presented by Ballantine Ale.

Command Performance, AFRS, May 14, 1942, Thursday evening, Armed Forces Radio.

Created by Louis G. Cowen; producers, Maury Holland, Vick Knight, Cal Kuhl; director, Glenn Wheaton; writers, Melvin Frank, Norman Panama; announcers, Ken Carpenter, Paul Douglas.

CAST: Edward G. Robinson (Host), Hedy Lamarr, Milton Berle, Glenn Miller Orchestra, Ginny Simms, Ray Eberle, Cliff Edwards "Ukelele Ike," etc. (Guest Stars).

Presented by Campbell Soups.

Lux Radio Theatre, CBS, "H.M. Pulham, Esq." July 13, 1942. 60 minutes. Monday, 9:00–10:00 P.M., from Hollywood. Eighth Season.

Presented by Lever Brothers–Lux Toilet Soap (Kathleen Fritz as "Libby Collins" in Lux commercials).

Producer, Cecil B. DeMille; director, Sanford Barnett; music, Louis Silver; writers, George Wells, Sanford Barnett, based on the book by John P. Marquand, screenplay by King Vidor and Elizabeth Hill; set decorator, George Sawley; special effects, Max Uhlig, David Light, Walter Person, Charlie Forsyth; announcer, Melville Ruick.

CAST: Hedy Lamarr (Marvin Myles), Robert Young (H.M. Pulham Jr.), Josephine Hutchinson (Kay Motford), Norman Field (Mr. Pulham Sr.), Verna Feldon (Mrs. Pulham/Nurse), Jack Mather (Bo-Jo/Driver), Tris Coffin (Ridge/Artist), Leo Cleary (Bullard/Conductor), Charles Seel (Kaufman), Eugene Forsyth (Page Boy), Cecil B. DeMille (Host).

Based on the 1941 M-G-M film *H.M. Pulham, Esq.*

The Voice of Broadway, WABC, August 8, 1942. 15 minutes.

Tuesday 6:15–6:30 P.M.

CAST: Hedy Lamarr (Guest).

Command Performance, AFRS, August 30, 1942. 30 minutes. Thursday evening. Recorded in Washington, D.C. Armed Forces Radio.

Created by Louis G. Cowen; producers, Maury Holland, Vick Knight, Cal Kuhl; director, Glenn Wheaton; writers, Melvin Frank, Norman Panama; announcers, Ken Carpenter, Paul Douglas.

CAST: Bing Crosby (Host), Hedy Lamarr, Connee Boswell, Ginny Simms, Abbott and Costello, Dr. Frank Black Orchestra.

Presented by Campbell Soups.

The Edgar Bergen / Charlie McCarthy Show, NBC, September 27, 1942. 30 minutes. Sunday, 8:00–8:30 P.M., from Hollywood.

Director, Earl Ebi; music, Ray Noble and His Orchestra; writers, Carroll Carroll, Dick Mack, Shirley Ward, Stanley Quinn, Joe Bigelow, Joe Connelly, Bob Mosher, Alan Smith, Zeno Klinker, Royal Foster, Roland MacLane, etc.; sound effects, John Glennon, etc.

SONG: "Let Freedom Ring," music by Thesarus Nusicus, lyrics by Samuel F. Smith.

CAST: Edgar Bergen, Charlie McCarthy, Bud Abbott, Lou Costello, Don Ameche, Dale Evans, Jane Powell, Hedy Lamarr (Guest Star), Buddy Twiss (Announcer).

Presented by Chase and Sanborn Coffee.

Lux Radio Theatre, CBS, "Love Crazy," October 5, 1942. 60 minutes.

Monday, 9:00–10:00 P.M., from Hollywood. Eighth Season.

Presented by Lever Brothers–Lux Toilet Soap (Kathleen Fritz as "Libby Collins" in Lux commercials).

Producer, Cecil B. DeMille; director, Sanford Barnett; music, Louis Silver; writers, George Wells, Sanford Barnett, based on a screenplay by William Ludwig, Charles Lederer, and David Hertz; set decorator, George Sawley; special effects, Max Uhlig, David Light, Walter Person, Charlie Forsyth; announcer, John Milton Kennedy.

CAST: Hedy Lamarr (Susan Ireland), William Powell (Steve Ireland), Gale Gordon (Ward Willoughby), Dorothy Lovett (Isabel Kimble Grayson), Verna Felton (Mrs. Bessie Cooper), Joseph Kearns (Dr. David Klugle), Fred MacKaye ("Pinkie" Grayson), Arthur Q. Bryan (George Renny), Boyd Davis (Dentist), Norman Field (Man), Cecil B. DeMille (Host).

Based on the 1941 M-G-M. film *Love Crazy*.

The Lady Esther Screen Guild Theater, WABC, "Come Live with Me." August 2, 1943. 30 minutes. Monday, 10:00–10:30 P.M., from Hollywood.

Producer, Bill Lawrence; director, Bill Lawrence; writers, Bill Hampton, Harry Kronman; based on the story by Virginia van Upp and on the screenplay "Come Live with Me" by Patterson McNutt.

Music by The Oscar Bradley Orchestra.

CAST: Truman Bradley (Host), Hedy Lamarr (Johanna Janns [Johnny Jones]), John Loder (Bill Smith), Vincent Price (Barton Kendrick).

Presented by Lady Esther Cosmetics.

The Edgar Bergen / Charlie McCarthy Show, NBC, September 26, 1943. 30 minutes. Sunday, 8:00–8:30 P.M., from Hollywood.

Director, Earl Ebi; music, Ray Noble and His Orchestra; writers, Carroll Carroll, Dick Mack, Shirley Ward, Stanley Quinn, Joe Bigelow, Joe Connelly, Bob Mosher, Alan Smith, Zeno Klinker, Royal Foster, Roland MacLane, etc.; sound effects, John Glennon, etc.

SONGS: "Ice Cold Katie," music by Arthur Schwartz, lyrics by Frank Loesser; "Put Your Arms Around Me, Honey, Hold Me Tight," music by Albert von Tilzer, lyrics by Junie McCree.

CAST: Edgar Bergen, Charlie McCarthy, Mortimer Snerd, Victor Moore, William Gaxton, Dale Evans, The Sportsmen, Hedy Lamarr (Guest Star), Bill Goodwin (Announcer).

Presented by Chase and Sanborn Coffee.

The Burns and Allen Show, CBS, October 26, 1943. 30 minutes.

Tuesday, 9:00–9:30 P.M., from Hollywood.

Directors, Ed Garner, Ralph Levy; writers, Paul Henning, Harvey Helm, Hal Block, Henry Garson, Keith Fowler, Aaron J. Ruben, Harmon J. Alexander, Helen Gould Harvey; music, Felix Mills and His Orchestra; sound effects, David Light, Al Span.

SONGS: "The Love Nest," by Louis Hirsch (theme song), "My Heart Tells," music by Harry Warren, lyrics by Mack Gordon; "They're Either Too Young or Too Old," music by Arthur Schwartz, lyrics by Frank Loesser.

CAST: George Burns, Gracie Allen, Hedy Lamarr, Elvia Allman, Lawrence Nash, Mel Blanc, Hans Conried, Jimmy Cash (Vocalist), Bill Goodwin (Announcer).

Skit: "Queen of the Fleet."

Presented by Lever Brothers–Swan Soap.

The Edgar Bergen / Charlie McCarthy Show, NBC, November 21, 1943. 30 minutes. Sunday, 8:00–8:30 P.M., from Hollywood. Broadcast from the United States Naval Air Station, at Terminal Island, California.

Director, Earl Ebi; music, Ray Noble and His Orchestra; writers, Carroll Carroll, Dick Mack, Shirley Ward, Stanley Quinn, Joe Bigelow, Joe Connelly, Bob Mosher, Alan Smith, Zeno Klinker, Royal Foster, Roland MacLane, etc.; sound effects, John Glennon, etc.

SONGS: "Someday My Prince Will Come," music by Frank Churchill, lyrics by Larry Morey; "You Discover You're in New York," music by Harry Warren, lyrics by Leo Robin.

CAST: Edgar Bergen, Charlie McCarthy, Jane Powell, Victor Moore, William Gaxton, The Pied Pipers, Hedy Lamarr (Guest Star), Bill Goodwin (Announcer).

Presented by Chase and Sanborn Coffee.

What's New, WJZ, December 11, 1943. 60 minutes. Saturday, 7:00–8:00 P.M., from Hollywood.

CAST: Don Ameche (Host), Hedy Lamarr, Arthur Treacher, Nancy Walker, Captain Charles Romaine, Andrew Higgins (Guests).

Soldiers with Wings, WEAF, December 12, 1943. 30 minutes.

Sunday, 12:00–12:30 P.M., from Hollywood.

CAST: Bill Goodwin (Host), Hedy Lamarr (Guest Star).

Lux Radio Theatre, CBS, "Casablanca," January 24, 1944. 60 minutes.

Monday, 9:00–10:00 P.M., from Hollywood.

Producer, Cecil B. DeMille; director, Sanford Barnett; music, Louis Silver; writers, George Wells, Sanford Barnett, based on a screenplay by Julius J. and Philip Epstein, and Howard Koch; based on the play *Everybody Comes to Rick's,* by Murray Bennett and Joan Alison; set decorator, George Sawley; special effects, Max Uhlig, David Light, Walter Person, Charlie Forsyth; announcer, John Milton Kennedy.

CAST: Hedy Lamarr (Ilsa Lund), Alan Ladd (Rick Blaine), John Loder (Victor Lazlo), Edgar Barrier (Captain Renault), Norman Field (Major Strausser), Ernest Whitman (Sam), René Gacaire (Casselle), Ed Emerson (Voice), Charles Seel (Carl), Jay Novello (Hans Ugarte), Leo Cleary (Ferrari), Charles Lung (Sascha), Cecil B. DeMille (Host).

Based on the 1942 Warner Bros. film *Casablanca.*

Presented by Lever Brothers–Lux Toilet Soap (Doris Singleton as "Libby Collins" in Lux commercials).

Silver Theatre, WABC, "She Looked Like an Angel," February 20, 1944. 30 minutes. Sunday, 6:00–6:30 P.M., from Hollywood.

Director, Conrad Nagel.

CAST: Conrad Nagel (Host), Hedy Lamarr, John Loder, H. Charles (Announcer).

Presented by the International Silver Company

Stars and Their Stories, CBS, "Romance," July 23, 1944. 30 minutes.

Sunday, 8:00–8:30 P.M., from Hollywood.

CAST: Walter Pidgeon (Host), Hedy Lamarr (Guest Star).

Presented by the Goodyear Tire Company.

Radio Hall of Fame, NBC Blue, "Experiment Perilous," February 4, 1945. 60 minutes. Sunday, 6:00–7:00 P.M., from Hollywood.

Music, Paul Whiteman Orchestra; variety editor, Abel Green.

CAST: Al Pearce (Host), Hedy Lamarr (Allida Bedereaux), George Brent (Dr. Huntington Bailey), Andy Russell, Marjorie Main, Marlin Hurt (Beulah), Eileen Barton, Matty Melneck, Robert Maxwell, Glen Riggs (Announcer).

Presented by Philco.

The Charlie McCarthy Show, NBC, April 7, 1946. 30 minutes.

Sunday, 8:00–8:30 P.M., from Hollywood.

Director, Earl Ebi; music, Ray Noble and His Orchestra; writers, Carroll Carroll, Dick Mack, Shirley Ward, Stanley Quinn, Joe Bigelow, Joe Connelly, Bob Mosher, Alan Smith, Zeno Klinker, Royal Foster, Roland MacLane, etc.; sound effects, John Glennon, etc.

SONGS: "It's Anybody's Spring," music by Jimmy van Husen, lyrics by Johnny Burke.

CAST: Edgar Bergen, Charlie McCarthy, Ray Noble and His Orchestra, Mortimer Snerd, Martha Wentworth, Hedy Lamarr (Guest Star), Ken Carpenter (Announcer).

Presented by Chase and Sanborn Coffee.

The Bob Hope Show, NBC, "From Coronado Island," April 10, 1951. 30 minutes.

Tuesday, 9:00–9:30 P.M.

Music, Les Brown Orchestra.

CAST: Bob Hope, Hedy Lamarr (Guest Star), Frankie Laine, Jack Kirkwood, Marilyn Maxwell, Hi Averback (Announcer).

Presented by Chesterfield Cigarettes.

Lux Radio Theatre, CBS, "Samson and Delilah," November 19, 1951. 60 minutes. Monday, 9:00–10:00 P.M., from Hollywood. Seventeenth Season.

Producer, Cecil B. DeMille; director, Erle Erbi; musical director, Rudy Schrager; writer, George Wells; adapted by Sanford H. Barnett; set decorator, George Sawley; announcer, John Milton Kennedy.

CAST: Victor Mature (Samson), Hedy Lamarr (Delilah), Edgar Barrier (Saran), Leif Erickson (Ahtur), Herbert Rowlinson (Minoah), Hope Sansbury (Hisham), Norma Varden (Hazel), and Jonathan Hole, Theodore van Eltz, Robert Griffin, Bill Johnstone, Eddie Marr, Gale Gordon (Narrator), William Keighley (Host).

Based on the 1948 Paramount film *Samson and Delilah*.

Presented by Lever Brothers–Lux Toilet Soap (Kathleen Fritz as "Libby Collins" in Lux commercials).

Endnotes

ABBREVIATIONS

AC   Author's Collection
AMPAS   Academy of Motion Picture Arts and Sciences, Fairbanks Center for Motion
            Picture Study
ARC   Arlene Roxbury's Collection
BYU   Brigham Young University, Provo, Utah
DKB   Deutsche Kinemathek Museum für Film und Fernsehen, Berlin
DLDC   The Denise Loder-DeLuca Collection
MOMA   Museum of Modern Art, New York
NYPL   New York City Public Library, Library for the Performing Arts Lincoln Center
ONV   Österreichische Nationalbibliothek, Vienna
USC   University of Southern California Research Library

INTRODUCTION

1. Richard Schickel, *The Stars* (New York: Dial, 1962), 64.
2. Diane Negra, *Off-White Hollywood: American Culture and Ethnic Female Stardom* (New York: Routledge, 2001), 131.
3. Quoted in Negra, *Off-White Hollywood*, 133–34.
4. Billie Melba Fuller, conversations with author.
5. Hedy Lamarr, *Ecstasy and Me: My Life as a Woman* (New York: Bartholomew House, 1966), 273.

6. Quoted in Adam Bernstein, "Actress Hedy Lamarr, Star of 'Samson and Delilah' Dies; She Made More than 25 Movies, Helped Invent a Method to Prevent Jamming of Radio Communications," *The Washington Post,* January 20, 2000.

1. AUSTRIA

1. James Huneker, "The Gayest City in Europe—Not Paris, but Vienna," *The New York Times,* April 13, 1913.
2. Ibid.
3. It is known that Hedy was raised and married in the Catholic Church. According to her only granddaughter, Denise, Gertrud always displayed a cross on the wall of her dining room. Hedy, until the day she died, professed her Christianity.
4. Untitled article, n.d., NYPL (Hedy Lamarr files).
5. Gene Ringgold, untitled article, *Screen Facts,* July 1965.
6. Hedy Lamarr, "This Is Myself . . . Hedy Lamarr," *Movieland,* n.d., USC.
7. Igor Cassini, untitled article [March 18, 1949], AMPAS.
8. Gladys Hall, "Hedl in Hollywood," *Silver Screen,* August 1942.
9. Untitled article, n.d., MOMA.
10. Gertrud Kiesler quoted in Adele Whitely Fletcher, "Think with Your Heart," *Modern Screen,* April 1941.
11. Untitled article, n.d., MOMA.
12. Cassini, untitled article.
13. Lamarr, "This Is Myself."
14. Angela Lambert, *The Lost Life of Eva Braun* (New York: St. Martin's, 2007), 25.
15. Hedy Lamarr, "The Curse of Beauty," *Look,* June 5, 1951.
16. Untitled article, *The American Magazine,* n.d., DLDC.
17. Hedy Lamarr, "The Story of My Life," *Picturegoer,* November 15, 1941.
18. Hedy Lamarr, *Ecstasy and Me: My Life as a Woman* (New York: Bartholomew House, 1966), 99.
19. Robert Joseph, "Hedy's Here," *Silver Screen,* December 1938.
20. Untitled article, n.d., MOMA (Hedy Lamarr files).
21. Lamarr, *Ecstasy and Me,* 99.
22. Ibid., 278.
23. Ringgold, untitled article.
24. Hall, "Hedl in Hollywood."
25. Joseph, "Hedy's Here."
26. M-G-M, press release, June 8, 1942, AMPAS.
27. Gladys Hall, "As I See Myself—by Hedy Lamarr," *Motion Picture,* February 1942.
28. Untitled article, n.d., MOMA (Hedy Lamarr files).

29. Lamarr, *Ecstasy and Me*, 130.

30. Kay Proctor, "Play Truth or Consequences with Hedy Lamarr," *Photoplay,* November 1942.

31. Lamarr, "Curse of Beauty."

32. Ibid.

33. Hall, "Hedl in Hollywood."

34. Warner Bros., press release, October 1944, AMPAS.

35. Kay Proctor, "The Lure That's Lamarr," *Modern Screen,* November 1938.

36. Lamarr, "Curse of Beauty."

37. Hedy Lamarr, "Loneliest Woman in Hollywood," *Silver Screen,* February 1943.

38. Hall, "Hedl in Hollywood."

39. Lamarr, "Story of My Life."

40. Hall, "Hedl in Hollywood."

41. Lamarr, "This Is Myself."

42. Lamarr, "Story of My Life."

43. Ibid.

44. Lamarr, *Ecstasy and Me,* 17.

45. Ibid.

46. *Geld auf der Strasse* was photographed by one of the most respected European cinematographers of the silent era, Nicholas Farkas. His photography graced Maurice Tourneur's 1929 adventure film *Das Schiff der verlorenen Menschen* (*The Ship of Lost Men*), starring Marlene Dietrich. Rudolph Bernauer wrote the original play *Geld auf der Strasse*, a success in Central Europe, on which the film was based.

47. *Sturm im Wasserglas* was remade in England as *Storm in a Teacup* (1937), starring Rex Harrison and Vivien Leigh and directed by Victor Saville. Renate Müller (1906–37) became involved with a Jewish gentleman just as the Nazis began infiltrating the film industry in Germany. At the age of thirty-one, on October 1, 1937, she checked into a Berlin hospital, ostensibly for knee surgery, though rumors were spread later that it was for drug addiction. From a third-floor window she fell, or was pushed, to her death.

48. Christopher Young, *The Films of Hedy Lamarr* (Secaucus, NJ: Citadel Press, 1978), 82.

49. Arthur MacKenzie, "Is Hedy Lamarr Jinxed . . . ??" [incomplete title], *Hollywood,* November 1942, DLDC. According to Elizabeth Copeland, the young Ritter Franz von Hochestetten "blew his brains out." "Reel News From . . . Hollywood," *The Richmond (VA) News Leader,* January 6, 1939. Yet in her *Ecstasy and Me*, Hedy says, "he hung himself. That was one of my early indications about the tragic side of love" (20).

50. Scott Eyman, *Ernst Lubitsch: Laughter in Paradise* (New York: Simon & Schuster, 1993), 30.

51. Otto Preminger, *Preminger* (Bantam: New York, 1978), 49.

52. Lamarr, *Ecstasy and Me,* 18.

53. "Hedy Kiesler, Max Reinhardt, and Hollywood," n.d., ONV.

2. REINHARDT

1. Scott Eyman, *Ernst Lubitsch: Laughter in Paradise* (New York: Simon & Schuster, 1993), 30.

2. George Weller, "The Ecstatic Hedy Lamarr," *Ken* magazine (published by *Esquire*), January 26, 1939. Weller (1907–2002) was born in Boston and graduated from Roxbury Latin School in 1925 and from Harvard College in 1929. He studied acting under Reinhardt in Vienna, the only American member of Reinhardt's theatre company. In the 1930s he was assigned by *The New York Times* to its Balkan reporting team. Shortly after the outbreak of World War II, he joined *The Chicago Daily News* as a foreign-service corresponding reporter from Europe, for which in 1943 he won a Pulitzer Prize. Weller was one of the first foreign news correspondents at the end of the war to enter the bombed city of Nagasaki after Japan's surrender. He died in Italy in 2002.

3. Eyman, *Ernst Lubitsch*, 29–30.

4. Ludwig Stössel is best remembered as the commercial character the Little Old Wine Maker for Gallo wine.

5. Weller, "Ecstatic Hedy Lamarr."

6. Ibid.

7. Ibid.

8. Ibid.

9. Ibid.

10. Hedy Lamarr, *Ecstasy and Me: My Life as a Woman* (New York: Bartholomew House, 1966), 13.

11. Ibid., 18.

12. Quoted in Stephen D. Youngkin, Raymond G. Cabana Jr., and James Biguoco, *The Films of Peter Lorre* (Secaucus, NJ: Citadel Press, 1982), 70–71.

13. C. Hooper Trask, "Berlin Screen Notes," *The New York Times,* July 17, 1932.

14. Heinz Rühmann (1902–94) was a popular German film star. A favorite of Hitler and Goebbels, he was also beloved by a young Jewish girl named Anne Frank, who pasted his picture on her bedroom wall in her family's hiding place in Amsterdam during the war. The attic is now a museum, and Rühmann's picture remains on Anne's wall to this day.

15. In an uncredited bit was the young Lilia Skala, later an Oscar- and Emmy-nominated actress best remembered in Hollywood for 1965's *Ship of Fools,* which also featured Heinz Rühmann.

16. The rotund Kurt Gerron (1897–1944) was Germany's most respected character actor before the emergence of the Third Reich. In a small theatre in Berlin in 1928, performing as Tiger Brown in Bertolt Brecht's and Kurt Weill's *Dreigroschenoper* (*The Three Penny Opera*), Gerron introduced the song "Mack the Knife." When Germany invaded the Netherlands in 1940, Gerron was forced to appear in the propaganda film *Der ewige Jude* (*The Eternal Jew*), and in 1943 he and his wife were transported to the Theresienstadt concentration camp near Prague. There he was enticed to direct the pseudodocumen-

tary *Der Führer schenkt den Juden eine Stadt* (*The Führer Gives a City to the Jews*), completed on September 11, 1944, which showed an ideal internment camp to appease international criticism. Gerron had believed he and his wife would be spared deportation if he directed the film. But on its completion they were deported on the final transport out of Theresienstadt to Birkenau. Gerron was ordered to sing "Mack the Knife" one last time before being sent to death in the gas chamber with his wife on October 28, 1944.

17. Regina Crewe, "German Picture Affords Much of Pleasant Comedy," *The New York American*, November 10, 1932.

18. Quoted in Christopher Young, *The Films of Hedy Lamarr* (Secaucus, NJ: Citadel Press, 1978), 86.

19. H. T. S., "*Man braucht kein Geld* (1931): Fun and Finance," *The New York Times*, November 16, 1932.

20. Gene Ringgold, untitled article, *Screen Facts*, 1965.

21. Jeffrey Donovan, "The Agony and the *Extaze*," *The Prague Post*, February 2, 2000.

22. After his brief engagement to Hedy Kiesler, Fred D. Döderlein (1906–85) married the actress Ursula von Arnim. In 1952 the couple immigrated to Canada. He continued making brief film appearances, including a small role in *Hotel New Hampshire* (1984) before his death in 1985.

23. Michael Brooke (1904–78) was born Guy Fulke Greville, the 7th Earl of Warwick. Brooke acted in such films as DeMille's *The Buccaneer* (1938); *The Dawn Patrol* (1938), with Errol Flynn; and (uncredited) Samuel Goldwyn's *Zaza* (1939). Handsome and charming, Brooke was quite a "ladies' man," dating the actress Marlene Dietrich during the mid-1930s.

24. Ted Magree, "Never Again, Mr. Hayes!" *Picture Play*, November 1938.

25. Quoted in Donatella Dubini and Fosco Dubini, *Hedy Lamarr: Secrets of a Hollywood Star* (Dubini Filmproduktion, 2006).

3. ECSTASY

1. Lupita Tovar Kohner quoted in Donatella Dubini and Fosco Dubini, *Hedy Lamarr: Secrets of a Hollywood Star* (Dubini Filmproduktion, 2006).

2. Ibid. Lupita Tovar and Paul Kohner's daughter, the actress Susan Kohner, was nominated for a Best Supporting Actress Oscar for her role in *Imitation of Life* (Universal, 1959).

3. Hedy Lamarr, *Ecstasy and Me: My Life as a Woman* (New York: Bartholomew House, 1966), 19.

4. Ibid., 28.

5. Christopher Young, *The Films of Hedy Lamarr* (Secaucus, NJ: Citadel Press, 1978), 14.

6. Jan Christopher Horak, "High Class Whore," *CineAction*, March 2001.

7. Patrick Robinson, *Film Facts* (New York: Billboard, 2001), 66. Hedy was most definitely *not* the first leading lady to appear nude on film. That first is credited to the silent screen actress Audrey Munson, who disrobed for the melodrama *Inspiration*, a Thanhouser

Film Corporation picture released on November 8, 1915. A former well-known artist's model, she made a career out of taking her clothes off in the movies, as she did in *Purity* (1916) and *Heedless Moths* (1921). At the age of thirty-nine, after being linked to a famous murder trial, which destroyed her career, she was admitted to a psychiatric institution. She died there at 105 years of age. Also, the Australian swimmer-actress Annette Kellerman appeared nude in Hollywood's first million-dollar picture, *A Daughter of the Gods* (1916). Nudity was frequently glimpsed in innumerable American and European films during the 1920s, including M-G-M's own multimillion-dollar epic *Ben-Hur: A Tale of Christ* (1925), with Ramon Novarro, which included an extended scene (in early two-strip Technicolor) of bare-breasted women and (in black-and-white) the lingering view of the backside of a naked male galley slave.

8. Lamarr, *Ecstasy and Me,* 29.
9. Quoted by Gene Youngblood, *The Los Angeles Examiner,* January 28, 1966.
10. Lamarr, *Ecstasy and Me,* 30.
11. "Hedy Kiesler, Max Reinhardt, and Hollywood," n.d., ONV.
12. "Hedy Kiesler, Max Reinhardt, and Hollywood."
13. William L. Shirer, *The Nightmare Years, 1930–1940*, vol. 2 of *20th Century Journey* (Boston: Little, Brown, 1994), 48.
14. Lamarr, *Ecstasy and Me,* 30.
15. Ibid., 30–31.
16. Hedy Lamarr quoted in *Hedy Lamarr: Secrets of a Hollywood Star.*
17. "The Film Society," *The London Times,* March 12, 1933, NYPL.
18. Paula Wessely (1907–2000) was a popular German stage and screen actress. Her film work was studied by Bette Davis, and she was considered by Sir Laurence Olivier to have been the greatest actress in motion pictures.
19. In this early attempt at "multimedia" big-stage production, the inclusion of this short film, in silhouette motion and created as an "interlude" between the acts, caused a small sensation. Later Reiniger would gain lasting fame with *Die Geschichte des Prinzen Achmed (The Adventures of Prince Achmed)*, completed in 1926, the oldest surviving animated feature film now in existence. Escaping Germany in the mid-1930s, Reiniger and her husband, Carl Koch, survived the war in Europe, moving from country to country. Before her death in 1981, she became a British citizen.
20. Fritz Kreisler (1875–1962) was a Viennese-born Jewish violinist. He achieved worldwide popularity around the turn of the century. He also wrote several pieces for the violin, including solos and encores. His only two operettas were *Apple Blossoms* in 1919, which premiered on Broadway with Fred and Adele Astaire, and the Vienna-staged *Sissy* in 1932. In 1938 he fled Berlin for France, eventually coming to America in 1939. He died in New York on January 29, 1962.
21. The Jewish Sam Spiegel (1901–85) was born in Poland and later, as a producer, won three Academy Awards for Best Picture for *On the Waterfront* (1955), *The Bridge on the River Kwai* (1957), and *Lawrence of Arabia* (1962).

22. "The Cheerful Outlook," *Time,* June 11, 1945.

23. "Double Cross?" *Time,* April 15, 1945.

24. Joe May, an uncle of Fritz Mandl, had been born into wealth as Julius Otto Mandl in Vienna in 1880. He would direct several films in Hollywood after 1934, after he and his wife fled Europe, including *Music in the Air* (1934), *Confession* (1937), and *The Invisible Man Returns* (1940). May found it nearly impossible to adjust to Hollywood and ended his days running a Viennese restaurant with his wife, Mia, as cook. He died in 1954.

25. "Idol of Foreign Cinema Patrons Takes Her Life," *Los Angeles Times,* September 12, 1924.

26. Rob Walters, *Spread Spectrum: Hedy Lamarr and the Mobile Phone* (Charleston, SC: BookSurge, 2005), 79.

27. Hedy Lamarr, "The Curse of Beauty," *Look,* June 5, 1971.

28. Kenyon Lee, "The Men in Hedy Lamarr's Life," *Screen Guide,* November 1947.

29. Lamarr, *Ecstasy and Me,* 26.

4. MANDL

1. Kay Proctor, "The Lure That's Lamarr," *Modern Screen,* November 1938.

2. Kay Proctor, "Play Truth or Consequences with Hedy Lamarr," *Photoplay,* November 1942.

3. "Hedy's Persistent Husband," *The American Weekly,* February 12, 1948.

4. Christopher Young, *The Films of Hedy Lamarr* (Secaucus, NJ: Citadel Press, 1978), 18. Contrary to what has been written, Hedy never met Adolf Hitler. By 1933 it would have been impossible for Hitler to have knowingly been introduced to or to have been publicly entertained by Hedy or her husband, since both were of Jewish heritage.

5. Lon Murray, "Hedy Lamarr Has Had Too Much Ecstasy," *Modern Screen,* April 1939.

6. Arlene Roxbury, interview by author, July 11, 2008.

7. Hedy Lamarr, *Ecstasy and Me: My Life as a Woman* (New York: Bartholomew House, 1966), 26.

8. "Hedy's Persistent Husband."

9. Proctor, "Play Truth or Consequences."

10. Farley Granger, *Include Me Out: My Life from Goldwyn to Hollywood*, with Robert Calhoun (New York: St. Martin's, 2007), 73.

11. Scott Eyman, *Lion of Hollywood: The Life and Legend of Louis B. Mayer* (New York: Simon & Schuster, 2005), 198. The previous year, the Jewish-born Reinhardt left Germany, taking up residence in Austria. By 1934, he would come to the United States and stage, first as a live production at the Hollywood Bowl and then as a feature motion picture for Warner Bros., William Shakespeare's *A Midsummer Night's Dream.*

12. Charles Higham, *Merchant of Dreams: Louis B. Mayer, M.G.M. and the Secret Hollywood* (New York: Donald I. Fine, 1993), 224–25.

13. Lamarr, *Ecstasy and Me* (New York: Bartholomew House, 1966), 27.

14. Ibid.

15. "'Audacious' Film's Entry Pondered by Treasury," *Los Angeles Times,* January 1, 1935.

16. Ruth McKenney, "Ecstasy Is a Film, Not a Husband's State of Mind," NYPL.

17. "Treasury Bans Nude Scene Film," *The New York Times,* January 7, 1935.

18. Fred Stein, "New York Spectacle," *Hollywood Spectator,* May 23, 1936.

19. "Love Symbols in Banned Movie," *The New York American,* July 17, 1935.

20. "*Ecstasy* Burned Despite Appeal," *The New York Times,* August 8, 1935.

21. McKenney, "Ecstasy Is a Film, Not a Husband's State of Mind."

22. Granger, *Include Me Out* (New York: St. Martin's, 2007), 73.

23. Thomas M. Pryor, "New York vs. *Ecstasy,*" *The New York Times,* November 28, 1937. (*The Times* is quoting *The Boston Globe,* April 23, 1936.)

24. Stein, "New York Spectacle."

25. Rob Walters, *Spread Spectrum: Hedy Lamarr and the Mobile Phone* (Charleston, SC: BookSurge, 2005), 79.

26. "Death Notice," unknown newspaper, February 21, 1935, ONV.

27. Denise Loder-DeLuca, telephone interview by author, April 3, 2009.

28. Marian Rhea, "I Have Lived," *Movie Mirror,* February 1939.

29. Ibid.

30. Lamarr, *Ecstasy and Me,* 32.

31. Ibid.

32. Ibid., 33. In *Ecstasy and Me,* Hedy tells of allegedly attempting to flee Mandl by escaping into a brothel. Tasteless stories like this are frequent in the book and highly unlikely to have happened.

33. Kathryn R. Swift, "Austria Follows Her Romantic Prince," *The New York Times,* February 9, 1936.

34. Gertrude Schneider, *Exile and Destruction: The Fate of Austrian Jews, 1938–1945* (Westport, CT: Greenwood, 1995), 10.

35. "Austria May Seize the Arms Industry," *The New York Times,* May 23, 1936. Mandl and Starhemberg maintained a curiously intense relationship. In late 1937, Starhemberg wed the German film actress Nora Gregor, best known for her starring role in Jean Renoir's 1938 film *La regle de jeu* (*Rules of the Game*) and, with their four-year-old son, fled to Switzerland after the *Anschluss,* where he sold his vineyards in the Wachau to its tenants, creating the Wachau wine growers' cooperative, now the Freie Weingärtner Wachau. They then moved to France. There Mandl briefly joined them. During World War II, Starhemberg served in the British and the French armed forces, living in Argentina from 1942 to 1955. He eventually returned to Austria, where he died on March 15, 1956.

36. Rhea, "I Have Lived."

37. "'Ecstasy' Star to Quit Rich Mate for the Stage," New York *Daily News,* September 19, 1937, NYPL.

38. Young, *Films of Hedy Lamarr,* 18.

39. Lamarr, *Ecstasy and Me,* 311.

40. Higham, *Merchant of Dreams,* 267.

41. "'Ecstasy' Star to Quit Rich Mate for the Stage," New York *Daily News,* September 19, 1937.

42. In a different and more outrageous version in Hedy's alleged autobiography, she tells of drugging her maid with sleeping pills, dressing in the maid's clothing, and making good her escape. In another fanciful tale, it was winter and Hedy was forced to dive out a window—fairly unlikely from the Mandl's Vienna apartment—into a snowdrift on her rush to freedom and London with the assistance of a kindly Englishman.

43. "'Ecstasy' Star to Quit Rich Mate for Stage," New York *Daily News,* September 19, 1937. For years historians have theorized that Mandl actually financed and secured safe passage for his wife to London, where she would be free to divorce him. There is little evidence, however, to support this speculation. Regarding Hedy's flight from Mandl, one questions the situation as written about in *Ecstasy and Me.* Diane Negra writes, "More significantly, this fictionalized version of Lamarr's private history de-emphasized her urgency in choosing to come to the United States, re-orienting the terms of that decision to position Louis B. Mayer as her rescuer." *Off-White Hollywood: American Culture and Ethnic Female Stardom* (New York: Routledge, 2001), 122.

44. Higham, *Merchant of Dreams,* 265.

45. Raymond Sarlot and Fred E. Basten, *Life at the Marmont* (Santa Monica, CA: Roundtable, 1987), 55.

46. Ibid., 55.

47. Ibid., 56.

48. The silent film actress Barbara La Marr (1896–1926) was known as "the girl who was too beautiful" and starred in *The Prisoner of Zenda* in 1922. La Marr enjoyed Hollywood's wild party life and died of tuberculosis and nephritis on January 30, 1926. During her brief and turbulent life, La Marr married five times and had an illegitimate son. He grew up to become the actor Don Gallery and was once the frequent date of young Elizabeth Taylor.

49. Higham, *Merchant of Dreams,* 268.

50. Jane Ellen Wayne, *The Golden Girls of MGM* (New York: Carroll & Graf, 2002), 362.

51. Howard Dietz, *Dancing in the Dark: An Autobiography* (New York: Bantam, 1976), 172.

5. HOLLYWOOD

1. Raymond Sarlot and Fred E. Basten, *Life at the Marmont* (Santa Monica, CA: Roundtable, 1987), 55.

2. Gerold Frank, *Judy* (New York: Harper & Row, 1975), 67.

3. "Louis Mayer's $688,369 Pay Check Leads Nation," *Los Angeles Times,* July 1, 1940.

4. Hedy Lamarr, *Ecstasy and Me: My Life as a Woman* (New York: Bartholomew House, 1966), 52.

5. Sarlot and Basten, *Life at the Marmont,* 57.

6. Ibid.

7. Frank, *Judy,* 69.

8. John Scott, "Faces Cost Fortunes in Film Colony," *Los Angeles Times,* December 27, 1936.

9. Marian Rhea, "Hedy's Private Opinion of Men," *Motion Picture,* January 1941.

10. Sarlot and Basten, *Life at the Marmont,* 57.

11. Scott Eyman, *Lion of Hollywood: The Life and Legend of Louis B. Mayer* (New York: Simon & Schuster, 2005), 316.

12. Untitled article, n.d., *Screen Life,* DLDC.

13. Sheilah Graham, *Hollywood Revisited* (New York: St. Martin's, 1985), 78.

14. Untitled article, n.d., MOMA (Hedy Lamarr files).

15. Lamarr, *Ecstasy and Me,* 58.

16. Larry Swindell, *Charles Boyer: The Reluctant Lover* (Garden City, NY: Doubleday, 1983), 113–14.

17. Diane Negra, *Off-White Hollywood: American Culture and Ethnic Female Stardom* (New York: Routledge, 2001), 191.

18. Lamarr, *Ecstasy and Me,* 59.

19. Ibid., 59–60.

20. "Saga of 'Pepe le Moko'," *The New York Times,* March 2, 1941.

21. Eyman, *Lion of Hollywood,* 198.

22. A. Scott Berg, *Goldwyn: A Biography* (New York: Alfred A. Knopf, 1989), 320.

23. Matthew Bernstein, *Walter Wanger, Hollywood Independent* (Berkeley: University of California Press, 1994), 143.

24. William Lynch Vallee, "The Secret of Hedy's Appeal," *Screenland,* February 1952, 60.

25. Kyle Chrichton, "Escape to Hollywood," *Colliers,* November 5, 1938.

26. Hedy Lamarr, "This Is Myself . . . Hedy Lamarr," *Movieland,* n.d., USC.

27. *Cinema's Exiles,* PBS, 2008.

28. Perhaps one of the least successful exiles was Fritz Lang, director of *Metropolis* (UFA, 1927), *M* (Nero, 1931), and *The Testament of Dr. Mabuse* (Nero, 1933). His arrogance and stubbornness prevented him from learning Hollywood filmmaking ways and from adapting to American film techniques. In Germany he was omnipotent in the industry. In Hollywood he was assigned primarily B pictures. On the other hand, the most successful of the exiles would be the writer and director Billy Wilder, who was nominated for twenty-three Academy Awards, winning six.

29. Lamarr, *Ecstasy and Me,* 63.

30. Bernstein, *Walter Wanger, Hollywood Independent,* 11.

31. "Austrian Nazis Find Foe Took His Assets," *The New York Times,* May 8, 1938.

32. Gertrude Schneider, *Exile and Destruction: The Fate of Austrian Jews, 1938–1945* (Westport, CT: Greenwood, 1995), 10.

33. "Austrian Nazis Find Foe Took His Assets."

34. Ibid.

35. *The Daily Variety,* June 24, 1938.

36. "True Adaptation of French Success," *The Hollywood Reporter,* June 24, 1938.

37. Lamarr, *Ecstasy and Me,* 67.

38. Ibid.

39. Elena Binckley, "High Interest in Hedy LaMarr," July 14, 1938, USC.

40. Ed Sullivan, "Worlds of Exotic Women!" *Modern Screen,* September 1938.

41. Alma Whitaker, "Hedy Lamarr Justifies Judgment of Producer," *Los Angeles Times,* August 3, 1938.

42. *Time,* July 25, 1938.

43. Christopher Young, *The Films of Hedy Lamarr* (Secaucus, NJ: Citadel Press, 1978), 104.

44. *Algiers* cost $691,833 and grossed $951,801 (a $150,466 net) and would eventually earn $2.4 million in rentals in the United States. The fall of its release, 1938, Boyer starred in a radio adaptation of *Algiers* on *The Woodbury Playhouse.* In 1948 *Algiers* was remade as a musical, entitled *Casbah,* by Universal-International, starring Tony Martin, Marta Toren as Gaby, Yvonne De Carlo, and Peter Lorre.

45. Richard Hanley, "James Wong Howe Dies; Noted Cinematographer," *The New York Times,* July 16, 1976.

46. Margaret J. Bailey, *Those Glorious Glamour Years: Classic Hollywood Costume Design of the 1930's* (New York: Citadel Press, 1982), 191.

47. Richard Griffith and Arthur Mayer, *The Movies* (New York: Simon & Schuster, 1957), 365.

6. STARDOM

1. Gladys Hall, "Luxurious Lamarr," submission copy for *Motion Picture,* October 12, 1938, AMPAS.

2. Larry Swindell, *Spencer Tracy: A Biography* (Cleveland: World, 1969), 155.

3. Hall, "Luxurious Lamarr."

4. Hedy Lamarr, *Ecstasy and Me: My Life as a Woman* (New York: Bartholomew House, 1966), 68.

5. Ibid.

6. Hall, "Luxurious Lamarr." Also mentioned by the studio was the possibility of having Hedy portray Pocahontas.

7. Shortly after the filming of *Marie Antoinette,* Hedy recalled a party Norma Shearer had invited her to attend, thrown by William Randolph Hearst at the Santa Monica beach house of his mistress, the actress Marion Davies (who had longed to portray the French queen for Metro). "'Little Old New York' was the theme, but this didn't deter Norma, Ty Power, myself and a group of others from merrily raiding Metro's wardrobe department and appropriating the beautiful costumes used in 'Marie,'" Hedy said. "I'll never forget the expression on the host's face as our car pulled up the driveway—I thought Mr. Hearst would have apoplexy as we alighted and advanced toward him in our French finery." Bob Edison, "Hubba, Hubba, Hubba—It's Hedy!" *The New York Times,* September 26, 1971.

8. Swindell, *Spencer Tracy,* 153. After 1938 over three dozen properties (novels, plays, etc.) were purchased by M-G-M as possible vehicles for Tracy, but only *Edison the Man* and *Tortilla Flat* were ever produced from these starring the actor.

9. Patrick Agan, "Hedy Lamarr! Tragic Beauty Lives On," *Hollywood Studio Magazine,* November 1984.

10. Untitled article, *Movie Mirror,* February 1939.

11. Hall, "Luxurious Lamarr."

12. Ibid.

13. Ibid.

14. Hedda Hopper, Hedda Hopper's Hollywood, *Los Angeles Times,* October 21, 1938.

15. Dorothy Ducas, "Hollywood Bows to Exotic Allure of Hedy Lamarr," *The New York Daily News,* November 16, 1938.

16. Peter Hay, *MGM: When the Lion Roared* (Atlanta: Turner, 1991), 202.

17. Swindell, *Spencer Tracy,* 156.

18. Douglas W. Churchill, "Out Again In Again Corrigan," *The New York Times,* November 13, 1938.

19. Swindell, *Spencer Tracy,* 156.

20. Hopper, Hedda Hopper's Hollywood, *Los Angeles Times,* November 8, 1938.

21. Edison, "Hubba, Hubba, Hubba."

22. Hopper, Hedda Hopper's Hollywood, *Los Angeles Times,* December 23, 1938.

23. Hopper, Hedda Hopper's Hollywood, *Los Angeles Times,* February 6, 1939.

24. Hopper, Hedda Hopper's Hollywood, *Los Angeles Times,* February 6, 1939.

25. Hopper, Hedda Hopper's Hollywood, *Los Angeles Times,* February 29, 1939.

26. Martha Kerr, "Is Hedy Lamarr a Flop?" *Modern Screen,* June 1939.

27. Metro also purchased *They Call It Glamour,* by John Larkin and Jerry Horwin, for Taylor and Lamarr at the end of January 1939. It dealt with the lives of professional fashion models. Also mentioned in *The New York Times*: "Hedy Lamarr has been penciled in for the feminine lead in 'Wings over the Desert,' already scheduled for Clark Gable and James Stewart." "Screen News Here and in Hollywood," *The New York Times,* February 7, 1939.

28. Read Kendall, Around and About Hollywood, *Los Angeles Times,* January 28, 1939.

29. Kendall, Around and About Hollywood, *Los Angeles Times,* February 2, 1939.

30. Hopper, Hedda Hopper's Hollywood, *Los Angeles Times,* February 11, 1939.

31. "Columbia's Seniors Pick Hedy Lamarr," *Los Angeles Times,* February 19, 1939.

32. Hopper, Hedda Hopper's Hollywood, *Los Angeles Times,* January 31, 1939.

33. "Markey Weds Hedy Lamarr," *The Los Angeles Examiner,* March 5, 1939.

34. "Hedy Lamarr and Gene Markey Marry at Mexicali Palace," *Los Angeles Times,* March 5, 1939.

35. Adele Whitely Fletcher, "The Dilemma of Lamarr," *Photoplay,* June 1939.

36. Hopper, Hedda Hopper's Hollywood, *Los Angeles Times,* March 7, 1939.

37. Gene Markey to Hedda Hopper, March 8, 1939, AMPAS.

38. Ibid.

39. Kenyon Lee, "The Men in Hedy Lamarr's Life," *Screen Guide,* November 1947. Hedy sold her eight-room home with swimming pool and pavilion on Camden Drive for $35,000 to the British actor Leslie Howard in May 1939.

40. Lamarr, *Ecstasy and Me,* 91.

41. "Screen News Here and in Hollywood," *The New York Times,* March 15, 1939. Machatý did take revenge on Hitler and the Nazi Party when he wrote for the director G. W. Pabst *Es geschah am 20. Juli* (*It Happened on July 20*) for Arca/Ariston Films in 1955, about the failed assassination attempt on Hitler. On December 14, 1963, Gustav Machatý died after a long illness in Munich, Germany. He was sixty-three years old.

42. Kyle Chrichton, "Escape to Hollywood," *Collier's,* November 5, 1938. In September 1939, *Ecstasy* opened at the Cinema Theater in Los Angeles, and the *Los Angeles Times* film correspondent, Edwin Schallert, wrote in his column, "'Ecstasy' . . . proved once again that Hedy Lamarr is not only one of the most beautiful girls on the screen, but also an unusually good actress." September 14, 1939.

43. Jimmie Fidler, "Star Wears 25-Pound Gown," Jimmie Fidler in Hollywood, *Los Angeles Times,* September 6, 1939.

44. Hopper, Hedda Hopper's Hollywood, *Los Angeles Times,* May 6, 1939.

45. Edison, "Hubba, Hubba, Hubba."

46. "The New Pictures," *Time,* August 26, 1939.

47. Fletcher, "The Dilemma of Lamarr."

48. "Close-Ups and Long Shot," *Photoplay,* June 1939.

49. Fidler, Jimmie Fidler in Hollywood, *Los Angeles Times,* June 8, 1939.

50. "Reviews of Previews," *The Hollywood-Citizen News,* n.d., USC.

51. *Film Bulletin,* August 12, 1939.

52. Hopper, Hedda Hopper's Hollywood, *Los Angeles Times,* August 8, 1939.

53. Hedda Hopper Collection, AMPAS.

54. "Pocahontas' to Be Filmed," *The New York Times,* August 19, 1939, NYPL.

55. Jimmie Fidler, Fidlings, *Los Angeles Times,* September 30, 1939.

7. GLAMOUR

1. Jimmie Fidler, Fidlings, *Los Angeles Times,* October 12, 1939.

2. *The New York Times,* November 10, 1939, NYPL (Hedy Lamarr files).

3. Hedda Hopper, Hedda Hopper's Hollywood, *Los Angeles Times,* November 25, 1939.

4. Fidler, Jimmie Fidler in Hollywood, *Los Angeles Times,* November 23, 1939.

5. "Hedy Lamarr Ends Contract Dispute," *Los Angeles Times,* November 25, 1939.

6. Ibid.

7. Hedy Lamarr, *Ecstasy and Me: My Life as a Woman* (New York: Bartholomew House, 1966), 92.

8. Larry Swindell, *Spencer Tracy: A Biography* (Cleveland: World, 1969), 159.

9. Ibid.

10. Fidler, Jimmie Fidler in Hollywood, *Los Angeles Times,* January 10, 1940.

11. "Tracy, Hedy Lamarr Team in 'I Take This Woman,'" *Los Angeles Times,* January 27, 1940.

12. Richard Griffith, "'Of Mice and Men' Takes Lead in Critical Favor," *Los Angeles Times,* February 27, 1940.

13. Artur (Arthur) Guttman had composed the musical score for Hedy's earlier film, *Mein braucht kein Geld.* Along with Bronislau Kaper, Guttman did the music for *I Take This Woman* as well.

14. Diane Negra, *Off-White Hollywood: American Culture and Ethnic Female Stardom* (New York: Routledge, 2001), 112.

15. Swindell, *Spencer Tracy,* 159.

16. Ibid.

17. Edwin Schallert, "While the Films Reel By," *Los Angeles Times,* March 3, 1940.

18. Fidler, Jimmie Fidler in Hollywood, *Los Angeles Times,* February 28, 1940.

19. "The Amazing Mr. X" (1940), NYPL.

20. "The Amazing Mr. X" (1940). Mandl moved to Brazil in 1940 and then Argentina shortly afterward. Fritz would eventually become an Argentine citizen and later serve as an advisor to vice president and war minister Colonel Juan Domingo Perón, later the country's dictator. (Allegedly, Mandl also was a film producer, some of his pictures starring Perón's mistress and eventual wife, Eva Duarte.) Mandl founded the IMPA (Industria Metalúrgica y Plástica Argentina), an airplane-manufacturing company in Argentina, in 1944. It was seized in April 1945 by the Argentine government, six months after its opening, having been blacklisted by the Allies. Suspected of having been funded by the Nazis after he left Austria in 1938, Mandl was held under arrest until late July. Securing a release from President Edelmiro J. Farrell, Mandl arrived unexpectedly on July 27 in Colonia, Uruguay, where he was promptly arrested again and taken to Montevideo. He left by riverboat back to Buenos Aires when he was told he was not wanted in Uruguay. Back in Buenos Aires, Mandl was confined to his home by police.

On December 10, 1945, Arnaldo Cortesi wrote in *The New York Times* ("Peron Proved Bar to Inquiry on Foe"): "Colonel Peron intervened with particular energy in favor of . . . Fritz Mandl, Austrian by birth and Argentine by naturalization. . . . Mandl was an Austrian armaments manufacturer and prominent in European politics before his advent in Argentina, where he later acquired citizenship and launched various manufacturing enterprises. There is no direct proof that he ever handled Axis money or actively helped the Germans during the war, but he is on the United States and British blacklists and is considered a dangerous schemer. He played a prominent part as a technical advisor in the Argentine military government's rearmament program and is considered at least partly responsible for implanting in the minds of some Argentine militarists a dream of reuniting the territory of the old Spanish viceroyalty of the River Plate, which included Argentina, Bolivia, Paraguay, and Uruguay."

In November 1947, Mandl made news again when his wife, Herta, accused him of assaulting her in their fashionable Buenos Aires apartment. In early 1948, they divorced. It was estimated at that time that Mandl's worth had grown to over $7.5 million. A proud man who enjoyed an opulent lifestyle (he once owned 278 suits), Fritz fathered two children with Herta, Alexander and Gloria. Mandl's fourth marriage was to Gloria Vinelli, whom he married in Mexico City in 1951. He would father another child, a daughter called by the name of Pupp. His last wife was Monika Brücklmeier, the only daughter of the German diplomat, lawyer, and freedom fighter Eduard Brücklmeier (1903–44), who was involved in the July 20, 1944, assassination attempt on Adolf Hitler. Brücklmeier was found guilty as an accessory on October 20 and hanged the same day.

In 1940 Fritz purchased The White Castle, or El Castillo de Mandl as it has come to be called. In December 2006 the property became an elegant residential hotel.

Pupp Mandl in recent times was quoted as stating her father was an anti-Fascist, though it was true he was a close friend of Mussolini's. When Pupp attended secondary school in Switzerland, Fritz resided in the south of France to be near her. A very private person in his later years, Mandl would return to Austria, taking up residence in Vienna on Argentina Strasse, not far from the Karlskirche where he and Hedy had been married. He died on September 8, 1977, and is buried in the Hirtenberger cemetery.

21. Clark Gable alledgedly allowed Metro's top male star of the late 1920s, the homosexual William Haines, to satisfy his sexual desires with Gable to secure Gable's Metro contract. Gable was, however, latently heterosexual. He fathered Loretta Young's "adopted" daughter, Judy Lewis, in 1935, and a son (John Clark Gable) in 1961.

22. James Reid, "The Hedy Lamarr No One Knows," *Motion Picture*, June 1940.

23. The studio would spend over $37 million for its 1939–40 productions, averaging $777,283 a film. Metro would amass $68 million in total earnings, including $40 million gross from its 125 movie theatres, out of 16,250 U.S. theatres in operation at the time owned by Loew's Inc.

24. Jane Ellen Wayne, *Gable's Women* (New York: Prentice Hall, 1987), 171. In an interesting aside, in Larry Swindell's book on Lombard, he writes, "Spencer Tracy attempted to persuade Carole that she didn't have to worry about Clark staying true-blue, but Carole said, 'Spence, this is one time you're a less than convincing actor.'" *Screwball: The Life of Carole Lombard* (New York: William Morrow, 1975), 271.

25. Fidler, Jimmie Fidler in Hollywood, *Los Angeles Times*, July 15, 1940.

26. Louella Parsons quoted in Fidler, Jimmie Fidler in Hollywood, *Los Angeles Times*, July 15, 1940.

27. Fidler, Jimmie Fidler in Hollywood, *Los Angeles Times*, April 10, 1940.

28. Reid, "Hedy Lamarr No One Knows."

29. "Hedy Lamarr Admits Riff," *Los Angeles Times*, July 7, 1940.

30. Sidney Skolsky, *New York Post*, July 12, 1940.

31. "Heartlines of Hedy," *Photoplay–Movie Mirror*, January 1943.

32. Lamarr, *Ecstasy and Me*, 94.

33. Fidler, Jimmie Fidler in Hollywood, *Los Angeles Times,* July 31, 1940.
34. Chatterbox, *Los Angeles Times,* June 17, 1940.

8. DISCOVERY

1. Frederick Kiesler's two architectural structures were the Film Guild Cinema (1929) in New York and the Shrine of the Book (1954) in Jerusalem. His architectural designs and plans were unorthodox, called "polydimensional." In 1965 he died in New York. In Vienna, in 1997, The Austrian Frederick and Lillian Kiesler Private Foundation was established, and it annually grants the Kiesler Prize for Architecture and the Arts.
2. Gregg Smith, telephone interview by author, June 4, 2008. The Gregg Smith Singers would perform Antheil's 1951 choral piece "8 Fragments from Shelley" in later concerts.
3. George Antheil, *Bad Boy of Music* (Garden City, NY: Doubleday, Doran, 1945), 325.
4. Ibid., 327–28.
5. Ibid., 328–29.
6. Ibid., 330.
7. Ibid., 330–31.
8. Hedy Lamarr, untitled article, n.d., DLDC.
9. Hedy Lamarr, *Ecstasy and Me: My Life as a Woman* (New York: Bartholomew House, 1966), 100.
10. Louella O. Parsons, "'Boom Town' Oil Epic Renews Gable, Tracy Feud; It's a Gusher," *The Los Angeles Examiner,* August 2, 1940.
11. Philip K. Scheuer, *Los Angeles Times,* August 2, 1940.
12. Lawrence J. Quirk, *Claudette Colbert: An Illustrated Biography* (New York: Crown, 1985), 114.
13. Ibid., 113–14.
14. "Screen News Here and in Hollywood," *The New York Times,* August 12, 1940.
15. "Screen News Here and in Hollywood," *The New York Times,* August 22, 1940.
16. The director of such classic silent films for M-G-M as *The Big Parade* (1925) and the early talkie *Hallelujah* (1929), King Vidor was totally wrong for *Comrade X.* Wrote the film curator of the Museum of Modern Art in New York, Charles Silver, "Ten months after its release and following the Soviet entry into the war with Germany, M-G-M had to add an apologetic forward to the film stating, 'nothing in this story should be deemed derogatory to the brave Russian fighters.' Somebody should have apologized to King Vidor." Memo on King Vidor, September 12–November 13, 1972, MOMA.
17. Warren G. Harris, *Clark Gable: A Biography* (New York: Harmony, 2002), 229.
18. Ibid.
19. Bob Edison, "Hubba, Hubba, Hubba—It's Hedy!" *The New York Times,* September 26, 1971.
20. Jean Garceau, *"Dear Mr. G—": The Biography of Clark Gable,* with Inez Locke (Boston: Little, Brown, 1961), 123.

21. David Hough, "Away with Glamour," *Los Angeles Times,* May 31, 1942.

22. Ibid. So much for Hedy's vanity.

23. Florabel Muir, "Lady in The Dark," *Modern Screen,* n.d., USC.

24. "Hedy Lamarr Granted Divorce from Markey," *Los Angeles Times,* September 28, 1940.

25. Ibid.

26. Ibid.

27. During World War II, Markey was awarded the Bronze Star. He became a lieutenant commander, rising to the rank of commodore and eventually being promoted to rear admiral, before retiring from the navy in 1956. His first wife, Joan Bennett, married the producer of *Algiers,* Walter Wanger, on January 12, 1940. On January 3, 1942, Markey married Myrna Loy, who had divorced Arthur Hornblow Jr. In 1950 Markey and Loy divorced. His final marriage was in September 1952 to Lucille Wright, the widow of the baking-powder king Warren Wright, who owned Calumet Farms. Retiring to Kentucky, Markey died there on May 1, 1980.

28. Fidler, Jimmie Fidler in Hollywood, *Los Angeles Times,* September 18, 1940.

29. Philip K. Scheuer, "Town Called Hollywood," *Los Angeles Times,* September 29, 1940.

30. Hopper, Hedda Hopper's Hollywood, *Los Angeles Times,* January 25, 1941.

31. Edison, "Hubba, Hubba, Hubba."

32. Arlene Roxbury interview, May 13, 2008.

33. George Antheil papers, Columbia University, New York.

34. Fidler, Jimmie Fidler in Hollywood, *Los Angeles Times,* November 26, 1940.

35. *Film Daily,* quoted in Young, *The Films of Hedy Lamarr,* 127.

36. Ibid.

37. Edwin Schallert, "'Comrade X' Romps Lustily over Soviet Landscapes," *Los Angeles Times,* December 4, 1940.

9. CAREER

1. George Antheil to Hedy Lamarr, January 10, 1941. George Antheil papers, Columbia University.

2. Marc Eliot, *Jimmy Stewart: A Biography* (New York: Harmony, 2006), 161.

3. Hedy Lamarr, untitled article, n.d., DLDC.

4. John Douglas Eames, *The MGM Story* (New York: Crown, 1975), 168.

5. Donald Dewey, *James Stewart: A Biography* (Atlanta: Turner, 1996), 222.

6. Jeanine Basinger, *Lana Turner* (New York: Pyramid, 1976), 47.

7. Tony Martin, Cyd Charisse, Dick Kleiner, *The Two of Us* (New York: Mason Charter, 1976), 78.

8. Tony Martin, interview by author, May 7, 2007.

9. Lorna Luft, interview by author, July 31, 2009.

10. Dewey, *James Stewart,* 224.

11. David Shipman, *Judy Garland: The Secret Life of an American Legend* (New York: Hyperion, 1993), 120.

12. Dewey, *James Stewart*, 224.

13. Gladys Hall, "I Live for Today," *Silver Screen*, February 1941.

14. Hopper, Hedda Hopper's Hollywood, *Los Angeles Times*, January 25, 1941.

15. Christopher Young, *The Films of Hedy Lamarr* (Secaucus, NJ: Citadel Press, 1978), 131.

16. Jimmie Fidler, Jimmie Fidler in Hollywood, *Los Angeles Times*, February 7, 1941.

17. Hedy Lamarr, *Ecstasy and Me: My Life as a Woman* (New York: Bartholomew House, 1966), 107.

18. Fidler, Jimmie Fidler in Hollywood, *Los Angeles Times*, March 6, 1941.

19. F. M., "The Sound of Lamarr," *Forbes*, May 14, 1990.

20. Shaun Considine, *Bette and Joan: The Divine Feud* (New York: E. P. Dutton, 1984), 87.

21. Julie Goldsmith Gilbert, *Opposite Attraction: The Lives of Erich Maria Remarque and Paulette Goddard* (New York: Pantheon, 1995), 162.

22. Fidler, Jimmie Fidler in Hollywood, *Los Angeles Times*, March 22, 1941.

23. "Walt," *Variety*, April 16, 1941.

24. Hopper, Hedda Hopper's Hollywood, *Los Angeles Times*, April 18, 1941.

25. Young, *Films of Hedy Lamarr*, 143.

26. T. S., *The New York Times*, April 25, 1941.

27. Tony Thomas, *The Busby Berkeley Book* (New York: New York Graphic Society, 1973), 134.

28. Bob Edison, "Hubba, Hubba, Hubba—It's Hedy!" *The New York Times*, September 26, 1971.

29. George Antheil, *Bad Boy of Music* (Garden City, NY: Doubleday, Doran, 1945), 334.

30. Karin Hanta, "Beauty and the Brains," *Austrian Kultur*, May 1997.

31. Hans-Joachim Braun, "Advanced Weaponry of the Stars," *Invention and Technology Magazine*, Spring 1997.

32. "Lamarr Threat Suspect Seized," *The New York Daily Mirror*, July 5, 1941.

33. Fidler, Jimmie Fidler in Hollywood, *Los Angeles Times*, May 14, 1941.

34. Gladys Hall, "As I See Myself," *Motion Picture*, February 1942.

35. Lamarr, *Ecstasy and Me*, 111

36. Hedy's character was called Johnny Jones in *Come Live with Me*, Theodore in *Comrade X*, and Marvin in *H.M. Pulham, Esq.*, which led Hedy to remark, "Why, I wondered, did they give a supposedly sexy lady such weird names? Ah, Hollywood!" Edison, "Hubba, Hubba, Hubba."

37. Macdonald Carey, *The Days of My Life* (New York: St. Martin's, 1991), 82–83.

38. Lee Server, *Ava Gardner: "Love Is Nothing"* (New York: St. Martin's, 2006), 49–50.

10. ACTRESS

1. The King Vidor Collection, USC.

2. Gladys Hall, "As I See Myself—by Hedy Lamarr," *Motion Picture*, February 1942.

3. Douglas W. Churchill, "Matters of the Moment in Hollywood," *The New York Times*, September 7, 1941.

4. Ibid.

5. Frank Daugherty, "Hollywood at Work," *The Christian Science Monitor*, September 17, 1941.

6. The King Vidor Collection, USC.

7. The King Vidor Collection, USC.

8. Hall, "As I See Myself."

9. Hedda Hopper, Hedda Hopper's Hollywood, *Los Angeles Times*, July 21, 1941.

10. Jimmie Fidler, Jimmie Fidler in Hollywood, *Los Angeles Times*, September 12, 1941.

11. Muriel Reed, "Inventive Venus," [1942?], NYPL (Hedy Lamarr files).

12. "Hedy Lamarr Inventor," *The New York Times*, October 1, 1941.

13. Hopper, Hedda Hopper's Hollywood, *Los Angeles Times*, October 15, 1941.

14. John Kobal, *People Will Talk* (New York: Alfred A. Knopf, 1985), 379.

15. Ibid., 271

16. "I Am Hedy Lamarr," n.d., NYPL (Hedy Lamarr files).

17. Thomas Brady, "It Happened in Monterey," *The New York Times*, November 30, 1941.

18. Margaret O'Brien, interview by author, March 5, 2007.

19. Gladys Hall, "Hedy Lamarr's Diary," *Movies*, n.d., DLDC.

20. "You'll Pull for *Pulham*," Lion's Roar, *Los Angeles Times*, December 7, 1941.

21. *Daily Variety*, November 13, 1941.

22. "A Vidor Triumph: Young, Lamarr Tops," *The Hollywood Reporter*, November 13, 1942.

23. Bosley Crowther, The Screen in Review, *The New York Times*, December 19, 1941.

24. Christopher Young, *The Films of Hedy Lamarr* (Secaucus, NJ: Citadel Press, 1978), 148.

25. Ibid., 147.

26. Hopper, Hedda Hopper's Hollywood, *Los Angeles Times*, February 9, 1941.

27. Ibid. Metro dragged the property out again in 1943 as a vehicle for Joan Fontaine. And in 1945 the studio attempted unsuccessfully to combine *Forever* with another property, *Flight from Youth*. Tyrone Power shopped it around to his many actress girlfriends, including Judy Garland. Dick Haymes wanted the vehicle for Rita Hayworth, then his wife. And at one time even Richard Rodgers and Oscar Hammerstein II were interested in turning it into a stage musical. Metro spent a small fortune bringing it to light one more time, in 1959, as a property for their newest hot item, George Hamilton. The picture has yet to be made.

28. Gladys Hall, "Hedl in Hollywood," *Silver Screen*, August 1942.

29. Hedy Lamarr, "Loneliest Woman in Hollywood," *Silver Screen*, February 1943.

30. Hopper, Hedda Hopper's Hollywood, *Los Angeles Times*, April 22, 1942.

31. "A Word on George Montgomery, Recently of Mr. Zanuck's Finishing School," *The New York Times*, May 24, 1942.

32. Hall, "Hedl in Hollywood."

33. Ibid.

34. Kay Proctor, "Play Truth or Consequences with Hedy Lamarr," *Photoplay*, November 1942.

35. "Heartlines of Hedy," *Photoplay,* January 1943.

36. Hedy Lamarr, *Ecstasy and Me: My Life as a Woman* (New York: Bartholomew House, 1966), 116.

37. Lamarr, "Loneliest Woman in Hollywood."

38. Hobe, *Variety,* April 22, 1942.

39. Kenneth McCaleb, "'Tortilla Flat' Wears It Well," *The New York Sunday Mirror,* May 17, 1942.

40. Bosley Crowther, The Screen in Review, *The New York Times,* May 22, 1942.

41. Louella O. Parsons, "'Tortilla Flat' Wins Praise as Film Play," June 5, 1942, USC.

42. Hopper, Hedda Hopper's Hollywood, *Los Angeles Times,* January 2, 1951.

43. Rudy Behlmer, *Inside Warner Brothers 1935–1951* (New York: Viking, 1985), 164.

44. On April 17, 1942, the director Vincent Sherman tested Jean-Pierre Aumont for the role of Victor, portrayed eventually by Paul Henreid.

11. BATTLE

1. *White Cargo* papers, AMPAS.

2. Hedy Lamarr, *Ecstasy and Me: My Life as a Woman* (New York: Bartholomew House, 1966), 118.

3. Internet Movie Database, listing for Walter Pidgeon, http://www.imdb.com.

4. Hedda Hopper, Hedda Hopper's Hollywood, *Los Angeles Times,* n.d., DLDC.

5. Christopher Young, *The Films of Hedy Lamarr* (Secaucus, NJ: Citadel Press, 1978), 161.

6. Ibid., 159.

7. Ibid., 161.

8. Lamarr, *Ecstasy and Me,* 113.

9. Hedy Lamarr, "Loneliest Woman in Hollywood," *Silver Screen,* February 1943.

10. Hearst newsreel, UCLA Film and Television Archive.

11. "Hedy Lamarr Sells $4,547,000 Bonds," *The New York Times,* September 2, 1942.

12. Untitled article, n.d., DLDC.

13. Hedy Lamarr, "Hedy Lamarr Tells About War Bond Tour," *The Cleveland Plain Dealer,* September 13, 1942.

14. Lamarr, "Loneliest Woman in Hollywood."

15. "Star Saleslady "Hedy Enjoys Bond Selling," *Los Angeles Examiner,* n.d., USC.

16. "'White Cargo' Sure of Hit," *The Hollywood Reporter,* September 15, 1942.

17. "Scho," *Variety,* September 16, 1942.

18. Bosley Crowther, The Screen in Review, *The New York Times,* November 27, 1942.

19. Bosley Crowther, "Better and/or Worse," *The New York Times,* November 29, 1942.

20. Lamarr, *Ecstasy and Me,* 118.

21. Bob Edison, "Hubba, Hubba, Hubba—It's Hedy!" *The New York Times,* September 26, 1971.

22. Lamarr, *Ecstasy and Me,* 118.

23. Peter Hay, *MGM: When the Lion Roared* (Atlanta: Turner, 1991), 202.

24. Edwin Schallert, "Aumont, Lamarr Will Costar as Guerillas," *Los Angeles Times,* November 3, 1942.

25. Aumont made only one more picture for the studio, *Cross of Lorraine,* before enlisting as a French resistance fighter in the Free French Forces, and, while assigned to North Africa, he participated in Operation Torch in Tunisia. He was wounded twice while in Europe moving with the Allied armies in France and Italy and received the Legion d'Honneur and the Croix de Guerre. He married the actress Maria Montez shortly before leaving Hollywood in 1943, married another actress, Marisa Pavan, after Montez's death, and continued making films up until his death in January 2001.

26. The Hollywood Canteen, inspired by the success of the Stage Door Canteen in New York, would cost around $3,000 a week to run, the motion picture and entertainment industry supplying the funds. It closed its doors on Thanksgiving Day, November 22, 1945.

27. Lamarr, "Loneliest Woman in Hollywood."

28. Untitled article, n.d., DLDC.

29. Robin Loder later became an agent and was the husband of the late actress Hilary Tindall, who starred in the 1970s British BBC television series *The Brothers.*

30. "Of Love and Donuts," *Modern Screen,* September 1943.

31. Ibid.

32. Sidney Skolsky, "Handbook on Hedy," *Photoplay,* May 1944.

33. John Loder, *Hollywood Hussar: The Life and Times of John Loder* (London: Howard Baker, 1977), 131.

34. Hedda Hopper, Looking at Hollywood, *Los Angeles Times,* April 15, 1943.

35. Irene Collection, scrapbook, AMPAS.

36. Florabel Muir, "Lady in the Dark," *Modern Screen,* n.d., USC.

37. Fearless, "Crazy In Love," *Photoplay,* February 1944.

38. Loder, *Hollywood Hussar,* 132–33.

39. The picture would not be released until 1946.

40. Skolsky, "Handbook on Hedy."

41. "Hedy Becomes a Bride," *Photoplay,* n.d., USC.

12. MARRIAGE

1. John Loder, *Hollywood Hussar: The Life and Times of John Loder* (London: Howard Baker, 1977), 133.

2. Kitty Callahan, *Family Circle,* September 24, 1943.

3. Diana Barrymore and Gerold Frank, *Too Much, Too Soon* (New York: Holt, 1957), 193.

4. Kay Proctor, "My Son and I," n.d., NYPL.

5. Loder, *Hollywood Hussar,* 133.

6. Hedy Lamarr, *Ecstasy and Me: My Life as a Woman* (New York: Bartholomew House, 1966), 123.

7. Bob Edison, "Hubba, Hubba, Hubba—It's Hedy!" *The New York Times,* September 26, 1971.

8. Burt Prelutsky, "In the Balcony with 'Laura,'" *Los Angeles Times,* June 13, 1976.

9. Bob Edison, *Films in Review,* June–July 1974, 351.

10. Loder, *Hollywood Hussar,* 137.

11. James Lee, *American Weekly* (1941), NYPL (Hedy Lamarr files).

12. "Hedy Lamarr's Mate Now Legally Free of Ex-Wife," *Los Angeles Times,* September 28, 1943.

13. Edwin Schallert, "Hedy Seeks Dream Role," *Los Angeles Times,* October 17, 1943.

14. Loder, *Hollywood Hussar,* 134.

15. Edison, *Films in Review,* June–July 1974, 351.

16. Hal B. Wallis, interoffice memo to Roy Obringer, *The Conspirators* papers, USC.

17. Warner Bros. archives, interoffice memo, February 18, 1944 (USC). In the final outcome, John Garfield would only make one M-G-M film per this contract, *The Postman Always Rings Twice,* in 1945, with Lana Turner. On May 21, 1952, the thirty-nine-year-old Garfield died of a heart attack.

18. Stephen D. Youngkin, Raymond G. Cabana Jr., and James Biguoco, *The Films of Peter Lorre* (Secaucus, NJ: Citadel Press, 1982), 172.

19. Loder, *Hollywood Hussar,* 135.

20. *Silver Screen,* n.d., DLDC.

21. Stephen D. Youngkin, *The Lost One: A Life of Peter Lorre* (Lexington, KY: University Press of Kentucky, 2005), 220.

22. *Silver Screen,* n.d., DLDC.

23. *Harrison's Reports,* n.d., MOMA.

24. Christopher Young, *The Films of Hedy Lamarr* (Secaucus, NJ: Citadel Press, 1982), 173.

25. "Hedy Lamarr Files Denial in Author's Suit," *Los Angeles Times*, April 22, 1944.

26. Production notes for *The Conspirators,* USC.

27. Hedda Hopper, Looking at Hollywood, *Los Angeles Times,* April 22, 1944.

28. Lamarr, *Ecstasy and Me,* 124.

29. James Robert Parish and Don E. Stanke, *The Debonairs* (New Rochelle, NY: Arlington, 1975), 49.

13. INDEPENDENCE

1. James Lamarr Loder quoted in *Hedy Lamarr: Secrets of a Hollywood Star,* 2005.

2. Edwin Schallert, "Hedy Seeks Dream Role," *Los Angeles Times,* October 17, 1943.

3. Macdonald Carey, *The Days of My Life* (New York: St. Martin's, 1991), 164.

4. "Hedgerow—Exclusive Color Pictures of the Hilltop Home of Hedy Lamarr and John Loder," Kodachromes by Len Weissman, *Motion Picture,* July 1944.

5. Ibid.

6. John Loder, *Hollywood Hussar: The Life and Times of John Loder* (London: Howard Baker, 1977), 135.

7. Ibid., 135–36.

8. Jody Jacobs, "St. Laurent Fans Catch the Scent," *Los Angeles Times,* September 25, 1978.

9. Hedy Lamarr, *Ecstasy and Me: My Life as a Woman* (New York: Bartholomew House, 1966), 126.

10. Lamarr, *Ecstasy and Me*, 127.

11. Bosley Crowther, The Screen, *The New York Times,* October 21, 1944.

12. Stephen D. Youngkin, *The Lost One: A Life of Peter Lorre* (Lexington, KY: University of Kentucky Press, 2005), 221.

13. Jean Negulesco, *Things I Did and Things I Think I Did: A Hollywood Memoir* (New York: Simon & Schuster, 1984), 122.

14. Scott Eyman, *Lion of Hollywood: The Life and Legend of Louis B. Mayer* (New York: Simon & Schuster, 2005), 366.

15. Lorania K. Francis, "Louis B. Mayer Again Holds Income List Lead," *Los Angeles Times,* October 13, 1944.

16. Eyman, *Lion of Hollywood,* 365.

17. Lamarr, *Ecstasy and Me,* 133.

18. Edward Z. Epstein, *Portrait of Jennifer* (New York: Simon & Schuster, 1996), 146.

19. Christopher Young, *The Films of Hedy Lamarr* (Secaucus, NJ: Citadel Press, 1978), 182.

20. Ibid., 183.

21. T. M. P., *The New York Times,* December 30, 1944.

22. Young, *Films of Hedy Lamarr,* 183.

23. Chris Fujiwara, *Jacques Tourneur: The Cinema of Nightfall* (Baltimore: Johns Hopkins University Press, 1998).

24. After turning in brilliant performances in Metro's *The Clock* (1945), with Judy Garland, and *Song of Love* (1947), with Katharine Hepburn, Walker suffered a nervous breakdown. He died unexpectedly on August 28, 1951, from a reaction to alcohol and sodium amytal administered by his psychiatrist. He was thirty-two years old.

25. June Allyson, *June Allyson*, with Frances Spatz Leighton (New York: Putnam, 1982), 53.

26. Ibid., 52.

27. Bob Edison, "Hubba, Hubba, Hubba—It's Hedy!" *The New York Times,* September 26, 1971.

28. Arlene Roxbury, interview by author, July 11, 2008.

29. Lamarr, *Ecstasy and Me,* 128.

30. Ibid., 129.

31. "Thorpe Does Well with Lean Script," *The Hollywood Reporter,* July 11, 1945.

32. Young, *Films of Hedy Lamarr,* 187.

33. Ibid.

34. "The New Pictures" *Time,* October 1, 1945.

35. T. M. P., "'Her Highness and Bellboy' with Robert Walker and Hedy Lamarr in Principal Roles, Opens at Capitol Theatre," *The New York Times,* September 28, 1945.

36. Hedy Lamarr, "This Is Myself," *Movieland,* n.d., USC.

37. In *Her Highness and the Bellboy,* Allyson blows her one big chance in her one big scene requiring tears. Not a drop. The champ "sob sister" at Metro would always undeniably remain Margaret O'Brien.

38. Todd S. Purdum, "Children of Paradise," *Vanity Fair,* March 2009. Denise Loder-DeLuca recalled that *Her Highness and the Bellboy* was the very first of Hedy's films that her mother ever took her and her younger brother Anthony to see. Because it had a fairy-tale plot, Hedy assumed that it was something children would enjoy. But when Hedy's character Veronica is arrested and slapped into jail, the fun stopped. "And we got hysterical," Denise recalled. "We saw Mommy behind bars and we just went crazy."

39. *The Los Angeles Examiner,* n.d., USC.

40. George Antheil, *Bad Boy of Music* (Garden City, NY: Doubleday, Doran, 1945), 346.

41. Also in discussion was *White Jade,* a property owned by the director Tay Garnett using ten-year-old leftover footage from United Artists' 1938 *Trade Winds,* which would have saved the company about $100,000.

42. Errol Flynn, *My Wicked, Wicked Ways: The Autobiography of Errol Flynn* (New York: Cooper Square, 2003), 255.

43. Ibid.

44. Ibid., 256. *William Tell* would have actually been the very first CinemaScope feature film. For his female lead Flynn settled for the actress Antonella Lualdi. After a few weeks of shooting, the picture folded and was never completed.

45. Louella O. Parsons, "Hedy Lamarr," In Hollywood, n.d., USC.

46. Ibid.

47. Ibid.

48. Anthony Summers and Robbyn Swan, "The Hidden Life of Hedy Lamarr," *Talk,* March 3, 2001.

14. PRODUCER

1. Hedy Lamarr, *Ecstasy and Me: My Life as a Woman* (New York: Bartholomew House, 1966), 143–44.

2. Ibid. Actually, Hedy must have been referring to the seduction scene at Ephraim's shack during a raging rainstorm. And no robe slips off.

3. Lamarr, *Ecstasy and Me,* 143.

4. Anthony Summers and Robbyn Swan, "The Hidden Life of Hedy Lamarr," *Talk,* March 3, 2001.

5. "Hedy Lamarr Confirms Quarrel and Parting," *Los Angeles Times,* January 19, 1946.

6. Ibid.

7. Louella O. Parsons, "The Strange Case of Hedy Lamarr," *Photoplay*, September 1947.

8. John Loder, *Hollywood Hussar: The Life and Times of John Loder* (London: Howard Baker, 1977), 136.

9. "Hedy Lamarr Sobs over Young Burglary Suspect," *Los Angeles Times*, May 20, 1946.

10. Ibid.

11. In 1940, Hitchcock announced that he would direct *The Paradine Case* for Selznick, which would star Leslie Howard and Hedy. The deal fell through. The project lay in limbo until 1946, when Hitchcock, at the time working independently, was casting a new version, set to star Laurence Olivier as the barrister. When Olivier bowed out, Ronald Colman was offered the role, with Ingrid Bergman as Mrs. Paradine. Then Bergman became unavailable and Hedy was reconsidered. Donald Spoto, *The Dark Side of Genius: The Life of Alfred Hitchcock* (Boston: Back Bay, 1993), 294.

12. In 1950 the definitive *Madeleine*, directed by David Lean and starring Ann Todd, was filmed, and it was based on the Smith case.

13. Joseph I. Breen, memo, February 23, 1946, *Dishonored Lady* papers, AMPAS.

14. Robert Stevenson was brought to Hollywood by David O. Selznick after Stevenson directed several small British films, the most important being Gaumont Pictures' 1937 *King Solomon's Mines*, which starred Paul Robeson and John Loder. Under contract with Selznick for ten years, Stevenson was consistently loaned out and never actually directed a film for the producer. Stevenson, a quiet, effective director, was forty-two years old when he directed *Dishonored Lady*. He signed a contract with Walt Disney Productions in 1956 and directed twenty films for the company, including *Old Yeller* (1957), *The Absent-Minded Professor* (1961), and *Mary Poppins* (1964), for which he was nominated for a Best Director Oscar (the only Disney director ever to be so honored). All his Disney-directed films were major blockbusters. Stevenson holds the distinctive honor of possibly being *the* most profitable film director in motion picture history. He died in 1986.

15. Untitled article, n.d., DLDC.

16. Loder, *Hollywood Hussar*, 136.

17. Lamarr, *Ecstasy and Me*, 162.

18. "Hedy Lamarr Sues Company for Property," *Los Angeles Times*, July 21, 1946.

19. Loder, *Hollywood Hussar*, 136.

20. "Hedy Lamarr and John Loder Expect Stork in Spring," *Los Angeles Times*, April 22, 1946.

21. Lamarr, *Ecstasy and Me*, 138.

22. Lamarr, *Ecstasy and Me*, 138.

23. Kay Proctor, "Was Hedy Jinxed?" n.d., NYPL (Hedy Lamarr files).

24. "Bogart Pair Setting Gay Pace for Hollywoodians," *Los Angeles Times*, September 15, 1946. The Bogarts officially purchased Hedgerow on July 6, 1948. It would later be sold by Bacall after Bogart's death in 1957, to a writer, and then in 1979 to Ann-Margret and her husband, the actor Roger Smith.

25. George Antheil, *Bad Boy of Music* (Garden City, NY: Doubleday, Doran, 1945), 332.

26. Brog, *Variety*, October 26, 1946.

27. Philip K. Scheuer, "Hedy Plays Evil Woman," *Los Angeles Times,* December 21, 1946.

28. Jack D. Grant, "Hedy Makes Strong Academy Award Bid," *The Hollywood Reporter,* October 28, 1946.

29. "Plea Concerning Stork Fails to Aid Hedy Lamarr," *Los Angeles Times,* January 11, 1947.

30. Thomas F. Brady, "Garfield Signed for Role at Fox," *The New York Times,* May 21, 1947.

31. Earl Wilson, "'Mr. Hedy Lamarr' Revolts, Will Make a Name for Himself," *New York Post,* April 6, 1947.

32. Jack D. Grant, "Lamarr in Second Unit Arts Hit," *The Hollywood Reporter,* April 21, 1947.

33. Christopher Young, *The Films of Hedy Lamarr* (Secaucus, NJ: Citadel Press, 1978), 197.

34. Edward Margulis, "Bad Movies We Love," *Movieline,* July 1996.

35. Loder, *Hollywood Hussar,* 138.

36. Florabel Muir, "Lady in the Dark," *Modern Screen,* n.d., USC.

37. "Hedy Lamarr Sues to Divorce John Loder," *Los Angeles Times,* July 4, 1947.

38. "Hedy Lamarr Divorces 'Indifferent' Husband," *Los Angeles Times,* July 18, 1947.

39. Ibid.

40. Muir, "Lady in the Dark."

41. Internet Movie Database, listing for Hedy Lamarr, http://www.imdb.com.

15. DELILAH

1. Louella O. Parsons, "The Strange Case of Hedy Lamarr," *Photoplay,* September 1947, USC.

2. Loder would later marry Evelyn Carolan Auffmordt, the mother of a seven-year-old daughter, on November 23, 1949, in New York. He divorced Auffmordt in 1955 and was married for the fifth and last time to the thirty-eight-year-old South American beauty Alba Julia Lagomarsino (Larden) near London in a civil ceremony on September 22, 1958. They would remain wed until Loder's death on December 26, 1988. On August 17, 2006, a one-act play called *Hedy Lamarr and the Easter Rising* was staged at Bewley's Café Theatre in Dublin, written by its star, Michael James Ford, staged by Trevor Knight, and designed by Jack Kirwan. It was a one-man show, a long fifty-minute monologue in which Ford, portraying Loder, reminisces about his life and loves.

3. Florabel Muir, "Out of Happiness," *Modern Screen,* n.d., USC.

4. Ibid.

5. Annelle Hayes divorced Stevens and named Hedy in her complaint. Stevens died in Spain in 1994.

6. Parsons, "Strange Case of Hedy Lamarr."

7. Frank Brady, *Citizen Welles: A Biography of Orson Welles* (New York: Scribner, 1989), 417.

8. Hedy Lamarr, *Ecstasy and Me: My Life as a Woman* (New York: Bartholomew House, 1966), 166–67.

9. Hedda Hopper, Looking at Hollywood, *Los Angeles Times,* December 26, 1947.

10. Thomas F. Brady, "Hollywood Memos," *Los Angeles Times,* March 21, 1948.

11. Ibid.

12. Hopper, Looking at Hollywood, *Los Angeles Times*, March 17, 1948.

13. James Lamarr Loder quoted in Donatella Dubini and Fosco Dubini, *Hedy Lamarr: Confessions of a Hollywood Star*, Dubini Filmproduktion, 2006.

14. Anthony Summers and Robbyn Swan, "The Hidden Life of Hedy Lamarr," *Talk*, March 3, 2001.

15. Parsons, "The Strange Case of Hedy Lamarr."

16. Louella O. Parsons, *Los Angeles Examiner*, n.d., USC.

17. Parsons, "The Strange Case of Hedy Lamarr."

18. "Hedy Lamarr Asks Damages of $200,000," *Los Angeles Times*, April 16, 1948.

19. Lamarr, *Ecstasy and Me*, 168.

20. Ibid., 170.

21. Ibid., 171.

22. Gabe Essoe and Raymond Lee, *DeMille: The Man and His Pictures* (Cranbury, NJ: A.S. Barnes, 1970), 195.

23. Phil Koury, "Haircut by DeMille," *The New York Times*, June 20, 1948.

24. Cecil B. DeMille Collection, BYU. Yet another possibility for Samson was the bodybuilder Steve Reeves. DeMille viewed Reeves's test and noted, "I expected to say send him back, but you can't say it. He has a magnificent body and voice. He is not good, but he is better than I thought he would be. Give him three hours a day of intensive coaching." DeMille reviewed another film test of Reeves in modern dress and noted, "He's a lot better than he was last time." Eventually, Reeves failed to make the grade. DeMille also viewed tests of John Bromfield and Rory Calhoun in a scene from *Johnny Belinda*. Neither actor was good. On February 20, 1948, Lex Barker was added as a possibility. DeMille sent a telegram to Paramount stating, "John Bromfield still my first choice for Samson." Eventually, DeMille chose to go with a more seasoned actor. Cecil B. DeMille Collection, BYU.

25. Others on the list were Murvyn Vye, Bill Bishop, Glenn Langan, John Ireland, and, once again, John Bromfield. Cecil B. DeMille Collection, BYU.

26. Also on that list were Claude Rains, Howard da Silva, John Hoyt, Ralph Richardson, Robert Morley, Leo Genn, Roland Culver, Lee J. Cobb, José Ferrer, Alan Napier, Marcel Journet, and Vincent Price. Cecil B. DeMille Collection, BYU.

27. Robert S. Birchard, *Cecil B. DeMille's Hollywood* (Lexington, KY: University Press of Kentucky, 2004), 336.

28. DeMille, surprisingly, considered wholesome Nancy Olson. Other actresses listed were Ann Sheridan, Diana Lynn, Mona Freeman, Joan Fontaine, Jane Russell, Ella Raines, Maureen O'Hara, Gene Tierney, Wanda Hendrix, Jane Greer, Barbara Bel Geddes (who wanted $100,000 per picture—$5,000 a week), Vivian Blaine, Evelyn Keyes, Ruth Hussey, Maria Montez, Lizabeth Scott, and Viveca Lindfors. Hedy was not DeMille's first choice for Delilah. On May 15, 1948, DeMille sent a telegram to Paramount's Donald Hayne in New York at the Plaza Hotel, knowing that Rita Hayworth was unhappy with her new

picture assignment at her home studio: "I am wondering if [Russell] Holman could now get Columbia to loan her to us for Delilah." Apparently Holman and no one else could pry Rita away from Columbia studio boss Harry Cohn. Cecil B. DeMille Collection, BYU.

29. Other actresses listed were Alexis Smith, Virginia Grey, Andrea King, and Hillary Brooke. Ilona Massey was once considered for the part of Semadar but did not make the list, as was Geraldine Brooks (wrote one assistant: "opens mouth habit"). And Elizabeth Taylor was briefly considered for the role of Miriam, as were Jeanne Cagney and Cathy Downs. Cecil B. DeMille Collection, BYU.

30. Both Hedy's stand-in Sylvia Lamarr (Hollis) and Mature's stand-in Kay Bell were paid $100 a week for twelve weeks. George Sanders, who signed in July, received $75,000— $7,500 per week. And Angela Lansbury, borrowed from Metro in September, was paid $40,000 for seven weeks, with one week free if necessary, then pro rata at $5,714.28 per week. Rusty (Russ) Tamblyn was paid $750 a week, and the dwarfs in the arena sequence were paid $75 a week. Cecil B. DeMille Collection, BYU.

31. Edwin Schallert, "Hollywood in Review," *Los Angeles Times,* January 22, 1950.

32. Ibid.

33. Hopper, Looking at Hollywood, *Los Angeles Times,* June 25, 1948.

34. Hedy Lamarr, telegram to Cecil B. DeMille, July 7, 1948, Cecil B. DeMille Collection, BYU.

35. Cecil B. DeMille, letter to Hedy Lamarr, July 8, 1948, Cecil B. DeMille Collection, BYU.

36. David Chierichetti, *The Life and Times of Hollywood's Celebrated Costume Designer Edith Head* (New York: HarperCollins, 2003), 116.

37. Lamarr, *Ecstasy and Me,* 173–74.

38. Ibid., 174.

39. Chierichetti, *Life and Times,* 81–83.

40. Ibid., 84.

41. Cecil B. DeMille, Western Union telegram to Hedy Lamarr, August 20, 1948, Cecil B. DeMille Collection, BYU.

42. Hedy Lamarr, telegram to Cecil B. DeMille, August 22, 1948, Cecil B. DeMille Collection, BYU.

43. Birchard, *Cecil B. DeMille's Hollywood,* 337.

44. James Robert Parish and Don E. Stanke, *The Swashbucklers* (New Rochelle, NY: Arlington, 1976), 453.

45. Ibid., 450.

46. Robert Osborne, interview by author, June 6, 2007.

47. Birchard, *Cecil B. DeMille's Hollywood,* 337.

48. Anthony Cassa, "Hedy Lamarr: The Heavenly Body," *Hollywood Studio,* February– March 1981.

49. Bob Edison, "Hubba, Hubba, Hubba—It's Hedy!" *The New York Times,* September 26, 1971.

50. It landed Farnum a $1,000 guarantee; he made $2,833. Olsen was given $1,500 for one week's guarantee. Varconi was paid $500 a week, with two weeks' guarantee. He had starred in DeMille's *The Volga Boatman* in 1926 and *The King of Kings* in 1927. Nils As-

ther was paid $500 for one week's work. *Samson and Delilah* was Mayo's last film. He was once married to the screen vamp Dagmar Godowsky.

51. Julia Faye made $500 a week, ending up with a total of $4,333.

16. PARAMOUNT

1. *Daily Variety,* October 26, 1948.
2. Philip K. Scheuer, "Hedy Lamarr, As Bedevil Robert Cummings," *Los Angeles Times,* December 23, 1948.
3. The Robert Cummings Papers, L. Tom Perry Special Collections, BYU.
4. Hedda Hopper, "Hedy's a Homebody," Looking at Hollywood.
5. Cecil B. DeMille Papers, L. Tom Perry Special Collections, BYU.
6. Osborne interview.
7. Macdonald Carey, *The Days of My Life* (New York: St. Martin's, 1991), 164.
8. Harry Carey Jr., telephone interview by author, June 14, 2008.
9. "Hedy Lamarr Unnoticed by 200 at Airport," *Los Angeles Times,* August 28, 1949.
10. Cecil B. DeMille, telegram to Hedy Lamarr, September 7, 1949, Cecil B. DeMille Papers, L. Tom Perry Special Collections, BYU.
11. Cecil B. DeMille, *The Autobiography of Cecil B. DeMille* (Englewood Cliffs, NJ: Prentice Hall, 1959), 401.
12. Ivan Spear, *Boxoffice,* October 22, 1949.
13. Christopher Young, *The Films of Hedy Lamarr* (Secaucus, NJ: Citadel Press, 1978), 209.
14. Bosley Crowther, "Lavish De Mille Film Arrives," *The New York Times,* December 22, 1949.
15. Internet Movie Database, listing for *Samson and Delilah,* http://www.imdb.com.
16. *Newsweek,* "Hedy Lamarr as Delilah," November 28, 1949.
17. Bob Edison, "Hubba, Hubba, Hubba—It's Hedy!" *The New York Times,* September 26, 1971.
18. DeMille, *Autobiography,* 400.
19. Hedy Lamarr, *Ecstasy and Me: My Life as a Woman* (New York: Bartholomew House, 1966), 185.
20. Ibid., 186.
21. Ibid., 186–87.
22. Arlene Dahl, interview by author, June 14, 2008.
23. John Hodiak, "Hedy Really Surprised Me," *Screenland,* July 1950.
24. Hedda Hopper, Drama, "Widmark Will Rest Before Marine Story," *Los Angeles Times,* February 13, 1950.
25. Edwin Schallert, "Hollywood in Review," *Los Angeles Times,* January 22, 1950.
26. Ibid.
27. Hedy Lamarr, telegram to Cecil B. DeMille, March 14, 1950, BYU.
28. Cecil B. DeMille, telegram to Hedy Lamarr, March 15, 1950, BYU.
29. Igor Cassini, "New Yorker Dates Hedy," *The Los Angeles Examiner,* June 21, 1950.

30. Ibid.

31. Denise Loder-DeLuca, interview with author, 2008.

32. Hodiak, "Hedy Really Surprised Me."

33. Dahl interview.

17. ADRIFT

1. Cecil B. DeMille, letter to Hedy Lamarr, July 13, 1950, BYU.

2. G. K., "Hedy Enacts 'Lady Without Passport,'" *Los Angeles Times,* September 15, 1950.

3. Christopher Young, *The Films of Hedy Lamarr* (Secaucus, NJ: 1978), 213.

4. Perhaps the best reflection on *A Lady Without Passport* appears in the definitive book, *Film Noir: An Encyclopedic Reference to the American Style*: "Utilizing a number of noir conventions ranging from the exotic *femme fatale*, to decadent villainy and hard-boiled heroes, without any real noir insight, this production falls into that category of films made during the noir period that reproduce the look but without the complex ethos of true noir." Carl Macek, "A Lady Without Passport," in Alain Silver and Elizabeth Ward, eds., with the assistance of Carl Macek and Robert Porfirio (New York: Outlook, 1993), 168.

5. Louella O. Parsons, "Hedy Lamarr Reveals She'll Retire from Films," *Los Angeles Examiner,* January 24, 1951.

6. Paulette Goddard was certain the role of Angel would be hers once Hedy had declined the part. Goddard did not land it, and the part was then offered to Lucille Ball. Ball then discovered she was pregnant, and her contract was mutually canceled by DeMille and Paramount on December 19. Once again DeMille's past stars were advised the film was commencing. Some who were desperate were not used—like Mary Earle, Edna Bennett, and Cleo Ridgely. A more tragic figure was sixty-seven-year-old Francis X. Bushman (he had played Messala to Ramon Novarro's Ben-Hur in Metro's 1924 film epic), an actor who had not had a job in pictures since 1944. Bushman begged DeMille for a few days' work and wrote he was about to lose his house. He did not get a part. But DeMille's ever faithful, tiny-footed Julia Faye was hired at $500 a week to portray the circus "wardrobe mistress" Birdie. *The Greatest Show on Earth* would eventually outgross *Samson and Delilah* and bring DeMille his only Oscar win for Best Picture.

7. Hedy Lamarr, *Ecstasy and Me: My Life as a Woman* (New York: Bartholomew House, 1966), 191.

8. Edwin Schallert, "'Copper Canyon' Keeps Westerns on the March," *Los Angeles Times,* November 17, 1950.

9. Bosley Crowther, *The New York Times,* November 16, 1950.

10. James Robert Parish and Don E. Stanke, *The Debonairs* (New Rochelle, NY: Arlington, 1975), 267.

11. Lamarr, *Ecstasy and Me,* 193.

12. Parsons, "Hedy Lamarr Reveals She'll Retire from Films."

13. Hedy Lamarr, letter to Cecil B. DeMille, March 14, 1951, BYU.

14. Hedda Hopper, Drama, "Studios Offered Idea for 'American Story'," *Los Angeles Times,* April 10, 1951.

15. Lamarr, *Ecstasy and Me,* 208.

16. Hedda Hopper, "Old Stellar System Passe, Says Zanuck," *Los Angeles Times,* June 11, 1951.

17. "Hedy Lamarr Weds Night Club Owner," *Los Angeles Times,* June 12, 1951.

18. Pete Martin, "Hedy Sells Her Past," *Saturday Evening Post,* September 29, 1951.

19. Ibid.

20. Lamarr, *Ecstasy and Me,* 177.

21. Ibid., 203.

22. Christopher Young, *The Films of Hedy Lamarr* (Secaucus, NJ: Citadel Press, 1978), 221.

23. Ibid.

24. Lawrence J. Quirk, *Bob Hope: The Road Less Traveled* (New York: Applause Theater & Cinema Books, 1998), 222.

25. Lamarr, *Ecstasy and Me,* 214.

18. ITALY

1. "Hedy Lamarr Files for 4th Decree," *Los Angeles Times,* February 14, 1952.

2. Farley Granger, telephone interview by author, November 6, 2007.

3. Hedy Lamarr, *Ecstasy and Me: My Life as a Woman* (New York: Bartholomew House, 1966), 218.

4. "Hedy Lamarr Says Husband Beat Her," *Los Angeles Times,* March 18, 1952. On March 13, 1953, Teddy Stauffer married Anne Nekel Brown of New York. Hedy and Teddy's divorce was final ten days later. Teddy eventually wed three more times, all the unions ending in divorce. With his last wife, Patricia Morgan, in 1952, he fathered a daughter, Melinda. At his Villa Vera hotel, Teddy catered the wedding of Mike Todd and Elizabeth Taylor in February 1957. For years Stauffer spearheaded the Acapulco Film Festival. He passed away from heart failure on August 27, 1991. His ashes were scattered at sea, off the coast of his beloved Acapulco.

5. José, *Variety,* June 18, 1952.

6. Louella O. Parsons, "Hedy Lamarr to Make TV Series in Mexico," *Los Angeles Examiner,* June 6, 1952.

7. Lamarr, *Ecstasy and Me,* 312.

8. Ibid., 218.

9. Giovanni Secchi, letter to author, November 2008.

10. Edwin Schallert, "Benagoss Seeking Cobb, Ryan, O'Brien for films; Monster Story on Way," *Los Angeles Times,* September 11, 1954.

11. Hedy Lamarr quoted in Donatella Dubini and Fosco Dubini, *Hedy Lamarr: Secrets of a Hollywood Star,* Dubini Filmproduktion, 2006.

12. John Fraser, *Close-Up: An Actor Telling Tales* (London: Oberon, 2005), 104.

13. Ibid.

14. Ibid., 105–06.

15. Genevieve's costume as it appears in the film is actually a simple number, with a plain vest covering her blouse. In an e-mail to the author in 2007, John Fraser said, "In 1952 Hedy was neurotic and completely unable to communicate socially. In company, she was unaware of anyone but herself. Her need to be the centre of attention meant that whenever she appeared in public, she launched into a meaningless monologue. She was accompanied by her PA, Frankie Dawson and sometimes by her psychiatrist, who wasn't doing her much good." John Fraser, e-mail to author, October 30, 2007.

16. Peter Boyle, "Hedy's Glittering Too Much for Ulmer," *The London Sunday Pictorial*, October 18, 1953.

17. *The New York World-Telegram and Sun*, November 3, 1953.

18. Giovanni Secchi, letter to author, November 2008.

19. Lamarr, *Ecstasy and Me*, 220.

20. Denise Loder-DeLuca interview.

21. Lamarr, *Ecstasy and Me*, 269–70.

22. Ibid., 220–21.

23. Ibid., 26.

24. Ibid., 264.

25. Edwin Schallert, "Hedy Again Finds Films Luring Her," *Los Angeles Times*, November 28, 1954.

26. "Hedy Lamarr Settles Suit on Lawyers Fees," *Los Angeles Times*, September 10, 1957.

27. "Hedy Upset Cannot Tell a Lie Detector," New York *Daily News*, May 28, 1955.

28. "Gem Mystery on Shelf: Hedy Finds 'Em There," New York *Daily News*, June 17, 1957.

29. Lamarr, *Ecstasy and Me*, 264.

30. Production notes for *The Story of Mankind*, USC.

31. William Schallert, interview by author, October 29, 2007.

32. James Robert Parish and Don E. Stanke, *The Swashbucklers* (New Rochelle, NY: Arlington, 1976), 164.

19. TELEVISION

1. Sid Krofft, interview by author, October 24, 2007.

2. Helm, Tele Review, *Daily Variety*, March 15, 1957.

3. Aline Mosby, "Hedy Lamarr: Housewife!" *The Beverly Hills Citizen-News*, March 15, 1957.

4. Ibid.

5. *The Female Animal* papers, USC.

6. Madeleine Merrill, interview by author, June 20, 2008.

7. John Gavin, interview by author, June 10, 2008.

8. John Carlyle, *Under the Rainbow: An Intimate Memoir of Judy Garland, Rock Hudson and My Life in Old Hollywood* (New York: Da Capo, 2006), 170.

9. Nader made a successful transition into a top box-office star overseas, starring in a series of German-made spy films. After a serious automobile accident in the mid-1970s, which severely damaged his eyes, Nader took to writing and, in 1978, penned a groundbreaking science fiction novel, *Chrome,* the first sci-fi novel dealing with homosexual love. His health declining, Nader and his longtime partner, Mark Miller, returned to the United States in the early 1980s, settling in Palm Springs. Nader died in Woodland Hills on February 4, 2002, and his ashes were scattered at sea.

10. Jane Powell, *The Girl Next Door . . . and How She Grew* (New York: Berkley Books, 1990), 144–45.

11. Helena Kane, "Hedy Lamarr Is Ill and Tired at 43," *The Newark Evening News,* August 27, 1959.

12. Just three years later, Eddie Fisher would rival Richard Burton for the affections of Fisher's wife, Elizabeth Taylor, during the filming Twentieth Century–Fox's *Cleopatra* (1963).

13. Kove, Telepix Reviews, *Daily Variety,* October 28, 1957.

14. Christopher Young, *The Films of Hedy Lamarr* (Secaucus, NJ: Citadel Press, 1978), 229.

15. Harry Medved and Randy Dreyfuss, *The 50 Worst Films of All Time (And How They Got That Way)* (New York: Popular Library, 1978), 225.

16. Philip K. Scheuer, "'Mankind' Comes Out as Vulgarized History," *Los Angeles Times,* November 14, 1959, quoted in Medved and Dreyfuss, *50 Worst Films of All Time.*

17. Untitled article, February 1958, MOMA.

18. Untitled article, n.d., MOMA.

19. H. H. T., "Screen: U.-I. Double Bill," *The New York Times,* January 23, 1958.

20. Osborne interview.

21. Hedda Hopper, "Mitchum Will Star in True Spy Story," *Los Angeles Times,* July 7, 1958.

22. "Hedy, Mate Split," *The Los Angeles Examiner,* August 9, 1958.

23. "Hedy Broke," *The Los Angeles Examiner,* January 24, 1959.

24. "Hedy Lamarr Ill, Sues for Financial Aid," *The Hollywood Citizen-News,* January 22, 1959.

25. "'Only Man I Ever Loved' Says Suing Hedy," *New York Post,* January 22, 1959.

26. "Hedy Lamarr Sued for Divorce in Texas," *Los Angeles Times,* April 4, 1959.

27. Paul H. Jeffers, *Sal Mineo: His Life, Murder, and Mystery* (New York: Carroll & Graf, 2000), 8.

20. PURGATORY

1. Untitled article, n.d., AMPAS.

2. Helena Kane, "Hedy Lamarr Is Ill and Tired at 43," *The Newark Evening News,* August 27, 1959.

3. Walter Ames, "Hedy Wins $500,000 Divorce Settlement," *Los Angeles Times,* April 23, 1960.

4. Charles E. Davis Jr., "Hedy Says Fifth Husband 'Only Man I Ever Loved,'" *The Los Angeles Examiner,* April 22, 1960.

5. "Court Wants Closeup, Not Hedy's Stand-In," *The Los Angeles Examiner,* April 20, 1960.

6. Ibid.

7. Ames, "Hedy Wins $500,000 Divorce Settlement."

8. Ibid.

9. "Auction of Modern Art Will Aid Israel Museum," *The New York Times,* April 29, 1962.

10. Hedda Hopper, "Paula Prentiss Set As Rock's Co-star," *Los Angeles Times,* November 6, 1962.

11. Hedy Lamarr, *Ecstasy and Me: My Life as a Woman* (New York: Bartholomew House, 1966), 272.

12. Carl Reiner, interview by author, June 23, 2008.

13. Denise Loder-DeLuca interview.

14. Hopper, "Actress Laughs Off Rockefeller Rumors," *Los Angeles Times,* April 14, 1962.

15. Lamarr, *Ecstasy and Me,* 304. Hedy recalled once reading a copy of a letter Tony had written to his father, pleading with him for a meeting.

16. Lamarr, *Ecstasy and Me,* 273.

17. Stephen Birmingham, "Would You Believe I Was Once a Famous Star? It's the Truth," *The New York Times,* August 23, 1970.

18. "Hedy—'I'm Broke': Ex-Mate 'Ditto,'" *The Los Angeles Herald-Examiner,* August 10, 1965.

19. Osborne interview.

20. Ibid.

21. Ed Rambeau, interview by author, June 18, 2008.

22. Osborne interview.

23. John Carlyle, *Under the Rainbow: An Intimate Memoir of Judy Garland, Rock Hudson and My Life in Old Hollywood* (New York: Da Capo, 2006), 202.

24. Laura Bascombe, "Hedy Lamarr: The Men Who Made Her Suffer," *Modern Screen,* n.d. USC.

25. *Los Angeles Times,* January 28, 1966, and *The Los Angeles Herald-Examiner,* January 28, 1966.

26. Art Berman, "Hedy 'Mystified' over Arrest," *Los Angeles Times,* January 29, 1966.

27. Osborne interview.

28. Harry Tessel and Dick Horning, "'A Slap in the Face: Hedy's Son," *The Los Angeles Herald-Examiner,* January 28, 1966.

29. Berman, "Hedy 'Mystified' over Arrest."

30. Peter Bart, "Hedy Lamarr, After the Fall," *The New York Times,* February 6, 1966.

31. Ibid.

32. Bascombe, "Hedy Lamarr: The Men Who Made Her Suffer."

33. Berman, "Hedy 'Mystified' over Arrest." Andy Warhol quickly shot a cheap seventy-minute, grainy, black-and-white film at his New York Greenwich Village Factory Studio. It was called *Hedy* (or, *Hedy the Shoplifter* or, *The 14-Year-Old Girl*), which was screened in New York on March 3, 1966. Warhol hired a Hispanic transvestite drag queen called Mario Montez to portray a demented young character called Hedy. Both John Cale and Lou Reed contributed to the music in the film.

21. SCANDAL

1. "Actress Seeks Trial," *Los Angeles Times,* April 20, 1966.
2. Osborne interview.
3. Rudy Villasenor, "Hedy Lamarr Jurors Told of Events Leading to Her Arrest," *Los Angeles Times,* April 21, 1966.
4. Ibid.
5. Ibid.
6. Ibid.
7. Rudy Villasenor, "Psychiatrist Takes Stand for Hedy," *Los Angeles Times,* April 22, 1966.
8. Ibid.
9. Laura Bascombe, "Hedy Lamarr: The Men Who Made Her Suffer," *Modern Screen,* n.d., USC.
10. Rudy Villasenor, "She Was Broke and Sick When Arrested, Hedy Lamarr Says," *Los Angeles Times,* April 23, 1966.
11. Len Lesser, letter to author, July 15, 2008.
12. Rudy Villasenor, "Doctors, Son Tell of Hedy's Mental Stress," *Los Angeles Times,* April 24, 1966.
13. Ibid.
14. Villasenor, "She Was Broke and Sick When Arrested."
15. "Hedy Lamarr Denies Intent to Steal Goods from Store," *The New York Times,* April 26, 1966.
16. "State Demands Guilty Verdict," *The Los Angeles Herald-Examiner,* April 26, 1966.
17. Celia Rasmussen, "Tech Invention, Shoplifting Trial Set Hedy Lamarr Apart," *Los Angeles Times,* November 10, 2002.
18. "State Demands Guilty Verdict."
19. Ibid.
20. "Hedy Lamarr Wins Shoplift Acquittal After Coast Trial," *The New York Times,* April 27, 1966.
21. Rasmussen, "Tech Invention, Shoplifting Trial Set Hedy Lamarr Apart."
22. Osborne interview.
23. Osborne interview.

24. John Carlyle, *Under the Rainbow: An Intimate Memoir of Judy Garland, Rock Hudson and My Life in Old Hollywood* (New York: Da Capo, 2006), 170.

25. "Hedy Lamarr Sues Store," *Los Angeles Times*, May 13, 1966.

26. Sheilah Graham, "Beautiful Hedy Bewildered Lady," *The Hollywood Citizen-News*, September 13, 1966.

27. Graham, "Beautiful Hedy Bewildered Lady."

28. Osborne interview.

29. "Hedy Lamarr Loses Suit to Halt Book," *The New York Times*, September 27, 1966.

30. "Hedy Lamarr Sues to Quash Autobiog," *Variety*, September 27, 1966.

31. Howard Hertel, "Judge Refuses to Halt Hedy Lamarr Book," *Los Angeles Times*, September 27, 1966.

32. Ibid.

33. Ibid.

34. "Shed More Light on Hedy Autobiog," *Variety*, September 28, 1966.

35. Bob Edison, "Interview with Hedy Lamarr," *Films in Review*, June–July 1974.

36. "Hedy Seeking $499,000 in Loss of Role," *The Hollywood Citizen-News*, December 17, 1966.

37. *The Hollywood Reporter*, March 20, 1967.

38. "Hedy Lamarr Drops Assault Charges," *Los Angeles Times*, August 23, 1967.

39. "Man Accused by Hedy Sues for $1 Million," *Los Angeles Times*, September 26, 1967.

40. The ghostwriter Leo Guild once said, "I think I know what sells a book on a personality. Frankness . . . perhaps the strangest ghost-writing assignment I ever had was on '*Ecstasy and Me*.' Because there are still legal complications I cannot go into details. But to zero in on it, I wrote the book as a ghostwriter without the subject ever knowing I was writing it. The publisher signed me to write the book and Cy Rice did the interviewing on tape. The translated tapes were then turned over to me and copy sent daily to New York as I wrote. But it worked well, according to royalty statements from MacFadden-Bartell, the publishers." Leo Guild, "Confessions of a Celebrity Ghost Writer," *The New York Times*, November 5, 1967.

41. "Hedy on Her Firing: Goodbye, Hollywood," *New York Post*, February 4, 1966.

42. Osborne interview.

43. Gaeton Fonzi, "Hedy and Who?" *Philadelphia*, January 1968.

44. Ibid.

45. Ibid.

46. Ibid.

47. Ibid.

48. Ibid.

49. Henry Sutherland, "Auction Crowded as Hedy Lamarr's Effects Go on Sale," *Los Angeles Times*, January 29, 1968.

50. Advertisement, *Los Angeles Times*, January 28, 1968.

51. Mamie Van Doren, interview by author, November 2008.

52. "Hedy Lamarr Charges Nine with Plot (Hers)," *Variety*, February 19, 1969.

53. Ibid.

54. Hedy Lamarr, quoted in Donatella Dubini and Fosco Dubini, *Hedy Lamarr: Secrets of a Hollywood Star*, Dubini Filmproduktion, 2006.

55. Ava Gardner, *Ava: My Story* (New York: Bantam, 1990), 147.

22. SECLUSION

1. Kenneth Anger, quoted in Donatella Dubini and Fosco Dubini, *Hedy Lamarr: Secrets of a Hollywood Star*, Dubini Filmproduktion, 2006.

2. Ibid.

3. Patrick Agan, "Hedy Lamarr in 1973: 'Fame Is Something You Never Really Own,'" *Movie World*, 1973.

5. Paul H. Jeffers, *Sal Mineo: His Life, Murder, and Mystery* (New York: Carroll & Graf, 2000), 81.

4. Larry Colton would become a successful writer in the 1990s. His autobiographical 1993 novel *The Goat Brothers,* about the coming of age of fraternity brothers, was a modest literary success.

5. Peter Bond, "Lamarr's Secret System Widely Used," *The National Post (Ontario, Canada),* September 22, 2001.

6. Viola Hegyi Swisher, "Anthony Loder's 'Still Movies' Run Deep," *After Dark,* February 1978.

7. *Blazing Saddles*, commentary, 30th Anniversary DVD Edition, Warner Home Video, 2004.

8. "Hedy Lamarr Files Suit for $1 Million," *Los Angeles Times,* June 17, 1974.

9. "The Rostropoviches Get Freedom Award," *The New York Times,* April 18, 1975.

10. Jennings Parrott, "Wed 75 Years, They Find It Catching," *Los Angeles Times,* April 18, 1975.

11. James Bacon, "Hedy Lamarr's Sad Story," *The Los Angeles Herald-Examiner,* February 15, 1980.

12. "Hedy: 'He Gave Me My Eyes,'" New York *Daily News,* May 22, 1981.

13. Arlene Roxbury interview, May 13, 2008.

14. Ibid.

15. Ibid.

16. Ibid.

17. Arlene and Lawrence Roxbury, interview by author, July 11, 2008.

18. Ibid.

19. "Elegant Egghead," *People,* February 7, 2000.

20. Cindy Adams, *New York Post,* June 19, 1987.

21. Ibid.

22. Jim MacDonald (compiled from wire reports), "Theft Reported, Hedy Lamarr Reports Jewelry Stolen," *Orlando Sentinel,* September 4, 1988.

23. Arlene and Lawrence Roxbury interview.

24. "To Whom It May Concern," letter of illness verification, ARC.

25. James Lamarr Loder quoted in *Hedy Lamarr: Secrets of a Hollywood Star.*

26. Ibid.

27. "Hedy Lamarr's Fans Pledge Help After Arrest," *St. Petersburg* (FL) *Times,* August 3, 1991.

28. Ibid.

29. Sharon McBreen, "Hedy Lamarr Unwillingly in the Limelight Again; Actress Tells Daughter, Friend She Merely Forgot to Pay for Items; She Is Charged with Shoplifting," *Orlando Sentinel,* August 3, 1991.

30. "Hedy Lamarr Won't Be Charged," *The Washington Post,* October 25, 1991.

31. Aleene MacMinn, "Hedy Lamarr Case Comes to a Close," *Los Angeles Times,* October 25, 1991.

32. George Gerardo, "Hedy Lamarr's Sad and Lonely Last Days," November 5, 1996.

33. Anthony Summers and Robbyn Swan, "The Hidden Life of Hedy Lamarr." *Talk,* March 3, 2001.

34. Arlene and Lawrence Roxbury interview.

35. Madeleine Merrill interview.

36. Ibid.

37. Ibid.

38. Ibid.

23. LEGACY

1. Hedy Lamarr quoted in Donatella Dubini and Fosco Dubini, *Hedy Lamarr: Secrets of a Hollywood Star,* Dubini Filmproduktion, 2006.

2. "Salute to Inventors," *Los Angeles Times,* February 7, 1974.

3. Ibid.

4. Robert Boyd, untitled article, *Orlando Sentinel,* February 28, 1989.

5. Flemina Meeks, "guess they just take and forget about a person," *Forbes,* May 14, 1990.

6. Mark Boslet, "Cast Against Type," *The Wall Street Journal,* February 21, 1997.

7. Elizabeth Weiss, "Sultry Star Lamarr Did More Than Act, She Also Invented," *Salt Lake Tribune,* March 8, 1997.

8. "Recognition at Last," *Microtimes,* June 25, 1997.

9. Peter Y. Hong, *The Sacramento Bee,* September 7, 1997.

10. "Just Another Pretty Face," Internet website, January 8, 2006.

11. Debbie Salamone Wickham, "Ex-Star Wants Image Blocked: Once a Hollywood Beauty, Hedy Lamarr Isn't Keen on Being a Software Queen," *Orlando Sentinel,* October 30, 1998.

12. Debbie Salamone Wickham, "Actress Hedy Lamarr Fights Use of Image in Corel, McGraw-Hill Ads," *Orlando Sentinel,* October 29, 1998.

13. Nicholas Booth, "Film Beauty Stars Again," *The* (London) *Times,* December 9, 1998.
14. Cindy Adams, "Lamarr Less Heady About '90s Beauty Icons," *New York Post,* June 18, 1998.
15. "Proust Questionnaire," *Vanity Fair,* April 1999.
16. Madeleine Merrill interview.
17. Ibid.
18. Ibid.
19. Ibid.
20. Ibid.
21. Ibid.
22. Denise Loder-DeLuca interview.
23. Merrill interview.
24. Arlene and Lawrence Roxbury interview.
25. Robin Pettis, quoted in *Hedy Lamarr: Secrets of a Hollywood Star.*
26. Arlene Roxbury interview, May 13, 2008.
27. Arlene and Lawrence Roxbury interview.
28. Merrill interview.
29. Ibid.
30. Merrill interview.
31. Doris Bloodworth, "Sundays with Hedy," *Sun Sentinel (Orlando),* April 30, 2000.
32. Arlene Roxbury interview.
33. Arlene Roxbury interview.
34. Untitled article, January 19, 2000, DLDC.
35. Merrill interview.
36. Ibid.
37. Arlene and Lawrence Roxbury interview.
38. Ibid.
39. Denise Loder-DeLuca interview.

EPILOGUE

1. Carrie Rickey, "Hollywood Beauty and Grandmother of Cellphone Technology Hedy Lamarr Dies at 86," *The Philadelphia Inquirer,* January 19, 2000.
2. Mary Greene, "Hedy's Brainwave," London *Daily Mail,* February 5, 2005.
3. Michael T. Jarvis, "The Hollywood Industrial Complex: Boeing Hitches Its Star to Hedy," *Los Angeles Times,* January 4, 2004.
4. Hal Boedeker, "TCM Celebrates Beauty, Genius of Hedy Lamarr," *The Pittsburgh Tribune,* April 2, 2008.
5. John Fraser, *Close-Up: An Actor Telling Tales* (London: Oberon, 2005), 107.

6. Osborne interview.

7. Ibid.

8. Hedy Lamarr, *Ecstasy and Me: My Life as a Woman* (New York: Bartholomew House, 1966), 233.

9. Denise Loder-DeLuca interview.

10. Ibid.

Bibliography

Allyson, June. *June Allyson*. With Frances Spatz Leighton. New York: Putnam, 1982.

Amory, Cleveland, gen. ed. *International Celebrity Registry (U.S. Edition)*. New York: Celebrity Register, 1959.

Antheil, George. *Bad Boy of Music*. Garden City, NY: Doubleday, 1945.

Aumont, Jean-Pierre. *Sun and Shadow: An Autobiography*. W. W. Norton, 1977.

Bach, Steven. *Marlene Dietrich: Life and Legend*. New York: William Morrow, 1992.

Bailey, Margaret I. *Those Glorious Glamorous Years: Classic Costume Design of the 1930s*. Secaucus, NJ: Citadel Press, 1982.

Barrymore, Diana, and Gerold Frank. *Too Much Too Soon*. New York: Henry Holt, 1957.

Basinger, Jeanine. *Lana Turner*. New York: Pyramid, 1976.

Beaver, James N., Jr. *John Garfield: His Life and Films*. Cranbury, NJ: A.S. Barnes, 1978.

Behlmer, Rudy. *Inside Warner Brothers (1935–1951)*. New York: Viking-Penguin, 1985.

Berg, A. Scott. *Goldwyn: A Biography*. New York: Alfred A. Knopf, 1989.

Bergan, Ronald. *The United Artists Story*. New York: Crown, 1986.

Bernstein, Matthew. *Walter Wanger: Hollywood Independent*. Berkeley: University of California Press, 1994.

Billips, Connie, and Arthur Pierce. *Lux Presents Hollywood: A Show by Show History of the Lux Radio Theatre & The Lux Video Theatre, 1934–1957*. Jefferson, NC: McFarland, 1995.

Birchard, Robert S. *Cecil B. DeMille's Hollywood*. Lexington, KY: University Press of Kentucky, 2004.

Brady, Frank. *Citizen Welles: A Biography of Orson Welles*. New York: Scribner, 1989.

Brooks, Tom, and Earle Marsh. *The Complete Directory to Prime Time Network and Cable TV Shows, 1946–Present*. New York: Ballantine, 1999.

Bugliosi, Vincent, and Curt Gentry. *Helter Skelter*. New York: Bantam, 1975.

Cadden, Tom Scott. *What a Bunch of Characters! An Entertaining Guide to Who Played What in the Movies.* Englewood Cliffs, NJ: Prentice-Hall Publishers, 1984.

Calistro, Paddy. *Edith Head's Hollywood.* New York: Putnam, 1983.

Carey, Gary. *All the Stars in Heaven: Louis B. Mayer and M.G.M.* London: Robson, 1981.

Carey, Macdonald. *The Days of My Life.* New York: St. Martin's, 1991.

Carlyle, John. *Under the Rainbow: An Intimate Memoir of Judy Garland, Rock Hudson and My Life in Old Hollywood.* New York: Da Capo, 2006.

Chierichetti, David. *The Life and Times of Hollywood's Celebrated Costume Designer Edith Head.* New York: HarperCollins, 2003.

Considine, Shaun. *Bette and Joan: The Divine Feud.* New York: Dutton, 1984.

Crowther, Bosley. *The Lion's Share: The Story of an Entertainment Empire.* New York: Dutton, 1957.

Davidson, Bill. *Spencer Tracy: Tragic Idol.* New York: Dutton, 1987.

Davis, Ronald L. *Hollywood Beauty: Linda Darnell and the American Dream.* Norman, OK: University Press of Oklahoma, 1991.

Davis, Ronald L. *The Glamour Factory: Inside Hollywood's Big Studio System.* Dallas: Southern Methodist University Press, 1993.

DeMille, Cecil B. *Autobiography.* Englewood Cliffs, NJ: Prentice-Hall, 1959.

Deschner, Donald. *The Films of Spencer Tracy.* New York: Citadel Press, 1968.

Dewey, Donald. *James Stewart: A Biography.* Atlanta: Turner, 1996.

Dietz, Howard. *Dancing in the Dark: An Autobiography.* New York: Bantam, 1976.

Domont, Herve. *Frank Borzage: The Life and Films of a Hollywood Romantic.* Jefferson, NC: McFarland, 2006.

Donati, William. *Ida Lupino: A Biography.* Lexington, KY: University Press of Kentucky, 1996.

Drew, William M. *At the Center of the Frame: Leading Ladies of the Twenties and the Thirties.* Lanham, MD: Vestal, 1999.

Dunning, John. *On the Air: The Encyclopedia of Old-Time Radio.* New York: Oxford University Press, 1998.

Eames, John Douglas. *The MGM Story.* New York: Crown, 1975.

———. *The Paramount Story.* New York: Crown, 1985.

Edwards, Anne. *The DeMilles: An American Family.* New York: Harry N. Abrams, 1988.

Eliot, Marc. *Jimmy Stewart: A Biography.* New York: Harmony, 2006.

Epstein, Edward Z. *Portrait of Jennifer.* New York: Simon & Schuster, 1996.

Essoe, Gabe. *The Films of Clark Gable.* New York: Citadel Press, 1970.

Essoe, Gabe, and Raymond Lee. *DeMille: The Man and His Pictures.* Cranbury, NJ: A.S. Barnes, 1970.

Eyman, Scott. *Ernst Lubitsch: Laughter in Paradise.* New York: Simon & Schuster, 1993.

———. *Lion of Hollywood: The Life and Legend of Louis B. Mayer.* New York: Simon & Schuster, 2005.

Fidelman, Geoffrey Mark. *The Lucy Book: A Complete Guide to Her Five Decades on Television.* Los Angeles: Renaissance, 1999.

Fishgall, Gary. *Pieces of Time: The Life of James Stewart.* New York: Scribner, 1997.

Flagg, James M. *Roses and Buckshot: Autobiography of James Montgomery Flagg.* New York: Putnam, 1946.

Fleming, E.J. *The Fixers: Eddie Mannix, Howard Strickling and the MGM Publicity Machine.* Jefferson, NC: McFarland, 2004.

Flynn, Errol. *My Wicked, Wicked Ways: The Autobiography of Errol Flynn.* New York: Cooper Square, 2003.

Frank, Gerold. *Judy.* New York: Harper & Row, 1975.

Fraser, John. *Close Up: An Actor Telling Tales.* London: Oberon, 2005.

Fraser-Cavassoni, Natasha. *Sam Speigel.* New York: Simon & Schuster, 2003.

Fujiwara, Chris. *Jacques Tourneur: The Cinema of Nightfall.* Baltimore, MD: John Hopkins University Press, 1998.

Garceau, Jean. *"Dear Mr. G.": The Biography of Clark Gable.* With Inez Locke. Boston: Little, Brown, 1961.

Gardner, Ava. *Ava: My Story.* New York: Bantam, 1990.

Gelman, Howard. *The Films of John Garfield.* Secaucus, NJ: Citadel Press, 1975.

Gilbert, Julie Goldsmith. *Opposite Attraction: The Lives of Erich Maris Remarque and Paulette Goddard.* New York: Pantheon, 1995.

Gilmore, John. *Laid Bare: A Memoir of Wrecked Lives and the Hollywood Death Trip.* Los Angeles: AMOK, 1997.

Goldman, Herbert G. *Fanny Brice The Original Funny Girl.* New York: Oxford University Press, 1992.

Graham, Sheilah. *Hollywood Revisited.* New York: St. Martin's, 1985.

Granger, Farley. *Include Me Out: My Life from Goldwyn to Broadway.* With Robert Calhoun. New York: St. Martin's, 2007.

Granger, Stewart. *Sparks Fly Upwards.* New York: Putnam, 1981.

Griffith, Richard, and Arthur Mayer. *The Movies.* New York: Simon & Schuster, 1957.

Gutner, Howard. *Gowns by Adrian: The MGM Years, 1928–1941.* New York: Harry N. Abrams, 2001.

Harmetz, Aljean. *The Making of "The Wizard of Oz."* New York: Limelight, 1984.

Harris, Warren G. *Clark Gable: A Biography.* New York: Harmony, 2002.

———. *Gable and Lombard.* New York: Simon & Schuster, 1974.

Hay, Peter. *MGM: When the Lion Roared.* Atlanta: Turner, 1991.

Higham, Charles. *Ava.* New York: Dell, 1973.

———. *Merchant of Dreams: Louis B. Mayer, MGM, and the Secret Hollywood.* New York: Donald I. Fine, 1993.

———. *Cecil B. DeMille.* New York: Scribner, 1973.

———. *Sisters: The Story of Olivia de Havilland and Joan Fontaine.* New York: Dell, 1986.

Hirschhorn, Clive. *The Warner Brothers Story.* New York: Crown, 1979.

Hitler, Adolf. *Mein Kampf.* Translated by Ralph Manheim. New York: Houghton, Mifflin & Harcourt, 1998.

Hollander, Frederick. *Those Torn from Earth*. New York: Liveright, 1941.

Horne, Lena, and Richard Schickel. *Lena*. New York: Doubleday, 1965.

Jeffers, H. Paul. *Sal Mineo: His Life, Murder, and Mystery*. New York: Carroll & Graf, 2000.

Jewell, Richard B., and Vernon Harbin. *The RKO Story*. New York: Arlington House, 1982.

Jordan, Rene. *Clark Gable*. New York: Pyramid, 1973.

Kanfer, Stefan. *Ball of Fire: The Tumultuous Life and Comic Art of Lucille Ball*. New York: Alfred A. Knopf, 2003.

Kobal, John. *People Will Talk*. New York: Alfred A. Knopf, 1985.

Kreimeier, Klaus. *The UFA Story: A History of Germany's Greatest Film Company 1918–1945*. New York: Farrar, Straus and Giroux, 1996.

Lally, Kevin. *Wilder Times: The Life of Billy Wilder*. New York: Henry Holt, 1996.

Lamarr, Hedy. *Ecstasy and Me: My Life as A Woman*. New York: Bartholomew House, 1966.

Lambert, Angela. *The Lost Life of Eva Braun*. New York: St. Martin's, 2007.

Lamparski, Richard. *Whatever Became of. . . .* Vol. 2. New York: Bantam, 1977.

Leamer, Laurence. *As Time Goes By: The Life of Ingrid Bergman*. New York: HarperCollins, 1986.

Leese, Elizabeth. *Costume Design in the Movies*. New York: Frederick Ungar, 1977.

Loder, John. *Hollywood Hussar: The Life and Times of John Loder*. London: Howard Baker, 1977.

Louvish, Simon. *Cecil B. DeMille: A Life in Art*. New York: Thomas Dunne, 2007.

MacAdams, William. *Ben Hecht*. New York: Scribner, 1990.

Macdonald, Anne L. *Feminine Ingenuity: How Women Inventors Changed America*. New York: Ballantine, 1994.

Madsen, Axel. *The Sewing Circle: Hollywood's Greatest Secret Female Stars Who Loved Other Women*. New York: Birch Lane, 1995.

Martin, Pete. *Pete Martin Calls On. . . .* New York: Simon & Schuster, 1962.

Martin, Tony, and Cyd Charisse. *The Two of Us*. With Dick Kleiner. New York: Mason Charter, 1976.

Medved, Harry, and Randy Dreyfuss. *The 50 Worst Films of All Time (And How They Got That Way)*. New York: Popular Library, 1978.

Meredith, Burgess. *So Far So Good: A Memoir*. New York: Little, Brown, 1994.

Metro-Goldwyn-Mayer. *Who's Who at Metro-Goldwyn-Mayer, 1941*. MGM Studios, 1941.

Metro-Goldwyn-Mayer. *Who's Who at Metro-Goldwyn-Mayer, 1940*. MGM Studios, 1940.

Michael, Paul, ed. *The American Movies Reference Book: The Sound Era*. Englewood Cliffs, NJ: Prentice-Hall, 1968.

Milland, Ray. *Wide-Eyed in Babylon*. New York: William Morrow, 1974.

Miller, Frank. *Casablanca: As Time Goes By . . . 50th Anniversary Commemorative*. Atlanta: Turner, 1992.

Monush, Barry. *The Encyclopedia of Hollywood Film Actors: From the Silent Era to 1965*. New York: Applause Theater & Cinema, 2003.

Mordden, Ethan. *The Hollywood Studios: House Style in the Golden Age of Movies*. New York: Alfred A. Knopf, 1988.

Negra, Diane. *Off-White Hollywood: American Culture and Ethnic Female Stardom*. New York: Routledge, 2001.

Negulesco, Jean. *Things I Did and Things I Think I Did: A Hollywood Memoir*. New York: Simon & Schuster, 1984.

Paris, Barry. *Garbo*. New York: Alfred A. Knopf, 1995.

Parish, James Robert. *Good Dames*. Cranbury, NJ: A.S. Barnes, 1974.

———. *Hollywood Divas: The Good, the Bad, and the Fabulous*. New York: Contemporary, 2002.

Parish, James Robert, and Ronald L. Bowers. *The Golden Era: MGM Stock Company*. New Rochelle: Arlington House, 1973.

Parish, James Robert, and William T. Leonard. *The Funsters*. New Rochelle: Arlington House, 1979.

Parish, James Robert, and Gregory W. Mack. *The Best of MGM: The Golden Years, 1928–1959*. Westport, CT: Arlington House, 1981.

———. *The Hollywood Reliables*. Westport, CT: Arlington House, 1980.

Parish, James Robert, Gregory W. Mack, and Don E. Stanke. *The Hollywood Beauties*. New Rochelle: Arlington House, 1978.

Parish, James Robert, and Don E. Stanke. *The All-Americans*. New Rochelle: Arlington House, 1977.

———. *The Debonairs*. New Rochelle: Arlington House, 1975.

———. *The Forties Gals*. Westport: Arlington House, 1980.

———. *The Glamour Girls*. New Rochelle: Arlington House, 1975.

———. *The Swashbucklers*. New Rochelle: Arlington House, 1976.

Powell, Jane. *The Girl Next Door . . . and How She Grew*. New York: Berkley Books, 1990.

Preminger, Otto. *Preminger*. New York: Bantam, 1978.

Prouty, Howard H., ed. *Variety Television Reviews. Vol. 15*. New York: Garland, 1991.

Quirk, Lawrence J. *Bob Hope: The Road Less Traveled*. New York: Applause Theater & Cinema, 1998.

———. *Claudette Colbert: An Illustrated Biography*. New York: Crown, 1985.

———. *The Complete Films of William Powell*. Secaucus, NJ: Citadel Press, 1986.

———. *The Films of Robert Taylor*. Secaucus, NJ: Citadel Press, 1975.

———. *The Films of Ronald Colman*. Secaucus, NJ: Citadel Press, 1977.

Ragan, David. *Movie Stars of the '40s*. Englewood Cliffs, NJ: Prentice-Hall, 1985.

Ringgold, Gene, and DeWitt Bodeen. *The Films of Cecil B. DeMille*. New York: Cadillac, 1969.

Robbins, Trina. *Hedy Lamarr and a Secret Communication System*. Mankato, MN: Capstone, 2007.

Romani, Cinzia. *Tainted Goddesses: Female Film Stars of the Third Reich*. New York: Sarpedon, 1992.

Sanders, George. *Memoirs of a Professional Cad*. New York: Putnam, 1960.

Sarlot, Raymond, and Fred E. Basten. *Life at the Marmont*. Santa Monica: Roundtable, 1987.

Sarvady, Andrea. *Leading Ladies: The 50 Most Unforgettable Actresses of the Studio Era*. With a foreword by Robert Osborne and an introduction by Molly Haskell. San Francisco: Chronicle, 2006.

Schary, Dore. *Heyday*. New York: Berkeley Books, 1981.

Schneider, Gertrude. *Exile and Destruction: The Fate of the Austrian Jews, 1938–1945*. Westport, CT: Greenwood, 1995.

Schickel, Richard. *The Stars*. New York: Dial, 1962.

Server, Lee. *Ava Gardner: "Love Is Nothing."* New York: St. Martin's, 2006.

Shearer, Stephen Michael. *Patricia Neal: An Unquiet Life*. Lexington, KY: University Press of Kentucky, 2006.

Shipman, David. *Judy Garland: The Secret Life of an American Legend*. New York: Hyperion, 1993.

Shirer, William L. *20th Century Journey*. Vol. 2, *The Nightmare Years, 1930–1940*. Boston: Little, Brown, 1994.

Silver, Alain, and Elizabeth Ward, eds. *Film Noir: An Encyclopedic Reference to the American Style*. With Carl Macek and Robert Porfirio. New York: Outlook, 1993.

Skaerved, Malene Sheppard. *Dietrich*. London: Haus, 2003.

Sperber, Ann, and Eric Lax. *Bogart*. New York: Harper Perennial, 1998.

Spoto, Donald. *The Dark Side of Genius: The Life of Alfred Hitchcock*. Boston: Back Bay, 1993.

Staggs, Sam. *All About "All About Eve."* New York: St. Martin's, 2001.

———. *Close-Up on Sunset Boulevard*. New York: St. Martin's, 2002.

Swindell, Larry. *Charles Boyer: The Reluctant Lover*. Garden City, NY: Doubleday, 1983.

———. *Screwball: The Life of Carole Lombard*. New York: William Morrow, 1975.

Thomas, Bob. *Selznick: The Man Who Produced "Gone With the Wind."* Beverly Hills: New Millennium, 2001.

Thomas, Tony. *The Busby Berkeley Book*. New York: The New York Graphic Society, 1973.

Thomson, David. *Showman: The Life of David O. Selznick*. New York: Alfred A. Knopf, 1992.

———. *The New Biographical Dictionary of Film*. New York: Alfred A. Knopf, 2002.

Tierney, Gene, and Mickey Herskowitz. *Self-Portrait*. New York: Peter H. Wyden, 1979.

Toland, John. *Adolf Hitler*. Garden City, NY: Doubleday, 1976.

Tozzy, Romano. *Spencer Tracy*. New York: Pyramid, 1973.

Troyan, Michael. *A Rose for Mrs. Miniver: The Life of Greer Garson*. Lexington, KY: University Press of Kentucky, 1999.

Tyler, Parker. *Classics of the Foreign Film: A Pictorial Treasury*. New York: Cadillac, 1962.

Valentino, Lou. *The Films of Lana Turner*. Secaucus, NJ: Citadel Press, 1979.

Vermilye, Jerry. *The Films of the Thirties*. New York: Citadel Press, 1982.

Walters, Rob. *Spread Spectrum: Hedy Lamarr and the Mobile Phone*. Charleston, SC: BookSurge, 2005.

Wayne, Jane Ellen. *Ava's Men: The Private Life of Ava Gardner*. New York: St. Martin's, 1990.

———. *Gable's Women*. New York: Prentice Hall, 1987.

———. *The Leading Men of MGM*. New York: Carroll & Graf, 2004.

———. *The Golden Girls of MGM*. New York: Carroll & Graf, 2002.

Weinberg, Herman G. *The Lubitsch Touch: A Critical Study*. New York: Dover, 1968.

Wiley, Mason, and Damien Bond. *Inside Oscar: The Unofficial History of the Academy Awards*. New York: Ballantine, 1986.

Young, Christopher. *The Films of Hedy Lamarr*. Secaucus, NJ: Citadel Press, 1978.

Youngkin, Stephen D. *The Lost One: A Life of Peter Lorre*. Lexington, KY: University Press of Kentucky, 2005.

Youngkin, Stephen D., Raymond G. Cabana Jr., and James Biguoco. *The Films of Peter Lorre*. Secaucus, NJ: Citadel Press, 1982.

Daily Variety Television Reviews. Vol. 1, *1946–1956*. New York: Garland, 1989.

Daily Variety Television Reviews. Vol. 2, *1957–1960*. New York: Garland, 1989.

Variety Television Reviews. Vol. 3, *1923–1950*. New York: Garland, 1989.

Variety Television Reviews. Vol. 4, *1951–1953*. New York: Garland, 1989.

Variety Television Reviews. Vol. 9, *1966–1969*. New York: Garland, 1989.

Variety Television Reviews. Vol. 15, *Index to "Daily Variety" and "Variety."* New York: Garland, 1991.

Acknowledgments

A biography is a collaborative effort. The author does the research, conducts the interviews, views the material, designs the project, and then writes the manuscript. But there are untold others who contribute to the work, and these people and sources are more than vital if any book is to have merit.

The children of Hedy Lamarr I must thank for their encouragement and support throughout the development of this project. From recent documentaries and published articles, Hedy's adopted son, James Lamarr Loder, is quoted at length regarding his relationship with his mother, recalling compelling moments of both love and loss. Hedy's two other children by actor John Loder, Denise Loder-DeLuca (and her husband Vincent DeLuca) and Anthony Loder, have been extremely and exceptionally generous to me with their time and memories. They have graciously responded to sometimes sensitive questions with honesty and candor. Both Denise and Anthony have generously lent many personal family photographs provided for use in this biography. For their trust and friendship, I thank them sincerely.

I approached the noted television host and film historian Robert Osborne with the idea for this book, as I had done with my concept for *Patricia Neal: An Unquiet Life*. His love and memory of Hedy Lamarr stem from his personal relationship with her. His interview was the first conducted for this project. Thank you, Robert, for your encouragement and valued association.

Other professional colleagues who have lent me their support over the years are Eve Golden, Leonard Maltin, Sam Staggs, the late Richard Bojarski, and William J. Mann.

For their help in translating archival materials, my deepest appreciation goes to my dear friend Trudy Collins, for her "teaching" me German; to my brilliant Italian colleague Giovanni Secchi, who researched materials in Italian archives; and to my oldest and closest friend, Tony Morris, who translated the French.

Archive and library study is always made more exciting when the researcher has the generous support of those who know their stuff and the historical holdings of the collections they oversee. For their diligent and comprehensive assistance, I wish to deeply thank the following:

In New York and New Jersey: Charles Silver at the Museum of Modern Art; the staff of the New York Public Library for the Performing Arts; Howard and Ronald Mandelbaum at Photofest; Jerry Ohlinger at the Movie Material Store; Eve Golden, Alison J. Rigney, Mohamed Sham, and Jeff Wendt of the Everett Collection, New York; Jennifer B. Lee and Tara C. Craig of the George Antheil Collection, Rare Book and Manuscript Library, Columbia University; Nicholas Taylor (reference librarian) and the staff at the Fort Lee Public Library; the staff at the Englewood Public Library; and Anthony Macchio, Lawrence and Arlene Roxbury, Arlene Dahl, Farley Granger, Tripet Rutanarugsa, Ed Rambeau, Marion Seldes, Patricia Neal, Elyse Singer, and Gregg Smith.

In California: Ned Comstock, for his diligent, unceasingly generous, and always masterful and invaluable assistance at the Cinema-TV Library of the University of Southern California (USC); Melinda Hayes and Michaela Ullmann of the Max Reinhardt Collection and Marta Mierendorff Collection at USC; Barbara Hall, Christine Kreuger, Jenny Romero, and the complete staff of the special collections holdings at the Margaret Herrick Library of the Academy of Motion Picture Arts and Sciences; the staff of the Warner Bros. Archives of USC; Mark Quigley at the University of California, Los Angeles (UCLA) Media Lab; Mike Hawks at Larry Edmunds Bookshop; B. Caroline Sisneros (Louis B. Mayer Library) at the American Film Institute; Dennis Wills, owner and proprietor "sans pareil" of D. G. Wills Books in La Jolla; and Julie Adams, Margaret O'Brien, Phyllis Diller, Harry Carey Jr., Norm Crosby, John Gavin, Shecky Greene, Pat Harrington, Sid Krofft, Len Lesser, Jerry Maren, Tony Martin, Lorna Luft, William Schallert, Jayne Meadows, Terry Moore, Gregg Palmer, Paul Picerni, Carl Reiner, Mamie Van Doren, and Morgan Woodward.

In Nevada: Sherman Frederick, owner, and Patricia Morgan, features editor, of *The Las Vegas Review-Journal*; David Stevenson, James Patton, Bart Williams, and the late Liz Renay.

In Utah: James D'Arc and the staff of the special collections holdings (The DeMille Archives and the Robert Cummings collection) of the L. Tom Perry Special Collections at Brigham Young University.

In Florida: Madeleine Merrill.

In Wisconsin: Maxine Ducey, Dorinda Hartman, Lee Grady, Heather Richmond, Max Lubansky, and Andy Kraushaar at the Wisconsin Center for Film and Theater Research, Film and Theater Archive, Wisconsin Historical Society, University of Wisconsin-Madison.

In South Carolina: Georgia Carroll Kyser.

In England: David Price-Hughes of AKG-Images (London); the staff of the British Film Institute (London); and John Fraser.

In France: Olivia de Havilland.

In Austria: Ilse Jung, Andreas Ruhrig, and Florian Kugler of the Kunsthistorisches Museum mit MVK und OTM Wissenschaftliche Anstalt Öffentlichen Rechts (Vienna); Haris

Balic, Eva Farberger, and Ursula Klein of the Österreichisches Theatermuseum (Vienna); the staff of the Filmarchiv Austria; Ingeborg Formann and Brigitte Merisch of the Sammlung von Handschriften und alten Drucken at the Österreichische Nationalbibliothek (Vienna); Dr. Susanne Eschwe of the Universitätsbibliothek der Universität für Musik und darstellende Kunst Wien (Vienna); Eleonore Bailer of the Amtsleiterin Standesamt Wien-Innere Stadt (Vienna).

In Hungary: Zsofia Gera of the National Archives of Hungary (Budapest).

In Germany: Lisa Roth at the Deutsche Kinemathek Museum für Film und Fernsehen (Berlin); Jonas Fansa of the Staatsbibliothek zu Berlin; Dr. Dagmar Walach of the Freie Universität Berlin Institut für Theaterwissenschaft Theaterhistorische Sammlungen (Berlin); and the staff of the Deutsches Filminstitut, F. W. Murnau Foundation.

In the Czech Republic: Karel Zima at the Národní filmový Archiv (Prague); Petra Zikmundova of the Theater Department of the National Museum; Marie Valtrova of the Theatre-Cinema Department, the Municipal Library of Prague; and the staff of the Bohuslav Martinů Institute, Audiovisual Archive.

In Italy: Giancarlo Concetti and Alberto Blasetti at the Fondazione Centro Sperimentale di Cinematografia–Biblioteca "Luigi Chiarini" (Rome); the staff of the Cinema Archives at the Biblioteca Sormani di Milano, the Milan Sormani Library (Milan); and the staff of the Archivio Audiovisivo del Movimento Operaio e Democratico.

I want to thank my niece, DeNisha Williams McCollum, for her time and expertise in reading the manuscript. She gives me another set of eyes. Also, I want to thank Watson Bosler in New York, not only for supplying me with materials for this book but also for leading me to proper source references, attending the play *Frequency Hopping* in New York, and lending me his acute observations. For those whom I may have failed to mention who have contributed to this work, my sincere gratitude.

I most certainly wish to thank my agent, Deborah Ritchken, of the Castiglia Literary Agency, for seeing the intrinsic need to tell Hedy Lamarr's story and trusting in my work. Her patience and ability I value very much. Thanks too to my editor at Thomas Dunne Books, Peter Joseph. His age belies his vast wisdom. To my family and my extended church families at Saint Peter's Lutheran Church in New York, Grace in the Desert Episcopal Church in Las Vegas, and Central Lutheran Church in Minneapolis, my deepest thanks for the support and the community they have given me.

Index